by
NAOKI URASAWA
STORY by
HOKUSEI KATSUSHIKA, NAOKI URASAWA

MASTER KEATON

8

by
NAOKI URASAWA
STORY by
HOKUSEI KATSUSHIKA, NAOKI URASAWA

MASTER
KEATON

CONTENTS

Chapter 1
Special Menu

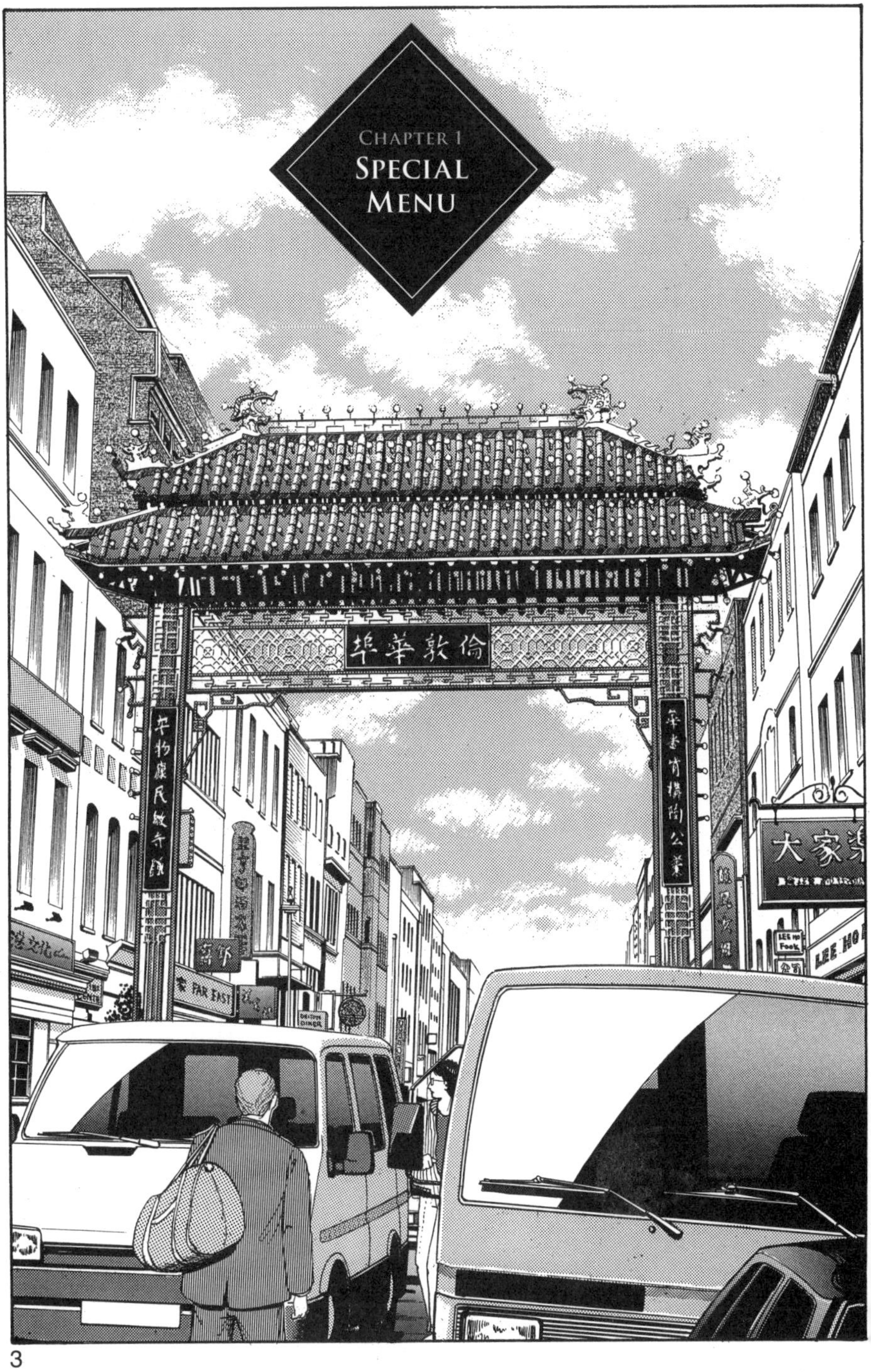

倫敦華埠
FAR EAST
LEE HO

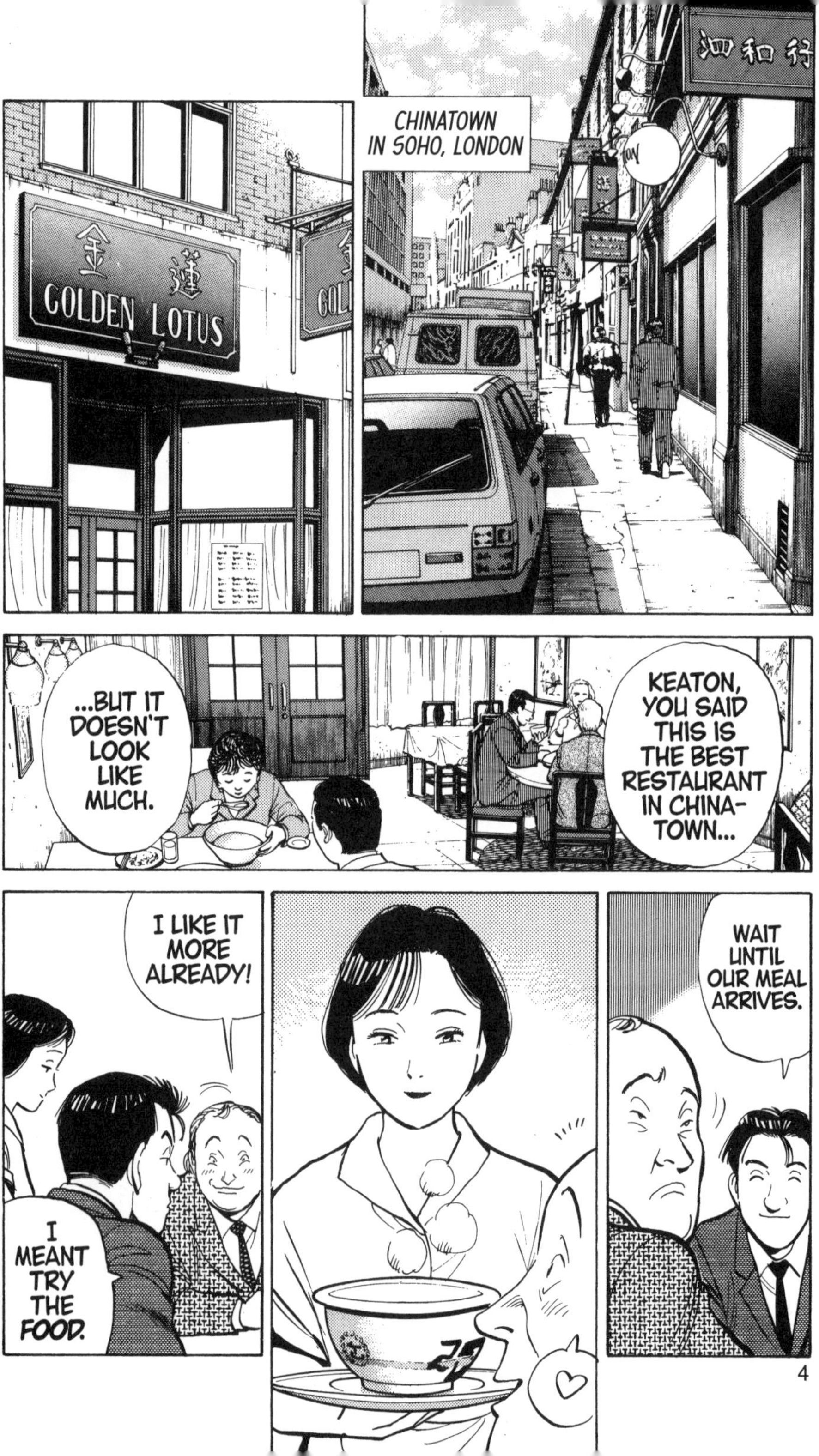
CHINATOWN IN SOHO, LONDON
金 蓮
GOLDEN LOTUS
KEATON, YOU SAID THIS IS THE BEST RESTAURANT IN CHINA-TOWN...
...BUT IT DOESN'T LOOK LIKE MUCH.
WAIT UNTIL OUR MEAL ARRIVES.
I LIKE IT MORE ALREADY!
I MEANT TRY THE *FOOD.*

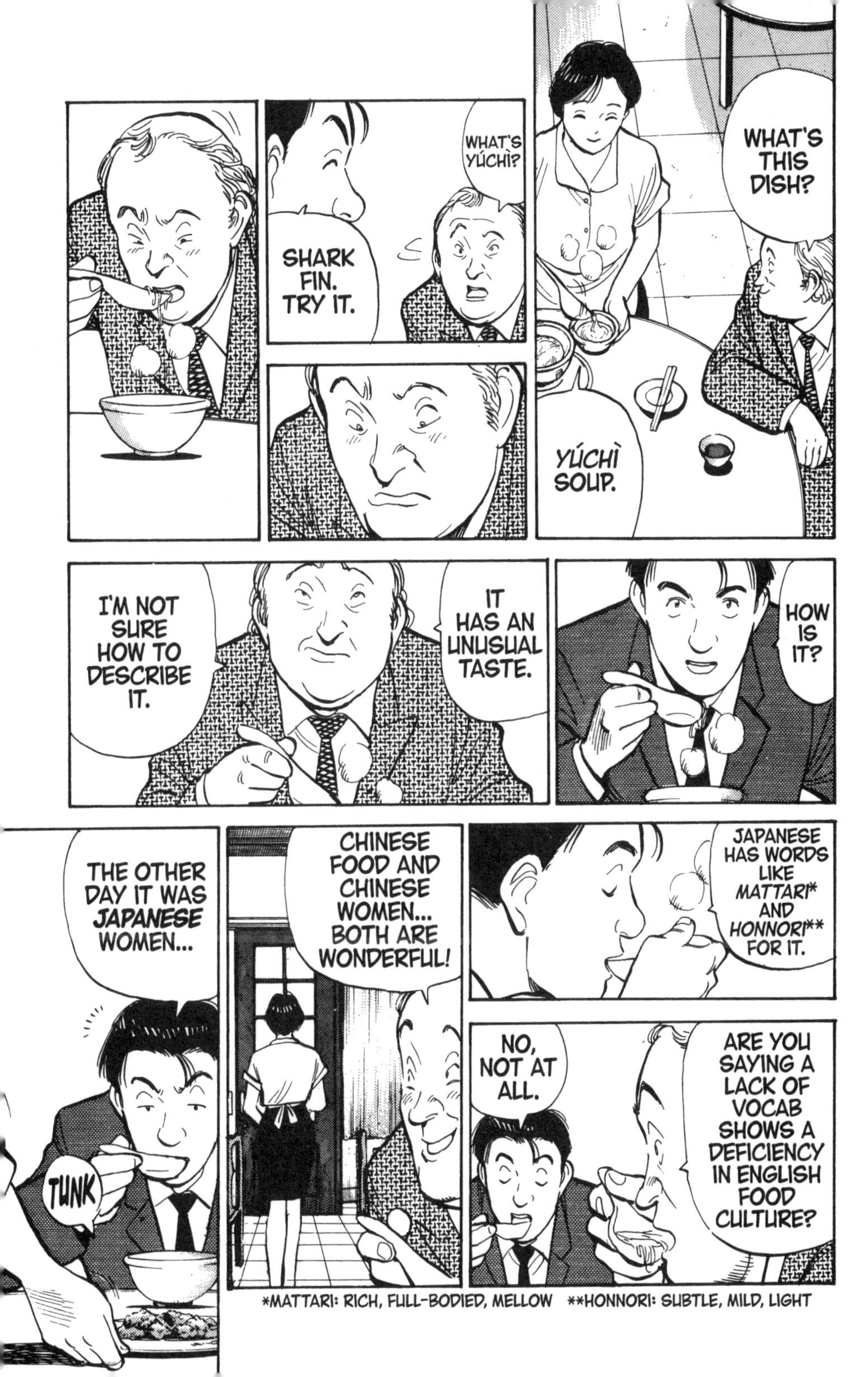
WHAT'S THIS DISH?
YÚCHÌ SOUP.
WHAT'S YÚCHÌ?
SHARK FIN. TRY IT.
HOW IS IT?
IT HAS AN UNUSUAL TASTE.
I'M NOT SURE HOW TO DESCRIBE IT.
JAPANESE HAS WORDS LIKE *MATTARI** AND *HONNORI*** FOR IT.
ARE YOU SAYING A LACK OF VOCAB SHOWS A DEFICIENCY IN ENGLISH FOOD CULTURE?
NO, NOT AT ALL.
CHINESE FOOD AND CHINESE WOMEN... BOTH ARE WONDERFUL!
THE OTHER DAY IT WAS **JAPANESE** WOMEN...
TUNK

*MATTARI: RICH, FULL-BODIED, MELLOW **HONNORI: SUBTLE, MILD, LIGHT

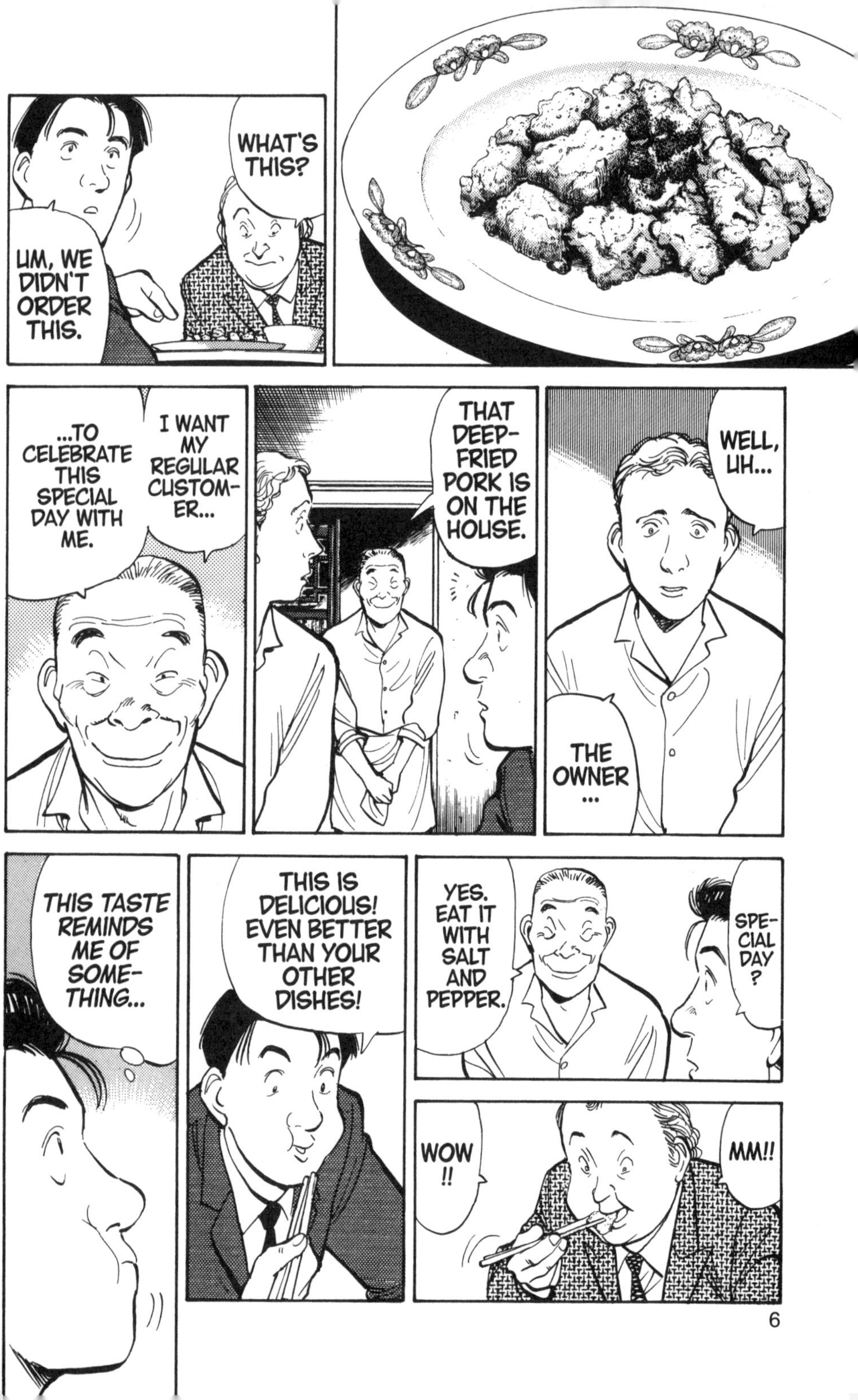
WHAT'S THIS?
UM, WE DIDN'T ORDER THIS.
WELL, UH...
THE OWNER ...
THAT DEEP-FRIED PORK IS ON THE HOUSE.
I WANT MY REGULAR CUSTOMER...
...TO CELEBRATE THIS SPECIAL DAY WITH ME.
SPECIAL DAY?
YES. EAT IT WITH SALT AND PEPPER.
MM!!
WOW !!
THIS IS DELICIOUS! EVEN BETTER THAN YOUR OTHER DISHES!
THIS TASTE REMINDS ME OF SOMETHING...

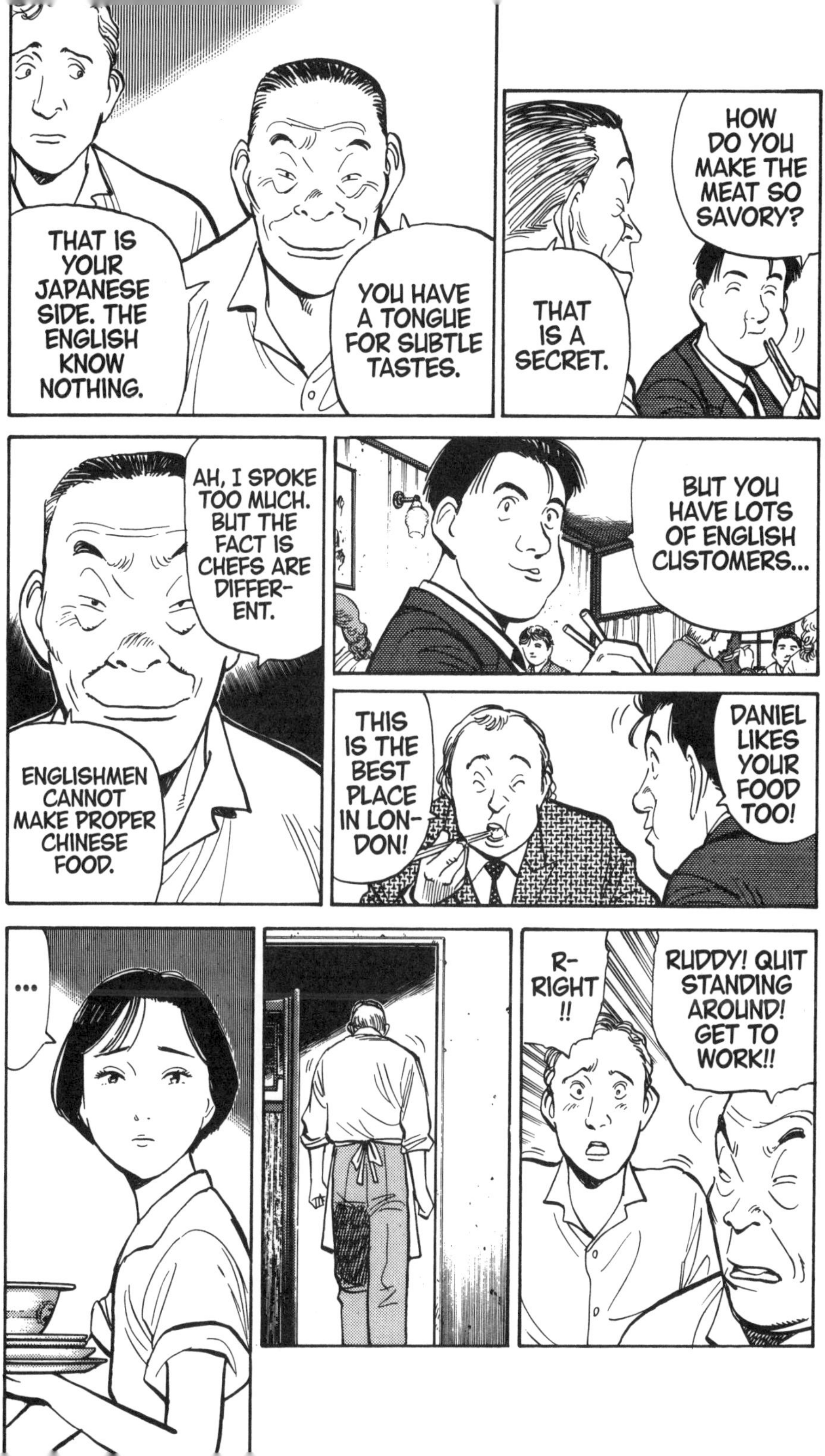
HOW DO YOU MAKE THE MEAT SO SAVORY?
THAT IS A SECRET.
YOU HAVE A TONGUE FOR SUBTLE TASTES.
THAT IS YOUR JAPANESE SIDE. THE ENGLISH KNOW NOTHING.
BUT YOU HAVE LOTS OF ENGLISH CUSTOMERS...
DANIEL LIKES YOUR FOOD TOO!
THIS IS THE BEST PLACE IN LON-DON!
AH, I SPOKE TOO MUCH. BUT THE FACT IS CHEFS ARE DIFFER-ENT.
ENGLISHMEN CANNOT MAKE PROPER CHINESE FOOD.
RUDDY! QUIT STANDING AROUND! GET TO WORK!!
R-RIGHT!!
...

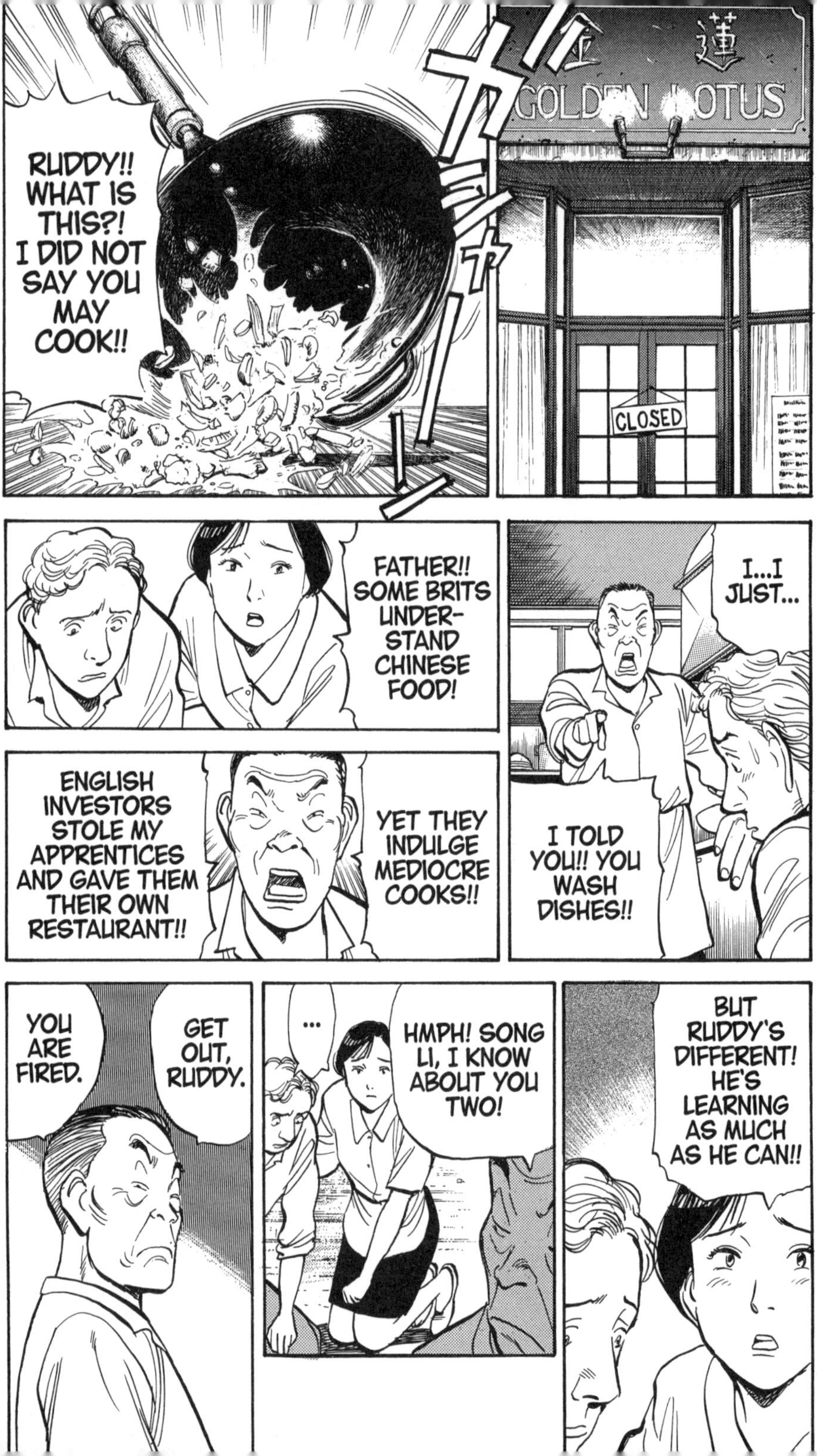
CLOSED
RUDDY!! WHAT IS THIS?! I DID NOT SAY YOU MAY COOK!!
I...I JUST...
I TOLD YOU!! YOU WASH DISHES!!
FATHER!! SOME BRITS UNDER-STAND CHINESE FOOD!
ENGLISH INVESTORS STOLE MY APPRENTICES AND GAVE THEM THEIR OWN RESTAURANT!!
YET THEY INDULGE MEDIOCRE COOKS!!
BUT RUDDY'S DIFFERENT! HE'S LEARNING AS MUCH AS HE CAN!!
HMPH! SONG LI, I KNOW ABOUT YOU TWO!
...
GET OUT, RUDDY.
YOU ARE FIRED.

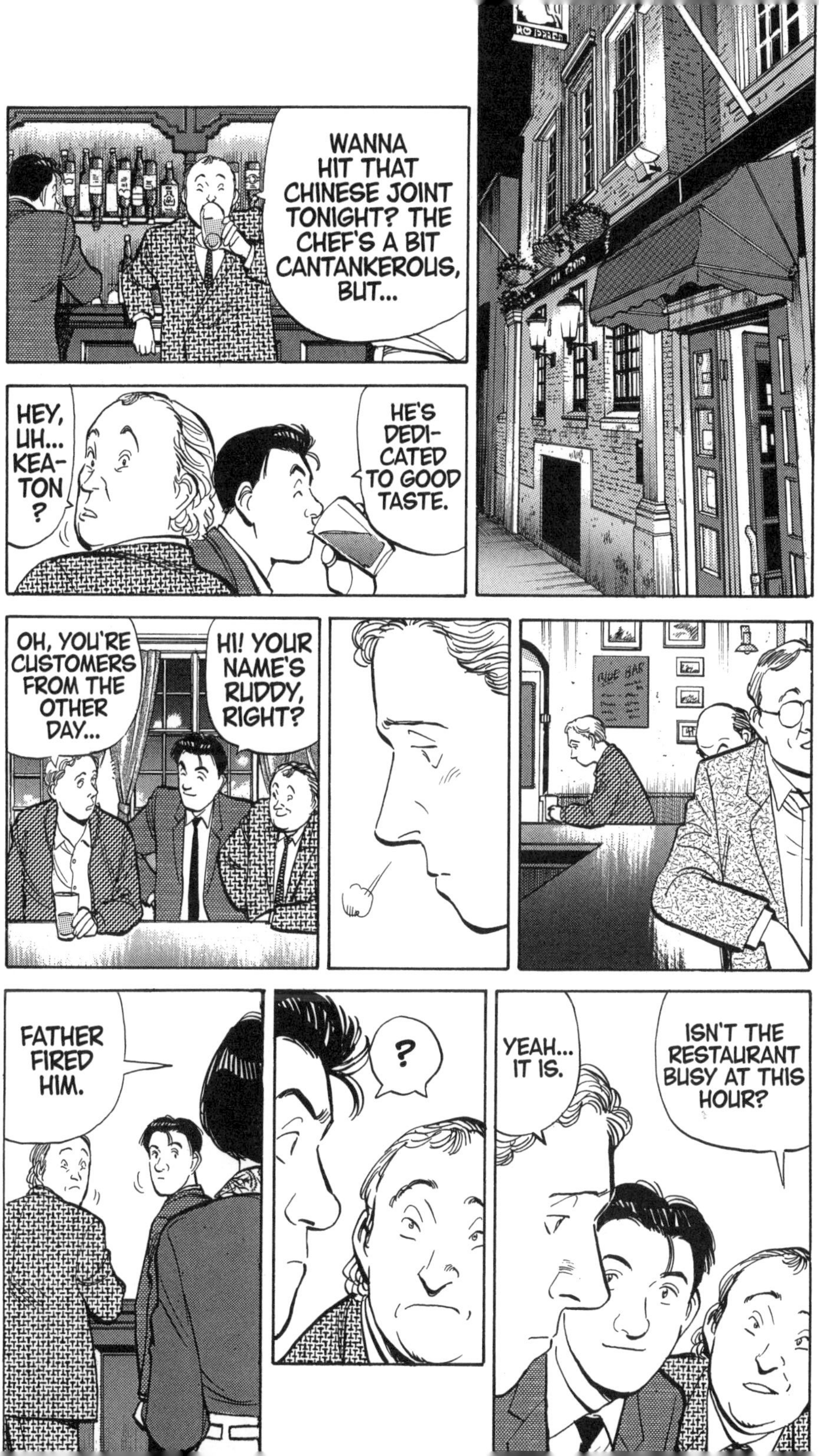
WANNA HIT THAT CHINESE JOINT TONIGHT? THE CHEF'S A BIT CANTANKEROUS, BUT...
HE'S DEDICATED TO GOOD TASTE.
HEY, UH... KEATON?
HI! YOUR NAME'S RUDDY, RIGHT?
OH, YOU'RE CUSTOMERS FROM THE OTHER DAY...
ISN'T THE RESTAURANT BUSY AT THIS HOUR?
YEAH... IT IS.
?
FATHER FIRED HIM.

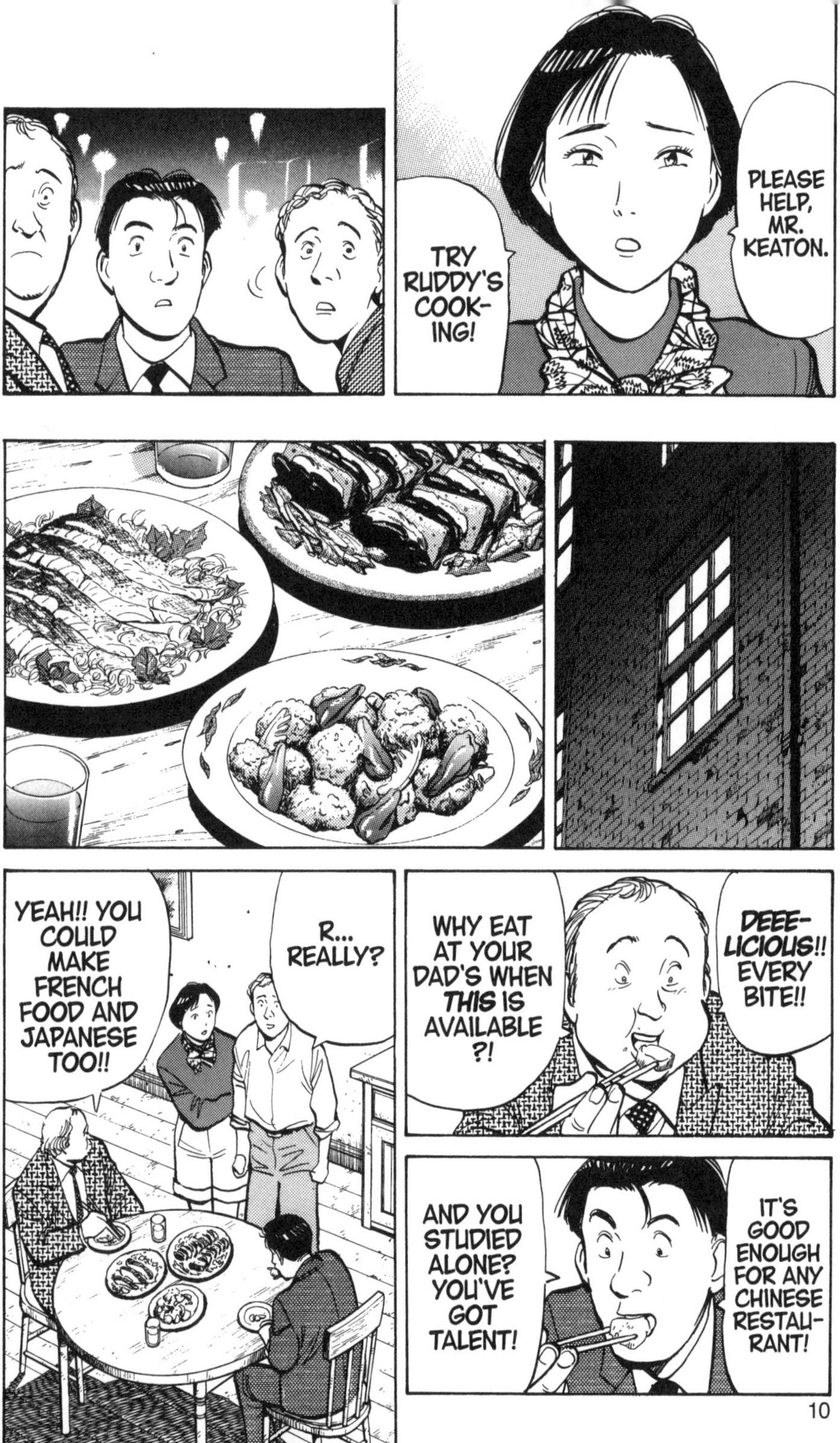
PLEASE HELP, MR. KEATON.
TRY RUDDY'S COOK-ING!
DEEE-LICIOUS!! EVERY BITE!!
WHY EAT AT YOUR DAD'S WHEN THIS IS AVAILABLE?!
IT'S GOOD ENOUGH FOR ANY CHINESE RESTAU-RANT!
AND YOU STUDIED ALONE? YOU'VE GOT TALENT!
R... REALLY?
YEAH!! YOU COULD MAKE FRENCH FOOD AND JAPANESE TOO!!

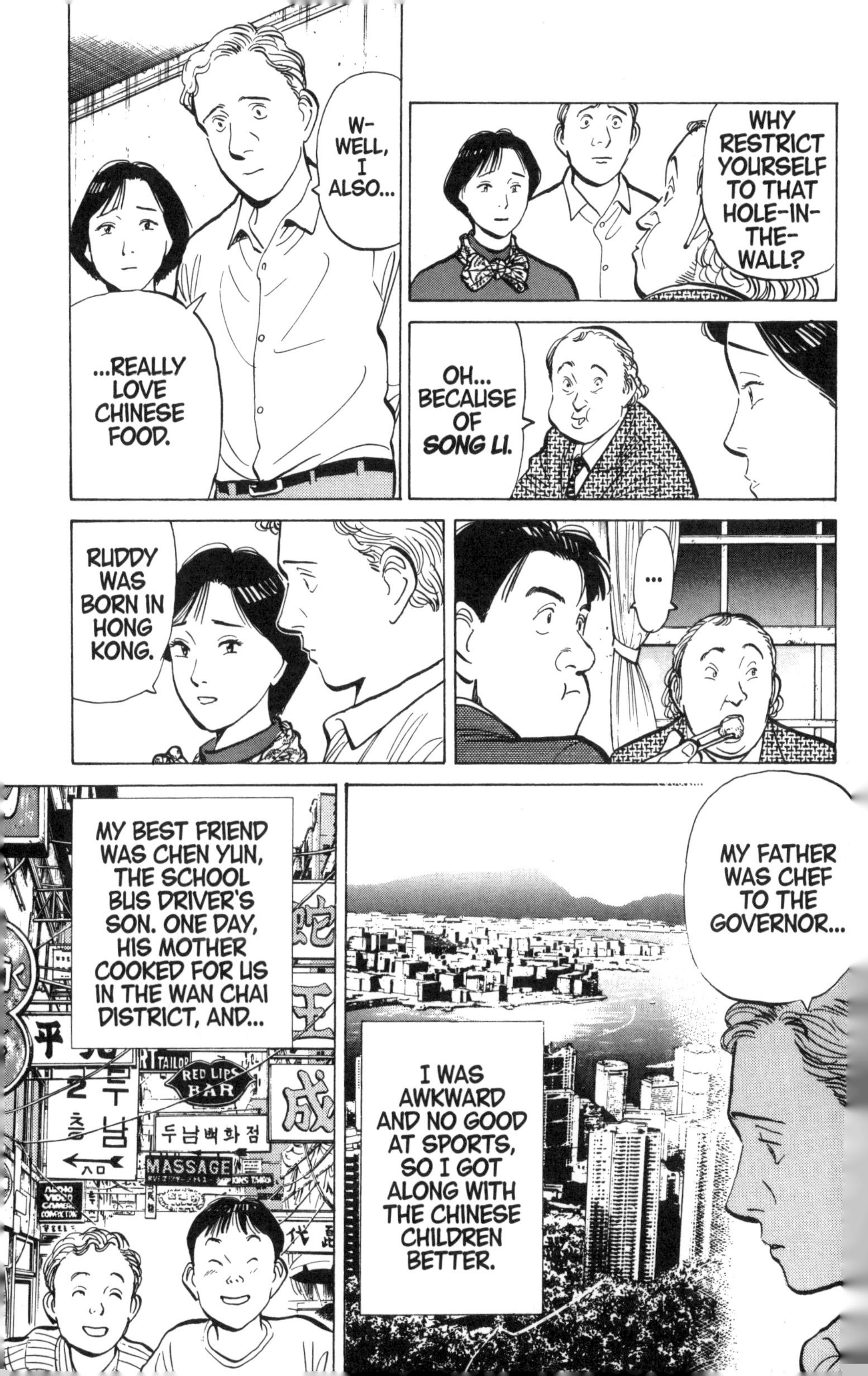
WHY RESTRICT YOURSELF TO THAT HOLE-IN-THE-WALL?
OH... BECAUSE OF SONG LI.
W-WELL, I ALSO...
...REALLY LOVE CHINESE FOOD.
...
RUDDY WAS BORN IN HONG KONG.
MY FATHER WAS CHEF TO THE GOVERNOR...
I WAS AWKWARD AND NO GOOD AT SPORTS, SO I GOT ALONG WITH THE CHINESE CHILDREN BETTER.
MY BEST FRIEND WAS CHEN YUN, THE SCHOOL BUS DRIVER'S SON. ONE DAY, HIS MOTHER COOKED FOR US IN THE WAN CHAI DISTRICT, AND...
RED LIPS BAR
TAILOR
MASSAGE
두남백화점

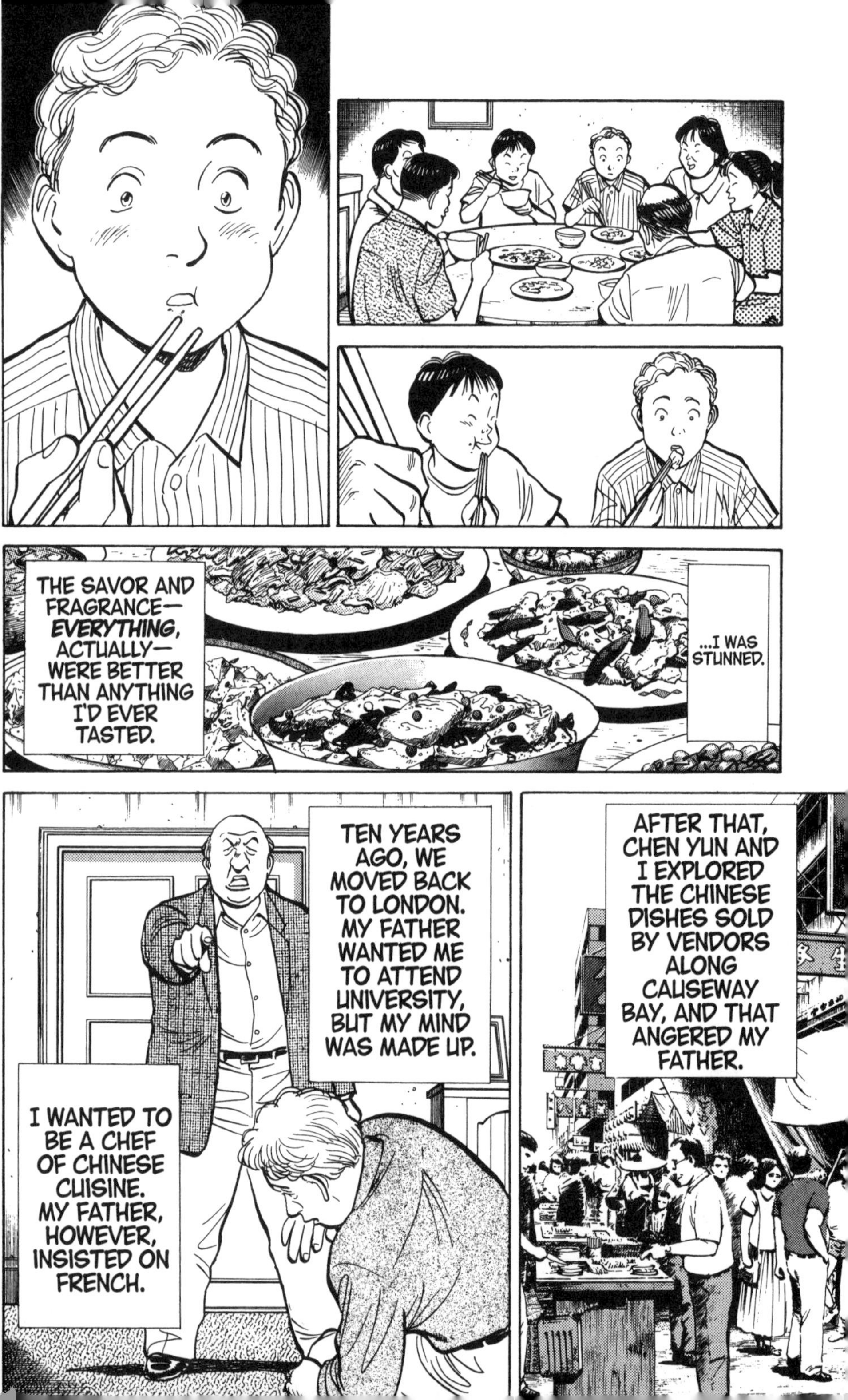
THE SAVOR AND FRAGRANCE—*EVERYTHING*, ACTUALLY—WERE BETTER THAN ANYTHING I'D EVER TASTED.
...I WAS STUNNED.
AFTER THAT, CHEN YUN AND I EXPLORED THE CHINESE DISHES SOLD BY VENDORS ALONG CAUSEWAY BAY, AND THAT ANGERED MY FATHER.
TEN YEARS AGO, WE MOVED BACK TO LONDON. MY FATHER WANTED ME TO ATTEND UNIVERSITY, BUT MY MIND WAS MADE UP.
I WANTED TO BE A CHEF OF CHINESE CUISINE. MY FATHER, HOWEVER, INSISTED ON FRENCH.

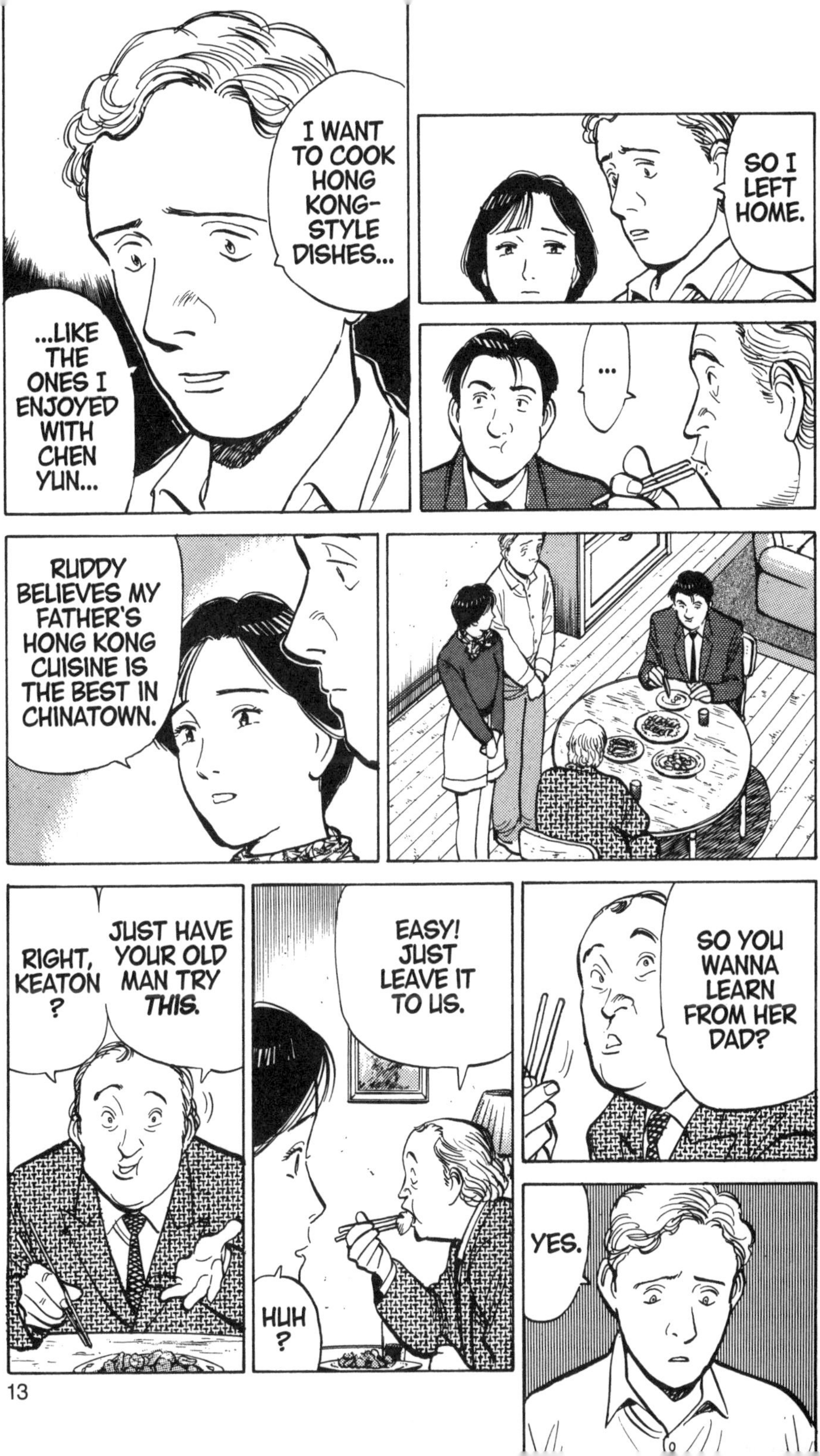
SO I LEFT HOME.
...
I WANT TO COOK HONG KONG-STYLE DISHES...
...LIKE THE ONES I ENJOYED WITH CHEN YUN...
RUDDY BELIEVES MY FATHER'S HONG KONG CUISINE IS THE BEST IN CHINATOWN.
SO YOU WANNA LEARN FROM HER DAD?
YES.
EASY! JUST LEAVE IT TO US.
HUH?
JUST HAVE YOUR OLD MAN TRY *THIS.*
RIGHT, KEATON?

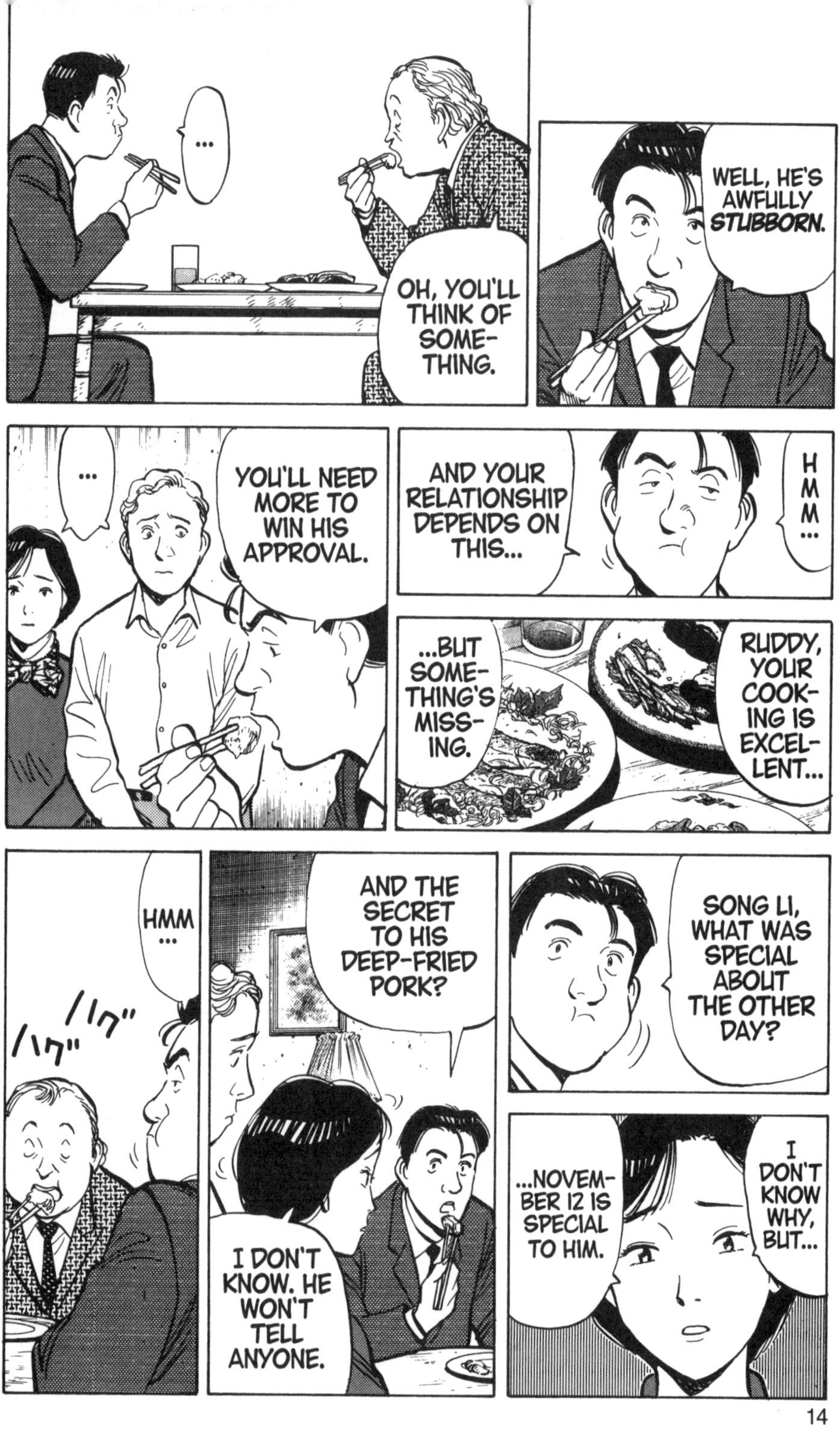
WELL, HE'S AWFULLY STUBBORN.
OH, YOU'LL THINK OF SOME-THING.
...
HMM...
AND YOUR RELATIONSHIP DEPENDS ON THIS...
RUDDY, YOUR COOK-ING IS EXCEL-LENT...
...BUT SOME-THING'S MISS-ING.
YOU'LL NEED MORE TO WIN HIS APPROVAL.
...
SONG LI, WHAT WAS SPECIAL ABOUT THE OTHER DAY?
I DON'T KNOW WHY, BUT...
...NOVEM-BER 12 IS SPECIAL TO HIM.
AND THE SECRET TO HIS DEEP-FRIED PORK?
I DON'T KNOW. HE WON'T TELL ANYONE.
HMM ...
ハグ
ハグ

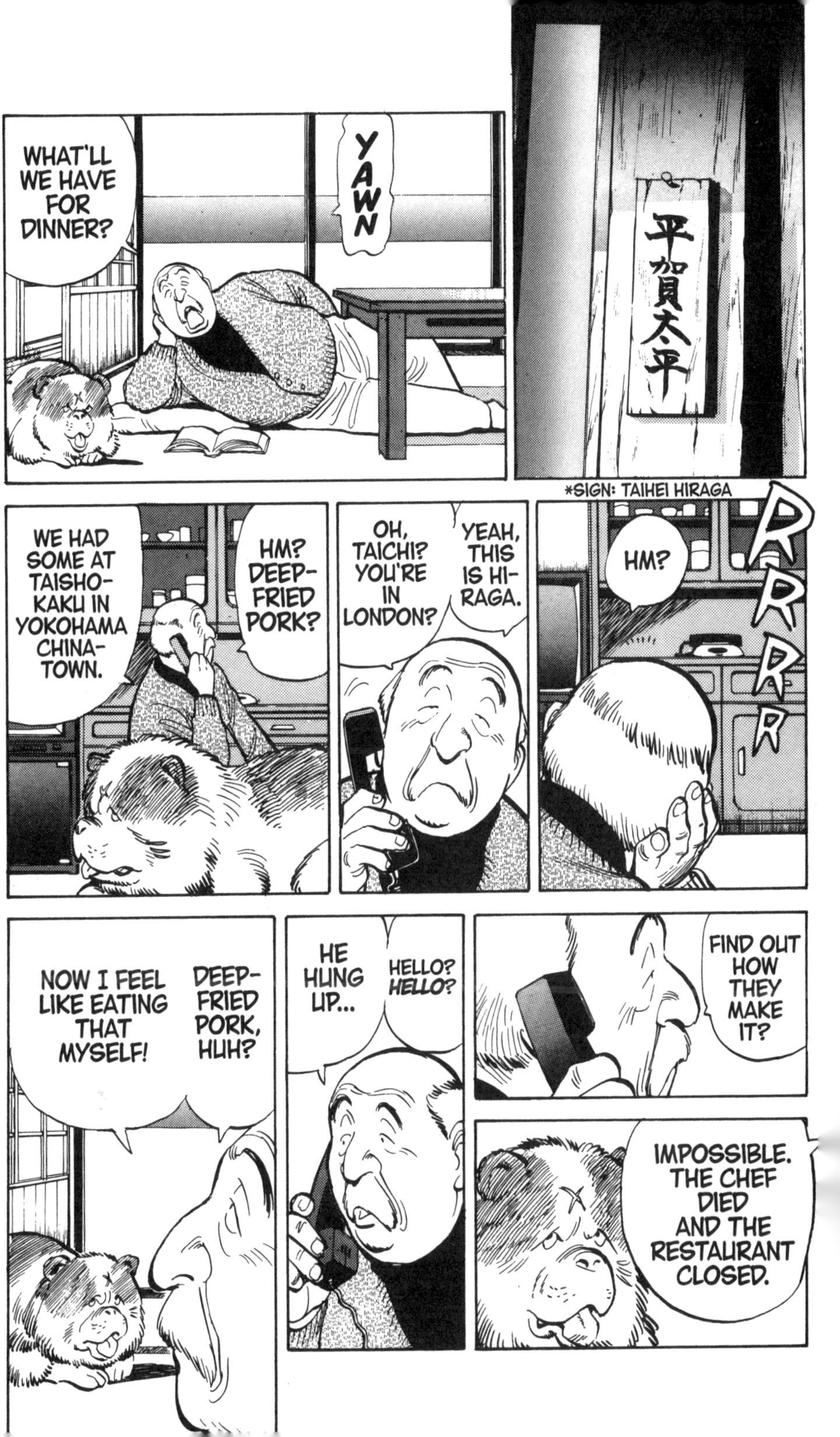
平賀太平
*SIGN: TAIHEI HIRAGA
YAWN
WHAT'LL WE HAVE FOR DINNER?
RRRR
HM?
YEAH, THIS IS HI-RAGA.
OH, TAICHI? YOU'RE IN LONDON?
HM? DEEP-FRIED PORK?
WE HAD SOME AT TAISHO-KAKU IN YOKOHAMA CHINA-TOWN.
FIND OUT HOW THEY MAKE IT?
IMPOSSIBLE. THE CHEF DIED AND THE RESTAURANT CLOSED.
HELLO? *HELLO?*
HE HUNG UP...
DEEP-FRIED PORK, HUH?
NOW I FEEL LIKE EATING THAT MYSELF!

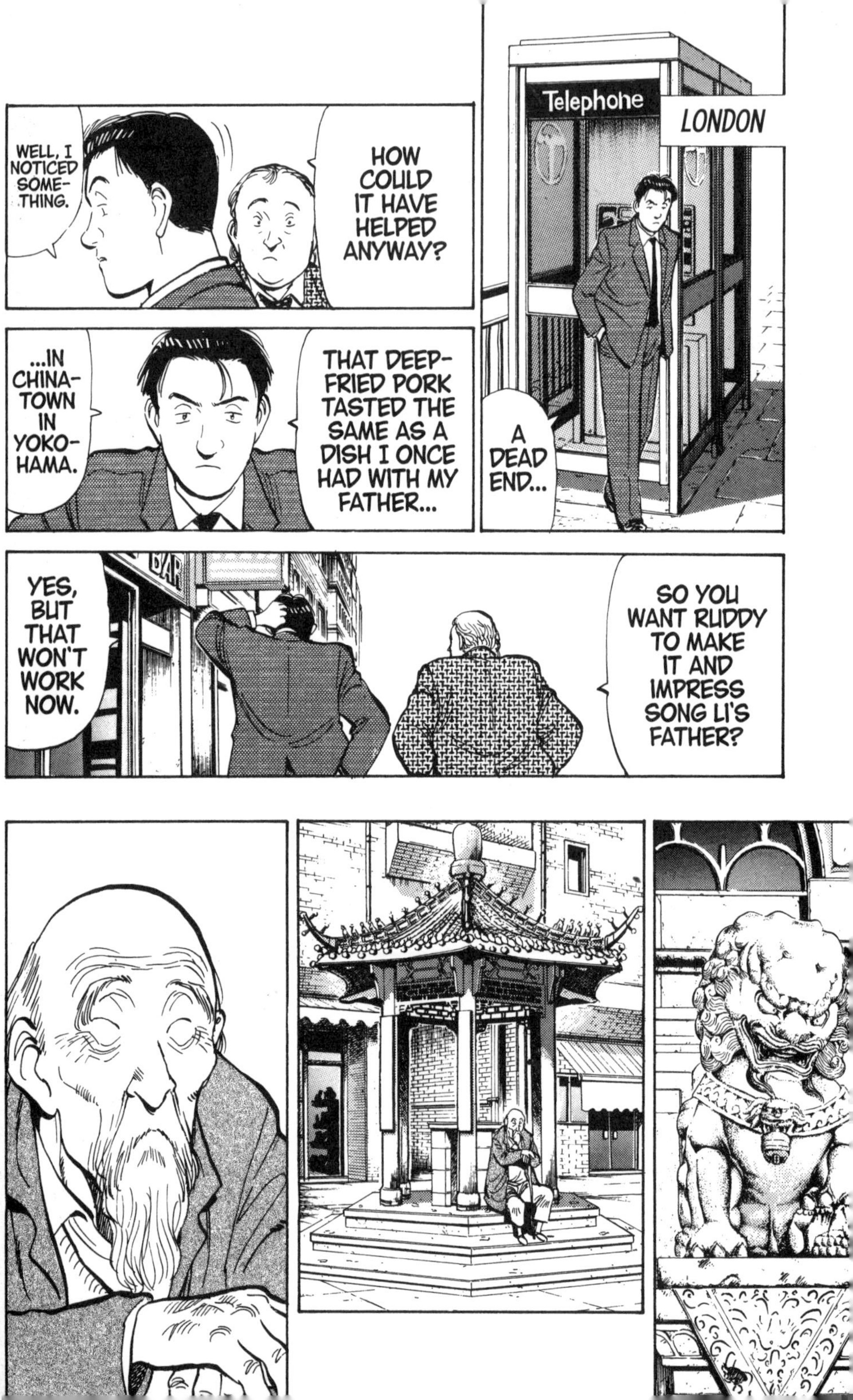
Telephone
LONDON
A DEAD END...
HOW COULD IT HAVE HELPED ANYWAY?
WELL, I NOTICED SOME-THING.
THAT DEEP-FRIED PORK TASTED THE SAME AS A DISH I ONCE HAD WITH MY FATHER...
...IN CHINA-TOWN IN YOKO-HAMA.
SO YOU WANT RUDDY TO MAKE IT AND IMPRESS SONG LI'S FATHER?
YES, BUT THAT WON'T WORK NOW.

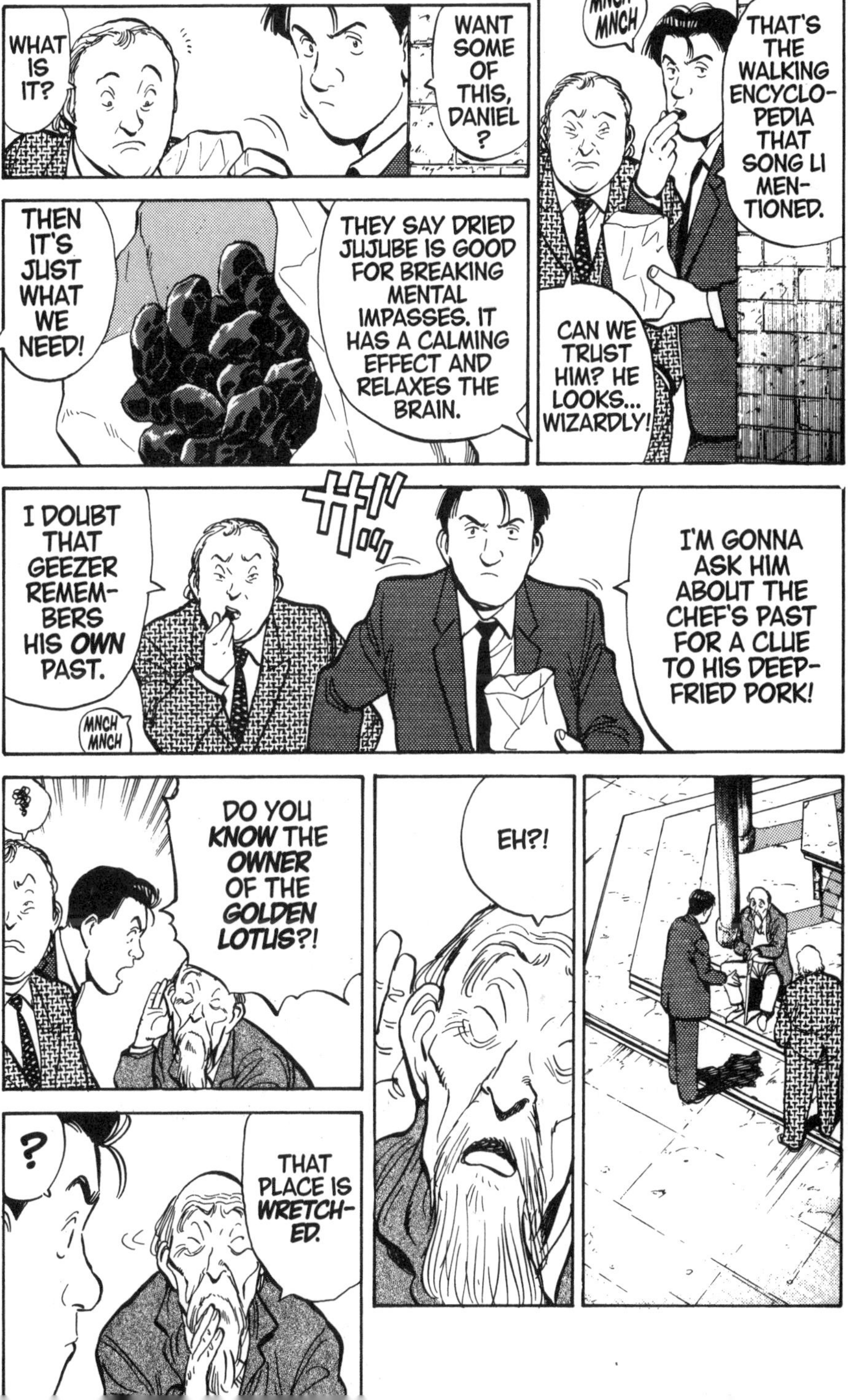
MNCH MNCH
THAT'S THE WALKING ENCYCLOPEDIA THAT SONG LI MENTIONED.
CAN WE TRUST HIM? HE LOOKS... WIZARDLY!
WANT SOME OF THIS, DANIEL?
WHAT IS IT?
THEY SAY DRIED JUJUBE IS GOOD FOR BREAKING MENTAL IMPASSES. IT HAS A CALMING EFFECT AND RELAXES THE BRAIN.
THEN IT'S JUST WHAT WE NEED!
I'M GONNA ASK HIM ABOUT THE CHEF'S PAST FOR A CLUE TO HIS DEEP-FRIED PORK!
I DOUBT THAT GEEZER REMEMBERS HIS **OWN** PAST.
MNCH MNCH
EH?!
DO YOU **KNOW** THE **OWNER** OF THE **GOLDEN LOTUS**?!
?
THAT PLACE IS **WRETCHED**.

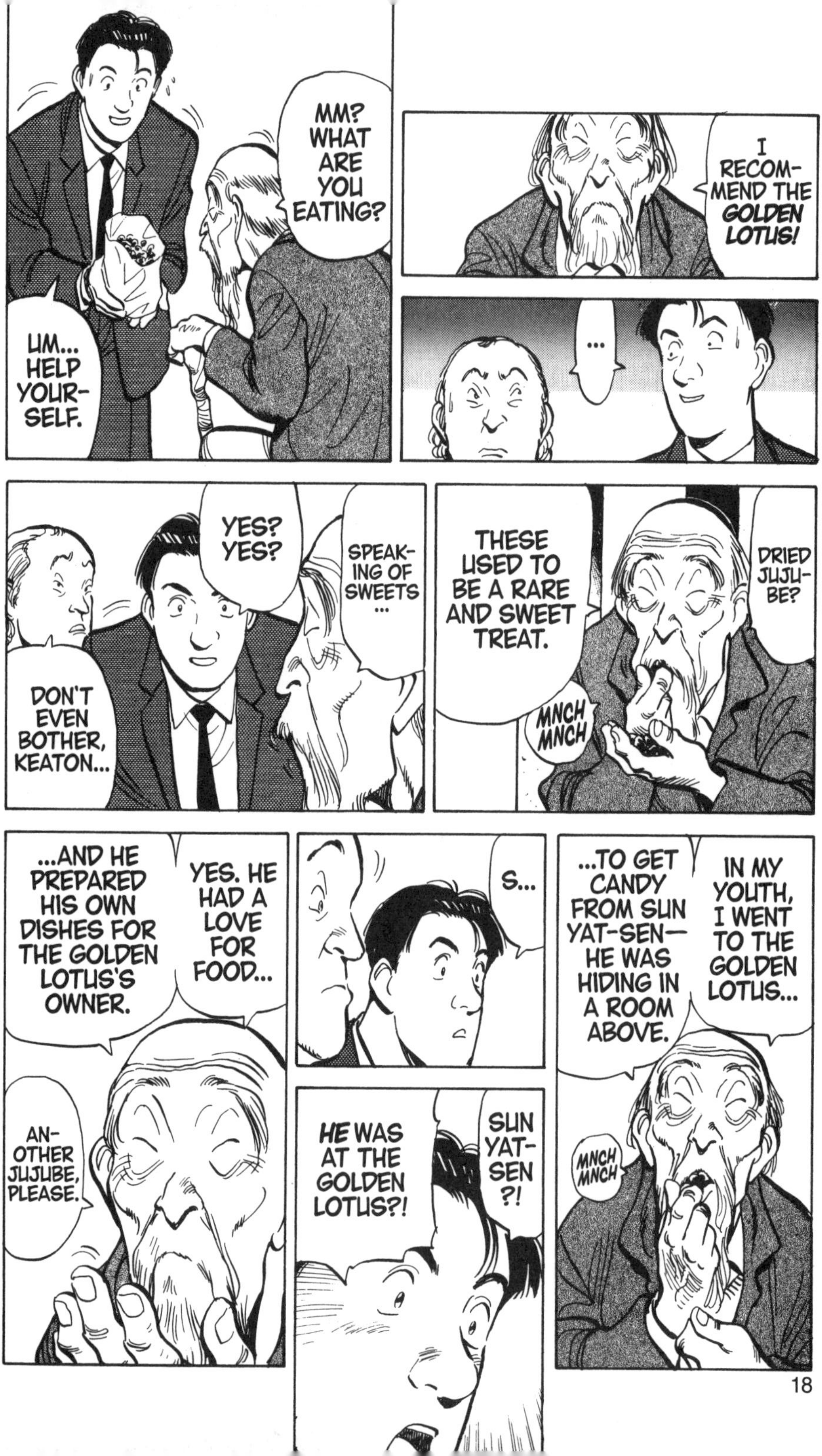
I RECOMMEND THE GOLDEN LOTUS!
...
MM? WHAT ARE YOU EATING?
UM... HELP YOURSELF.
DRIED JUJUBE?
THESE USED TO BE A RARE AND SWEET TREAT.
MNCH MNCH
SPEAKING OF SWEETS...
YES? YES?
DON'T EVEN BOTHER, KEATON...
IN MY YOUTH, I WENT TO THE GOLDEN LOTUS...
...TO GET CANDY FROM SUN YAT-SEN— HE WAS HIDING IN A ROOM ABOVE.
MNCH MNCH
S...
SUN YAT-SEN?!
HE WAS AT THE GOLDEN LOTUS?!
YES. HE HAD A LOVE FOR FOOD...
...AND HE PREPARED HIS OWN DISHES FOR THE GOLDEN LOTUS'S OWNER.
ANOTHER JUJUBE, PLEASE.

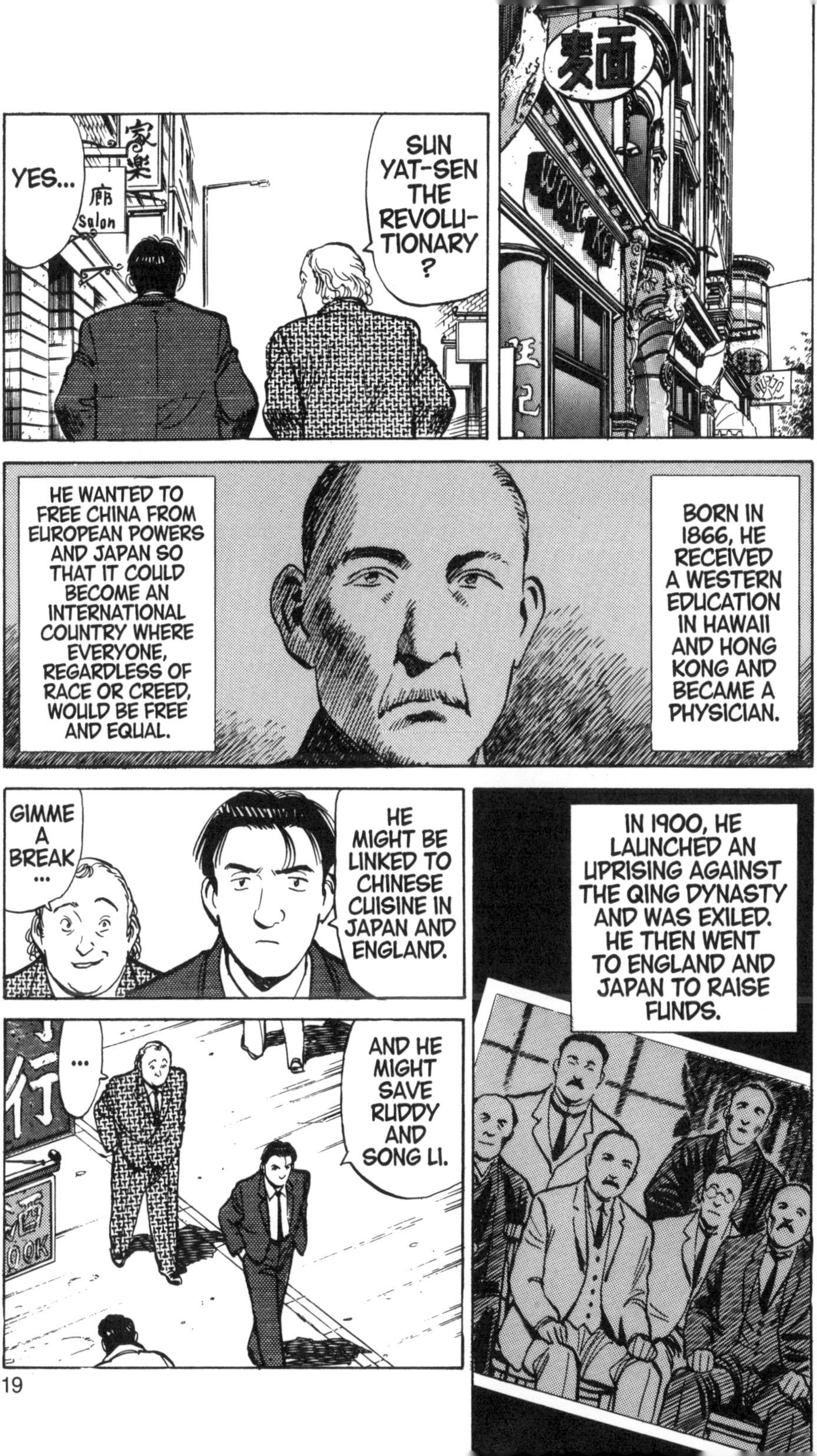
SUN YAT-SEN THE REVOLUTIONARY?
YES...
BORN IN 1866, HE RECEIVED A WESTERN EDUCATION IN HAWAII AND HONG KONG AND BECAME A PHYSICIAN.
HE WANTED TO FREE CHINA FROM EUROPEAN POWERS AND JAPAN SO THAT IT COULD BECOME AN INTERNATIONAL COUNTRY WHERE EVERYONE, REGARDLESS OF RACE OR CREED, WOULD BE FREE AND EQUAL.
IN 1900, HE LAUNCHED AN UPRISING AGAINST THE QING DYNASTY AND WAS EXILED. HE THEN WENT TO ENGLAND AND JAPAN TO RAISE FUNDS.
HE MIGHT BE LINKED TO CHINESE CUISINE IN JAPAN AND ENGLAND.
GIMME A BREAK...
AND HE MIGHT SAVE RUDDY AND SONG LI.
...

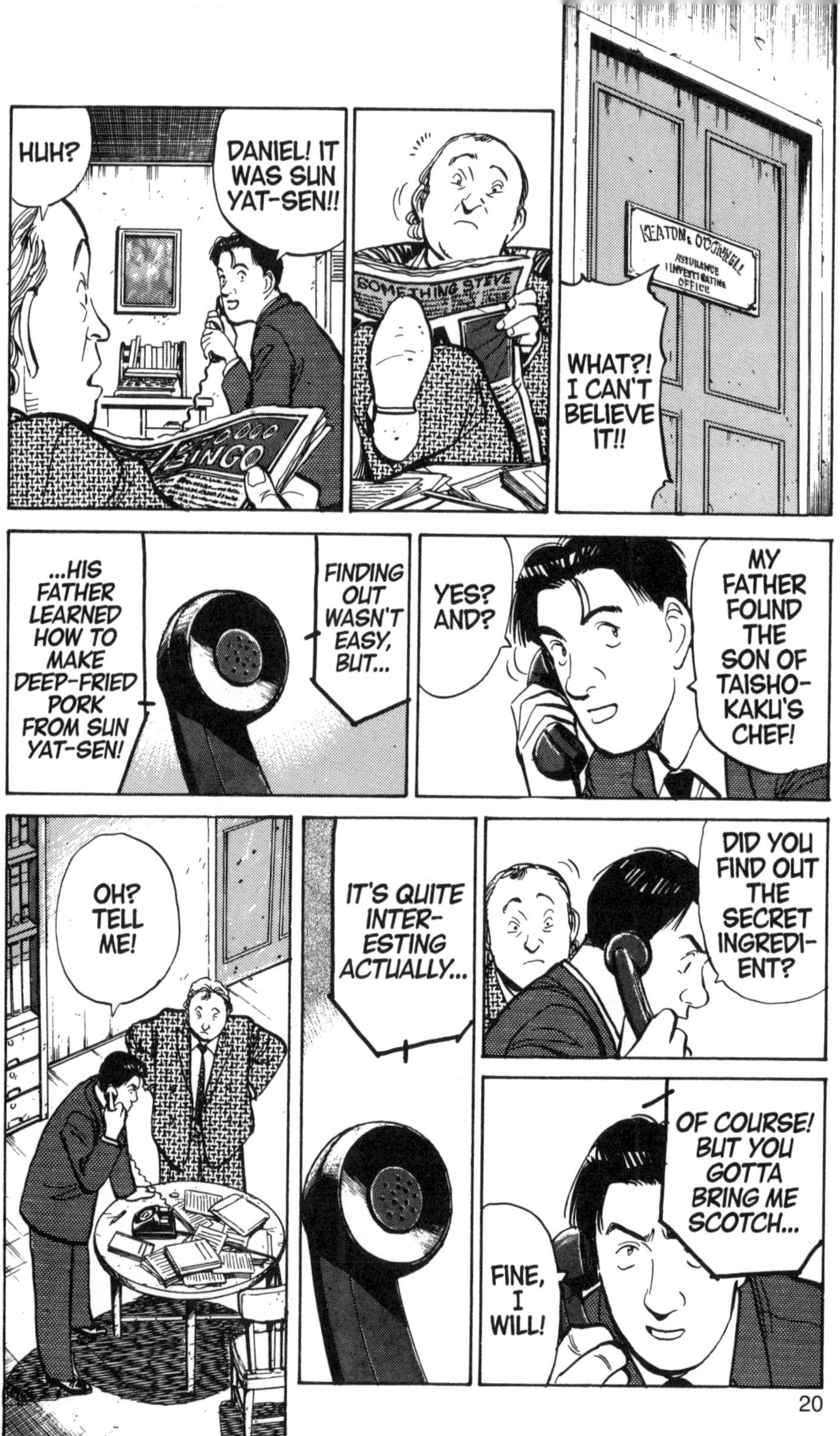
KEATON & O'CONNELL
ASSURANCE INVESTIGATING OFFICE
WHAT?! I CAN'T BELIEVE IT!!
SOMETHING STEVE
DANIEL! IT WAS SUN YAT-SEN!!
HUH?
BINGO
MY FATHER FOUND THE SON OF TAISHO-KAKU'S CHEF!
YES? AND?
FINDING OUT WASN'T EASY, BUT...
...HIS FATHER LEARNED HOW TO MAKE DEEP-FRIED PORK FROM SUN YAT-SEN!
DID YOU FIND OUT THE SECRET INGREDI-ENT?
OF COURSE! BUT YOU GOTTA BRING ME SCOTCH...
FINE, I WILL!
IT'S QUITE INTER-ESTING ACTUALLY...
OH? TELL ME!

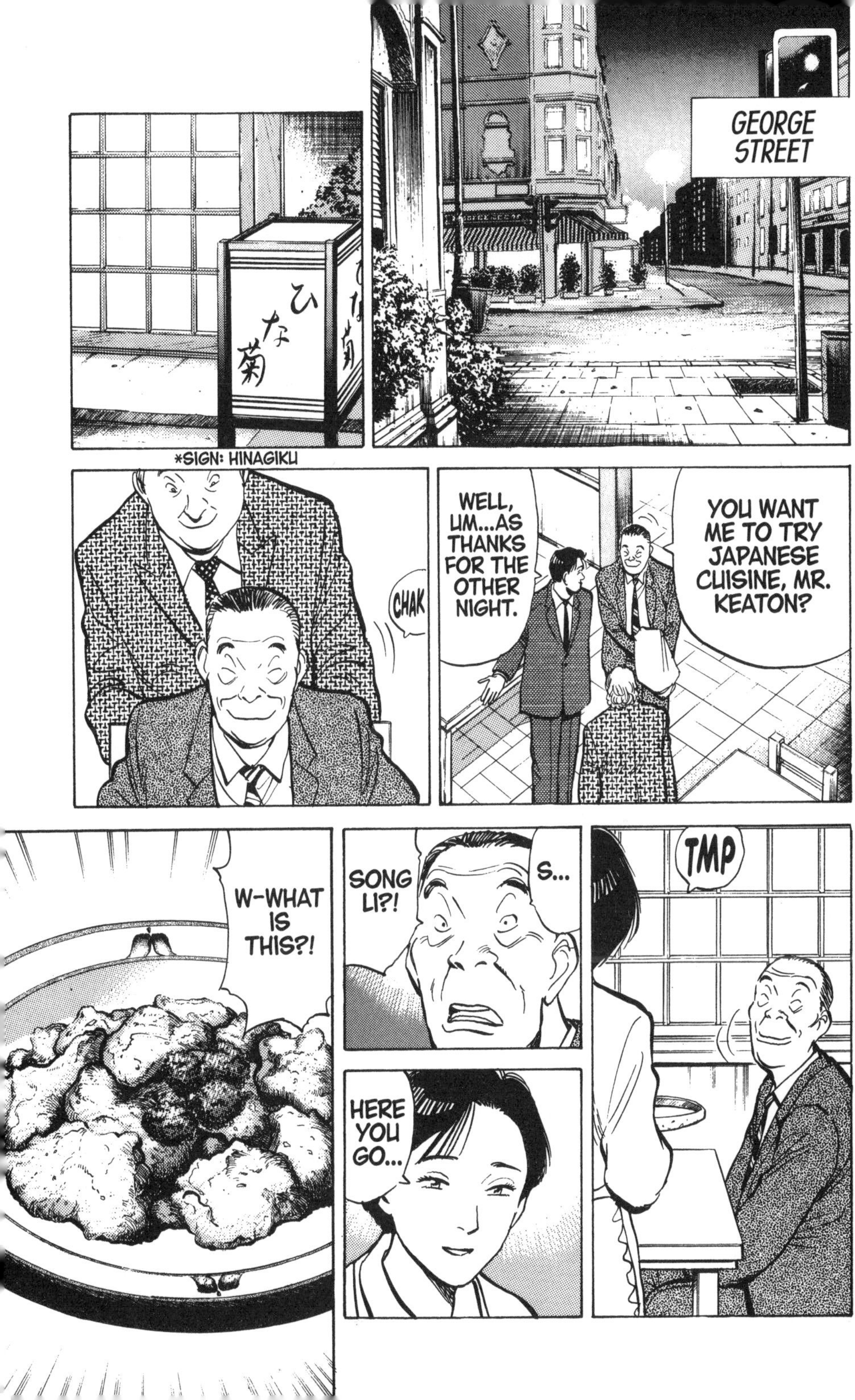
GEORGE STREET
ひな菊
*SIGN: HINAGIKU
YOU WANT ME TO TRY JAPANESE CUISINE, MR. KEATON?
WELL, UM...AS THANKS FOR THE OTHER NIGHT.
CHAK
TMP
S...
SONG LI?!
HERE YOU GO...
W-WHAT IS THIS?!

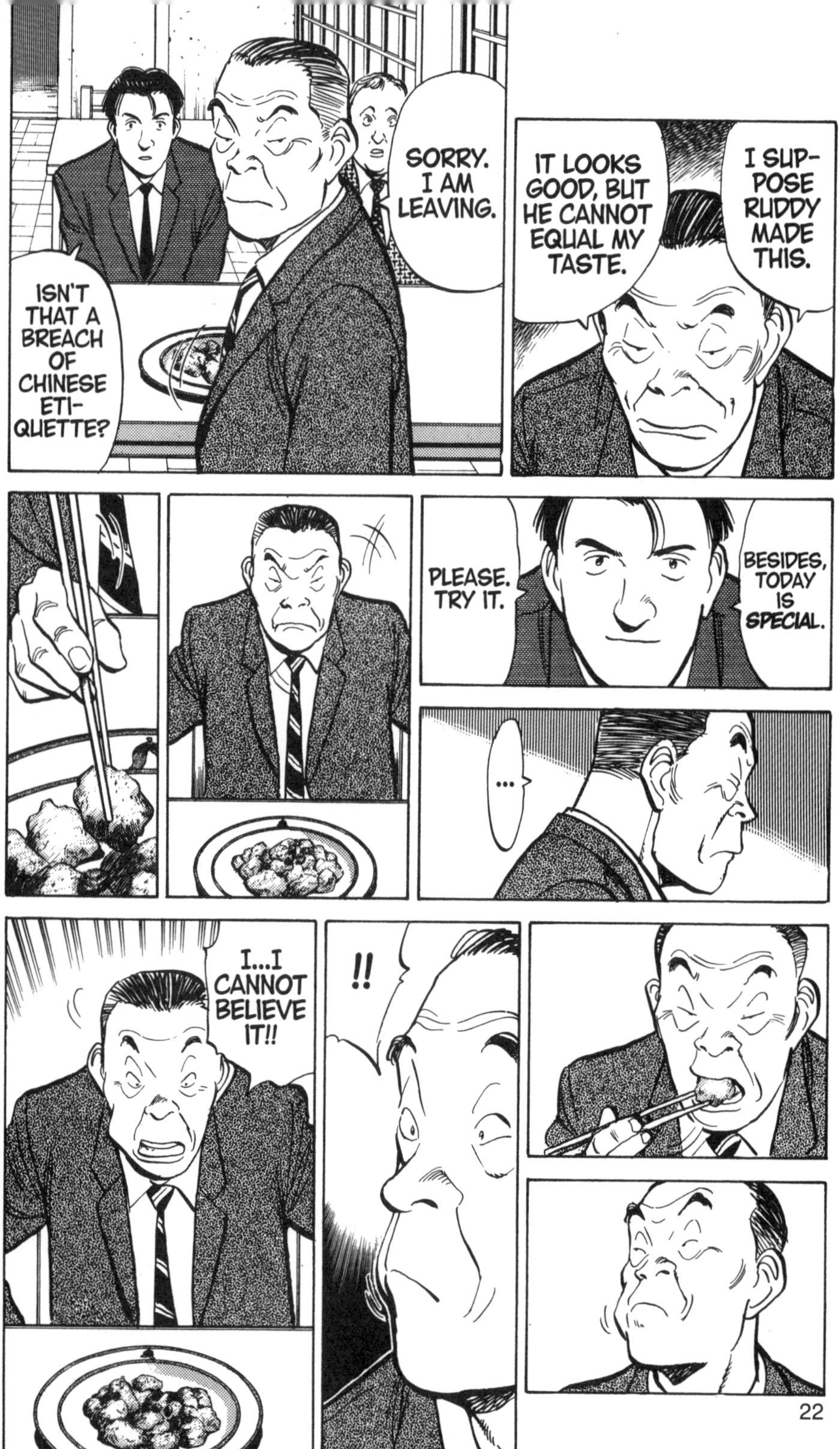
I SUP-
POSE
RUDDY
MADE
THIS.
IT LOOKS GOOD, BUT HE CANNOT EQUAL MY TASTE.
SORRY. I AM LEAVING.
ISN'T THAT A BREACH OF CHINESE ETI-
QUETTE?
BESIDES, TODAY IS SPECIAL.
PLEASE. TRY IT.
...
!!
I...I CANNOT BELIEVE IT!!

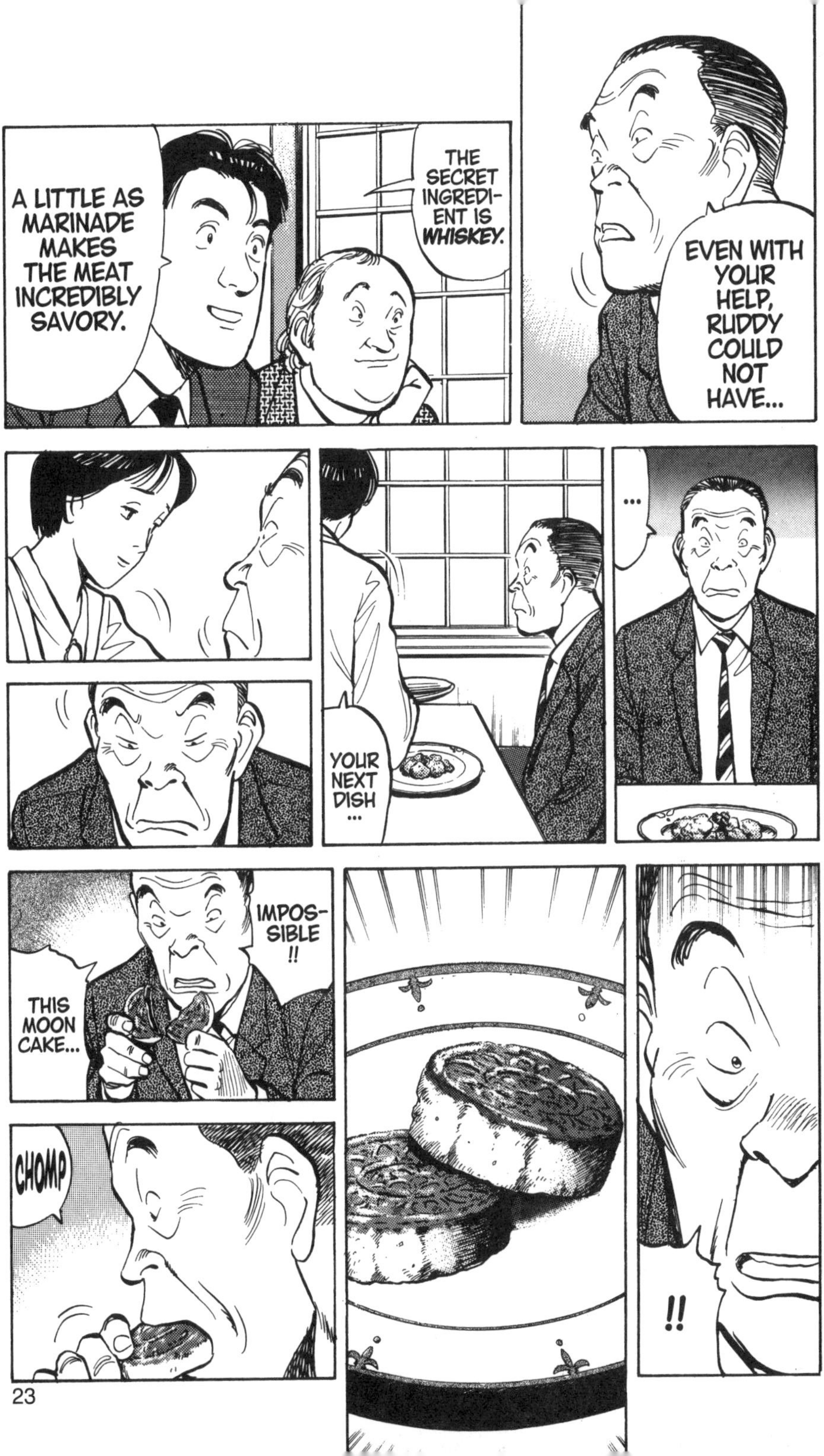
EVEN WITH YOUR HELP, RUDDY COULD NOT HAVE...
THE SECRET INGREDIENT IS WHISKEY.
A LITTLE AS MARINADE MAKES THE MEAT INCREDIBLY SAVORY.
...
YOUR NEXT DISH ...
!!
IMPOSSIBLE !!
THIS MOON CAKE...
CHOMP

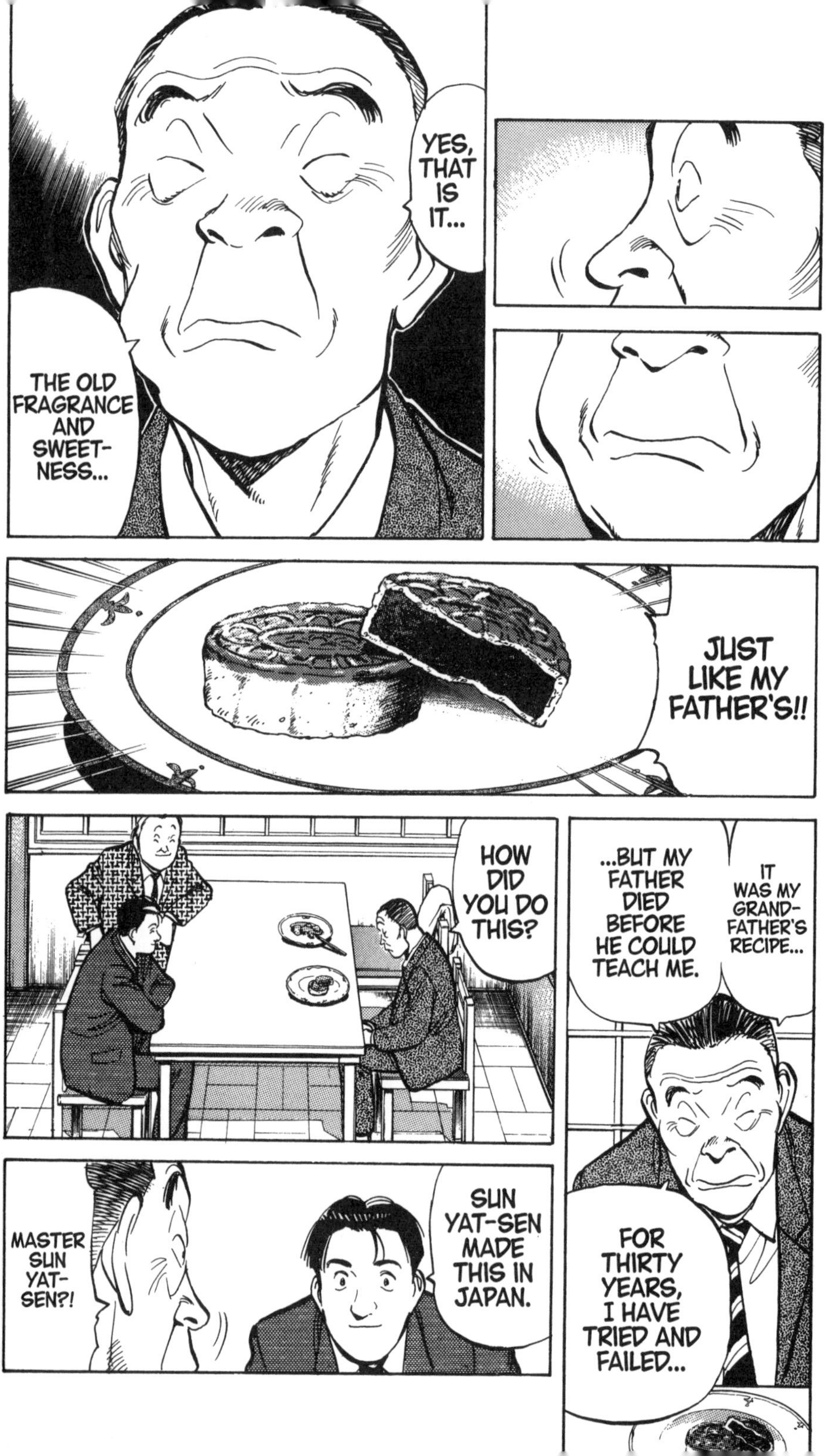
YES, THAT IS IT...
THE OLD FRAGRANCE AND SWEETNESS...
JUST LIKE MY FATHER'S!!
IT WAS MY GRANDFATHER'S RECIPE...
...BUT MY FATHER DIED BEFORE HE COULD TEACH ME.
FOR THIRTY YEARS, I HAVE TRIED AND FAILED...
HOW DID YOU DO THIS?
SUN YAT-SEN MADE THIS IN JAPAN.
MASTER SUN YAT-SEN?!

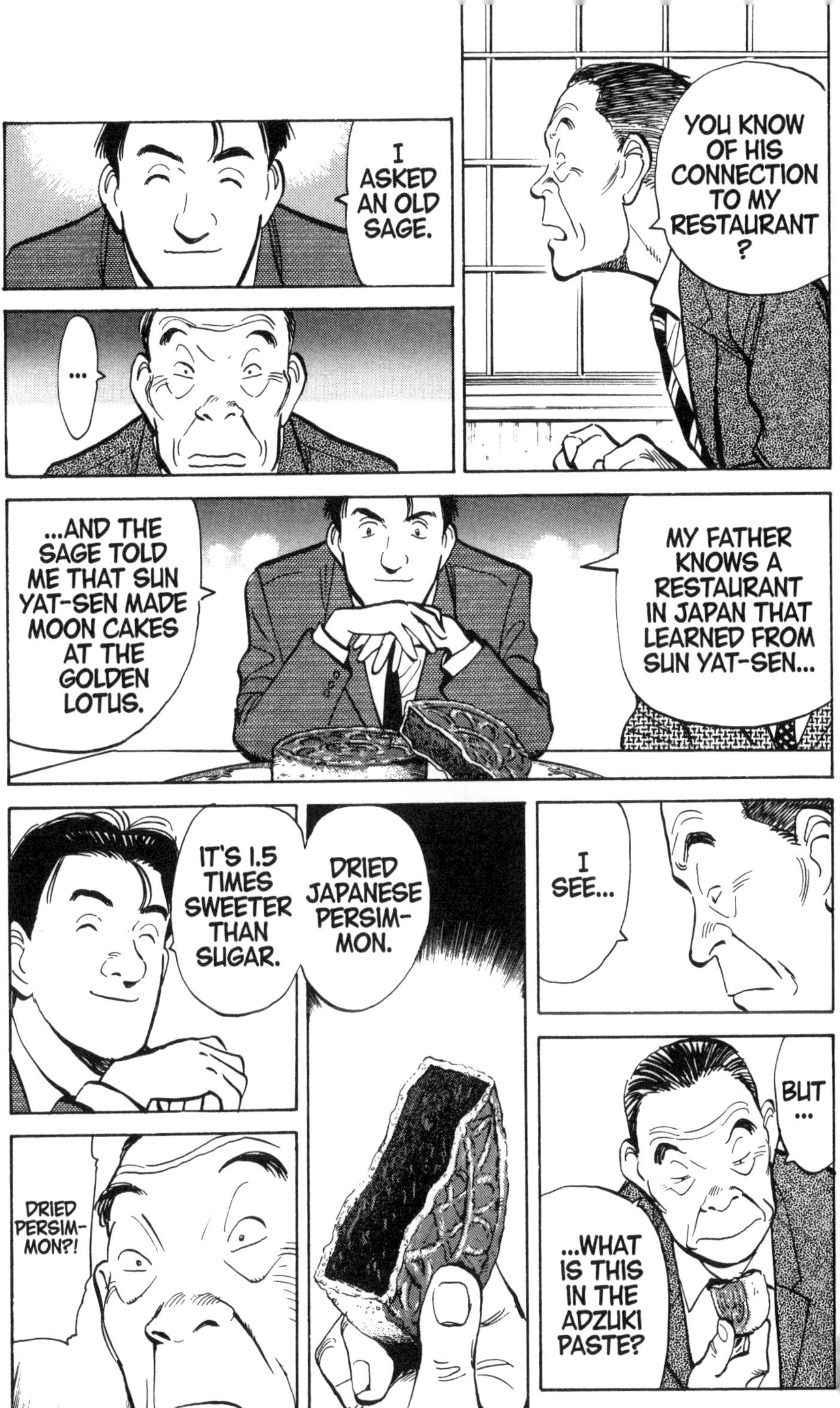
YOU KNOW OF HIS CONNECTION TO MY RESTAURANT ?
I ASKED AN OLD SAGE.
...
MY FATHER KNOWS A RESTAURANT IN JAPAN THAT LEARNED FROM SUN YAT-SEN...
...AND THE SAGE TOLD ME THAT SUN YAT-SEN MADE MOON CAKES AT THE GOLDEN LOTUS.
I SEE...
BUT ...
...WHAT IS THIS IN THE ADZUKI PASTE?
DRIED JAPANESE PERSIM-MON.
IT'S 1.5 TIMES SWEETER THAN SUGAR.
DRIED PERSIM-MON?!

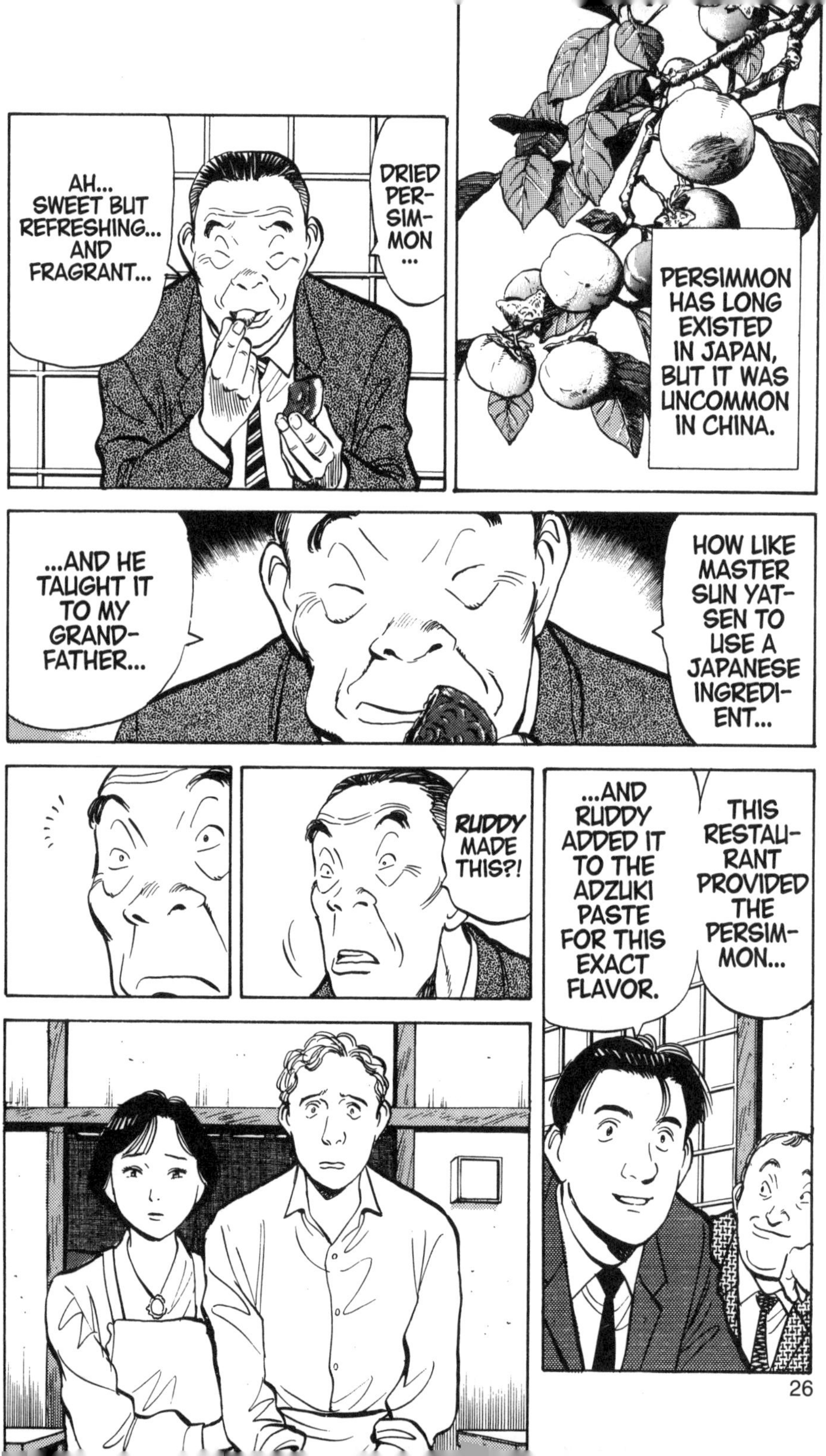
PERSIMMON HAS LONG EXISTED IN JAPAN, BUT IT WAS UNCOMMON IN CHINA.
DRIED PERSIMMON...
AH... SWEET BUT REFRESHING... AND FRAGRANT...
HOW LIKE MASTER SUN YAT-SEN TO USE A JAPANESE INGREDIENT...
...AND HE TAUGHT IT TO MY GRANDFATHER...
THIS RESTAURANT PROVIDED THE PERSIMMON...
...AND RUDDY ADDED IT TO THE ADZUKI PASTE FOR THIS EXACT FLAVOR.
RUDDY MADE THIS?!

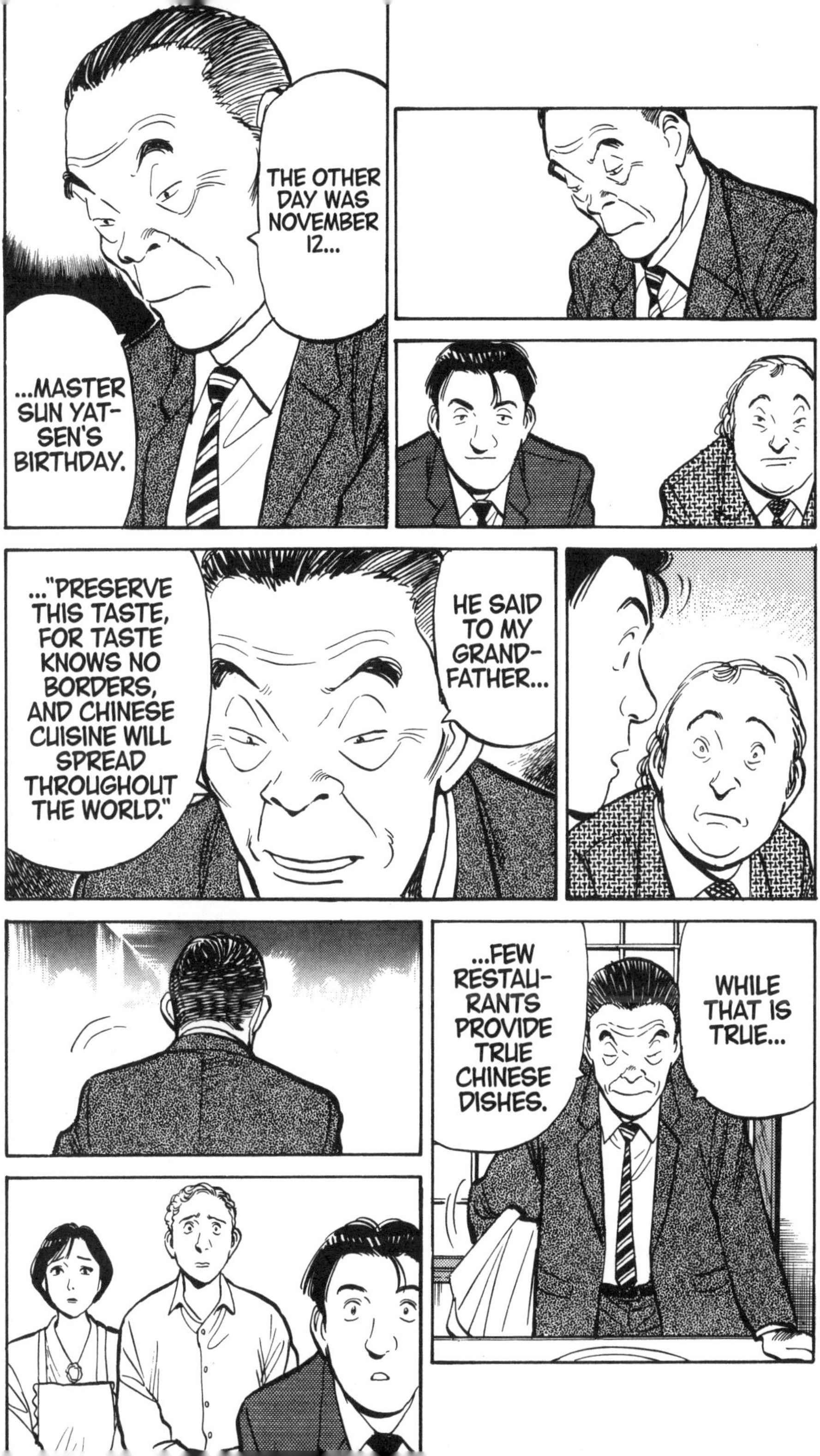
THE OTHER DAY WAS NOVEMBER 12...
...MASTER SUN YAT-SEN'S BIRTHDAY.
HE SAID TO MY GRAND-FATHER...
..."PRESERVE THIS TASTE, FOR TASTE KNOWS NO BORDERS, AND CHINESE CUISINE WILL SPREAD THROUGHOUT THE WORLD."
WHILE THAT IS TRUE...
...FEW RESTAU-RANTS PROVIDE TRUE CHINESE DISHES.

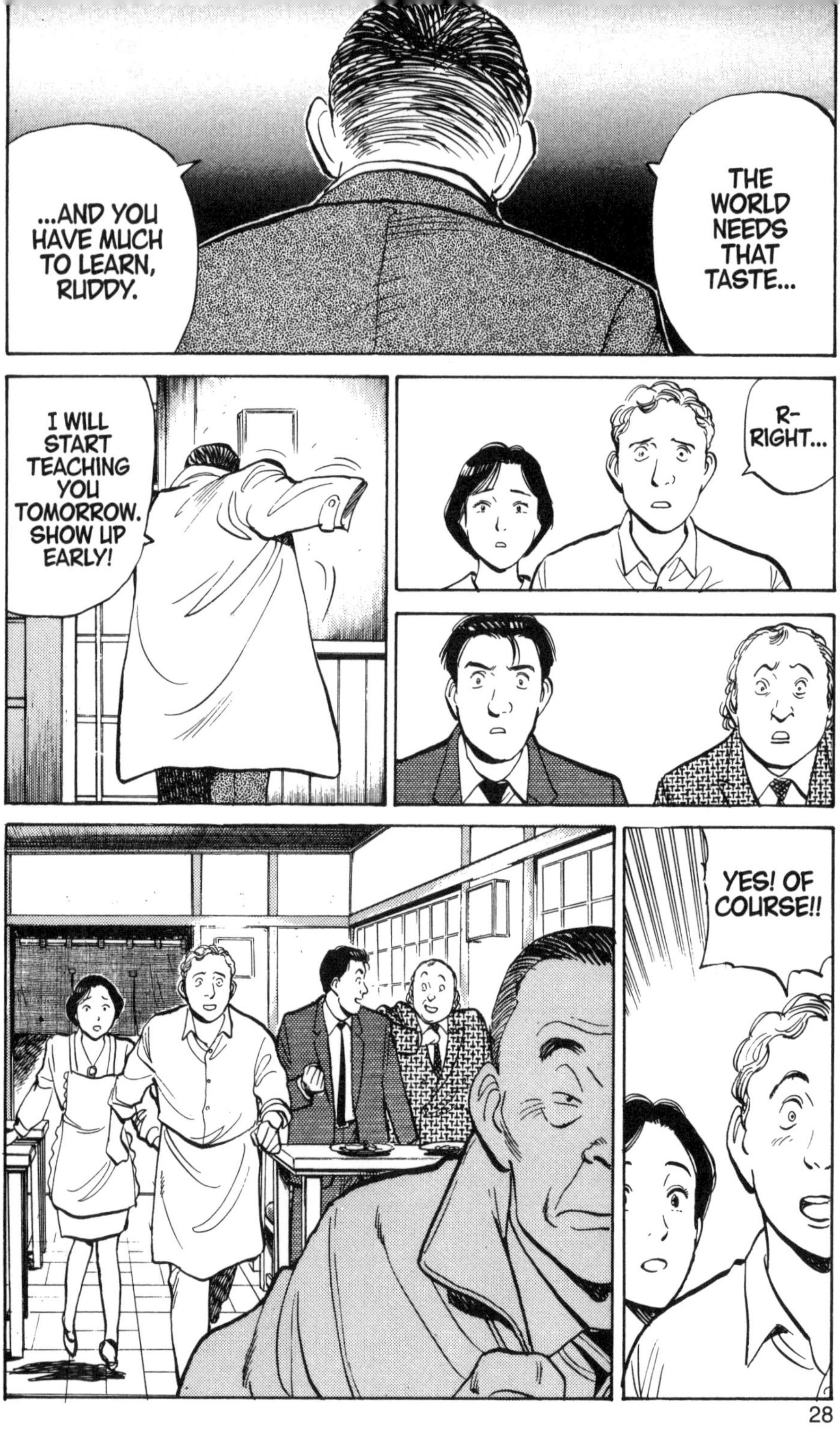
THE WORLD NEEDS THAT TASTE...
...AND YOU HAVE MUCH TO LEARN, RUDDY.
R- RIGHT...
I WILL START TEACHING YOU TOMORROW. SHOW UP EARLY!
YES! OF COURSE!!

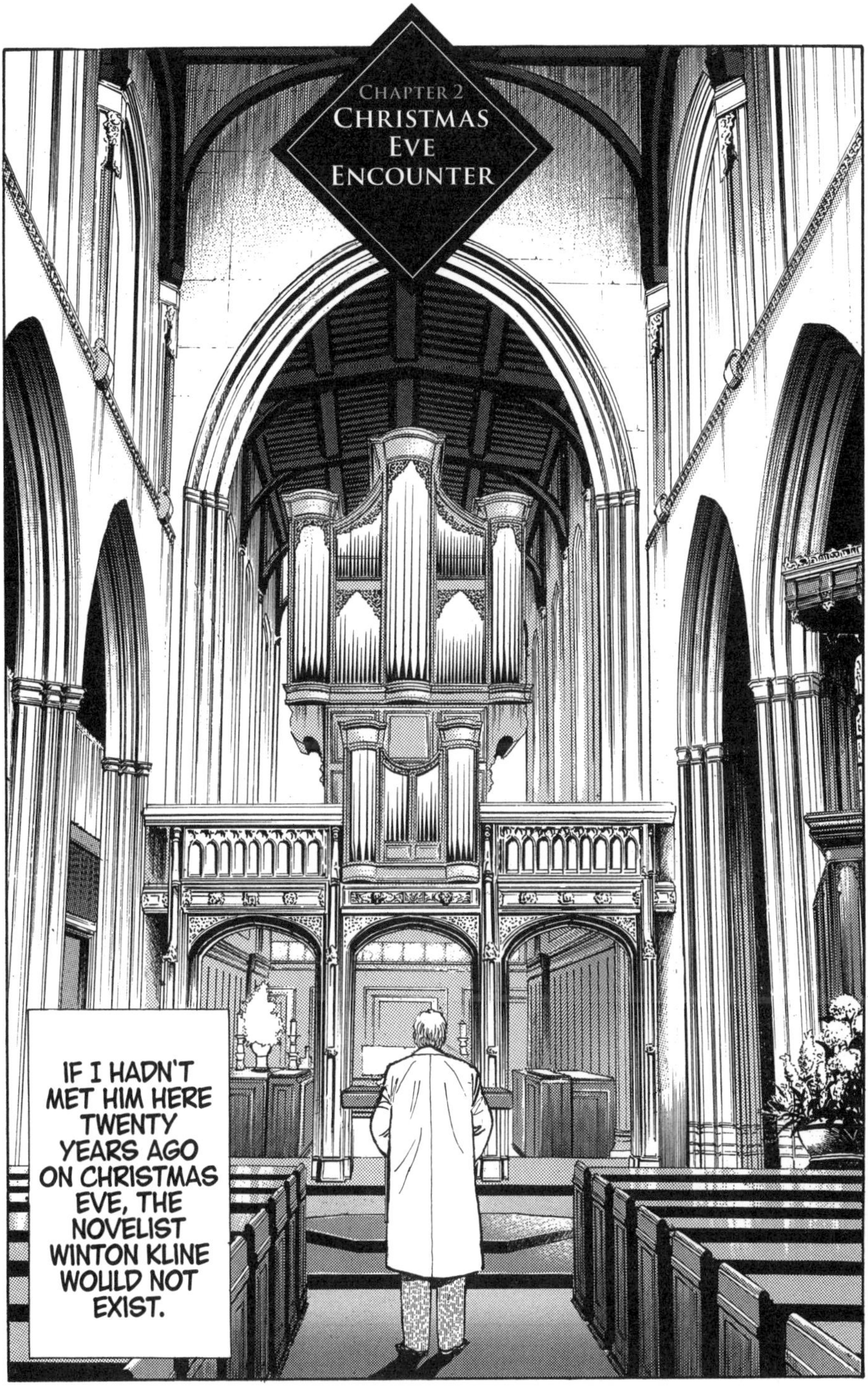
Chapter 2
Christmas Eve Encounter
IF I HADN'T MET HIM HERE TWENTY YEARS AGO ON CHRISTMAS EVE, THE NOVELIST WINTON KLINE WOULD NOT EXIST.

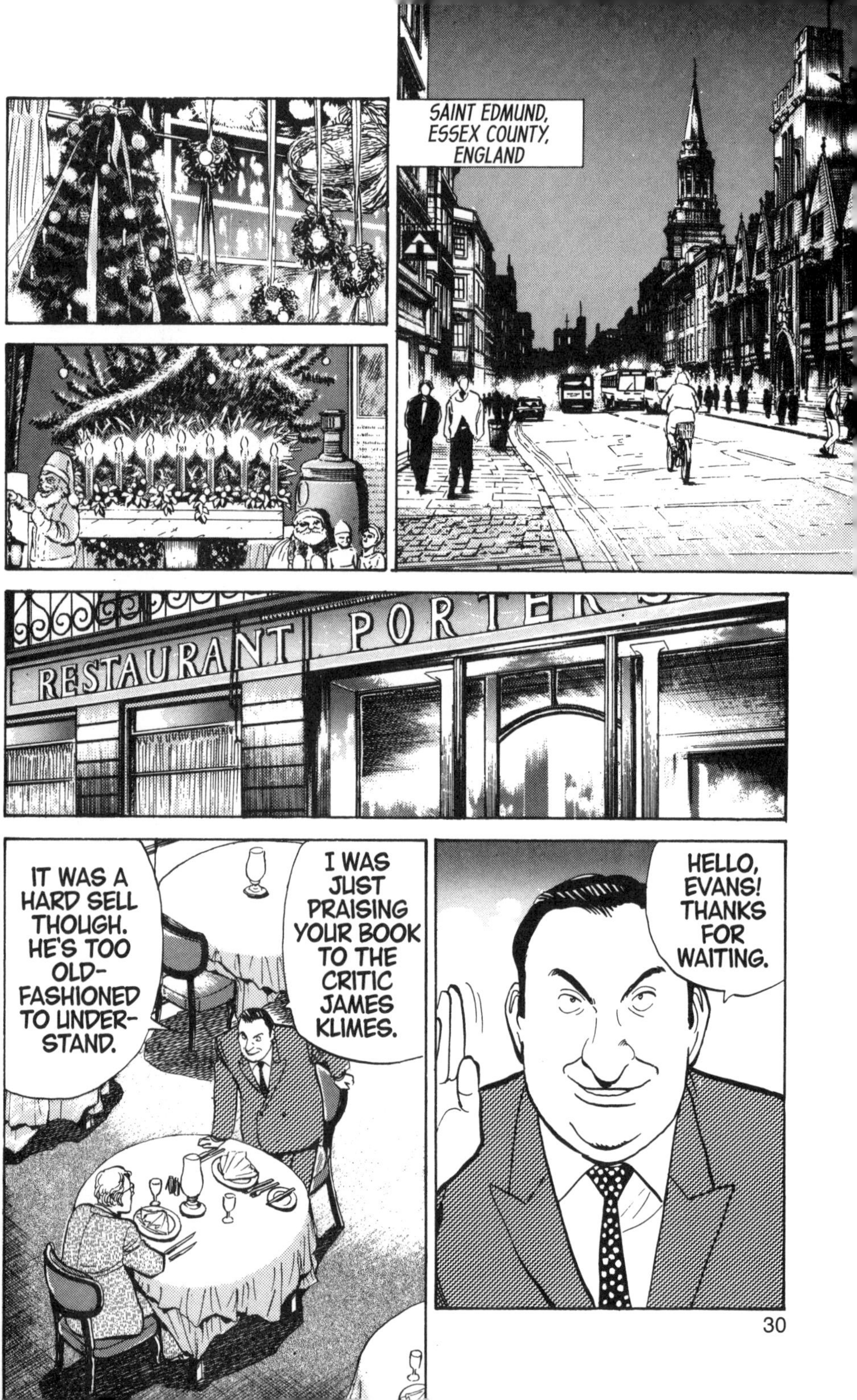
SAINT EDMUND, ESSEX COUNTY, ENGLAND
RESTAURANT PORTER
HELLO, EVANS! THANKS FOR WAITING.
I WAS JUST PRAISING YOUR BOOK TO THE CRITIC JAMES KLIMES.
IT WAS A HARD SELL THOUGH. HE'S TOO OLD-FASHIONED TO UNDER-STAND.

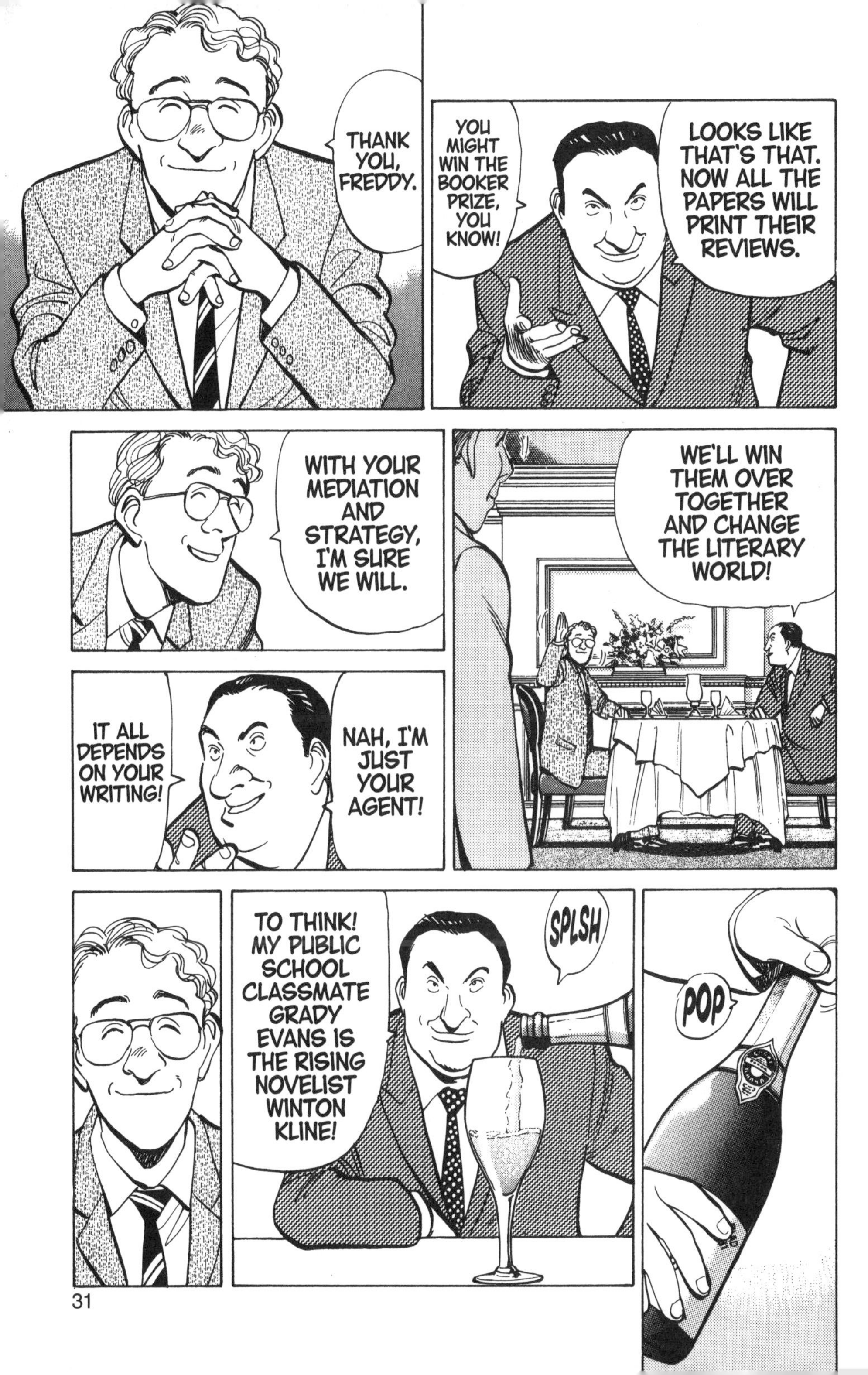
LOOKS LIKE THAT'S THAT. NOW ALL THE PAPERS WILL PRINT THEIR REVIEWS.
YOU MIGHT WIN THE BOOKER PRIZE, YOU KNOW!
THANK YOU, FREDDY.
WE'LL WIN THEM OVER TOGETHER AND CHANGE THE LITERARY WORLD!
WITH YOUR MEDIATION AND STRATEGY, I'M SURE WE WILL.
NAH, I'M JUST YOUR AGENT!
IT ALL DEPENDS ON YOUR WRITING!
POP
SPLSH
TO THINK! MY PUBLIC SCHOOL CLASSMATE GRADY EVANS IS THE RISING NOVELIST WINTON KLINE!

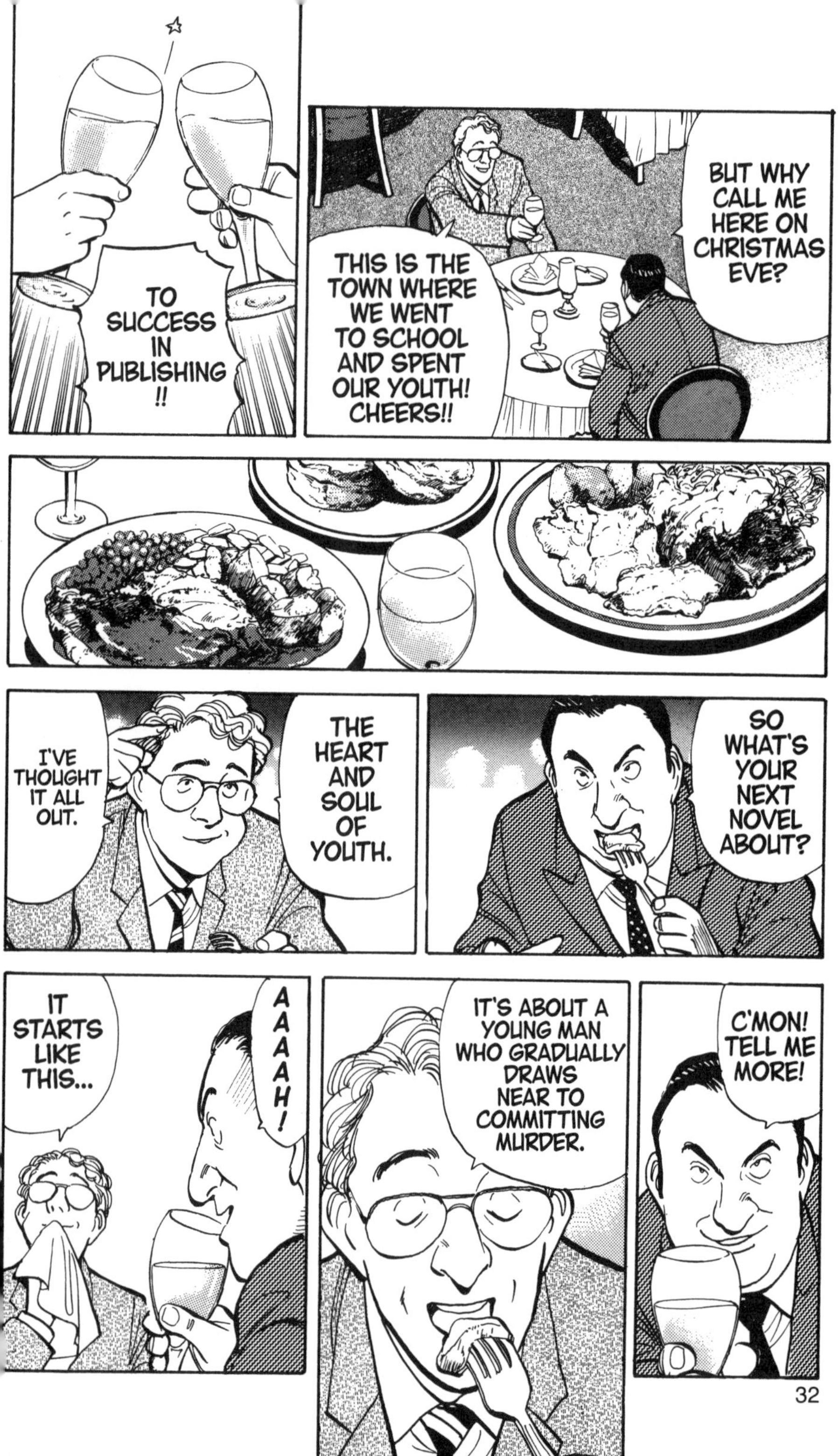
BUT WHY CALL ME HERE ON CHRISTMAS EVE?
THIS IS THE TOWN WHERE WE WENT TO SCHOOL AND SPENT OUR YOUTH! CHEERS!!
TO SUCCESS IN PUBLISHING!!
SO WHAT'S YOUR NEXT NOVEL ABOUT?
THE HEART AND SOUL OF YOUTH.
I'VE THOUGHT IT ALL OUT.
C'MON! TELL ME MORE!
IT'S ABOUT A YOUNG MAN WHO GRADUALLY DRAWS NEAR TO COMMITTING MURDER.
AAAAH!
IT STARTS LIKE THIS...

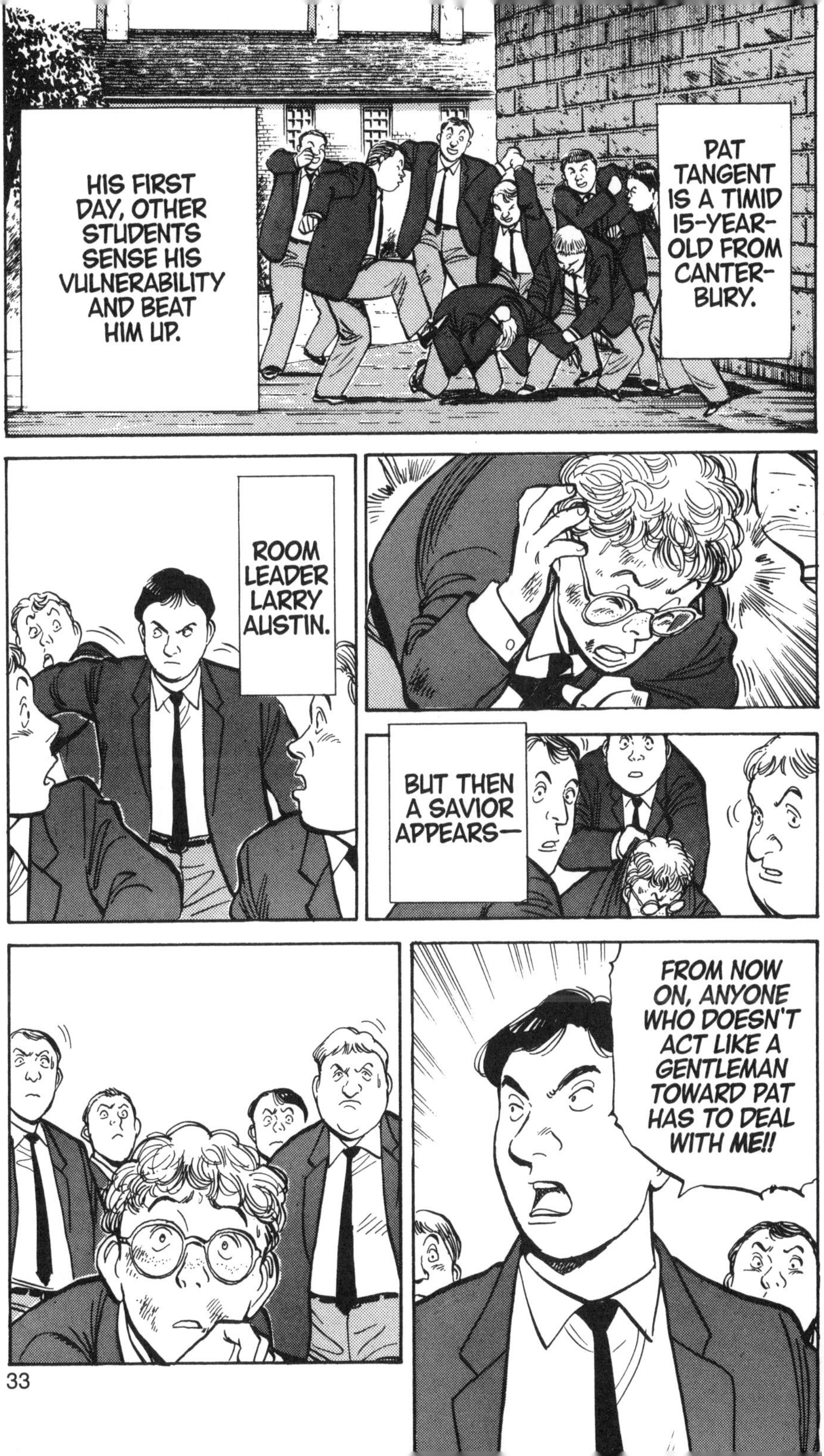
PAT TANGENT IS A TIMID 15-YEAR-OLD FROM CANTERBURY.
HIS FIRST DAY, OTHER STUDENTS SENSE HIS VULNERABILITY AND BEAT HIM UP.
BUT THEN A SAVIOR APPEARS—
ROOM LEADER LARRY AUSTIN.
FROM NOW ON, ANYONE WHO DOESN'T ACT LIKE A GENTLEMAN TOWARD PAT HAS TO DEAL WITH ME!!

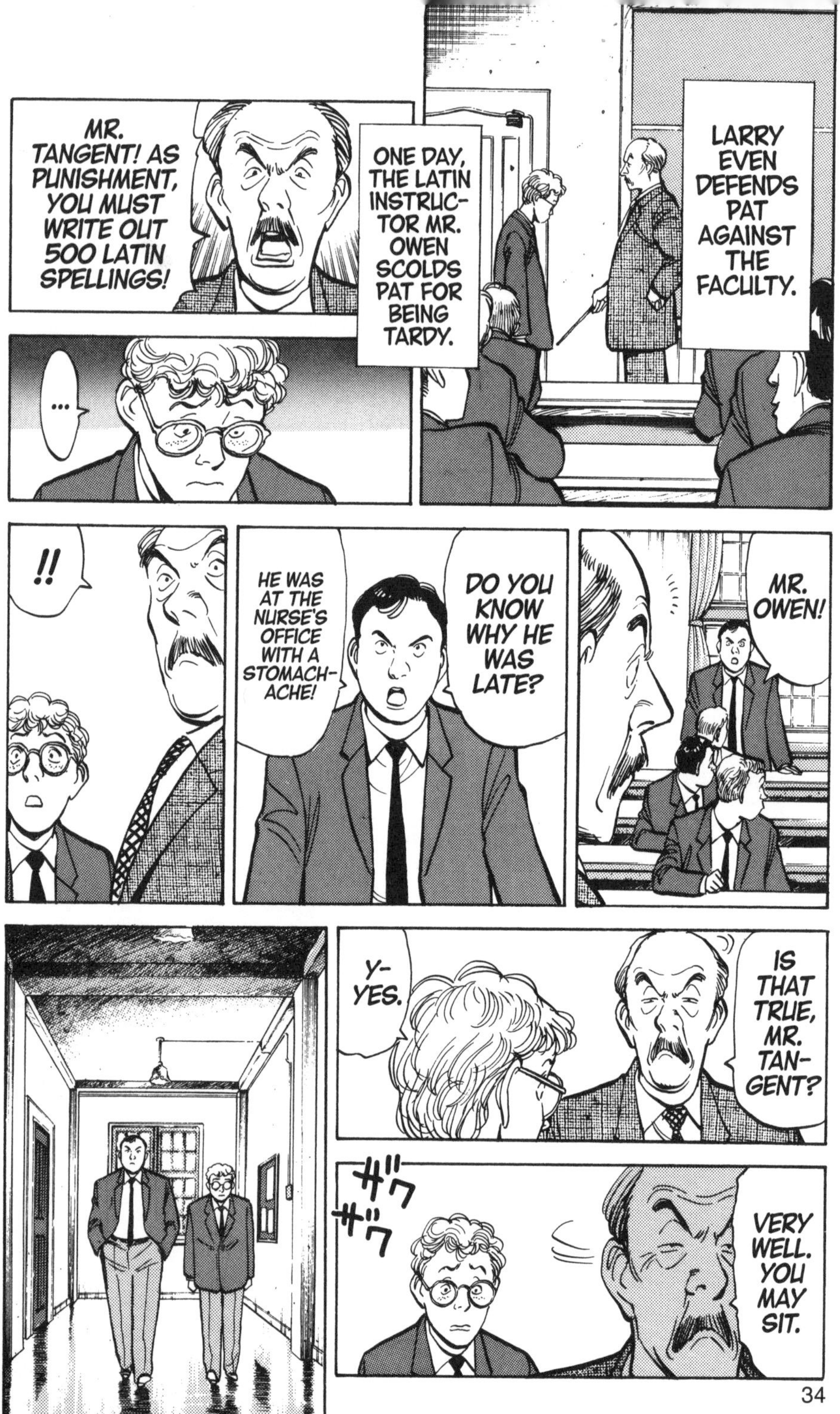
LARRY EVEN DEFENDS PAT AGAINST THE FACULTY.
ONE DAY, THE LATIN INSTRUCTOR MR. OWEN SCOLDS PAT FOR BEING TARDY.
MR. TANGENT! AS PUNISHMENT, YOU MUST WRITE OUT 500 LATIN SPELLINGS!
...
MR. OWEN!
DO YOU KNOW WHY HE WAS LATE?
HE WAS AT THE NURSE'S OFFICE WITH A STOMACHACHE!
!!
IS THAT TRUE, MR. TANGENT?
Y-YES.
VERY WELL. YOU MAY SIT.
ザワ
ザワ

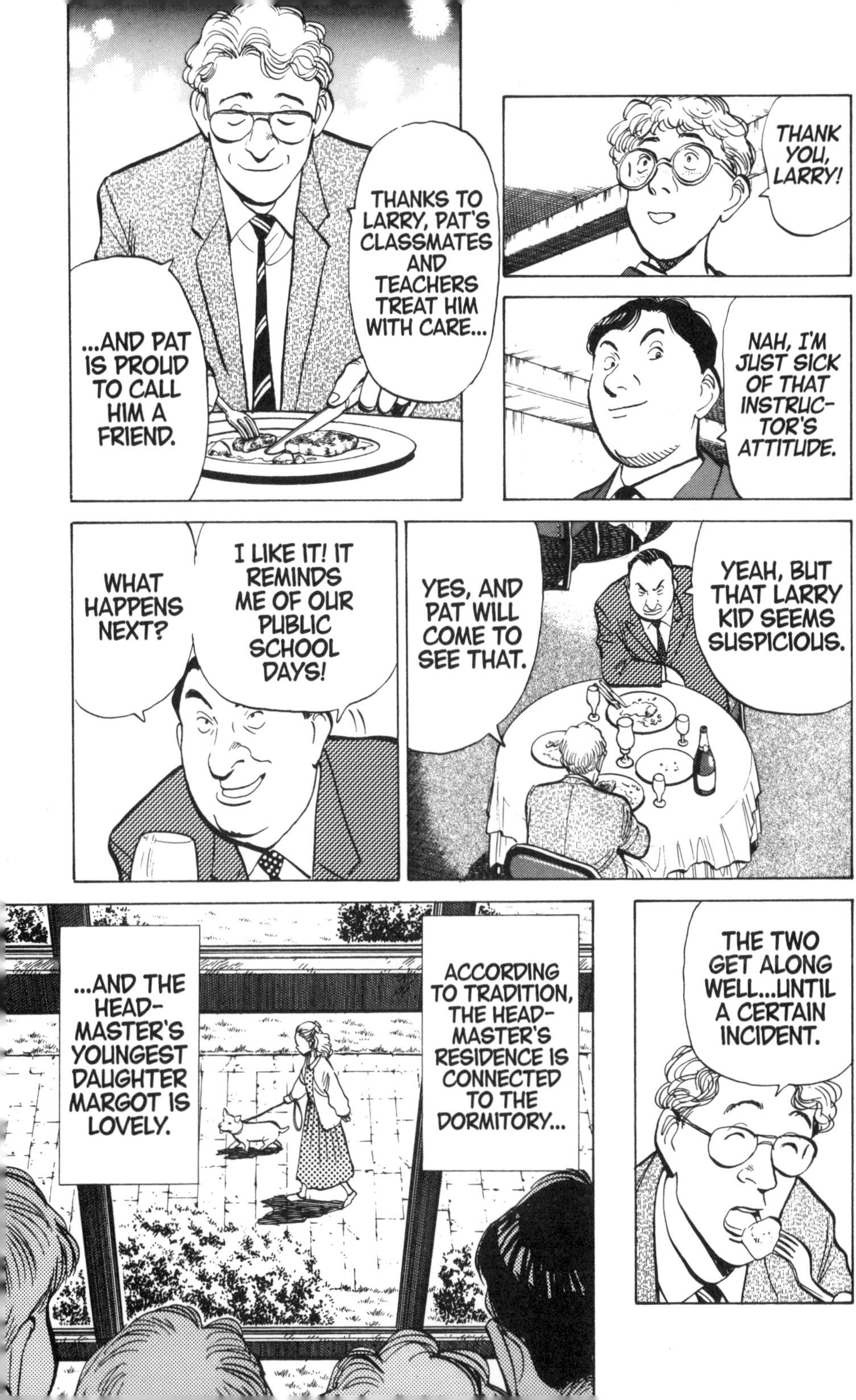
THANK YOU, LARRY!
NAH, I'M JUST SICK OF THAT INSTRUCTOR'S ATTITUDE.
THANKS TO LARRY, PAT'S CLASSMATES AND TEACHERS TREAT HIM WITH CARE...
...AND PAT IS PROUD TO CALL HIM A FRIEND.
YEAH, BUT THAT LARRY KID SEEMS SUSPICIOUS.
YES, AND PAT WILL COME TO SEE THAT.
I LIKE IT! IT REMINDS ME OF OUR PUBLIC SCHOOL DAYS!
WHAT HAPPENS NEXT?
THE TWO GET ALONG WELL...UNTIL A CERTAIN INCIDENT.
ACCORDING TO TRADITION, THE HEAD-MASTER'S RESIDENCE IS CONNECTED TO THE DORMITORY...
...AND THE HEAD-MASTER'S YOUNGEST DAUGHTER MARGOT IS LOVELY.

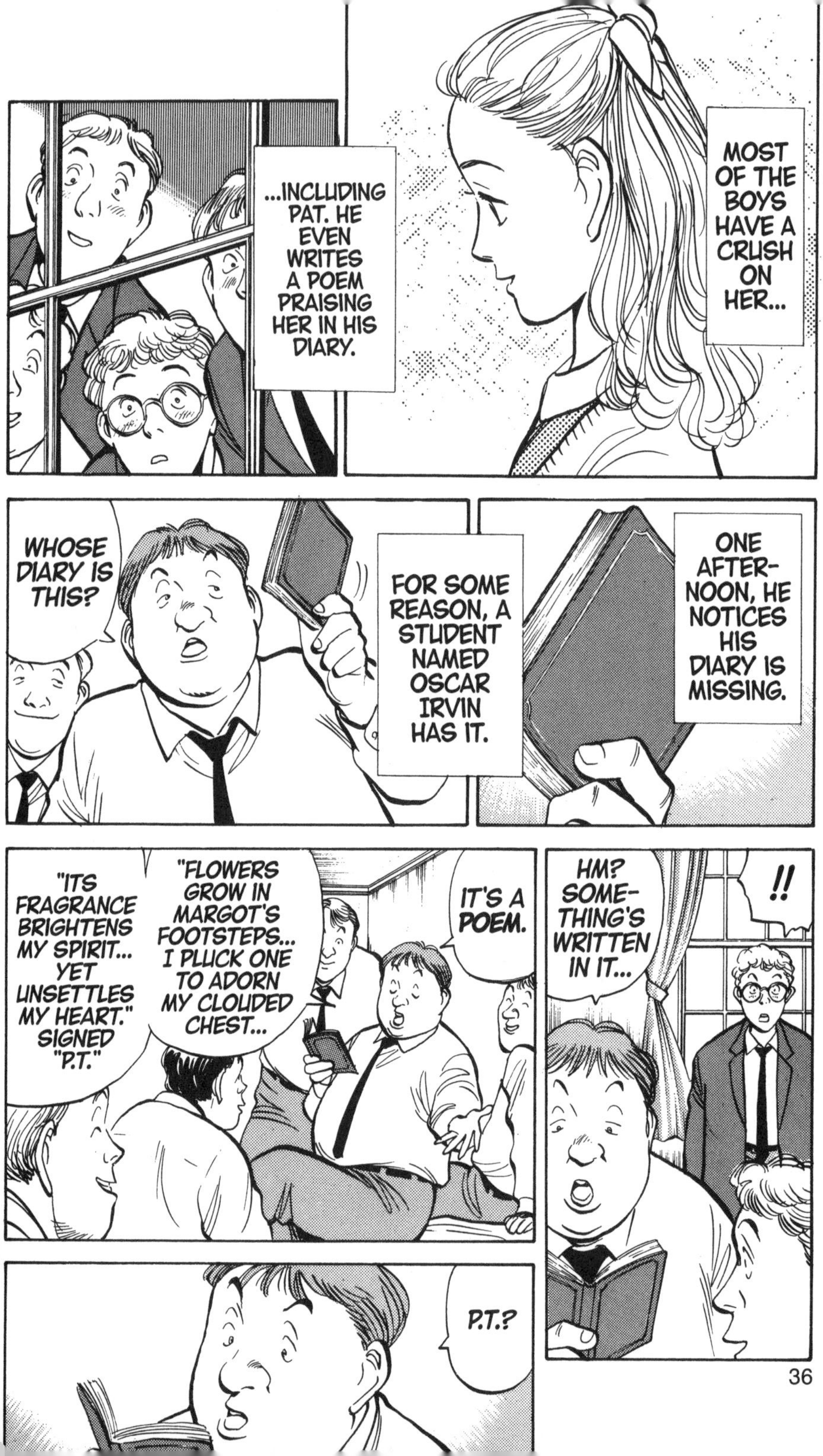
MOST OF THE BOYS HAVE A CRUSH ON HER...
...INCLUDING PAT. HE EVEN WRITES A POEM PRAISING HER IN HIS DIARY.
ONE AFTERNOON, HE NOTICES HIS DIARY IS MISSING.
FOR SOME REASON, A STUDENT NAMED OSCAR IRVIN HAS IT.
WHOSE DIARY IS THIS?
HM? SOMETHING'S WRITTEN IN IT...
!!
IT'S A POEM.
"FLOWERS GROW IN MARGOT'S FOOTSTEPS... I PLUCK ONE TO ADORN MY CLOUDED CHEST...
"ITS FRAGRANCE BRIGHTENS MY SPIRIT... YET UNSETTLES MY HEART." SIGNED "P.T."
P.T.?

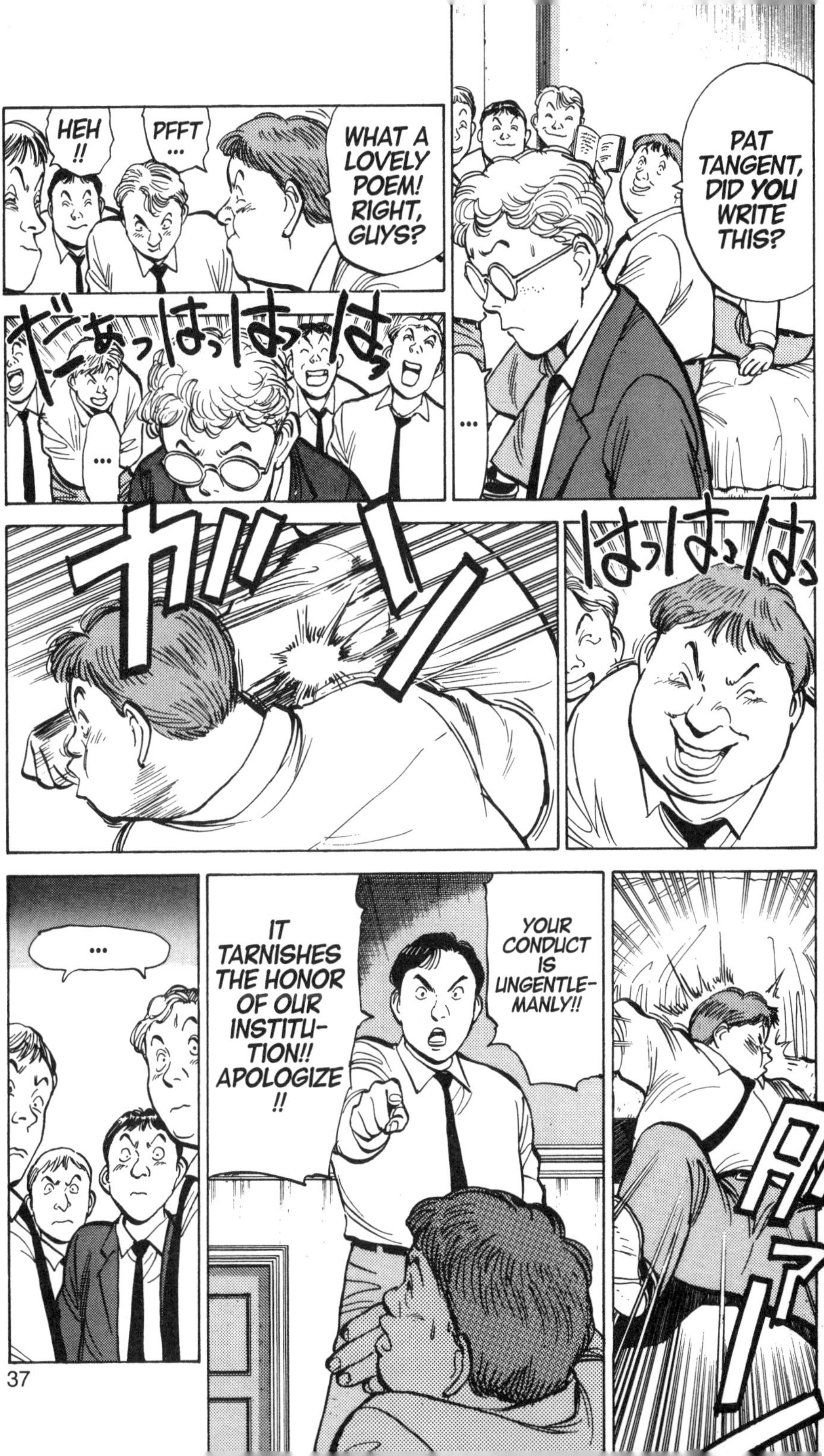
PAT TANGENT, DID YOU WRITE THIS?
...
WHAT A LOVELY POEM! RIGHT, GUYS?
PFFT ...
HEH !!
...
はっはっはっ
YOUR CONDUCT IS UNGENTLE-MANLY!!
IT TARNISHES THE HONOR OF OUR INSTITUTION!! APOLOGIZE !!
...

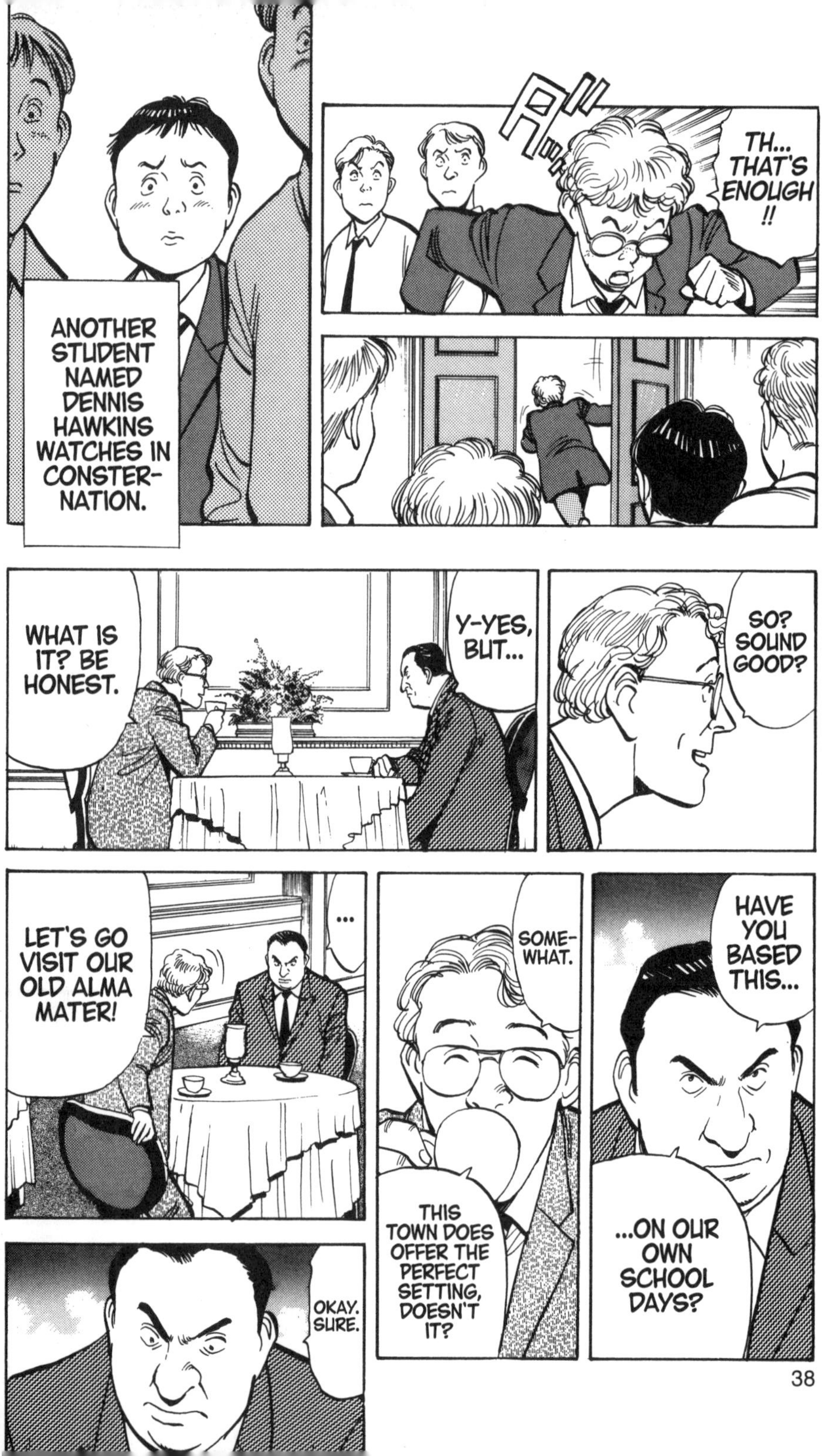
TH... THAT'S ENOUGH!!
ANOTHER STUDENT NAMED DENNIS HAWKINS WATCHES IN CONSTER-NATION.
SO? SOUND GOOD?
Y-YES, BUT...
WHAT IS IT? BE HONEST.
HAVE YOU BASED THIS...
...ON OUR OWN SCHOOL DAYS?
SOME-WHAT.
THIS TOWN DOES OFFER THE PERFECT SETTING, DOESN'T IT?
...
LET'S GO VISIT OUR OLD ALMA MATER!
OKAY. SURE.

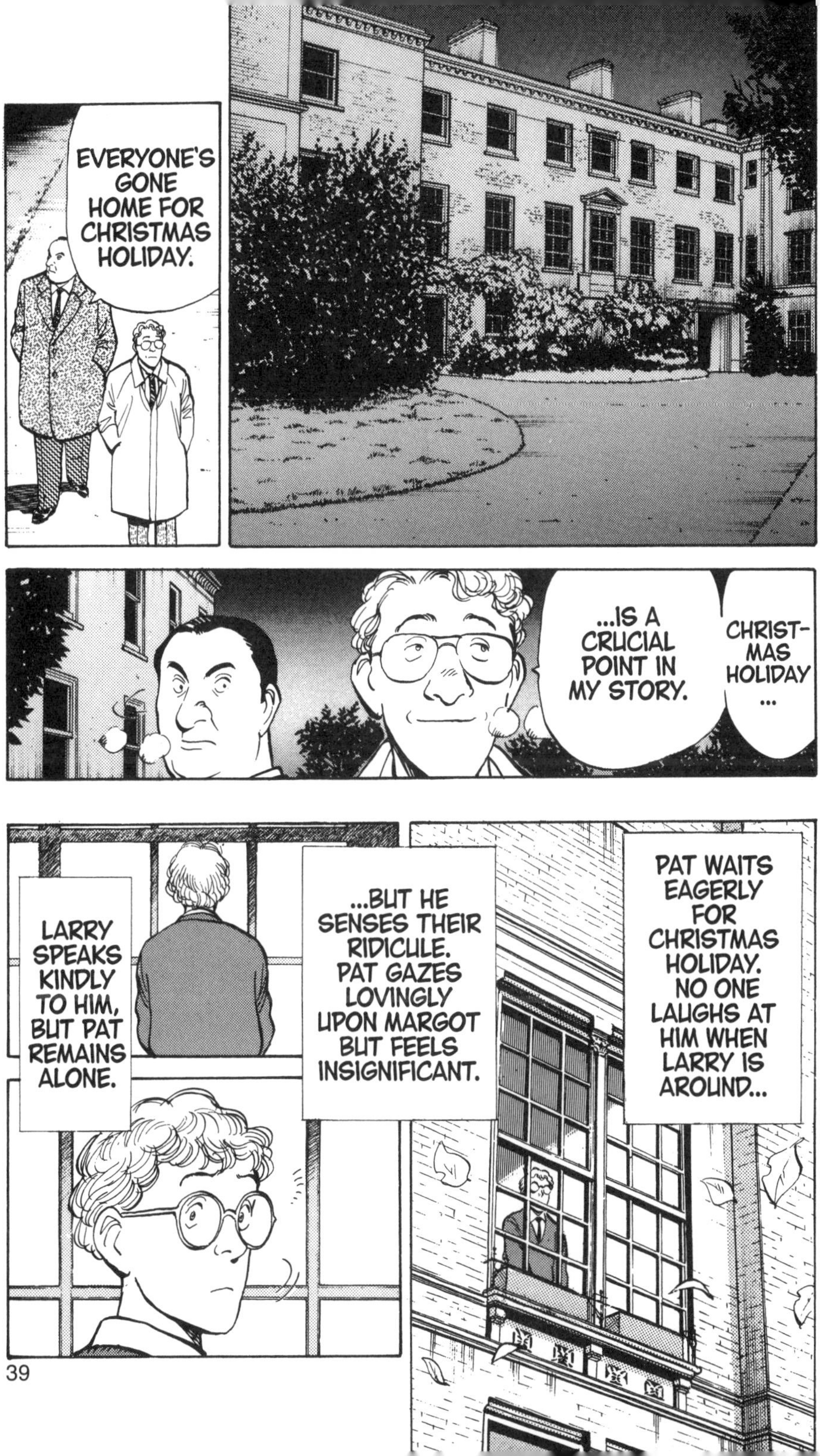
EVERYONE'S GONE HOME FOR CHRISTMAS HOLIDAY.
CHRIST-MAS HOLIDAY ...
...IS A CRUCIAL POINT IN MY STORY.
PAT WAITS EAGERLY FOR CHRISTMAS HOLIDAY. NO ONE LAUGHS AT HIM WHEN LARRY IS AROUND...
...BUT HE SENSES THEIR RIDICULE. PAT GAZES LOVINGLY UPON MARGOT BUT FEELS INSIGNIFICANT.
LARRY SPEAKS KINDLY TO HIM, BUT PAT REMAINS ALONE.

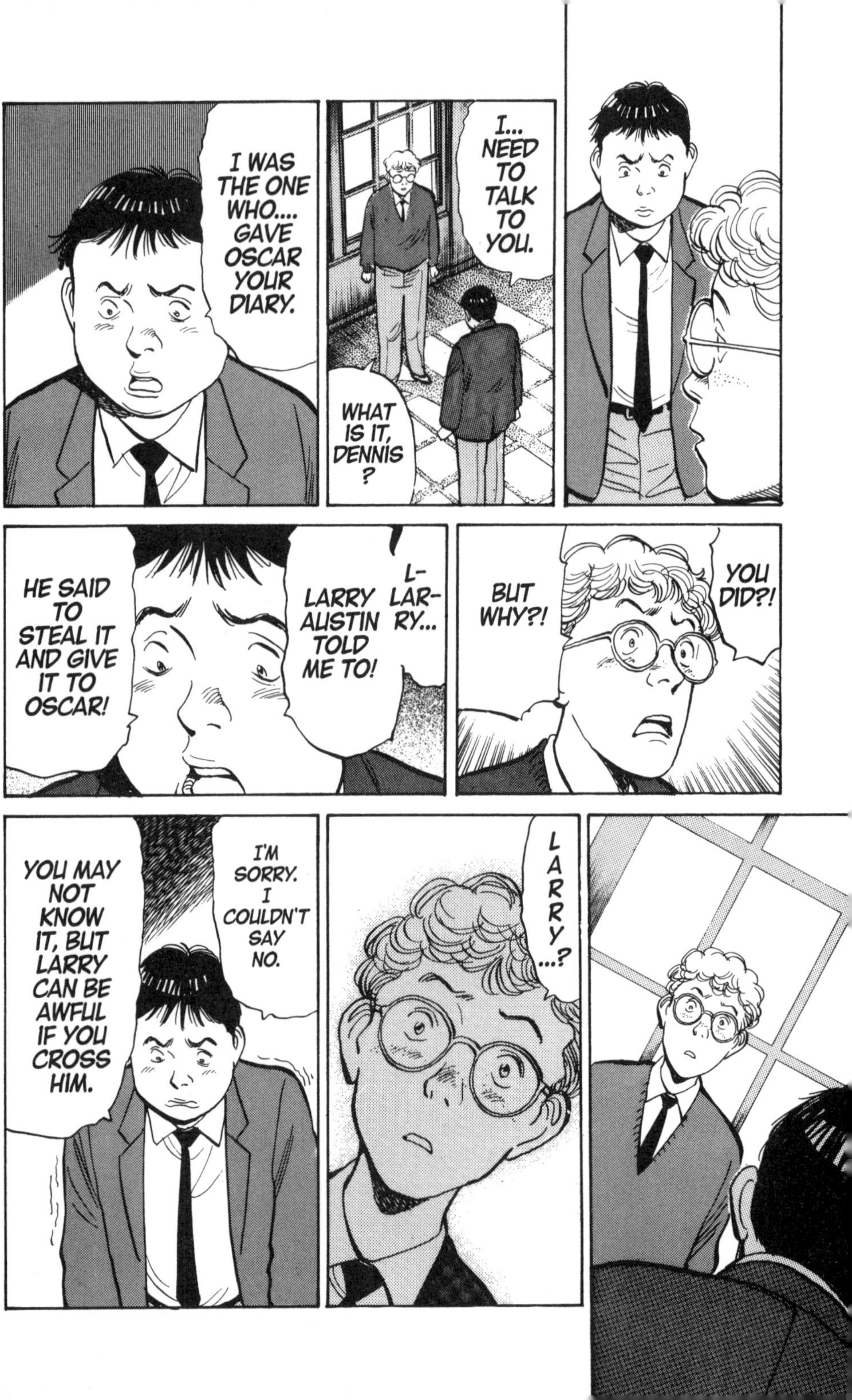
I... NEED TO TALK TO YOU.
WHAT IS IT, DENNIS?
I WAS THE ONE WHO.... GAVE OSCAR YOUR DIARY.
YOU DID?!
BUT WHY?!
L-LAR-RY...
LARRY AUSTIN TOLD ME TO!
HE SAID TO STEAL IT AND GIVE IT TO OSCAR!
LARRY...?
I'M SORRY. I COULDN'T SAY NO.
YOU MAY NOT KNOW IT, BUT LARRY CAN BE AWFUL IF YOU CROSS HIM.

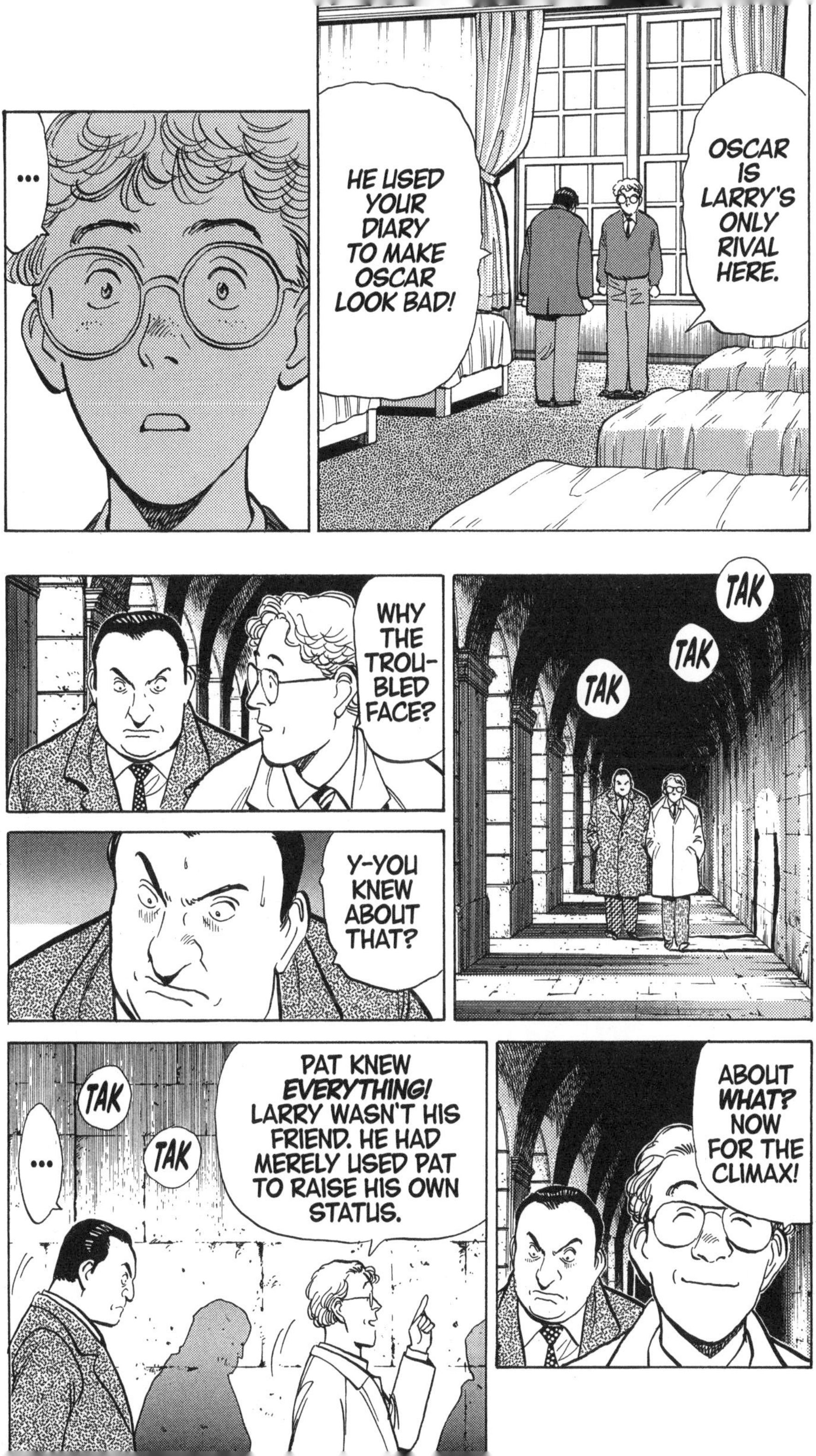

OSCAR IS LARRY'S ONLY RIVAL HERE.
HE USED YOUR DIARY TO MAKE OSCAR LOOK BAD!
...
TAK
TAK
TAK
WHY THE TROU-BLED FACE?
Y-YOU KNEW ABOUT THAT?
ABOUT *WHAT?* NOW FOR THE CLIMAX!
PAT KNEW *EVERYTHING!* LARRY WASN'T HIS FRIEND. HE HAD MERELY USED PAT TO RAISE HIS OWN STATUS.
TAK
TAK
...

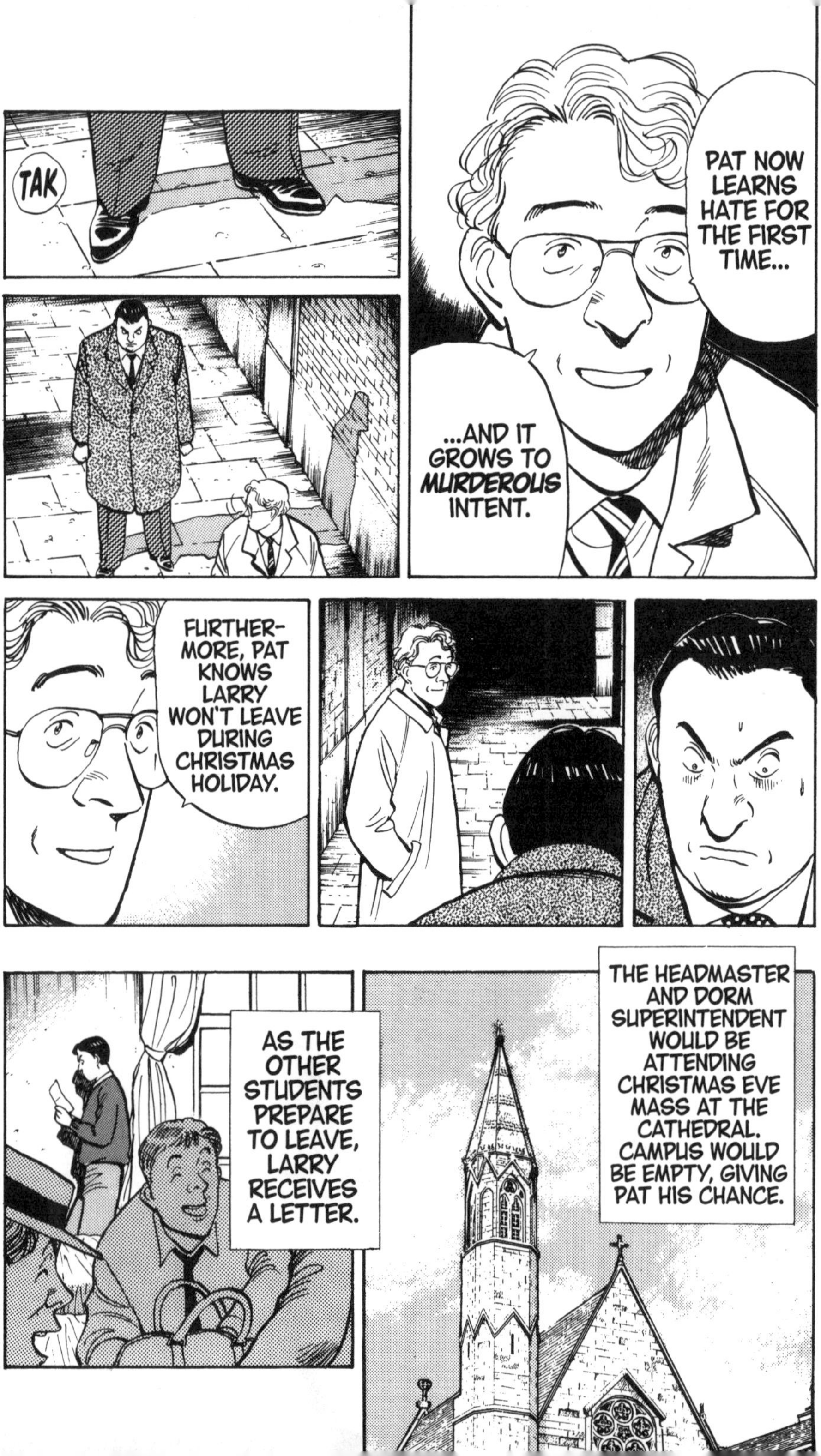
PAT NOW LEARNS HATE FOR THE FIRST TIME...
...AND IT GROWS TO *MURDEROUS* INTENT.
TAK
FURTHER-MORE, PAT KNOWS LARRY WON'T LEAVE DURING CHRISTMAS HOLIDAY.
THE HEADMASTER AND DORM SUPERINTENDENT WOULD BE ATTENDING CHRISTMAS EVE MASS AT THE CATHEDRAL. CAMPUS WOULD BE EMPTY, GIVING PAT HIS CHANCE.
AS THE OTHER STUDENTS PREPARE TO LEAVE, LARRY RECEIVES A LETTER.

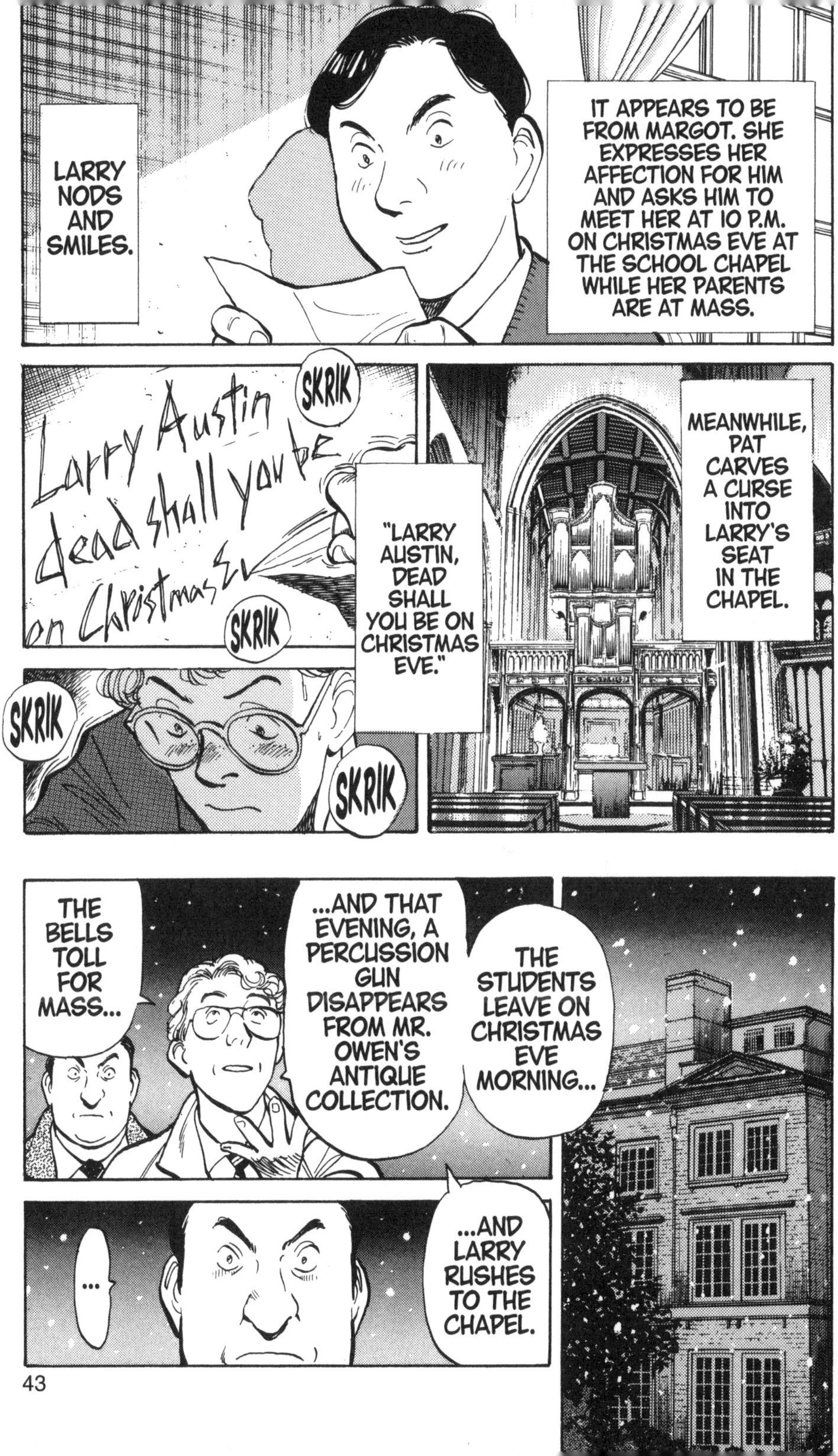
IT APPEARS TO BE FROM MARGOT. SHE EXPRESSES HER AFFECTION FOR HIM AND ASKS HIM TO MEET HER AT 10 P.M. ON CHRISTMAS EVE AT THE SCHOOL CHAPEL WHILE HER PARENTS ARE AT MASS.
LARRY NODS AND SMILES.
MEANWHILE, PAT CARVES A CURSE INTO LARRY'S SEAT IN THE CHAPEL.
"LARRY AUSTIN, DEAD SHALL YOU BE ON CHRISTMAS EVE."
SKRIK
Larry Austin dead shall you be on Christmas Ev
SKRIK
SKRIK
SKRIK
THE STUDENTS LEAVE ON CHRISTMAS EVE MORNING...
...AND THAT EVENING, A PERCUSSION GUN DISAPPEARS FROM MR. OWEN'S ANTIQUE COLLECTION.
THE BELLS TOLL FOR MASS...
...AND LARRY RUSHES TO THE CHAPEL.
...

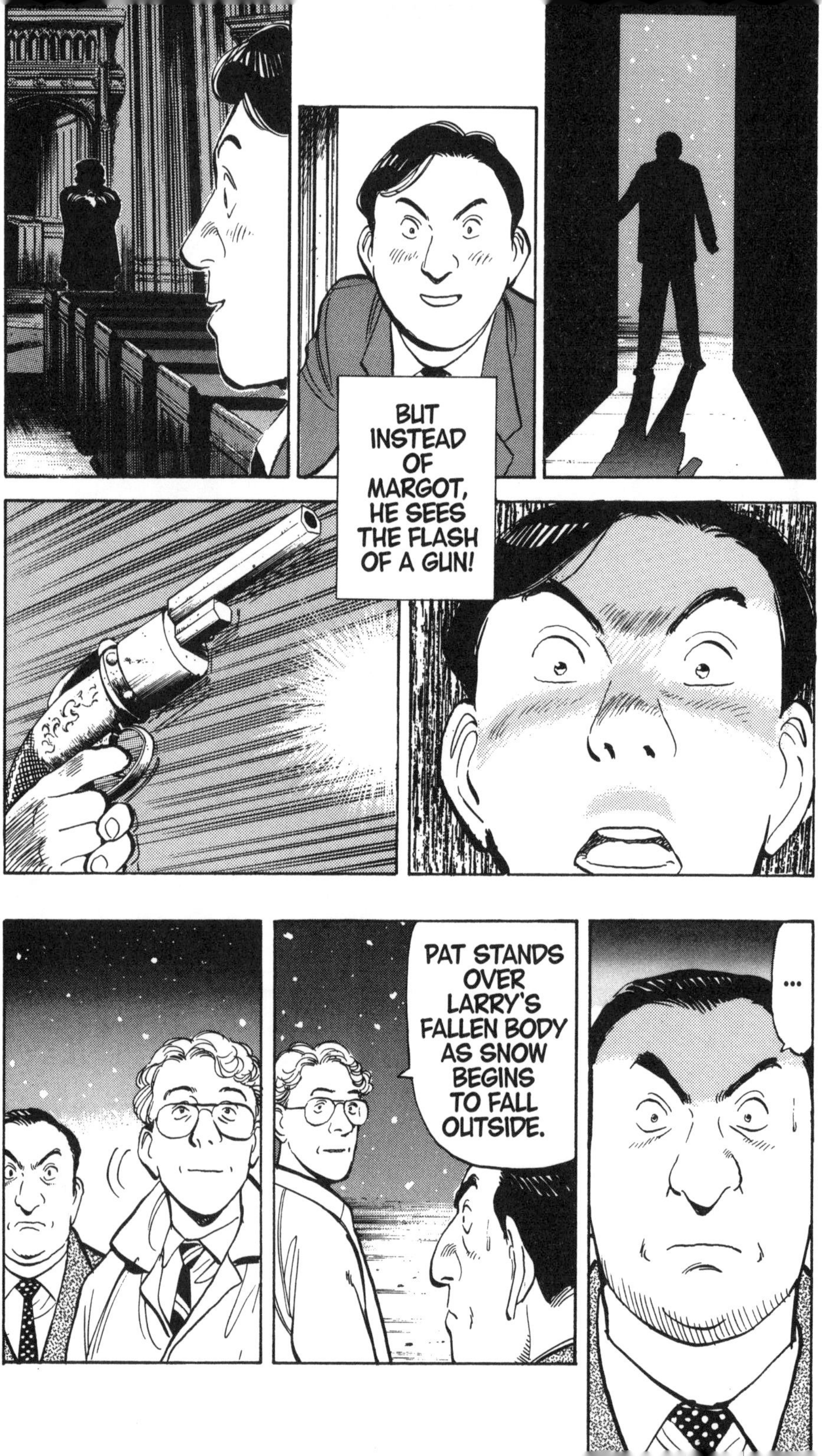
BUT INSTEAD OF MARGOT, HE SEES THE FLASH OF A GUN!
...
PAT STANDS OVER LARRY'S FALLEN BODY AS SNOW BEGINS TO FALL OUTSIDE.

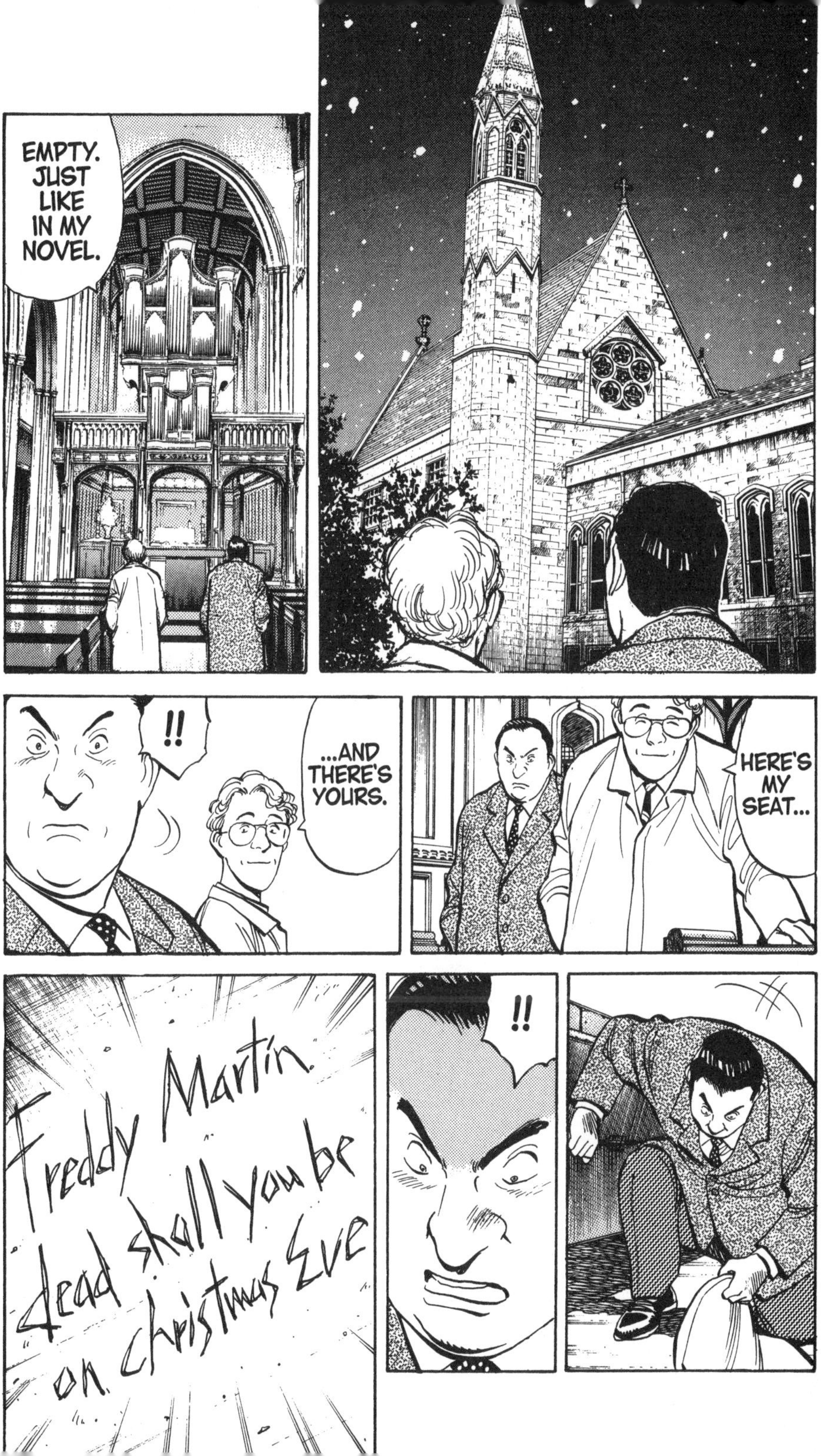
EMPTY. JUST LIKE IN MY NOVEL.
HERE'S MY SEAT...
...AND THERE'S YOURS.
!!
!!
Freddy Martin dead shall you be on christmas Eve

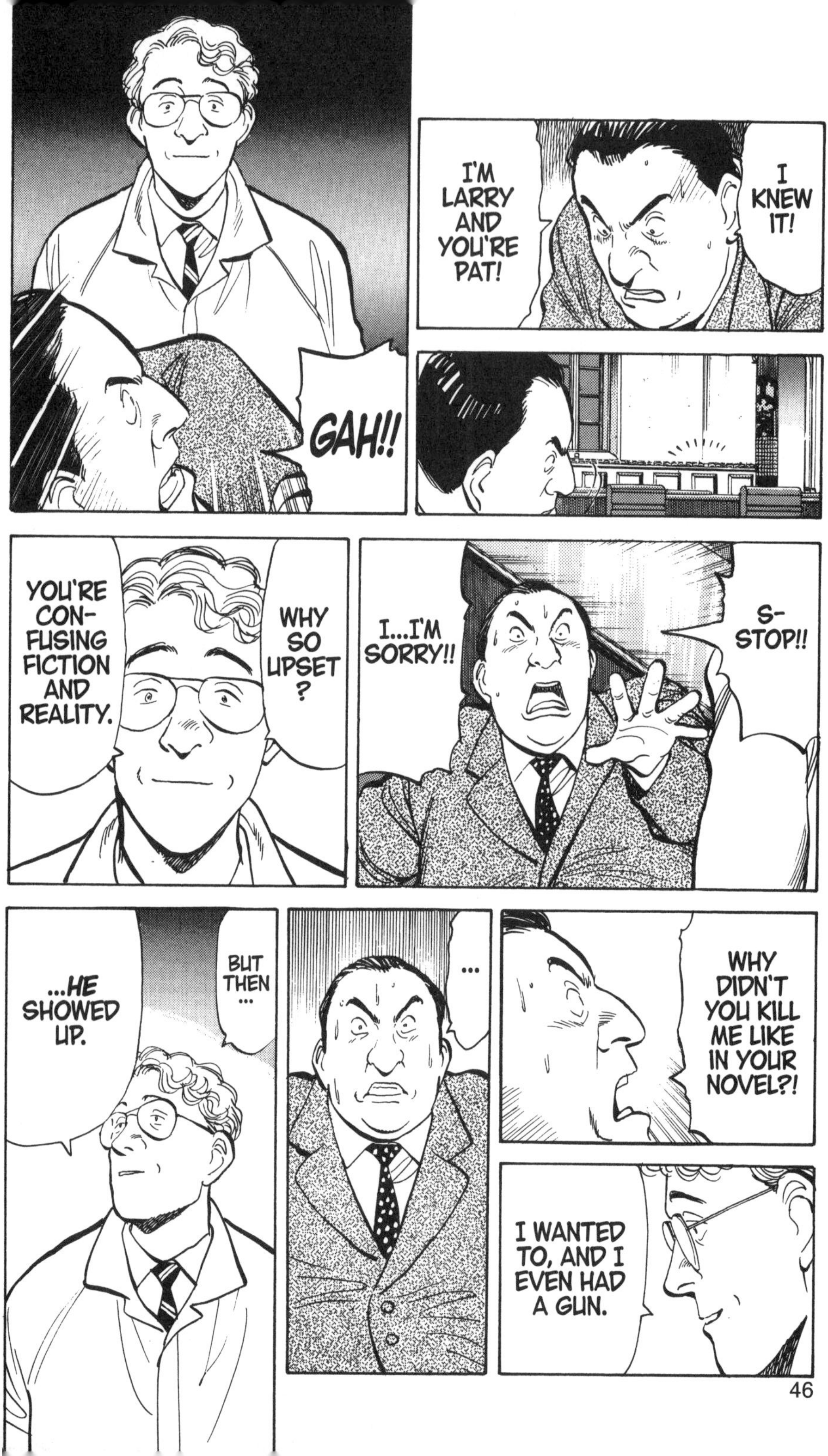
I KNEW IT!
I'M LARRY AND YOU'RE PAT!
GAH!!
S-STOP!!
I...I'M SORRY!!
WHY SO UPSET?
YOU'RE CONFUSING FICTION AND REALITY.
WHY DIDN'T YOU KILL ME LIKE IN YOUR NOVEL?!
I WANTED TO, AND I EVEN HAD A GUN.
...
BUT THEN...
...HE SHOWED UP.

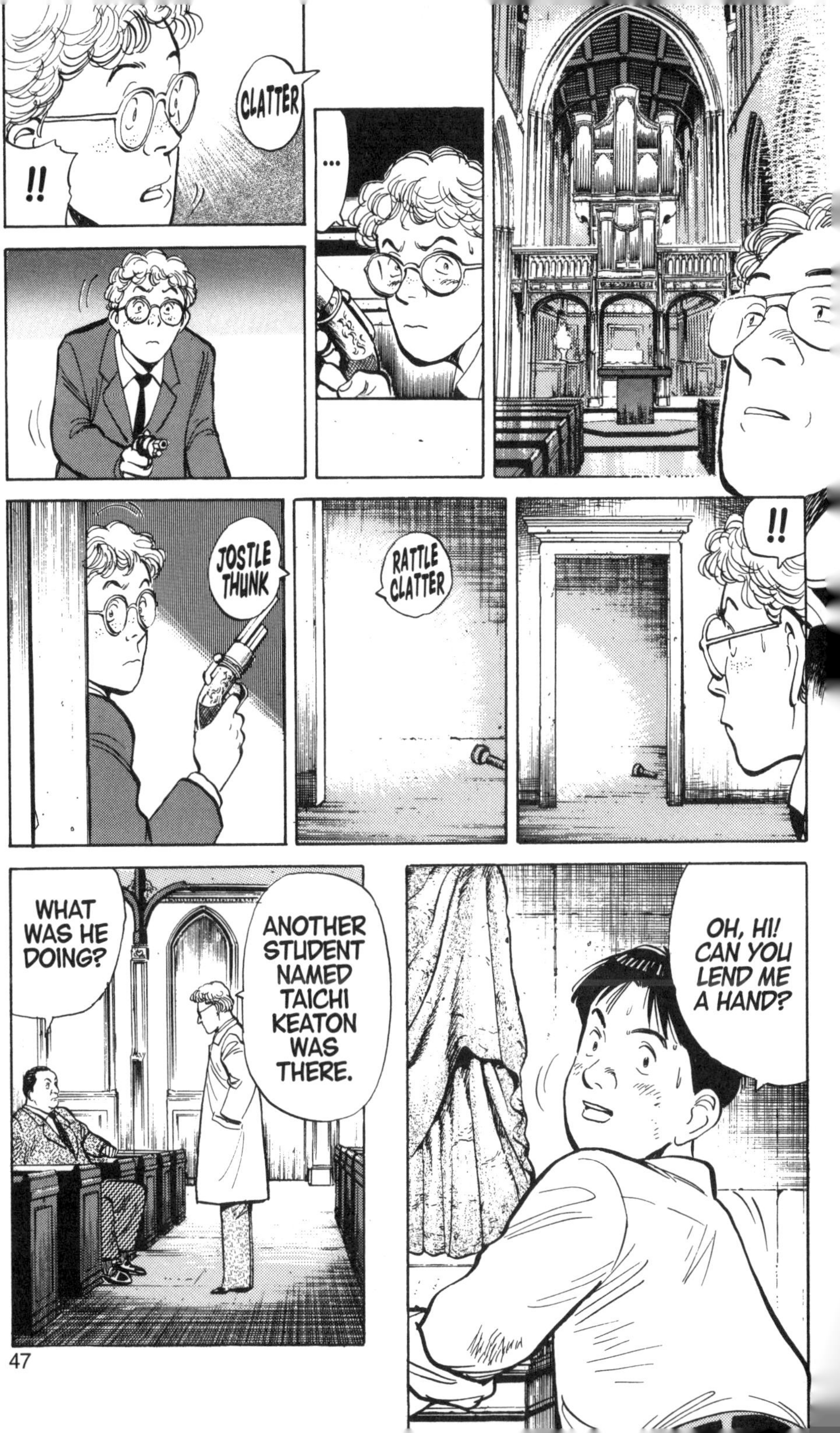
...
CLATTER
!!
!!
RATTLE CLATTER
JOSTLE THUNK
OH, HI! CAN YOU LEND ME A HAND?
ANOTHER STUDENT NAMED TAICHI KEATON WAS THERE.
WHAT WAS HE DOING?

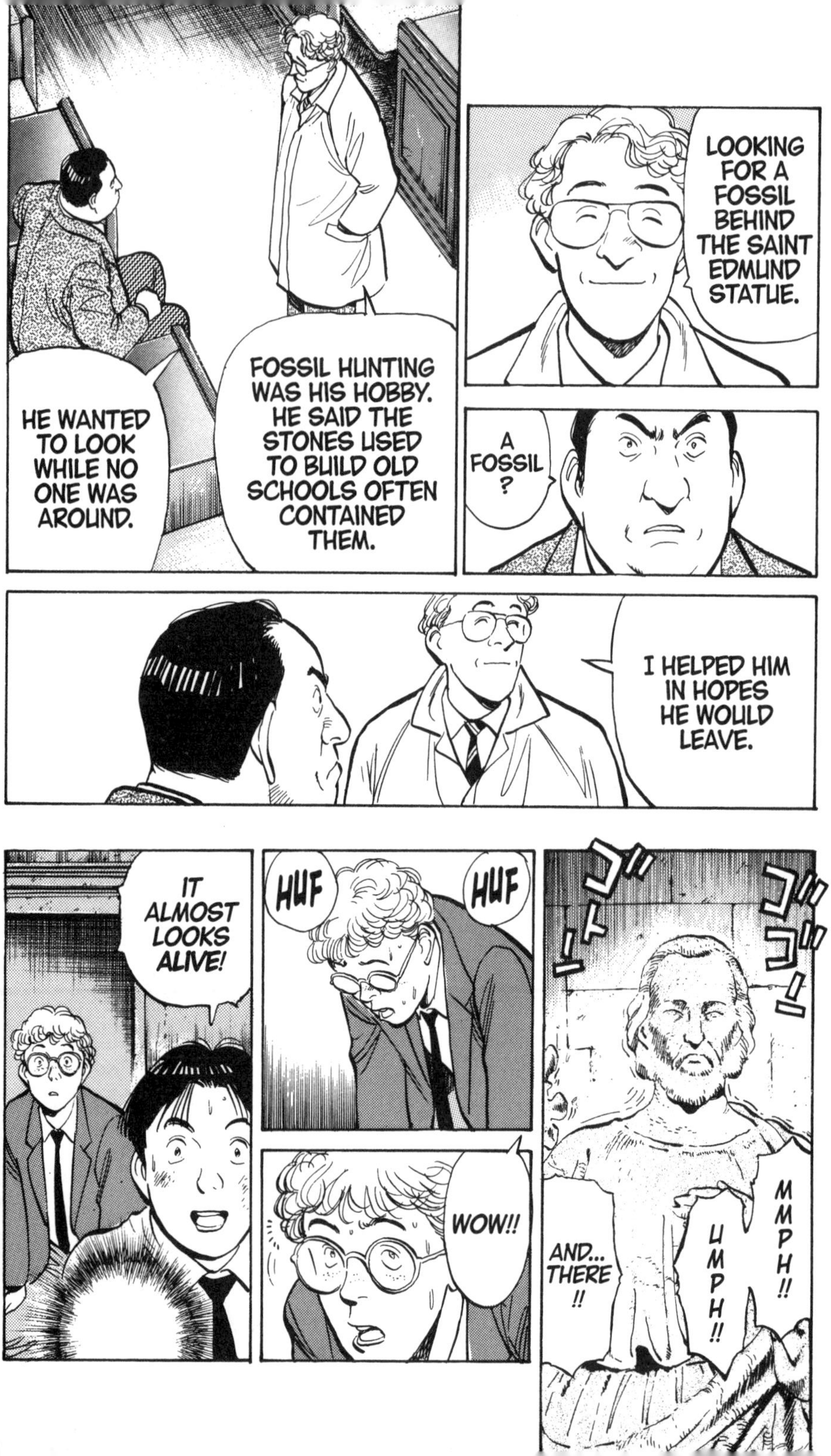
LOOKING FOR A FOSSIL BEHIND THE SAINT EDMUND STATUE.
A FOSSIL?
FOSSIL HUNTING WAS HIS HOBBY. HE SAID THE STONES USED TO BUILD OLD SCHOOLS OFTEN CONTAINED THEM.
HE WANTED TO LOOK WHILE NO ONE WAS AROUND.
I HELPED HIM IN HOPES HE WOULD LEAVE.
MMPH!!
UMPH!!
AND... THERE!!
HUF
HUF
WOW!!
IT ALMOST LOOKS ALIVE!

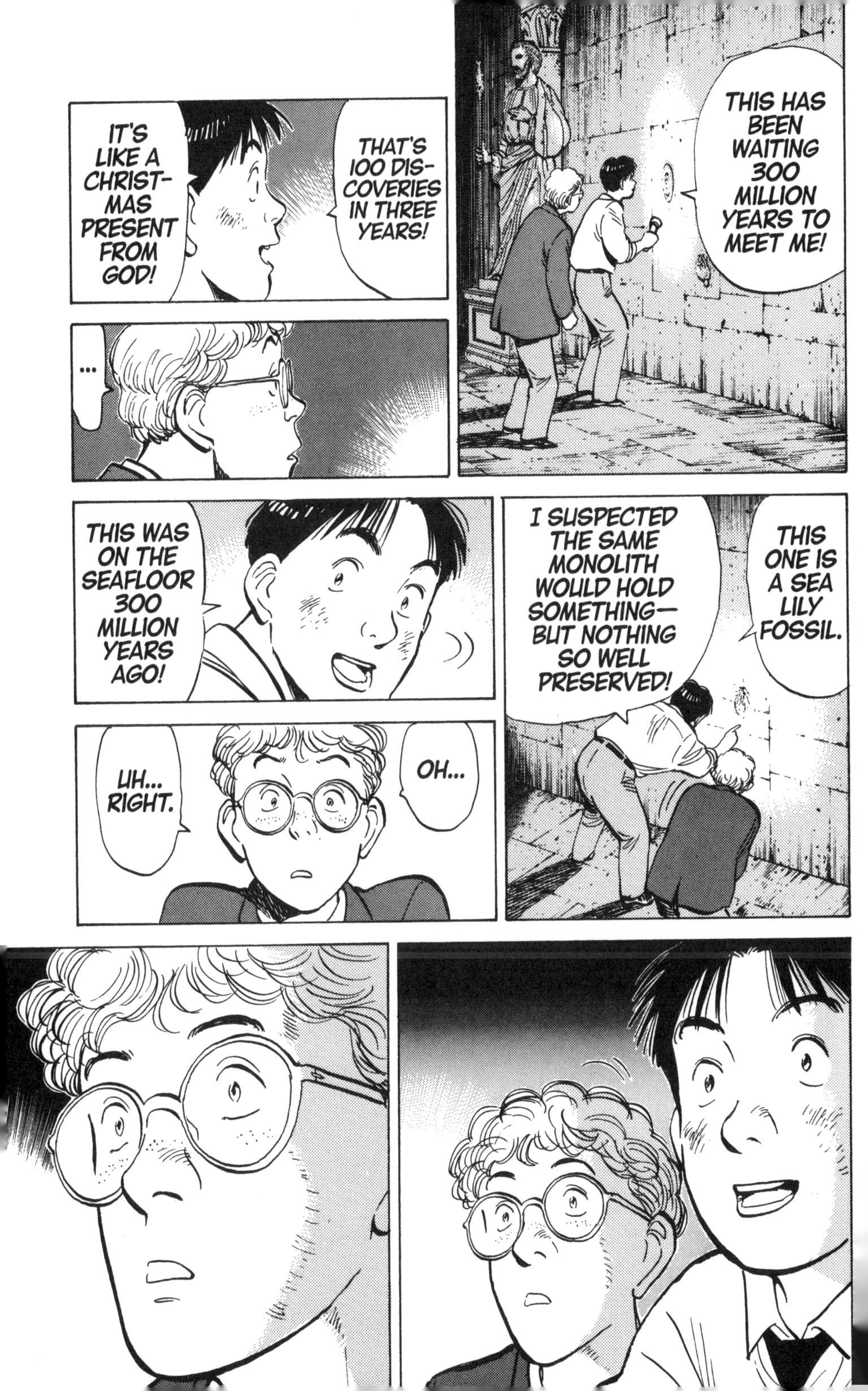
THIS HAS BEEN WAITING 300 MILLION YEARS TO MEET ME!
THAT'S 100 DIS-COVERIES IN THREE YEARS!
IT'S LIKE A CHRIST-MAS PRESENT FROM GOD!
...
THIS ONE IS A SEA LILY FOSSIL.
I SUSPECTED THE SAME MONOLITH WOULD HOLD SOMETHING— BUT NOTHING SO WELL PRESERVED!
THIS WAS ON THE SEAFLOOR 300 MILLION YEARS AGO!
OH...
UH... RIGHT.

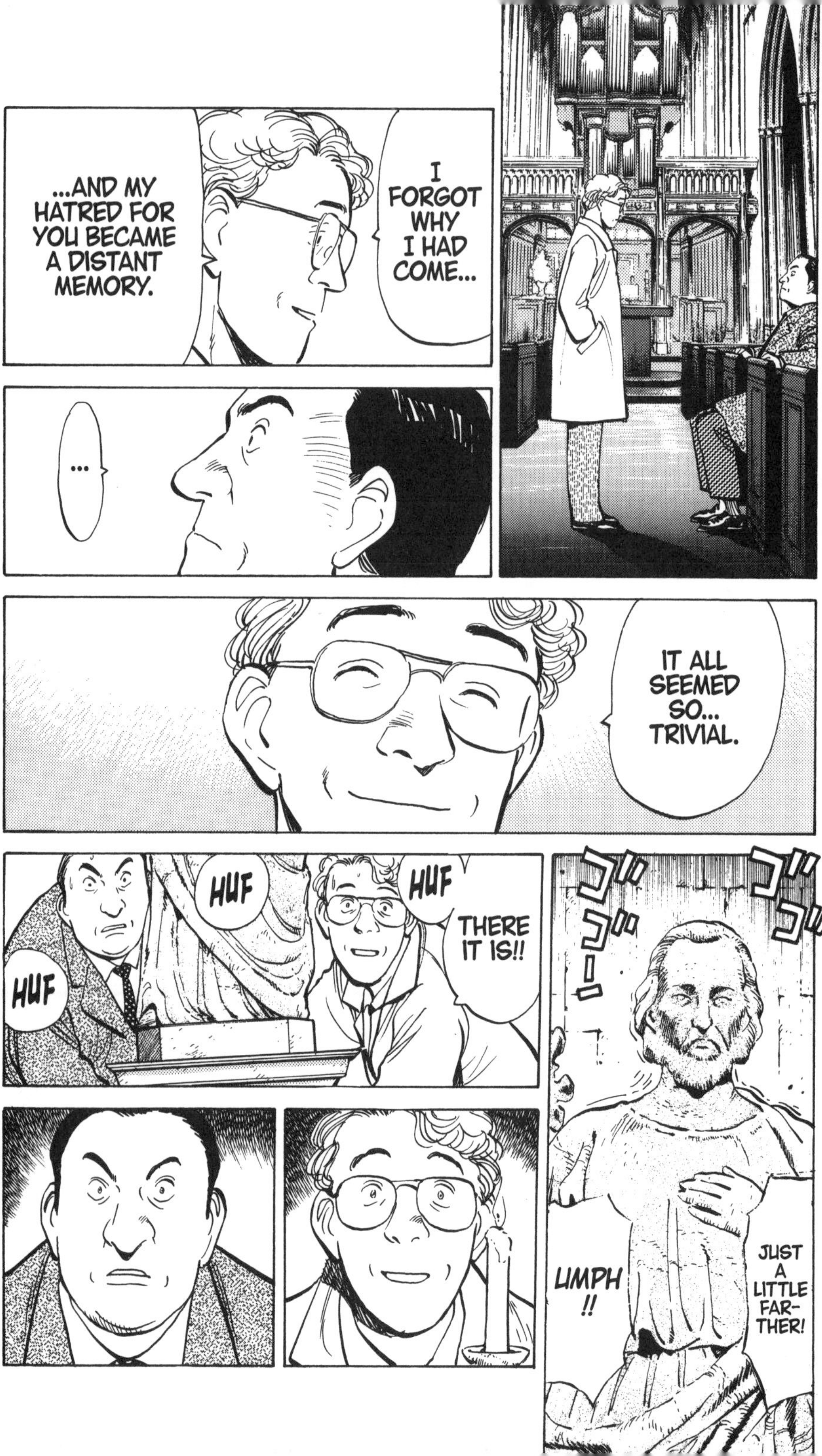
I FORGOT WHY I HAD COME...
...AND MY HATRED FOR YOU BECAME A DISTANT MEMORY.
...
IT ALL SEEMED SO... TRIVIAL.
ゴゴ
ゴゴー!
JUST A LITTLE FAR-THER!
UMPH !!
HUF
THERE IT IS!!
HUF
HUF

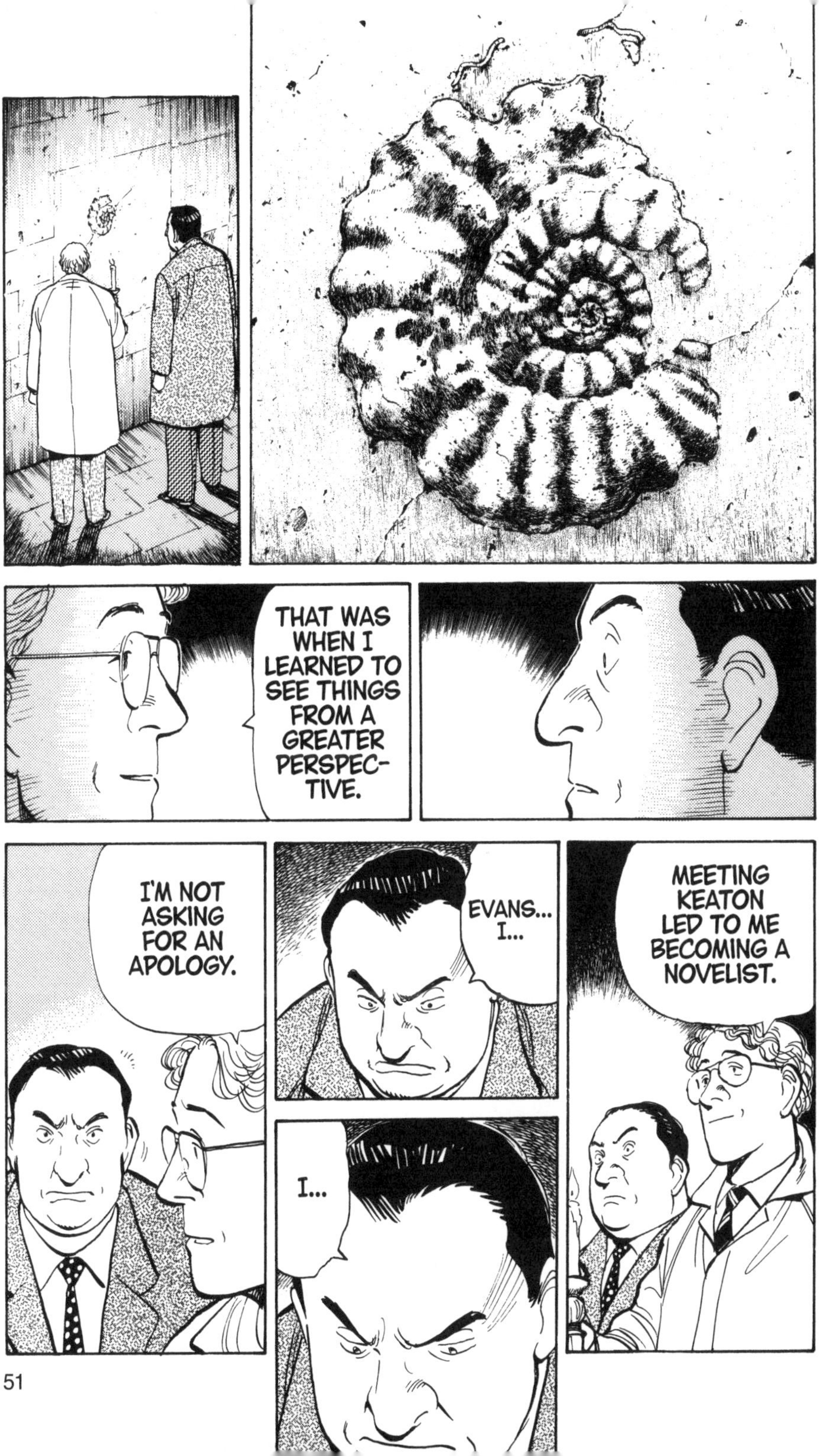
THAT WAS WHEN I LEARNED TO SEE THINGS FROM A GREATER PERSPEC-TIVE.
MEETING KEATON LED TO ME BECOMING A NOVELIST.
EVANS... I...
I...
I'M NOT ASKING FOR AN APOLOGY.

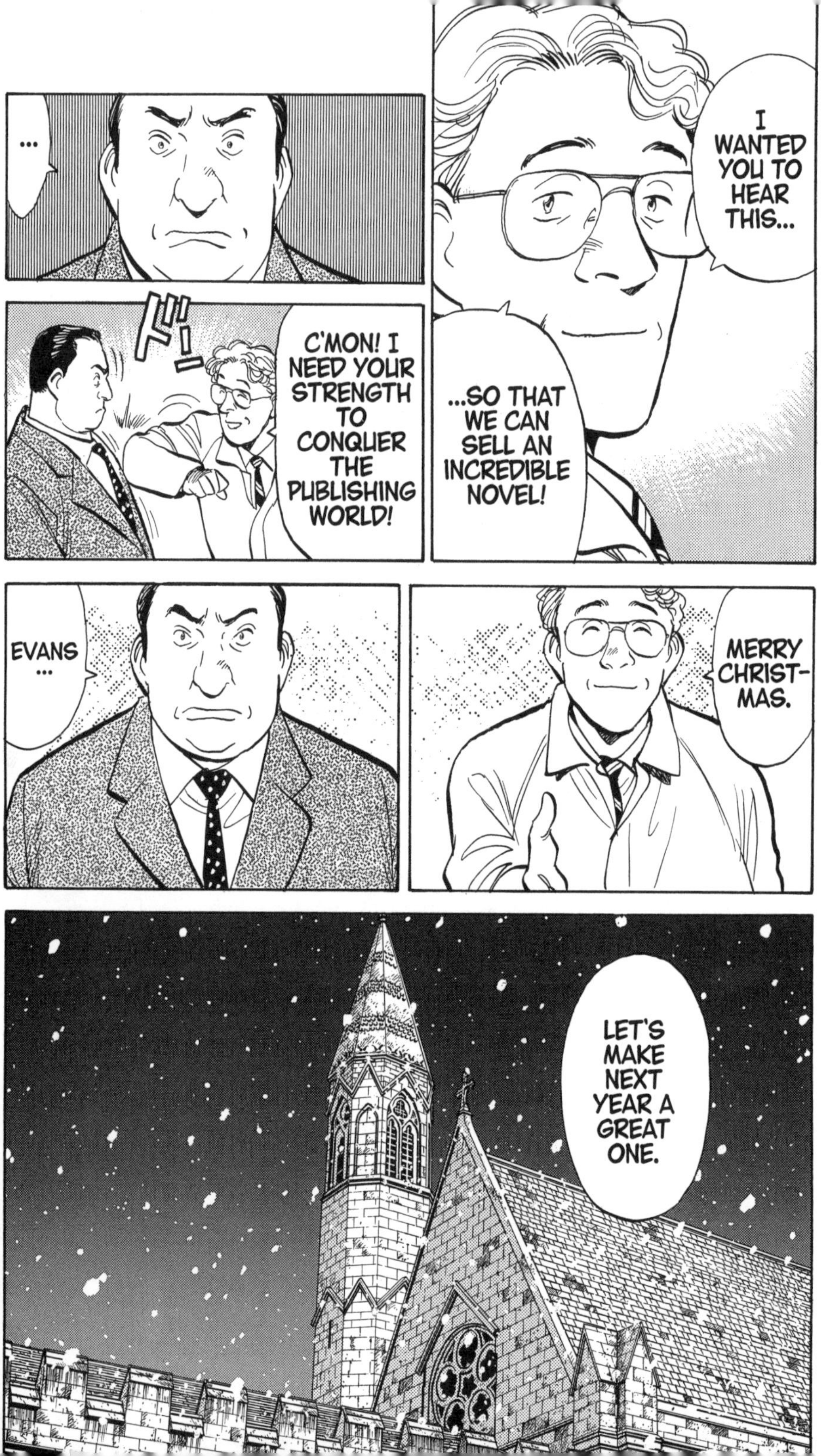
I WANTED YOU TO HEAR THIS...
...SO THAT WE CAN SELL AN INCREDIBLE NOVEL!
...
C'MON! I NEED YOUR STRENGTH TO CONQUER THE PUBLISHING WORLD!
MERRY CHRIST-MAS.
EVANS...
LET'S MAKE NEXT YEAR A GREAT ONE.

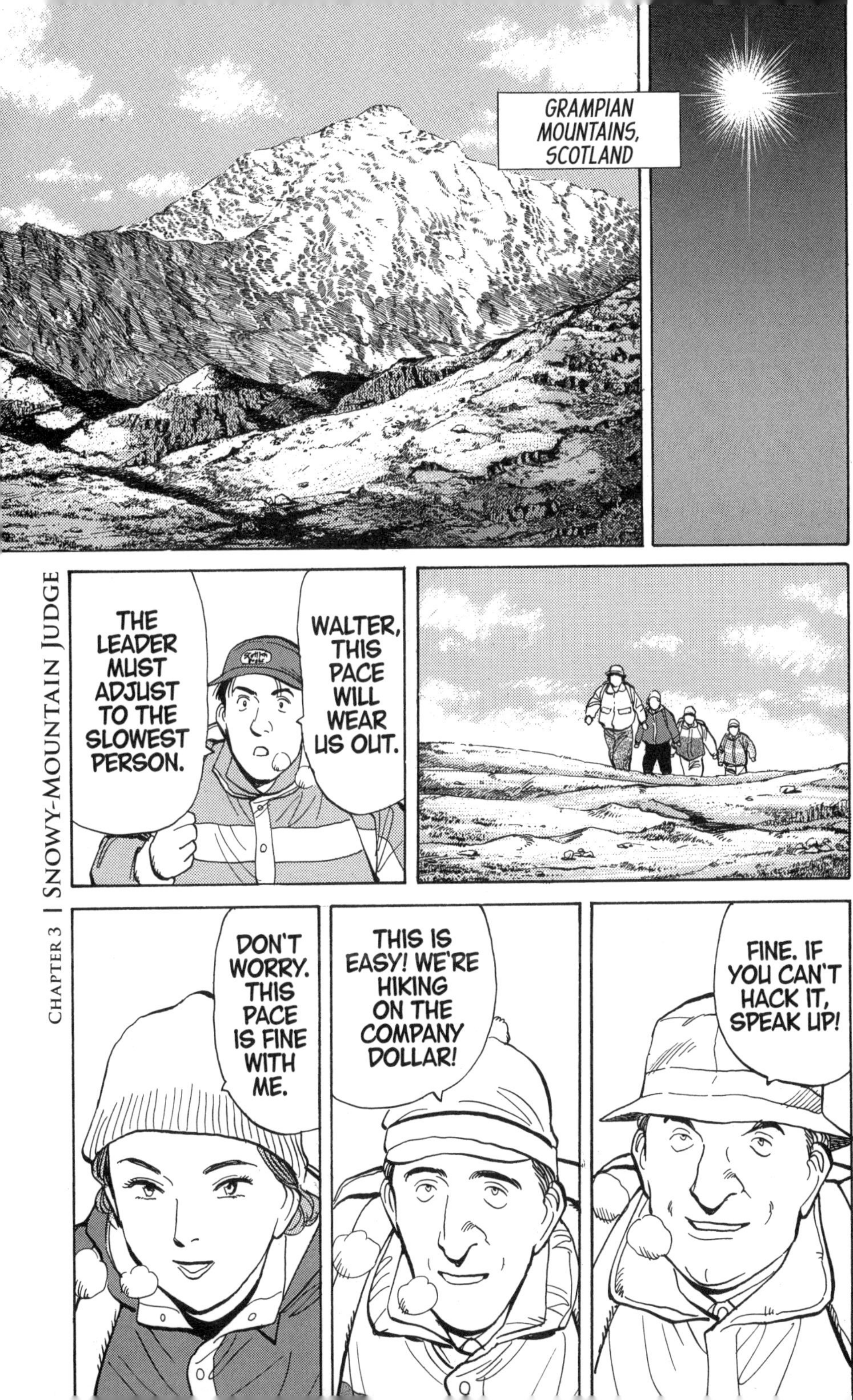
GRAMPIAN MOUNTAINS, SCOTLAND
WALTER, THIS PACE WILL WEAR US OUT.
THE LEADER MUST ADJUST TO THE SLOWEST PERSON.
FINE. IF YOU CAN'T HACK IT, SPEAK UP!
THIS IS EASY! WE'RE HIKING ON THE COMPANY DOLLAR!
DON'T WORRY. THIS PACE IS FINE WITH ME.

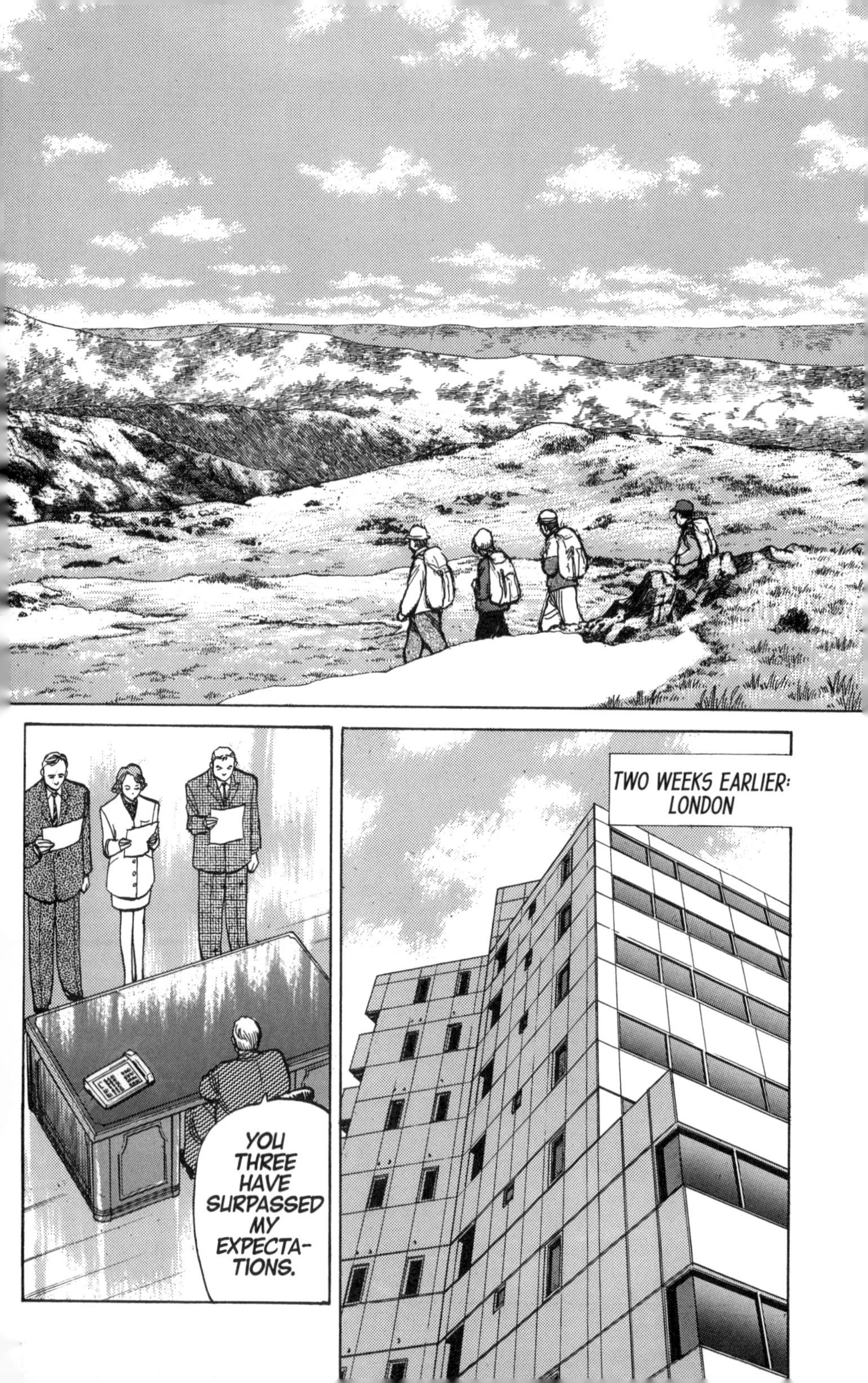
TWO WEEKS EARLIER: LONDON
YOU THREE HAVE SURPASSED MY EXPECTATIONS.

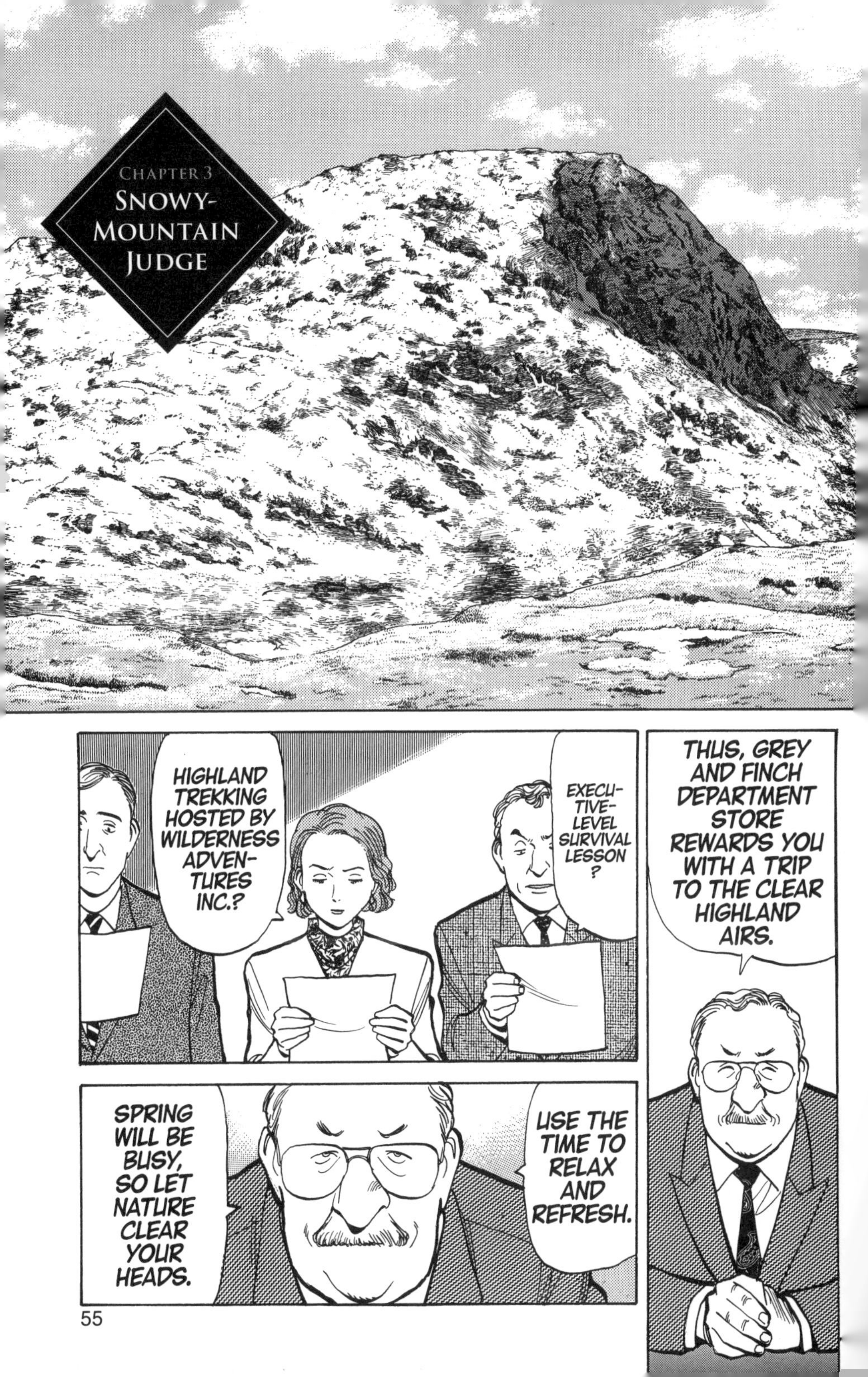
CHAPTER 3
SNOWY-MOUNTAIN JUDGE
THUS, GREY AND FINCH DEPARTMENT STORE REWARDS YOU WITH A TRIP TO THE CLEAR HIGHLAND AIRS.
EXECUTIVE-LEVEL SURVIVAL LESSON?
HIGHLAND TREKKING HOSTED BY WILDERNESS ADVENTURES INC.?
USE THE TIME TO RELAX AND REFRESH.
SPRING WILL BE BUSY, SO LET NATURE CLEAR YOUR HEADS.

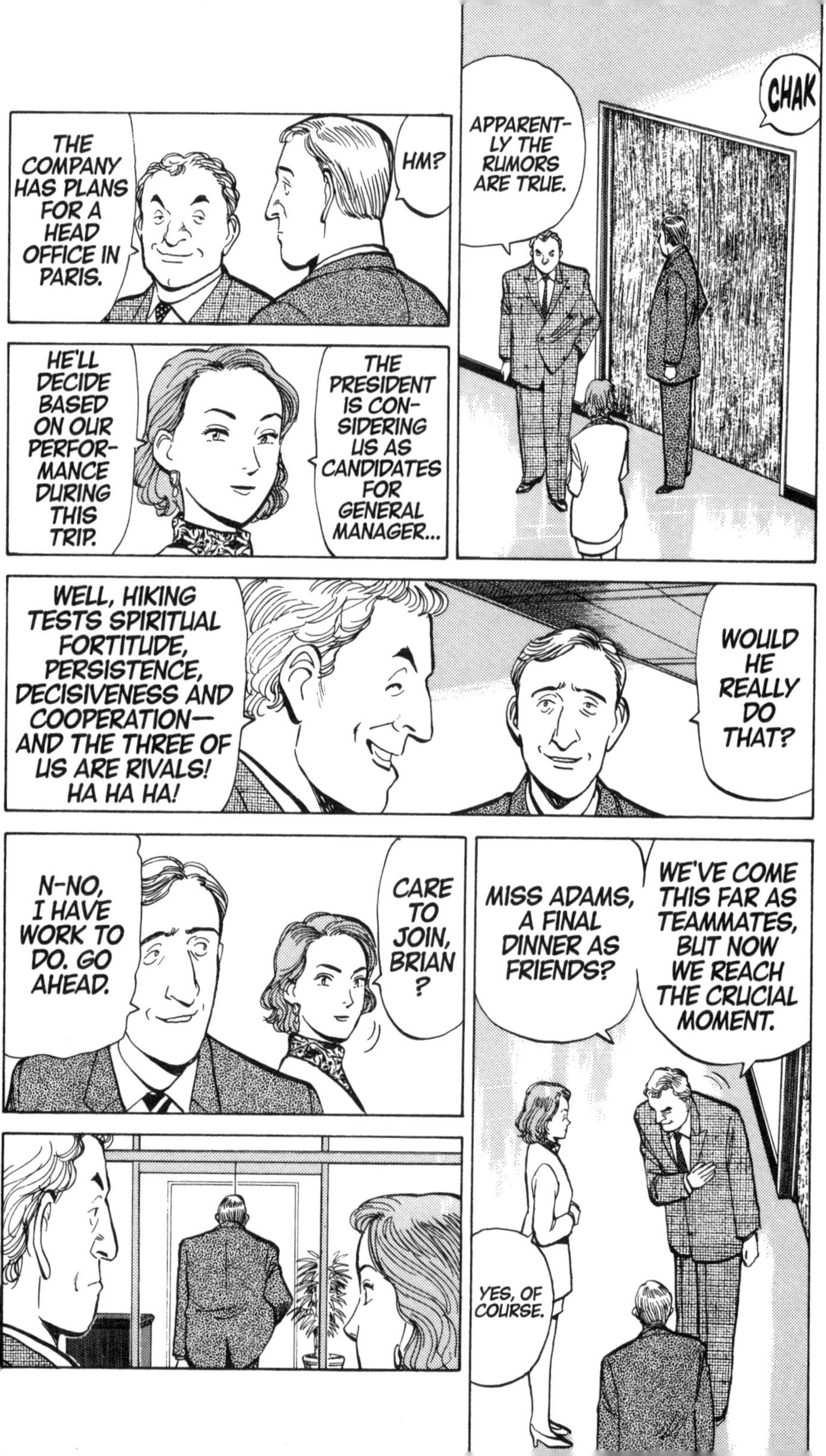
CHAK
APPARENTLY THE RUMORS ARE TRUE.
HM?
THE COMPANY HAS PLANS FOR A HEAD OFFICE IN PARIS.
THE PRESIDENT IS CONSIDERING US AS CANDIDATES FOR GENERAL MANAGER...
HE'LL DECIDE BASED ON OUR PERFORMANCE DURING THIS TRIP.
WOULD HE REALLY DO THAT?
WELL, HIKING TESTS SPIRITUAL FORTITUDE, PERSISTENCE, DECISIVENESS AND COOPERATION— AND THE THREE OF US ARE RIVALS! HA HA HA!
WE'VE COME THIS FAR AS TEAMMATES, BUT NOW WE REACH THE CRUCIAL MOMENT.
MISS ADAMS, A FINAL DINNER AS FRIENDS?
YES, OF COURSE.
CARE TO JOIN, BRIAN?
N-NO, I HAVE WORK TO DO. GO AHEAD.

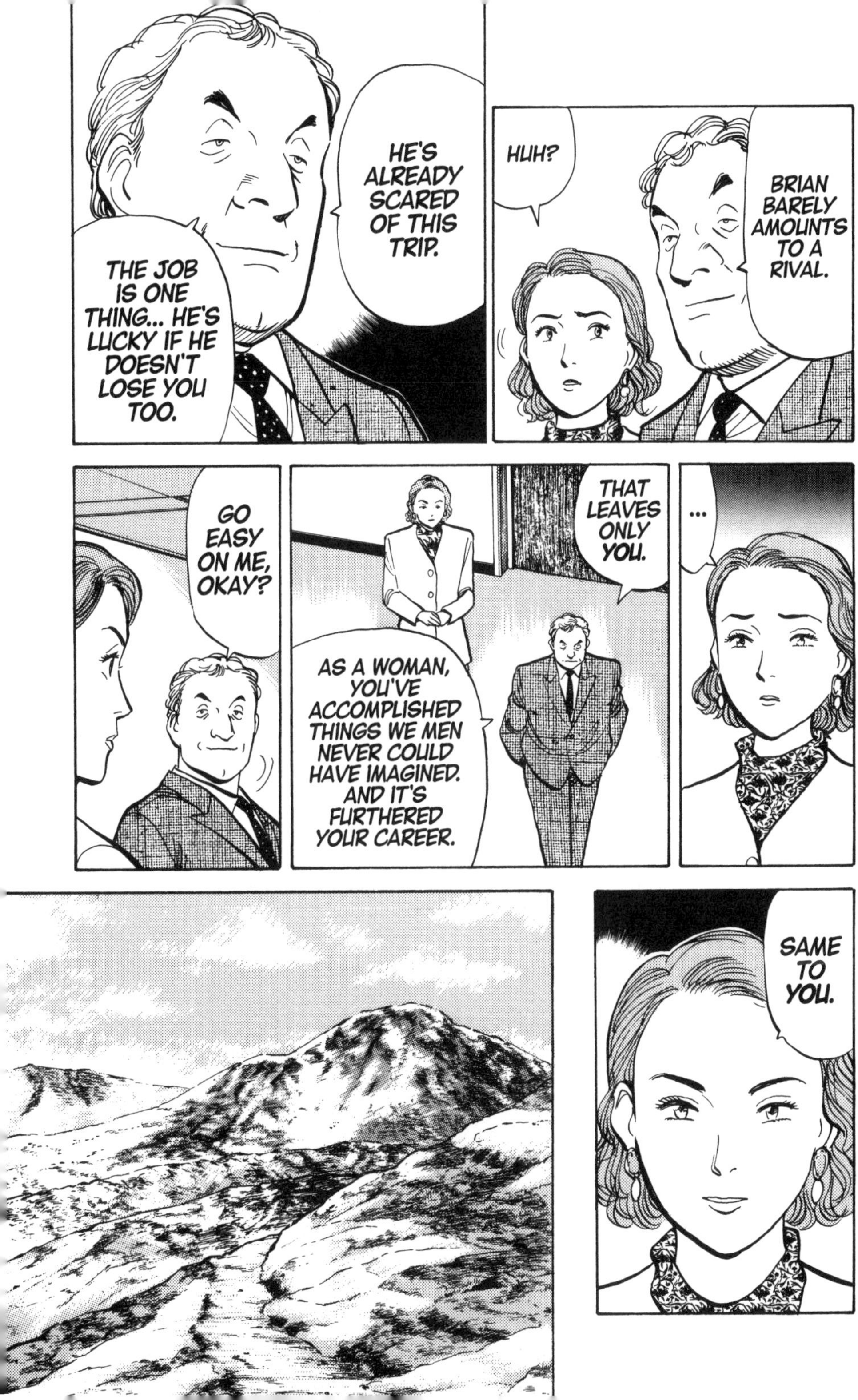
BRIAN BARELY AMOUNTS TO A RIVAL.
HUH?
HE'S ALREADY SCARED OF THIS TRIP.
THE JOB IS ONE THING... HE'S LUCKY IF HE DOESN'T LOSE YOU TOO.
...
THAT LEAVES ONLY YOU.
AS A WOMAN, YOU'VE ACCOMPLISHED THINGS WE MEN NEVER COULD HAVE IMAGINED. AND IT'S FURTHERED YOUR CAREER.
GO EASY ON ME, OKAY?
SAME TO YOU.

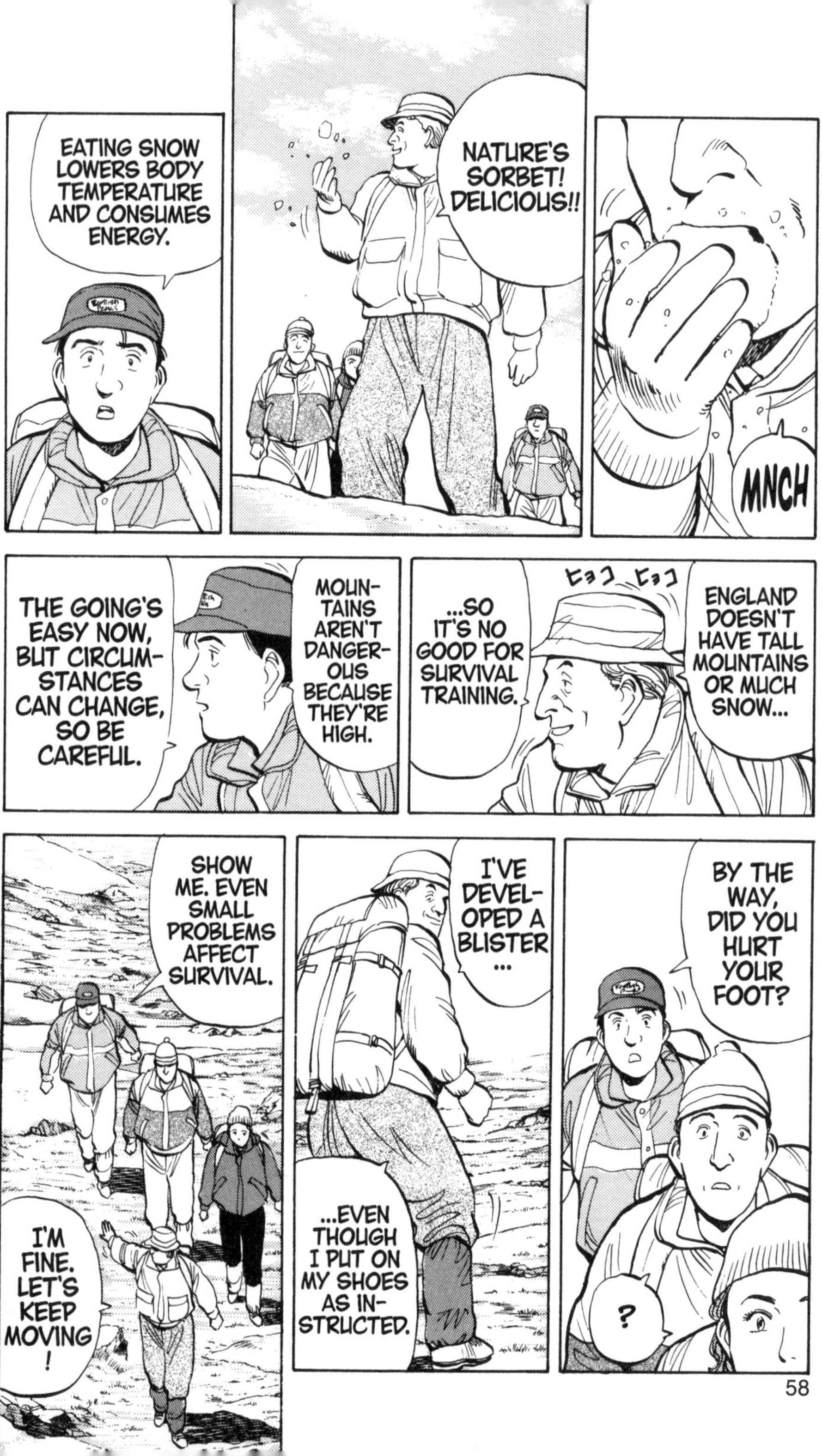
MNCH
NATURE'S SORBET! DELICIOUS!!
EATING SNOW LOWERS BODY TEMPERATURE AND CONSUMES ENERGY.
ヒョコ ヒョコ
ENGLAND DOESN'T HAVE TALL MOUNTAINS OR MUCH SNOW...
...SO IT'S NO GOOD FOR SURVIVAL TRAINING.
MOUNTAINS AREN'T DANGEROUS BECAUSE THEY'RE HIGH.
THE GOING'S EASY NOW, BUT CIRCUMSTANCES CAN CHANGE, SO BE CAREFUL.
BY THE WAY, DID YOU HURT YOUR FOOT?
?
I'VE DEVELOPED A BLISTER...
...EVEN THOUGH I PUT ON MY SHOES AS INSTRUCTED.
SHOW ME. EVEN SMALL PROBLEMS AFFECT SURVIVAL.
I'M FINE. LET'S KEEP MOVING!

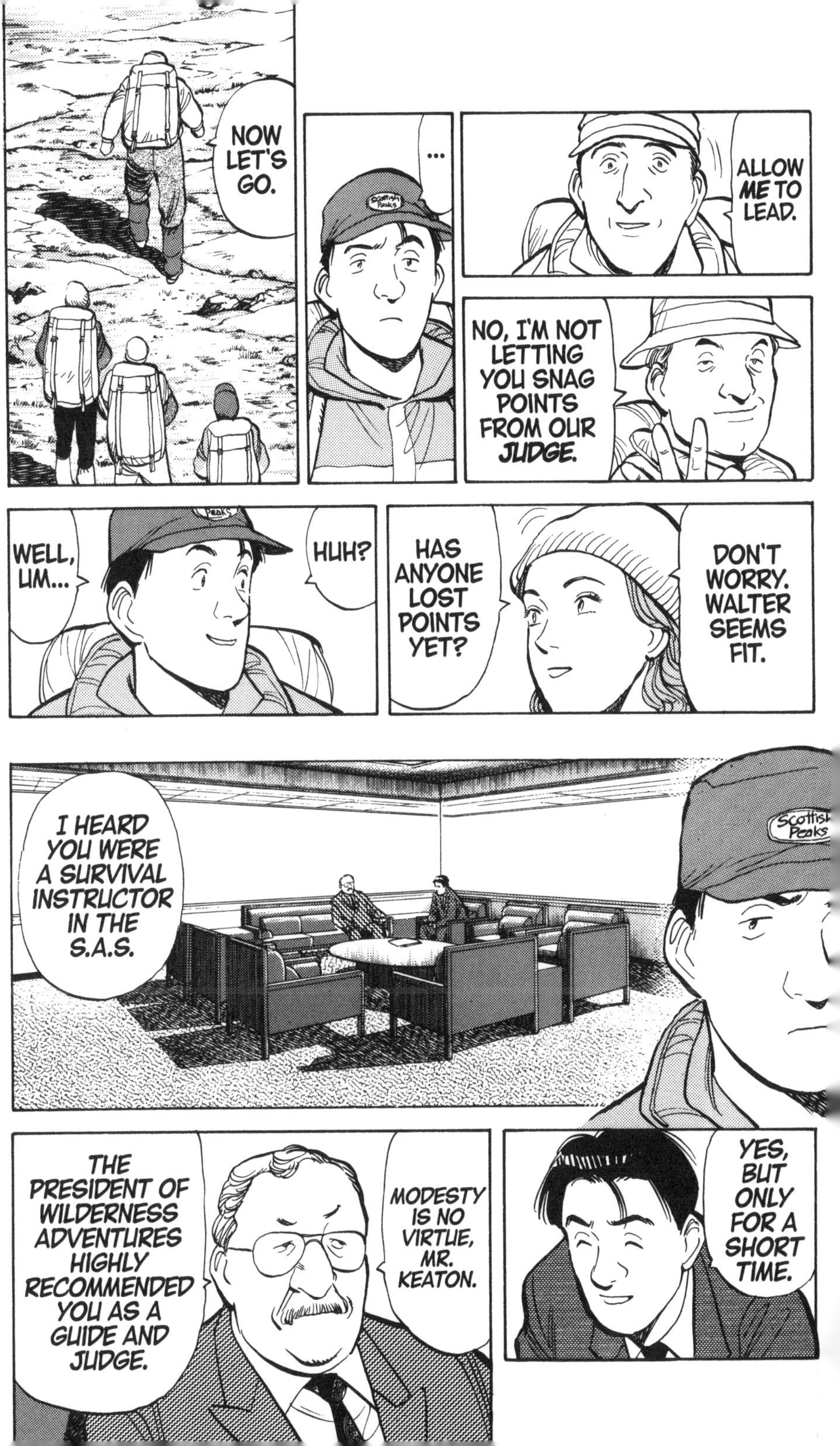
ALLOW ME TO LEAD.
NO, I'M NOT LETTING YOU SNAG POINTS FROM OUR JUDGE.
...
NOW LET'S GO.
DON'T WORRY. WALTER SEEMS FIT.
HAS ANYONE LOST POINTS YET?
HUH?
WELL, UM...
I HEARD YOU WERE A SURVIVAL INSTRUCTOR IN THE S.A.S.
YES, BUT ONLY FOR A SHORT TIME.
MODESTY IS NO VIRTUE, MR. KEATON.
THE PRESIDENT OF WILDERNESS ADVENTURES HIGHLY RECOMMENDED YOU AS A GUIDE AND JUDGE.

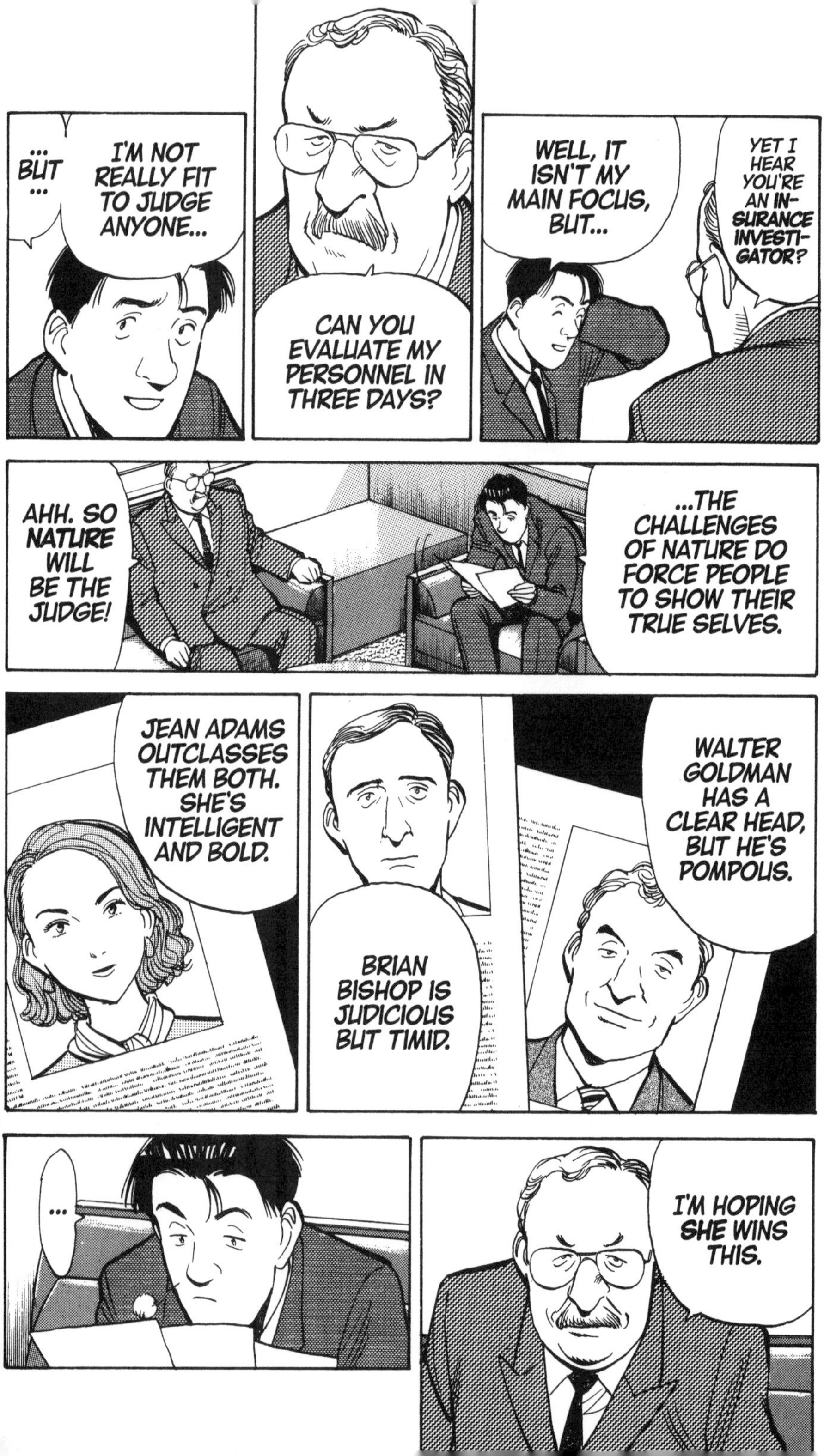
YET I HEAR YOU'RE AN INSURANCE INVESTIGATOR?
WELL, IT ISN'T MY MAIN FOCUS, BUT...
CAN YOU EVALUATE MY PERSONNEL IN THREE DAYS?
I'M NOT REALLY FIT TO JUDGE ANYONE...
...BUT...
...THE CHALLENGES OF NATURE DO FORCE PEOPLE TO SHOW THEIR TRUE SELVES.
AHH. SO NATURE WILL BE THE JUDGE!
WALTER GOLDMAN HAS A CLEAR HEAD, BUT HE'S POMPOUS.
BRIAN BISHOP IS JUDICIOUS BUT TIMID.
JEAN ADAMS OUTCLASSES THEM BOTH. SHE'S INTELLIGENT AND BOLD.
I'M HOPING SHE WINS THIS.
...

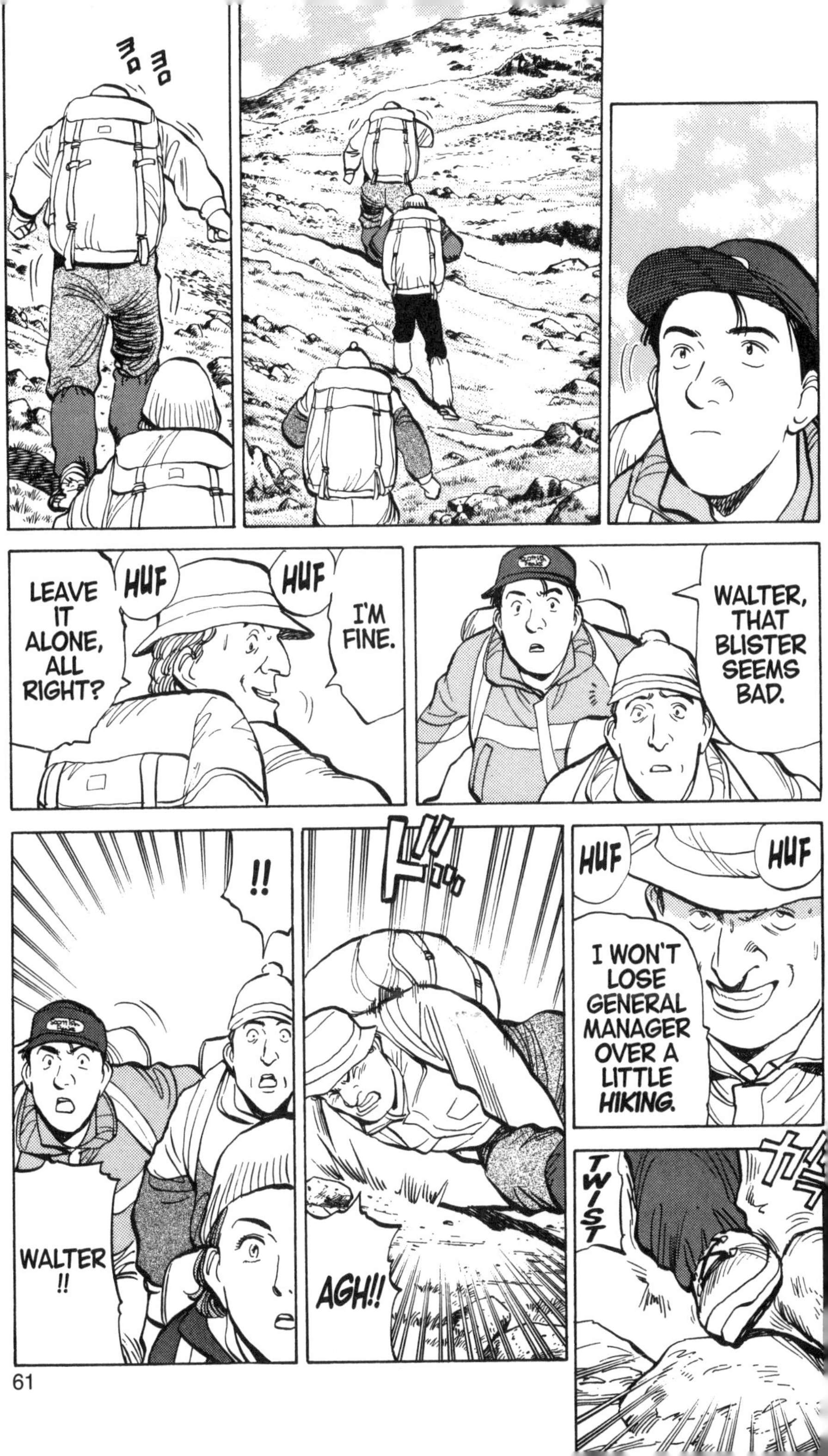
WALTER, THAT BLISTER SEEMS BAD.
HUF
I'M FINE.
HUF
LEAVE IT ALONE, ALL RIGHT?
HUF
HUF
I WON'T LOSE GENERAL MANAGER OVER A LITTLE HIKING.
TWIST
AGH!!
!!
WALTER !!

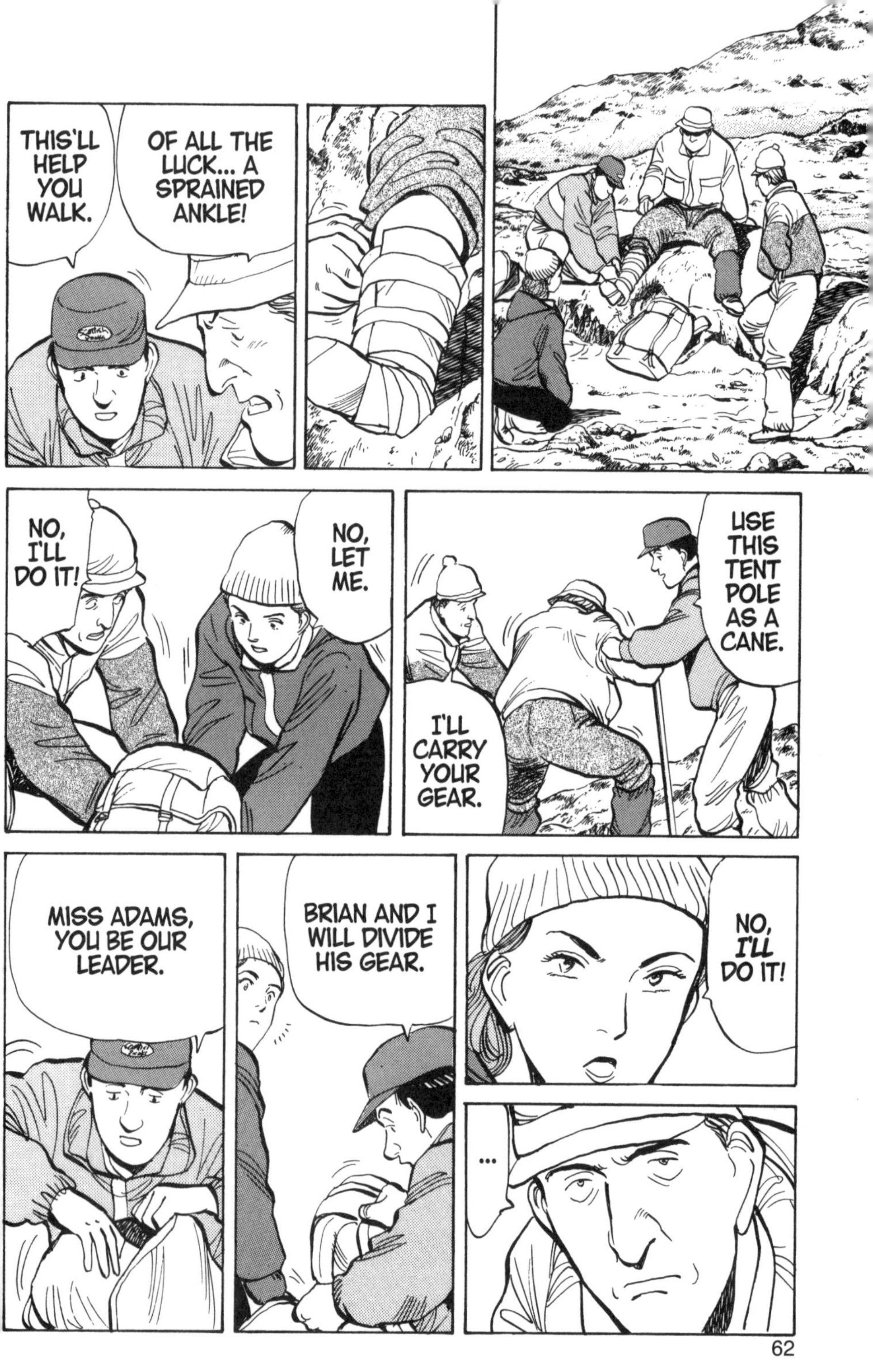
OF ALL THE LUCK... A SPRAINED ANKLE!
THIS'LL HELP YOU WALK.
USE THIS TENT POLE AS A CANE.
I'LL CARRY YOUR GEAR.
NO, LET ME.
NO, I'LL DO IT!
NO, I'LL DO IT!
...
BRIAN AND I WILL DIVIDE HIS GEAR.
MISS ADAMS, YOU BE OUR LEADER.

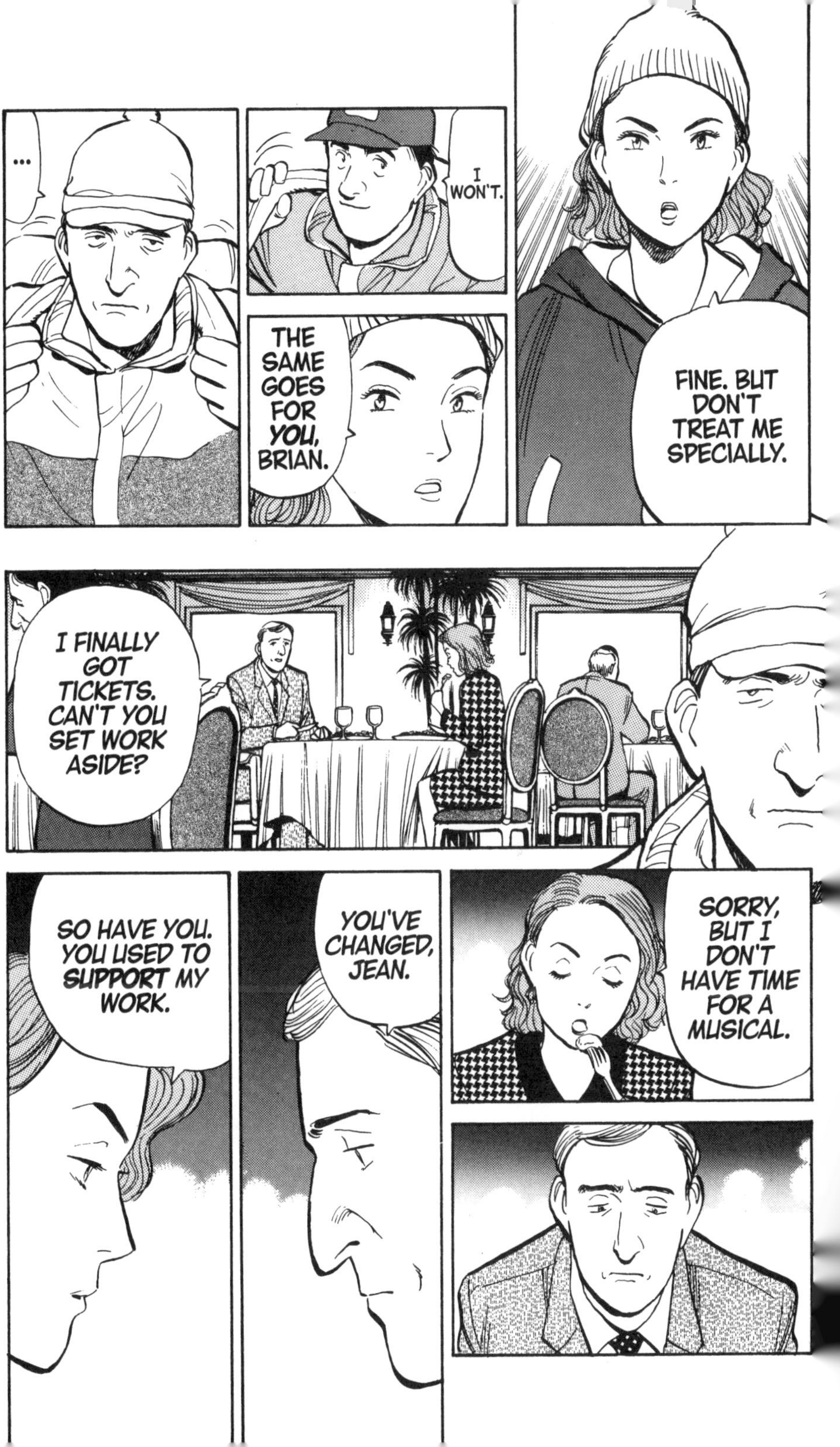
FINE. BUT DON'T TREAT ME SPECIALLY.
I WON'T.
THE SAME GOES FOR *YOU*, BRIAN.
...
I FINALLY GOT TICKETS. CAN'T YOU SET WORK ASIDE?
SORRY, BUT I DON'T HAVE TIME FOR A MUSICAL.
YOU'VE CHANGED, JEAN.
SO HAVE YOU. YOU USED TO **SUPPORT** MY WORK.

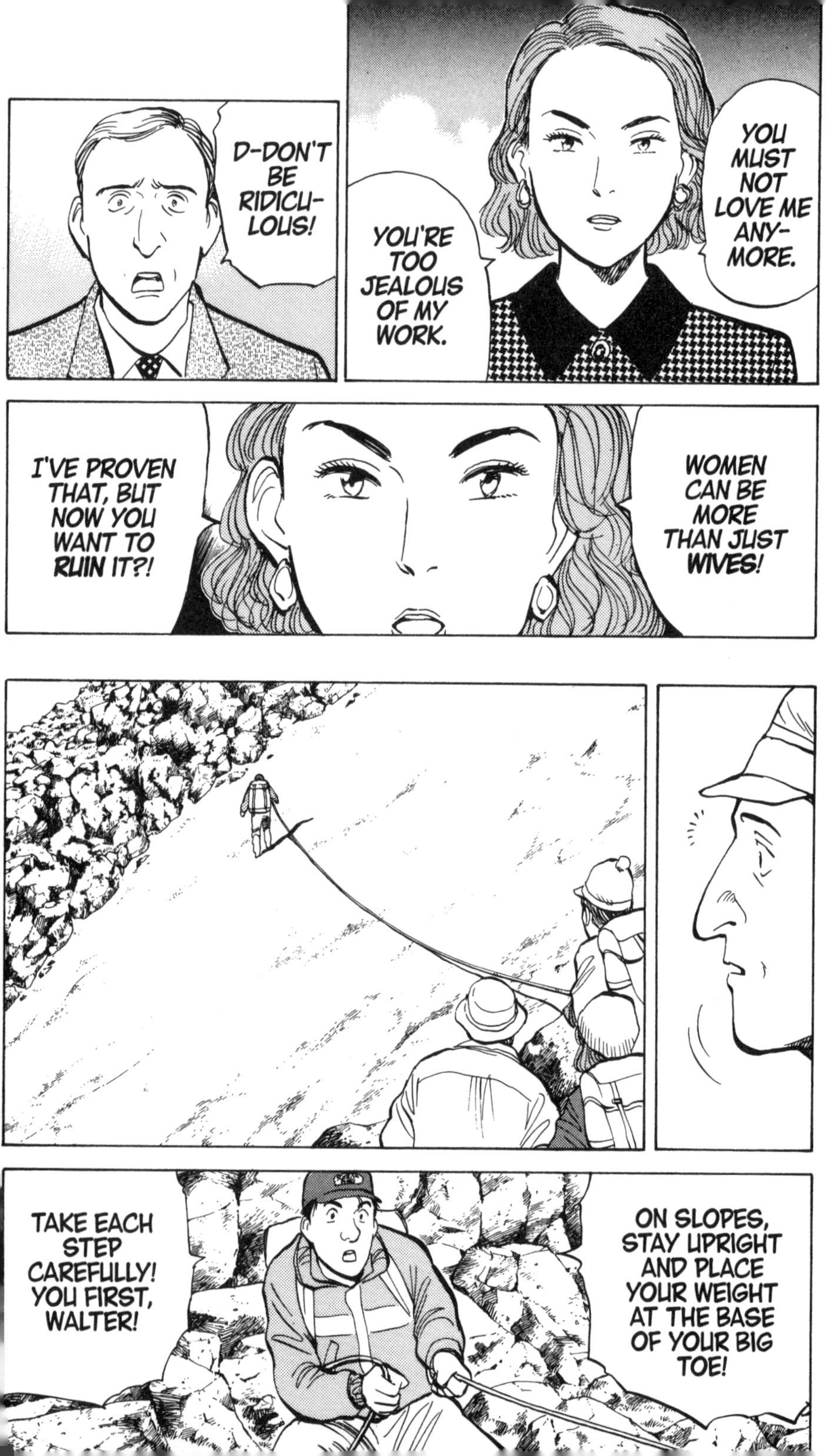
YOU MUST NOT LOVE ME ANYMORE.
YOU'RE TOO JEALOUS OF MY WORK.
D-DON'T BE RIDICULOUS!
WOMEN CAN BE MORE THAN JUST WIVES!
I'VE PROVEN THAT, BUT NOW YOU WANT TO RUIN IT?!
ON SLOPES, STAY UPRIGHT AND PLACE YOUR WEIGHT AT THE BASE OF YOUR BIG TOE!
TAKE EACH STEP CAREFULLY! YOU FIRST, WALTER!

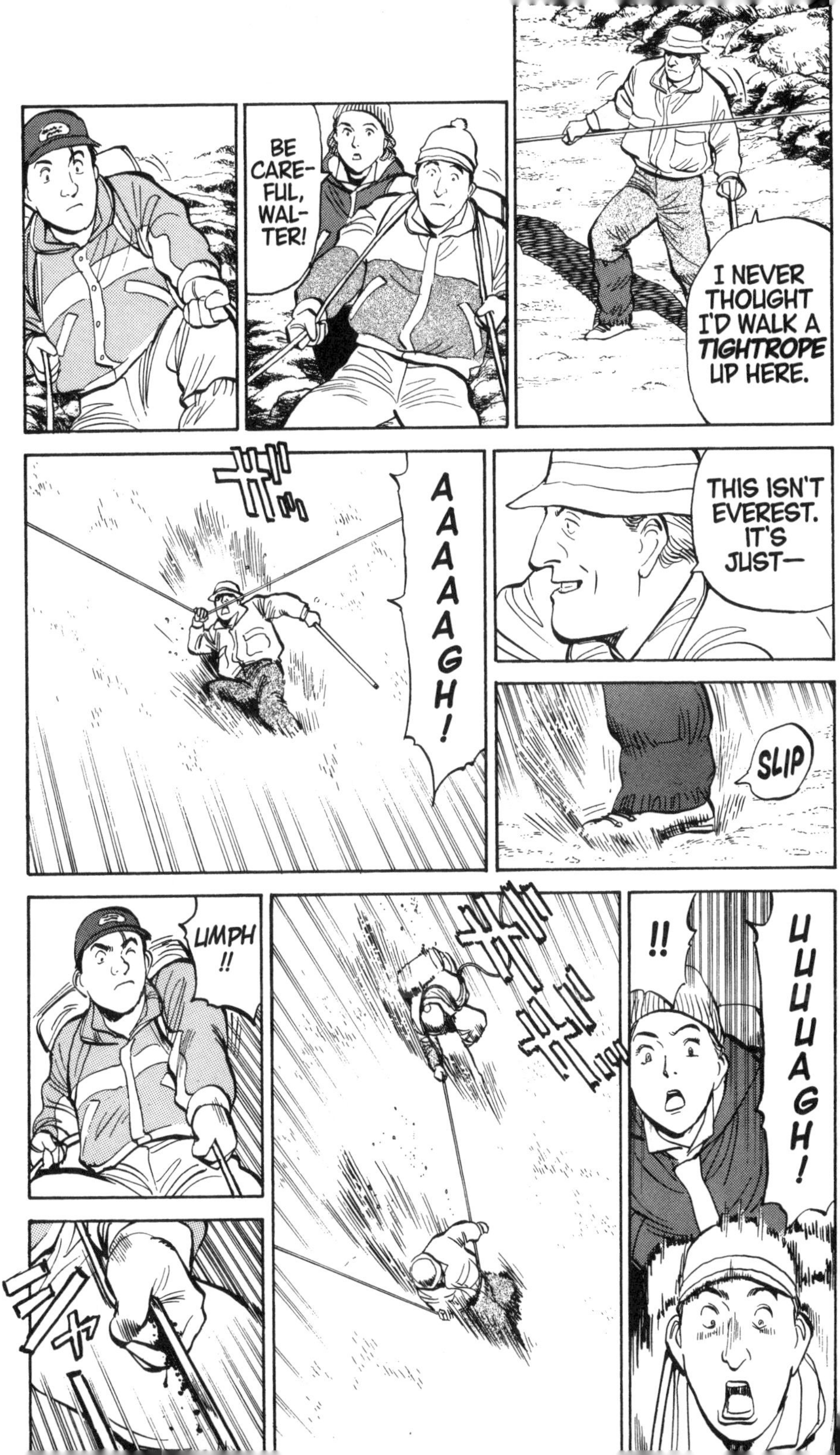

I NEVER THOUGHT I'D WALK A TIGHTROPE UP HERE.
BE CAREFUL, WALTER!
THIS ISN'T EVEREST. IT'S JUST—
SLIP
AAAAAAGH!
UUUUAGH!
!!
UMPH!!

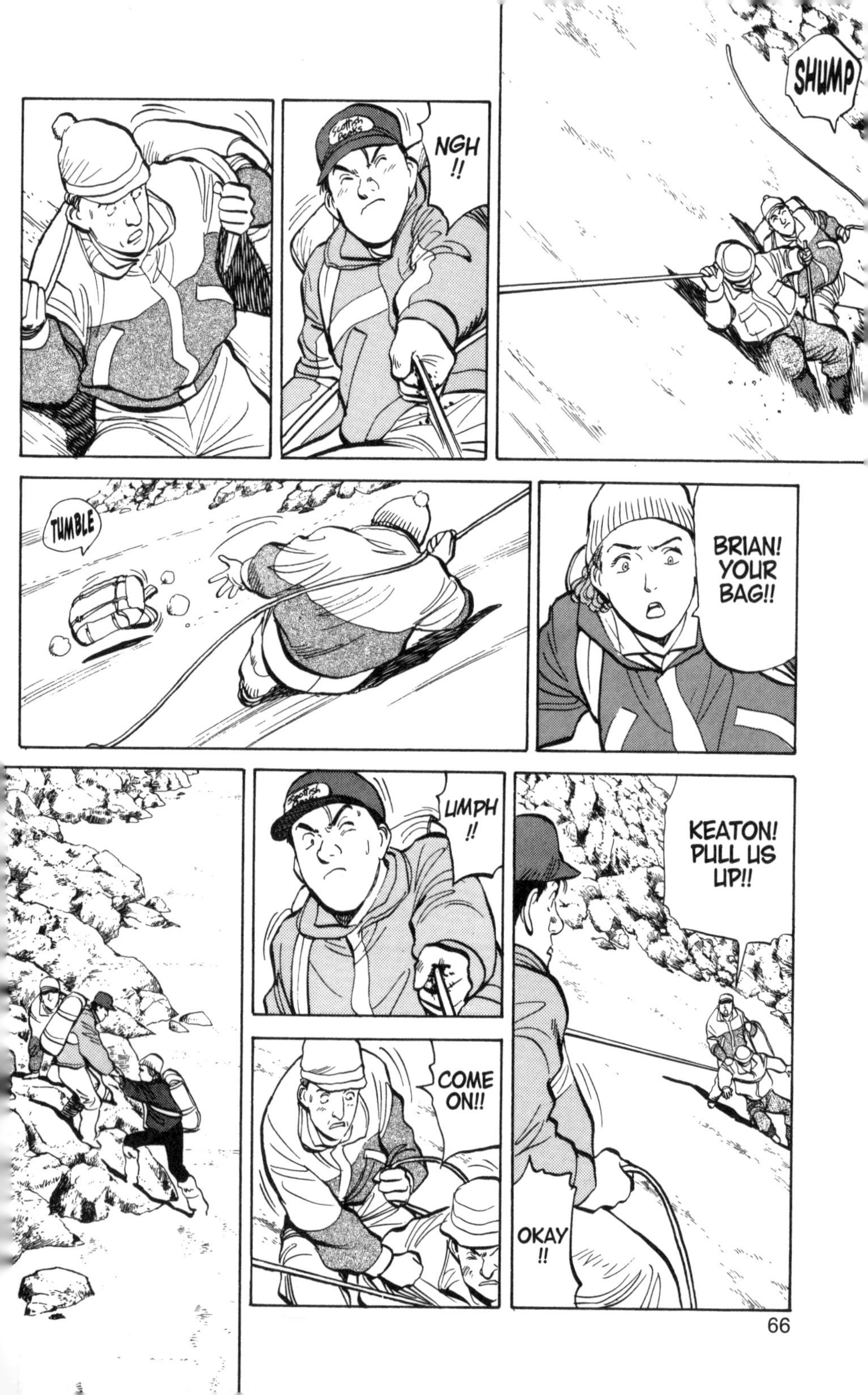
SHUMP
NGH!!
BRIAN! YOUR BAG!!
TUMBLE
KEATON! PULL US UP!!
OKAY!!
UMPH!!
COME ON!!

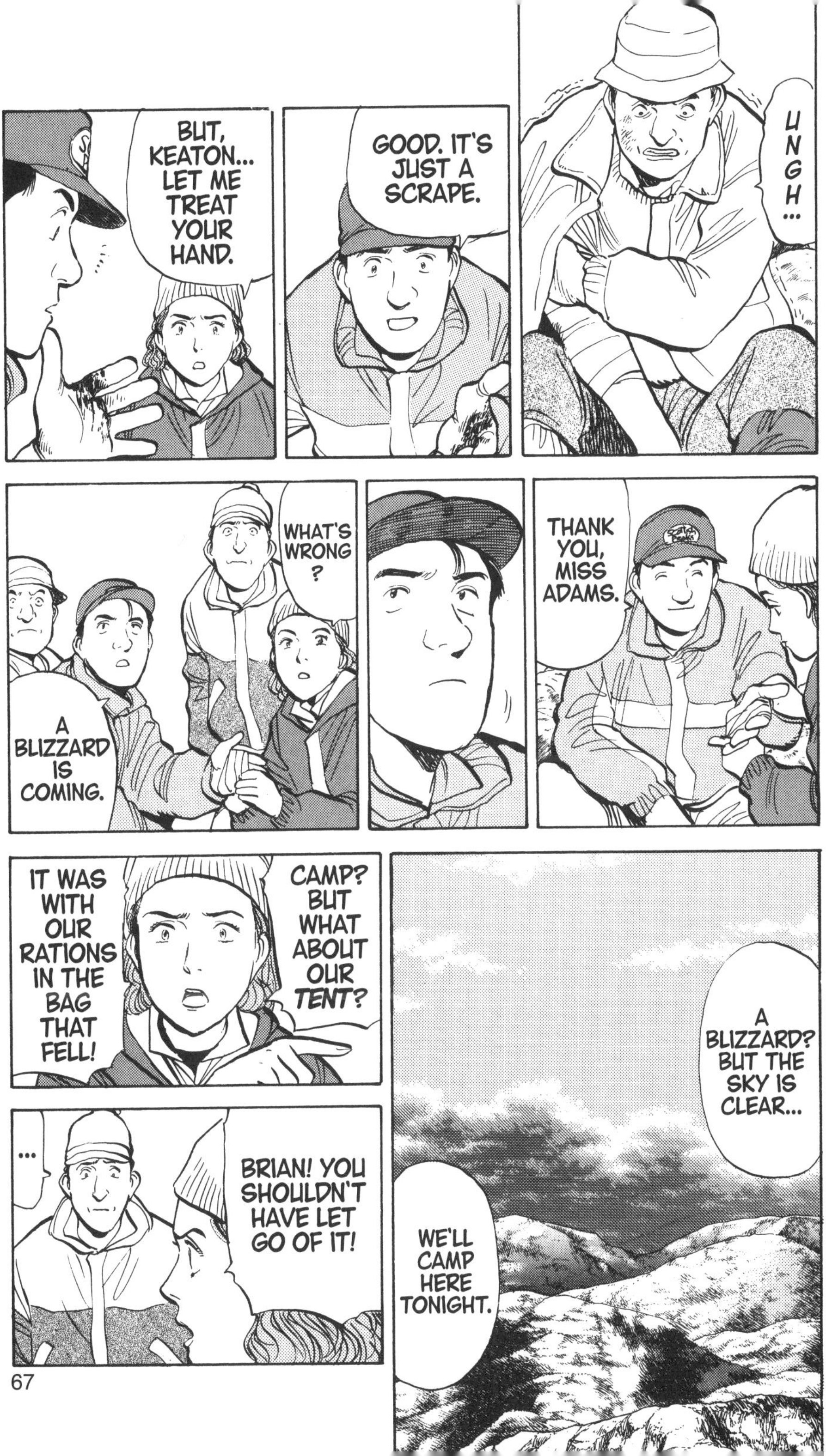
UNGH...
GOOD. IT'S JUST A SCRAPE.
BUT, KEATON... LET ME TREAT YOUR HAND.
THANK YOU, MISS ADAMS.
WHAT'S WRONG?
A BLIZZARD IS COMING.
A BLIZZARD? BUT THE SKY IS CLEAR...
WE'LL CAMP HERE TONIGHT.
CAMP? BUT WHAT ABOUT OUR *TENT*?
IT WAS WITH OUR RATIONS IN THE BAG THAT FELL!
BRIAN! YOU SHOULDN'T HAVE LET GO OF IT!
...

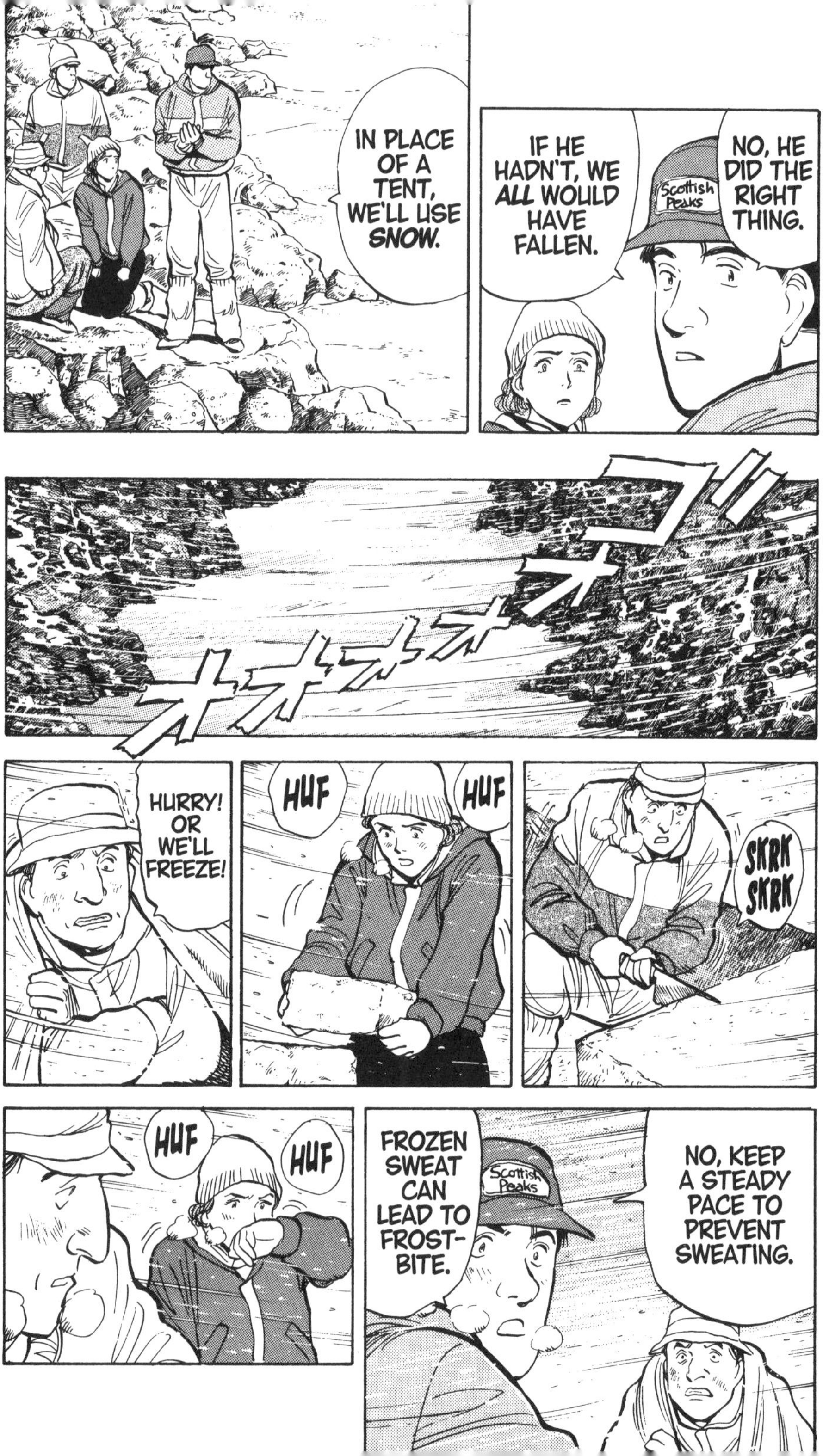
NO, HE DID THE RIGHT THING.
IF HE HADN'T, WE ALL WOULD HAVE FALLEN.
IN PLACE OF A TENT, WE'LL USE SNOW.
ゴオオオオオ
SKRK SKRK
HUF
HUF
HURRY! OR WE'LL FREEZE!
NO, KEEP A STEADY PACE TO PREVENT SWEATING.
FROZEN SWEAT CAN LEAD TO FROST-BITE.
HUF
HUF

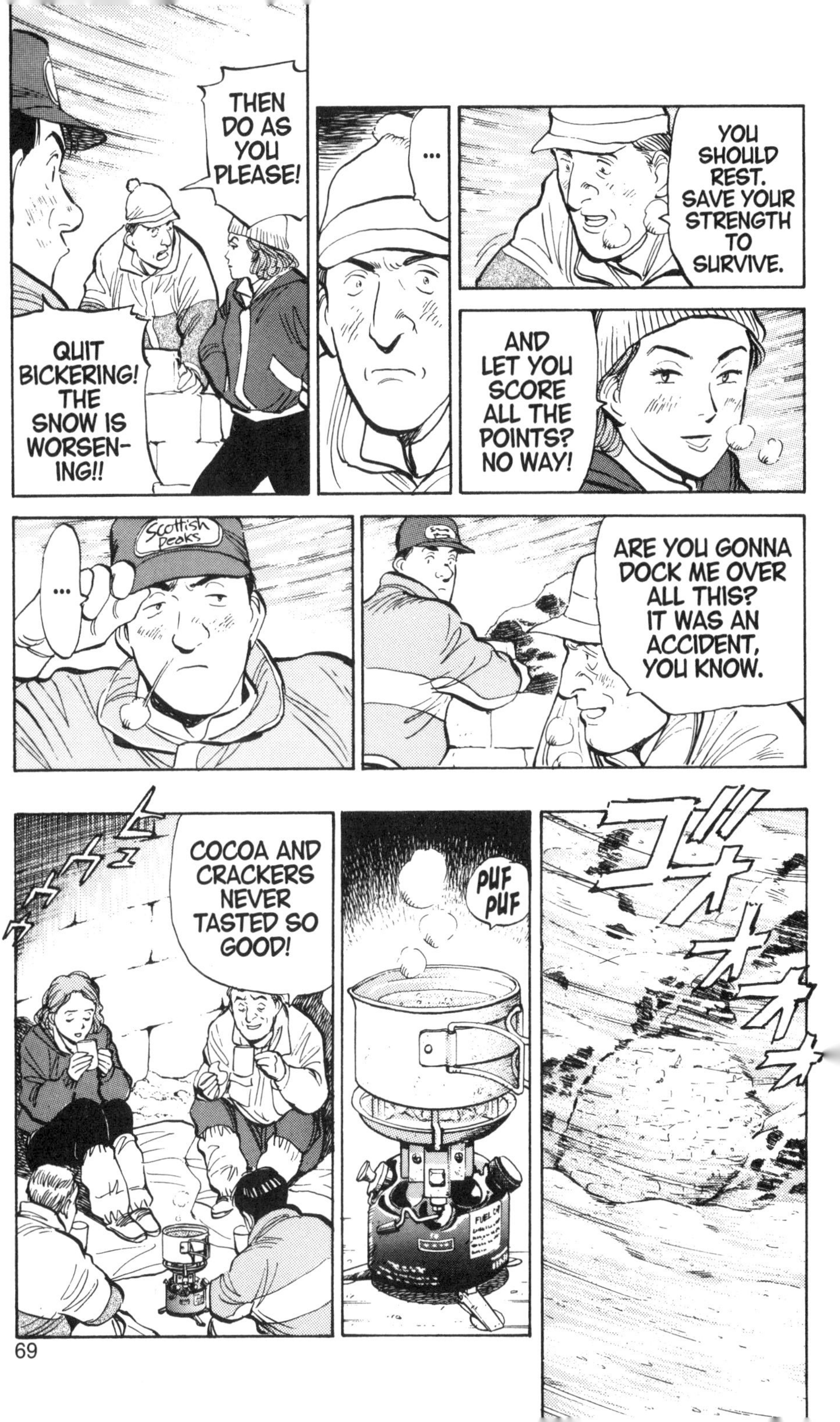
YOU SHOULD REST. SAVE YOUR STRENGTH TO SURVIVE.
AND LET YOU SCORE ALL THE POINTS? NO WAY!
...
THEN DO AS YOU PLEASE!
QUIT BICKERING! THE SNOW IS WORSEN-ING!!
ARE YOU GONNA DOCK ME OVER ALL THIS? IT WAS AN ACCIDENT, YOU KNOW.
...
Scottish Peaks
PUF PUF
COCOA AND CRACKERS NEVER TASTED SO GOOD!

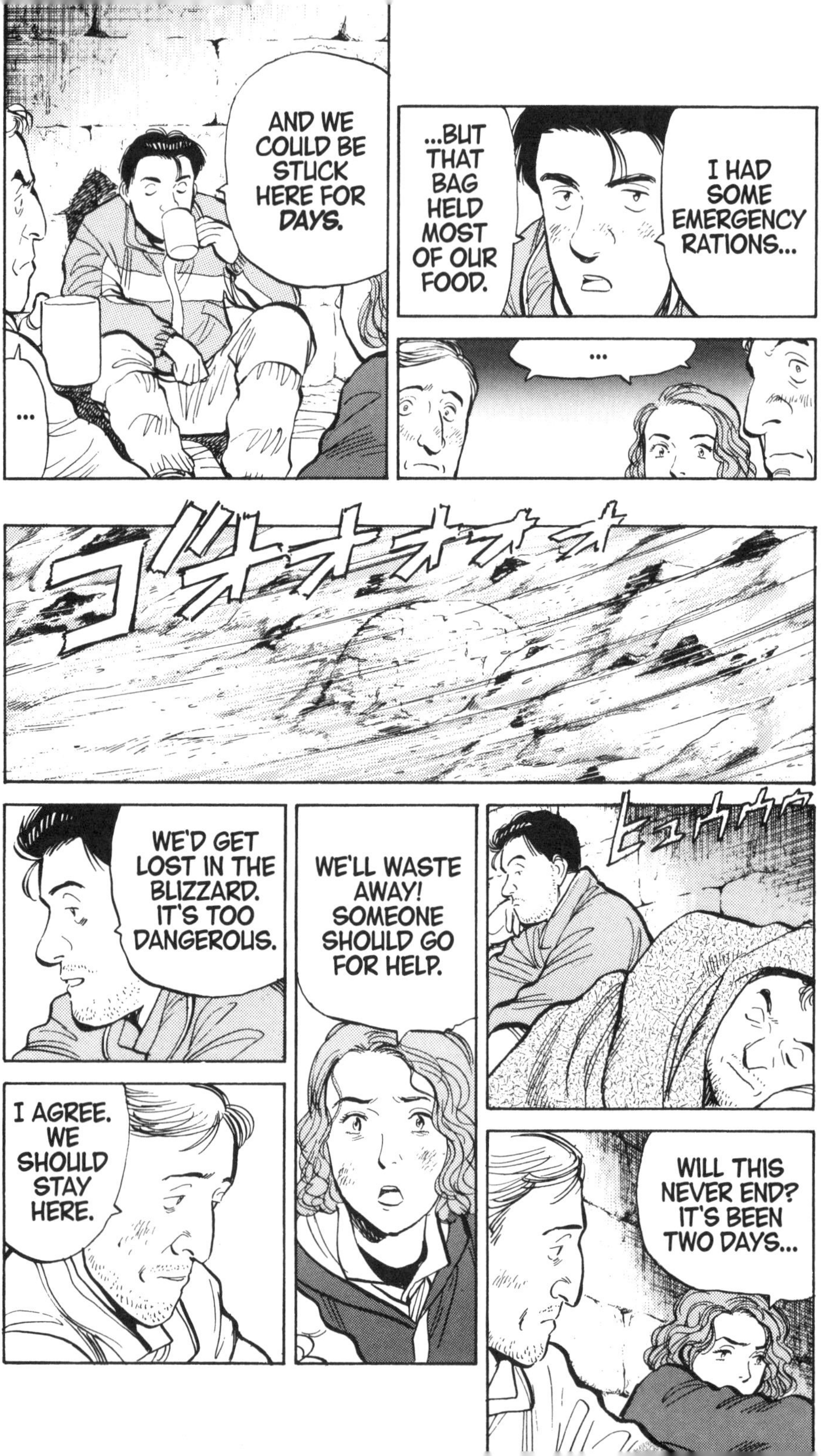
I HAD SOME EMERGENCY RATIONS...
...BUT THAT BAG HELD MOST OF OUR FOOD.
...
AND WE COULD BE STUCK HERE FOR DAYS.
...
ゴオオオオオ
ヒュウウウ
WILL THIS NEVER END? IT'S BEEN TWO DAYS...
WE'LL WASTE AWAY! SOMEONE SHOULD GO FOR HELP.
WE'D GET LOST IN THE BLIZZARD. IT'S TOO DANGEROUS.
I AGREE. WE SHOULD STAY HERE.

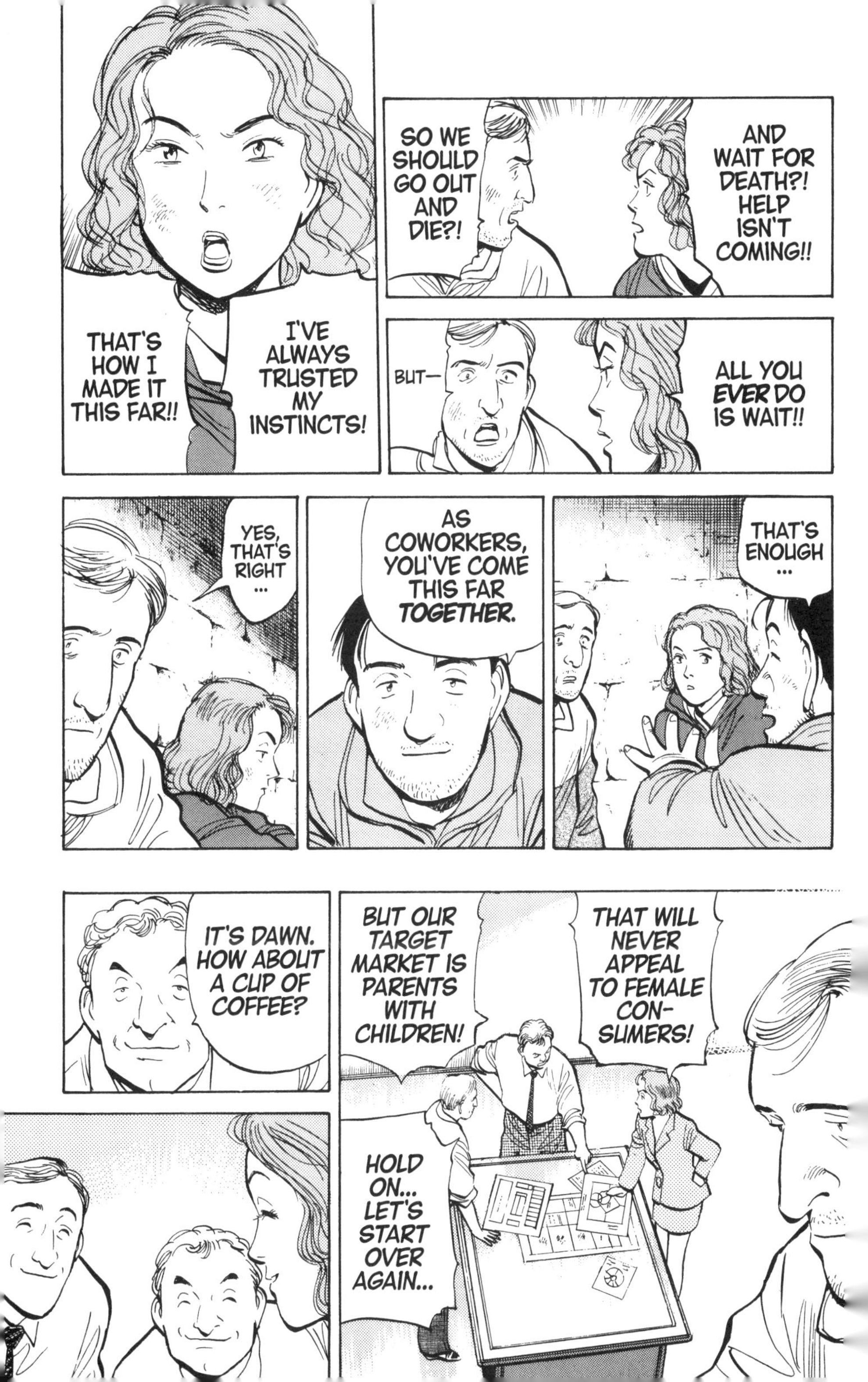
AND WAIT FOR DEATH?! HELP ISN'T COMING!!
SO WE SHOULD GO OUT AND DIE?!
ALL YOU *EVER* DO IS WAIT!!
BUT—
I'VE ALWAYS TRUSTED MY INSTINCTS!
THAT'S HOW I MADE IT THIS FAR!!
THAT'S ENOUGH...
AS COWORKERS, YOU'VE COME THIS FAR *TOGETHER.*
YES, THAT'S RIGHT...
THAT WILL NEVER APPEAL TO FEMALE CON-SUMERS!
BUT OUR TARGET MARKET IS PARENTS WITH CHILDREN!
HOLD ON... LET'S START OVER AGAIN...
IT'S DAWN. HOW ABOUT A CUP OF COFFEE?

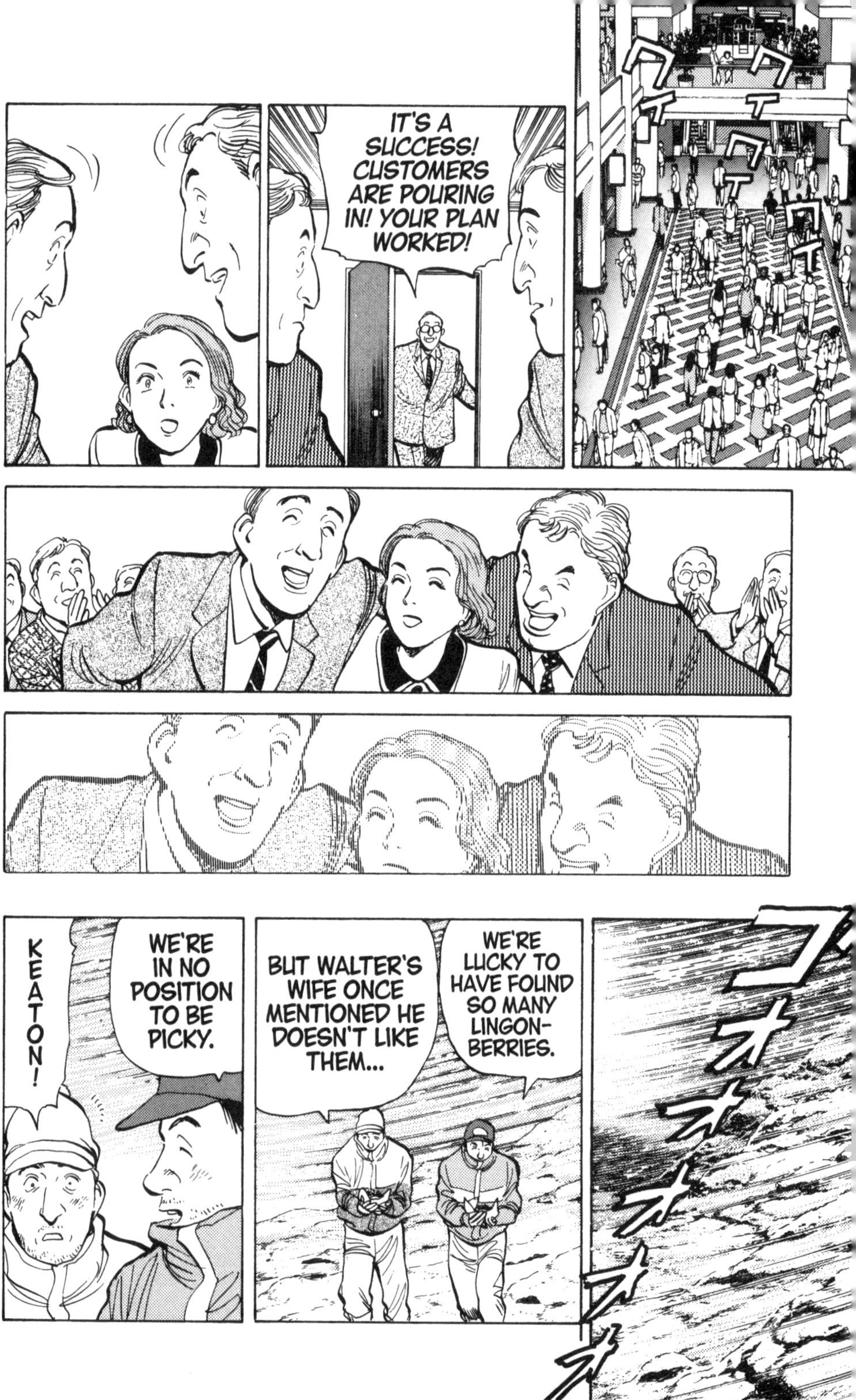
IT'S A SUCCESS! CUSTOMERS ARE POURING IN! YOUR PLAN WORKED!
WE'RE LUCKY TO HAVE FOUND SO MANY LINGON-BERRIES.
BUT WALTER'S WIFE ONCE MENTIONED HE DOESN'T LIKE THEM...
WE'RE IN NO POSITION TO BE PICKY.
KEATON!

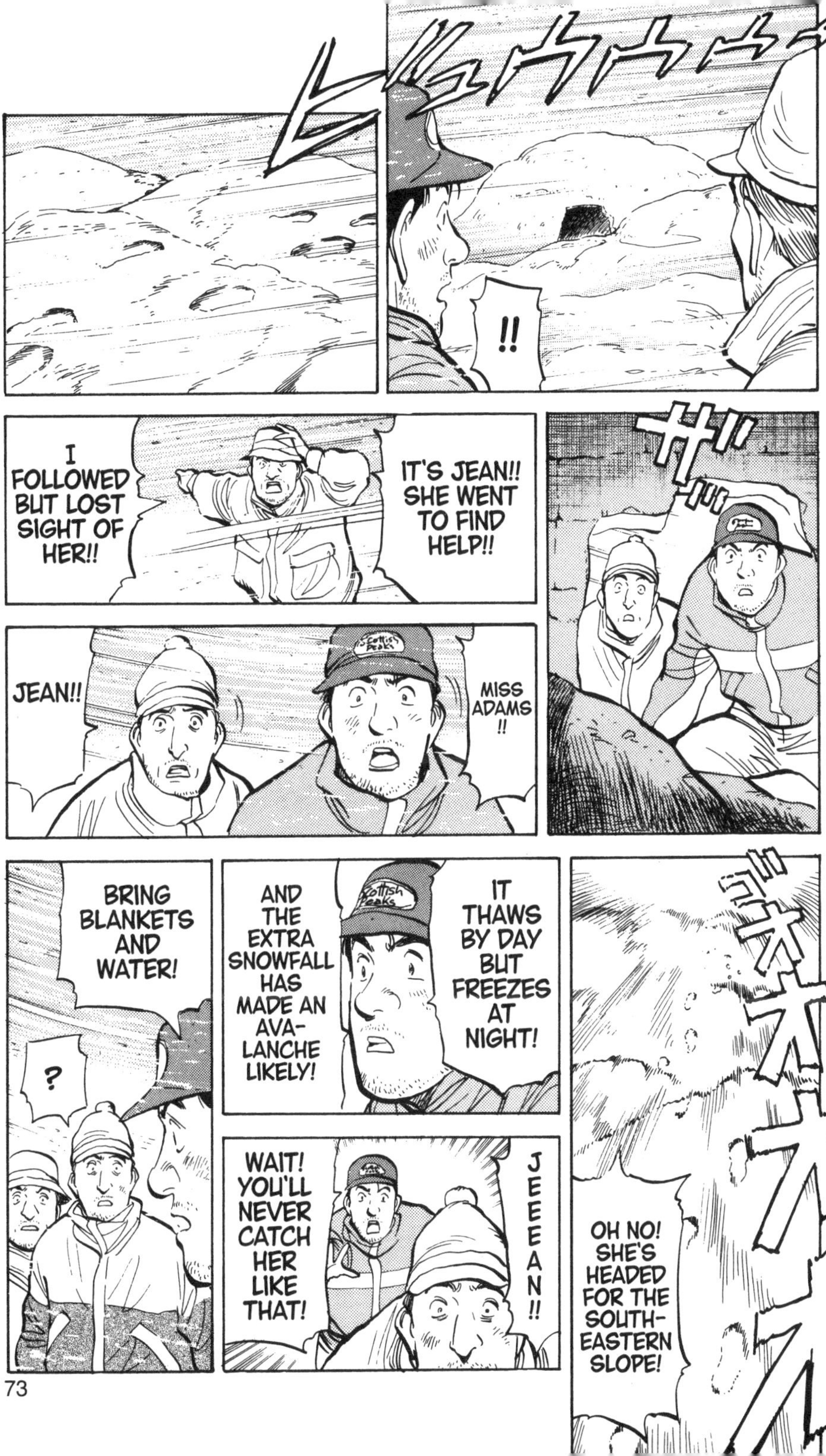
!!
IT'S JEAN!! SHE WENT TO FIND HELP!!
I FOLLOWED BUT LOST SIGHT OF HER!!
MISS ADAMS!!
JEAN!!
OH NO! SHE'S HEADED FOR THE SOUTH-EASTERN SLOPE!
IT THAWS BY DAY BUT FREEZES AT NIGHT!
AND THE EXTRA SNOWFALL HAS MADE AN AVA-LANCHE LIKELY!
JEEEEAN!!
WAIT! YOU'LL NEVER CATCH HER LIKE THAT!
BRING BLANKETS AND WATER!
?

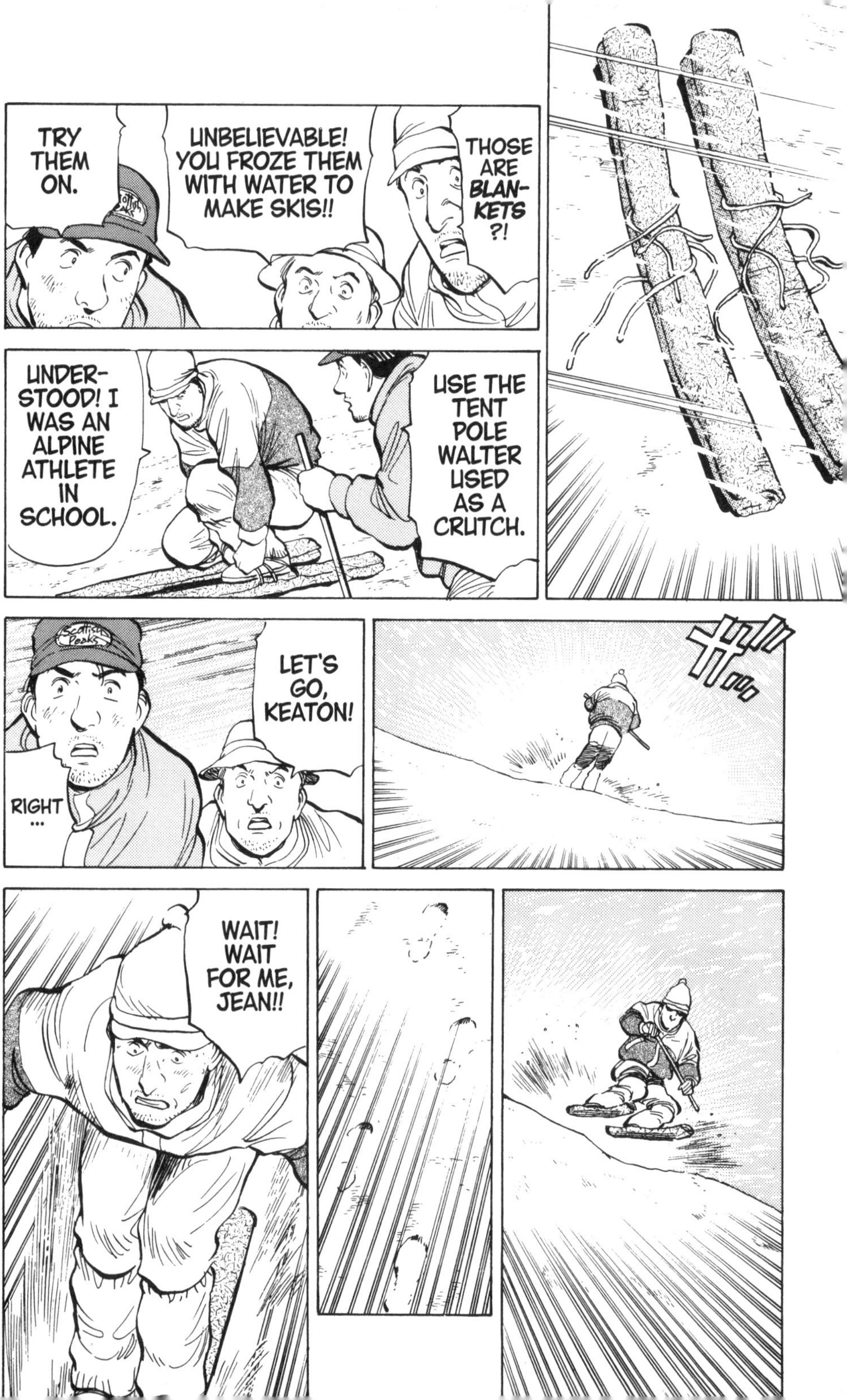
THOSE ARE BLANKETS?!
UNBELIEVABLE! YOU FROZE THEM WITH WATER TO MAKE SKIS!!
TRY THEM ON.
USE THE TENT POLE WALTER USED AS A CRUTCH.
UNDERSTOOD! I WAS AN ALPINE ATHLETE IN SCHOOL.
ザッ
LET'S GO, KEATON!
RIGHT...
WAIT! WAIT FOR ME, JEAN!!

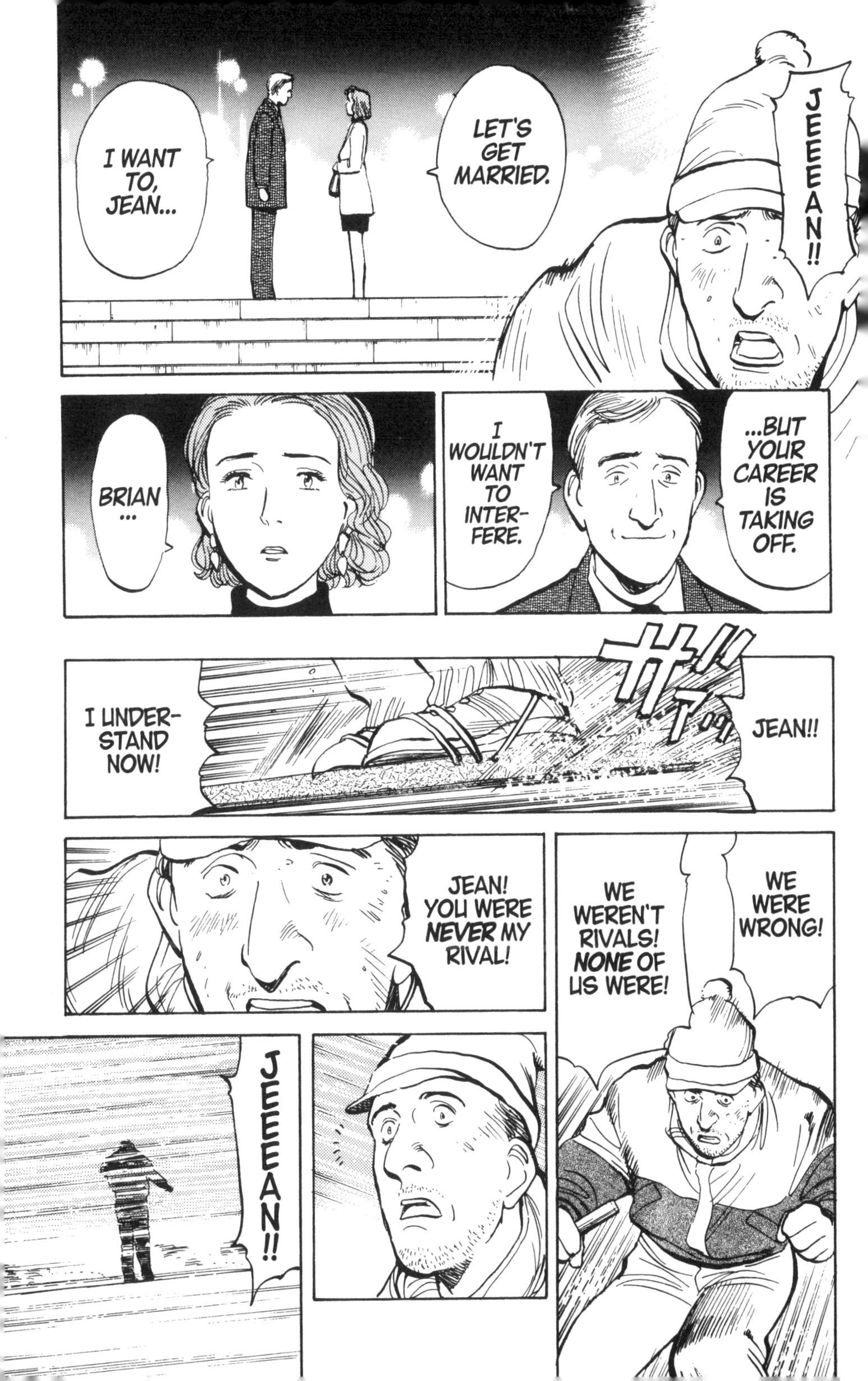
JEEEAN!!
LET'S GET MARRIED.
I WANT TO, JEAN...
...BUT YOUR CAREER IS TAKING OFF.
I WOULDN'T WANT TO INTERFERE.
BRIAN...
JEAN!!
ザザァッ
I UNDER-STAND NOW!
WE WERE WRONG!
WE WEREN'T RIVALS! NONE OF US WERE!
JEAN! YOU WERE NEVER MY RIVAL!
JEEEAN!!

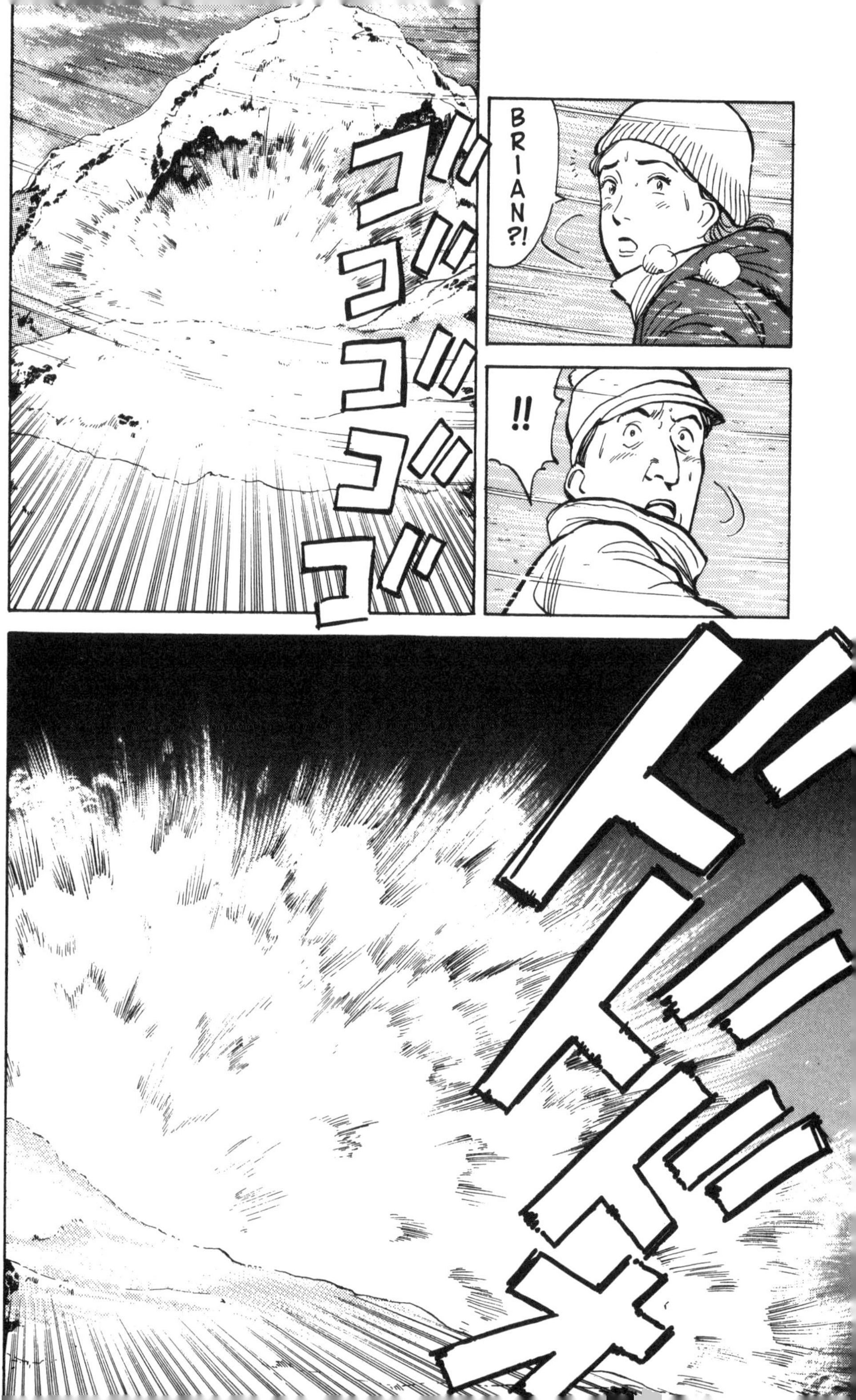
BRIAN?!
!!

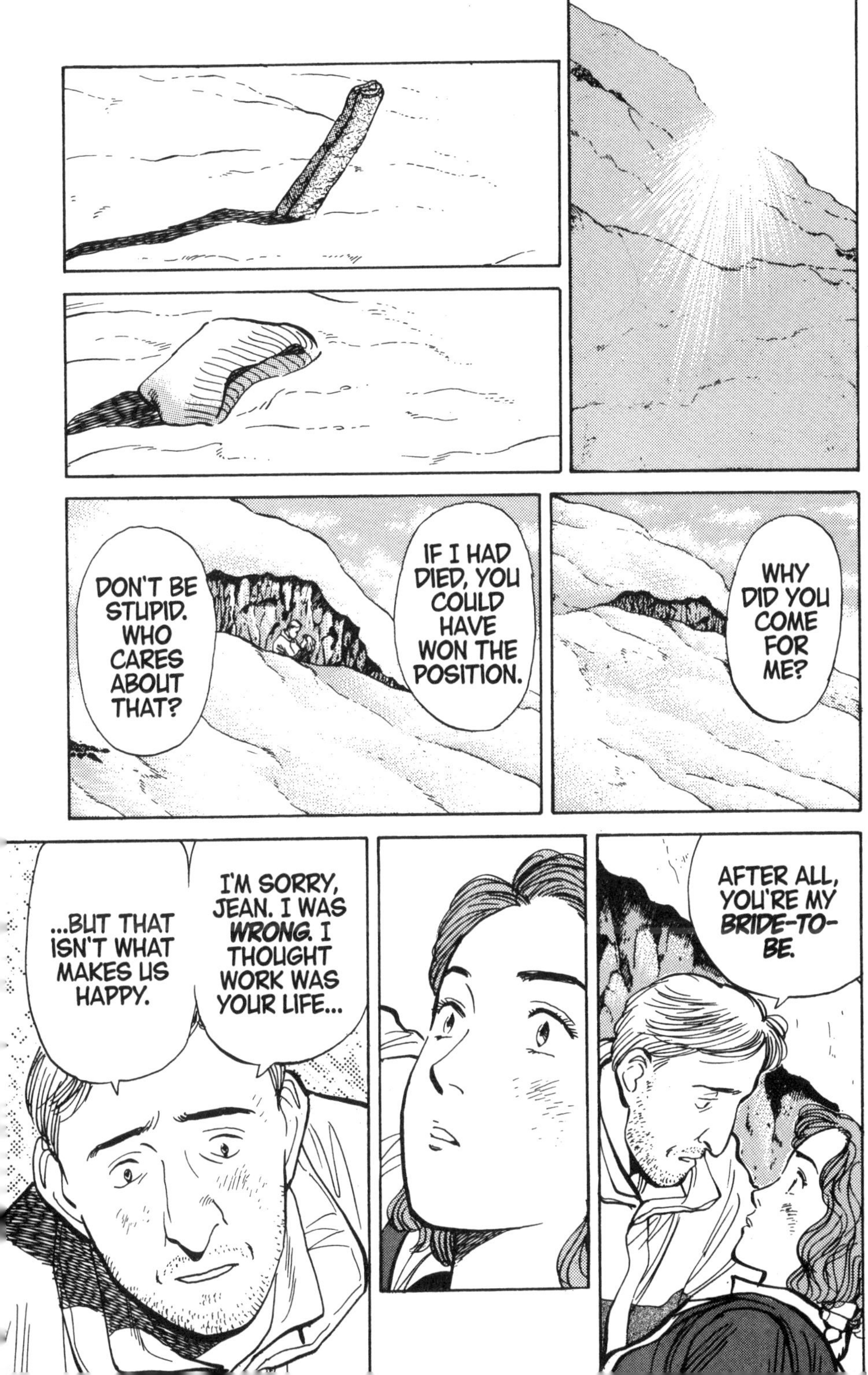
WHY DID YOU COME FOR ME?
IF I HAD DIED, YOU COULD HAVE WON THE POSITION.
DON'T BE STUPID. WHO CARES ABOUT THAT?
AFTER ALL, YOU'RE MY *BRIDE-TO-BE.*
I'M SORRY, JEAN. I WAS **WRONG.** I THOUGHT WORK WAS YOUR LIFE...
...BUT THAT ISN'T WHAT MAKES US HAPPY.

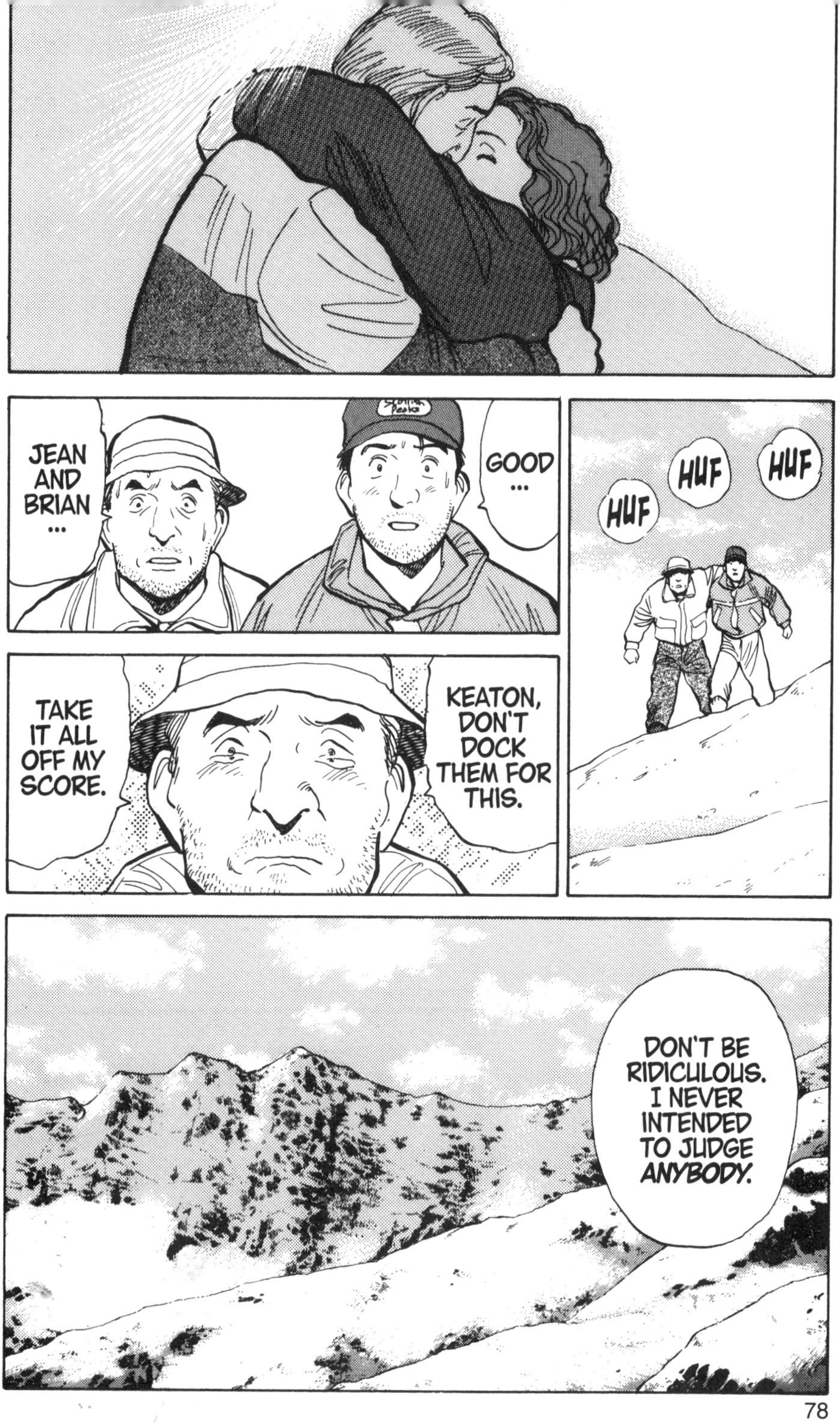
HUF
HUF
HUF
GOOD ...
JEAN AND BRIAN ...
KEATON, DON'T DOCK THEM FOR THIS.
TAKE IT ALL OFF MY SCORE.
DON'T BE RIDICULOUS. I NEVER INTENDED TO JUDGE ANYBODY.

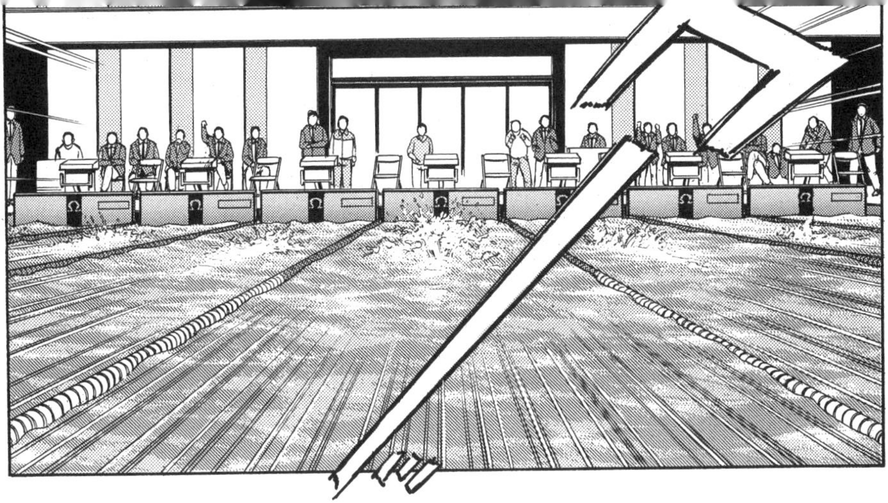

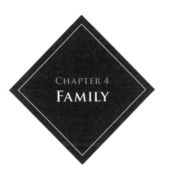

Chapter 4
Family

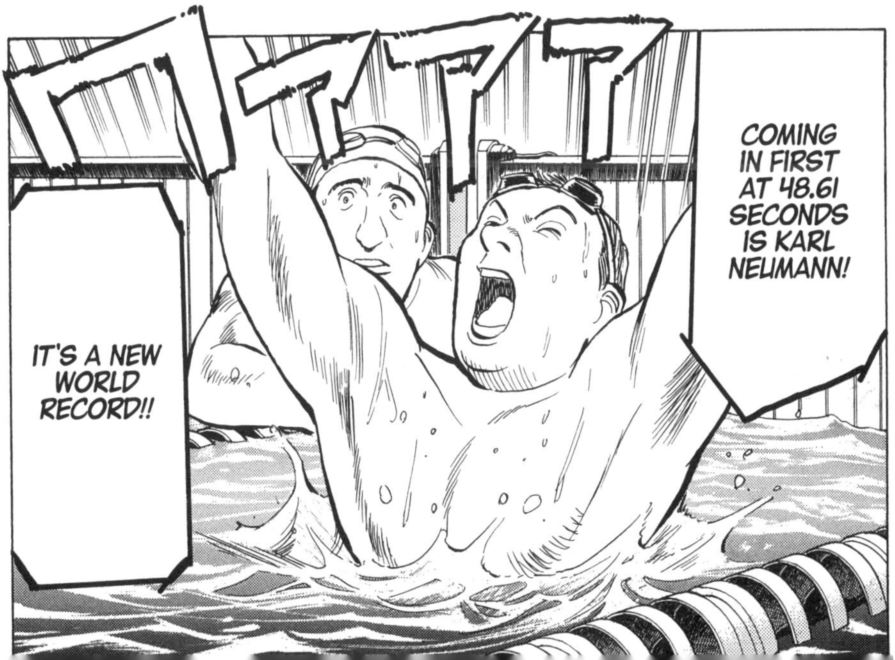
COMING IN FIRST AT 48.61 SECONDS IS KARL NEUMANN!
IT'S A NEW WORLD RECORD!!

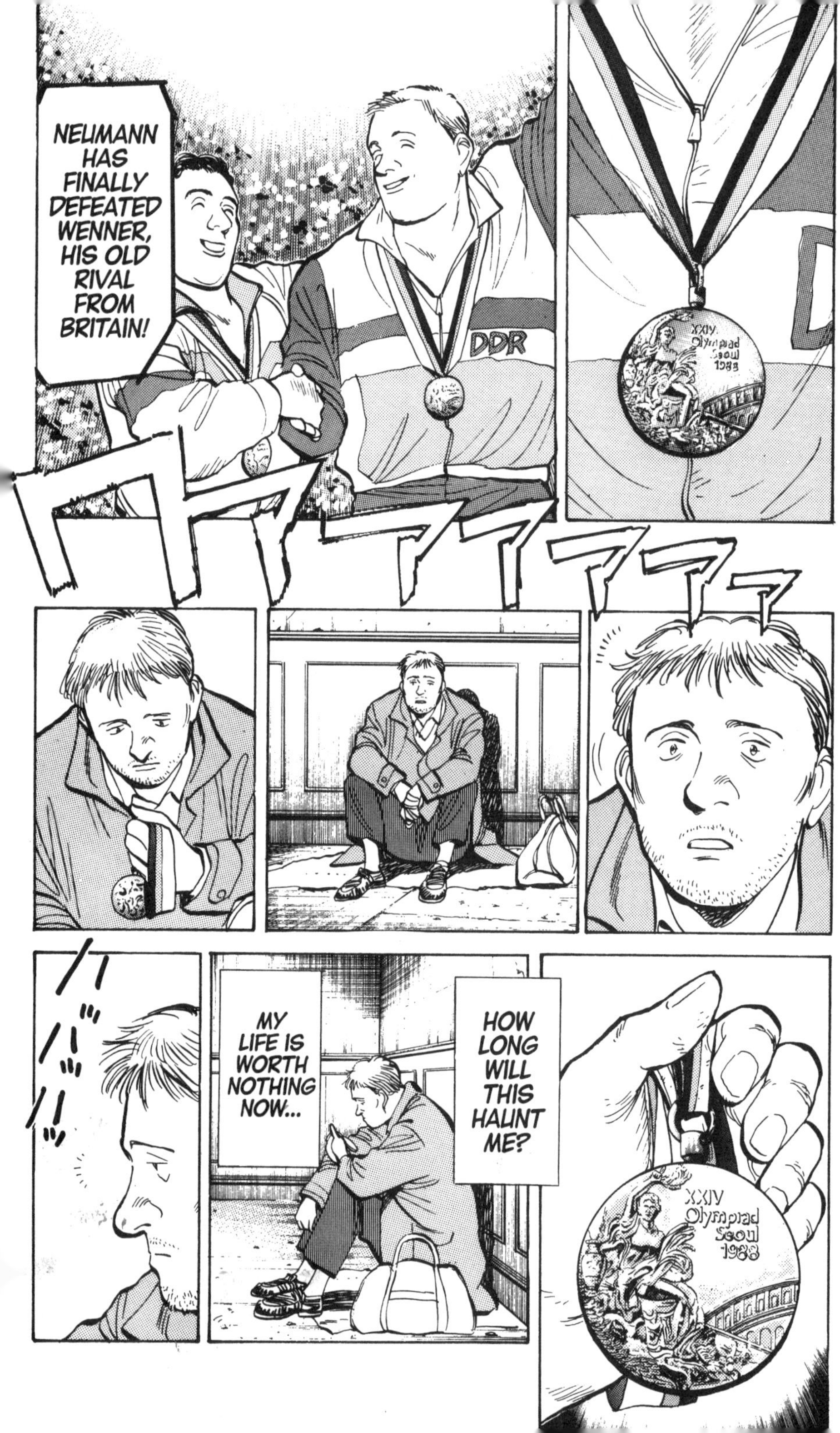
NEUMANN HAS FINALLY DEFEATED WENNER, HIS OLD RIVAL FROM BRITAIN!
ワァァァァァ
HOW LONG WILL THIS HAUNT ME?
MY LIFE IS WORTH NOTHING NOW...

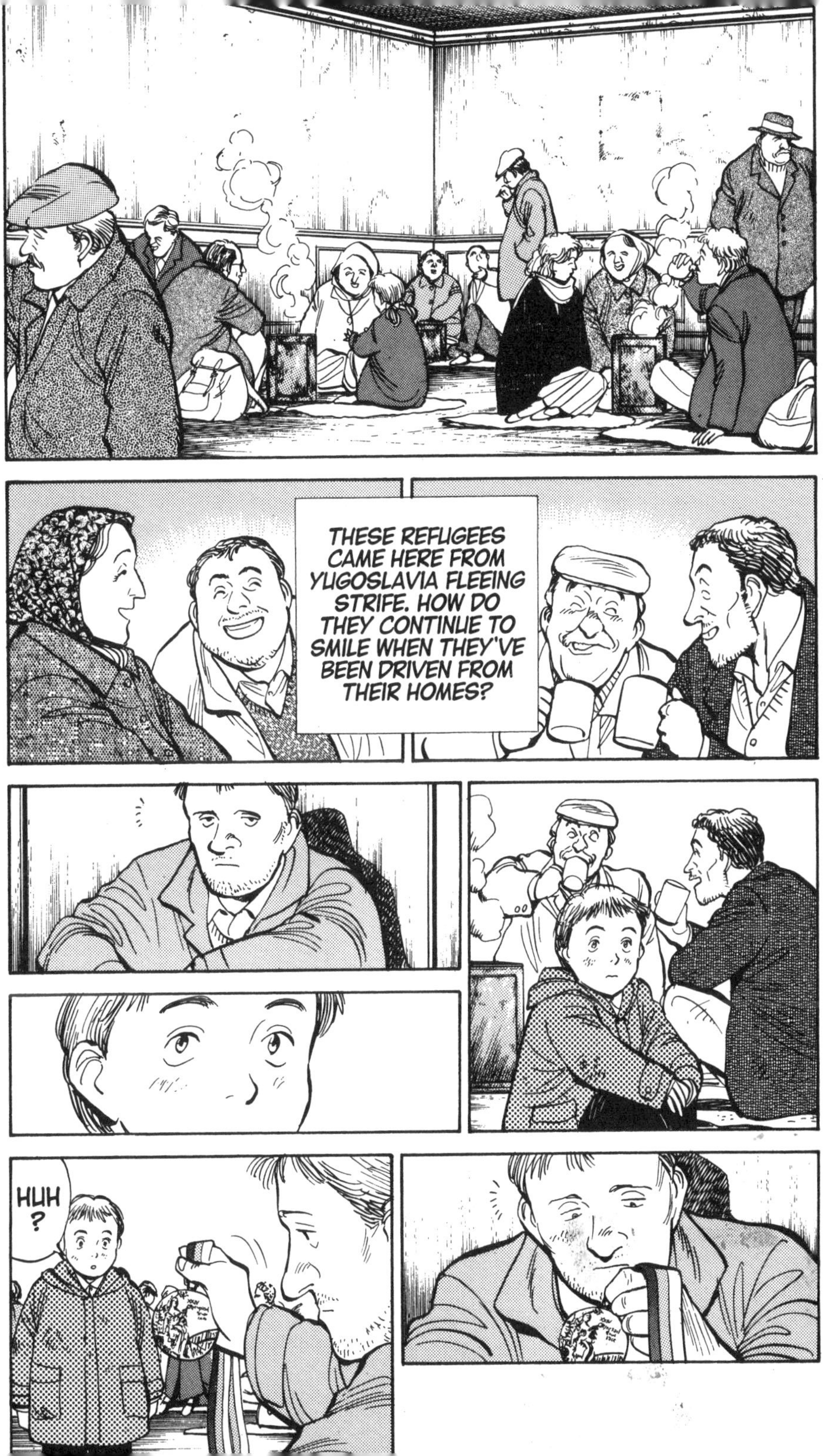
THESE REFUGEES CAME HERE FROM YUGOSLAVIA FLEEING STRIFE. HOW DO THEY CONTINUE TO SMILE WHEN THEY'VE BEEN DRIVEN FROM THEIR HOMES?
HUH ?

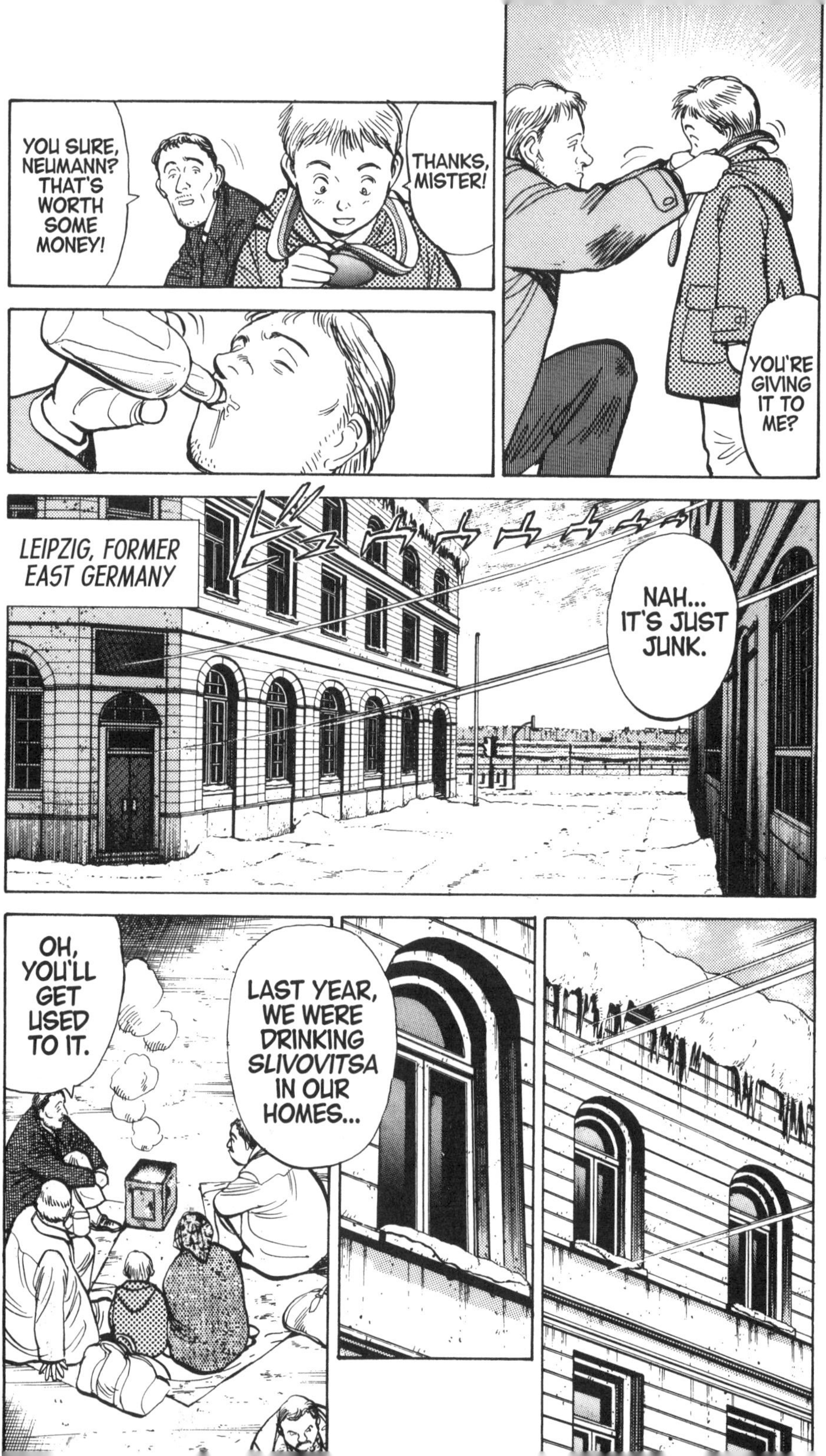
YOU'RE GIVING IT TO ME?
THANKS, MISTER!
YOU SURE, NEUMANN? THAT'S WORTH SOME MONEY!
NAH... IT'S JUST JUNK.
LEIPZIG, FORMER EAST GERMANY
LAST YEAR, WE WERE DRINKING *SLIVOVITSA* IN OUR HOMES...
OH, YOU'LL GET USED TO IT.

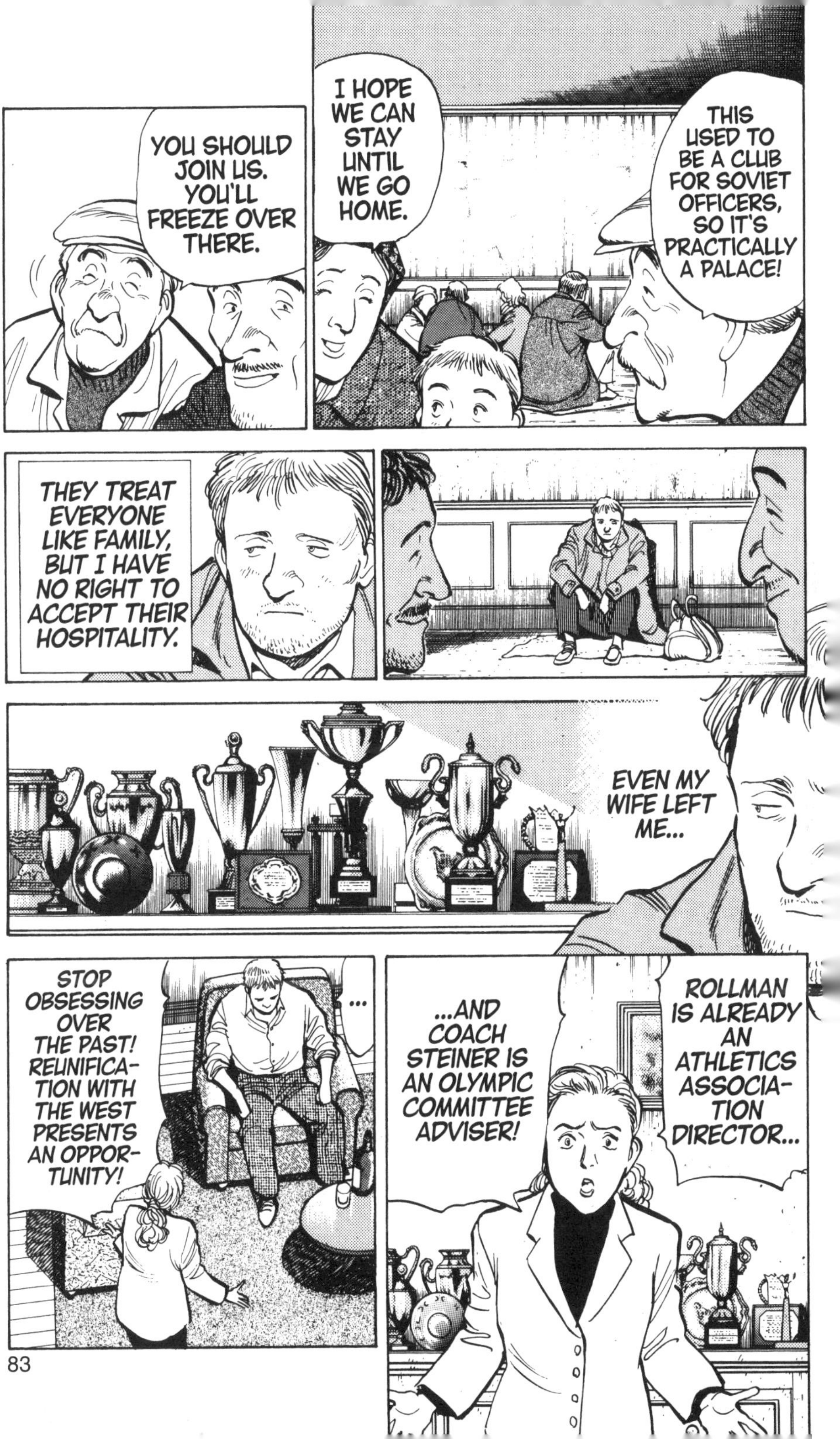
THIS USED TO BE A CLUB FOR SOVIET OFFICERS, SO IT'S PRACTICALLY A PALACE!
I HOPE WE CAN STAY UNTIL WE GO HOME.
YOU SHOULD JOIN US. YOU'LL FREEZE OVER THERE.
THEY TREAT EVERYONE LIKE FAMILY, BUT I HAVE NO RIGHT TO ACCEPT THEIR HOSPITALITY.
EVEN MY WIFE LEFT ME...
ROLLMAN IS ALREADY AN ATHLETICS ASSOCIATION DIRECTOR...
...AND COACH STEINER IS AN OLYMPIC COMMITTEE ADVISER!
...
STOP OBSESSING OVER THE PAST! REUNIFICATION WITH THE WEST PRESENTS AN OPPORTUNITY!

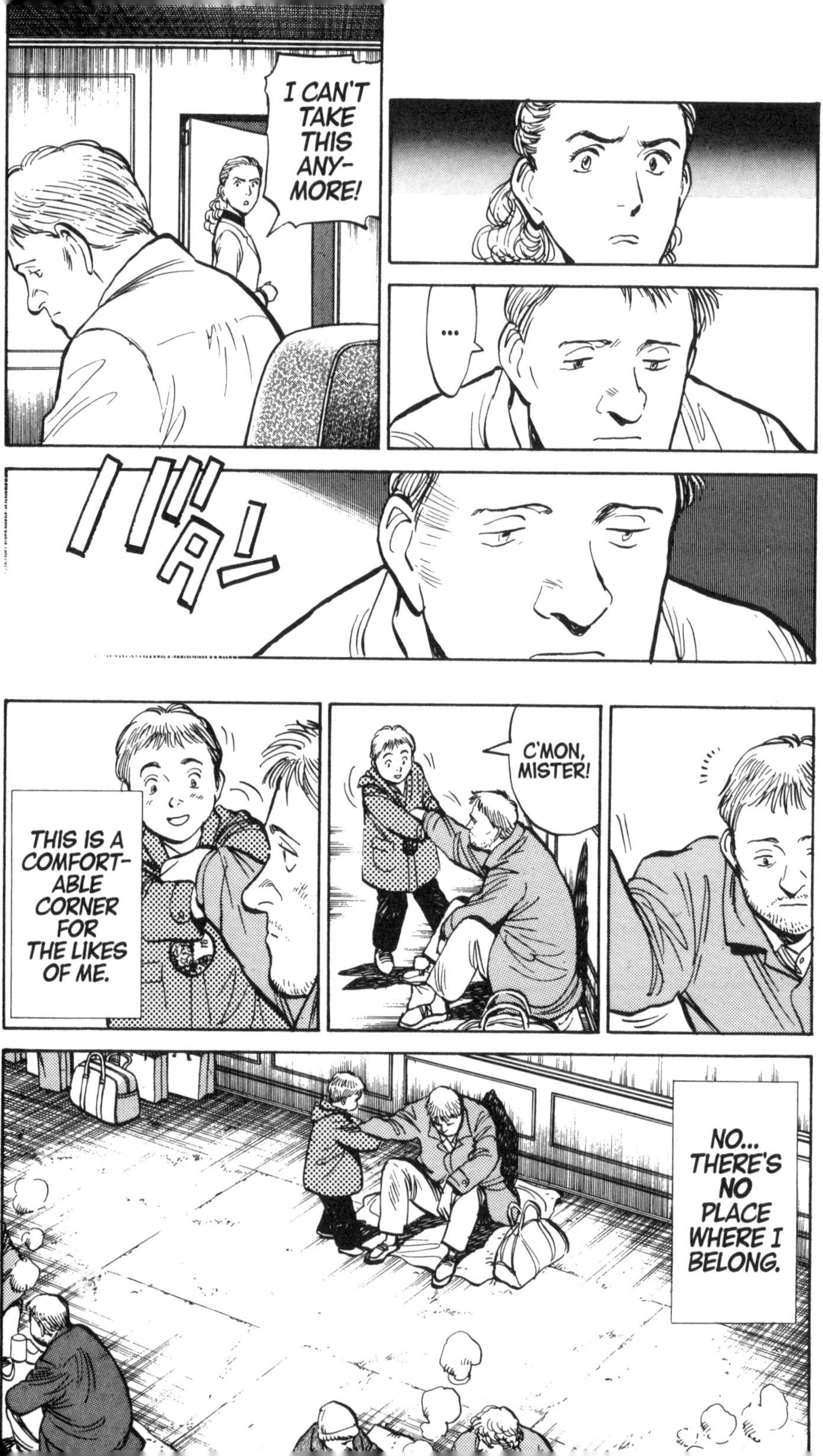
...
I CAN'T TAKE THIS ANYMORE!
バタン
C'MON, MISTER!
THIS IS A COMFORTABLE CORNER FOR THE LIKES OF ME.
NO... THERE'S NO PLACE WHERE I BELONG.

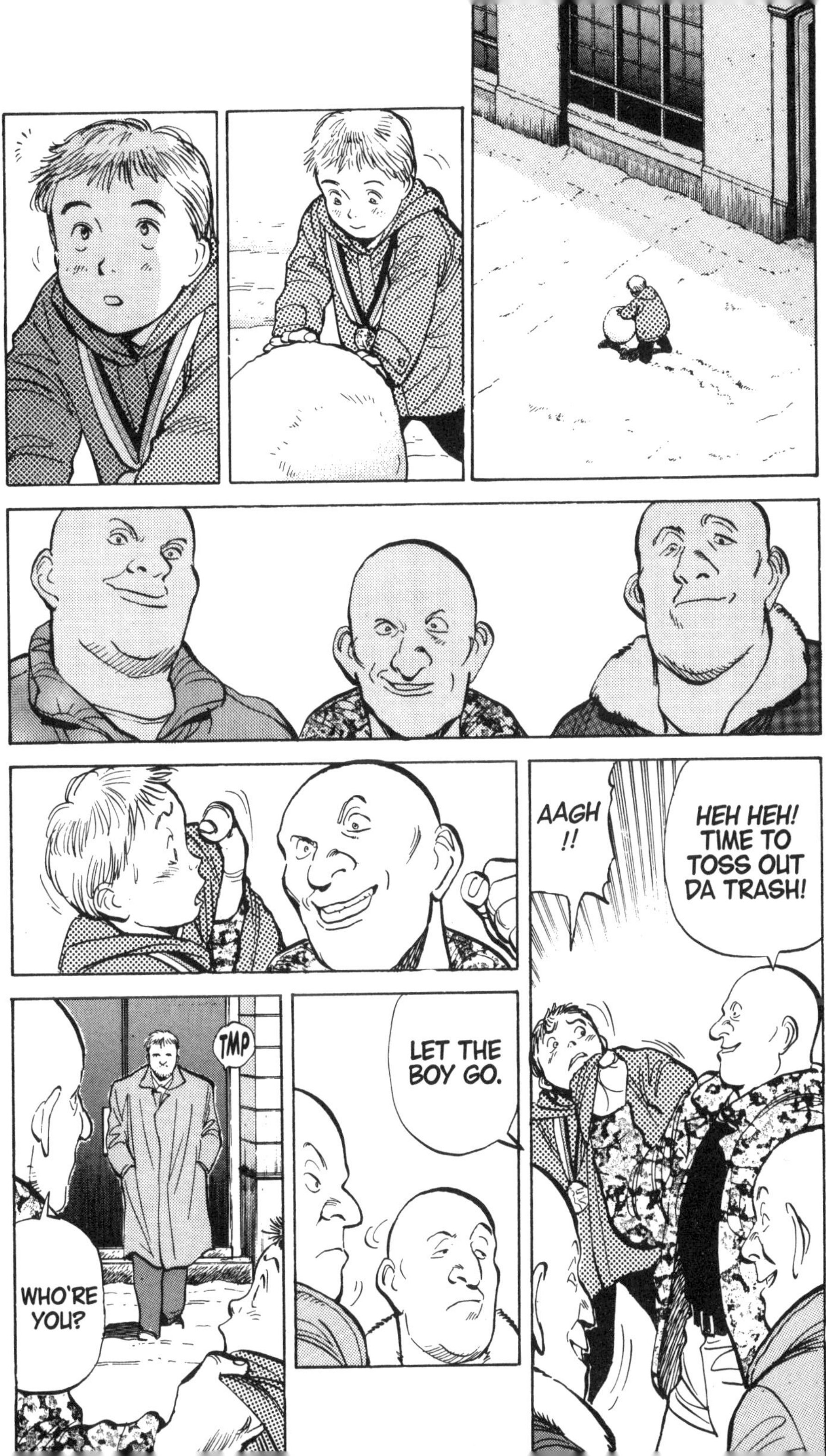
HEH HEH! TIME TO TOSS OUT DA TRASH!
AAGH !!
LET THE BOY GO.
TMP
WHO'RE YOU?

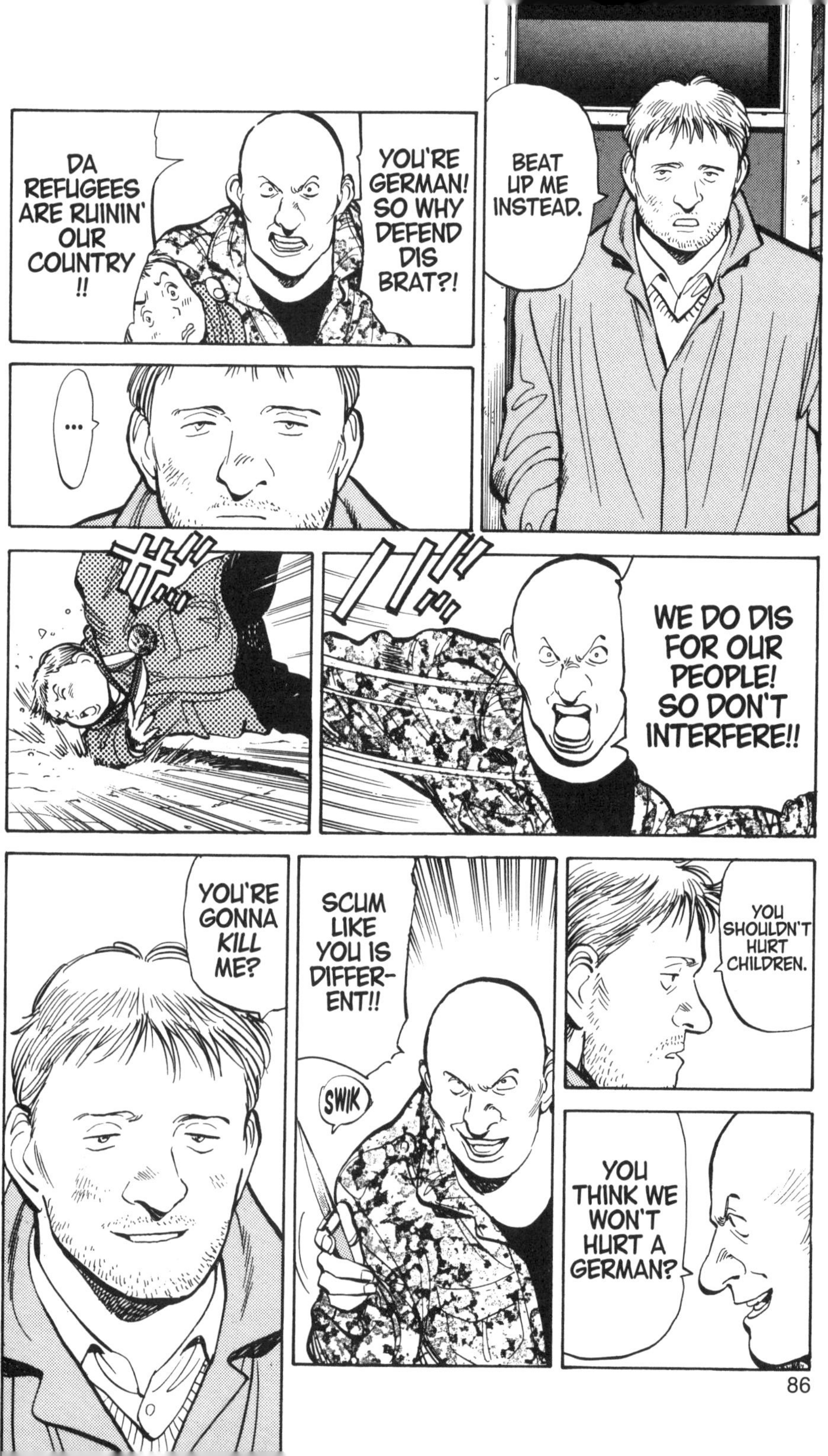
BEAT UP ME INSTEAD.
YOU'RE GERMAN! SO WHY DEFEND DIS BRAT?!
DA REFUGEES ARE RUININ' OUR COUNTRY !!
...
WE DO DIS FOR OUR PEOPLE! SO DON'T INTERFERE!!
YOU SHOULDN'T HURT CHILDREN.
YOU THINK WE WON'T HURT A GERMAN?
SCUM LIKE YOU IS DIFFER-ENT!!
SWIK
YOU'RE GONNA KILL ME?

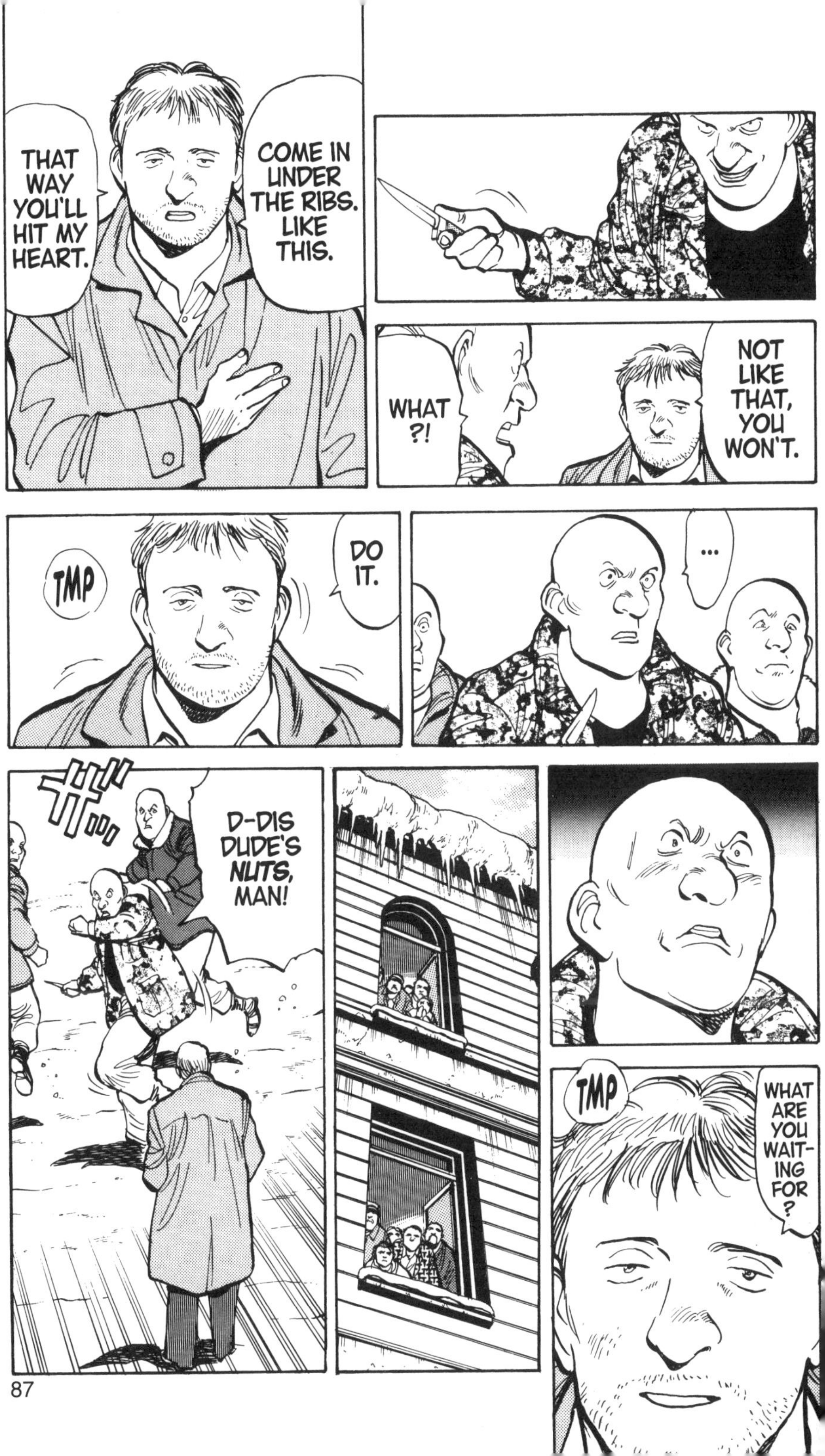
NOT LIKE THAT, YOU WON'T.
WHAT?!
COME IN UNDER THE RIBS. LIKE THIS.
THAT WAY YOU'LL HIT MY HEART.
...
DO IT.
TMP
WHAT ARE YOU WAITING FOR?
TMP
D-DIS DUDE'S NUTS, MAN!

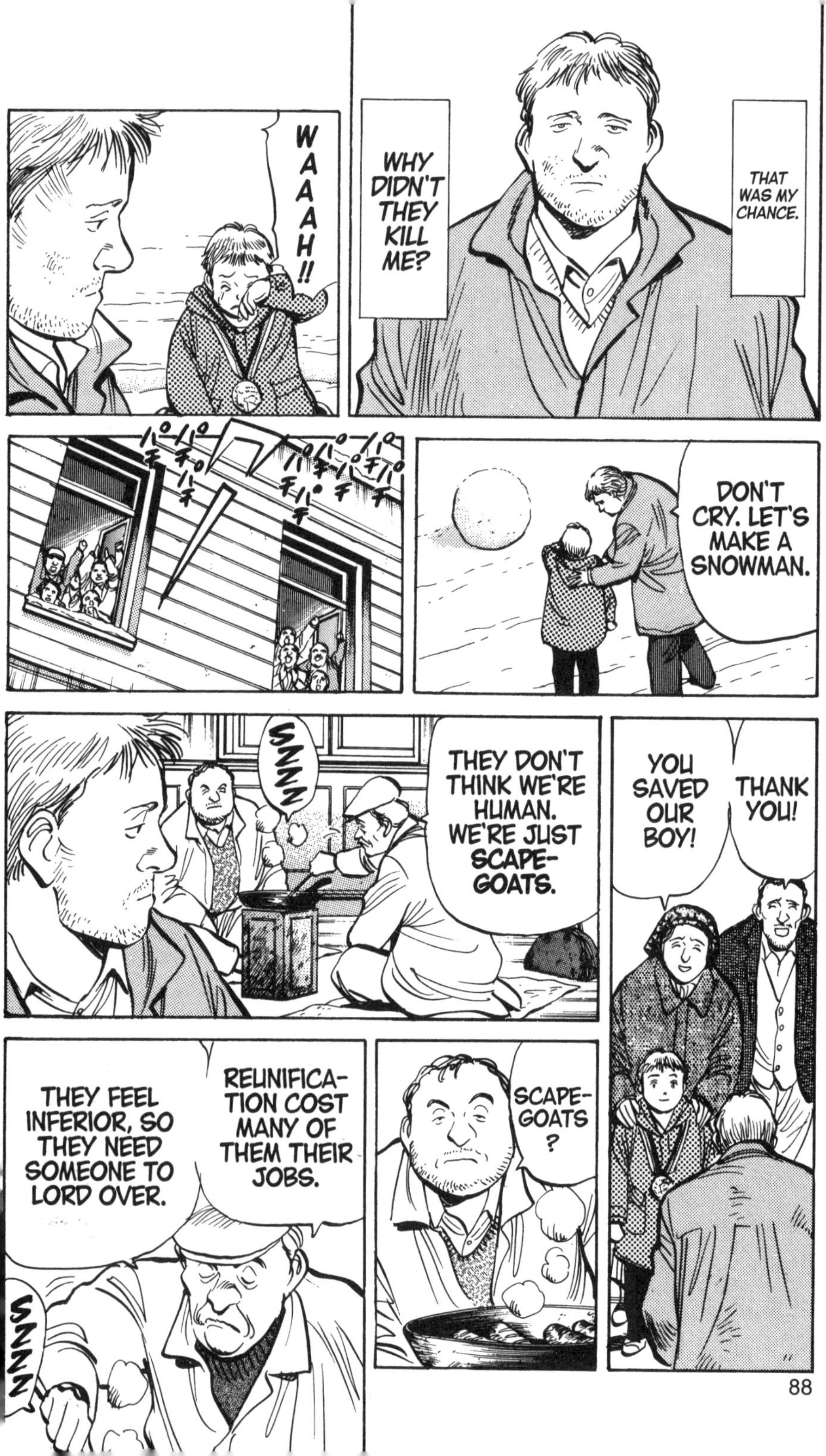
THAT WAS MY CHANCE.
WHY DIDN'T THEY KILL ME?
WAAAAH!!
DON'T CRY. LET'S MAKE A SNOWMAN.
THANK YOU!
YOU SAVED OUR BOY!
THEY DON'T THINK WE'RE HUMAN. WE'RE JUST SCAPE-GOATS.
SZZZ
SCAPE-GOATS?
REUNIFICA-TION COST MANY OF THEM THEIR JOBS.
THEY FEEL INFERIOR, SO THEY NEED SOMEONE TO LORD OVER.
SZZZ

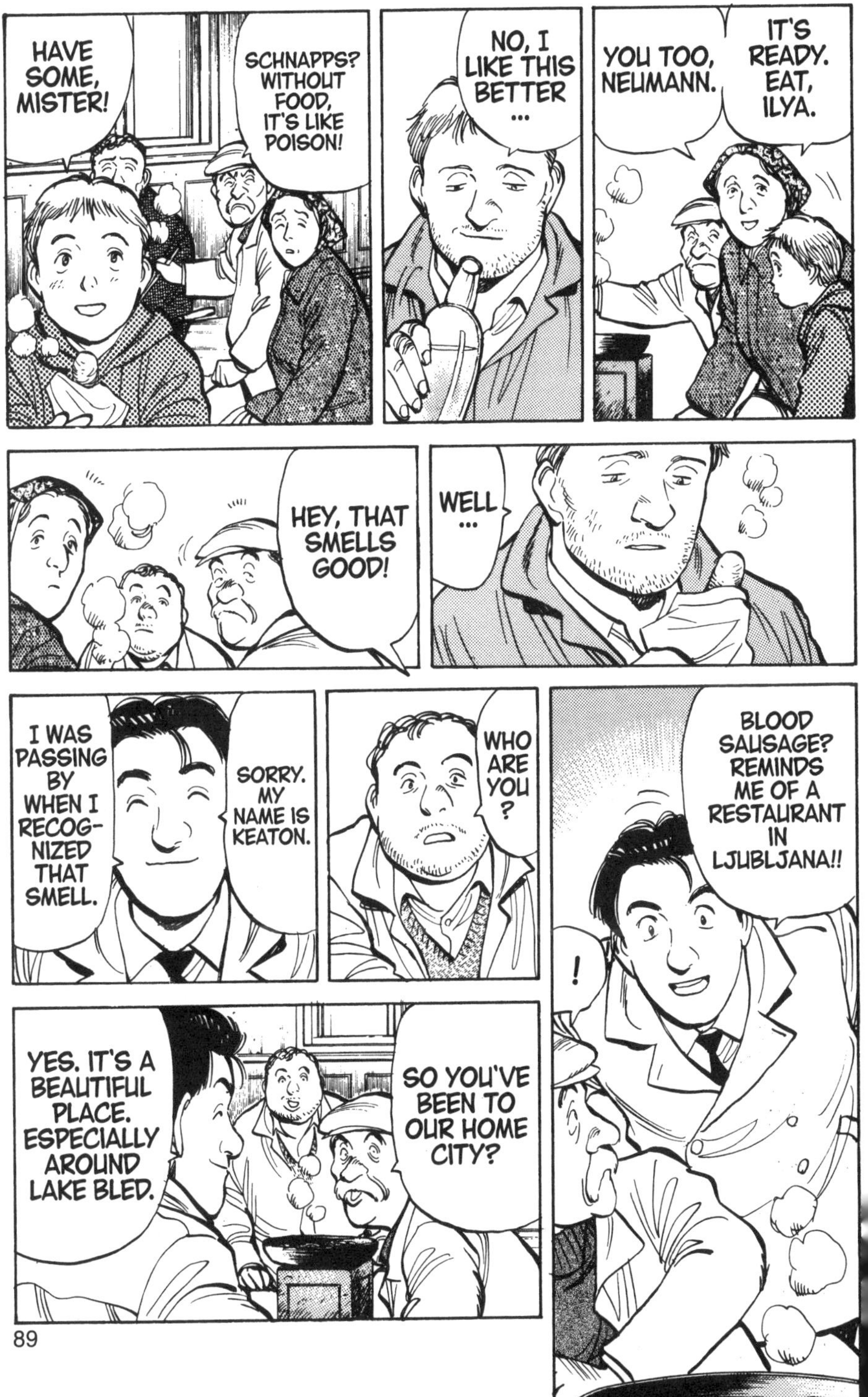
IT'S READY. EAT, ILYA.
YOU TOO, NEUMANN.
NO, I LIKE THIS BETTER ...
SCHNAPPS? WITHOUT FOOD, IT'S LIKE POISON!
HAVE SOME, MISTER!
WELL ...
HEY, THAT SMELLS GOOD!
BLOOD SAUSAGE? REMINDS ME OF A RESTAURANT IN LJUBLJANA!!
!
WHO ARE YOU?
SORRY. MY NAME IS KEATON.
I WAS PASSING BY WHEN I RECOGNIZED THAT SMELL.
SO YOU'VE BEEN TO OUR HOME CITY?
YES. IT'S A BEAUTIFUL PLACE. ESPECIALLY AROUND LAKE BLED.

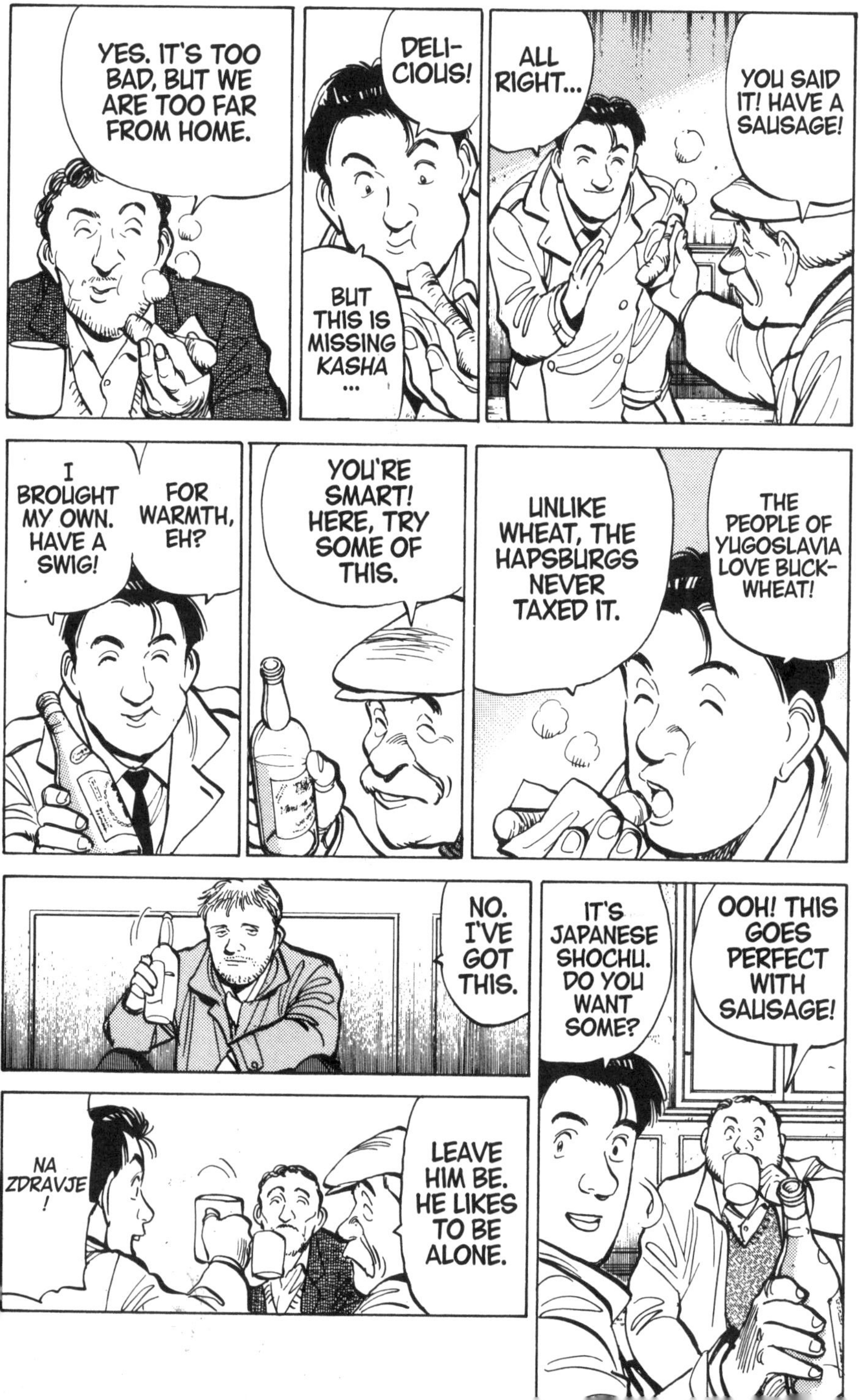
YOU SAID IT! HAVE A SAUSAGE!
ALL RIGHT...
DELI-CIOUS!
BUT THIS IS MISSING KASHA ...
YES. IT'S TOO BAD, BUT WE ARE TOO FAR FROM HOME.
THE PEOPLE OF YUGOSLAVIA LOVE BUCK-WHEAT!
UNLIKE WHEAT, THE HAPSBURGS NEVER TAXED IT.
YOU'RE SMART! HERE, TRY SOME OF THIS.
FOR WARMTH, EH?
I BROUGHT MY OWN. HAVE A SWIG!
OOH! THIS GOES PERFECT WITH SAUSAGE!
IT'S JAPANESE SHOCHU. DO YOU WANT SOME?
NO. I'VE GOT THIS.
LEAVE HIM BE. HE LIKES TO BE ALONE.
NA ZDRAVJE!

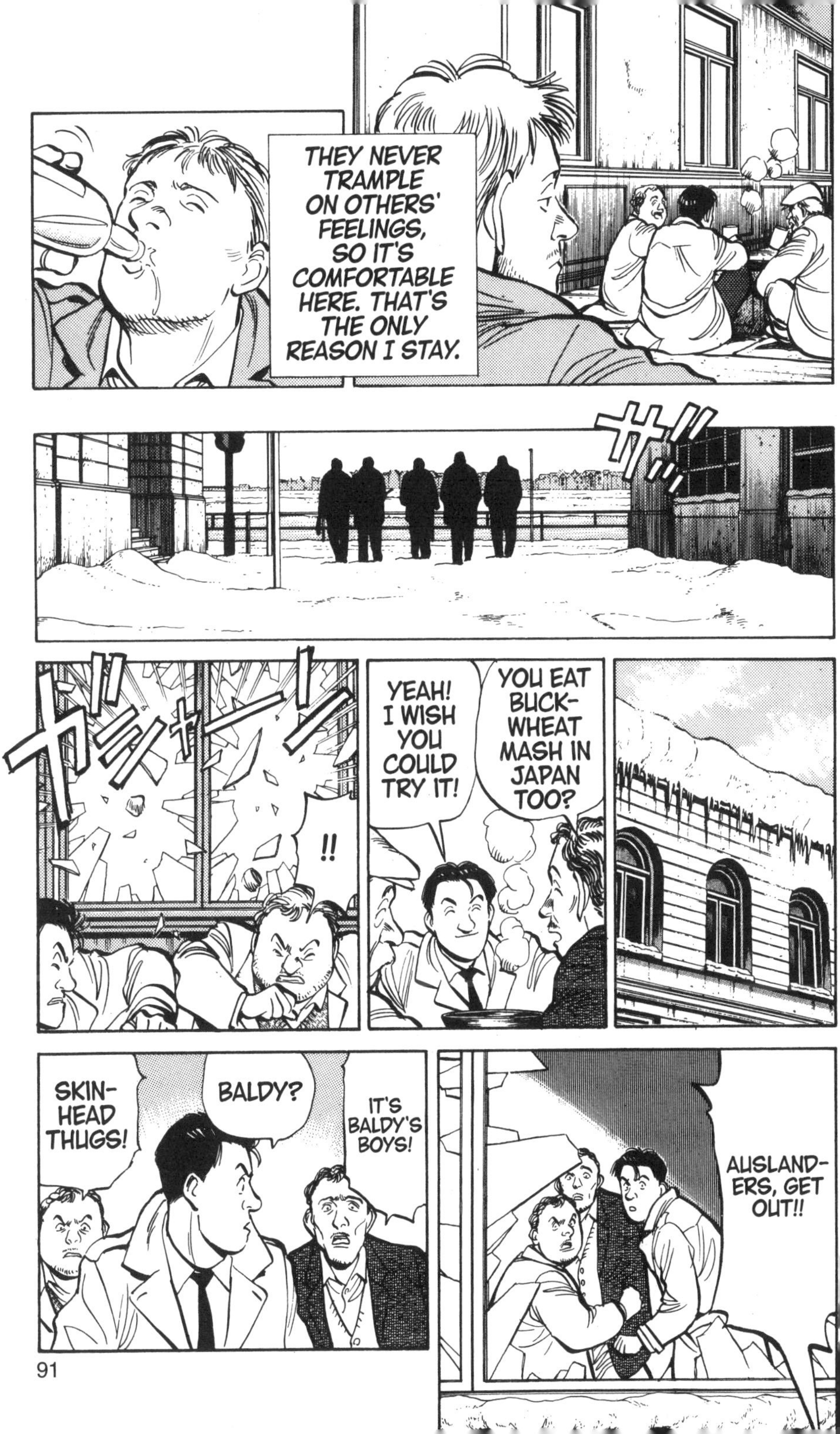
THEY NEVER TRAMPLE ON OTHERS' FEELINGS, SO IT'S COMFORTABLE HERE. THAT'S THE ONLY REASON I STAY.
ザッ
YOU EAT BUCK-WHEAT MASH IN JAPAN TOO?
YEAH! I WISH YOU COULD TRY IT!
ガシャーン
!!
AUSLANDERS, GET OUT!!
IT'S BALDY'S BOYS!
BALDY?
SKIN-HEAD THUGS!

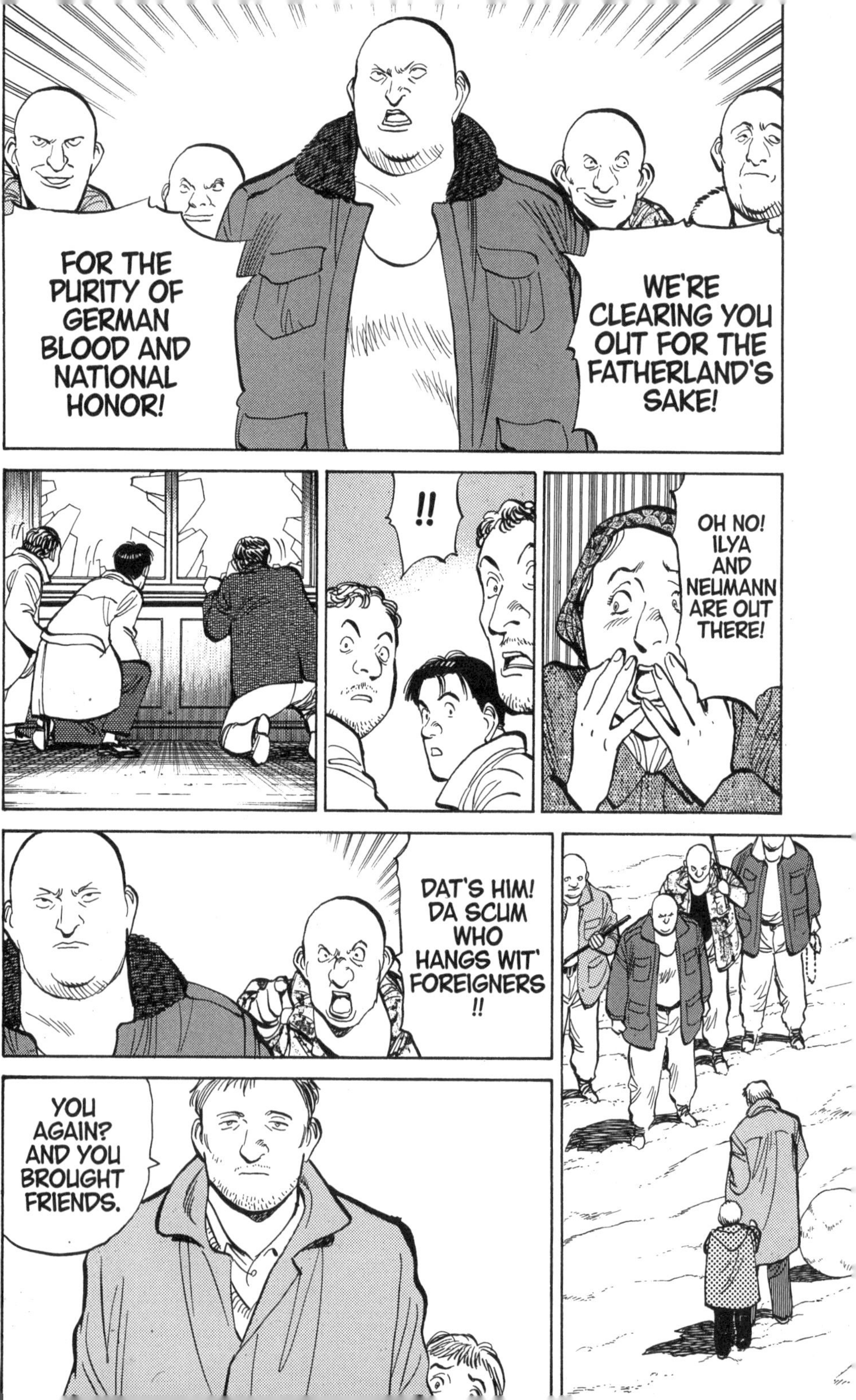
WE'RE CLEARING YOU OUT FOR THE FATHERLAND'S SAKE!
FOR THE PURITY OF GERMAN BLOOD AND NATIONAL HONOR!
OH NO! ILYA AND NEUMANN ARE OUT THERE!
!!
DAT'S HIM! DA SCUM WHO HANGS WIT' FOREIGNERS!!
YOU AGAIN? AND YOU BROUGHT FRIENDS.

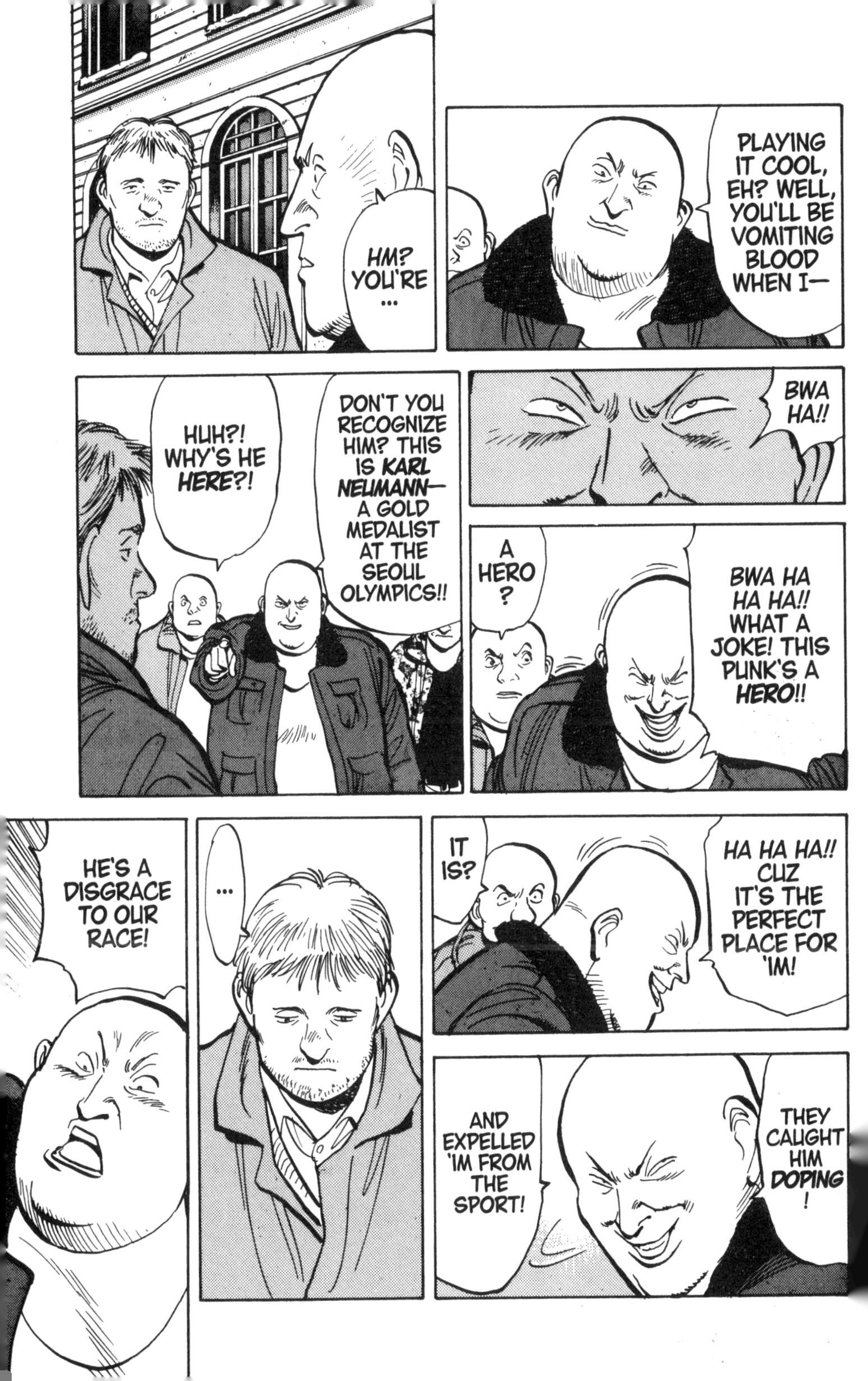
PLAYING IT COOL, EH? WELL, YOU'LL BE VOMITING BLOOD WHEN I—
HM? YOU'RE ...
BWA HA!!
BWA HA HA HA!! WHAT A JOKE! THIS PUNK'S A HERO!!
A HERO?
DON'T YOU RECOGNIZE HIM? THIS IS KARL NEUMANN— A GOLD MEDALIST AT THE SEOUL OLYMPICS!!
HUH?! WHY'S HE HERE?!
HA HA HA!! CUZ IT'S THE PERFECT PLACE FOR 'IM!
IT IS?
THEY CAUGHT HIM DOPING!
AND EXPELLED 'IM FROM THE SPORT!
...
HE'S A DISGRACE TO OUR RACE!

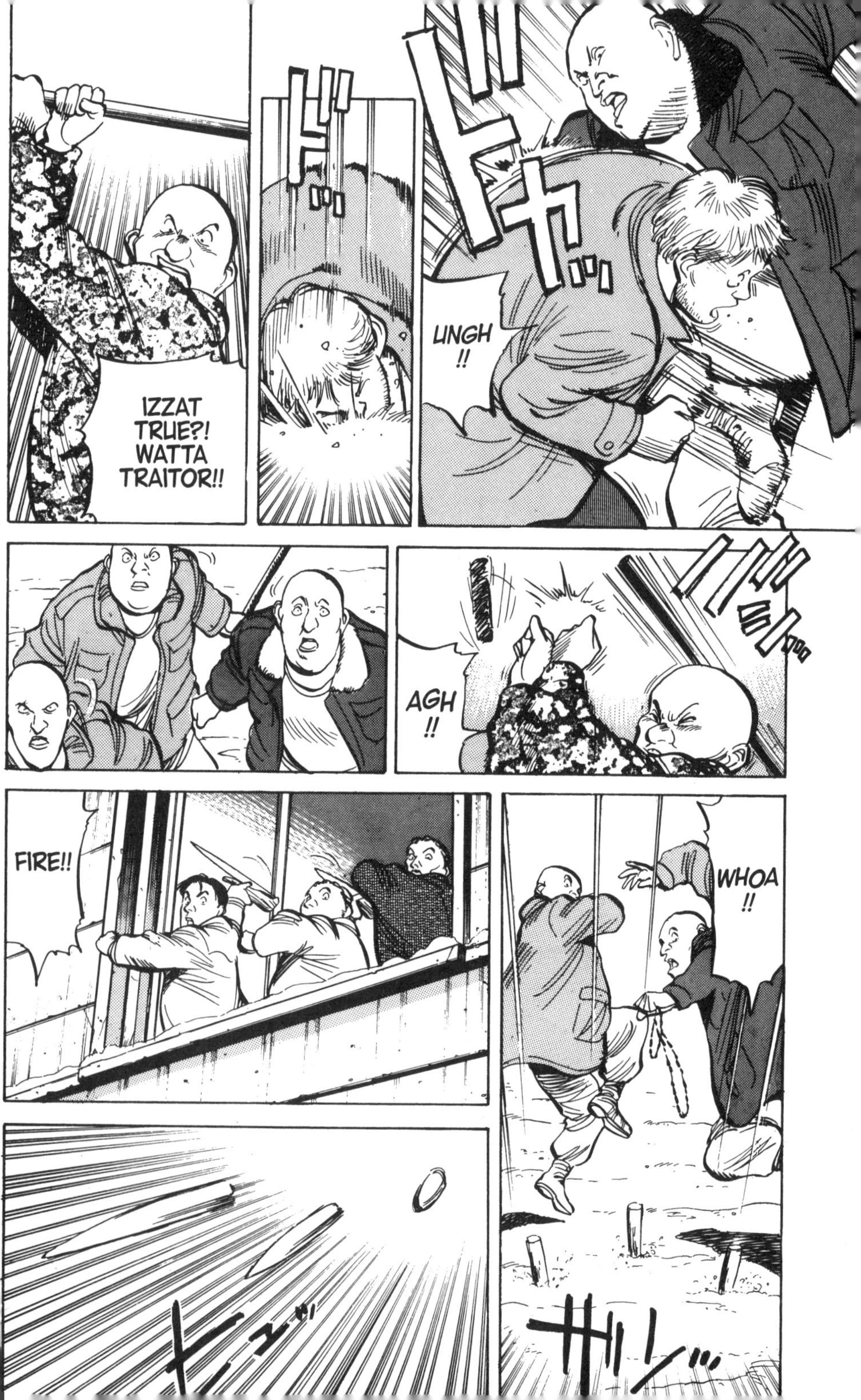
UNGH!!
IZZAT TRUE?! WATTA TRAITOR!!
AGH!!
WHOA!!
FIRE!!

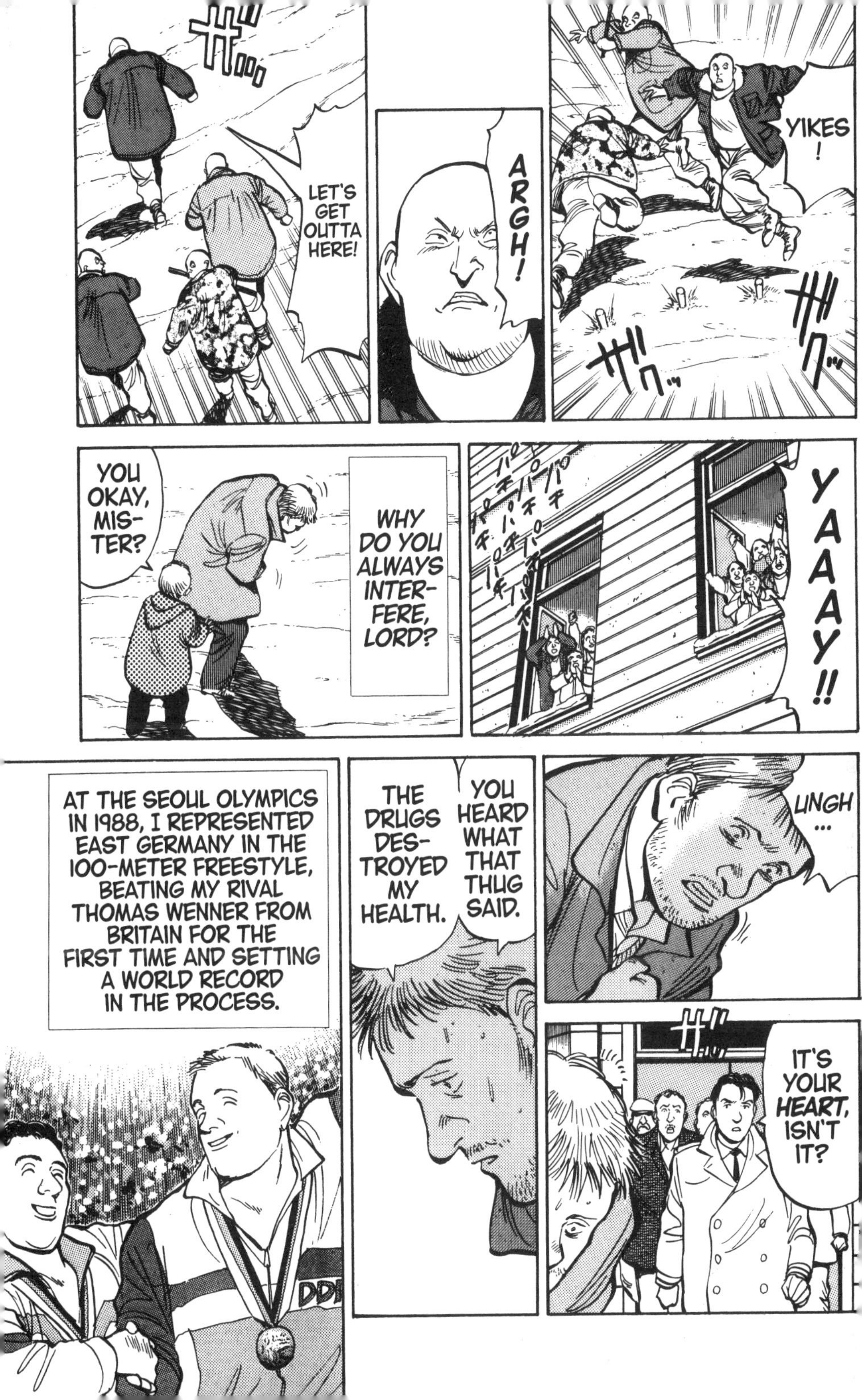
YIKES!
ARGH!
LET'S GET OUTTA HERE!
YAAAY!!
WHY DO YOU ALWAYS INTERFERE, LORD?
YOU OKAY, MISTER?
UNGH...
IT'S YOUR HEART, ISN'T IT?
YOU HEARD WHAT THAT THUG SAID.
THE DRUGS DESTROYED MY HEALTH.
AT THE SEOUL OLYMPICS IN 1988, I REPRESENTED EAST GERMANY IN THE 100-METER FREESTYLE, BEATING MY RIVAL THOMAS WENNER FROM BRITAIN FOR THE FIRST TIME AND SETTING A WORLD RECORD IN THE PROCESS.
DDR

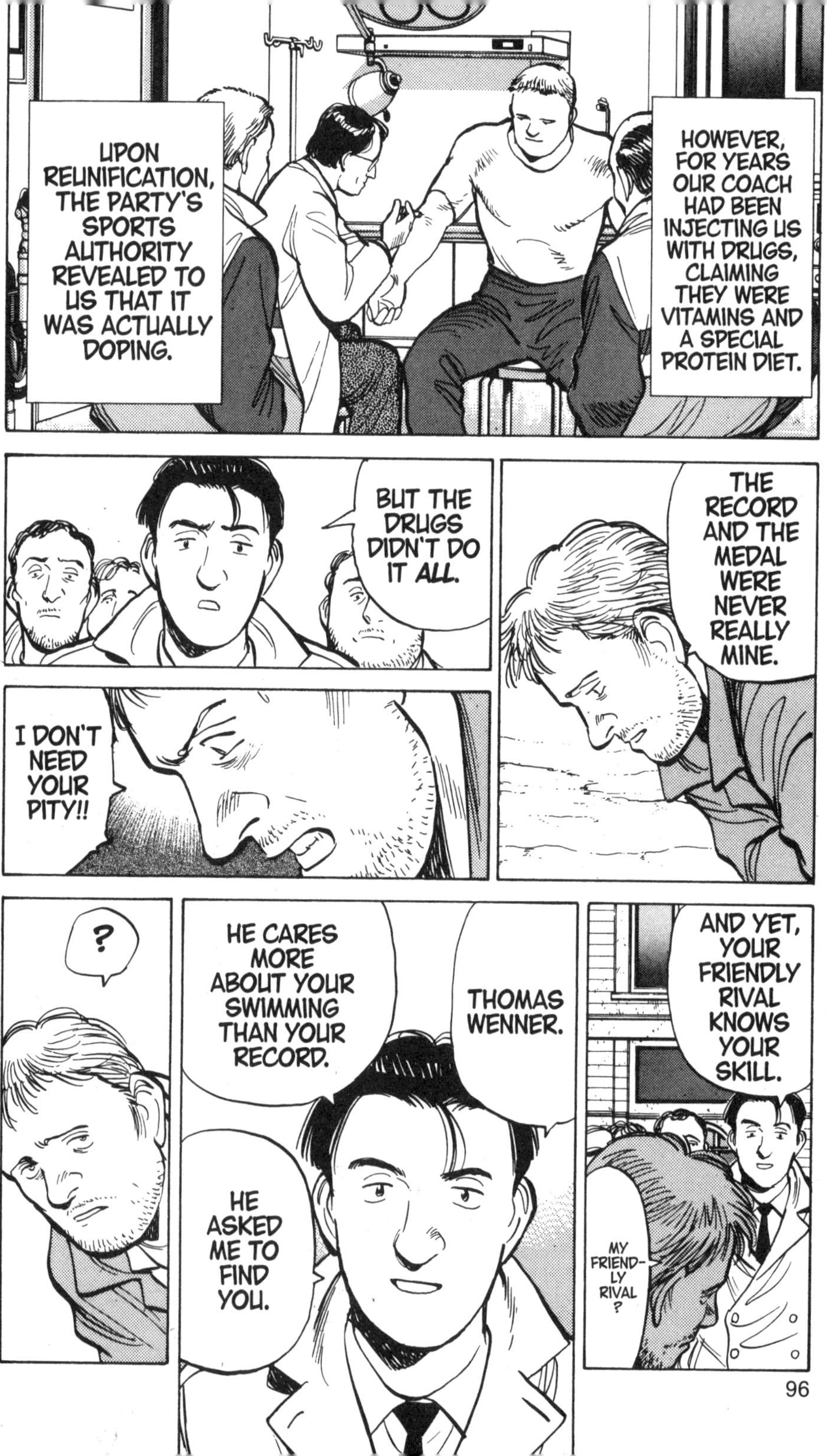
HOWEVER, FOR YEARS OUR COACH HAD BEEN INJECTING US WITH DRUGS, CLAIMING THEY WERE VITAMINS AND A SPECIAL PROTEIN DIET.
UPON REUNIFICATION, THE PARTY'S SPORTS AUTHORITY REVEALED TO US THAT IT WAS ACTUALLY DOPING.
THE RECORD AND THE MEDAL WERE NEVER REALLY MINE.
BUT THE DRUGS DIDN'T DO IT *ALL*.
I DON'T NEED YOUR PITY!!
AND YET, YOUR FRIENDLY RIVAL KNOWS YOUR SKILL.
MY FRIEND-LY RIVAL?
THOMAS WENNER.
HE CARES MORE ABOUT YOUR SWIMMING THAN YOUR RECORD.
HE ASKED ME TO FIND YOU.
?

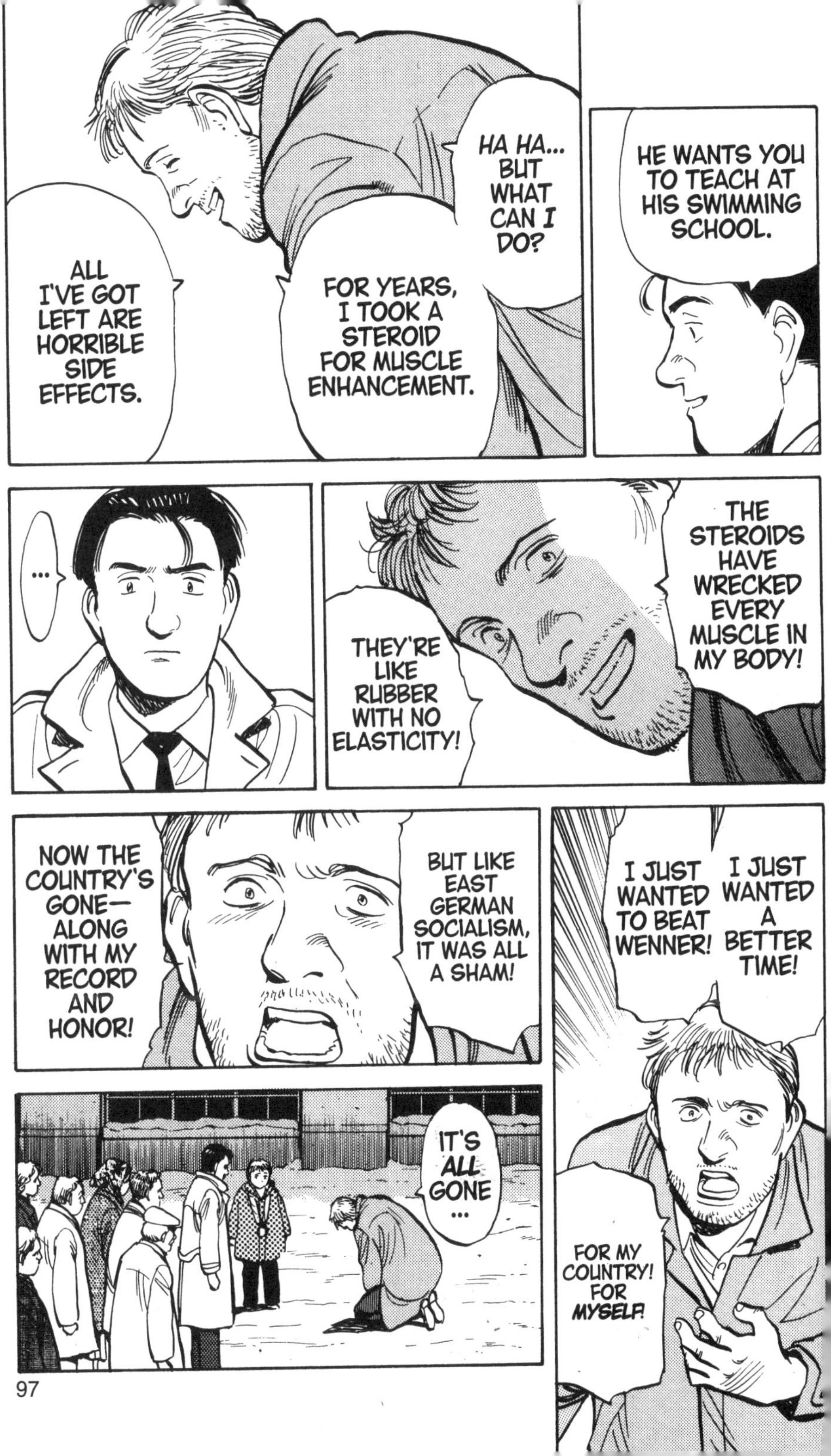
HE WANTS YOU TO TEACH AT HIS SWIMMING SCHOOL.
HA HA... BUT WHAT CAN I DO?
FOR YEARS, I TOOK A STEROID FOR MUSCLE ENHANCEMENT.
ALL I'VE GOT LEFT ARE HORRIBLE SIDE EFFECTS.
THE STEROIDS HAVE WRECKED EVERY MUSCLE IN MY BODY!
THEY'RE LIKE RUBBER WITH NO ELASTICITY!
...
I JUST WANTED A BETTER TIME!
I JUST WANTED TO BEAT WENNER!
FOR MY COUNTRY! FOR *MYSELF!*
BUT LIKE EAST GERMAN SOCIALISM, IT WAS ALL A SHAM!
NOW THE COUNTRY'S GONE—ALONG WITH MY RECORD AND HONOR!
IT'S *ALL* GONE...

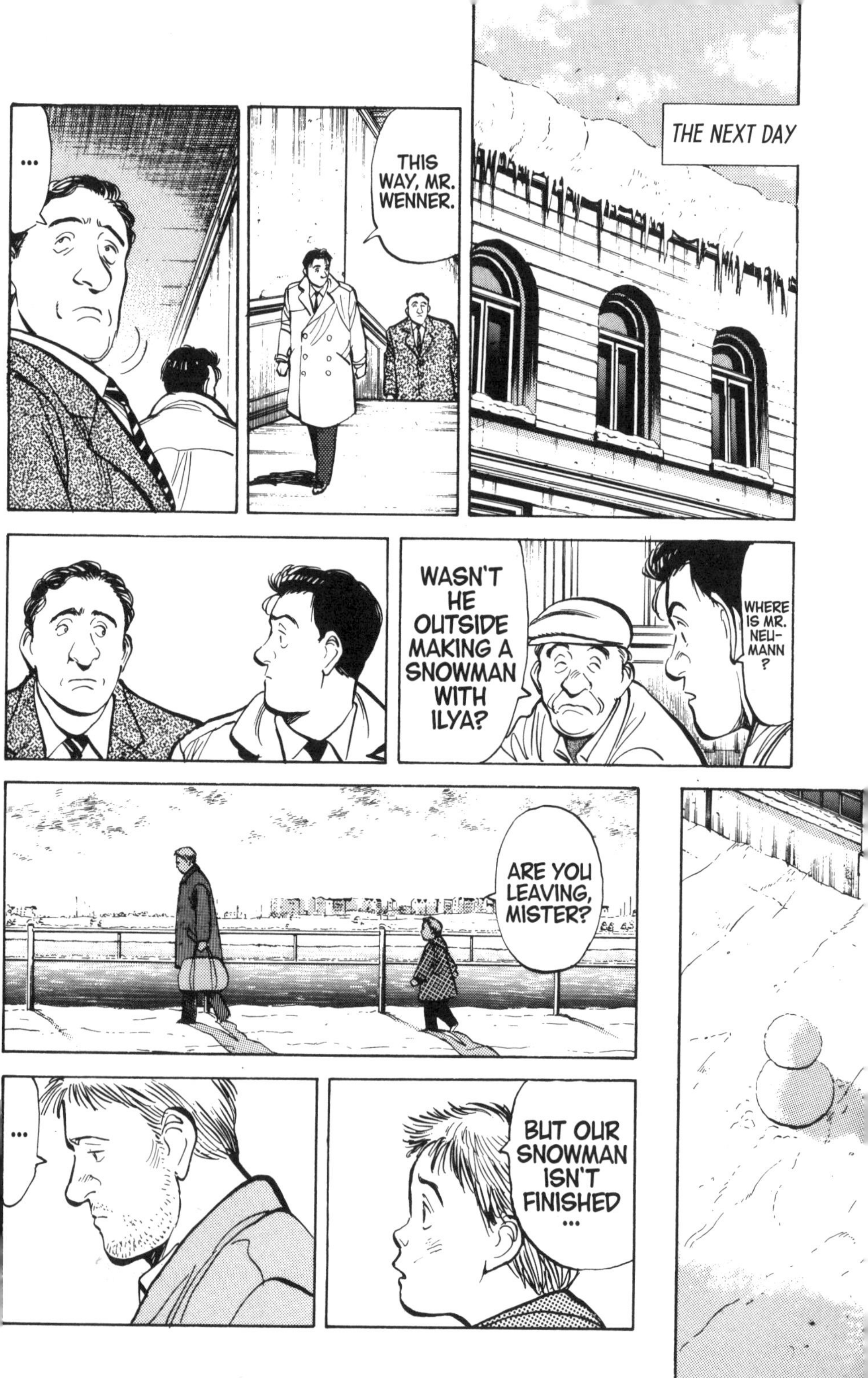
THE NEXT DAY
THIS WAY, MR. WENNER.
...
WHERE IS MR. NEUMANN?
WASN'T HE OUTSIDE MAKING A SNOWMAN WITH ILYA?
ARE YOU LEAVING, MISTER?
BUT OUR SNOWMAN ISN'T FINISHED ...
...

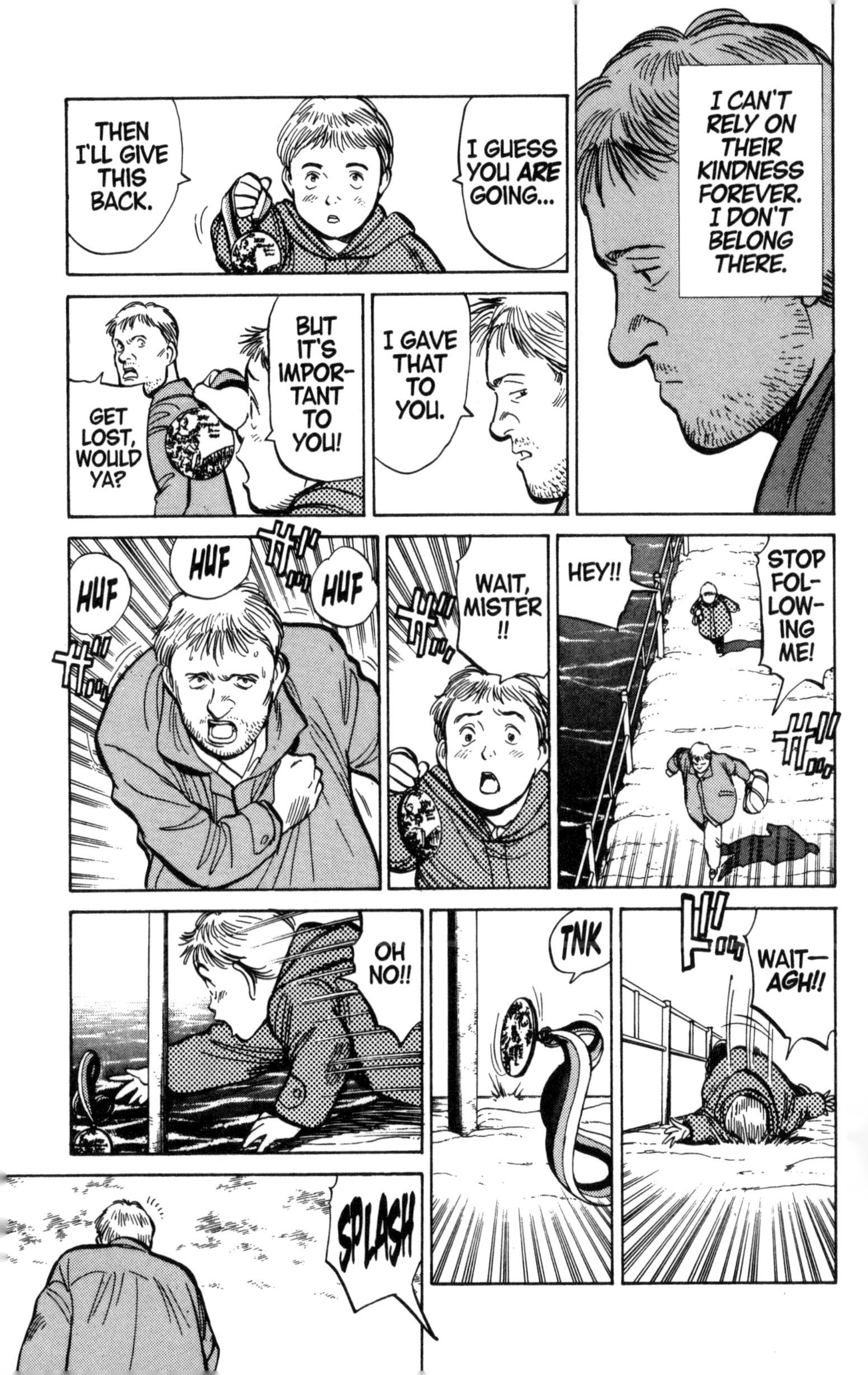
I CAN'T RELY ON THEIR KINDNESS FOREVER. I DON'T BELONG THERE.
I GUESS YOU ARE GOING...
THEN I'LL GIVE THIS BACK.
I GAVE THAT TO YOU.
BUT IT'S IMPORTANT TO YOU!
GET LOST, WOULD YA?
STOP FOL-LOW-ING ME!
HEY!!
WAIT, MISTER!!
HUF
HUF
HUF
WAIT—AGH!!
TNK
OH NO!!
SPLASH

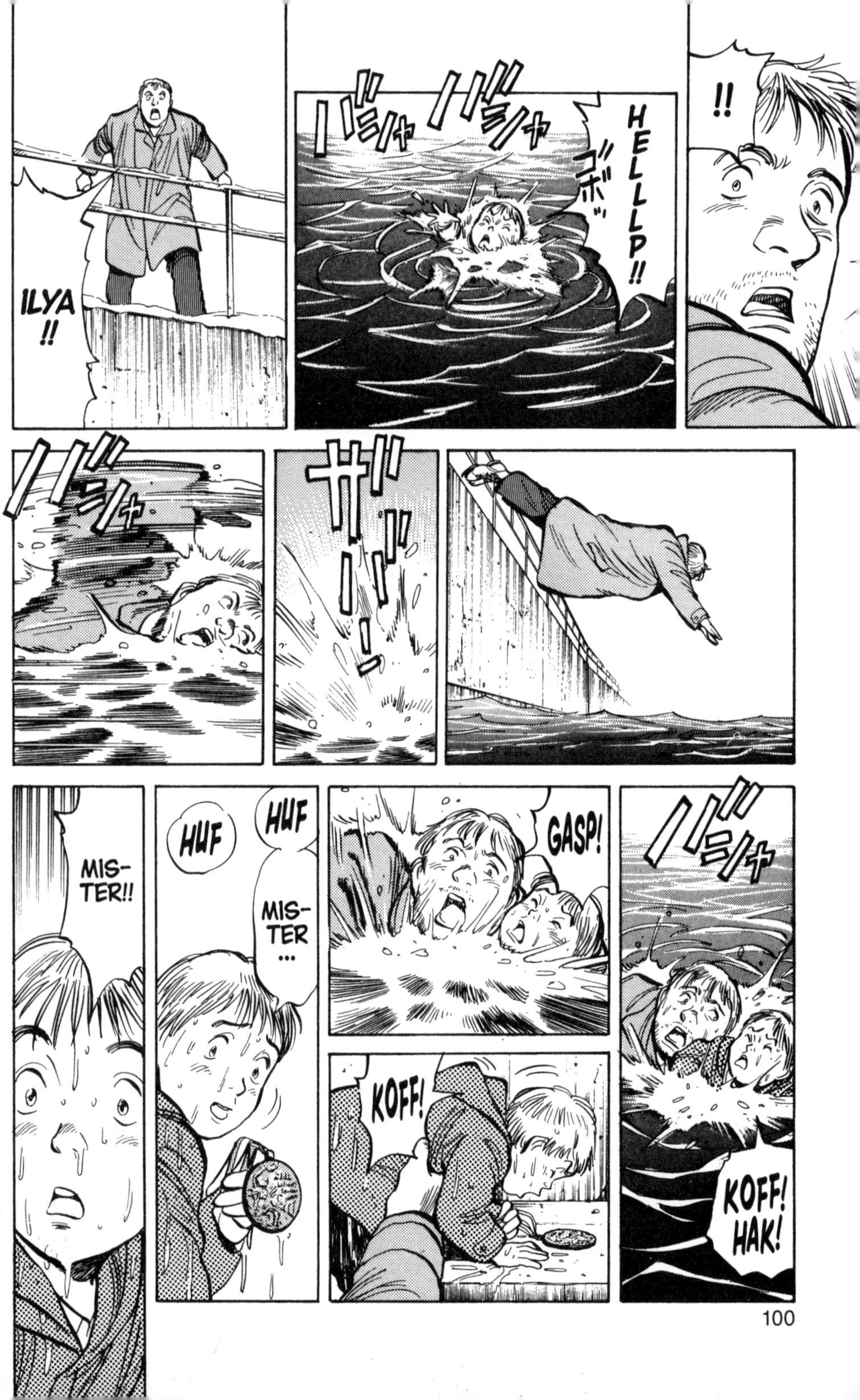
!!
バシャ
バシャ
HELLLP!!
ゴボッ
ILYA!!
バシャ
バシャ
KOFF! HAK!
GASP!
KOFF!
HUF
HUF
MISTER...
MISTER!!

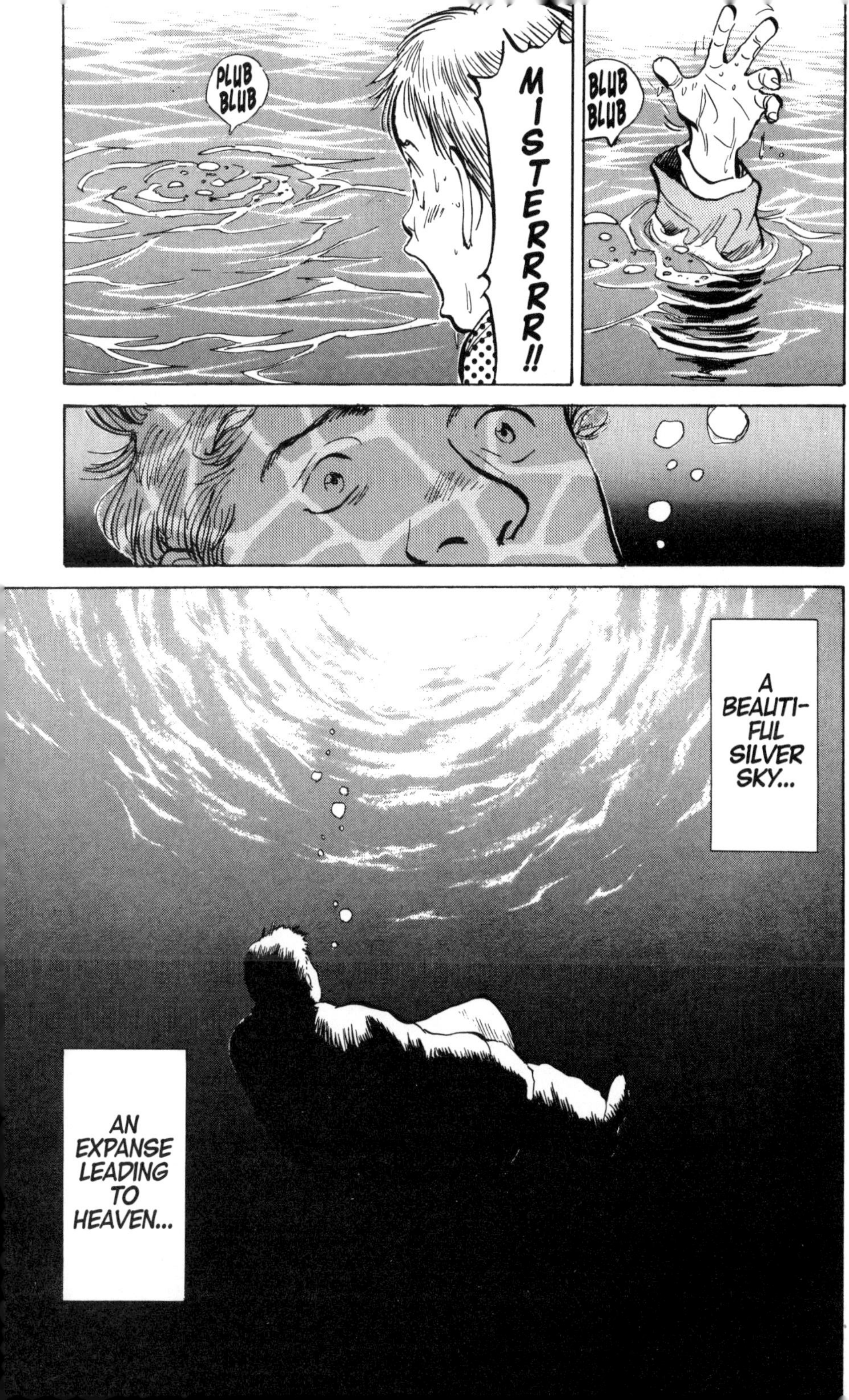
BLUB BLUB
MISTERRRR!!
PLUB BLUB
A BEAUTIFUL SILVER SKY...
AN EXPANSE LEADING TO HEAVEN...

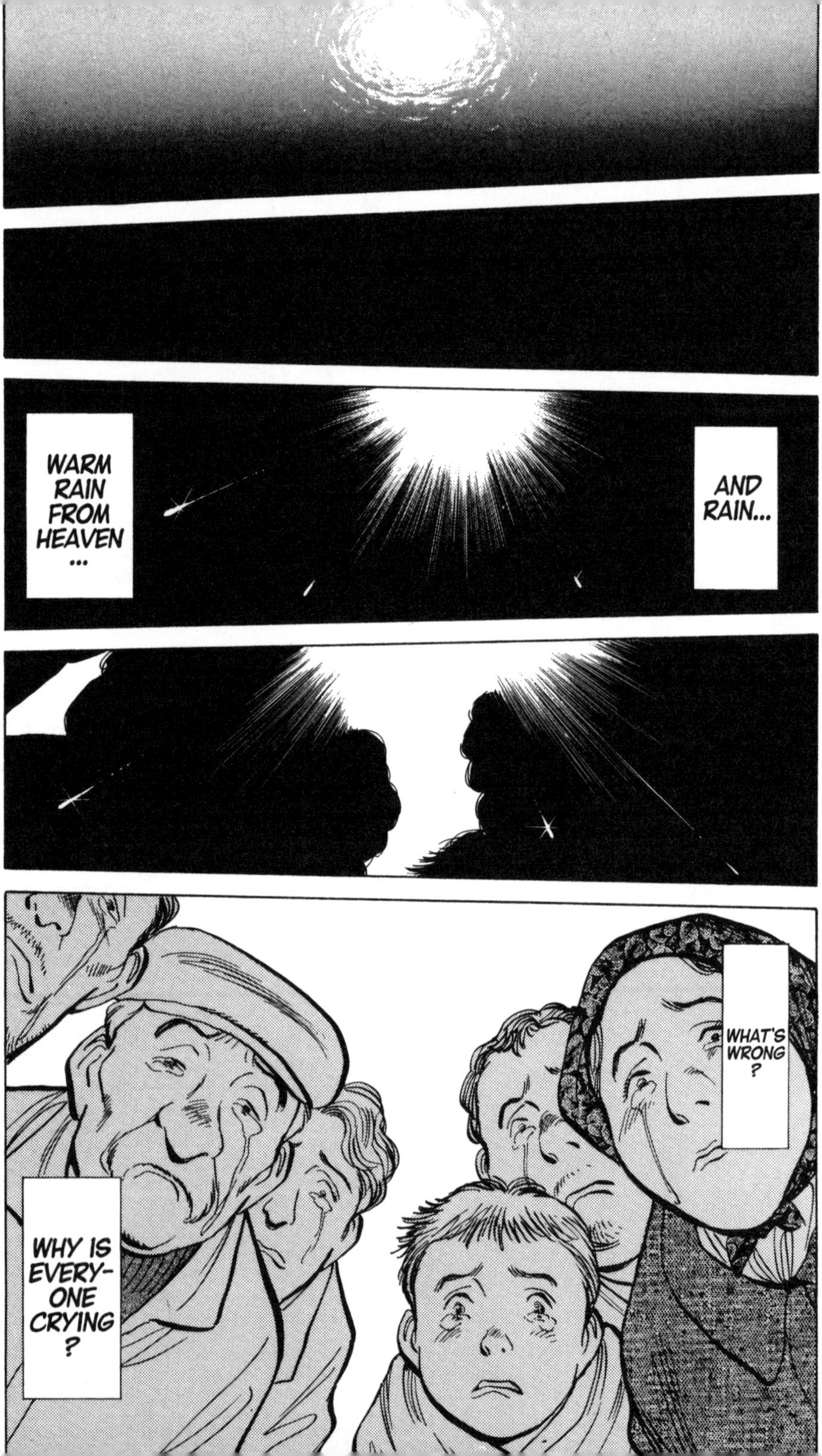
AND RAIN...
WARM RAIN FROM HEAVEN...
WHAT'S WRONG?
WHY IS EVERY-ONE CRYING?

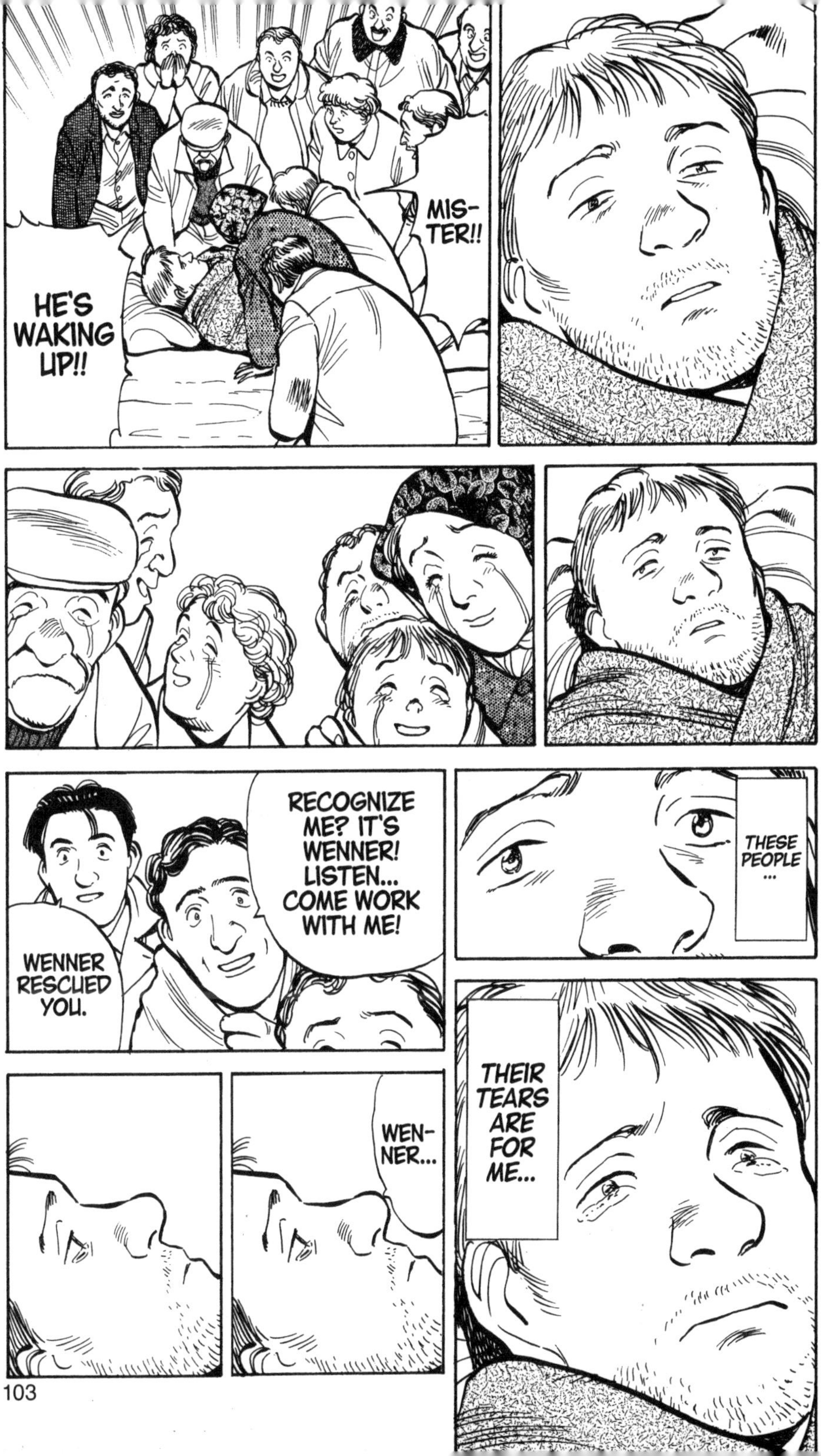
MIS-TER!!
HE'S WAKING UP!!
THESE PEOPLE ...
RECOGNIZE ME? IT'S WENNER! LISTEN... COME WORK WITH ME!
WENNER RESCUED YOU.
THEIR TEARS ARE FOR ME...
WEN-NER...

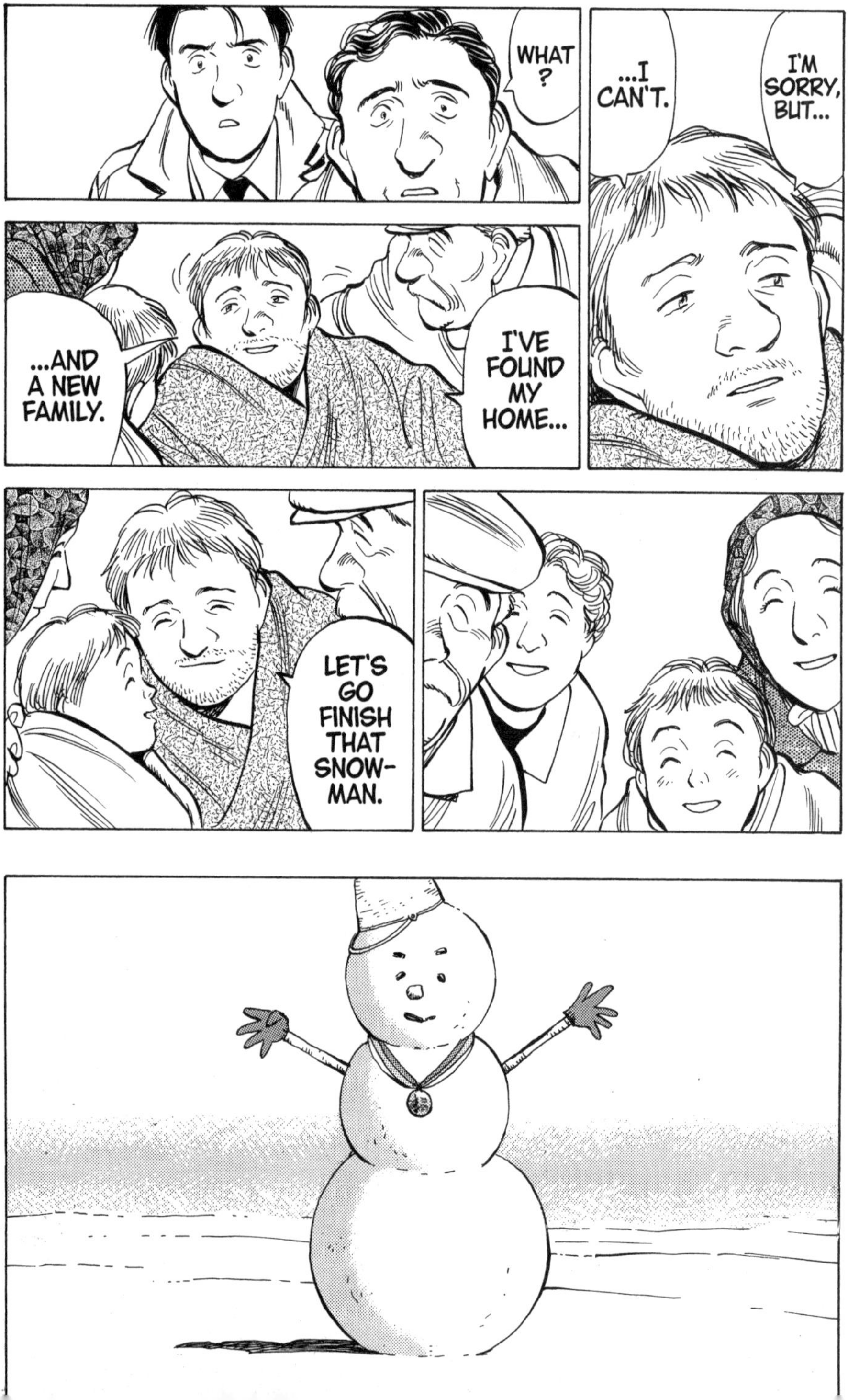
I'M SORRY, BUT...
...I CAN'T.
WHAT?
I'VE FOUND MY HOME...
...AND A NEW FAMILY.
LET'S GO FINISH THAT SNOWMAN.

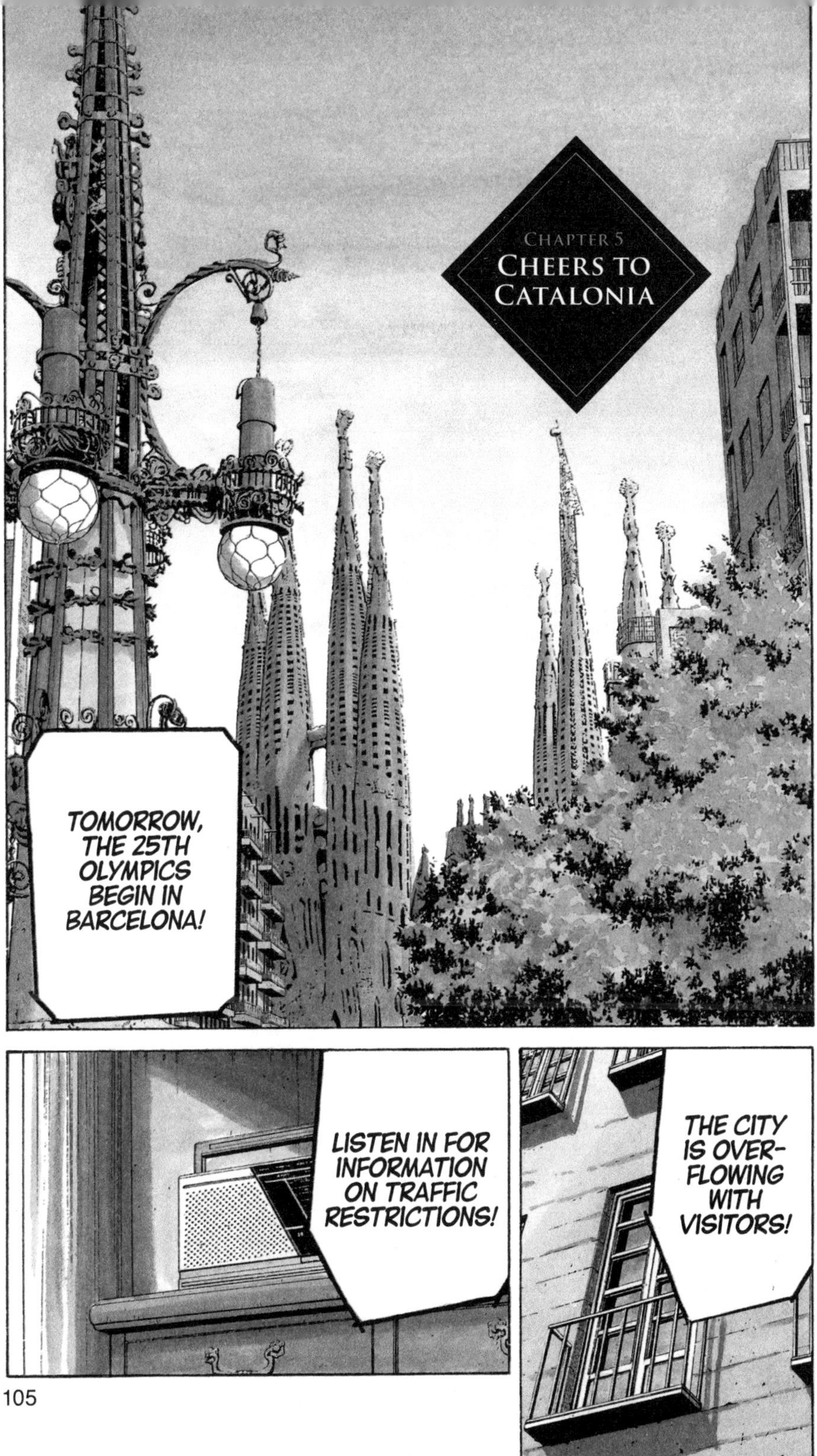
CHAPTER 5
CHEERS TO CATALONIA
TOMORROW, THE 25TH OLYMPICS BEGIN IN BARCELONA!
THE CITY IS OVER-FLOWING WITH VISITORS!
LISTEN IN FOR INFORMATION ON TRAFFIC RESTRICTIONS!

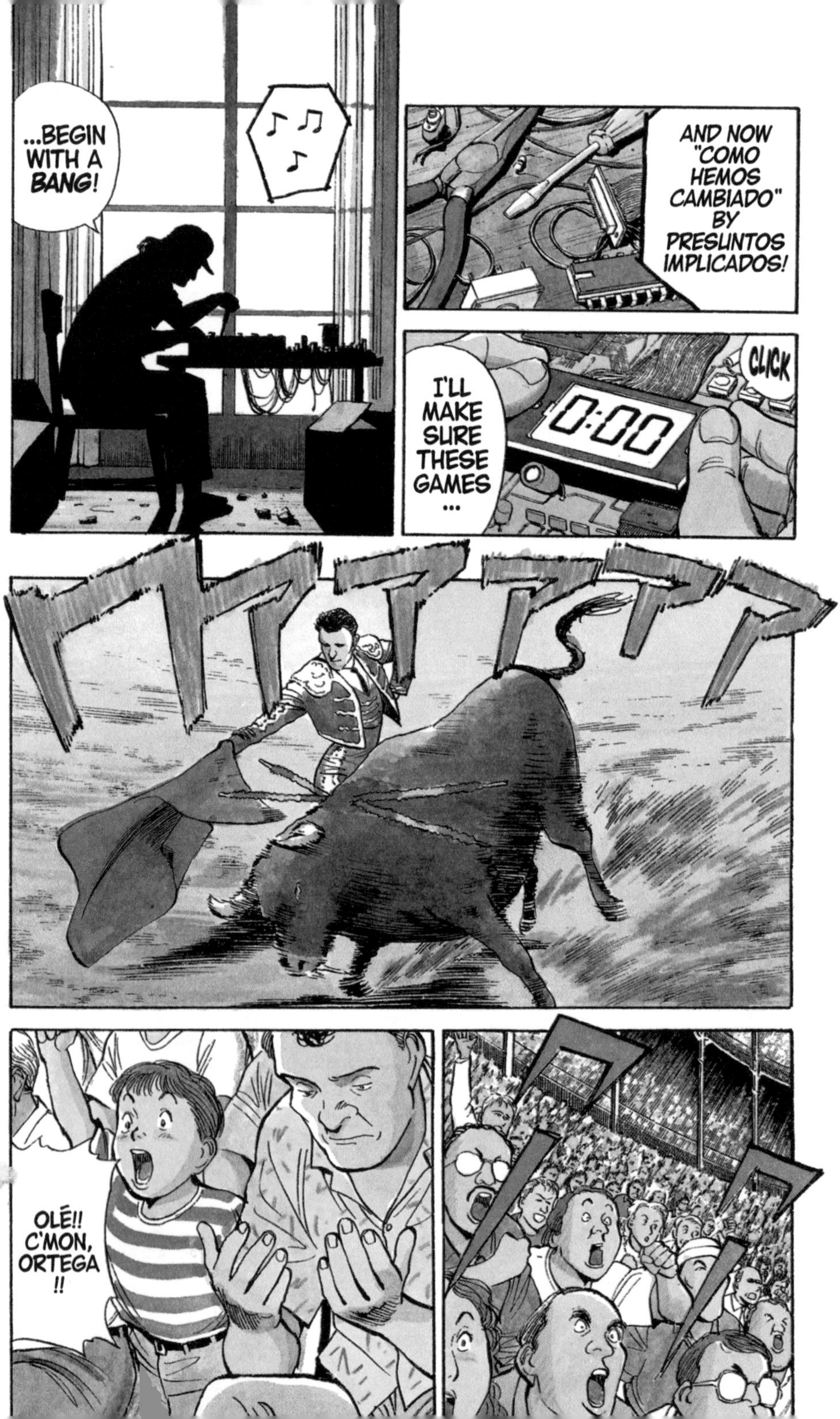
AND NOW "COMO HEMOS CAMBIADO" BY PRESUNTOS IMPLICADOS!
CLICK
I'LL MAKE SURE THESE GAMES...
0:00
...BEGIN WITH A BANG!
OLÉ!! C'MON, ORTEGA!!

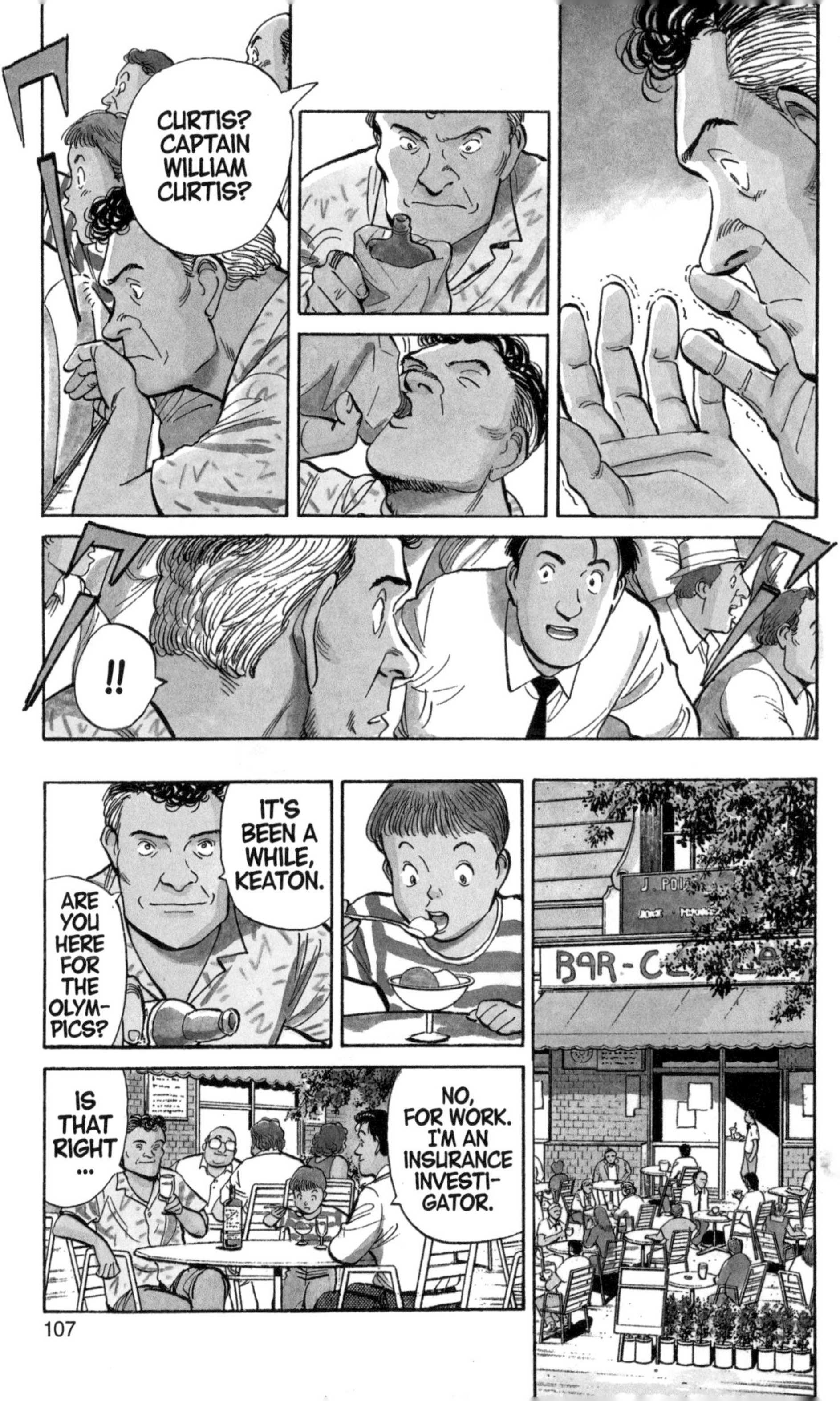
CURTIS? CAPTAIN WILLIAM CURTIS?
!!
IT'S BEEN A WHILE, KEATON.
ARE YOU HERE FOR THE OLYMPICS?
NO, FOR WORK. I'M AN INSURANCE INVESTIGATOR.
IS THAT RIGHT...

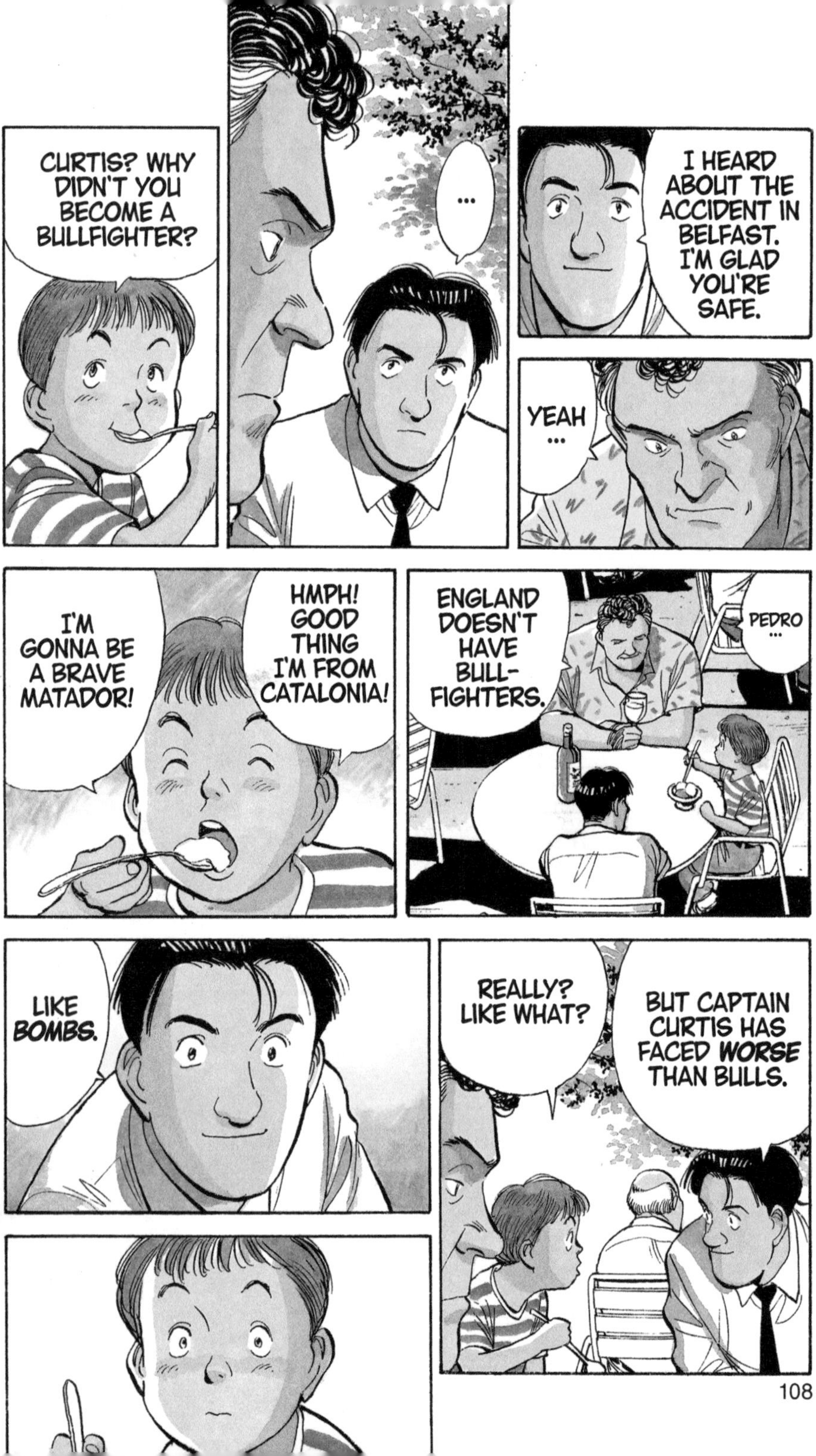
I HEARD ABOUT THE ACCIDENT IN BELFAST. I'M GLAD YOU'RE SAFE.
YEAH ...
...
CURTIS? WHY DIDN'T YOU BECOME A BULLFIGHTER?
PEDRO ...
ENGLAND DOESN'T HAVE BULL-FIGHTERS.
HMPH! GOOD THING I'M FROM CATALONIA!
I'M GONNA BE A BRAVE MATADOR!
BUT CAPTAIN CURTIS HAS FACED WORSE THAN BULLS.
REALLY? LIKE WHAT?
LIKE BOMBS.

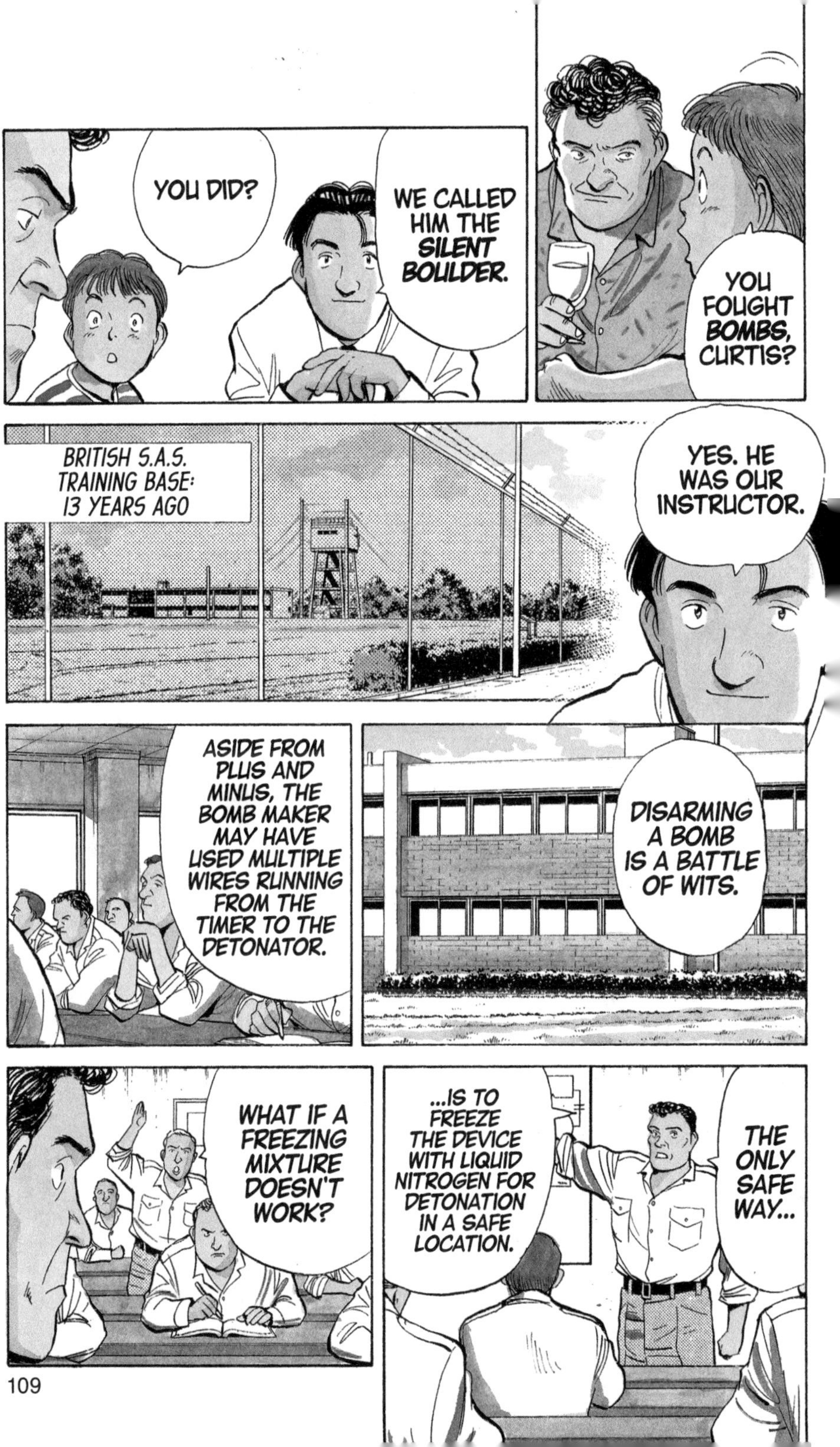
YOU FOUGHT BOMBS, CURTIS?
WE CALLED HIM THE SILENT BOULDER.
YOU DID?
YES. HE WAS OUR INSTRUCTOR.
BRITISH S.A.S. TRAINING BASE: 13 YEARS AGO
DISARMING A BOMB IS A BATTLE OF WITS.
ASIDE FROM PLUS AND MINUS, THE BOMB MAKER MAY HAVE USED MULTIPLE WIRES RUNNING FROM THE TIMER TO THE DETONATOR.
THE ONLY SAFE WAY...
...IS TO FREEZE THE DEVICE WITH LIQUID NITROGEN FOR DETONATION IN A SAFE LOCATION.
WHAT IF A FREEZING MIXTURE DOESN'T WORK?

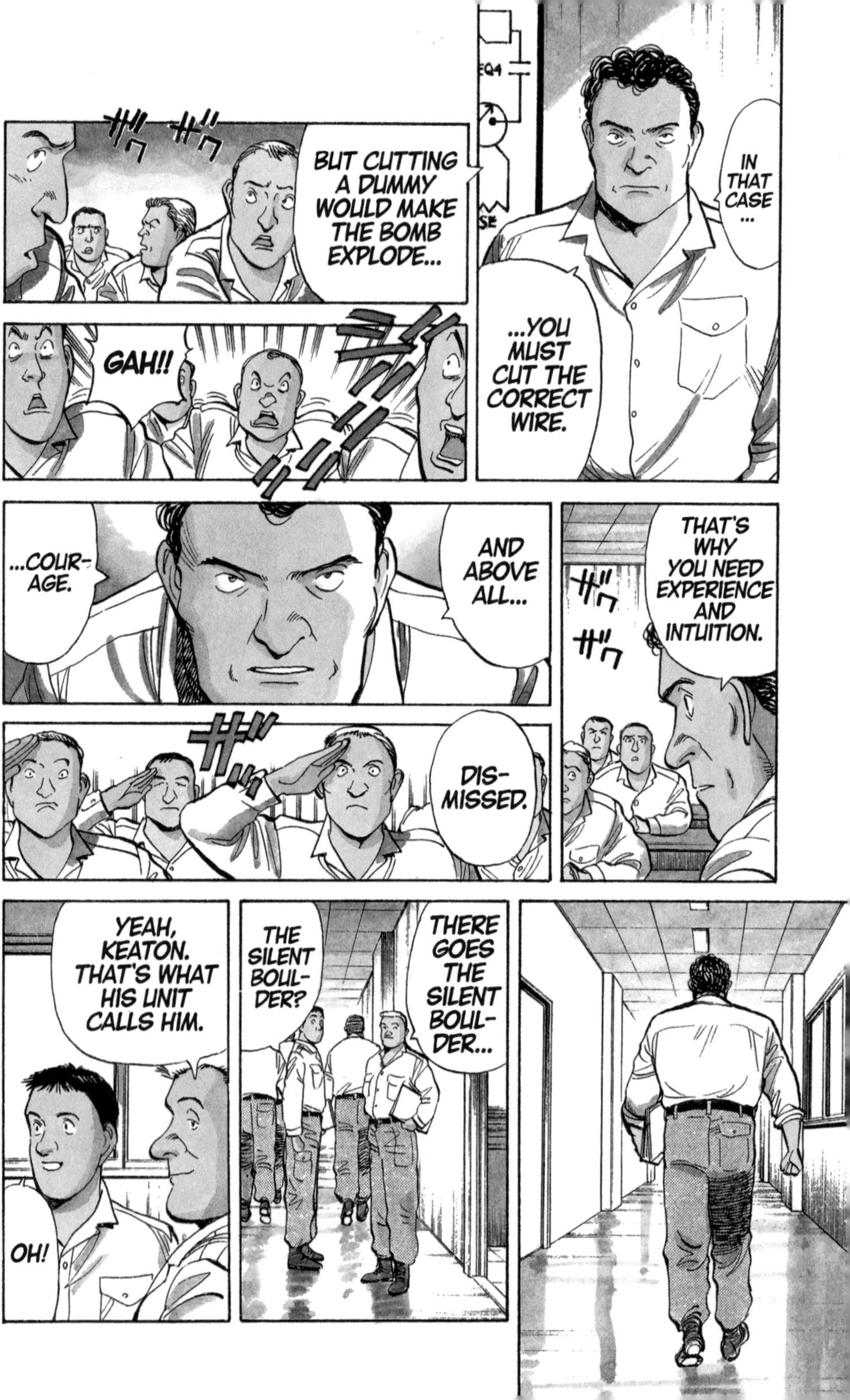
IN THAT CASE...
...YOU MUST CUT THE CORRECT WIRE.
BUT CUTTING A DUMMY WOULD MAKE THE BOMB EXPLODE...
GAH!!
THAT'S WHY YOU NEED EXPERIENCE AND INTUITION.
AND ABOVE ALL...
...COUR-AGE.
DIS-MISSED.
THERE GOES THE SILENT BOUL-DER...
THE SILENT BOUL-DER?
YEAH, KEATON. THAT'S WHAT HIS UNIT CALLS HIM.
OH!

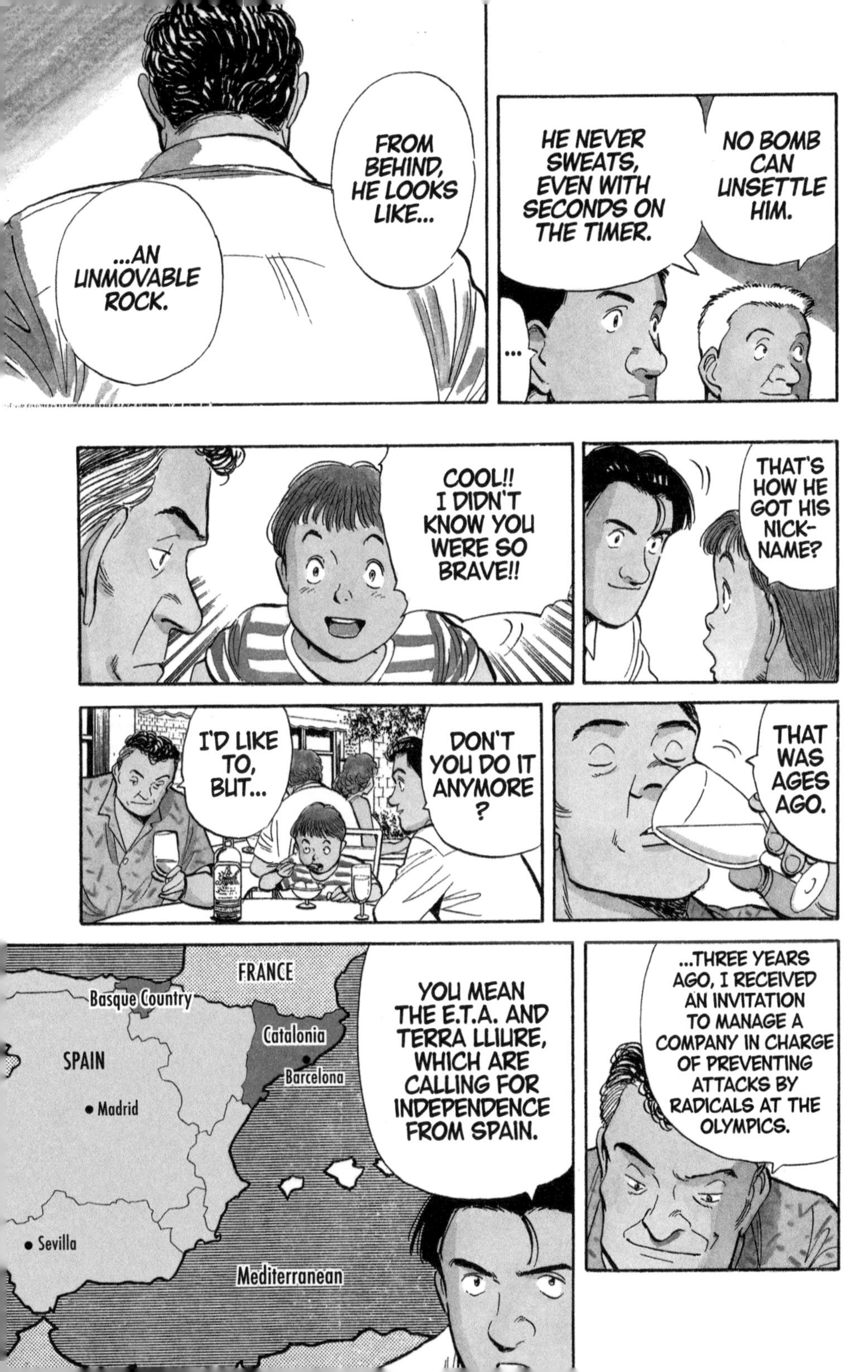
NO BOMB CAN UNSETTLE HIM.
HE NEVER SWEATS, EVEN WITH SECONDS ON THE TIMER.
...
FROM BEHIND, HE LOOKS LIKE...
...AN UNMOVABLE ROCK.
THAT'S HOW HE GOT HIS NICK-NAME?
COOL!! I DIDN'T KNOW YOU WERE SO BRAVE!!
THAT WAS AGES AGO.
DON'T YOU DO IT ANYMORE?
I'D LIKE TO, BUT...
...THREE YEARS AGO, I RECEIVED AN INVITATION TO MANAGE A COMPANY IN CHARGE OF PREVENTING ATTACKS BY RADICALS AT THE OLYMPICS.
YOU MEAN THE E.T.A. AND TERRA LLIURE, WHICH ARE CALLING FOR INDEPENDENCE FROM SPAIN.
FRANCE
Basque Country
Catalonia
Barcelona
SPAIN
Madrid
Sevilla
Mediterranean

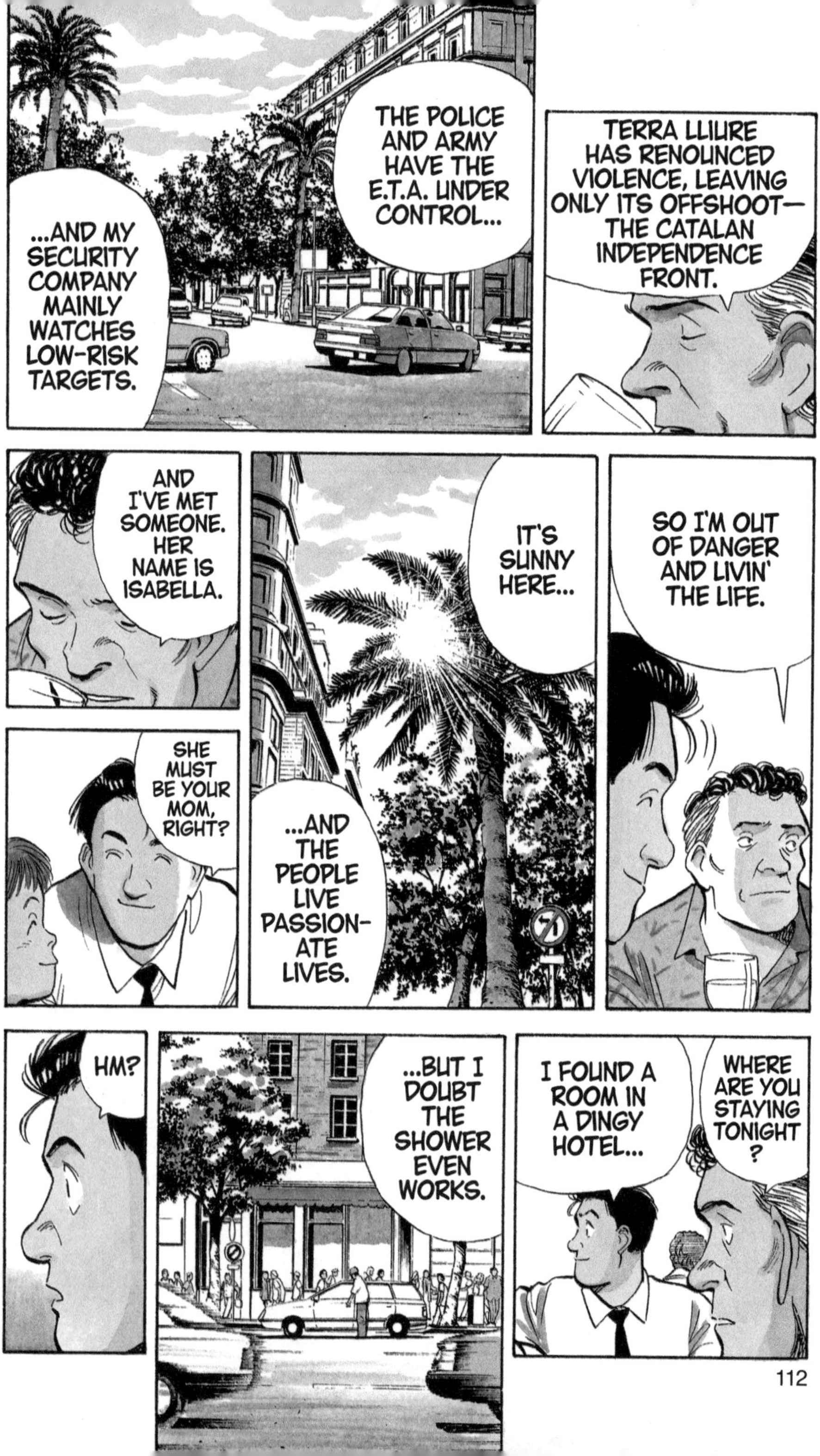
TERRA LLIURE HAS RENOUNCED VIOLENCE, LEAVING ONLY ITS OFFSHOOT— THE CATALAN INDEPENDENCE FRONT.
THE POLICE AND ARMY HAVE THE E.T.A. UNDER CONTROL...
...AND MY SECURITY COMPANY MAINLY WATCHES LOW-RISK TARGETS.
SO I'M OUT OF DANGER AND LIVIN' THE LIFE.
IT'S SUNNY HERE...
...AND THE PEOPLE LIVE PASSION-ATE LIVES.
AND I'VE MET SOMEONE. HER NAME IS ISABELLA.
SHE MUST BE YOUR MOM, RIGHT?
WHERE ARE YOU STAYING TONIGHT?
I FOUND A ROOM IN A DINGY HOTEL...
...BUT I DOUBT THE SHOWER EVEN WORKS.
HM?

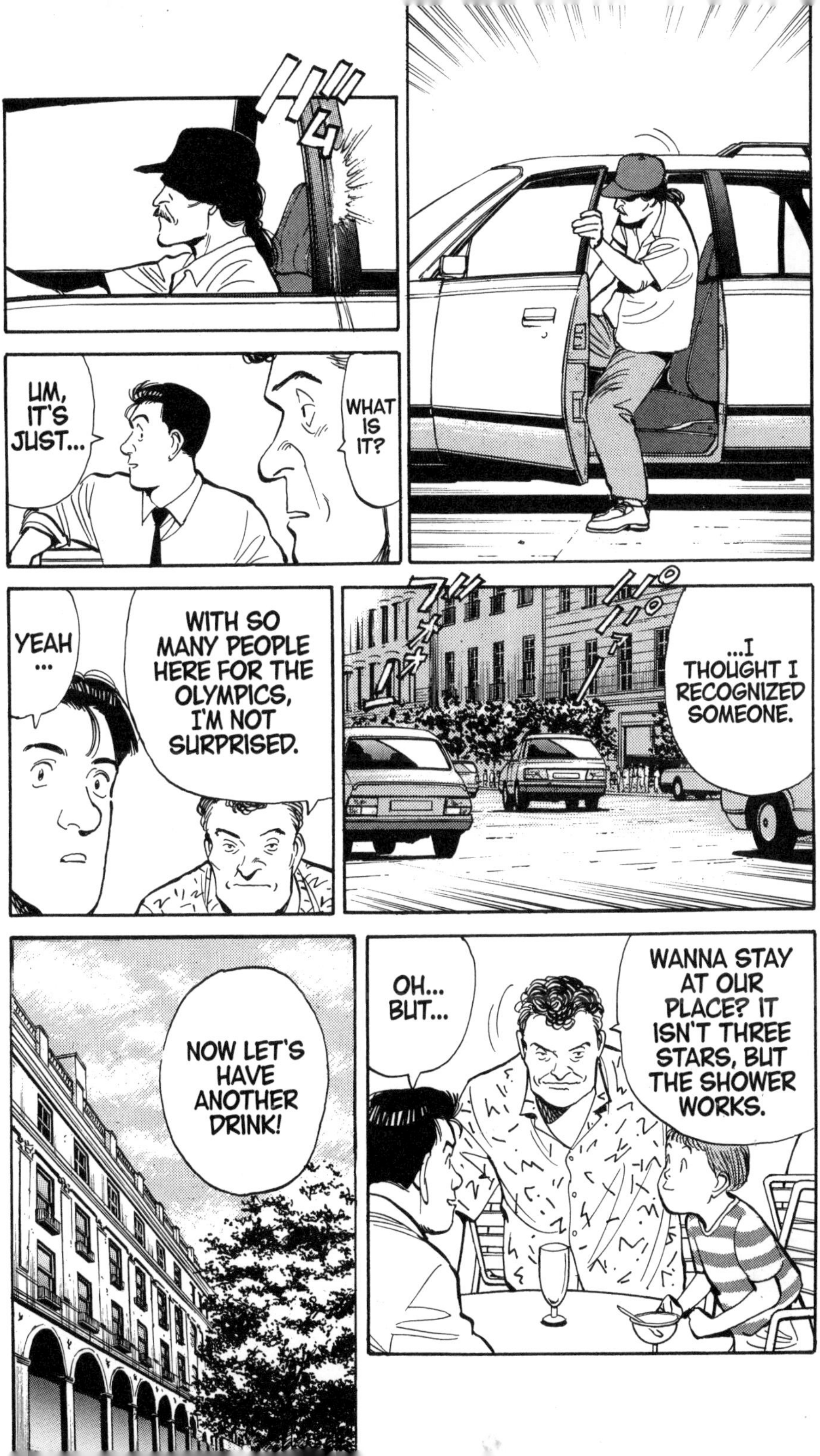
WHAT IS IT?
UM, IT'S JUST...
...I THOUGHT I RECOGNIZED SOMEONE.
WITH SO MANY PEOPLE HERE FOR THE OLYMPICS, I'M NOT SURPRISED.
YEAH ...
WANNA STAY AT OUR PLACE? IT ISN'T THREE STARS, BUT THE SHOWER WORKS.
OH... BUT...
NOW LET'S HAVE ANOTHER DRINK!

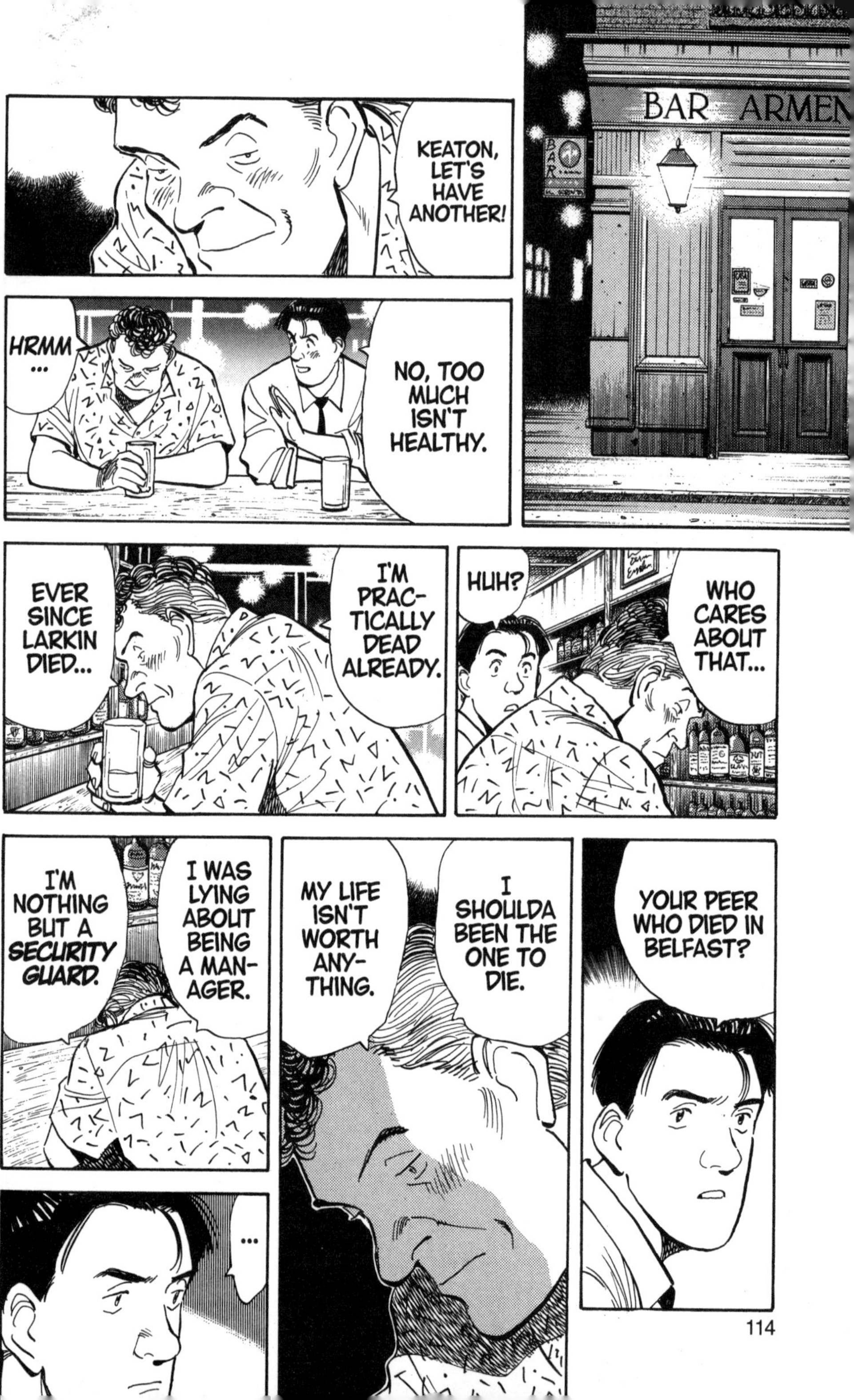
BAR ARMEN
KEATON, LET'S HAVE ANOTHER!
NO, TOO MUCH ISN'T HEALTHY.
HRMM...
WHO CARES ABOUT THAT...
HUH?
I'M PRAC-TICALLY DEAD ALREADY.
EVER SINCE LARKIN DIED...
YOUR PEER WHO DIED IN BELFAST?
I SHOULDA BEEN THE ONE TO DIE.
MY LIFE ISN'T WORTH ANY-THING.
I WAS LYING ABOUT BEING A MAN-AGER.
I'M NOTHING BUT A **SECURITY GUARD.**
...

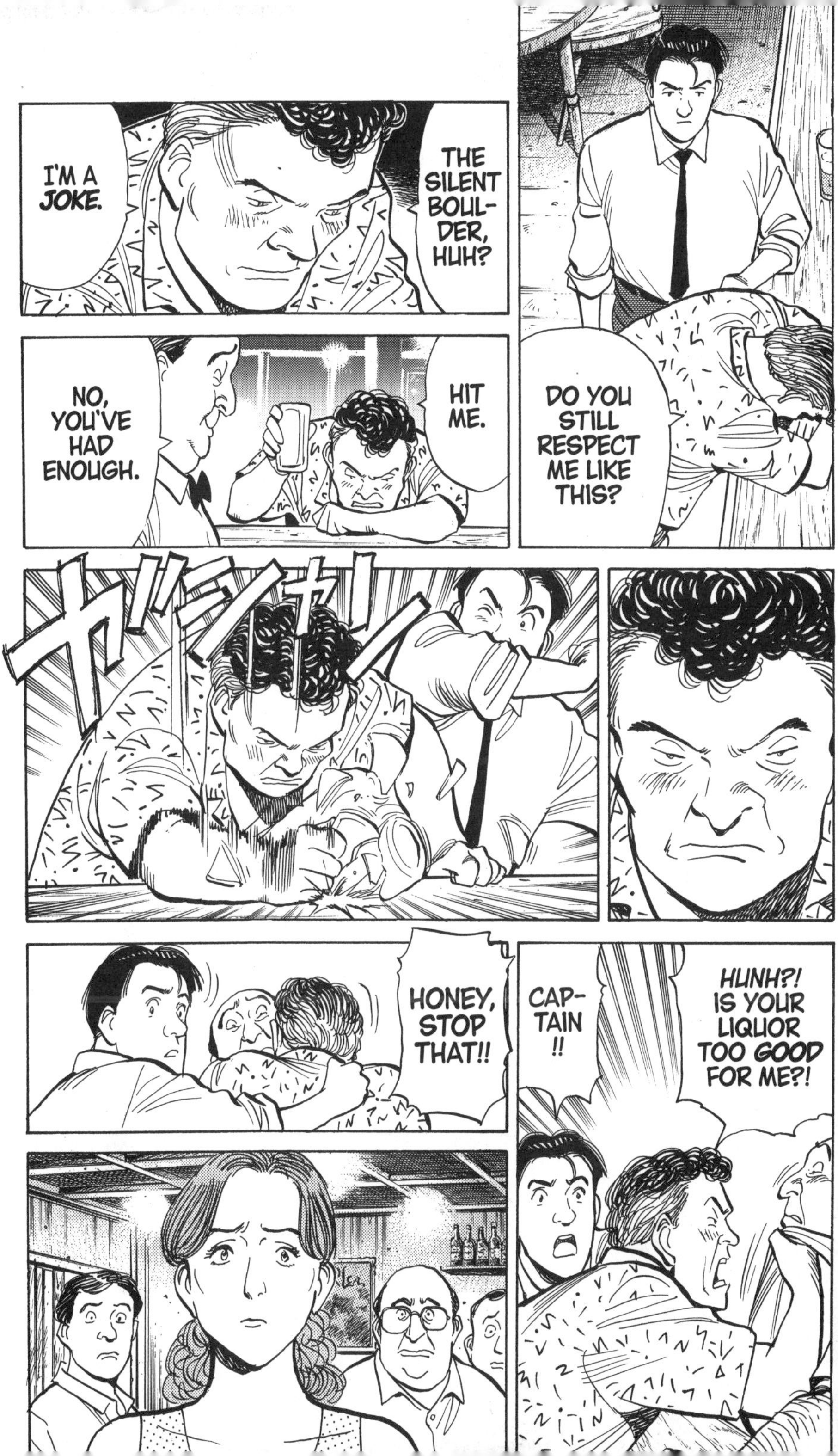
DO YOU STILL RESPECT ME LIKE THIS?
THE SILENT BOULDER, HUH?
I'M A JOKE.
HIT ME.
NO, YOU'VE HAD ENOUGH.
HUNH?! IS YOUR LIQUOR TOO GOOD FOR ME?!
CAPTAIN!!
HONEY, STOP THAT!!

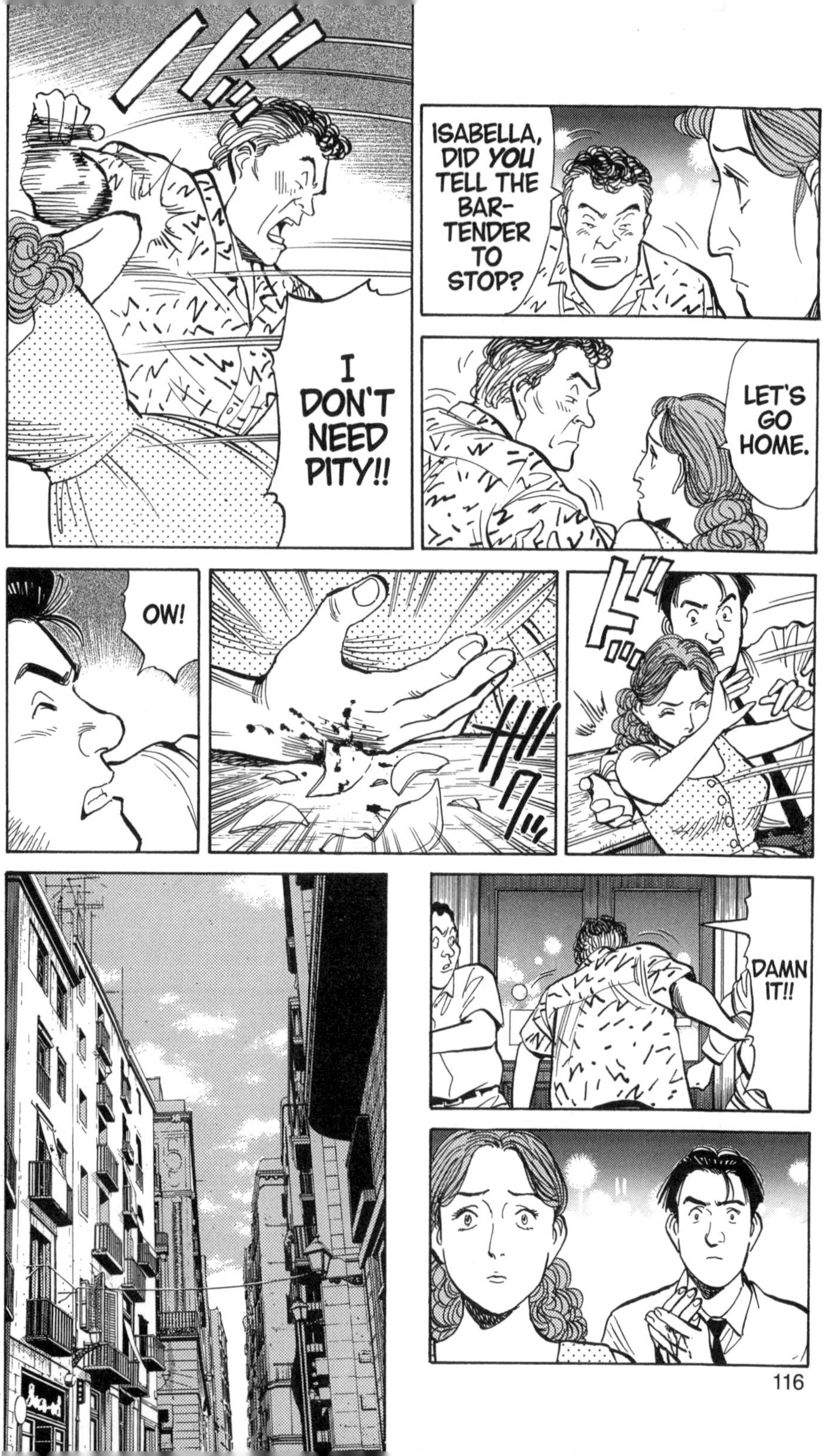
ISABELLA, DID YOU TELL THE BAR-TENDER TO STOP?
LET'S GO HOME.
I DON'T NEED PITY!!
OW!
DAMN IT!!

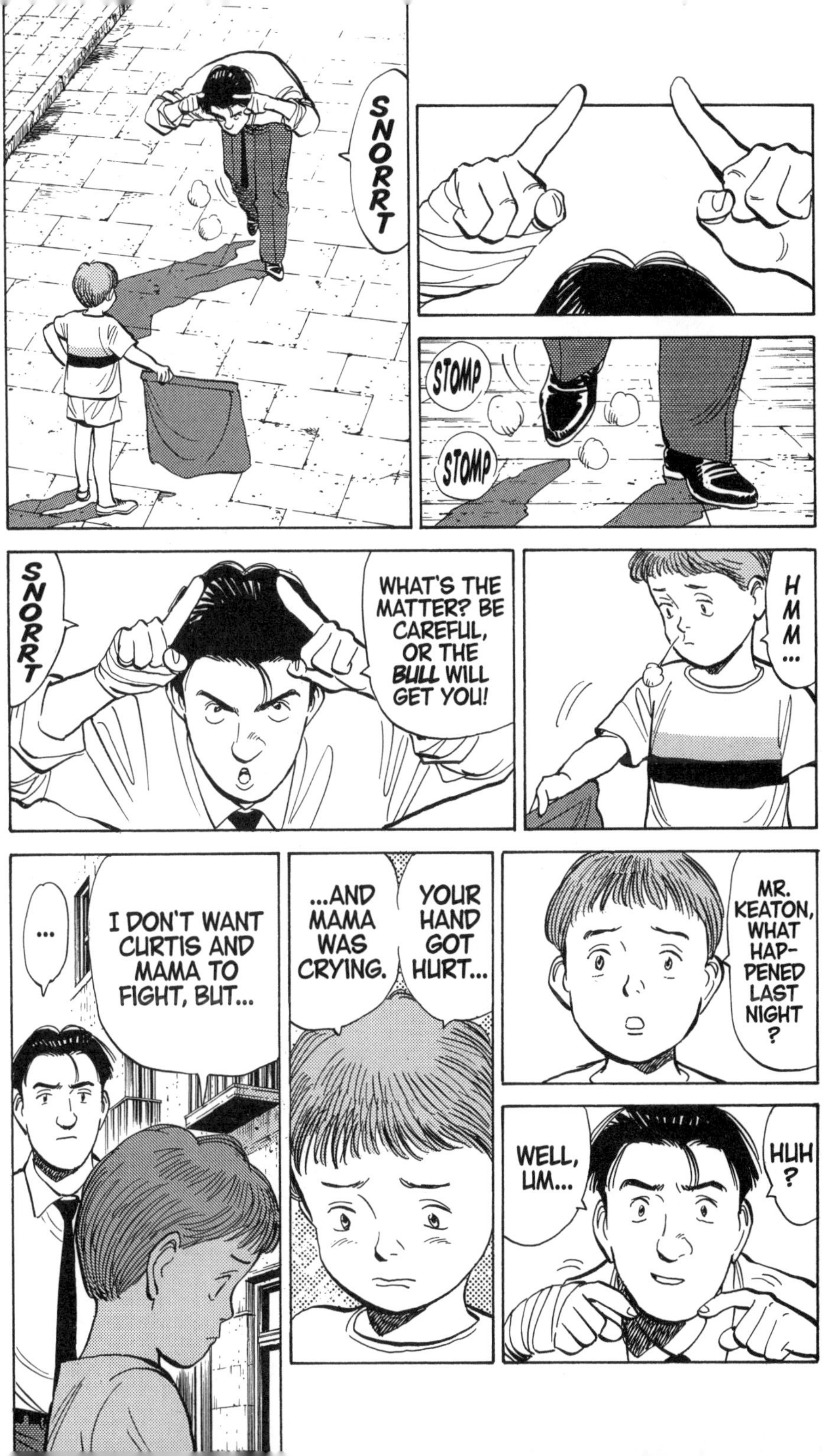
STOMP
STOMP
SNORRT
HMM...
WHAT'S THE MATTER? BE CAREFUL, OR THE BULL WILL GET YOU!
SNORRT
MR. KEATON, WHAT HAP-PENED LAST NIGHT?
HUH?
WELL, UM...
YOUR HAND GOT HURT...
...AND MAMA WAS CRYING.
I DON'T WANT CURTIS AND MAMA TO FIGHT, BUT...
...

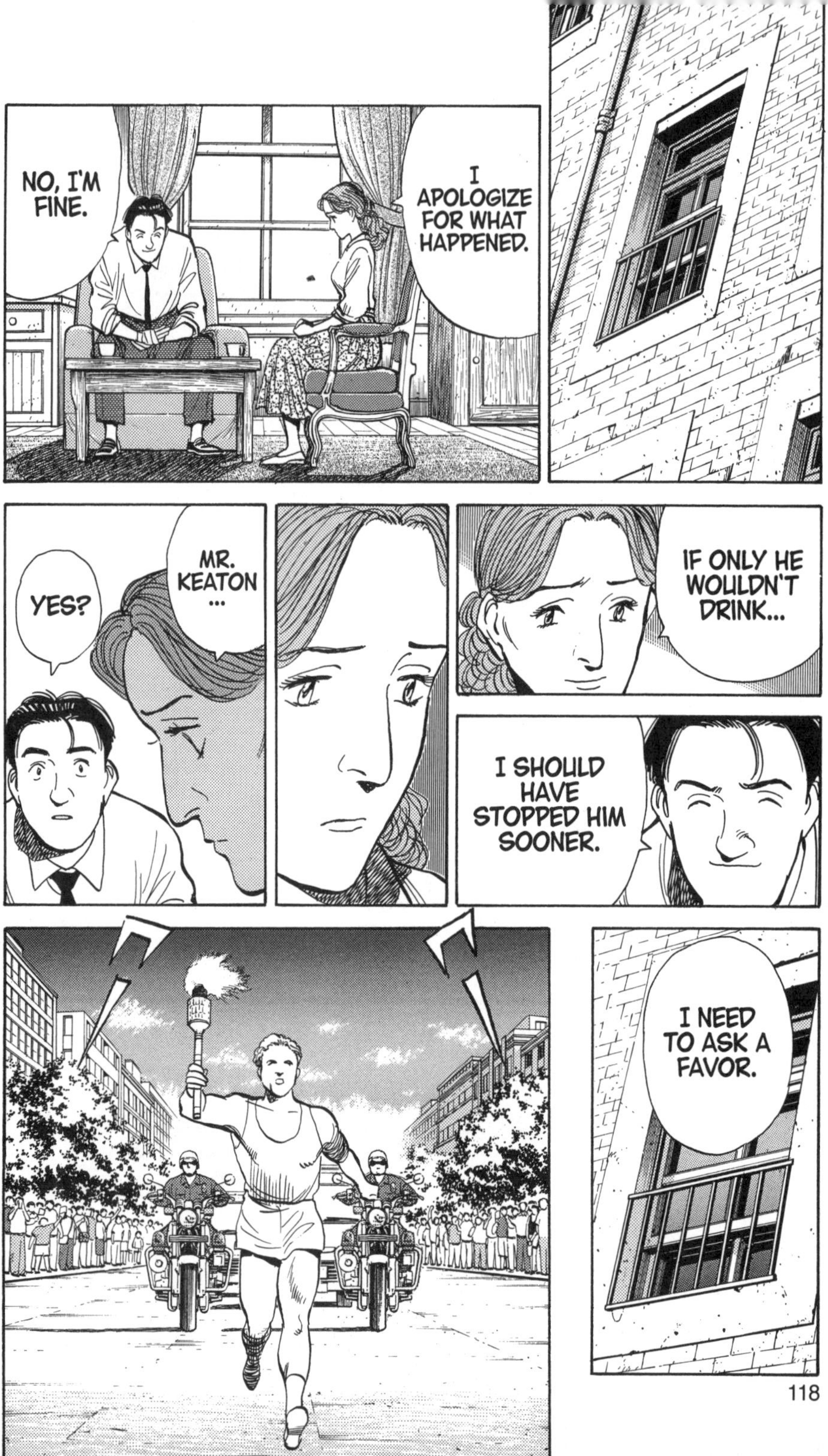
I APOLOGIZE FOR WHAT HAPPENED.
NO, I'M FINE.
IF ONLY HE WOULDN'T DRINK...
I SHOULD HAVE STOPPED HIM SOONER.
MR. KEATON ...
YES?
I NEED TO ASK A FAVOR.

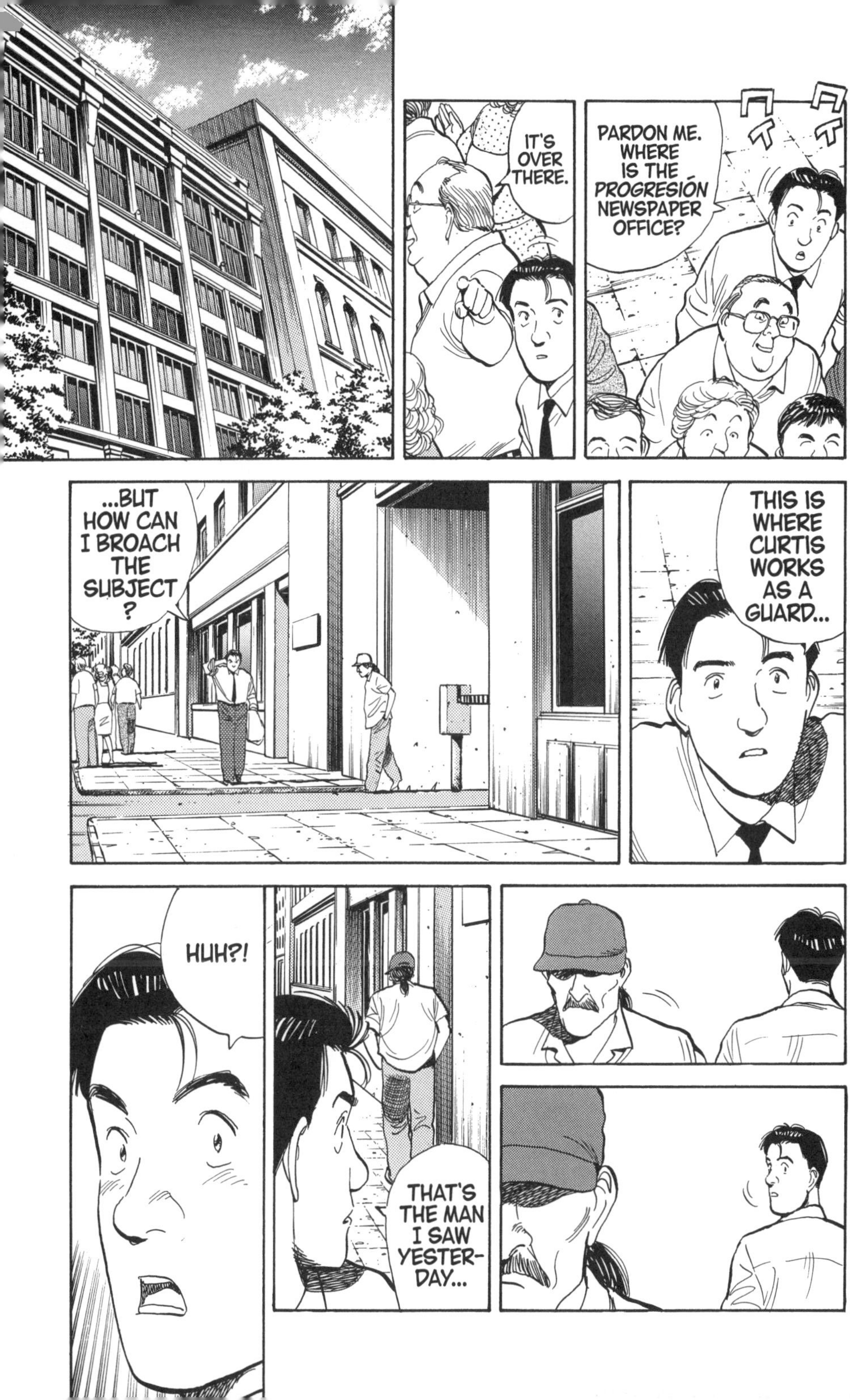
PARDON ME. WHERE IS THE PROGRESIÓN NEWSPAPER OFFICE?
IT'S OVER THERE.
THIS IS WHERE CURTIS WORKS AS A GUARD...
...BUT HOW CAN I BROACH THE SUBJECT?
THAT'S THE MAN I SAW YESTER-DAY...
HUH?!

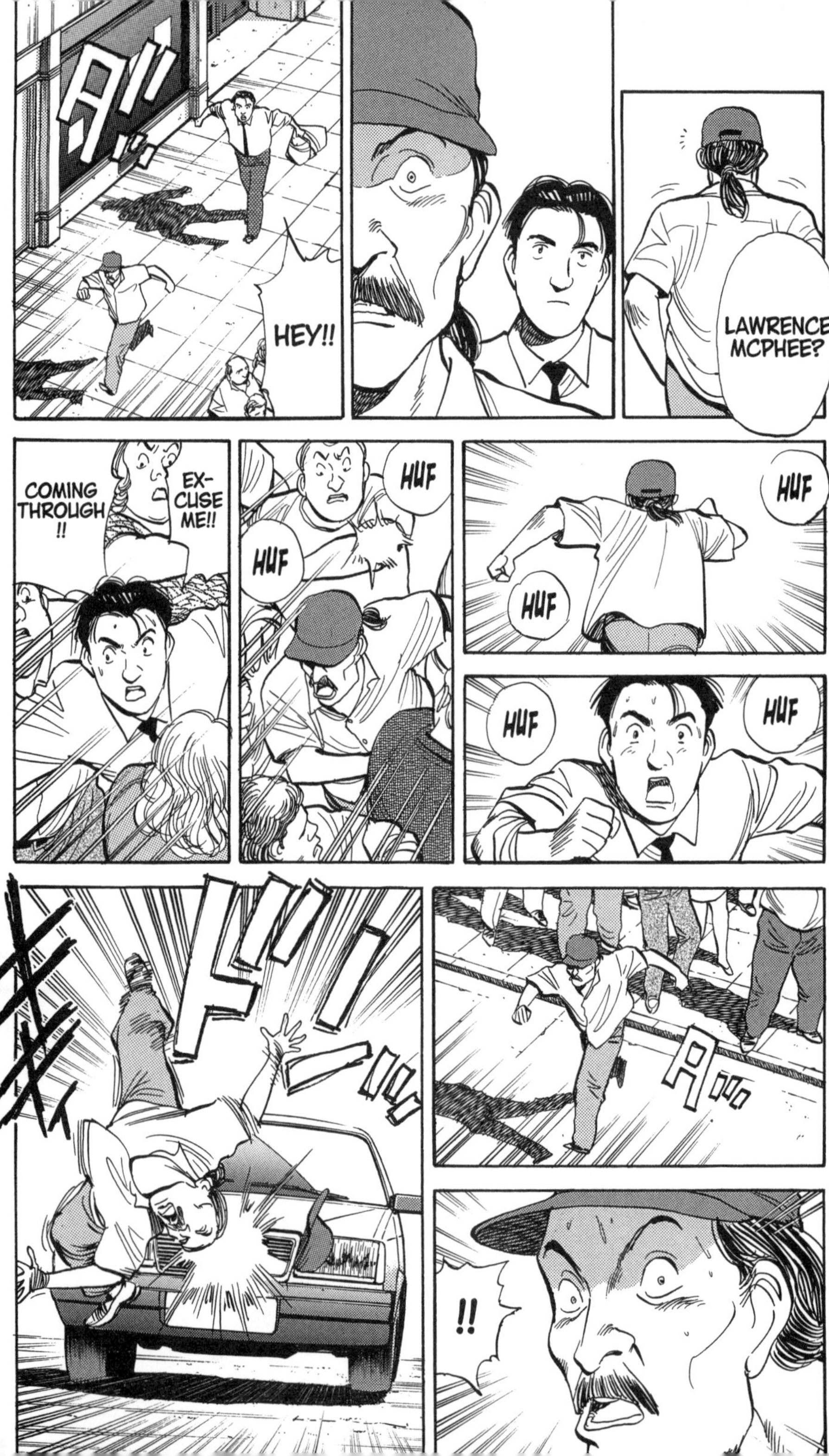
LAWRENCE MCPHEE?
HEY!!
HUF
HUF
HUF
HUF
HUF
HUF
EX-CUSE ME!!
COMING THROUGH !!
!!

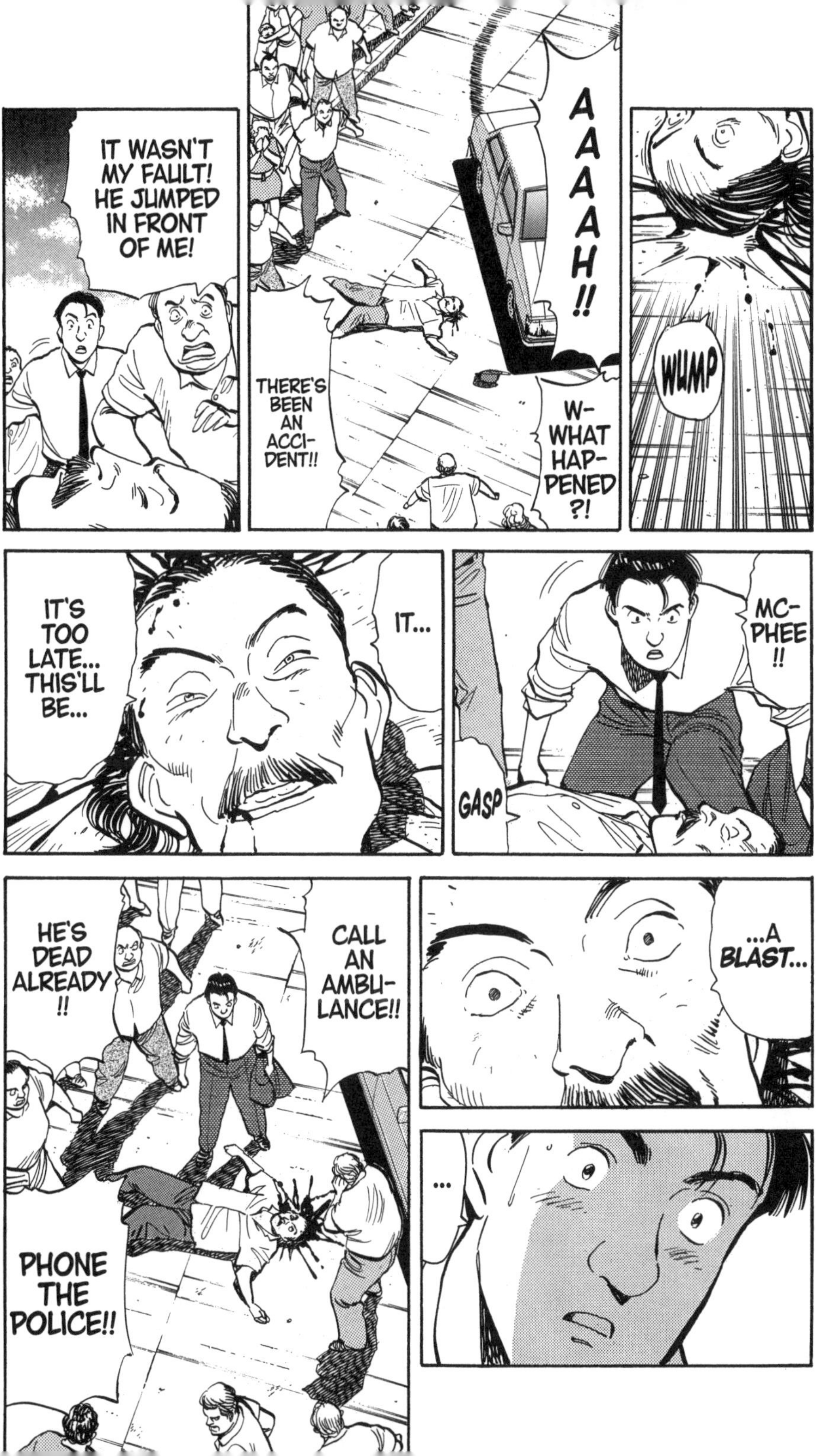
WUMP
AAAAAH!!
W-WHAT HAPPENED?!
THERE'S BEEN AN ACCIDENT!!
IT WASN'T MY FAULT! HE JUMPED IN FRONT OF ME!
MC-PHEE!!
GASP
IT...
IT'S TOO LATE... THIS'LL BE...
...A BLAST...
...
CALL AN AMBULANCE!!
HE'S DEAD ALREADY!!
PHONE THE POLICE!!

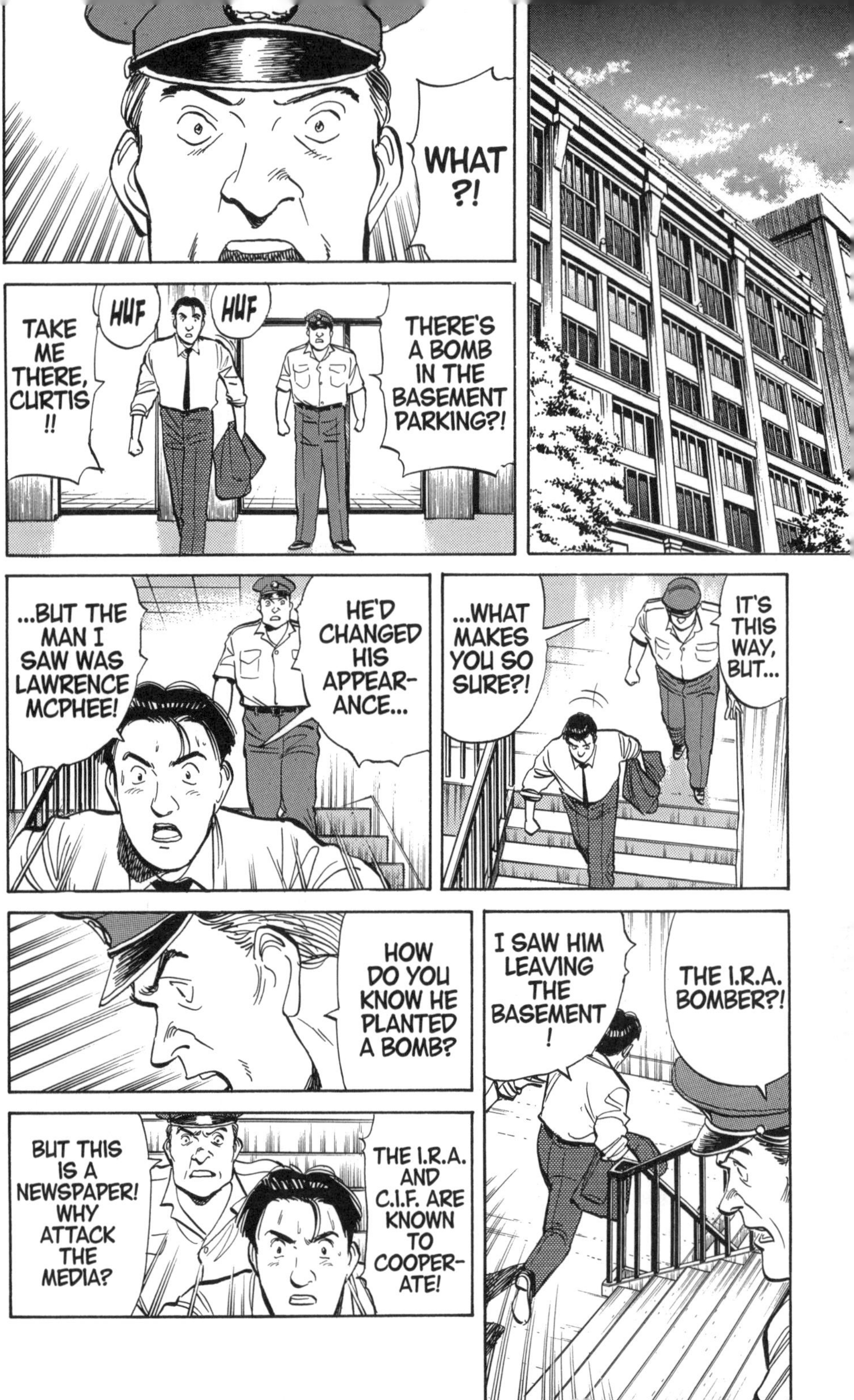
WHAT ?!
THERE'S A BOMB IN THE BASEMENT PARKING?!
HUF
HUF
TAKE ME THERE, CURTIS !!
IT'S THIS WAY, BUT...
...WHAT MAKES YOU SO SURE?!
HE'D CHANGED HIS APPEARANCE...
...BUT THE MAN I SAW WAS LAWRENCE MCPHEE!
THE I.R.A. BOMBER?!
I SAW HIM LEAVING THE BASEMENT !
HOW DO YOU KNOW HE PLANTED A BOMB?
THE I.R.A. AND C.I.F. ARE KNOWN TO COOPERATE!
BUT THIS IS A NEWSPAPER! WHY ATTACK THE MEDIA?

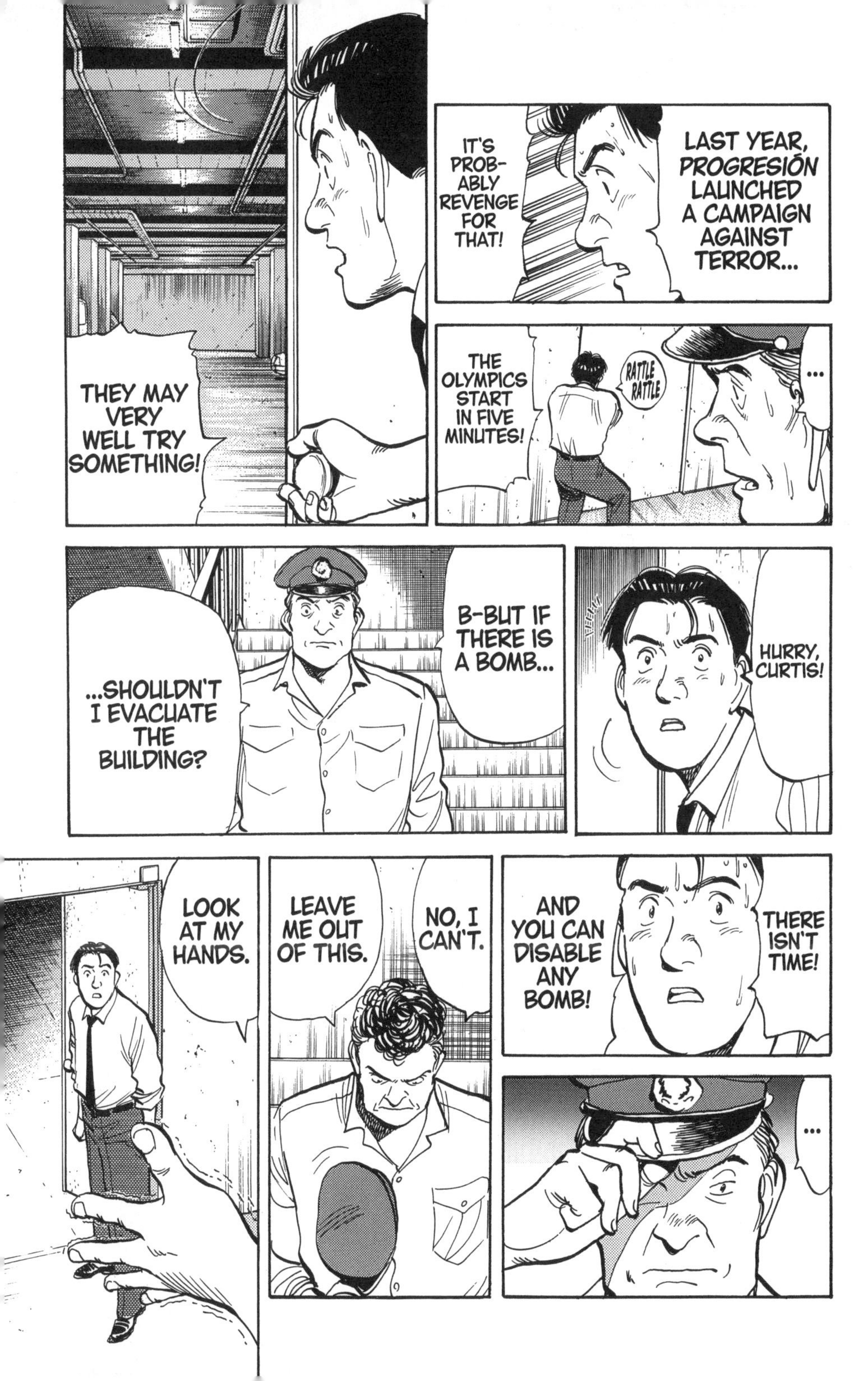
LAST YEAR, PROGRESIÓN LAUNCHED A CAMPAIGN AGAINST TERROR...
IT'S PROB-ABLY REVENGE FOR THAT!
...
RATTLE RATTLE
THE OLYMPICS START IN FIVE MINUTES!
THEY MAY VERY WELL TRY SOMETHING!
HURRY, CURTIS!
B-BUT IF THERE IS A BOMB...
...SHOULDN'T I EVACUATE THE BUILDING?
THERE ISN'T TIME!
AND YOU CAN DISABLE ANY BOMB!
...
NO, I CAN'T.
LEAVE ME OUT OF THIS.
LOOK AT MY HANDS.

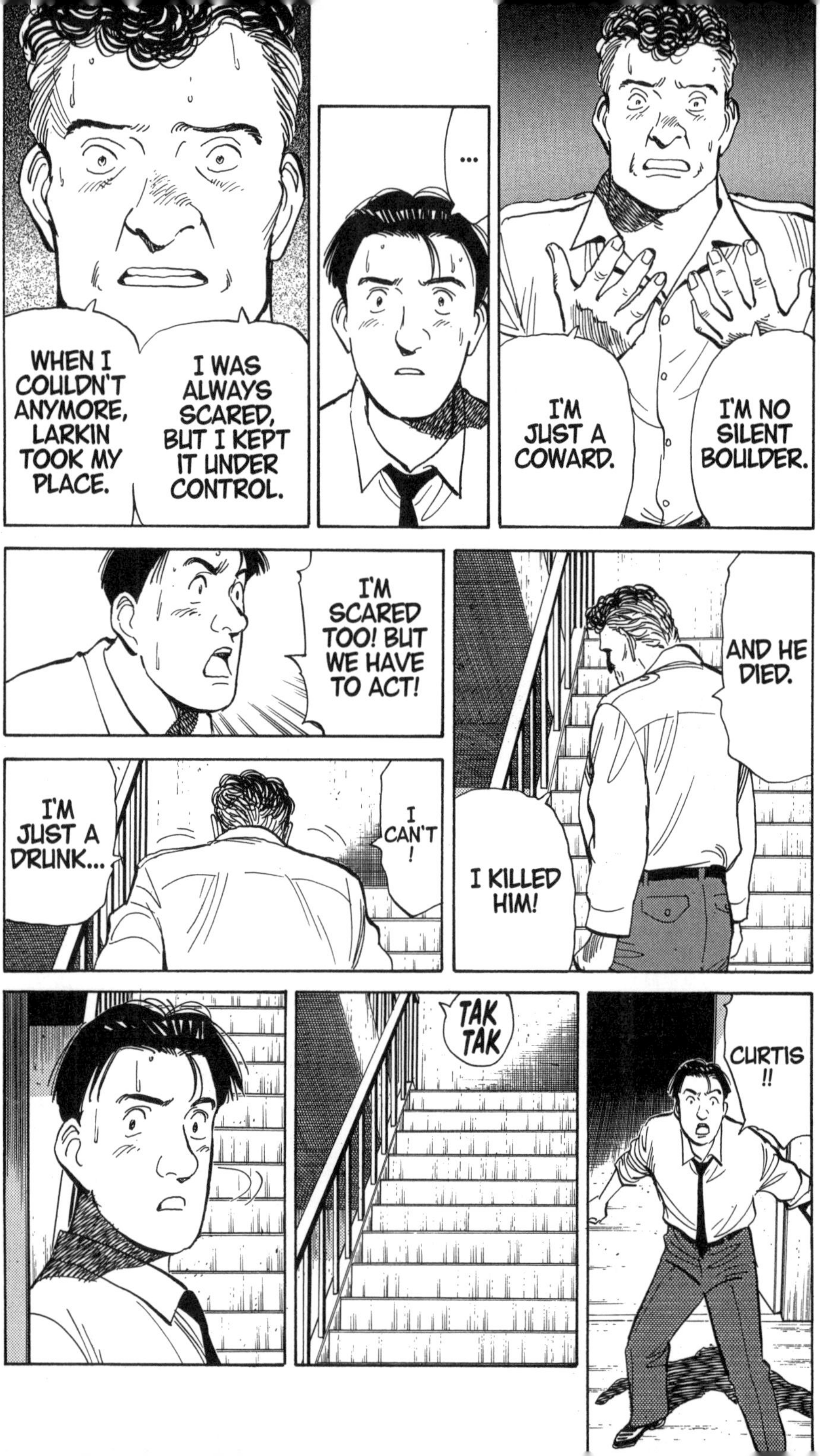
I'M NO SILENT BOULDER.
I'M JUST A COWARD.
...
I WAS ALWAYS SCARED, BUT I KEPT IT UNDER CONTROL.
WHEN I COULDN'T ANYMORE, LARKIN TOOK MY PLACE.
AND HE DIED.
I KILLED HIM!
I'M SCARED TOO! BUT WE HAVE TO ACT!
I CAN'T!
I'M JUST A DRUNK...
CURTIS!!
TAK TAK

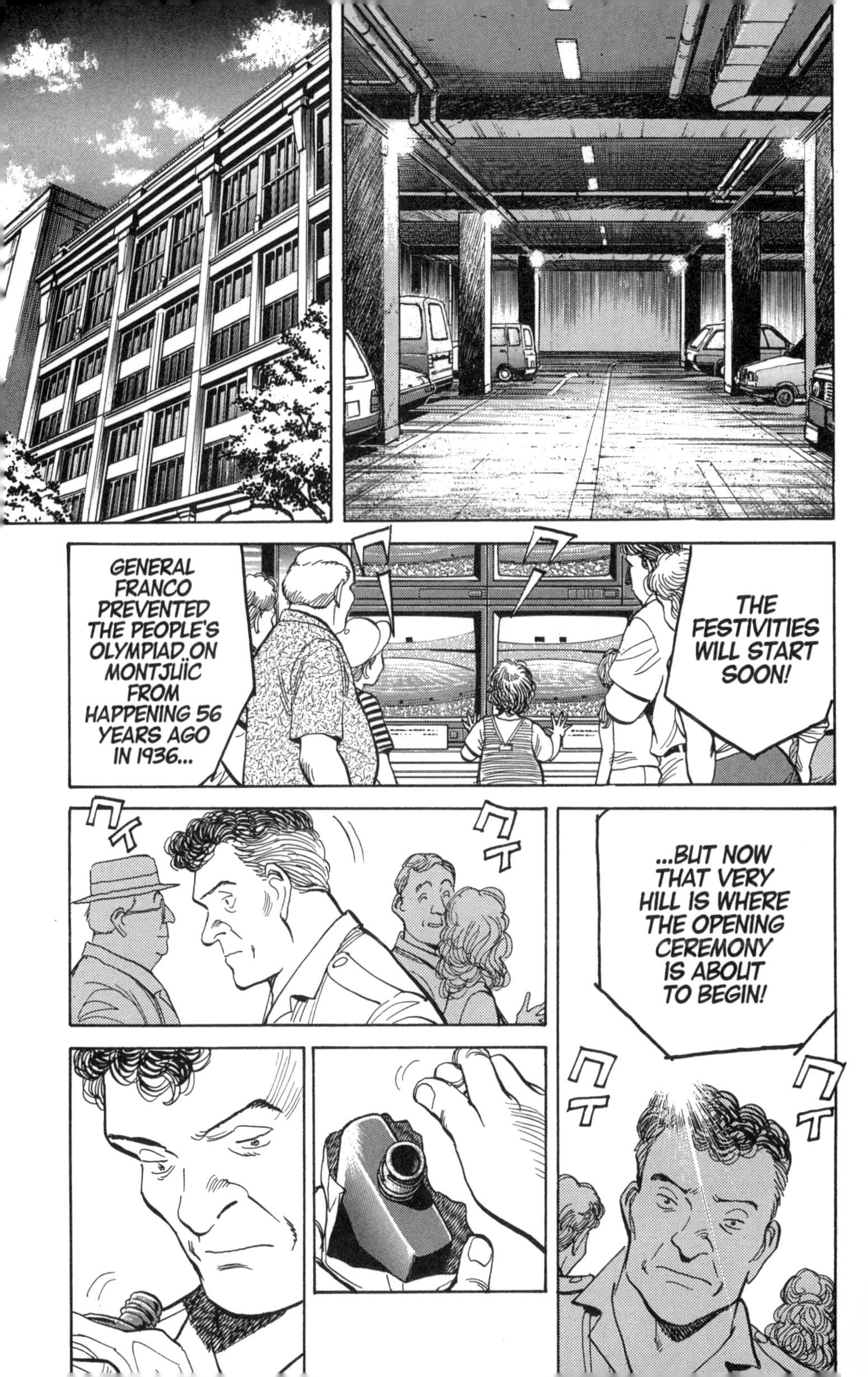
THE FESTIVITIES WILL START SOON!
GENERAL FRANCO PREVENTED THE PEOPLE'S OLYMPIAD ON MONTJUÏC FROM HAPPENING 56 YEARS AGO IN 1936...
...BUT NOW THAT VERY HILL IS WHERE THE OPENING CEREMONY IS ABOUT TO BEGIN!

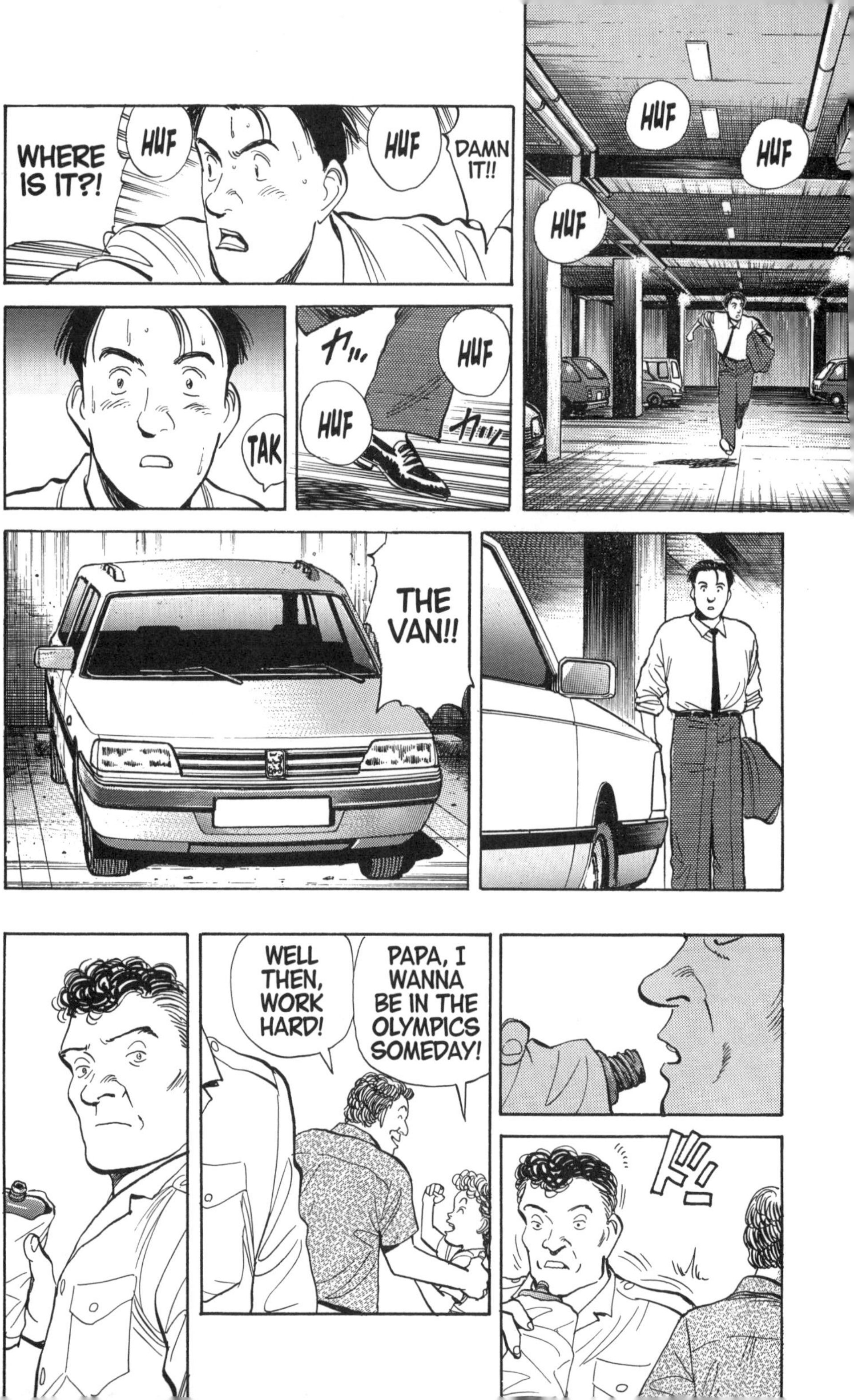
HUF
HUF
HUF
DAMN IT!!
HUF
HUF
WHERE IS IT?!
HUF
カッ
HUF
カッ
TAK
THE VAN!!
PAPA, I WANNA BE IN THE OLYMPICS SOMEDAY!
WELL THEN, WORK HARD!

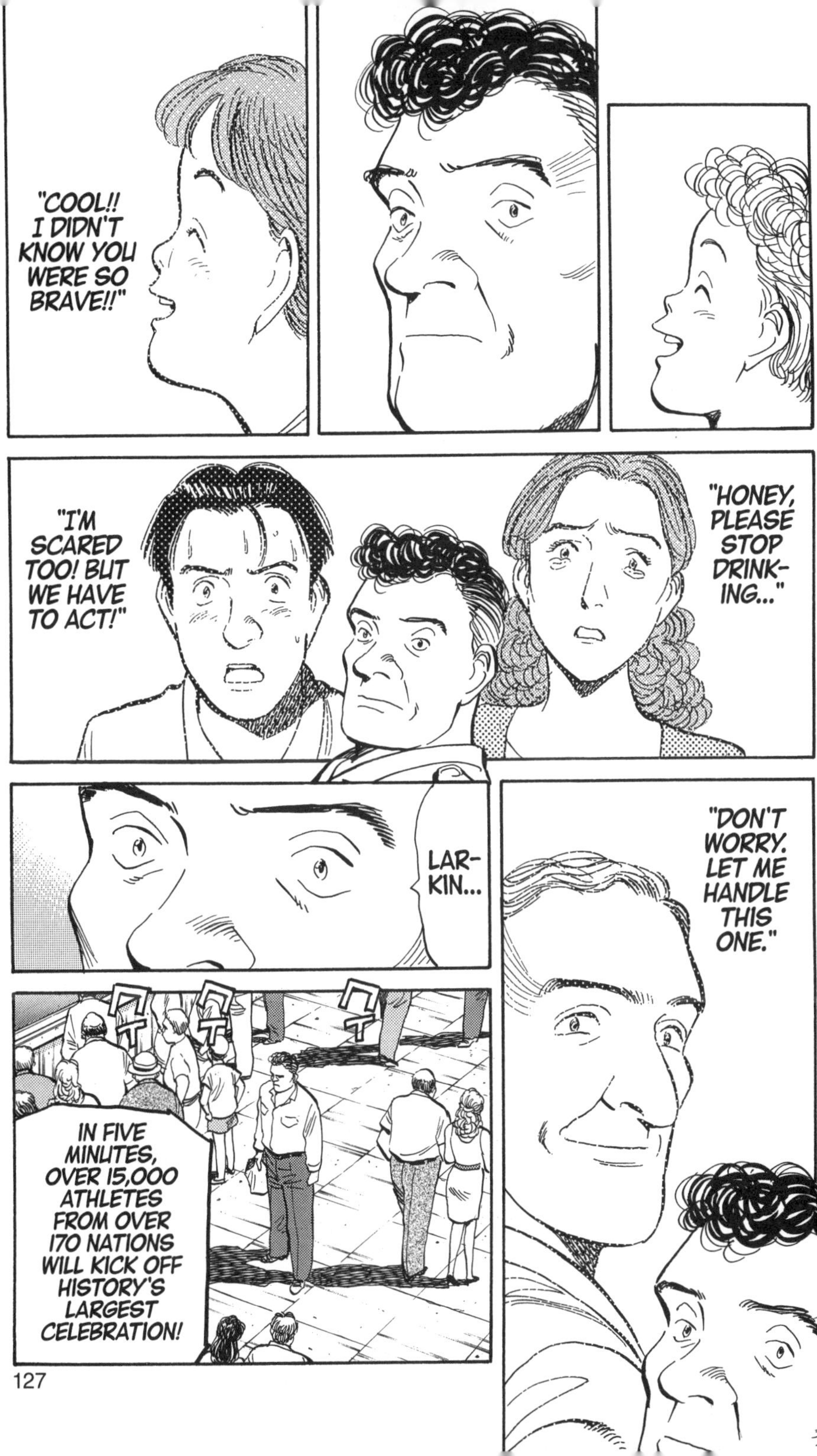
"COOL!! I DIDN'T KNOW YOU WERE SO BRAVE!!"
"HONEY, PLEASE STOP DRINK-ING..."
"I'M SCARED TOO! BUT WE HAVE TO ACT!"
"DON'T WORRY. LET ME HANDLE THIS ONE."
LAR-KIN...
IN FIVE MINUTES, OVER 15,000 ATHLETES FROM OVER 170 NATIONS WILL KICK OFF HISTORY'S LARGEST CELEBRATION!

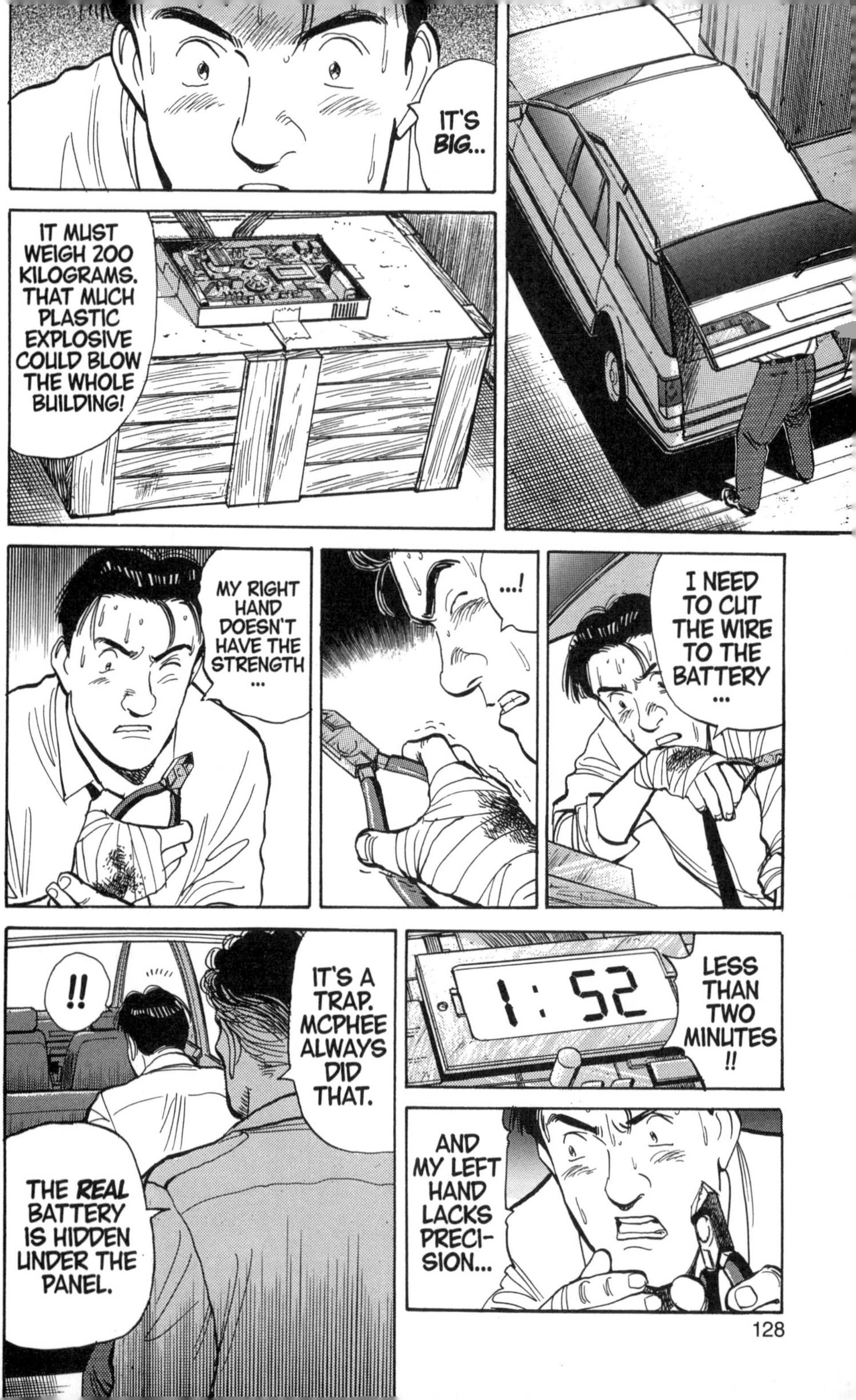
IT'S BIG...
IT MUST WEIGH 200 KILOGRAMS. THAT MUCH PLASTIC EXPLOSIVE COULD BLOW THE WHOLE BUILDING!
I NEED TO CUT THE WIRE TO THE BATTERY...
...!
MY RIGHT HAND DOESN'T HAVE THE STRENGTH...
1:52
LESS THAN TWO MINUTES!!
AND MY LEFT HAND LACKS PRECISION...
IT'S A TRAP. MCPHEE ALWAYS DID THAT.
!!
THE *REAL* BATTERY IS HIDDEN UNDER THE PANEL.

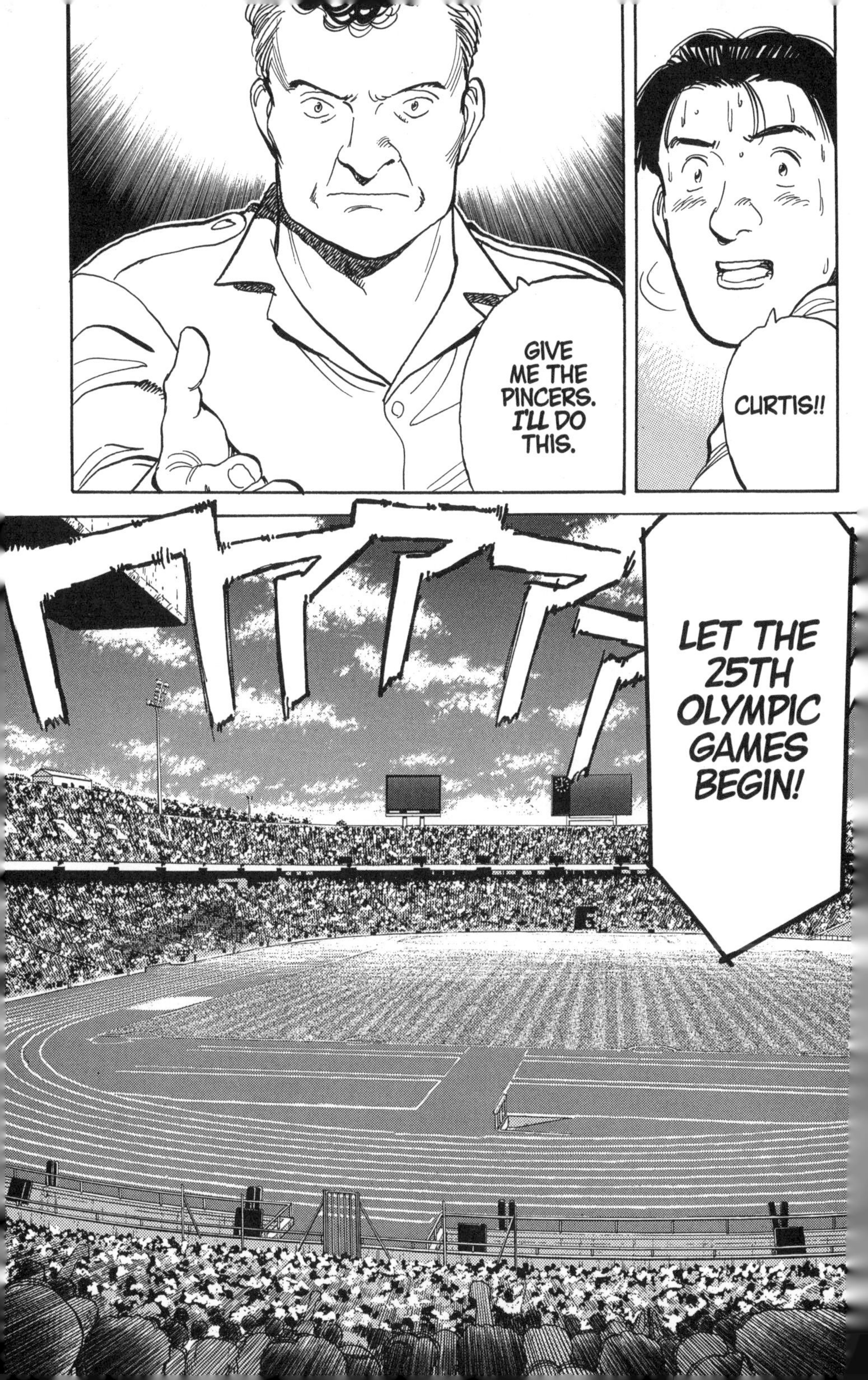
GIVE ME THE PINCERS. I'LL DO THIS.
CURTIS!!
LET THE 25TH OLYMPIC GAMES BEGIN!

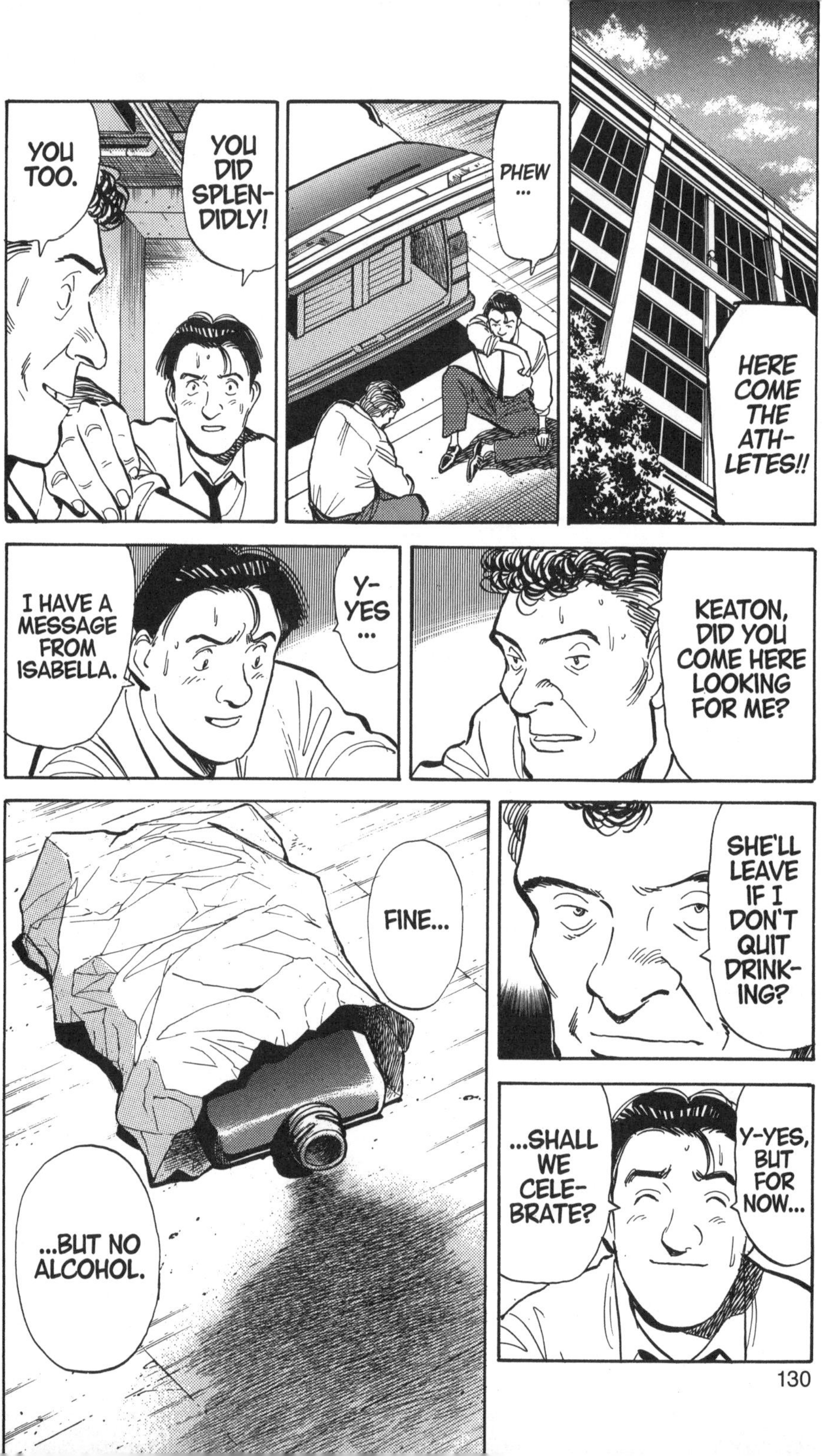
HERE COME THE ATH-LETES!!
PHEW ...
YOU DID SPLEN-DIDLY!
YOU TOO.
KEATON, DID YOU COME HERE LOOKING FOR ME?
Y-YES ...
I HAVE A MESSAGE FROM ISABELLA.
SHE'LL LEAVE IF I DON'T QUIT DRINK-ING?
Y-YES, BUT FOR NOW...
...SHALL WE CELE-BRATE?
FINE...
...BUT NO ALCOHOL.

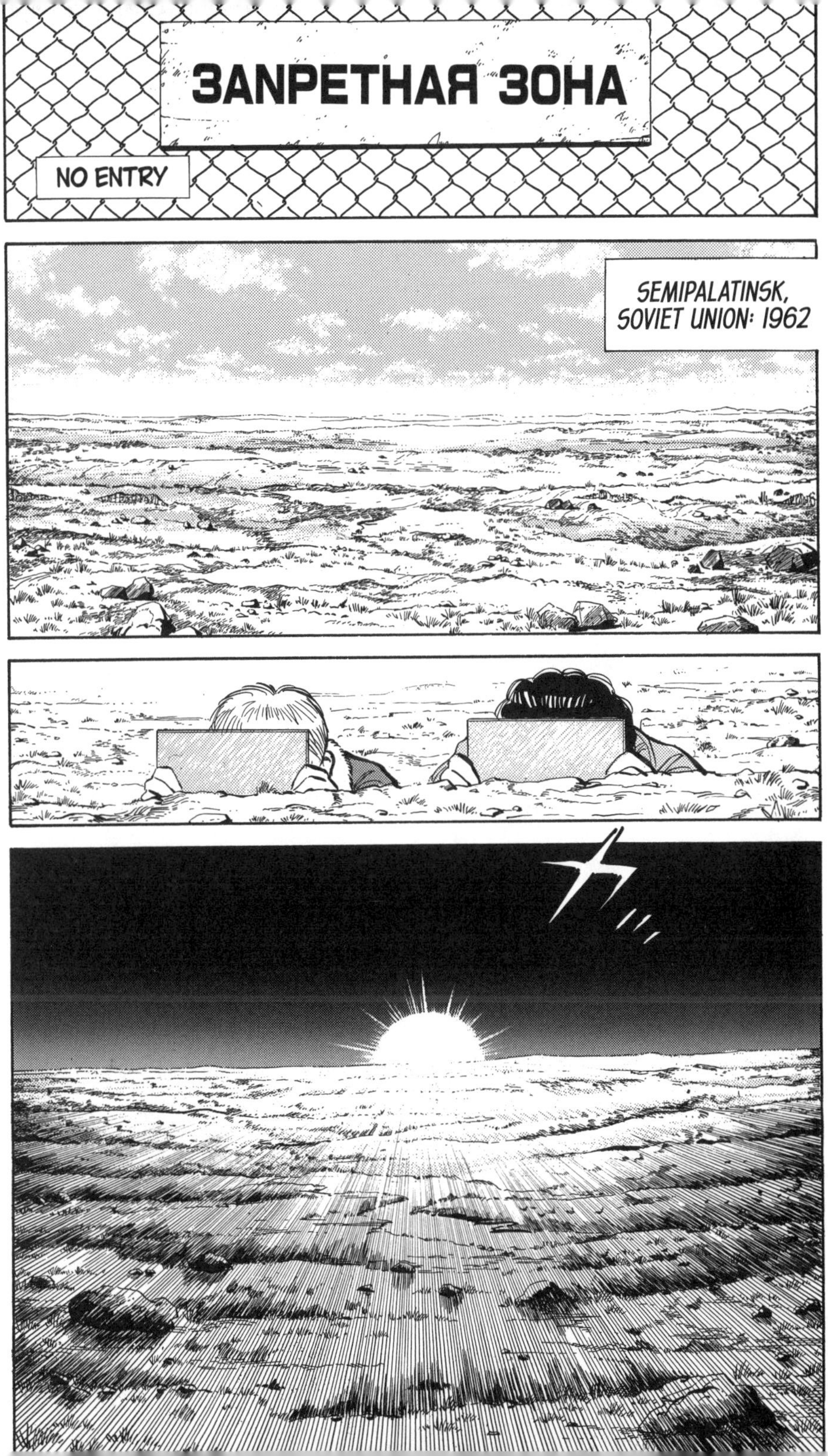
ЗАПРЕТНАЯ ЗОНА
NO ENTRY
SEMIPALATINSK, SOVIET UNION: 1962
カッ

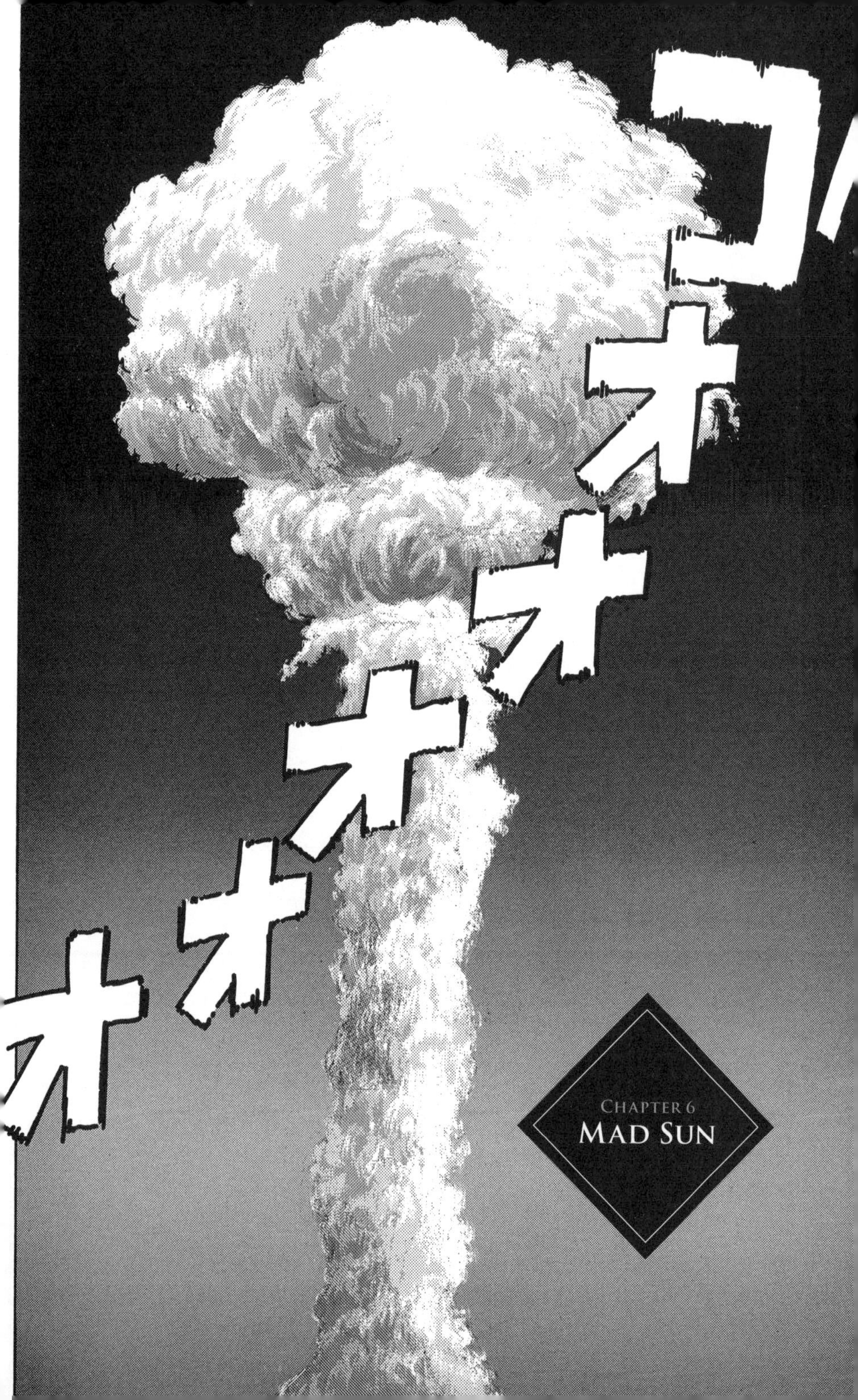
ゴオオオオオ

Chapter 6
Mad Sun

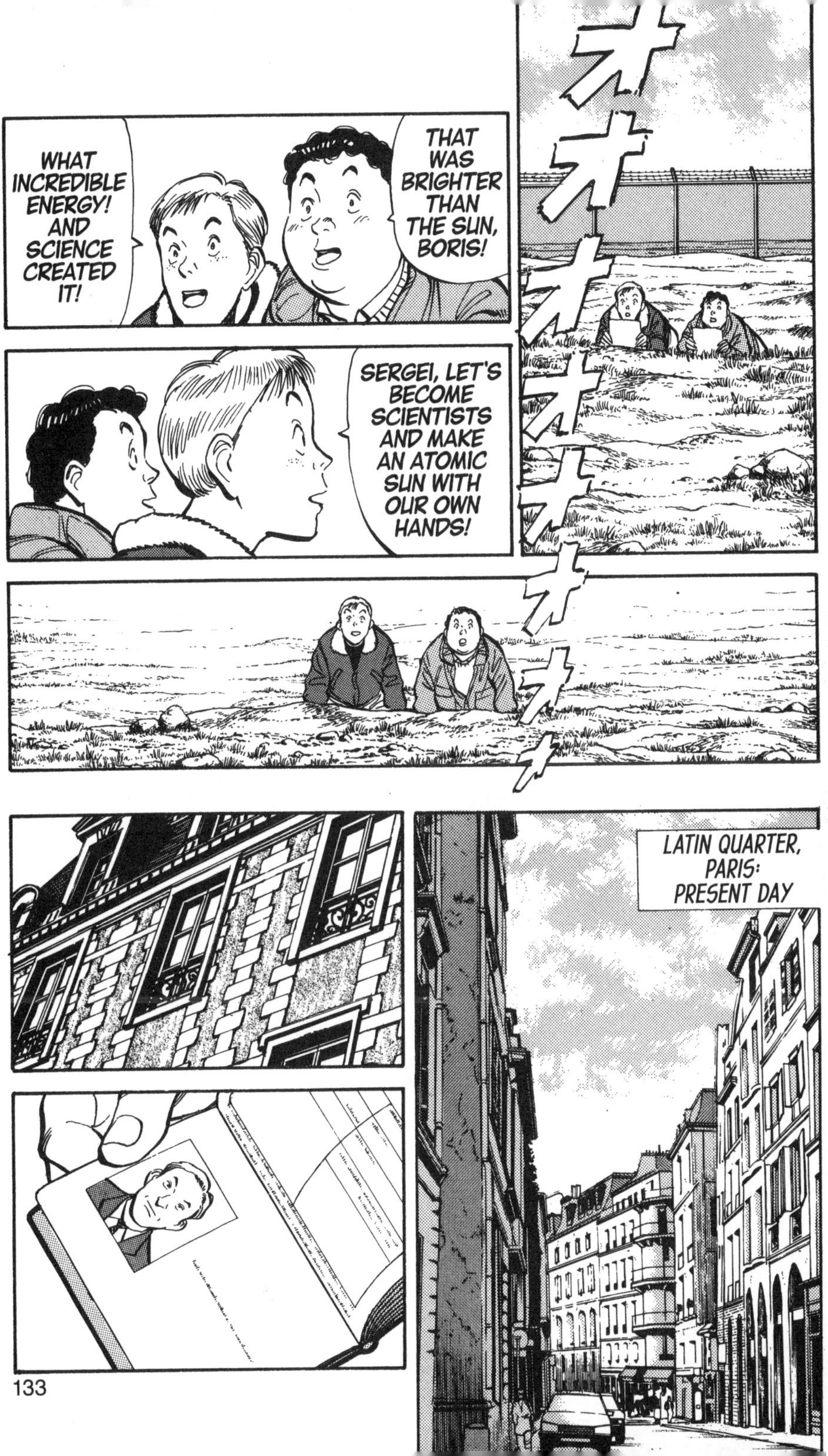
THAT WAS BRIGHTER THAN THE SUN, BORIS!
WHAT INCREDIBLE ENERGY! AND SCIENCE CREATED IT!
SERGEI, LET'S BECOME SCIENTISTS AND MAKE AN ATOMIC SUN WITH OUR OWN HANDS!
LATIN QUARTER, PARIS: PRESENT DAY

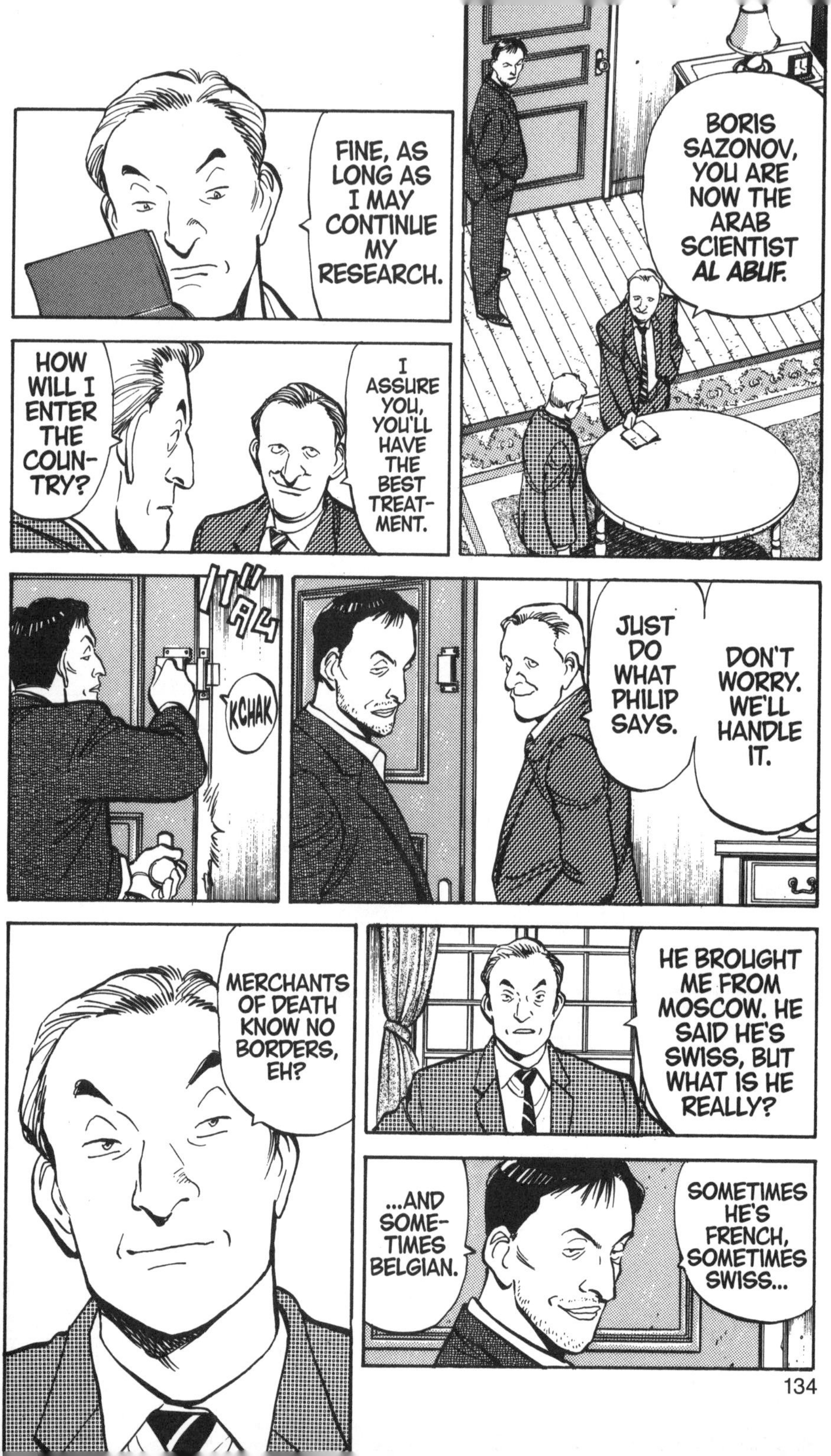
BORIS SAZONOV, YOU ARE NOW THE ARAB SCIENTIST *AL ABUF.*
FINE, AS LONG AS I MAY CONTINUE MY RESEARCH.
HOW WILL I ENTER THE COUN-TRY?
I ASSURE YOU, YOU'LL HAVE THE BEST TREAT-MENT.
DON'T WORRY. WE'LL HANDLE IT.
JUST DO WHAT PHILIP SAYS.
KCHAK
HE BROUGHT ME FROM MOSCOW. HE SAID HE'S SWISS, BUT WHAT IS HE REALLY?
SOMETIMES HE'S FRENCH, SOMETIMES SWISS...
...AND SOME-TIMES BELGIAN.
MERCHANTS OF DEATH KNOW NO BORDERS, EH?

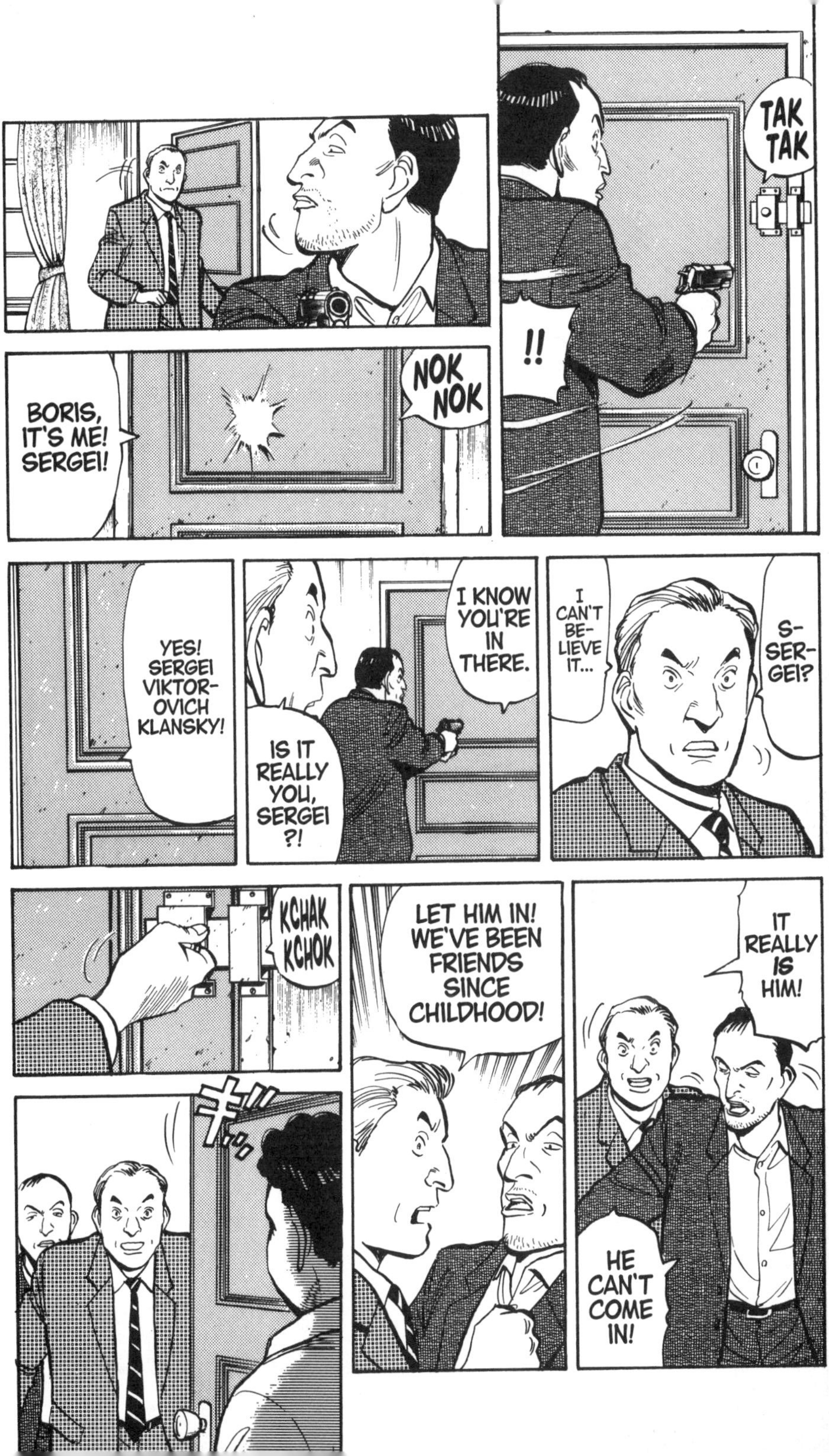
TAK TAK
!!
NOK NOK
BORIS, IT'S ME! SERGEI!
S-SERGEI?
I CAN'T BELIEVE IT...
I KNOW YOU'RE IN THERE.
IS IT REALLY YOU, SERGEI?!
YES! SERGEI VIKTOROVICH KLANSKY!
IT REALLY IS HIM!
HE CAN'T COME IN!
LET HIM IN! WE'VE BEEN FRIENDS SINCE CHILDHOOD!
KCHAK KCHOK

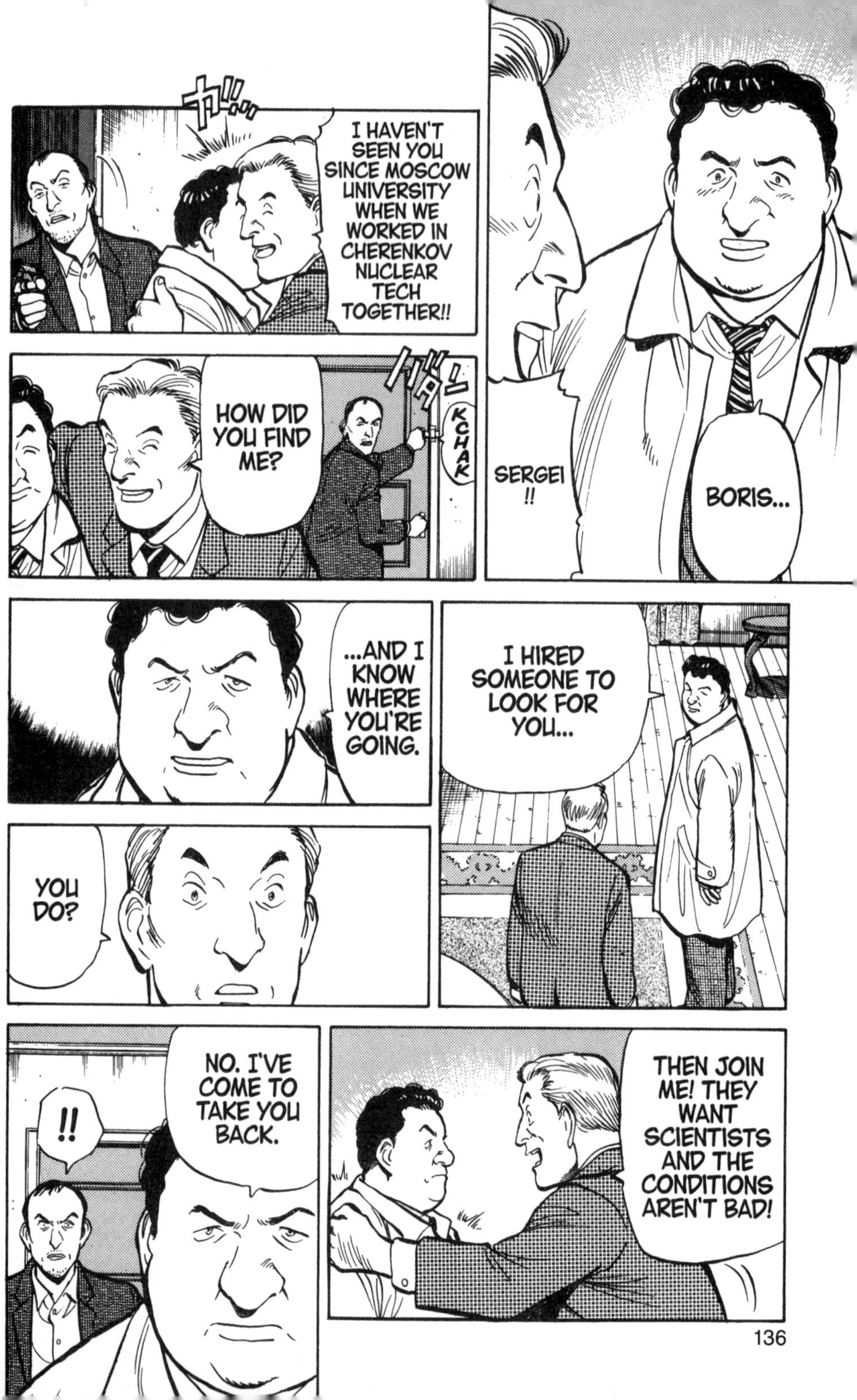
BORIS...
SERGEI !!
I HAVEN'T SEEN YOU SINCE MOSCOW UNIVERSITY WHEN WE WORKED IN CHERENKOV NUCLEAR TECH TOGETHER!!
KCHAK
HOW DID YOU FIND ME?
I HIRED SOMEONE TO LOOK FOR YOU...
...AND I KNOW WHERE YOU'RE GOING.
YOU DO?
THEN JOIN ME! THEY WANT SCIENTISTS AND THE CONDITIONS AREN'T BAD!
NO. I'VE COME TO TAKE YOU BACK.
!!

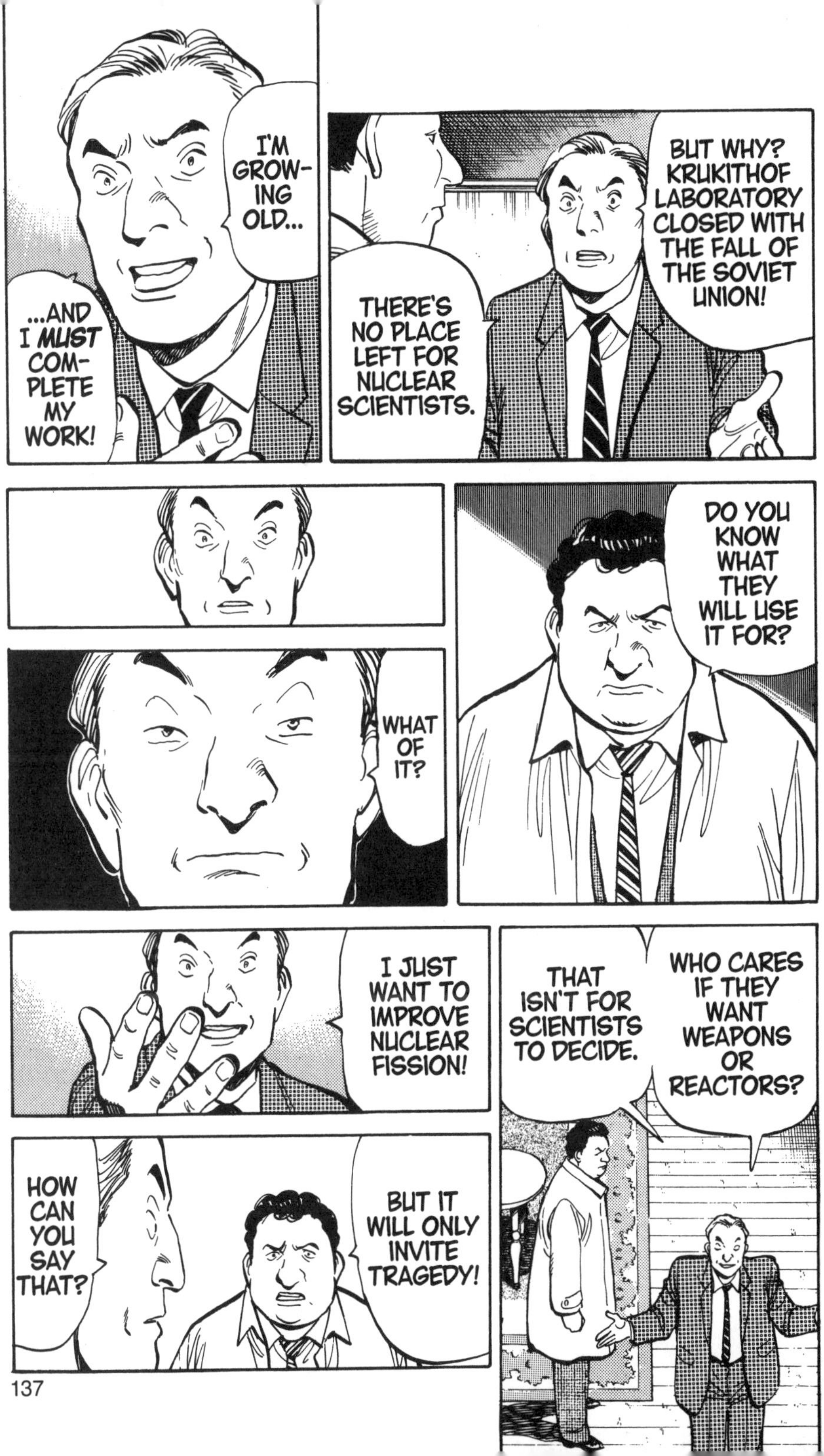
BUT WHY? KRUKITHOF LABORATORY CLOSED WITH THE FALL OF THE SOVIET UNION!
THERE'S NO PLACE LEFT FOR NUCLEAR SCIENTISTS.
I'M GROWING-ING OLD...
...AND I *MUST* COMPLETE MY WORK!
DO YOU KNOW WHAT THEY WILL USE IT FOR?
WHAT OF IT?
WHO CARES IF THEY WANT WEAPONS OR REACTORS?
THAT ISN'T FOR SCIENTISTS TO DECIDE.
I JUST WANT TO IMPROVE NUCLEAR FISSION!
BUT IT WILL ONLY INVITE TRAGEDY!
HOW CAN YOU SAY THAT?

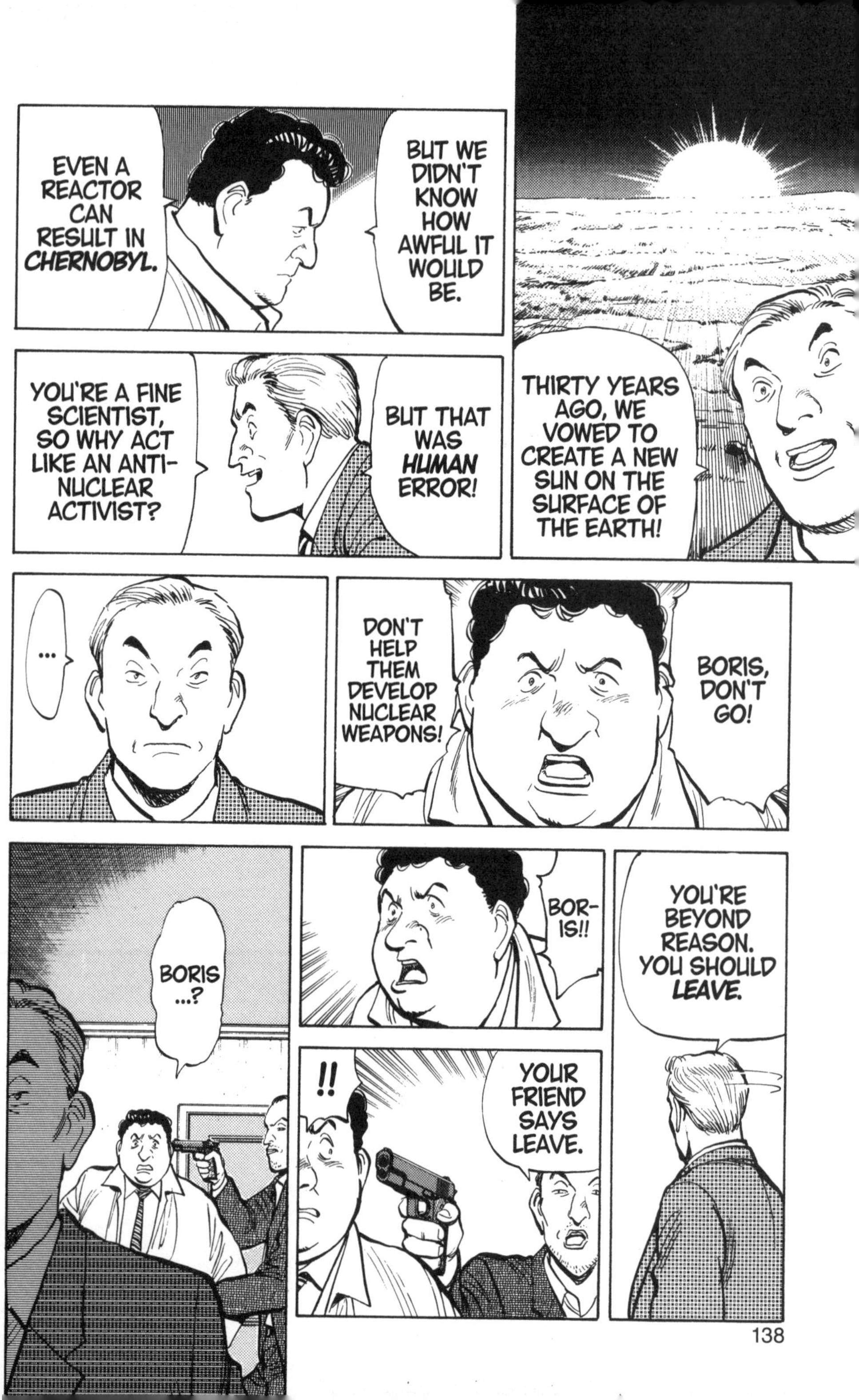
THIRTY YEARS AGO, WE VOWED TO CREATE A NEW SUN ON THE SURFACE OF THE EARTH!
BUT WE DIDN'T KNOW HOW AWFUL IT WOULD BE.
EVEN A REACTOR CAN RESULT IN CHERNOBYL.
BUT THAT WAS HUMAN ERROR!
YOU'RE A FINE SCIENTIST, SO WHY ACT LIKE AN ANTI-NUCLEAR ACTIVIST?
BORIS, DON'T GO!
DON'T HELP THEM DEVELOP NUCLEAR WEAPONS!
...
YOU'RE BEYOND REASON. YOU SHOULD LEAVE.
BOR-IS!!
YOUR FRIEND SAYS LEAVE.
!!
BORIS ...?

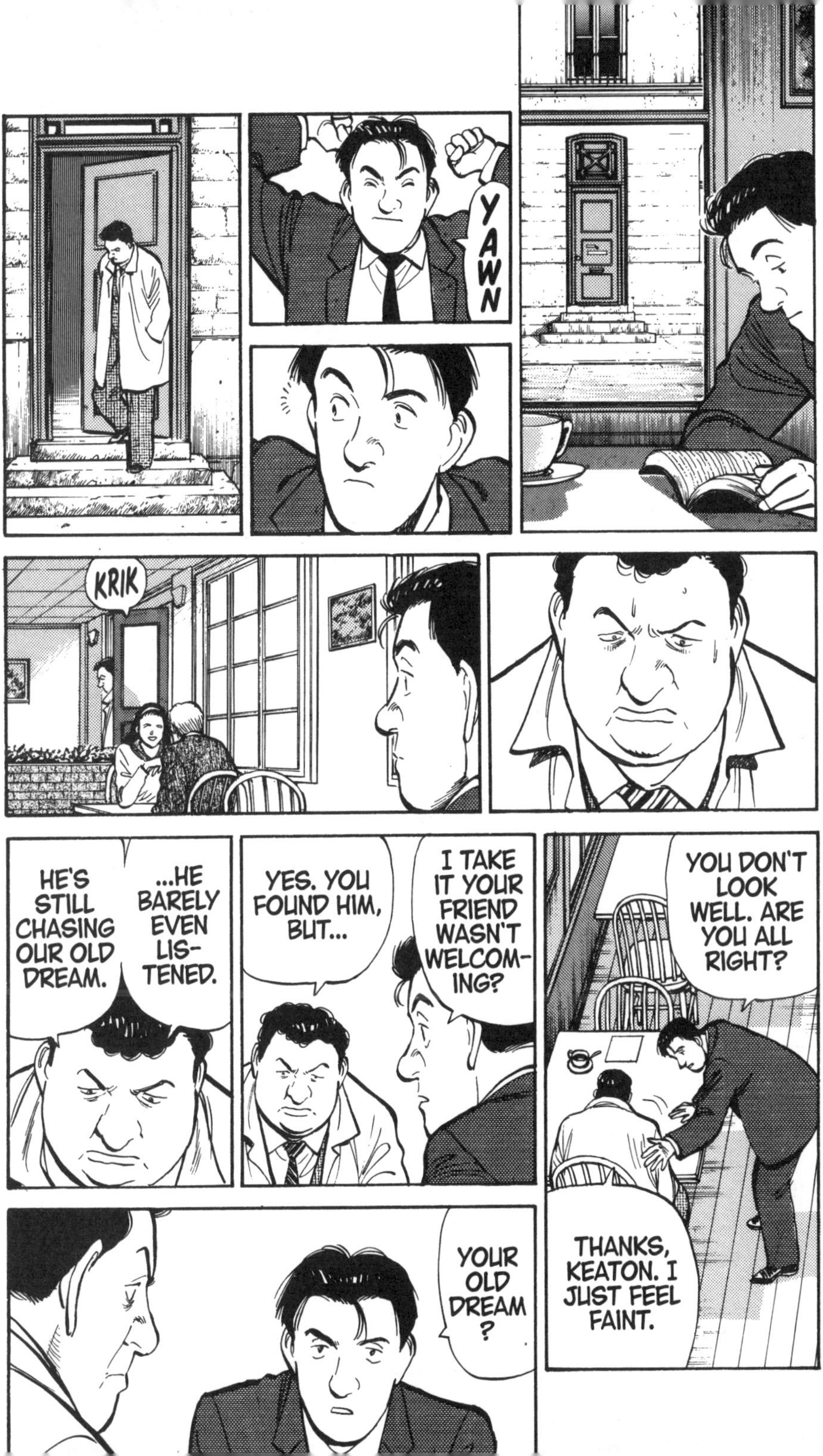
YAWN
KRIK
YOU DON'T LOOK WELL. ARE YOU ALL RIGHT?
THANKS, KEATON. I JUST FEEL FAINT.
I TAKE IT YOUR FRIEND WASN'T WELCOMING?
YES. YOU FOUND HIM, BUT...
...HE BARELY EVEN LISTENED.
HE'S STILL CHASING OUR OLD DREAM.
YOUR OLD DREAM?

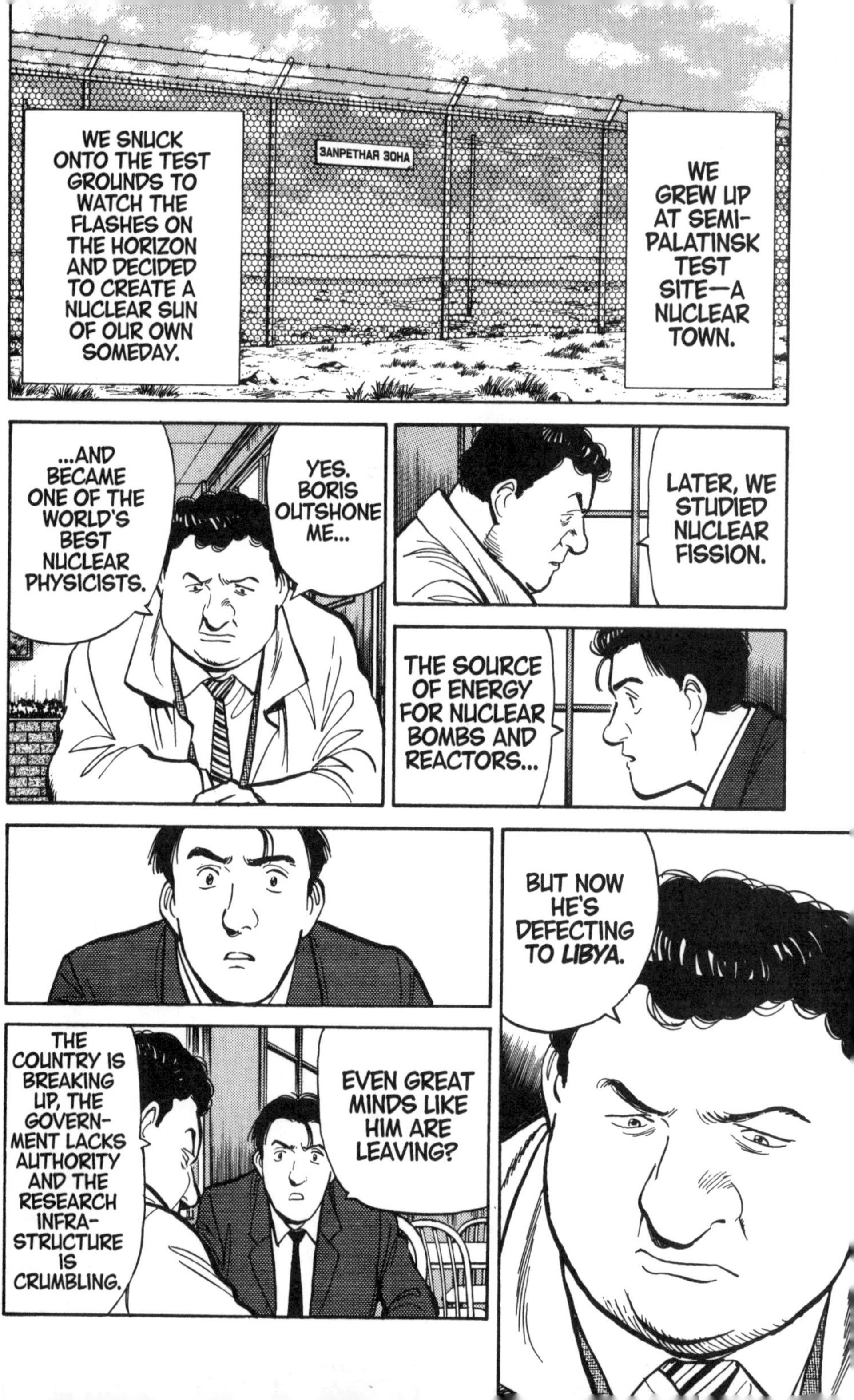
WE GREW UP AT SEMI-PALATINSK TEST SITE—A NUCLEAR TOWN.
ЗАПРЕТНАЯ ЗОНА
WE SNUCK ONTO THE TEST GROUNDS TO WATCH THE FLASHES ON THE HORIZON AND DECIDED TO CREATE A NUCLEAR SUN OF OUR OWN SOMEDAY.
LATER, WE STUDIED NUCLEAR FISSION.
THE SOURCE OF ENERGY FOR NUCLEAR BOMBS AND REACTORS...
YES. BORIS OUTSHONE ME...
...AND BECAME ONE OF THE WORLD'S BEST NUCLEAR PHYSICISTS.
BUT NOW HE'S DEFECTING TO *LIBYA*.
EVEN GREAT MINDS LIKE HIM ARE LEAVING?
THE COUNTRY IS BREAKING UP, THE GOVERNMENT LACKS AUTHORITY AND THE RESEARCH INFRA-STRUCTURE IS CRUMBLING.

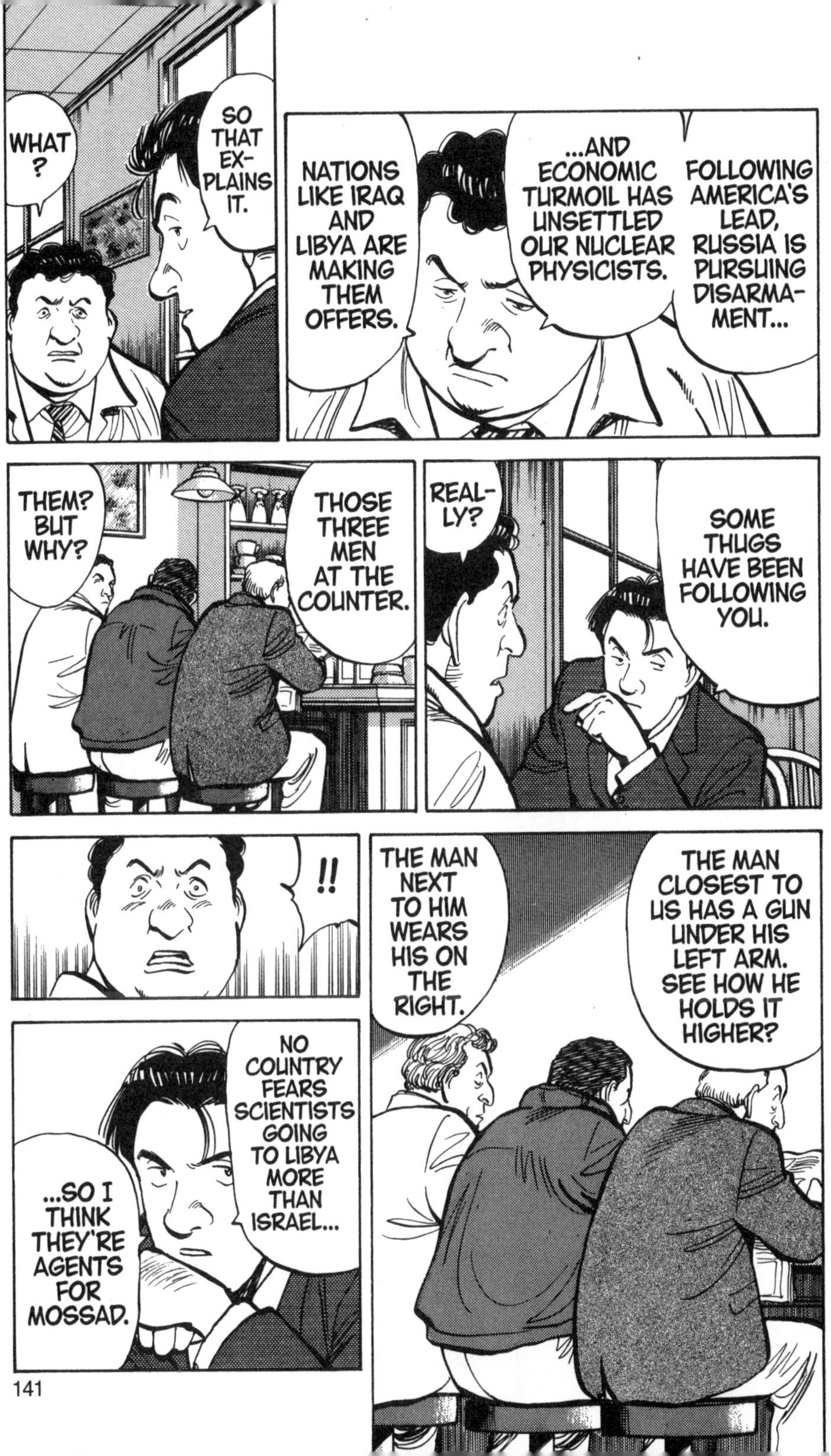
FOLLOWING AMERICA'S LEAD, RUSSIA IS PURSUING DISARMAMENT...
...AND ECONOMIC TURMOIL HAS UNSETTLED OUR NUCLEAR PHYSICISTS.
NATIONS LIKE IRAQ AND LIBYA ARE MAKING THEM OFFERS.
SO THAT EXPLAINS IT.
WHAT?
SOME THUGS HAVE BEEN FOLLOWING YOU.
REALLY?
THOSE THREE MEN AT THE COUNTER.
THEM? BUT WHY?
THE MAN CLOSEST TO US HAS A GUN UNDER HIS LEFT ARM. SEE HOW HE HOLDS IT HIGHER?
THE MAN NEXT TO HIM WEARS HIS ON THE RIGHT.
!!
NO COUNTRY FEARS SCIENTISTS GOING TO LIBYA MORE THAN ISRAEL...
...SO I THINK THEY'RE AGENTS FOR MOSSAD.

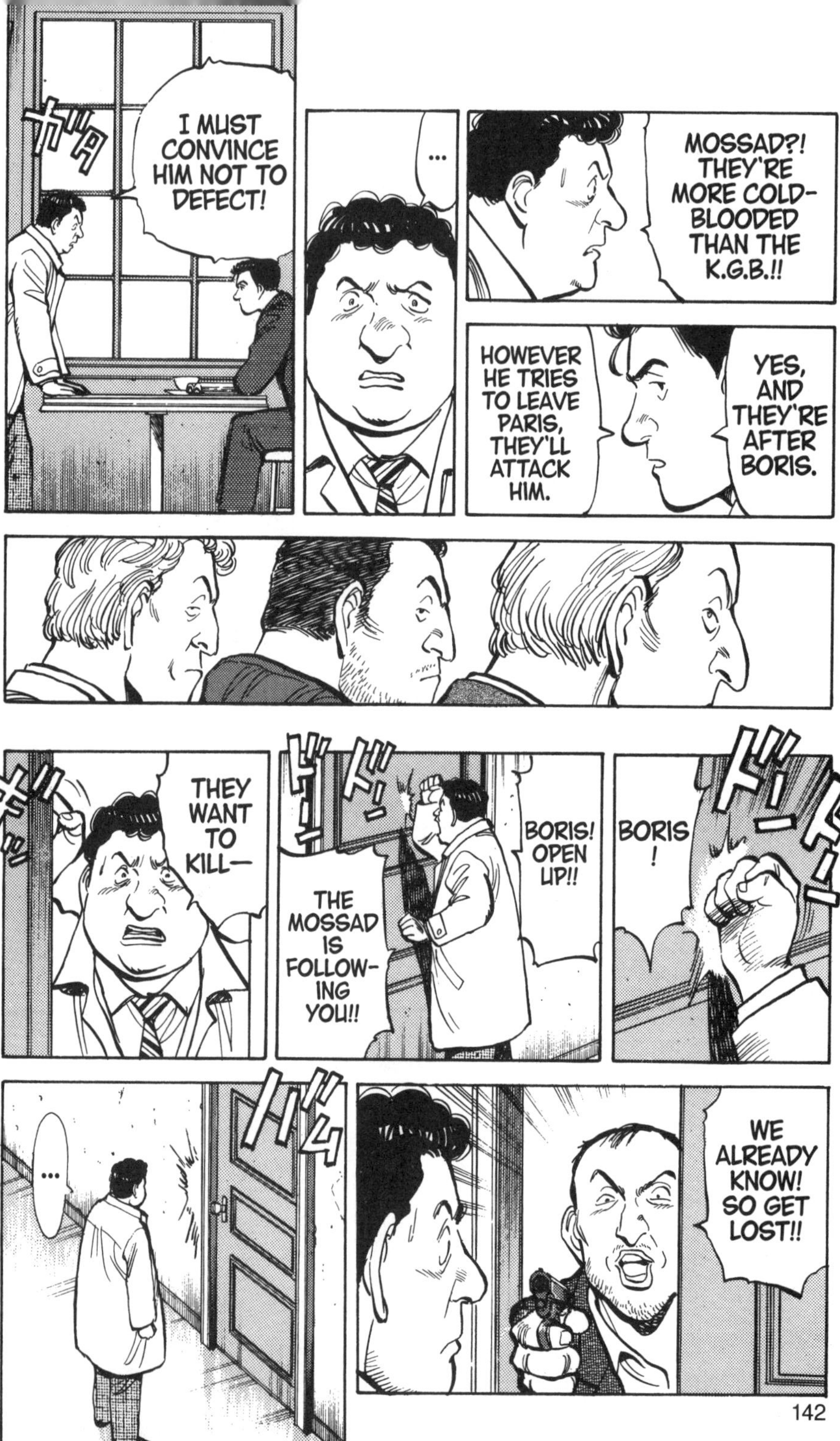
MOSSAD?! THEY'RE MORE COLD-BLOODED THAN THE K.G.B.!!
YES, AND THEY'RE AFTER BORIS.
HOWEVER HE TRIES TO LEAVE PARIS, THEY'LL ATTACK HIM.
...
I MUST CONVINCE HIM NOT TO DEFECT!
BORIS!
BORIS! OPEN UP!!
THE MOSSAD IS FOLLOWING YOU!!
THEY WANT TO KILL—
WE ALREADY KNOW! SO GET LOST!!
...

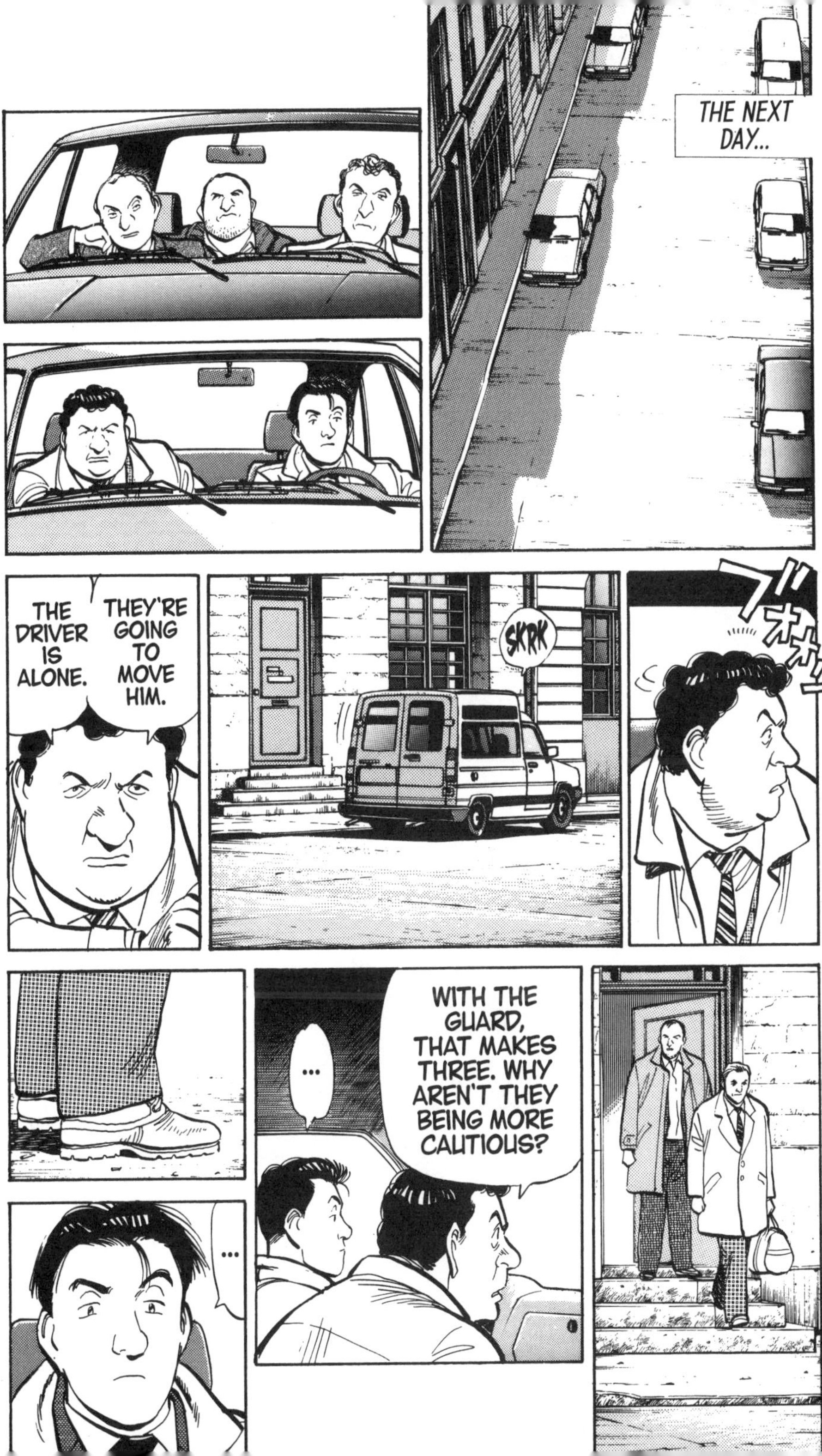
THE NEXT DAY...
SKRK
THEY'RE GOING TO MOVE HIM.
THE DRIVER IS ALONE.
WITH THE GUARD, THAT MAKES THREE. WHY AREN'T THEY BEING MORE CAUTIOUS?
...
...

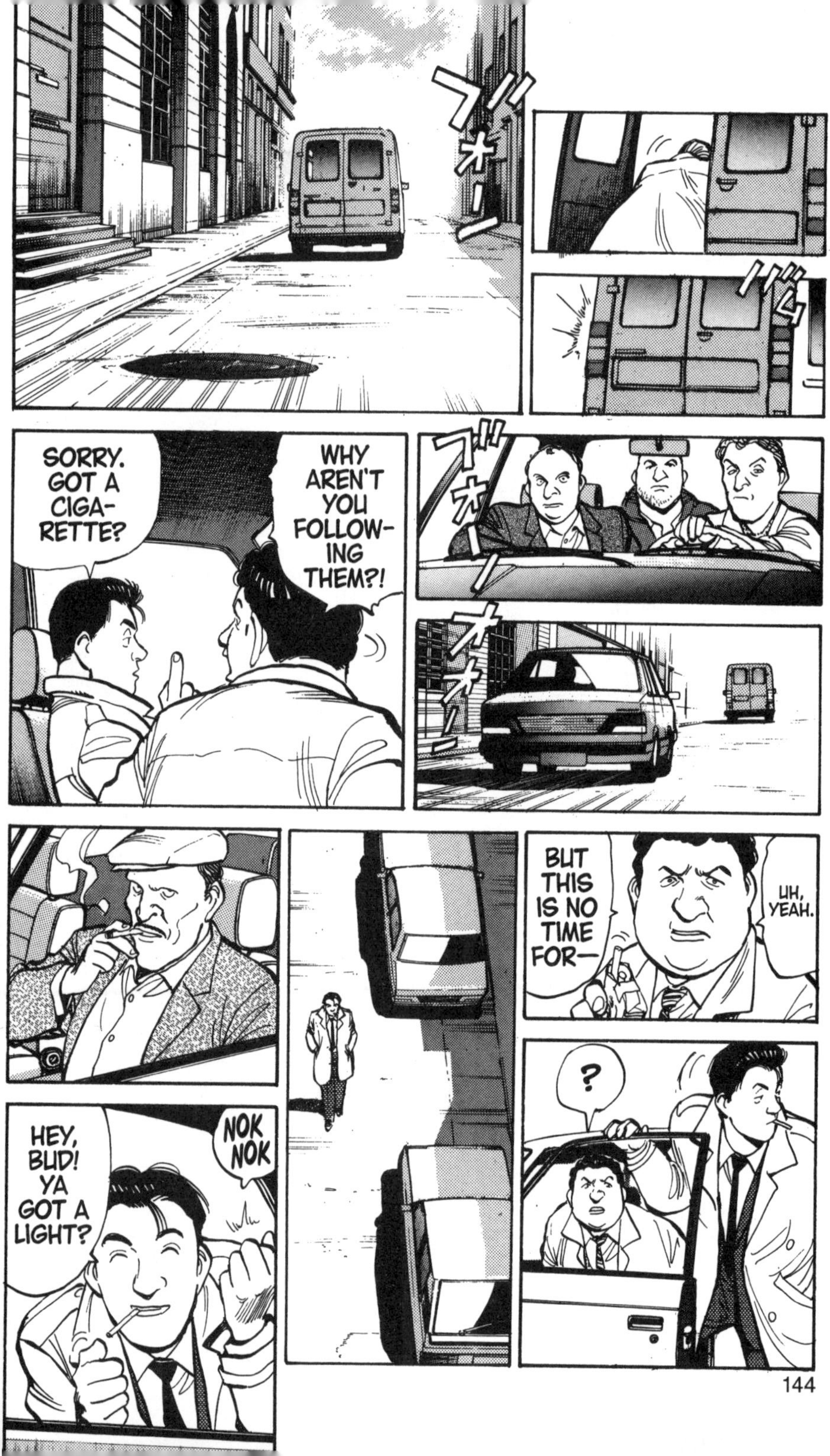

WHY AREN'T YOU FOLLOWING THEM?!
SORRY. GOT A CIGARETTE?
UH, YEAH.
BUT THIS IS NO TIME FOR—
?
NOK NOK
HEY, BUD! YA GOT A LIGHT?

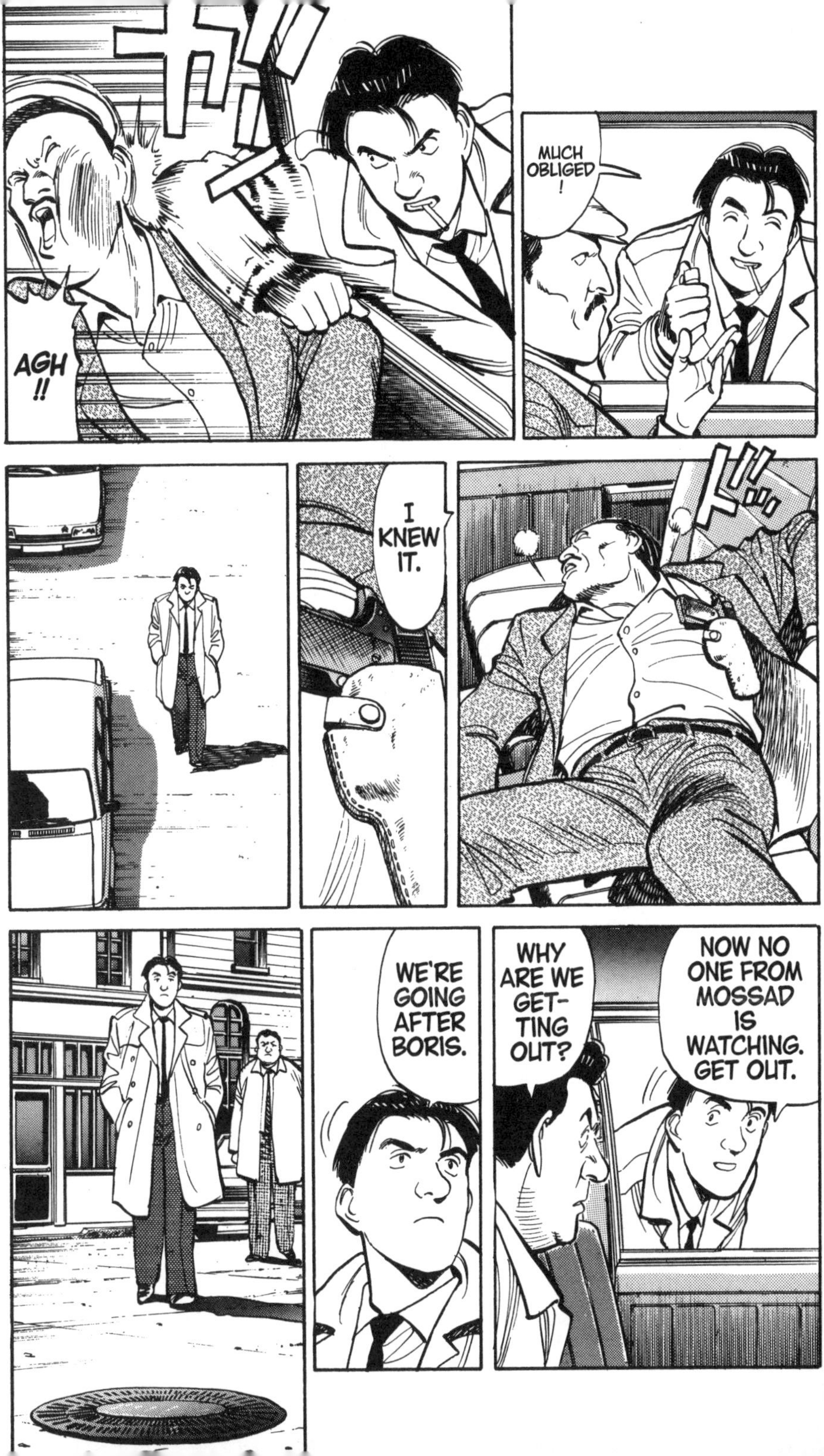
MUCH OBLIGED!
AGH!!
I KNEW IT.
NOW NO ONE FROM MOSSAD IS WATCHING. GET OUT.
WHY ARE WE GET-TING OUT?
WE'RE GOING AFTER BORIS.

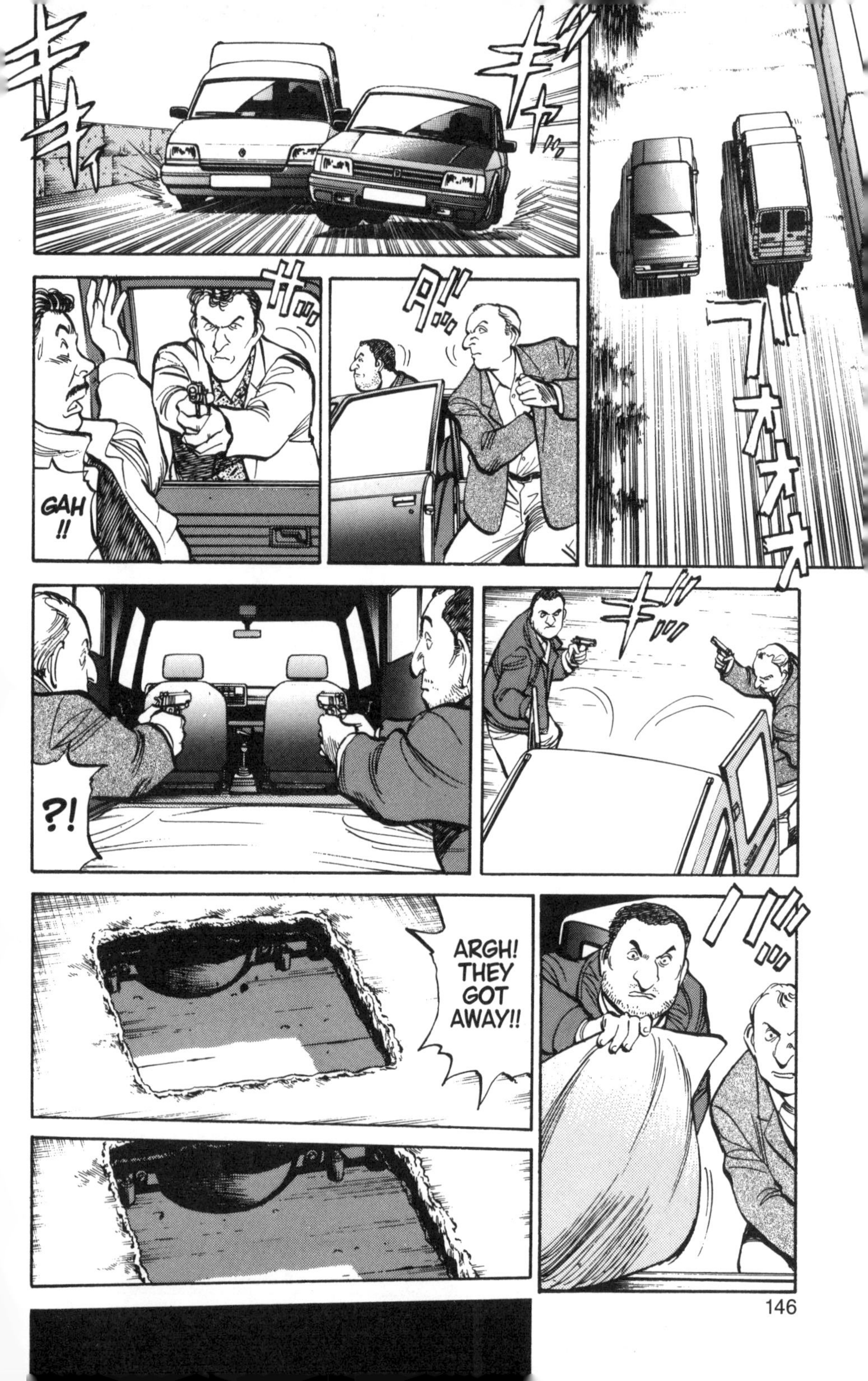
GAH!!
?!
ARGH! THEY GOT AWAY!!

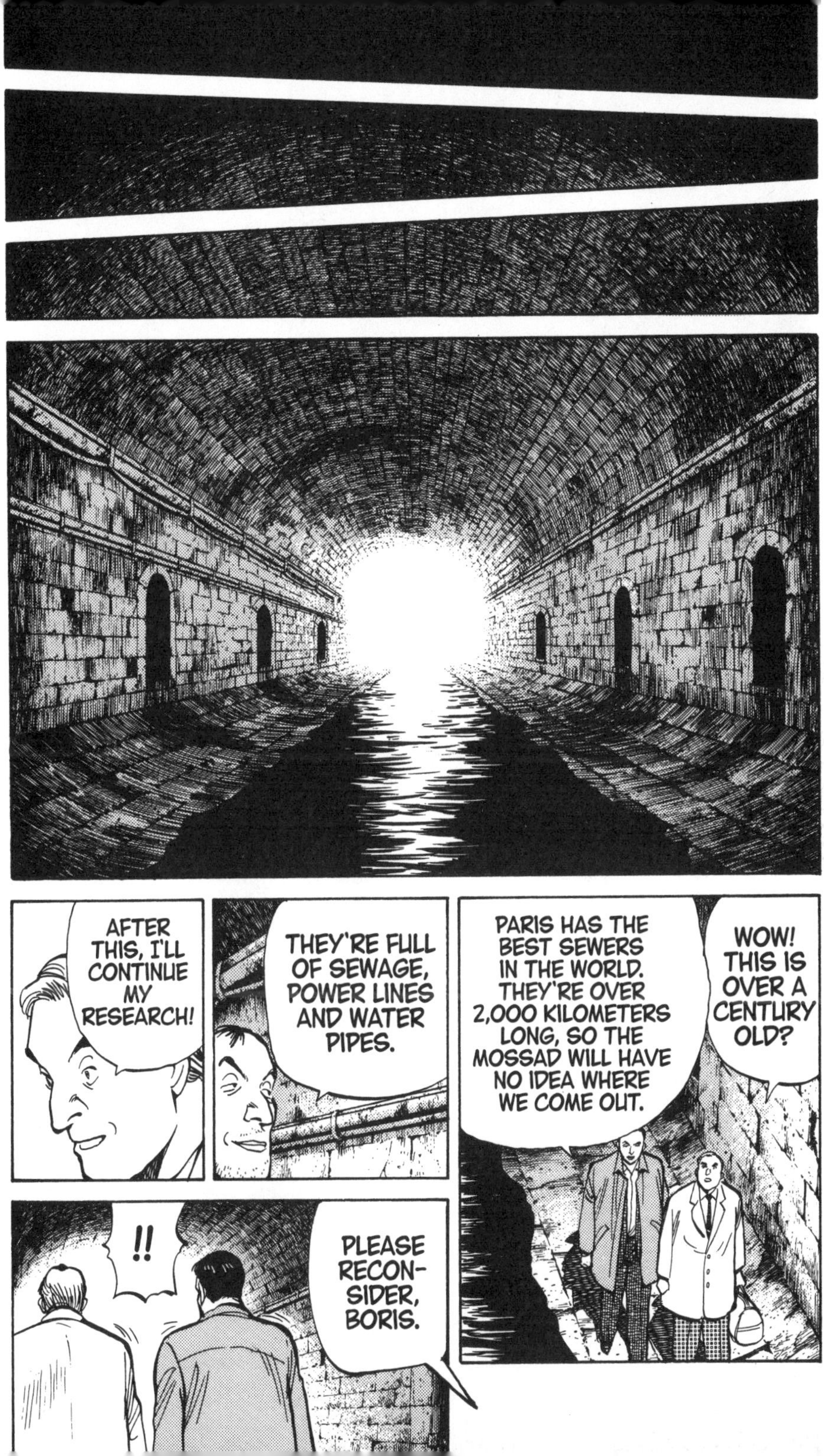
WOW! THIS IS OVER A CENTURY OLD?
PARIS HAS THE BEST SEWERS IN THE WORLD. THEY'RE OVER 2,000 KILOMETERS LONG, SO THE MOSSAD WILL HAVE NO IDEA WHERE WE COME OUT.
THEY'RE FULL OF SEWAGE, POWER LINES AND WATER PIPES.
AFTER THIS, I'LL CONTINUE MY RESEARCH!
PLEASE RECON-SIDER, BORIS.
!!

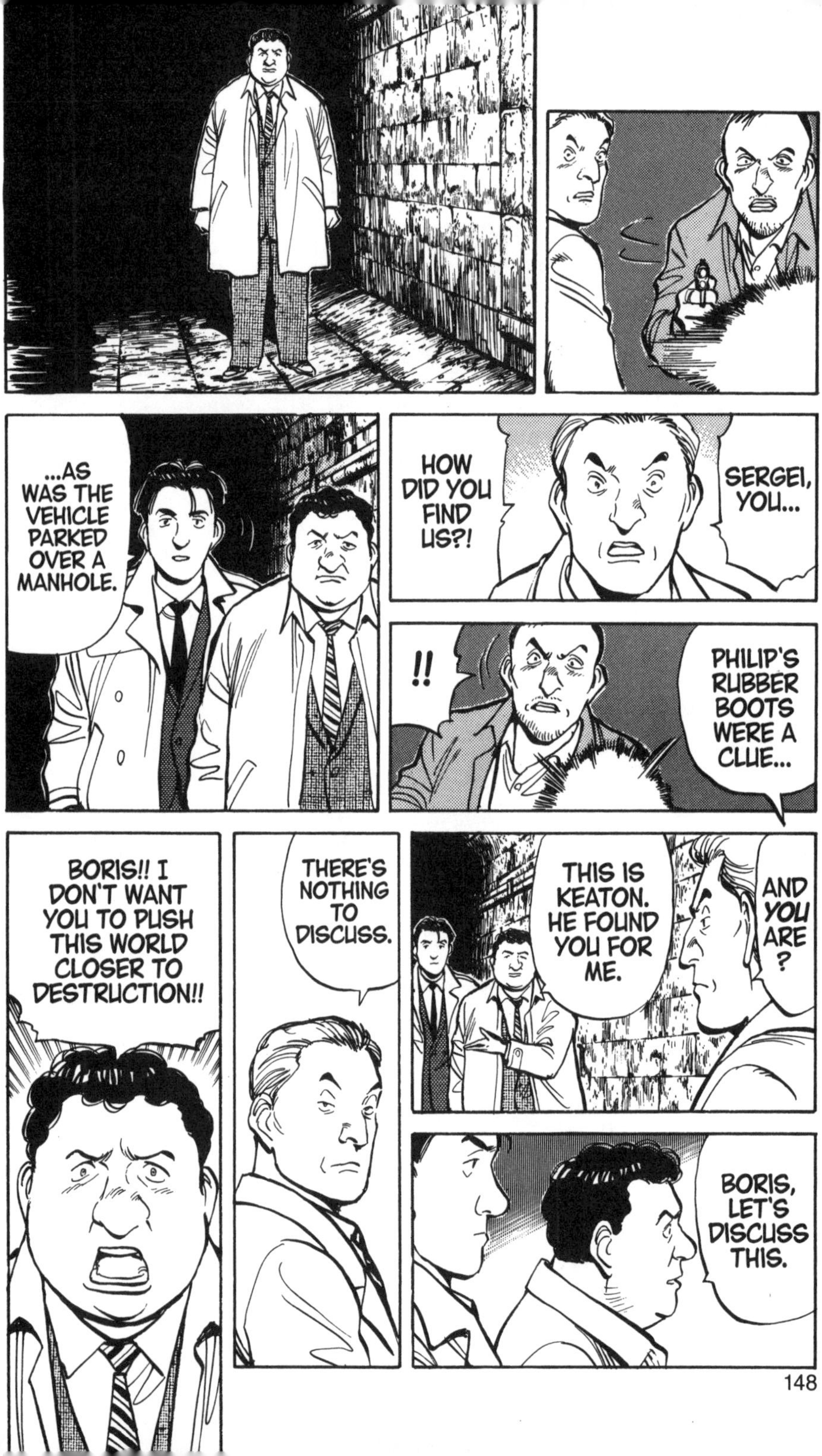
SERGEI, YOU...
HOW DID YOU FIND US?!
PHILIP'S RUBBER BOOTS WERE A CLUE...
!!
...AS WAS THE VEHICLE PARKED OVER A MANHOLE.
AND *YOU* ARE?
THIS IS KEATON. HE FOUND YOU FOR ME.
BORIS, LET'S DISCUSS THIS.
THERE'S NOTHING TO DISCUSS.
BORIS!! I DON'T WANT YOU TO PUSH THIS WORLD CLOSER TO DESTRUCTION!!

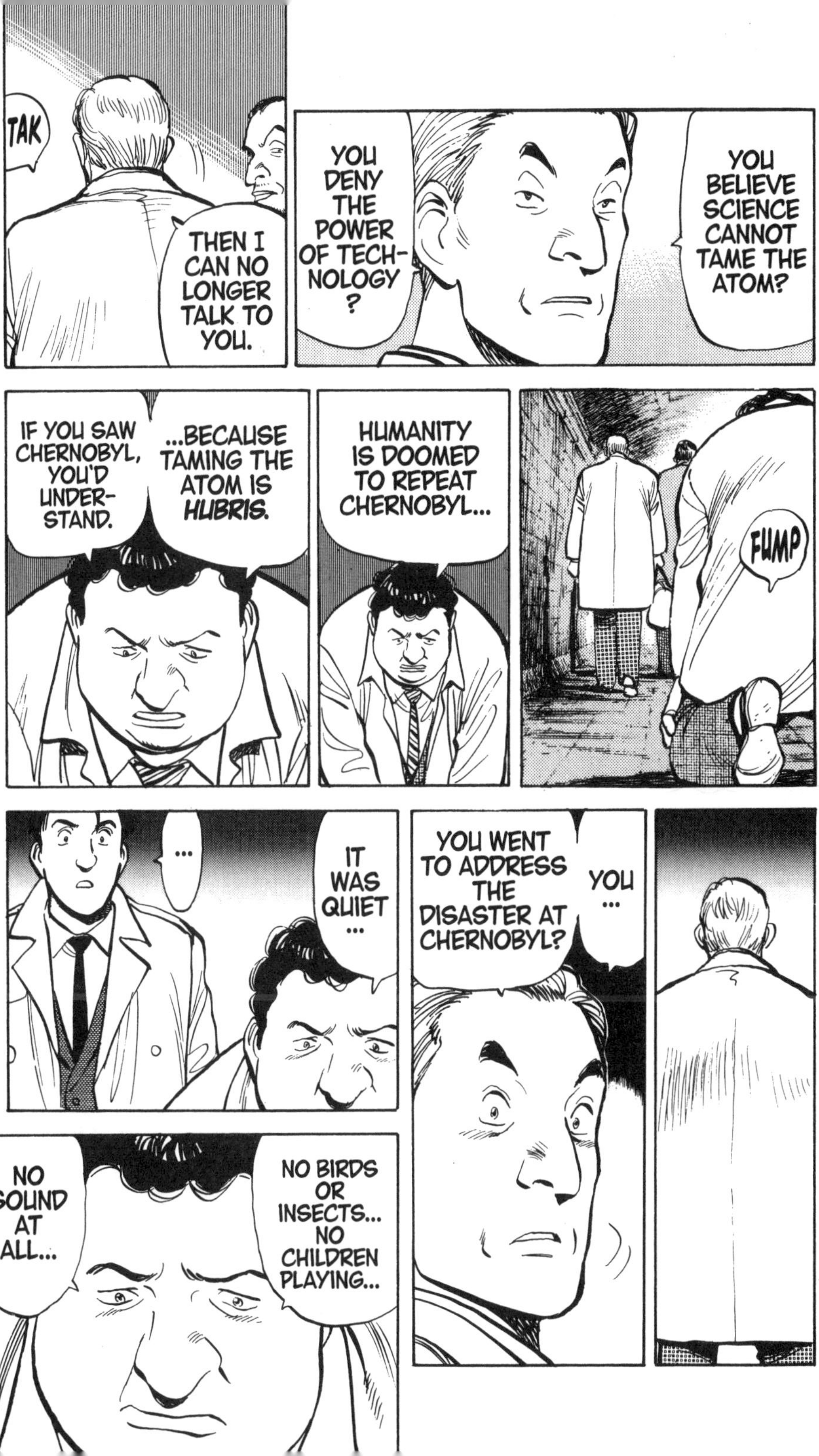
YOU BELIEVE SCIENCE CANNOT TAME THE ATOM?
YOU DENY THE POWER OF TECH-NOLOGY?
TAK
THEN I CAN NO LONGER TALK TO YOU.
FUMP
HUMANITY IS DOOMED TO REPEAT CHERNOBYL...
...BECAUSE TAMING THE ATOM IS *HUBRIS.*
IF YOU SAW CHERNOBYL, YOU'D UNDER-STAND.
YOU ...
YOU WENT TO ADDRESS THE DISASTER AT CHERNOBYL?
IT WAS QUIET ...
...
NO BIRDS OR INSECTS... NO CHILDREN PLAYING...
NO SOUND AT ALL...

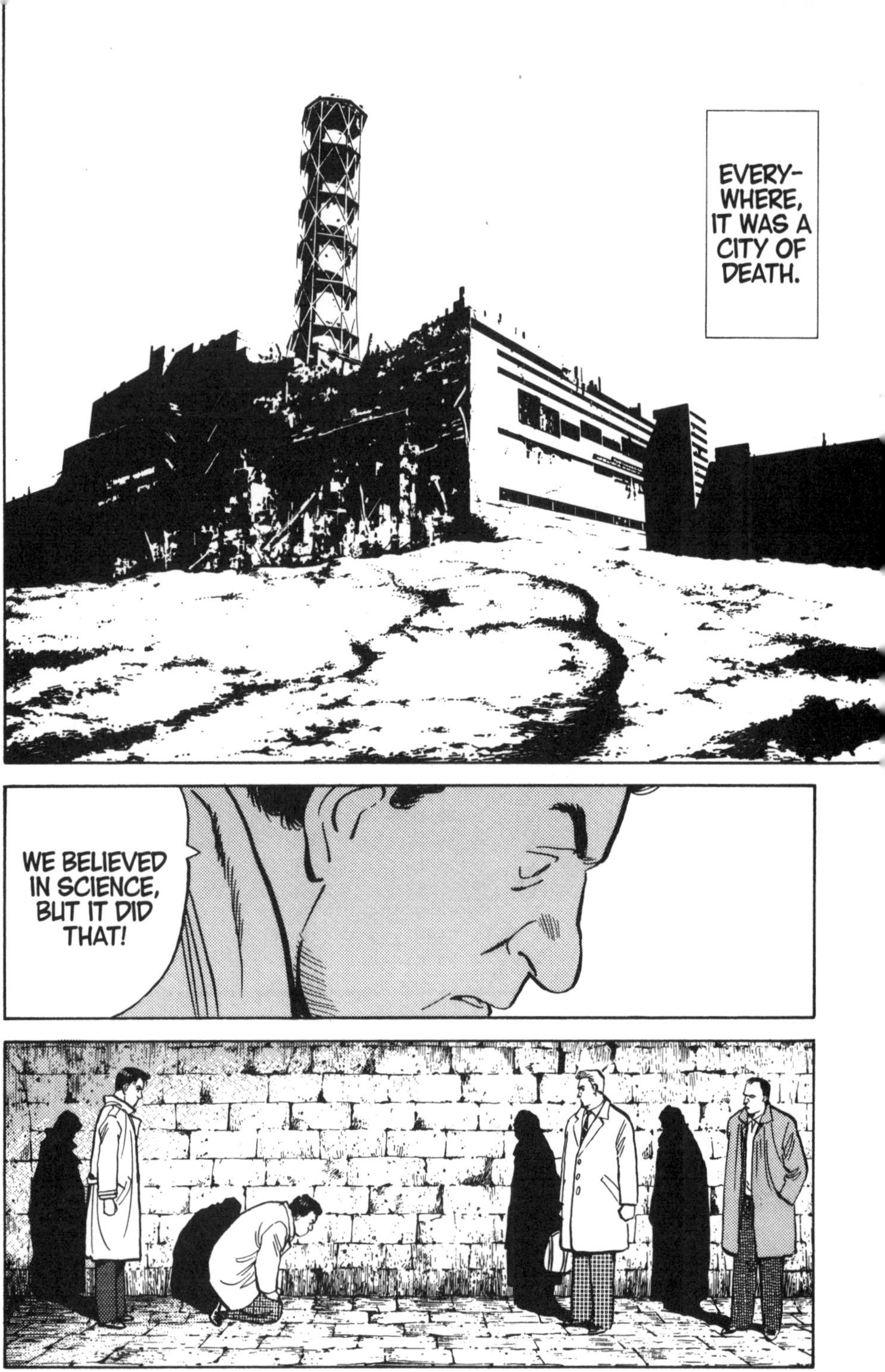
EVERY-WHERE, IT WAS A CITY OF DEATH.
WE BELIEVED IN SCIENCE, BUT IT DID THAT!

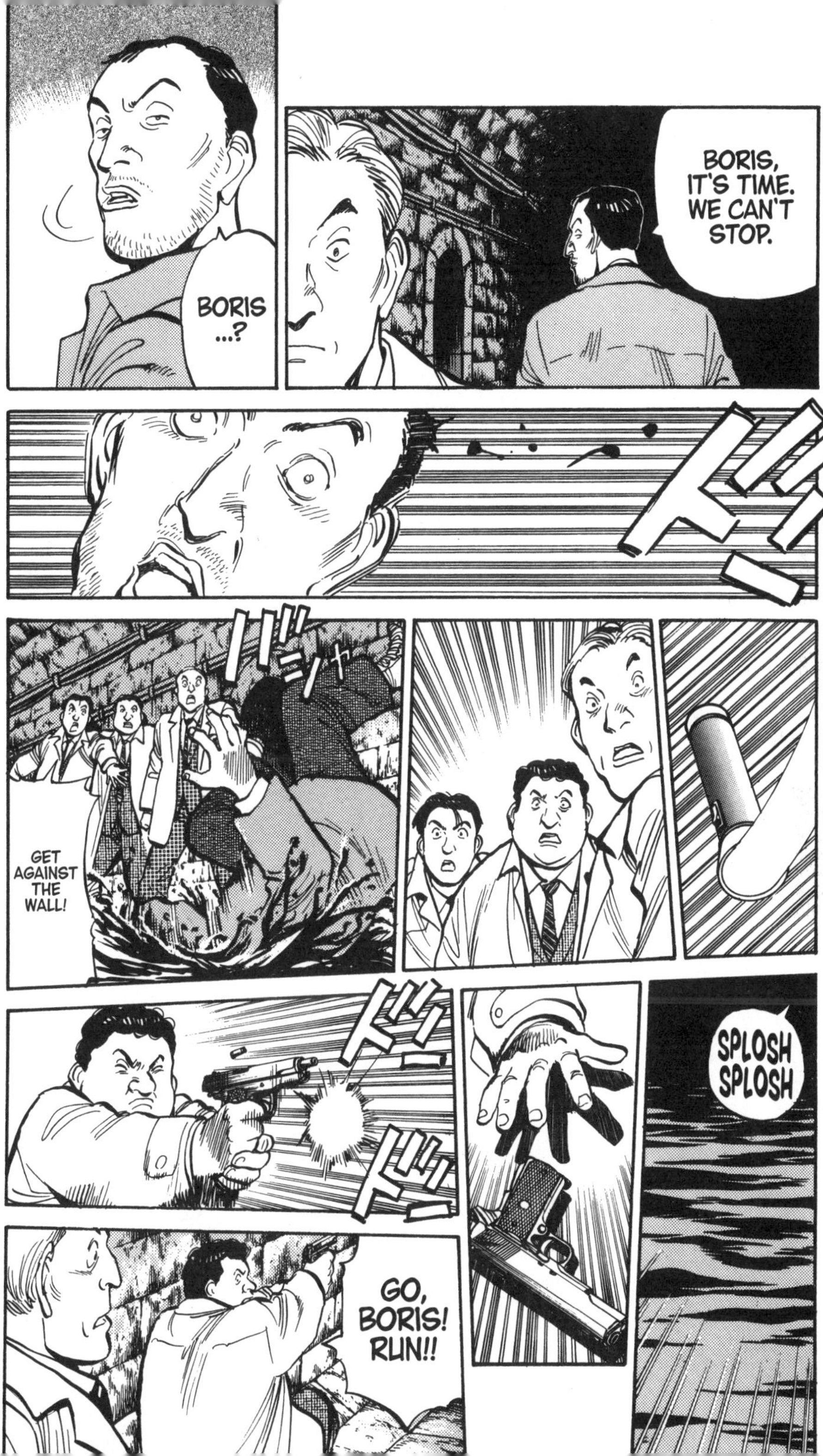
BORIS, IT'S TIME. WE CAN'T STOP.
BORIS ...?
GET AGAINST THE WALL!
SPLOSH SPLOSH
GO, BORIS! RUN!!

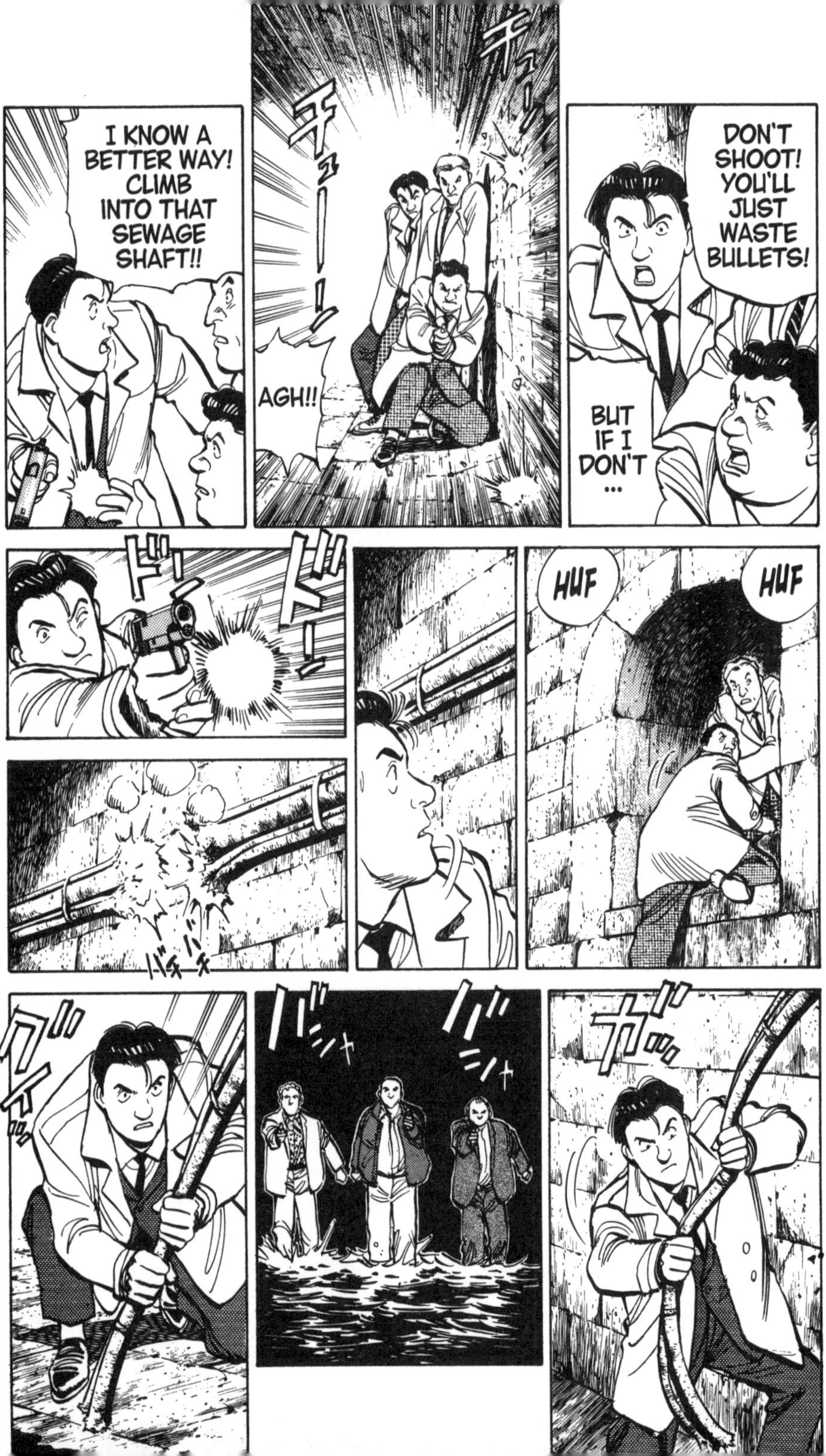
DON'T SHOOT! YOU'LL JUST WASTE BULLETS!
BUT IF I DON'T ...
AGH!!
I KNOW A BETTER WAY! CLIMB INTO THAT SEWAGE SHAFT!!
HUF
HUF

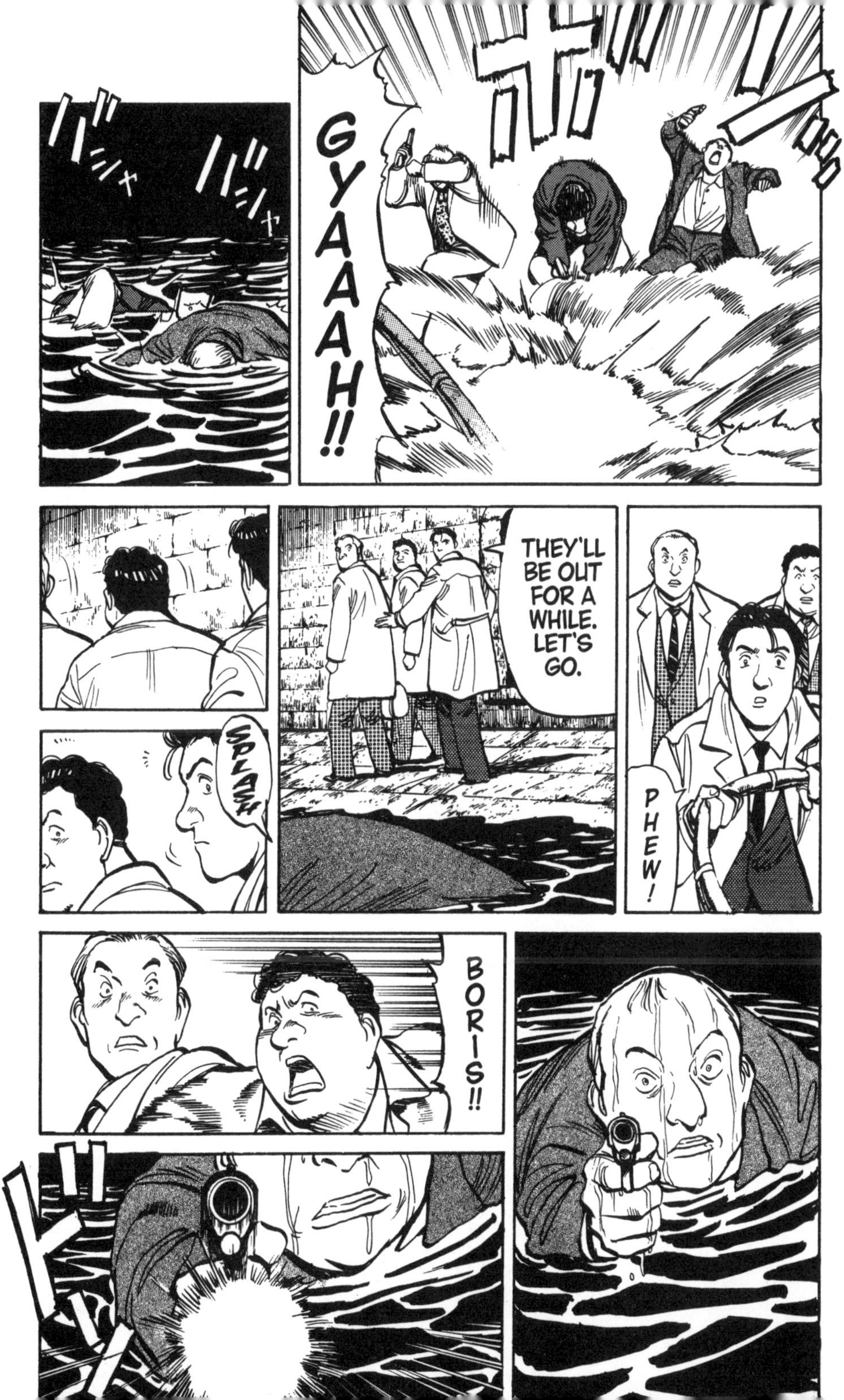
GYAAAH!!
バシャ
バシャ
PHEW!
THEY'LL BE OUT FOR A WHILE. LET'S GO.
SPLASH
BORIS!!

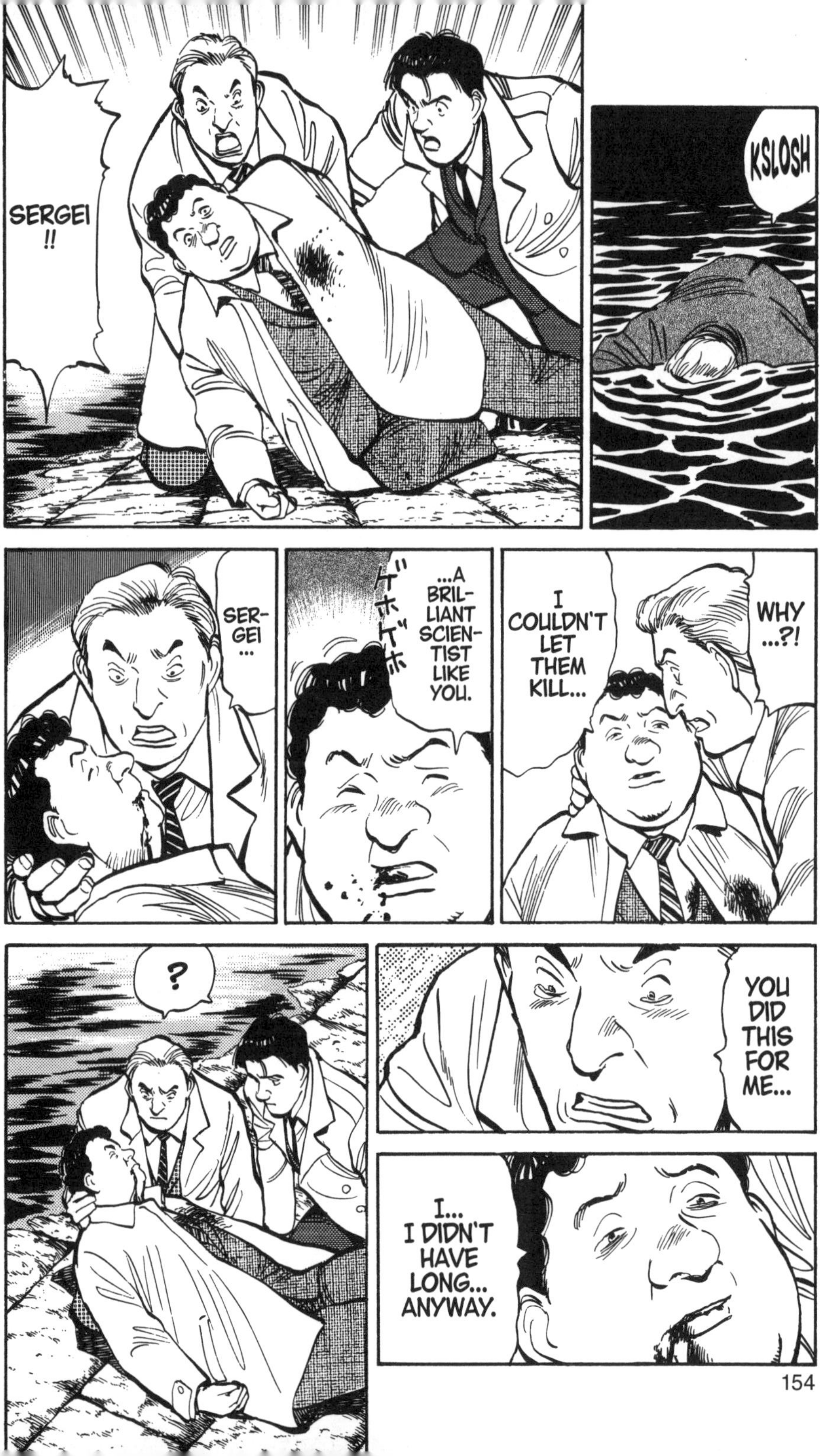
KSLOSH
SERGEI !!
WHY ...?!
I COULDN'T LET THEM KILL...
ゲホゲホ
...A BRILLIANT SCIENTIST LIKE YOU.
SERGEI ...
YOU DID THIS FOR ME...
I... I DIDN'T HAVE LONG... ANYWAY.
?

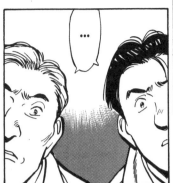

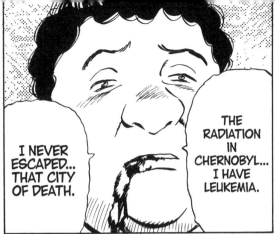

THE RADIATION IN CHERNOBYL... I HAVE LEUKEMIA.
I NEVER ESCAPED... THAT CITY OF DEATH.
...
DO YOU REMEMBER... THE FIRST TIME...WE SAW THAT LIGHT?
YES.
SO BRIGHT... LIKE THE SUN.
IT WAS NOT FOR US...TO TOUCH.
SER-GEI...

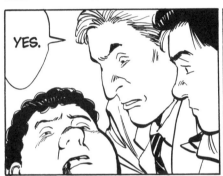

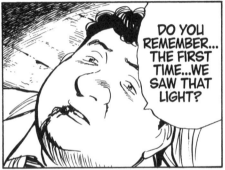

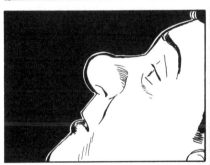

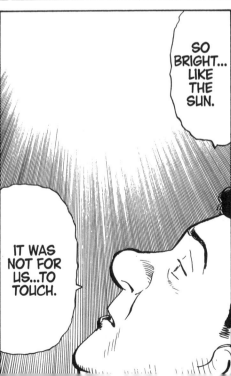

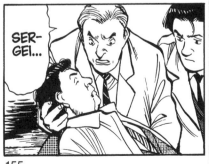

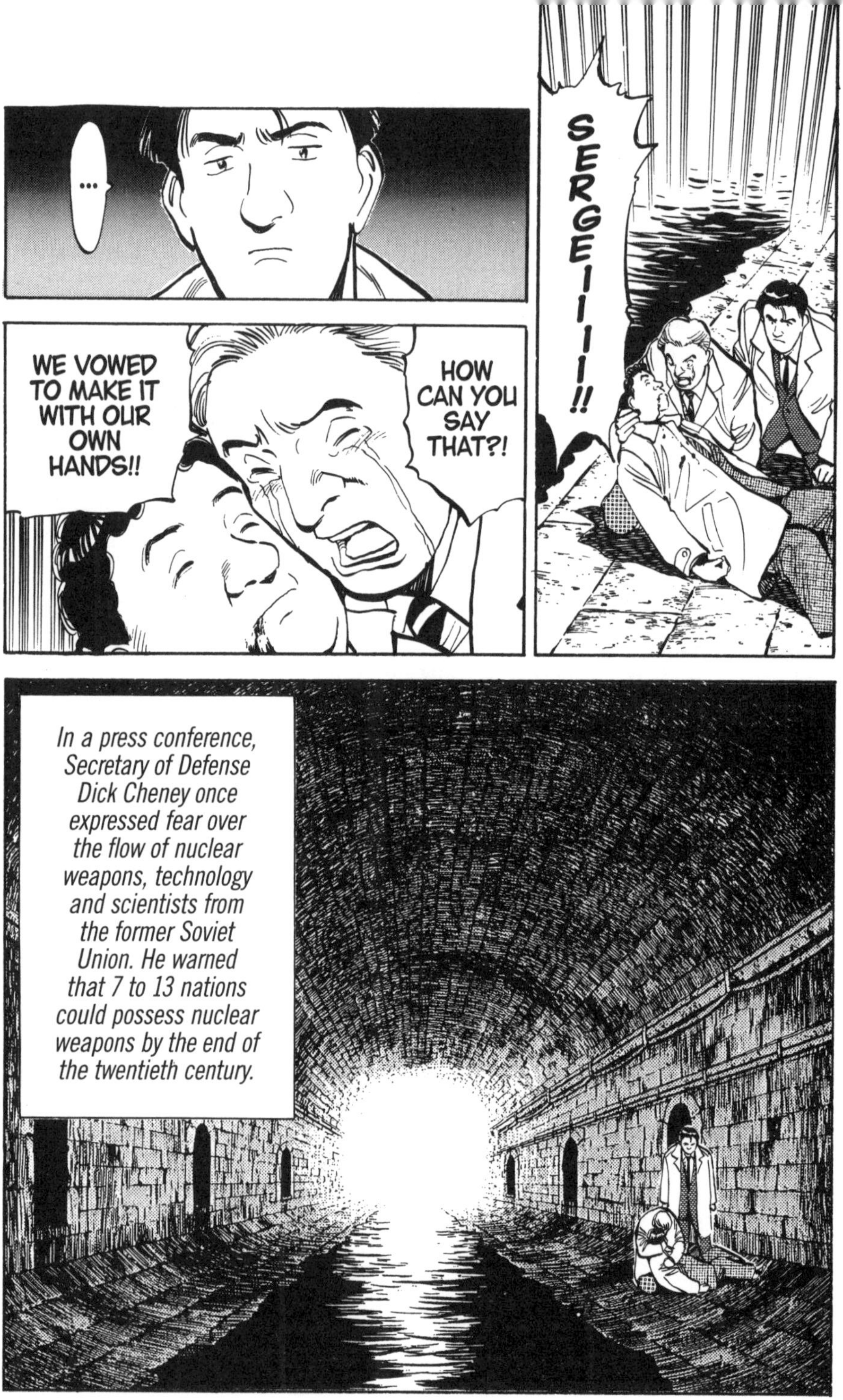
SERGEIIIII!!
...
HOW CAN YOU SAY THAT?!
WE VOWED TO MAKE IT WITH OUR OWN HANDS!!
In a press conference, Secretary of Defense Dick Cheney once expressed fear over the flow of nuclear weapons, technology and scientists from the former Soviet Union. He warned that 7 to 13 nations could possess nuclear weapons by the end of the twentieth century.

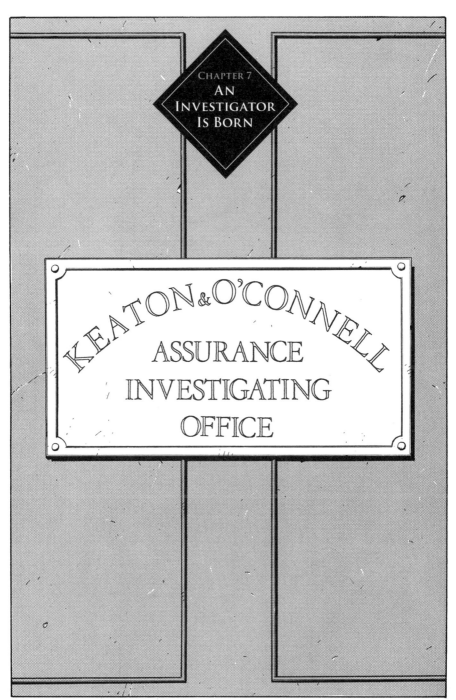

CHAPTER 7
AN
INVESTIGATOR
IS BORN

KEATON & O'CONNELL
ASSURANCE
INVESTIGATING
OFFICE

WHITE WELLS, YORKSHIRE COUNTY, ENGLAND: TEN YEARS AGO, 1982

Stewart Atkins, assistant professor of archaeology at East Yorkshire University, was found dead in the Ramsey River.

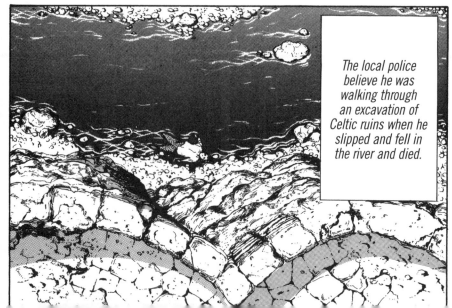

The local police believe he was walking through an excavation of Celtic ruins when he slipped and fell in the river and died.

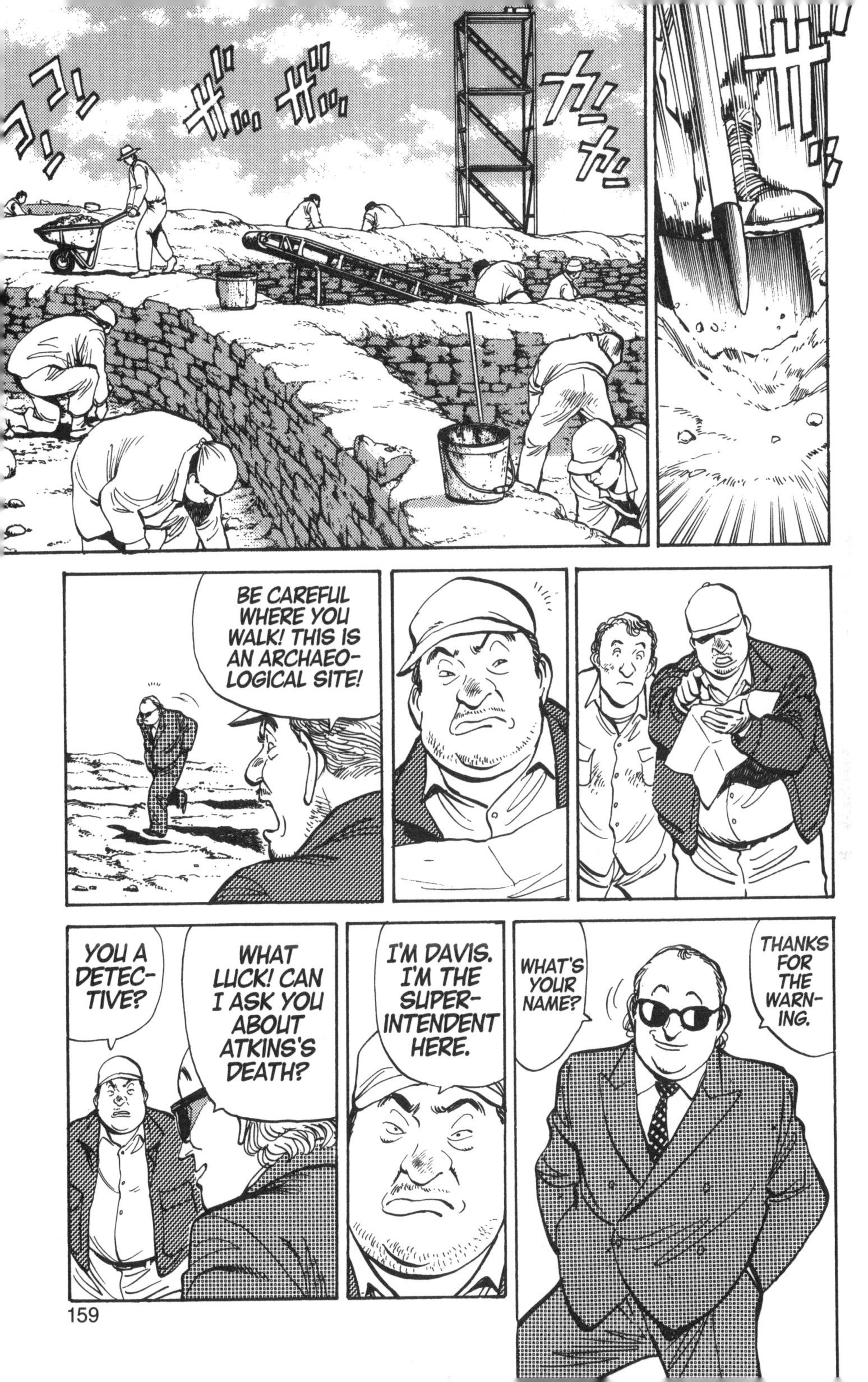
ザッ
コン コン
ザッ ザッ
カン カン
BE CAREFUL WHERE YOU WALK! THIS IS AN ARCHAEO-LOGICAL SITE!
THANKS FOR THE WARN-ING.
WHAT'S YOUR NAME?
I'M DAVIS. I'M THE SUPER-INTENDENT HERE.
WHAT LUCK! CAN I ASK YOU ABOUT ATKINS'S DEATH?
YOU A DETEC-TIVE?

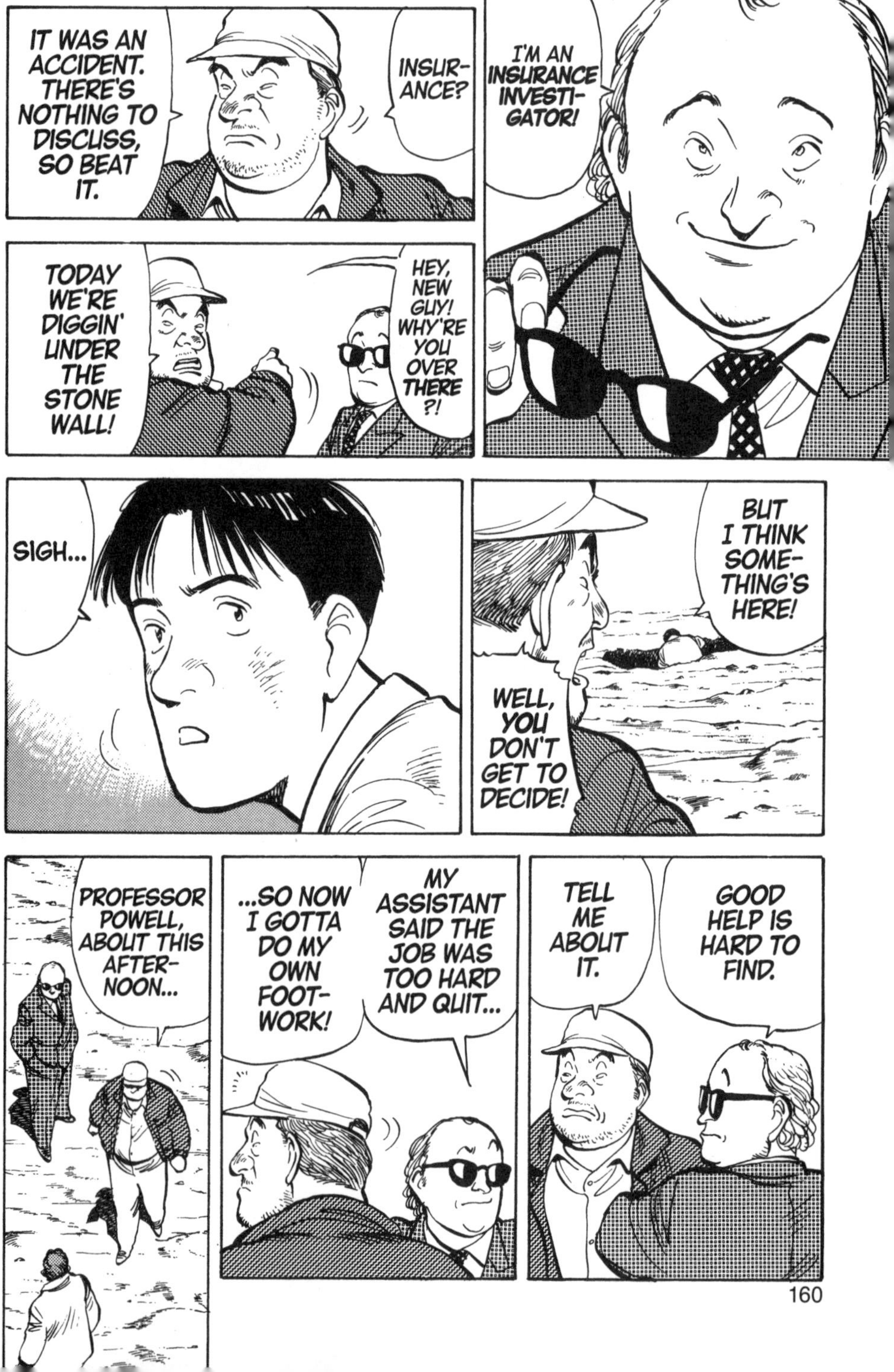
I'M AN INSURANCE INVESTIGATOR!
INSURANCE?
IT WAS AN ACCIDENT. THERE'S NOTHING TO DISCUSS, SO BEAT IT.
HEY, NEW GUY! WHY'RE YOU OVER THERE?!
TODAY WE'RE DIGGIN' UNDER THE STONE WALL!
BUT I THINK SOMETHING'S HERE!
WELL, YOU DON'T GET TO DECIDE!
SIGH...
GOOD HELP IS HARD TO FIND.
TELL ME ABOUT IT.
MY ASSISTANT SAID THE JOB WAS TOO HARD AND QUIT...
...SO NOW I GOTTA DO MY OWN FOOTWORK!
PROFESSOR POWELL, ABOUT THIS AFTERNOON...

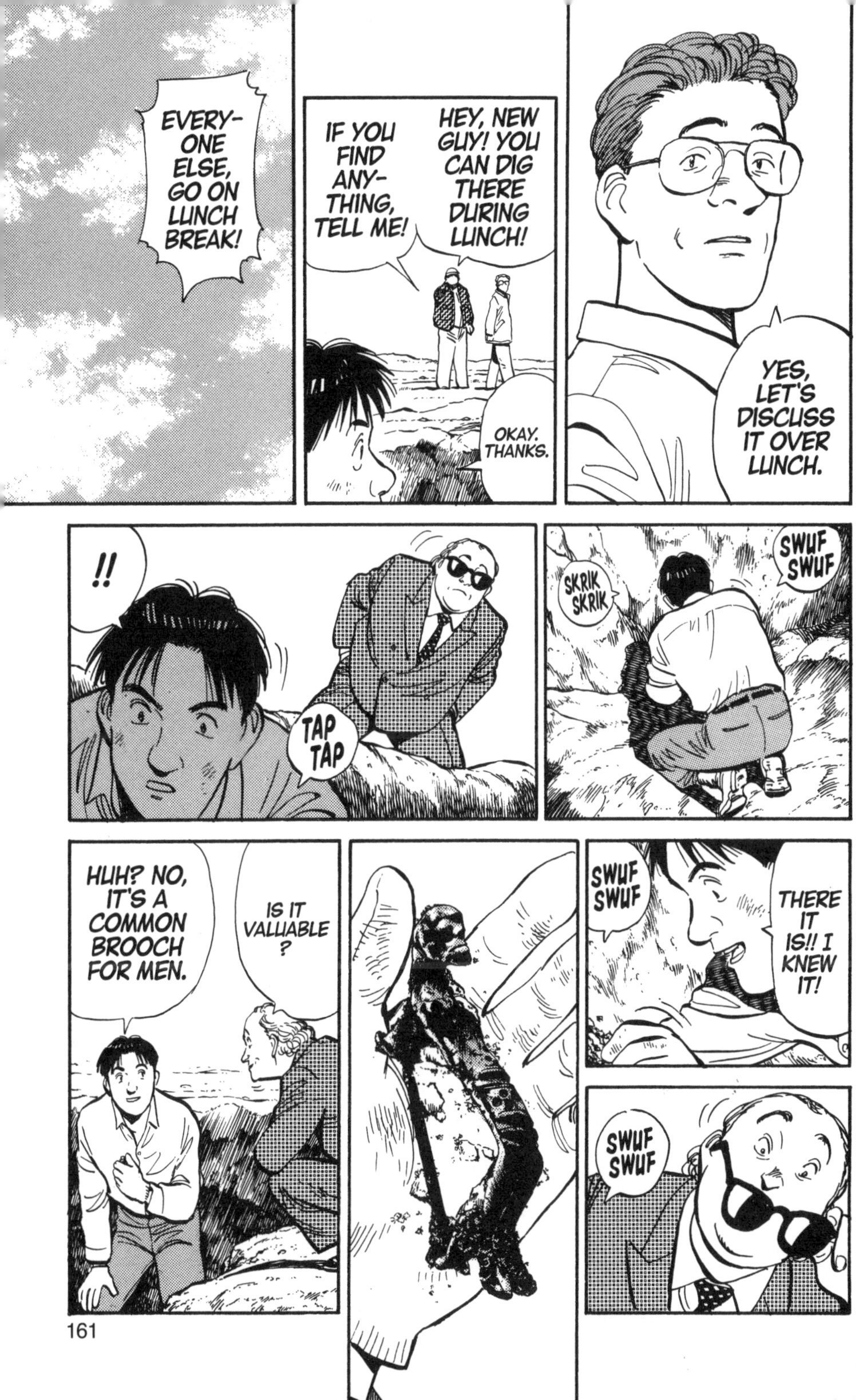
YES, LET'S DISCUSS IT OVER LUNCH.
HEY, NEW GUY! YOU CAN DIG THERE DURING LUNCH!
IF YOU FIND ANY-THING, TELL ME!
OKAY. THANKS.
EVERY-ONE ELSE, GO ON LUNCH BREAK!
SWUF SWUF
SKRIK SKRIK
!!
TAP TAP
THERE IT IS!! I KNEW IT!
SWUF SWUF
SWUF SWUF
IS IT VALUABLE?
HUH? NO, IT'S A COMMON BROOCH FOR MEN.

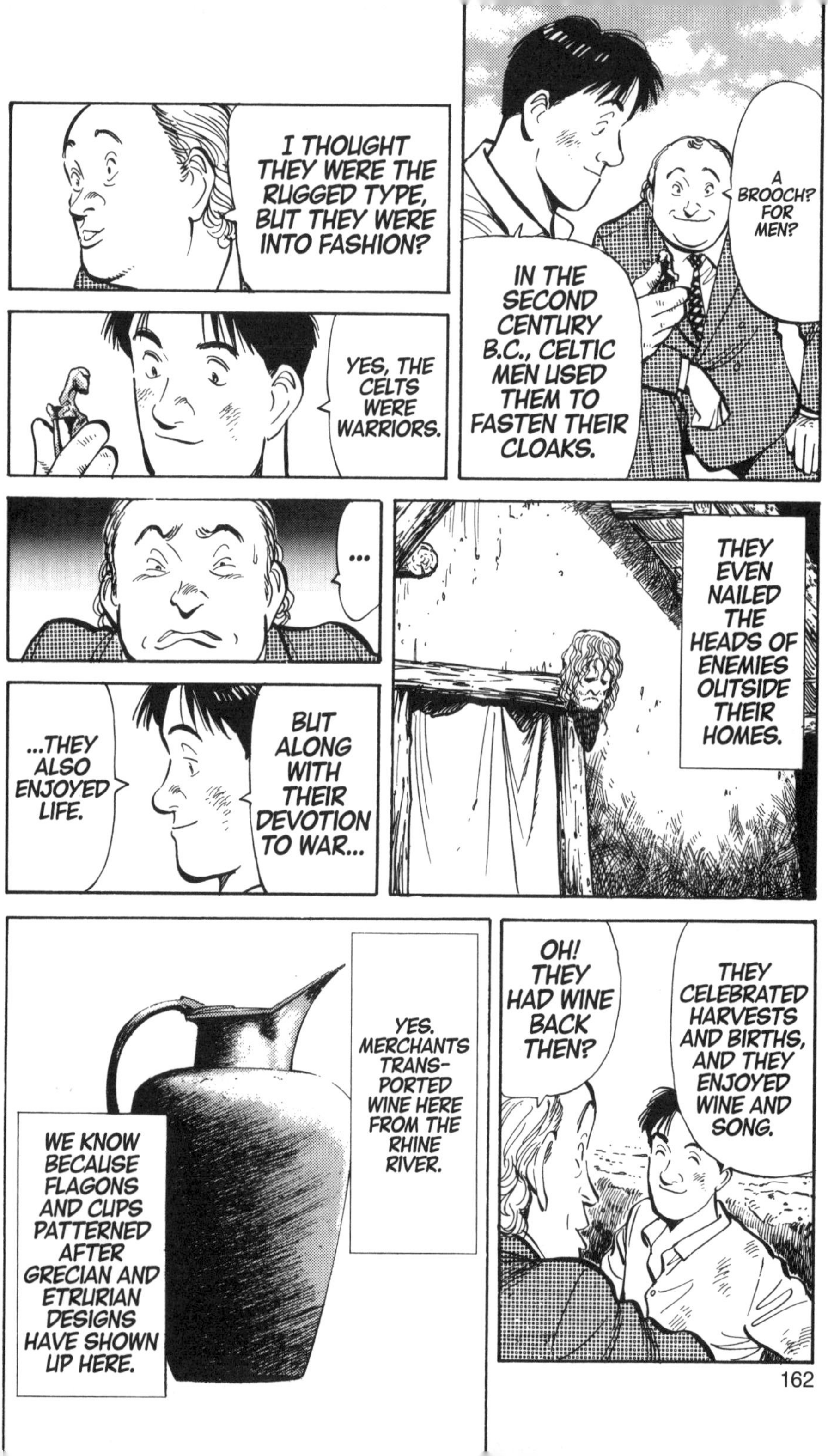
A BROOCH? FOR MEN?
IN THE SECOND CENTURY B.C., CELTIC MEN USED THEM TO FASTEN THEIR CLOAKS.
I THOUGHT THEY WERE THE RUGGED TYPE, BUT THEY WERE INTO FASHION?
YES, THE CELTS WERE WARRIORS.
THEY EVEN NAILED THE HEADS OF ENEMIES OUTSIDE THEIR HOMES.
...
BUT ALONG WITH THEIR DEVOTION TO WAR...
...THEY ALSO ENJOYED LIFE.
THEY CELEBRATED HARVESTS AND BIRTHS, AND THEY ENJOYED WINE AND SONG.
OH! THEY HAD WINE BACK THEN?
YES. MERCHANTS TRANS-PORTED WINE HERE FROM THE RHINE RIVER.
WE KNOW BECAUSE FLAGONS AND CUPS PATTERNED AFTER GRECIAN AND ETRURIAN DESIGNS HAVE SHOWN UP HERE.

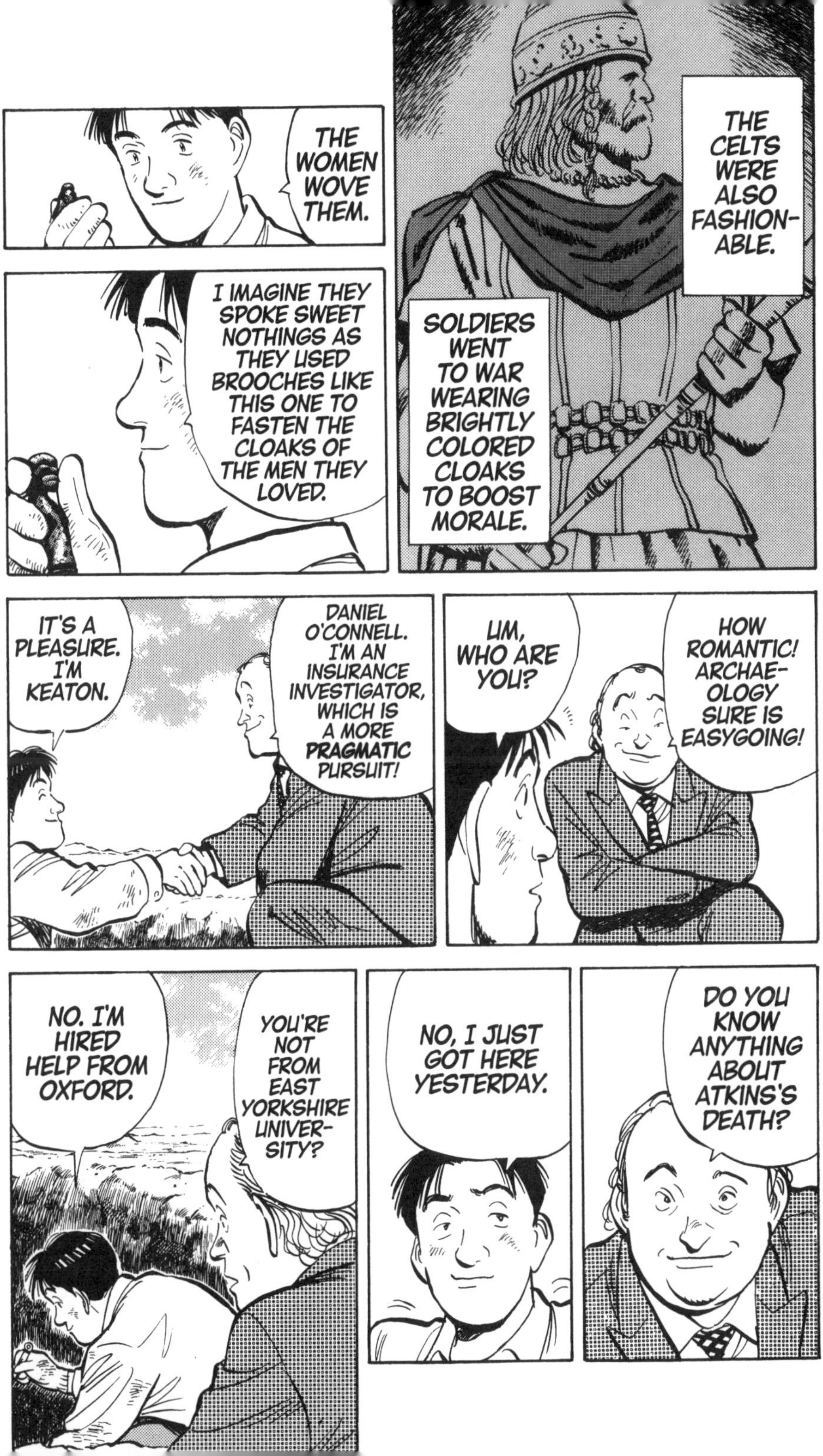
THE CELTS WERE ALSO FASHIONABLE.
SOLDIERS WENT TO WAR WEARING BRIGHTLY COLORED CLOAKS TO BOOST MORALE.
THE WOMEN WOVE THEM.
I IMAGINE THEY SPOKE SWEET NOTHINGS AS THEY USED BROOCHES LIKE THIS ONE TO FASTEN THE CLOAKS OF THE MEN THEY LOVED.
HOW ROMANTIC! ARCHAEOLOGY SURE IS EASYGOING!
UM, WHO ARE YOU?
DANIEL O'CONNELL. I'M AN INSURANCE INVESTIGATOR, WHICH IS A MORE **PRAGMATIC** PURSUIT!
IT'S A PLEASURE. I'M KEATON.
DO YOU KNOW ANYTHING ABOUT ATKINS'S DEATH?
NO, I JUST GOT HERE YESTERDAY.
YOU'RE NOT FROM EAST YORKSHIRE UNIVERSITY?
NO. I'M HIRED HELP FROM OXFORD.

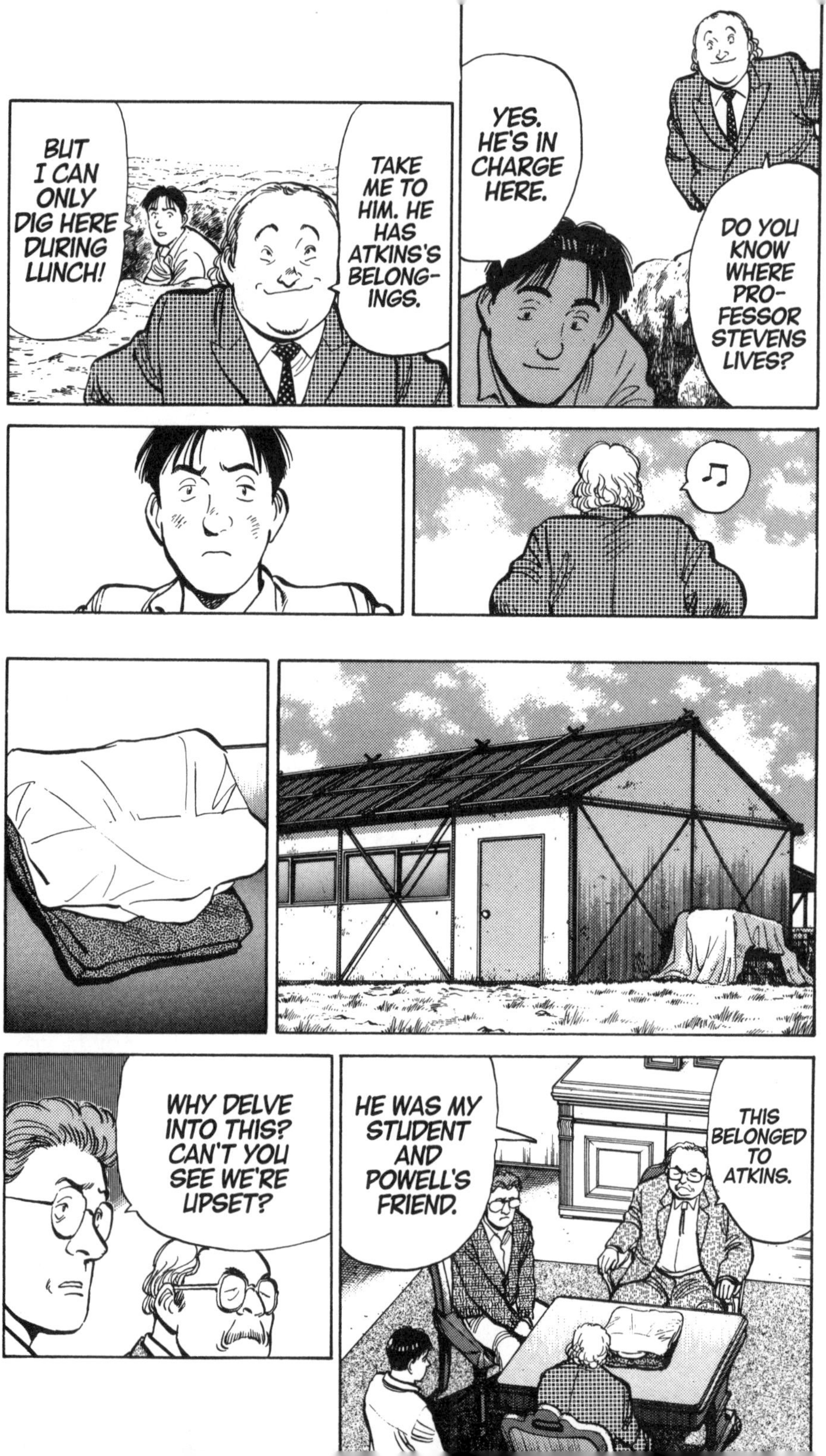
DO YOU KNOW WHERE PRO-FESSOR STEVENS LIVES?
YES. HE'S IN CHARGE HERE.
TAKE ME TO HIM. HE HAS ATKINS'S BELONG-INGS.
BUT I CAN ONLY DIG HERE DURING LUNCH!
♫
THIS BELONGED TO ATKINS.
HE WAS MY STUDENT AND POWELL'S FRIEND.
WHY DELVE INTO THIS? CAN'T YOU SEE WE'RE UPSET?

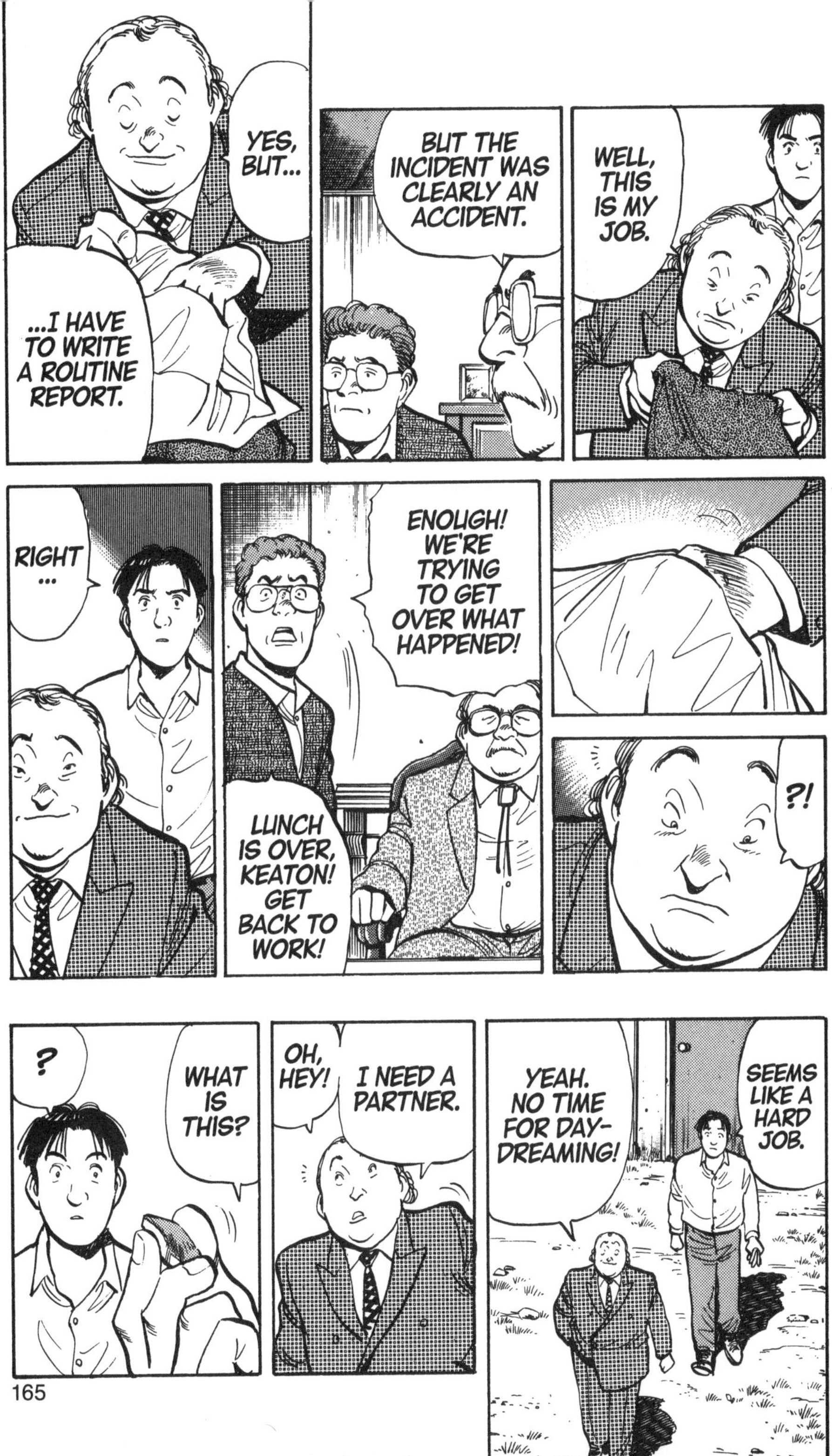
YES, BUT...
...I HAVE TO WRITE A ROUTINE REPORT.
BUT THE INCIDENT WAS CLEARLY AN ACCIDENT.
WELL, THIS IS MY JOB.
RIGHT ...
ENOUGH! WE'RE TRYING TO GET OVER WHAT HAPPENED!
LUNCH IS OVER, KEATON! GET BACK TO WORK!
?!
?
WHAT IS THIS?
OH, HEY!
I NEED A PARTNER.
YEAH. NO TIME FOR DAY-DREAMING!
SEEMS LIKE A HARD JOB.

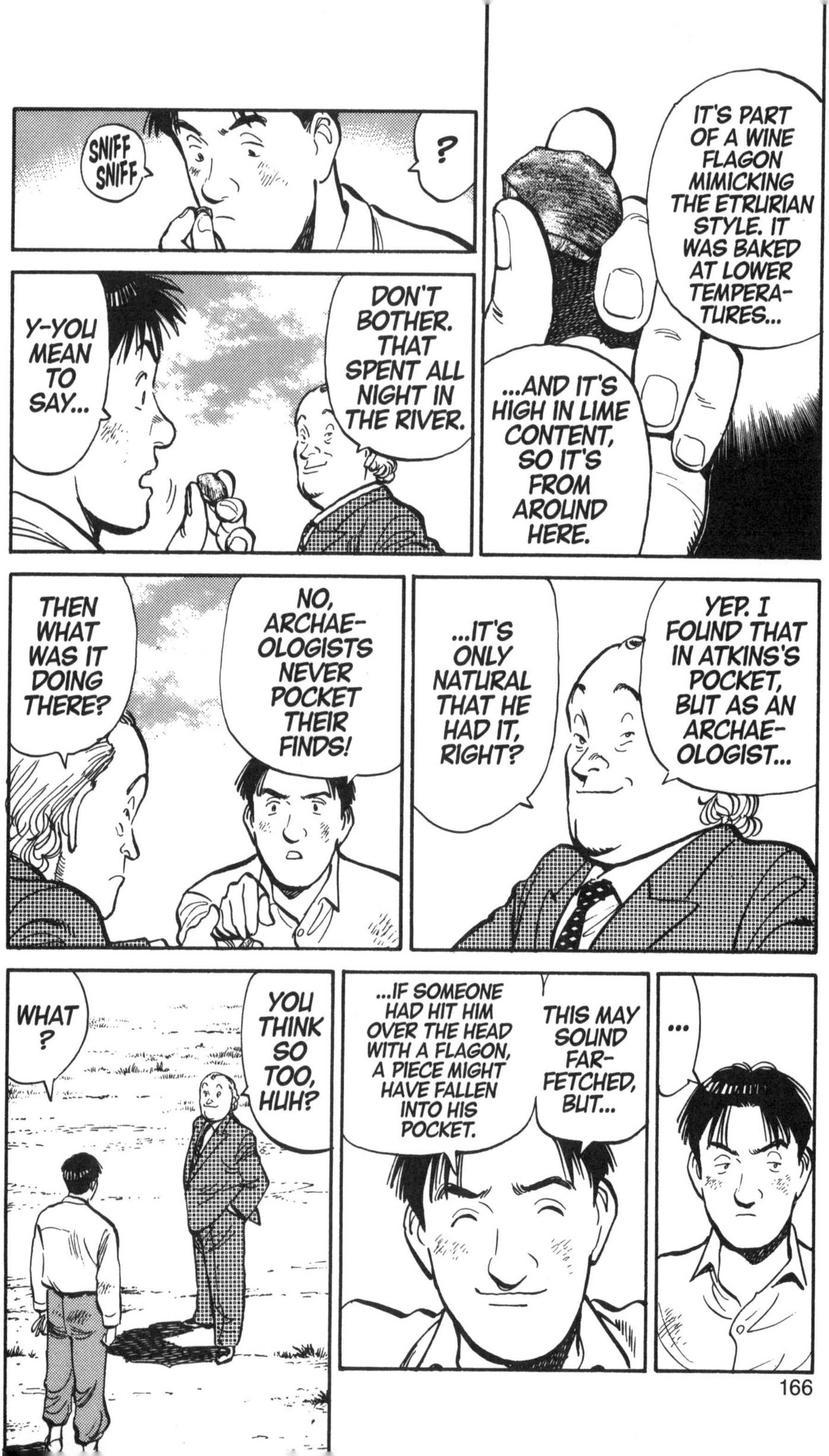
IT'S PART OF A WINE FLAGON MIMICKING THE ETRURIAN STYLE. IT WAS BAKED AT LOWER TEMPERA-TURES...
...AND IT'S HIGH IN LIME CONTENT, SO IT'S FROM AROUND HERE.
?
SNIFF SNIFF
DON'T BOTHER. THAT SPENT ALL NIGHT IN THE RIVER.
Y-YOU MEAN TO SAY...
YEP. I FOUND THAT IN ATKINS'S POCKET, BUT AS AN ARCHAE-OLOGIST...
...IT'S ONLY NATURAL THAT HE HAD IT, RIGHT?
NO, ARCHAE-OLOGISTS NEVER POCKET THEIR FINDS!
THEN WHAT WAS IT DOING THERE?
...
THIS MAY SOUND FAR-FETCHED, BUT...
...IF SOMEONE HAD HIT HIM OVER THE HEAD WITH A FLAGON, A PIECE MIGHT HAVE FALLEN INTO HIS POCKET.
YOU THINK SO TOO, HUH?
WHAT?

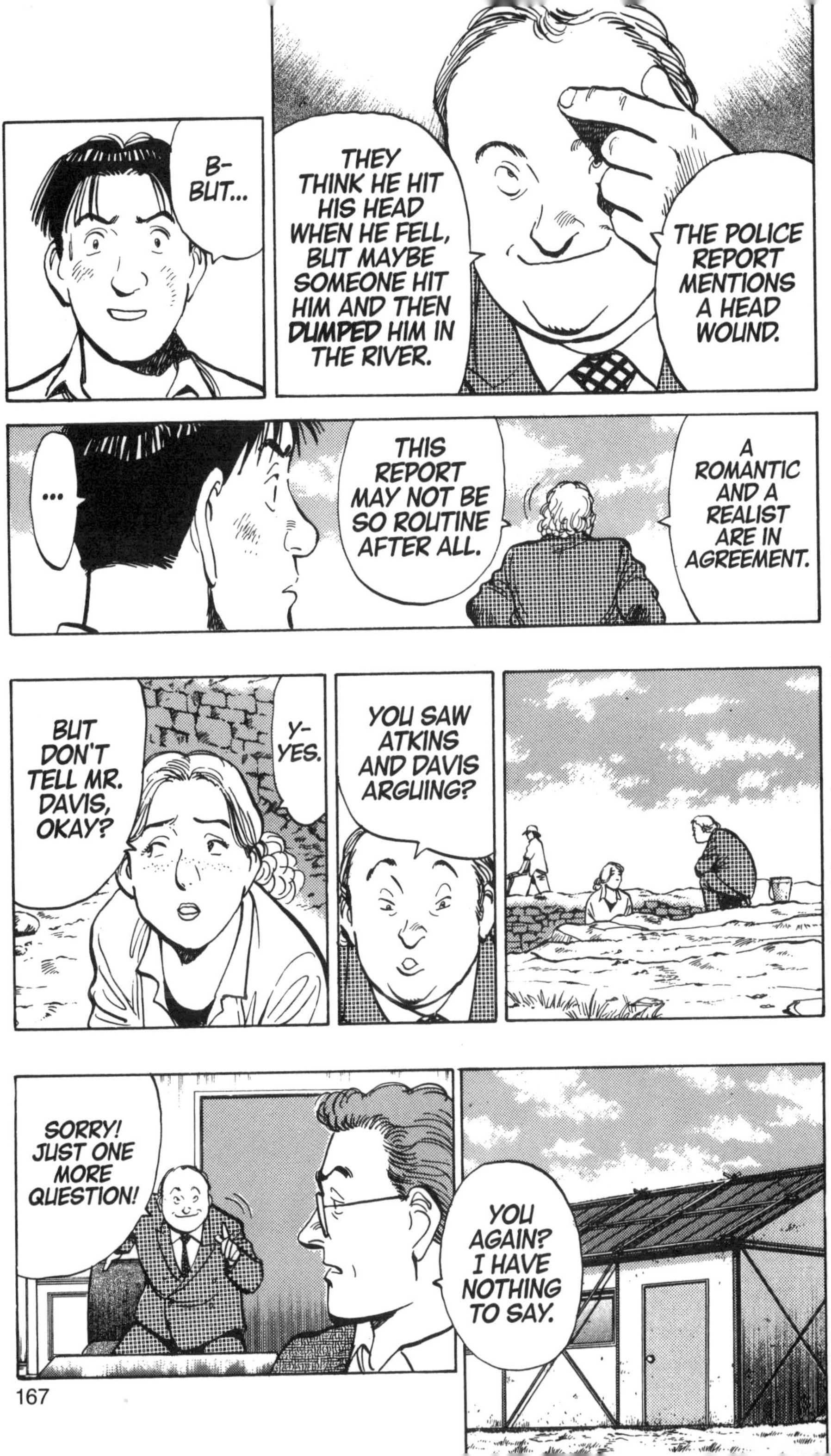
THE POLICE REPORT MENTIONS A HEAD WOUND.
THEY THINK HE HIT HIS HEAD WHEN HE FELL, BUT MAYBE SOMEONE HIT HIM AND THEN DUMPED HIM IN THE RIVER.
B- BUT...
A ROMANTIC AND A REALIST ARE IN AGREEMENT.
THIS REPORT MAY NOT BE SO ROUTINE AFTER ALL.
...
YOU SAW ATKINS AND DAVIS ARGUING?
Y- YES.
BUT DON'T TELL MR. DAVIS, OKAY?
YOU AGAIN? I HAVE NOTHING TO SAY.
SORRY! JUST ONE MORE QUESTION!

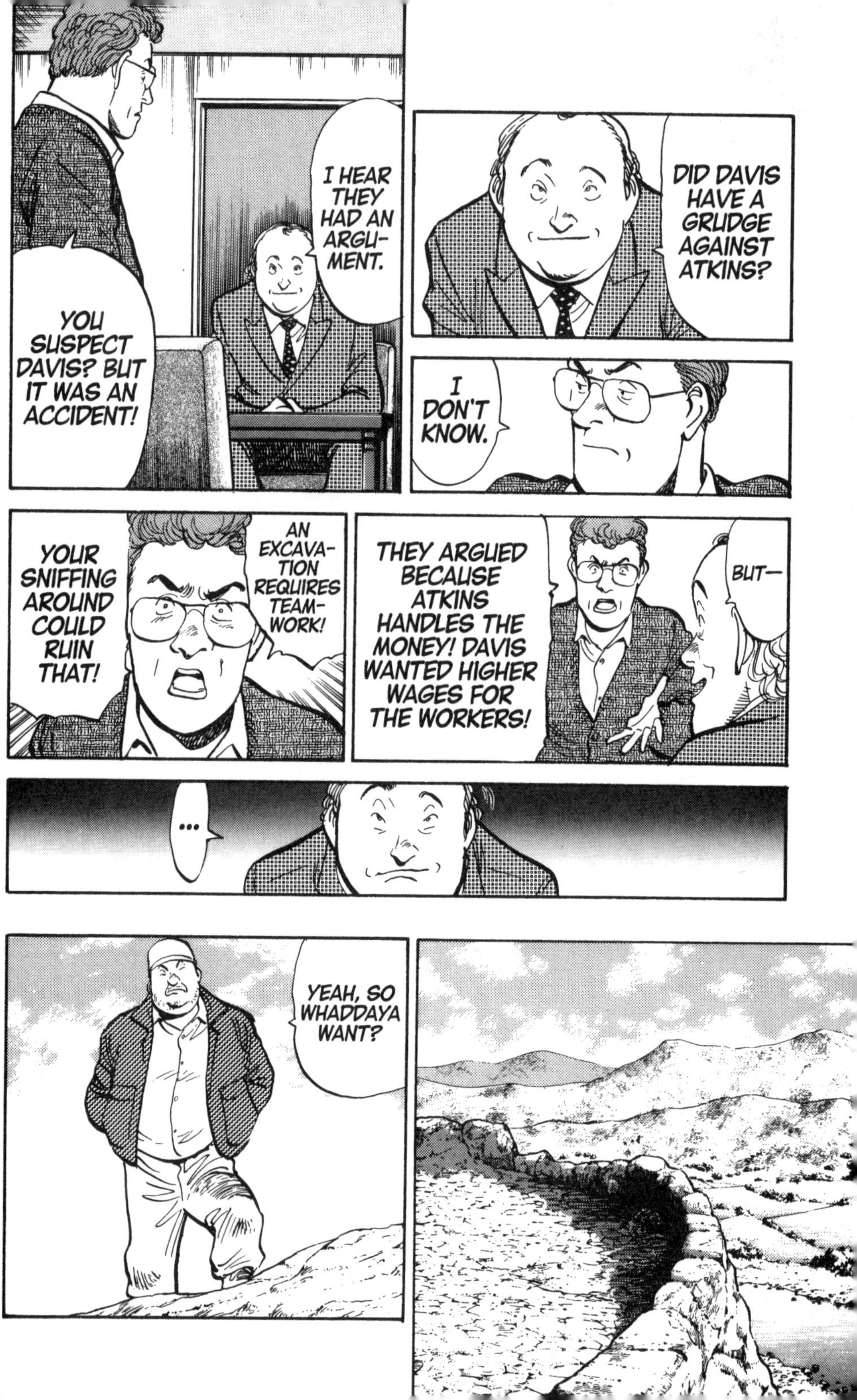
DID DAVIS HAVE A GRUDGE AGAINST ATKINS?
I DON'T KNOW.
I HEAR THEY HAD AN ARGUMENT.
YOU SUSPECT DAVIS? BUT IT WAS AN ACCIDENT!
THEY ARGUED BECAUSE ATKINS HANDLES THE MONEY! DAVIS WANTED HIGHER WAGES FOR THE WORKERS!
BUT—
AN EXCAVATION REQUIRES TEAMWORK!
YOUR SNIFFING AROUND COULD RUIN THAT!
...
YEAH, SO WHADDAYA WANT?

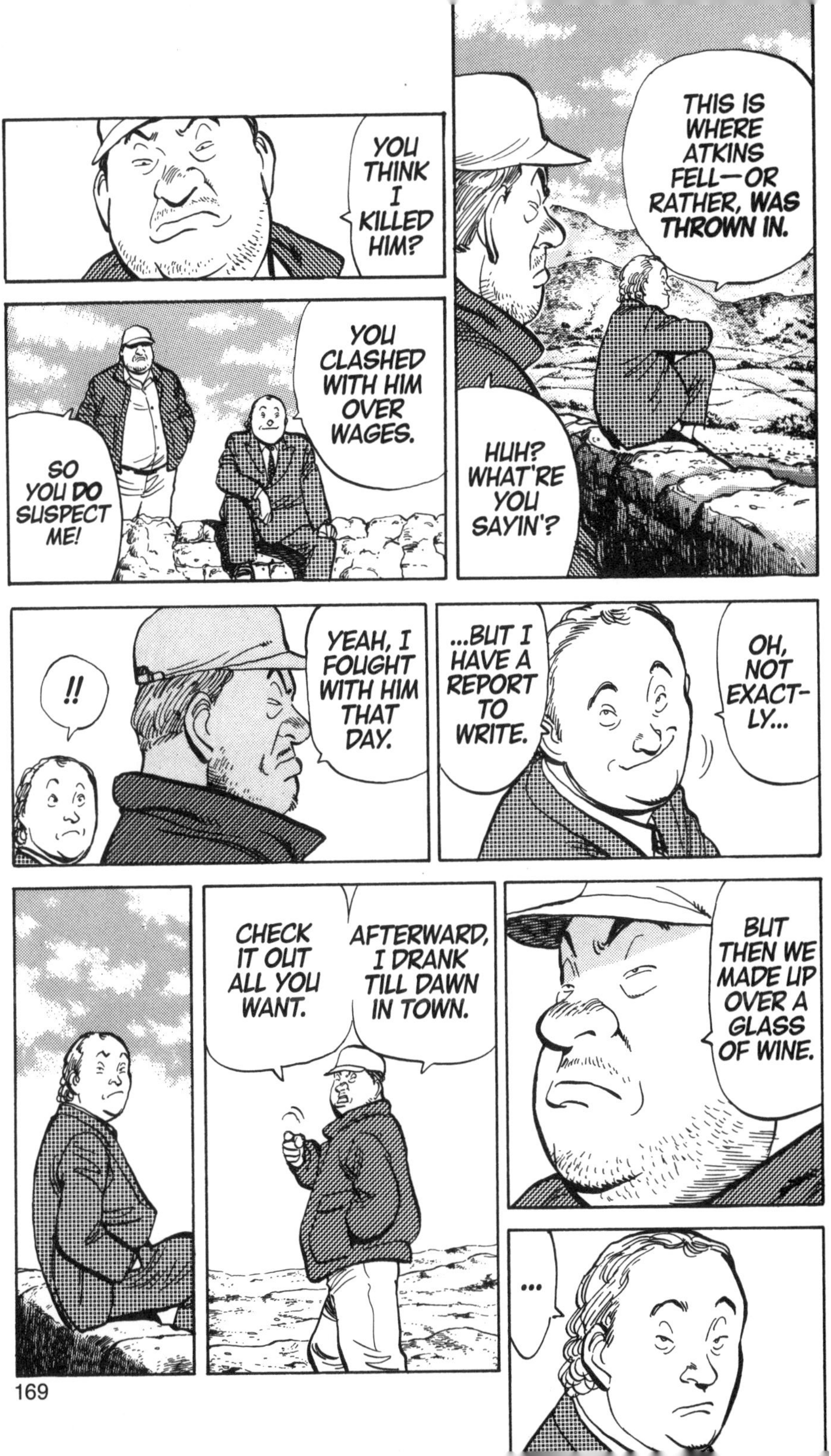
THIS IS WHERE ATKINS FELL—OR RATHER, WAS THROWN IN.
HUH? WHAT'RE YOU SAYIN'?
YOU THINK I KILLED HIM?
YOU CLASHED WITH HIM OVER WAGES.
SO YOU DO SUSPECT ME!
OH, NOT EXACTLY...
...BUT I HAVE A REPORT TO WRITE.
YEAH, I FOUGHT WITH HIM THAT DAY.
!!
BUT THEN WE MADE UP OVER A GLASS OF WINE.
...
AFTERWARD, I DRANK TILL DAWN IN TOWN.
CHECK IT OUT ALL YOU WANT.

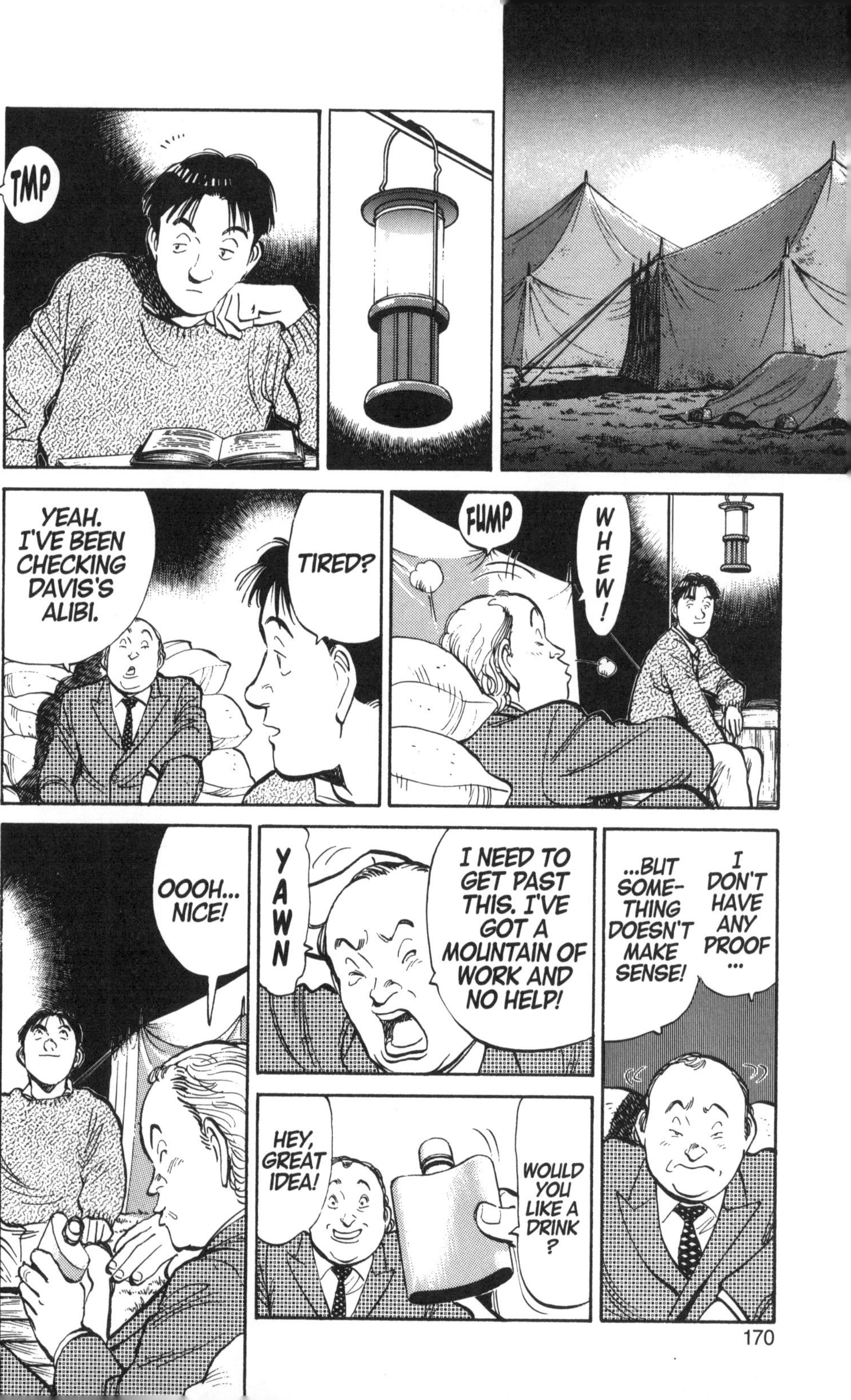
TMP
FUMP
WHEW!
TIRED?
YEAH. I'VE BEEN CHECKING DAVIS'S ALIBI.
I DON'T HAVE ANY PROOF...
...BUT SOME-THING DOESN'T MAKE SENSE!
I NEED TO GET PAST THIS. I'VE GOT A MOUNTAIN OF WORK AND NO HELP!
YAWN
WOULD YOU LIKE A DRINK?
HEY, GREAT IDEA!
OOOH... NICE!

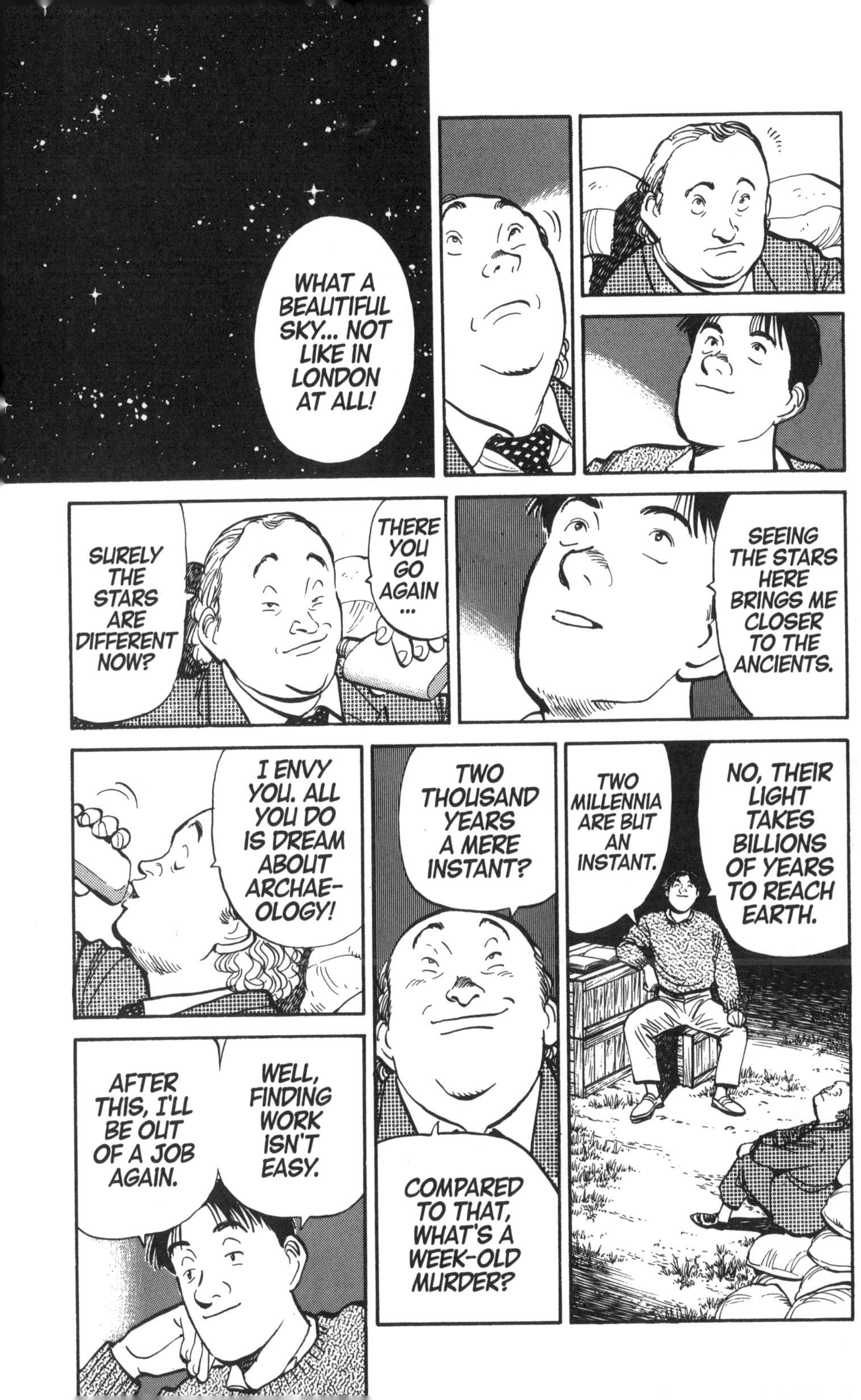
WHAT A BEAUTIFUL SKY... NOT LIKE IN LONDON AT ALL!
SEEING THE STARS HERE BRINGS ME CLOSER TO THE ANCIENTS.
THERE YOU GO AGAIN...
SURELY THE STARS ARE DIFFERENT NOW?
NO, THEIR LIGHT TAKES BILLIONS OF YEARS TO REACH EARTH.
TWO MILLENNIA ARE BUT AN INSTANT.
TWO THOUSAND YEARS A MERE INSTANT?
COMPARED TO THAT, WHAT'S A WEEK-OLD MURDER?
I ENVY YOU. ALL YOU DO IS DREAM ABOUT ARCHAE-OLOGY!
WELL, FINDING WORK ISN'T EASY.
AFTER THIS, I'LL BE OUT OF A JOB AGAIN.

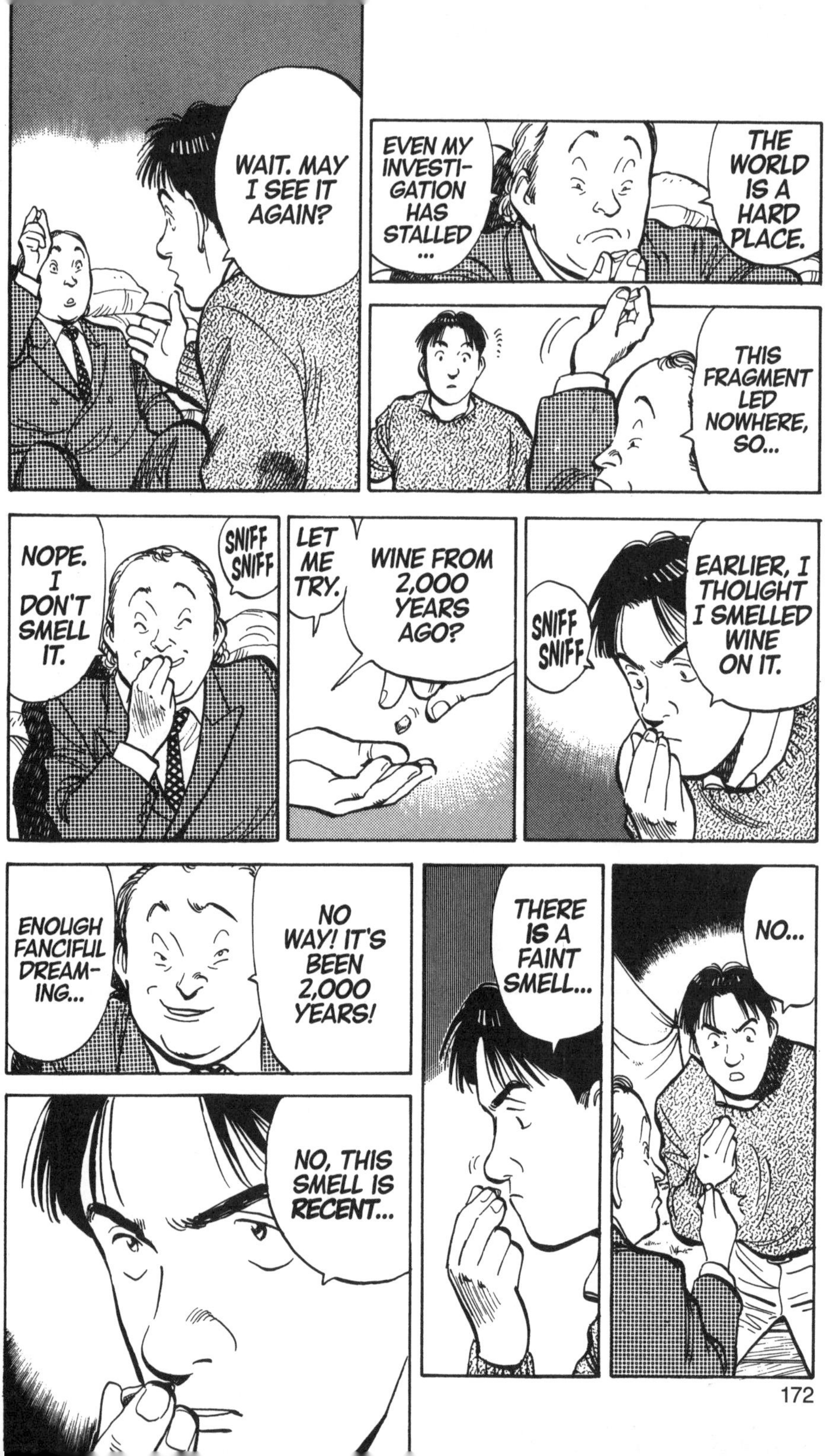
THE WORLD IS A HARD PLACE.
EVEN MY INVESTIGATION HAS STALLED...
THIS FRAGMENT LED NOWHERE, SO...
WAIT. MAY I SEE IT AGAIN?
EARLIER, I THOUGHT I SMELLED WINE ON IT.
SNIFF SNIFF
WINE FROM 2,000 YEARS AGO?
LET ME TRY.
SNIFF SNIFF
NOPE. I DON'T SMELL IT.
NO...
THERE IS A FAINT SMELL...
NO WAY! IT'S BEEN 2,000 YEARS!
ENOUGH FANCIFUL DREAMING...
NO, THIS SMELL IS RECENT...

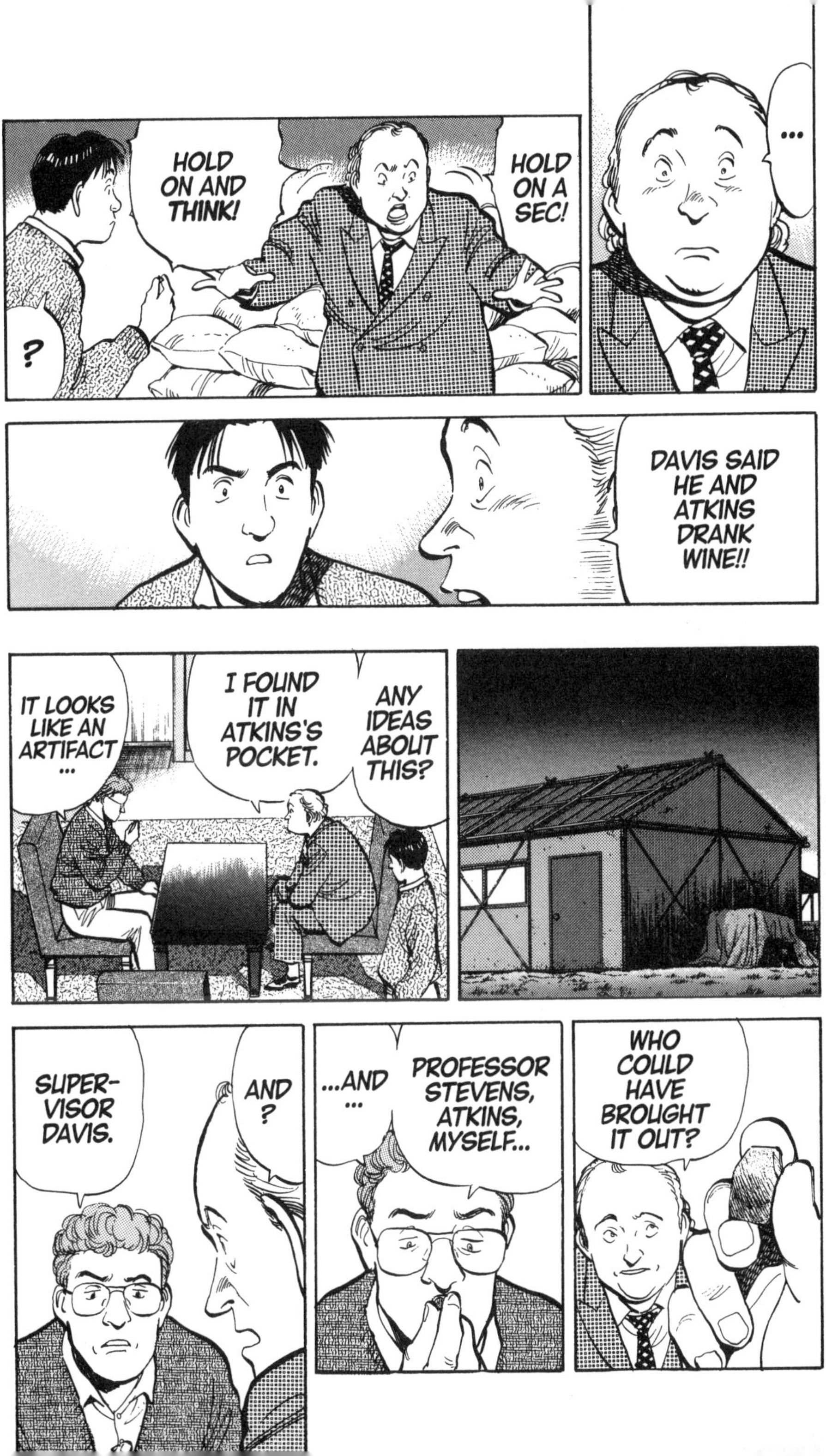
...
HOLD ON A SEC!
HOLD ON AND THINK!
?
DAVIS SAID HE AND ATKINS DRANK WINE!!
ANY IDEAS ABOUT THIS?
I FOUND IT IN ATKINS'S POCKET.
IT LOOKS LIKE AN ARTIFACT ...
WHO COULD HAVE BROUGHT IT OUT?
PROFESSOR STEVENS, ATKINS, MYSELF...
...AND ...
AND ?
SUPER-VISOR DAVIS.

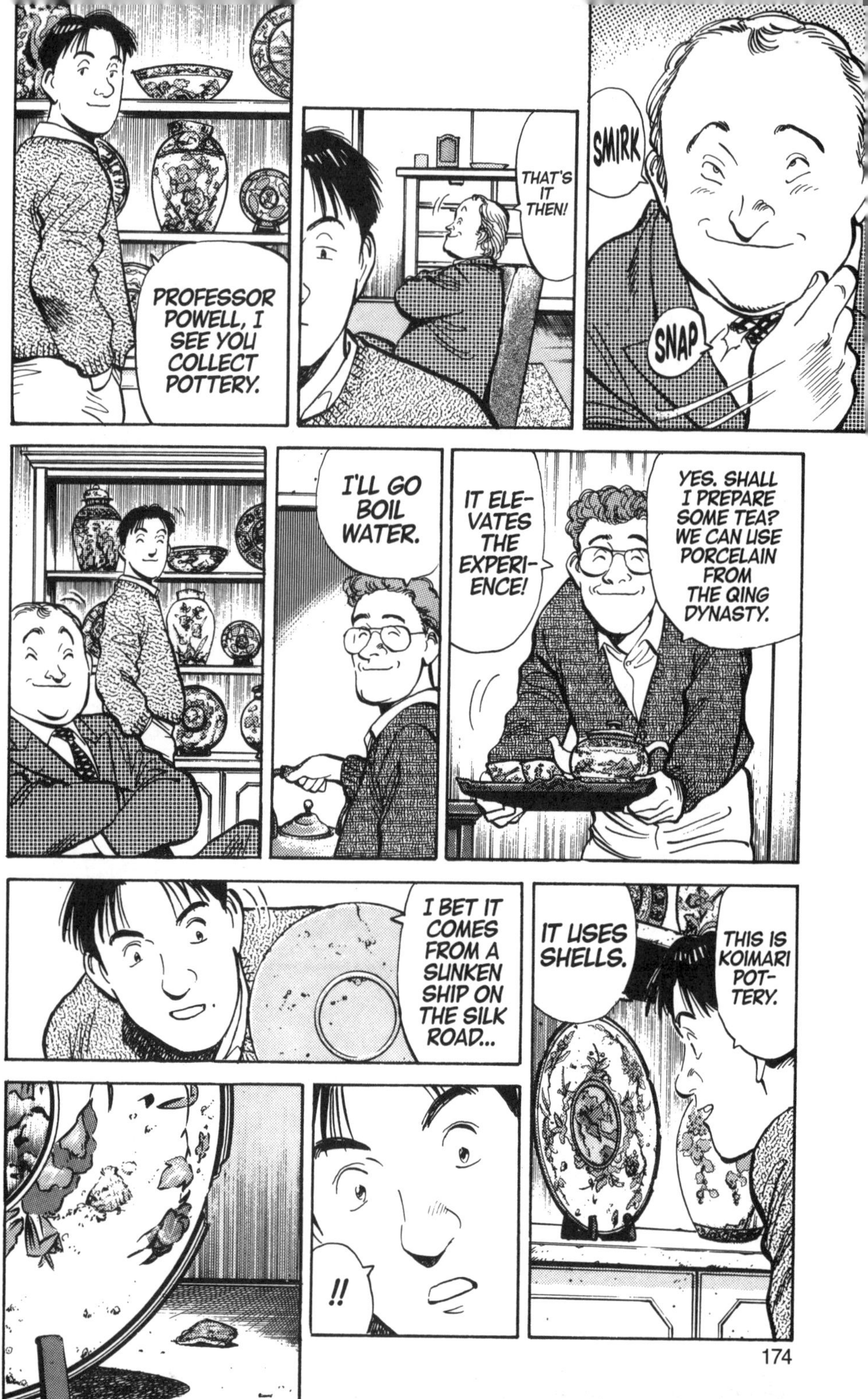
SMIRK
SNAP
THAT'S IT THEN!
PROFESSOR POWELL, I SEE YOU COLLECT POTTERY.
YES. SHALL I PREPARE SOME TEA? WE CAN USE PORCELAIN FROM THE QING DYNASTY.
IT ELE-VATES THE EXPERI-ENCE!
I'LL GO BOIL WATER.
THIS IS KOIMARI POT-TERY.
IT USES SHELLS.
I BET IT COMES FROM A SUNKEN SHIP ON THE SILK ROAD...
!!

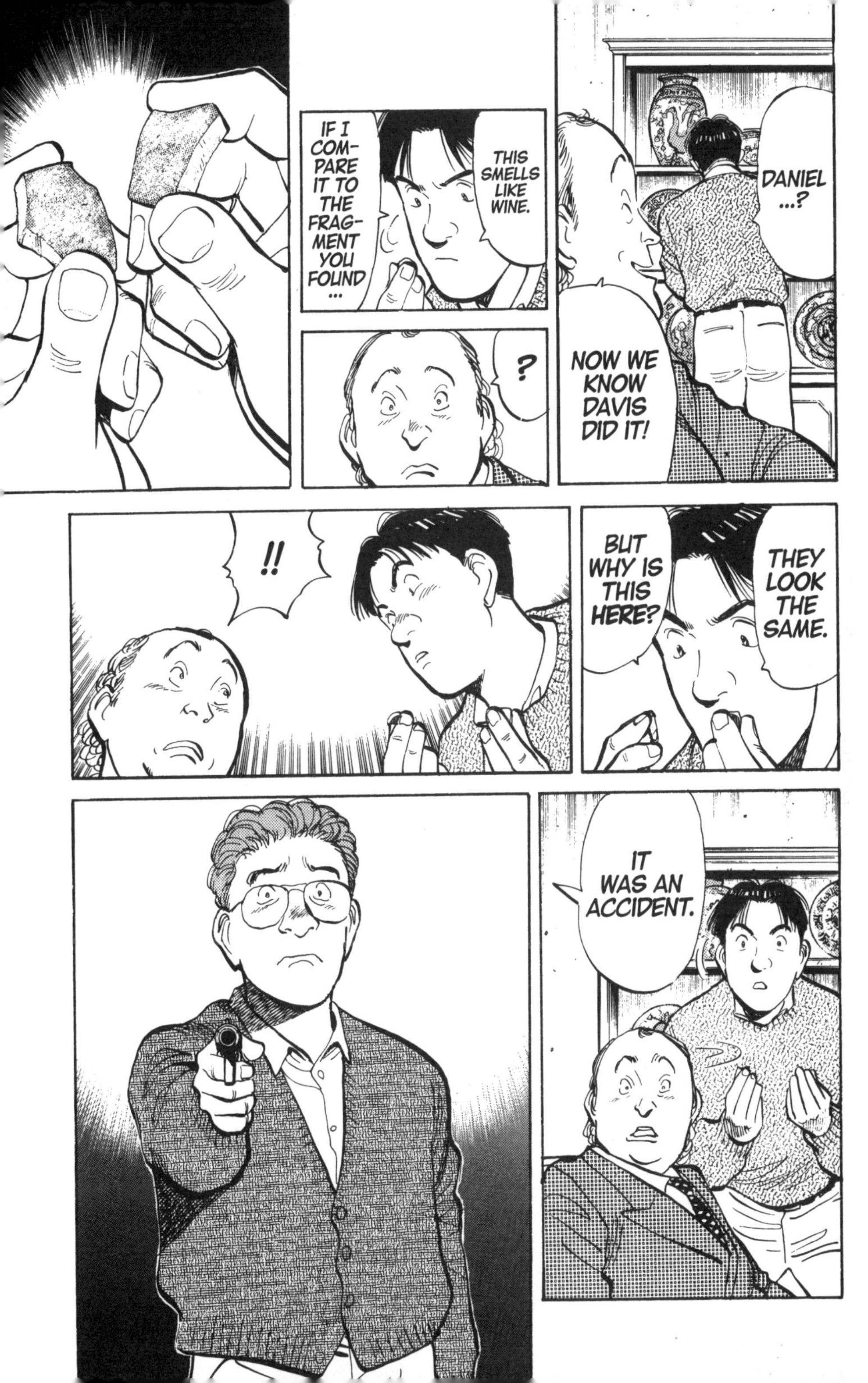
DANIEL ...?
NOW WE KNOW DAVIS DID IT!
THIS SMELLS LIKE WINE.
IF I COMPARE IT TO THE FRAGMENT YOU FOUND ...
?
THEY LOOK THE SAME.
BUT WHY IS THIS HERE?
!!
IT WAS AN ACCIDENT.

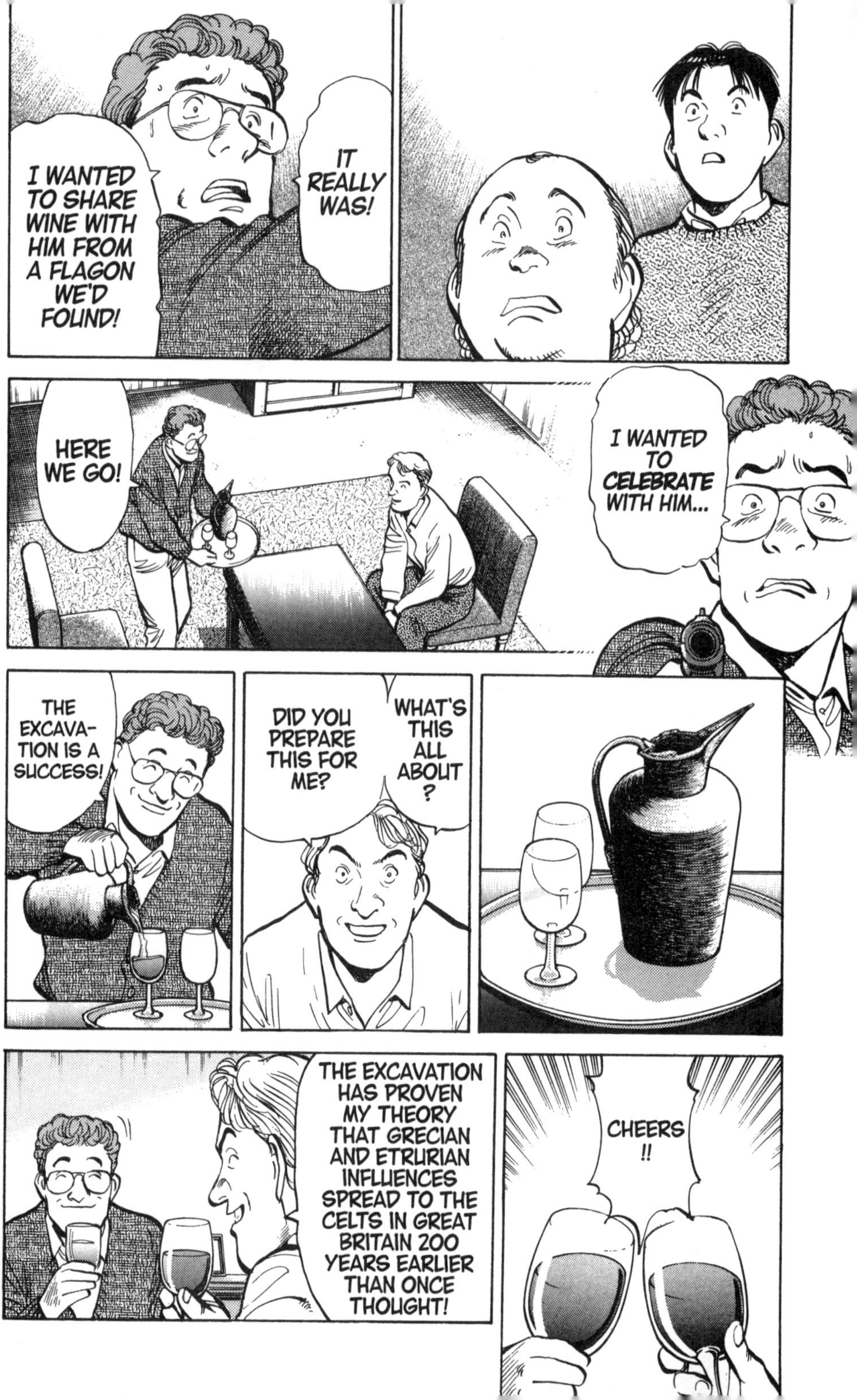
IT REALLY WAS!
I WANTED TO SHARE WINE WITH HIM FROM A FLAGON WE'D FOUND!
I WANTED TO CELEBRATE WITH HIM...
HERE WE GO!
WHAT'S THIS ALL ABOUT?
DID YOU PREPARE THIS FOR ME?
THE EXCAVATION IS A SUCCESS!
CHEERS!!
THE EXCAVATION HAS PROVEN MY THEORY THAT GRECIAN AND ETRURIAN INFLUENCES SPREAD TO THE CELTS IN GREAT BRITAIN 200 YEARS EARLIER THAN ONCE THOUGHT!

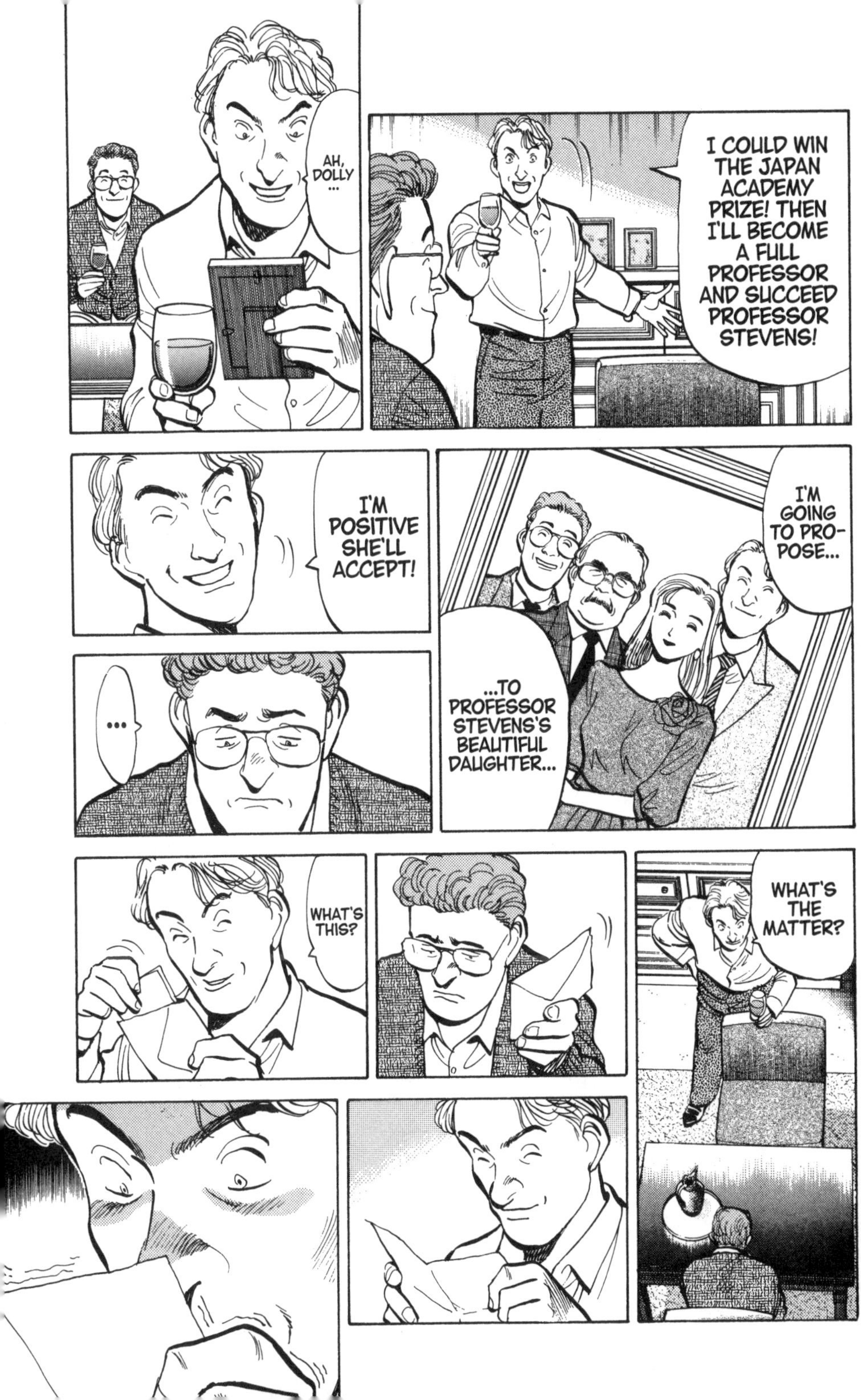
I COULD WIN THE JAPAN ACADEMY PRIZE! THEN I'LL BECOME A FULL PROFESSOR AND SUCCEED PROFESSOR STEVENS!
AH, DOLLY...
I'M GOING TO PRO-POSE...
...TO PROFESSOR STEVENS'S BEAUTIFUL DAUGHTER...
I'M POSITIVE SHE'LL ACCEPT!
...
WHAT'S THE MATTER?
WHAT'S THIS?

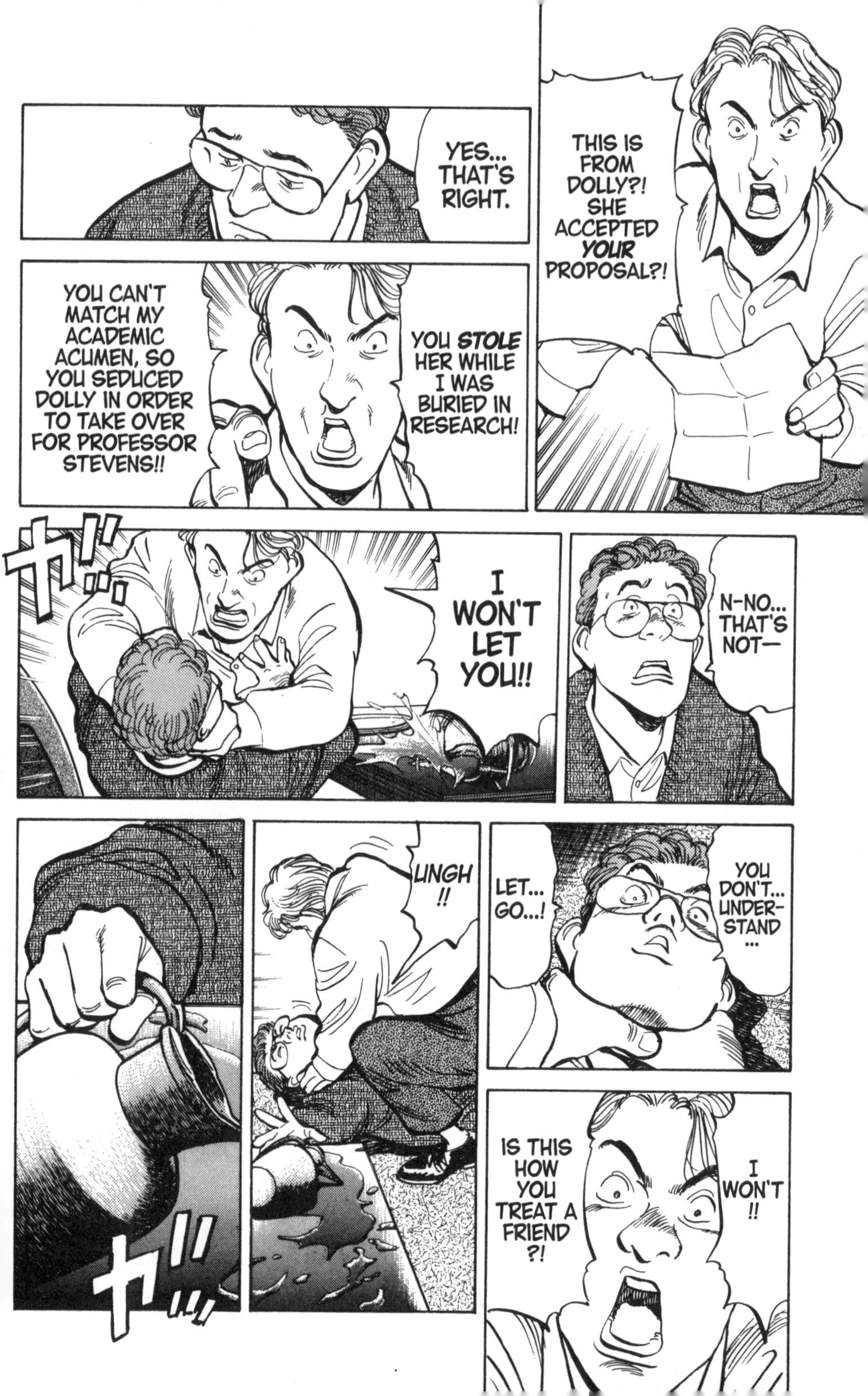
THIS IS FROM DOLLY?! SHE ACCEPTED YOUR PROPOSAL?!
YES... THAT'S RIGHT.
YOU STOLE HER WHILE I WAS BURIED IN RESEARCH!
YOU CAN'T MATCH MY ACADEMIC ACUMEN, SO YOU SEDUCED DOLLY IN ORDER TO TAKE OVER FOR PROFESSOR STEVENS!!
N-NO... THAT'S NOT—
I WON'T LET YOU!!
ガッ
YOU DON'T... UNDER-STAND...
LET... GO...!
I WON'T!!
IS THIS HOW YOU TREAT A FRIEND?!
UNGH!!
ガッ

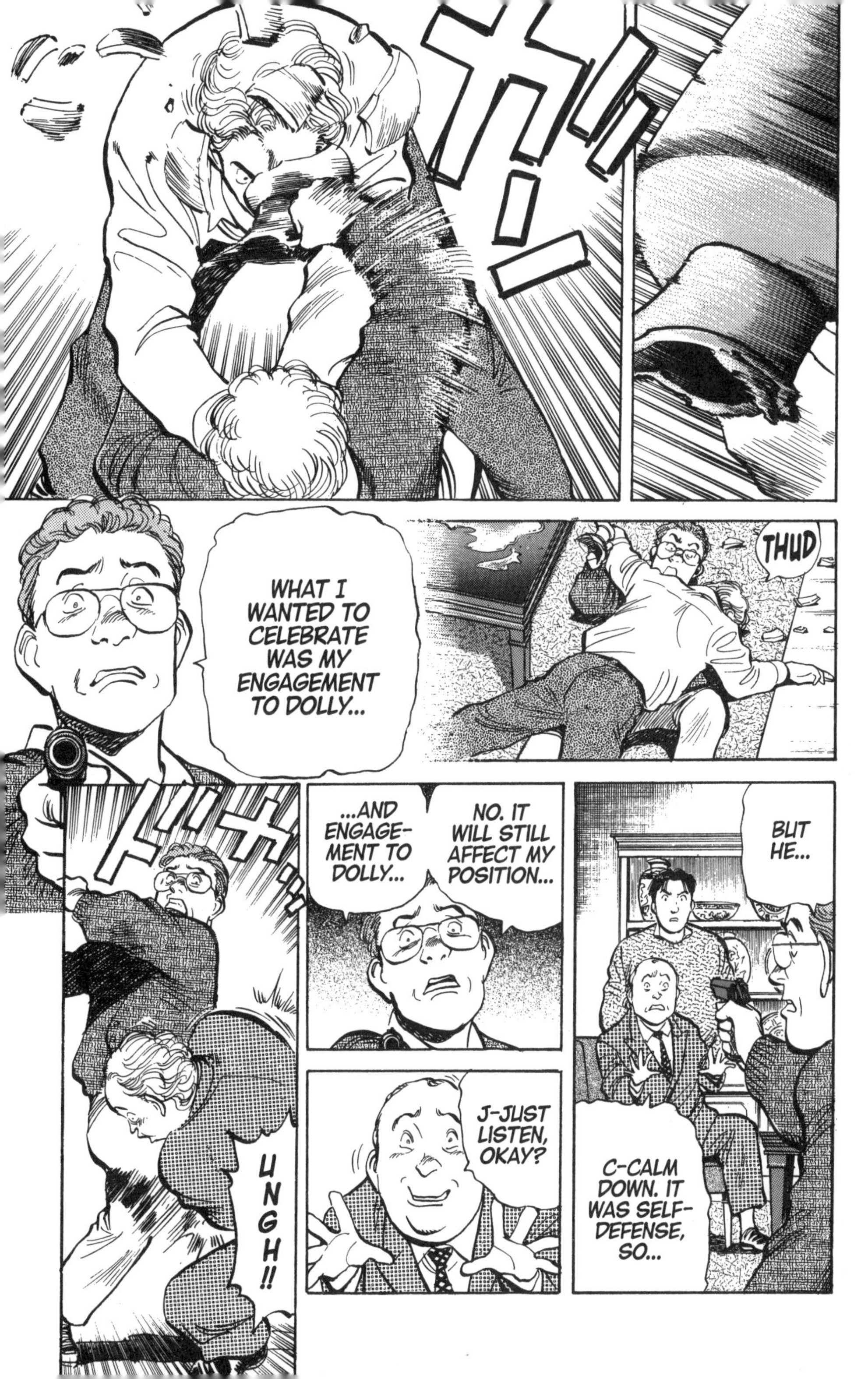
THUD
WHAT I WANTED TO CELEBRATE WAS MY ENGAGEMENT TO DOLLY...
BUT HE...
C-CALM DOWN. IT WAS SELF-DEFENSE, SO...
NO. IT WILL STILL AFFECT MY POSITION...
...AND ENGAGEMENT TO DOLLY...
J-JUST LISTEN, OKAY?
UNGH!!

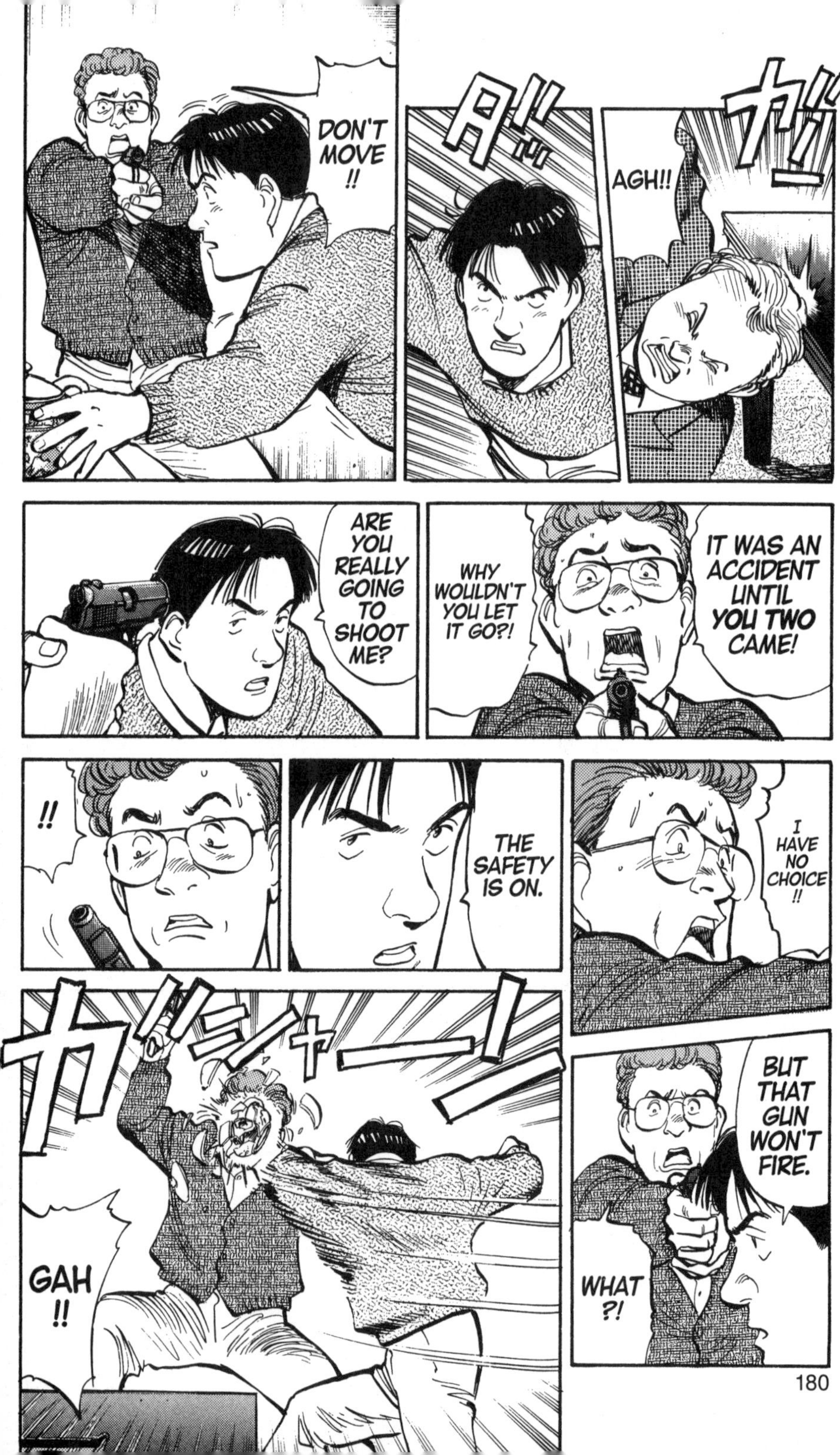
AGH!!
DON'T MOVE!!
IT WAS AN ACCIDENT UNTIL YOU TWO CAME!
WHY WOULDN'T YOU LET IT GO?!
ARE YOU REALLY GOING TO SHOOT ME?
I HAVE NO CHOICE!!
THE SAFETY IS ON.
!!
BUT THAT GUN WON'T FIRE.
WHAT?!
ガシャーン
GAH!!

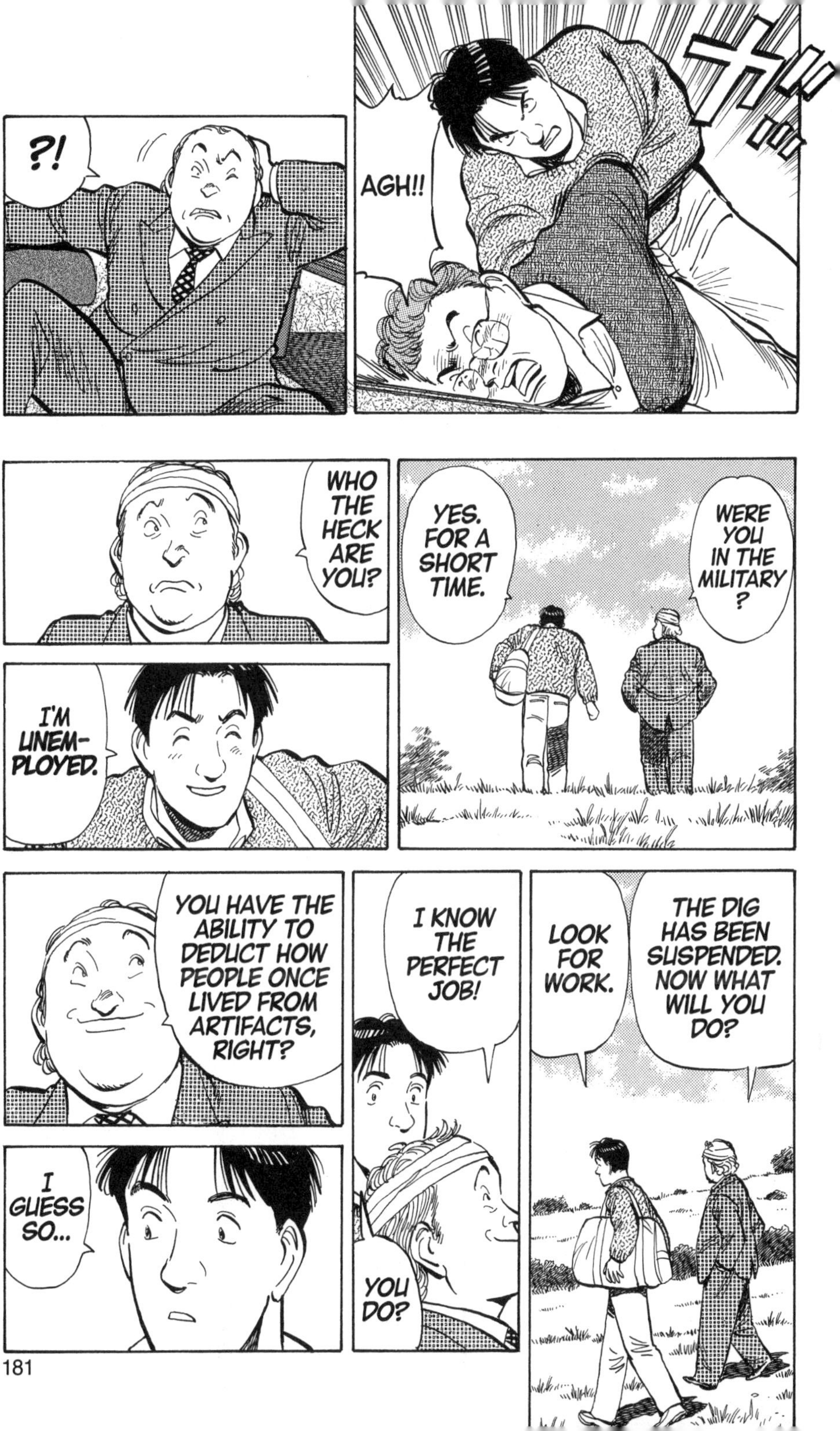
AGH!!
?!
WERE YOU IN THE MILITARY?
YES. FOR A SHORT TIME.
WHO THE HECK ARE YOU?
I'M UNEMPLOYED.
THE DIG HAS BEEN SUSPENDED. NOW WHAT WILL YOU DO?
LOOK FOR WORK.
I KNOW THE PERFECT JOB!
YOU DO?
YOU HAVE THE ABILITY TO DEDUCT HOW PEOPLE ONCE LIVED FROM ARTIFACTS, RIGHT?
I GUESS SO...

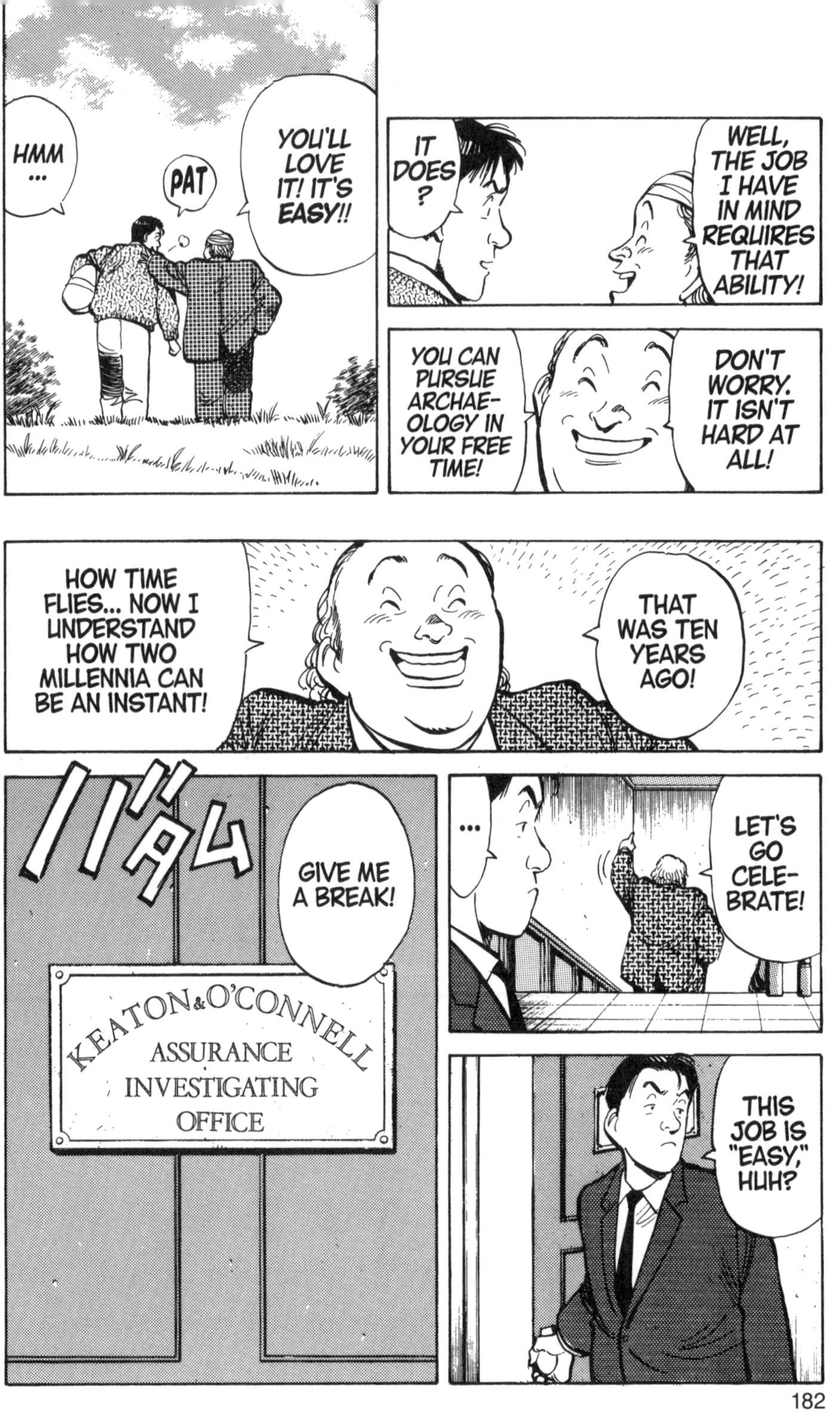
WELL, THE JOB I HAVE IN MIND REQUIRES THAT ABILITY!
IT DOES?
DON'T WORRY. IT ISN'T HARD AT ALL!
YOU CAN PURSUE ARCHAE-OLOGY IN YOUR FREE TIME!
YOU'LL LOVE IT! IT'S EASY!!
PAT
HMM ...
THAT WAS TEN YEARS AGO!
HOW TIME FLIES... NOW I UNDERSTAND HOW TWO MILLENNIA CAN BE AN INSTANT!
LET'S GO CELE-BRATE!
...
THIS JOB IS "EASY," HUH?
GIVE ME A BREAK!
バタム
KEATON & O'CONNELL
ASSURANCE
INVESTIGATING
OFFICE

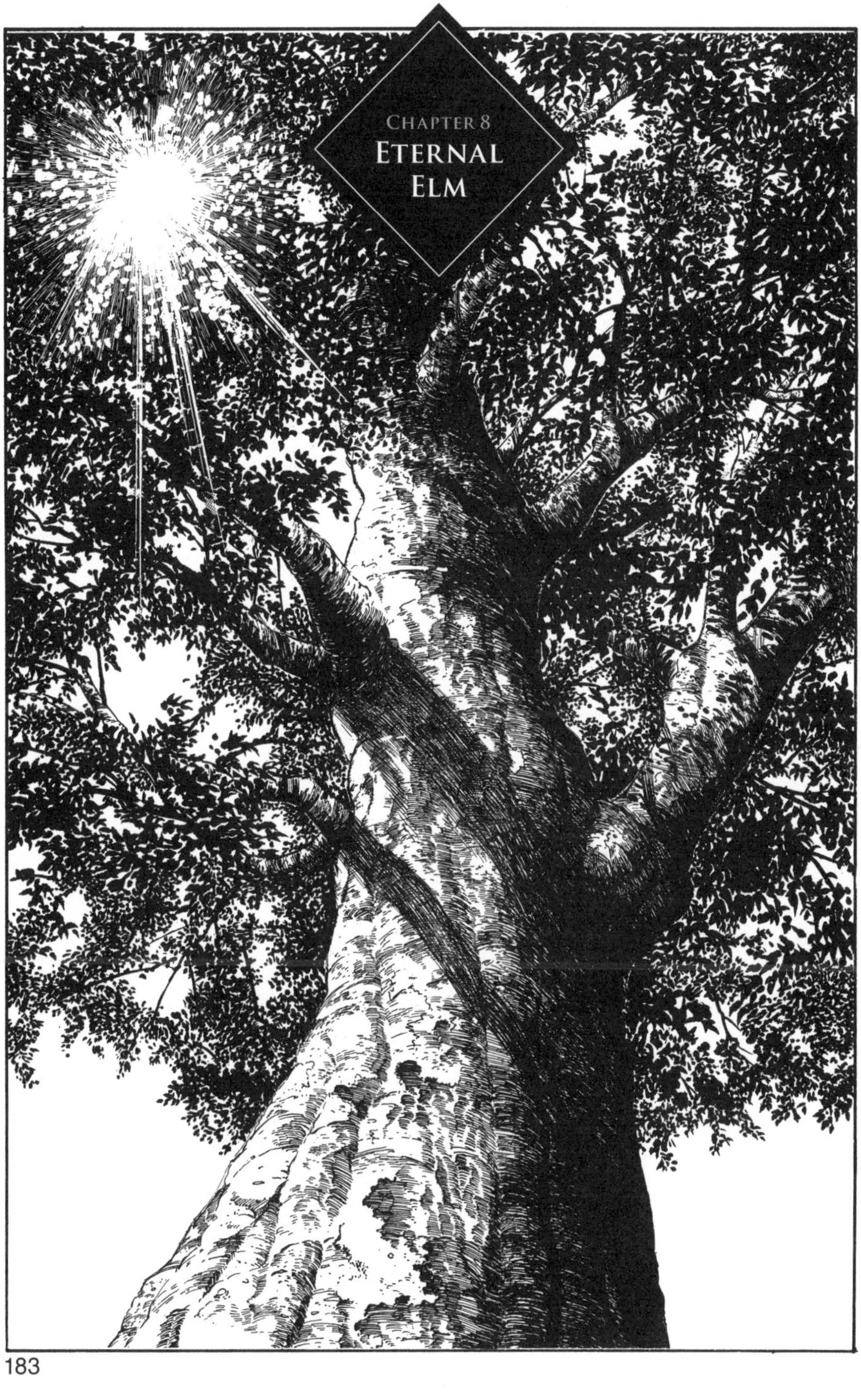
CHAPTER 8
ETERNAL ELM

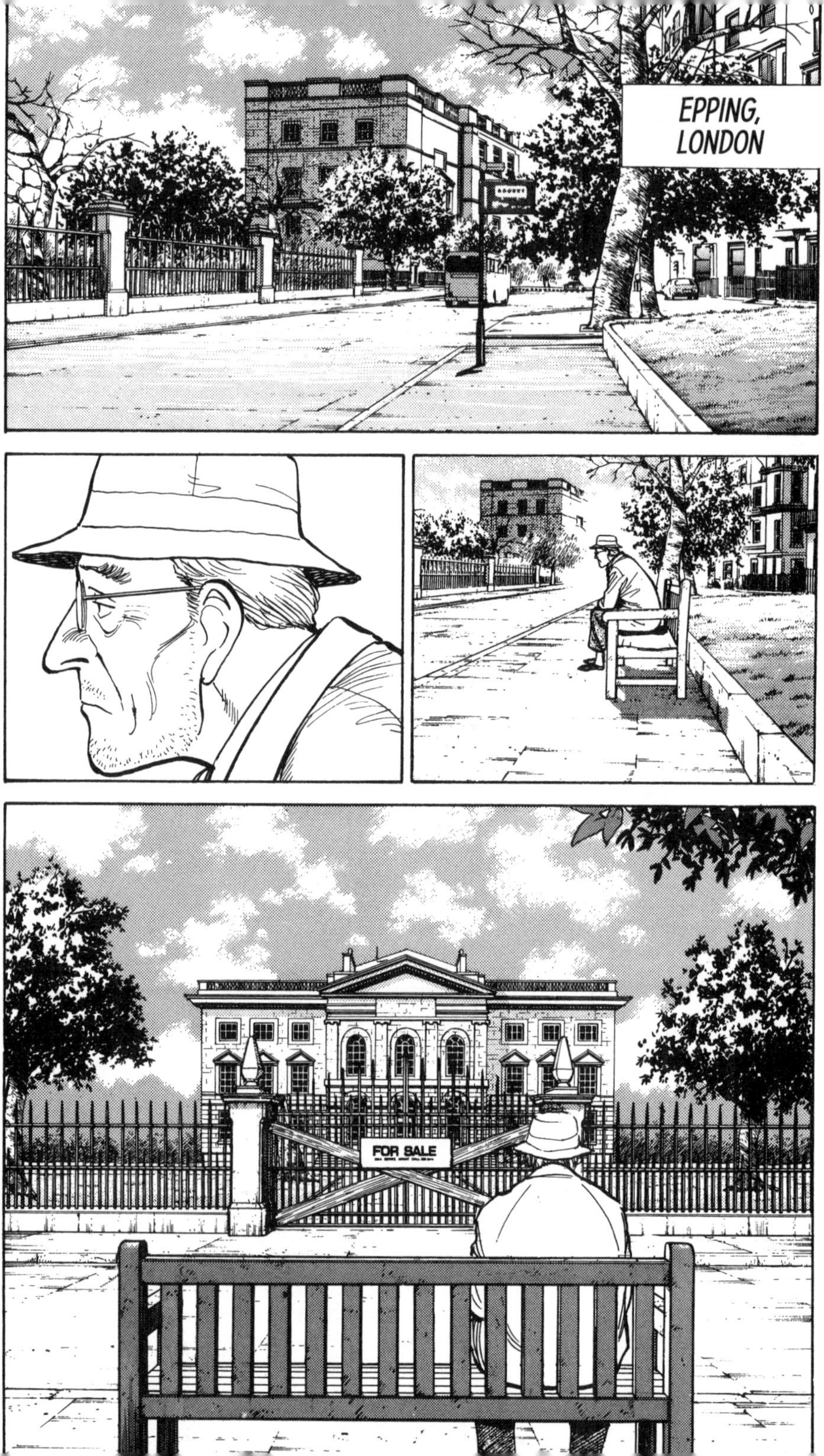
EPPING, LONDON
FOR SALE

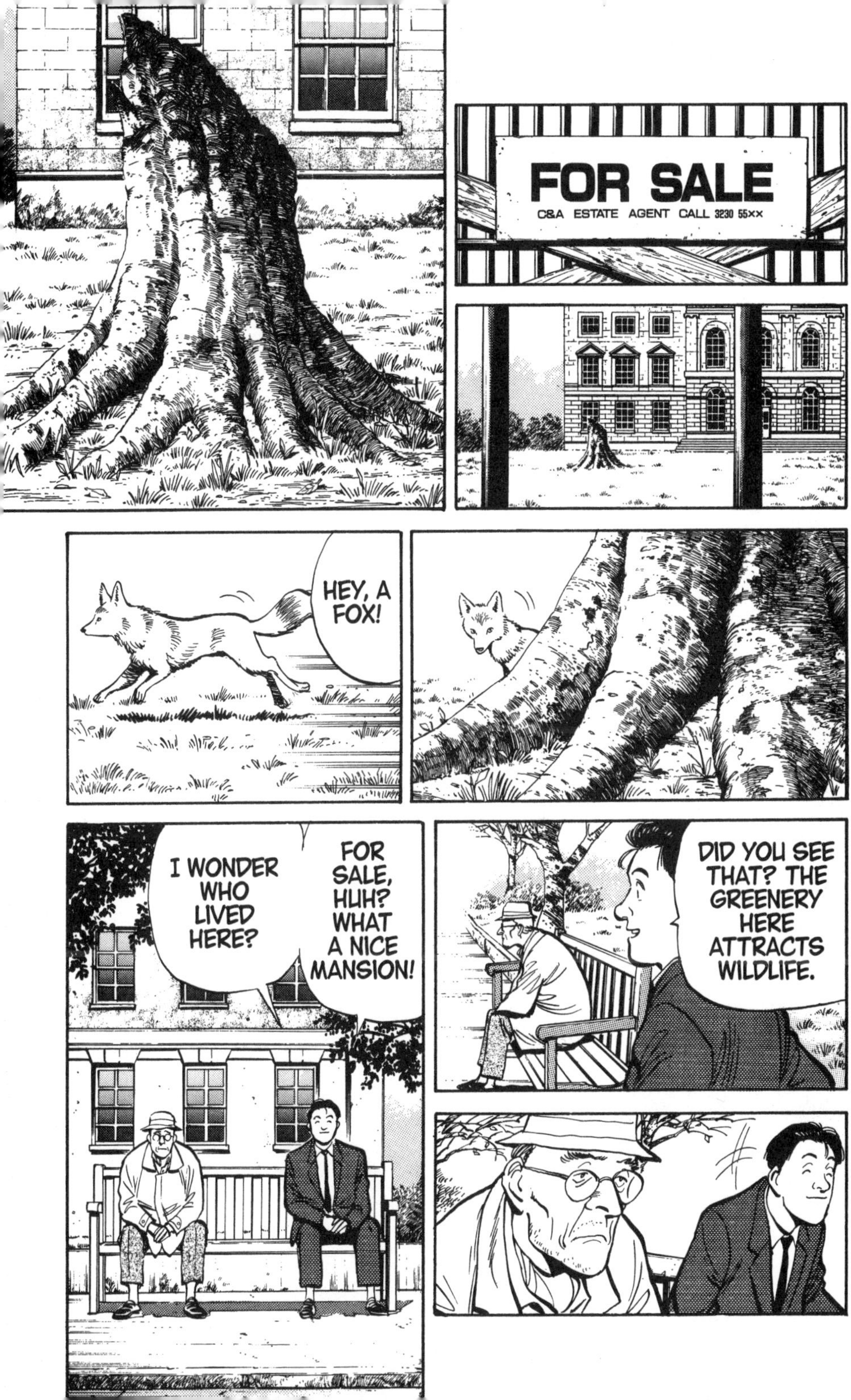
FOR SALE
C&A ESTATE AGENT CALL 3230 55××
HEY, A FOX!
DID YOU SEE THAT? THE GREENERY HERE ATTRACTS WILDLIFE.
FOR SALE, HUH? WHAT A NICE MANSION!
I WONDER WHO LIVED HERE?

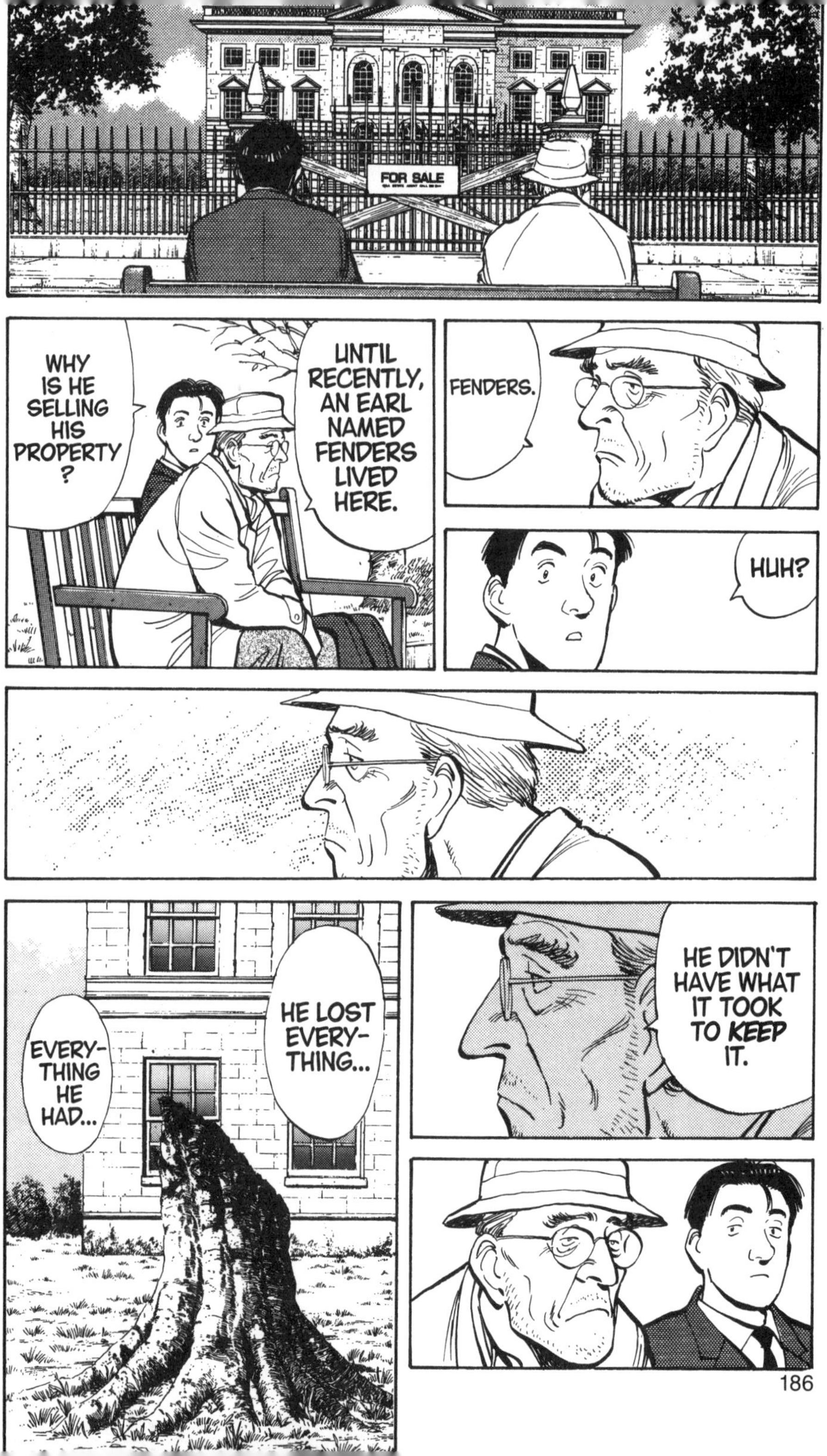

FOR SALE
WHY IS HE SELLING HIS PROPERTY?
UNTIL RECENTLY, AN EARL NAMED FENDERS LIVED HERE.
FENDERS.
HUH?
EVERYTHING HE HAD...
HE LOST EVERYTHING...
HE DIDN'T HAVE WHAT IT TOOK TO KEEP IT.

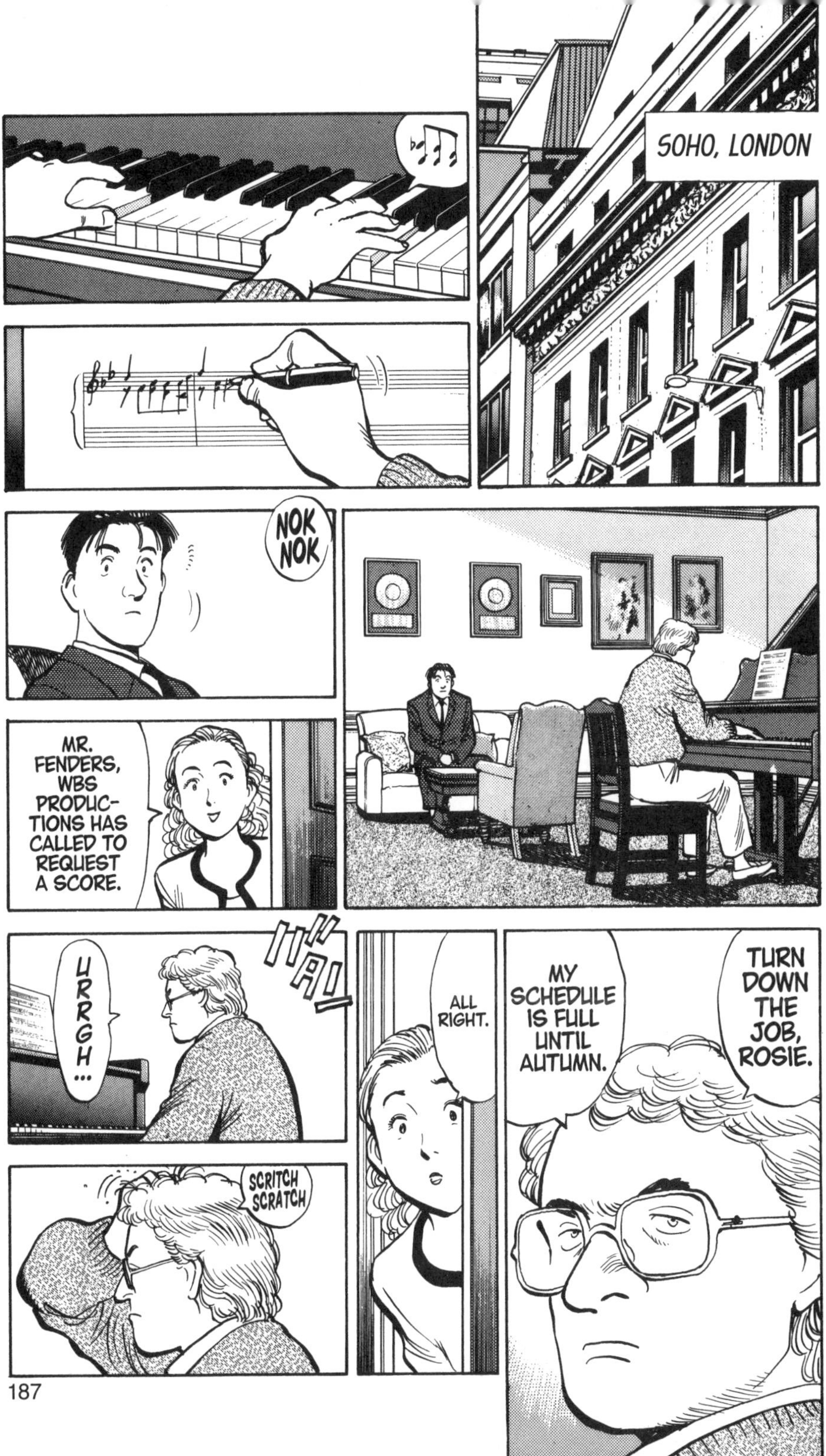
SOHO, LONDON
NOK NOK
MR. FENDERS, WBS PRODUCTIONS HAS CALLED TO REQUEST A SCORE.
TURN DOWN THE JOB, ROSIE.
MY SCHEDULE IS FULL UNTIL AUTUMN.
ALL RIGHT.
URRGH...
SCRITCH SCRATCH

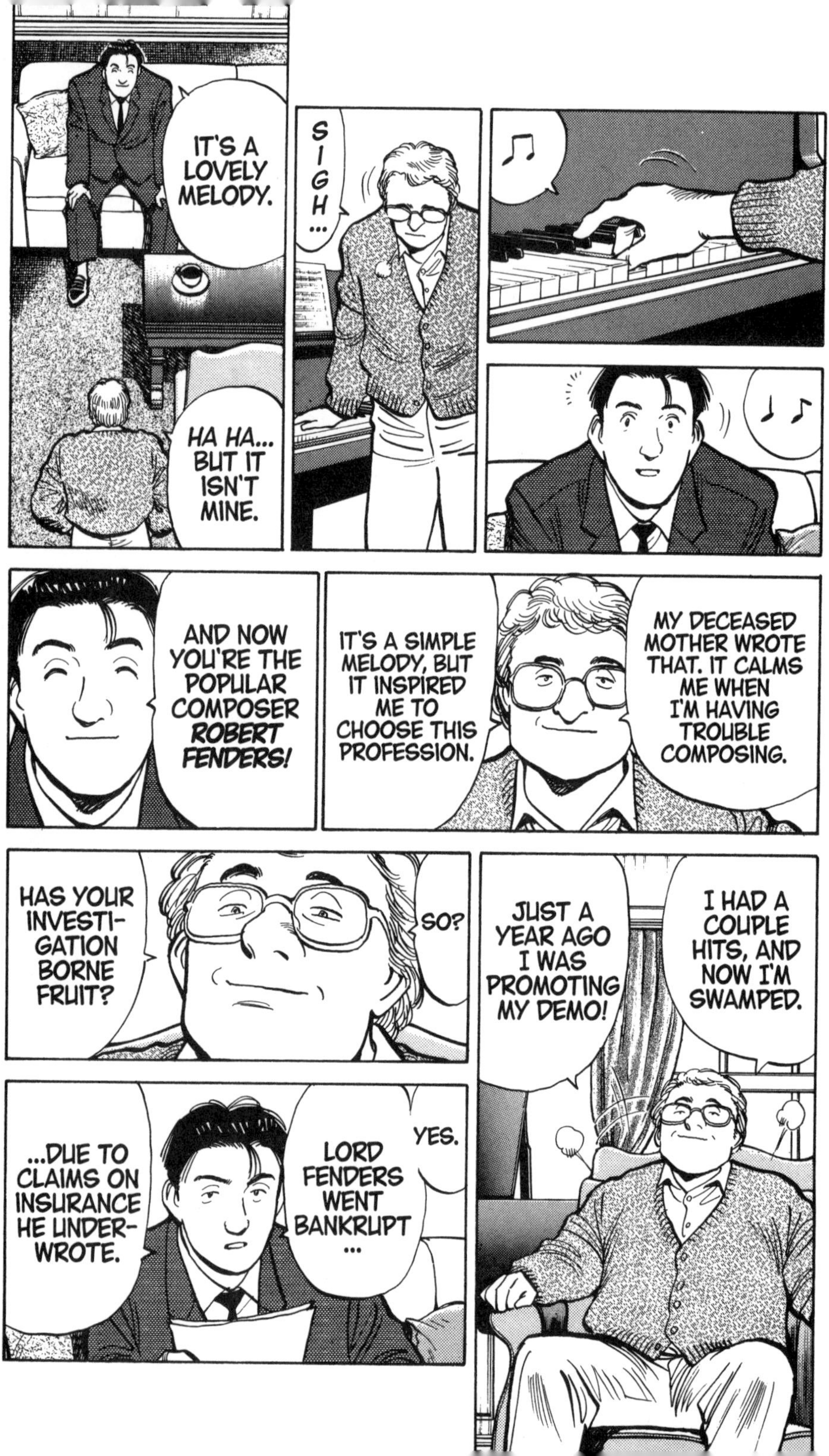
♫
♪ ♪
SIGH...
IT'S A LOVELY MELODY.
HA HA... BUT IT ISN'T MINE.
MY DECEASED MOTHER WROTE THAT. IT CALMS ME WHEN I'M HAVING TROUBLE COMPOSING.
IT'S A SIMPLE MELODY, BUT IT INSPIRED ME TO CHOOSE THIS PROFESSION.
AND NOW YOU'RE THE POPULAR COMPOSER ROBERT FENDERS!
I HAD A COUPLE HITS, AND NOW I'M SWAMPED.
JUST A YEAR AGO I WAS PROMOTING MY DEMO!
SO?
HAS YOUR INVESTI-GATION BORNE FRUIT?
YES.
LORD FENDERS WENT BANKRUPT...
...DUE TO CLAIMS ON INSURANCE HE UNDER-WROTE.

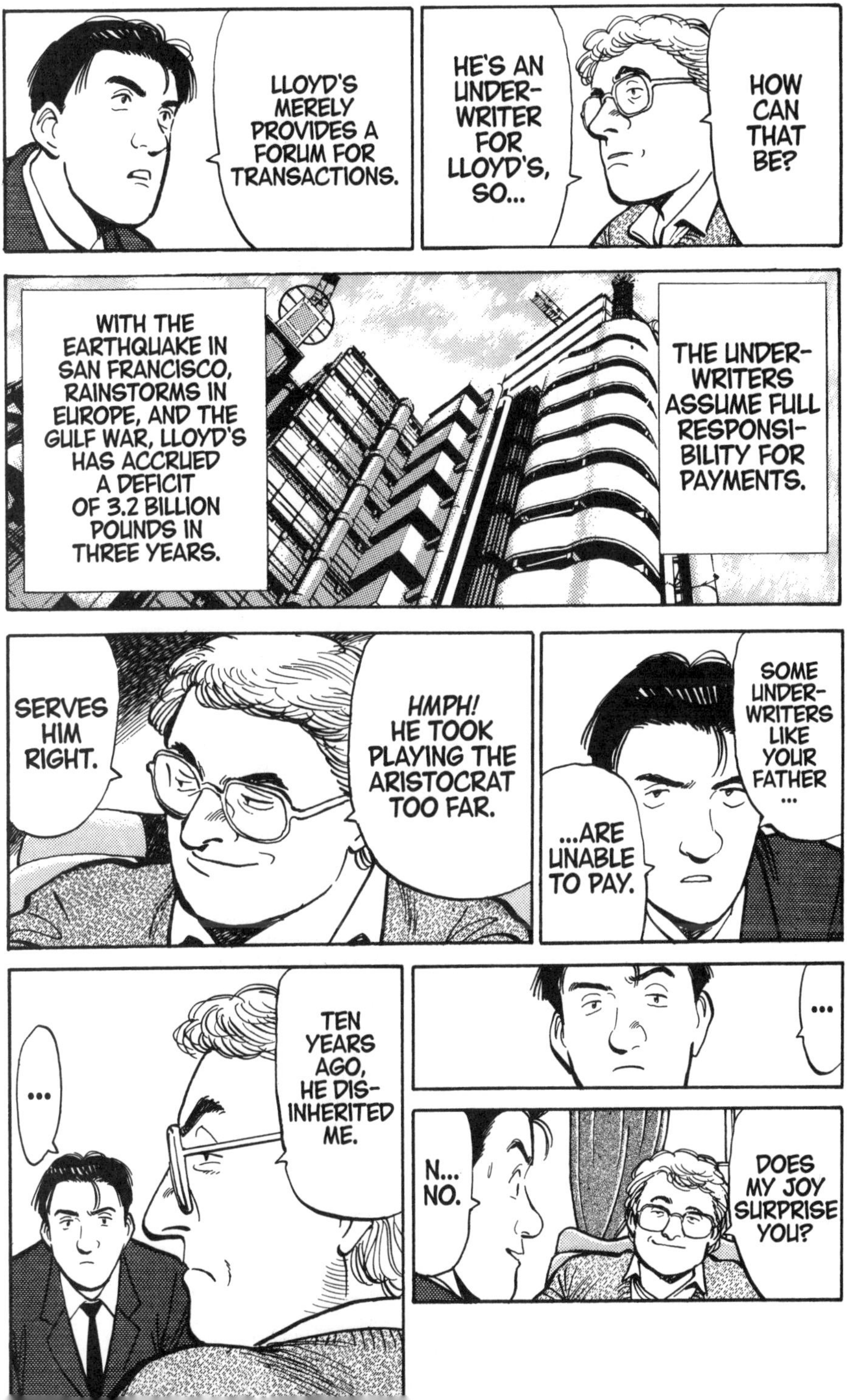
HOW CAN THAT BE?
HE'S AN UNDER-WRITER FOR LLOYD'S, SO...
LLOYD'S MERELY PROVIDES A FORUM FOR TRANSACTIONS.
THE UNDER-WRITERS ASSUME FULL RESPONSI-BILITY FOR PAYMENTS.
WITH THE EARTHQUAKE IN SAN FRANCISCO, RAINSTORMS IN EUROPE, AND THE GULF WAR, LLOYD'S HAS ACCRUED A DEFICIT OF 3.2 BILLION POUNDS IN THREE YEARS.
SOME UNDER-WRITERS LIKE YOUR FATHER ...
...ARE UNABLE TO PAY.
HMPH! HE TOOK PLAYING THE ARISTOCRAT TOO FAR.
SERVES HIM RIGHT.
...
DOES MY JOY SURPRISE YOU?
N... NO.
TEN YEARS AGO, HE DIS-INHERITED ME.
...

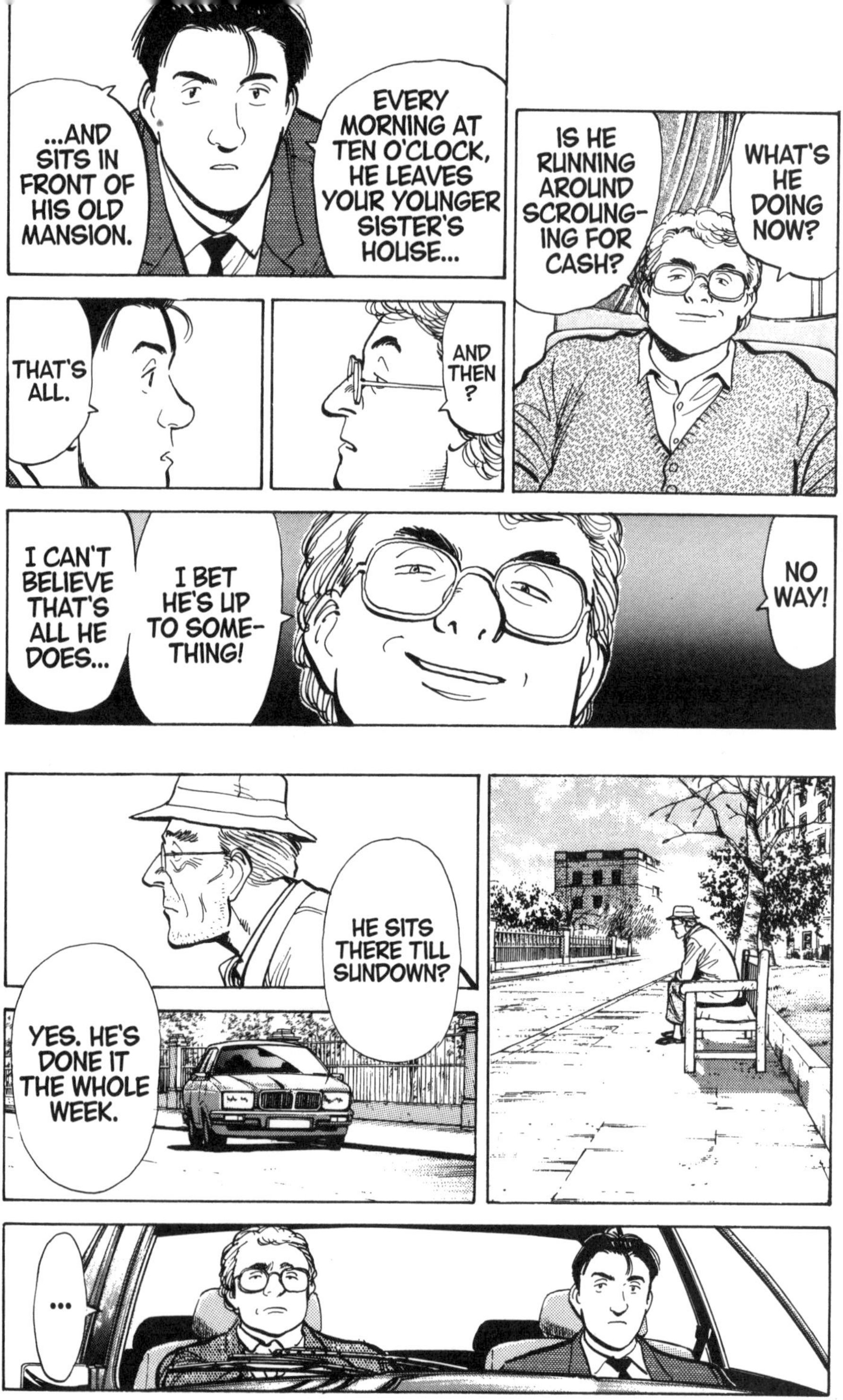
WHAT'S HE DOING NOW?
IS HE RUNNING AROUND SCROUNGING FOR CASH?
EVERY MORNING AT TEN O'CLOCK, HE LEAVES YOUR YOUNGER SISTER'S HOUSE...
...AND SITS IN FRONT OF HIS OLD MANSION.
AND THEN?
THAT'S ALL.
NO WAY!
I BET HE'S UP TO SOMETHING!
I CAN'T BELIEVE THAT'S ALL HE DOES...
HE SITS THERE TILL SUNDOWN?
YES. HE'S DONE IT THE WHOLE WEEK.
...

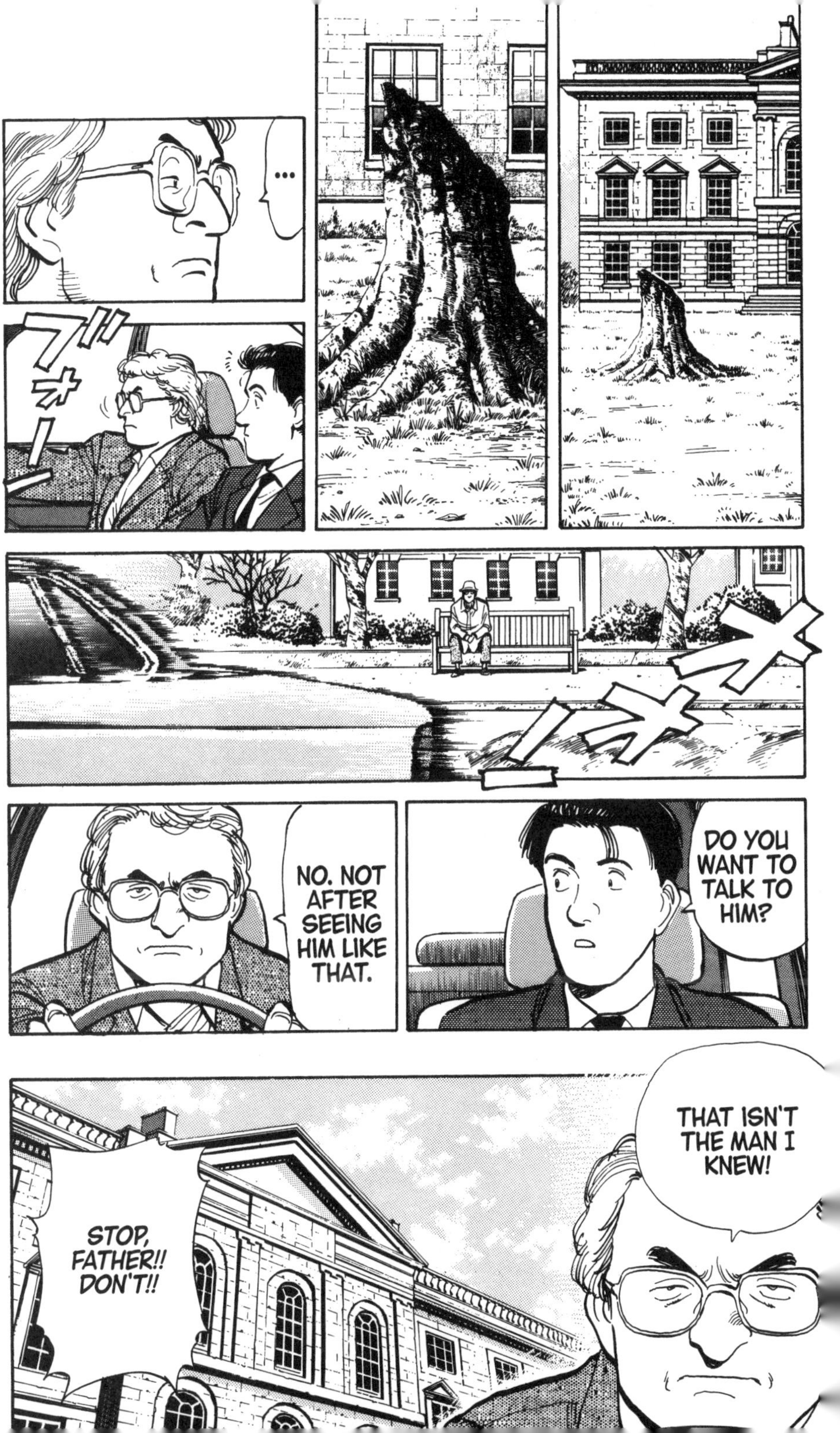
...
ブォー
DO YOU WANT TO TALK TO HIM?
NO. NOT AFTER SEEING HIM LIKE THAT.
THAT ISN'T THE MAN I KNEW!
STOP, FATHER!! DON'T!!

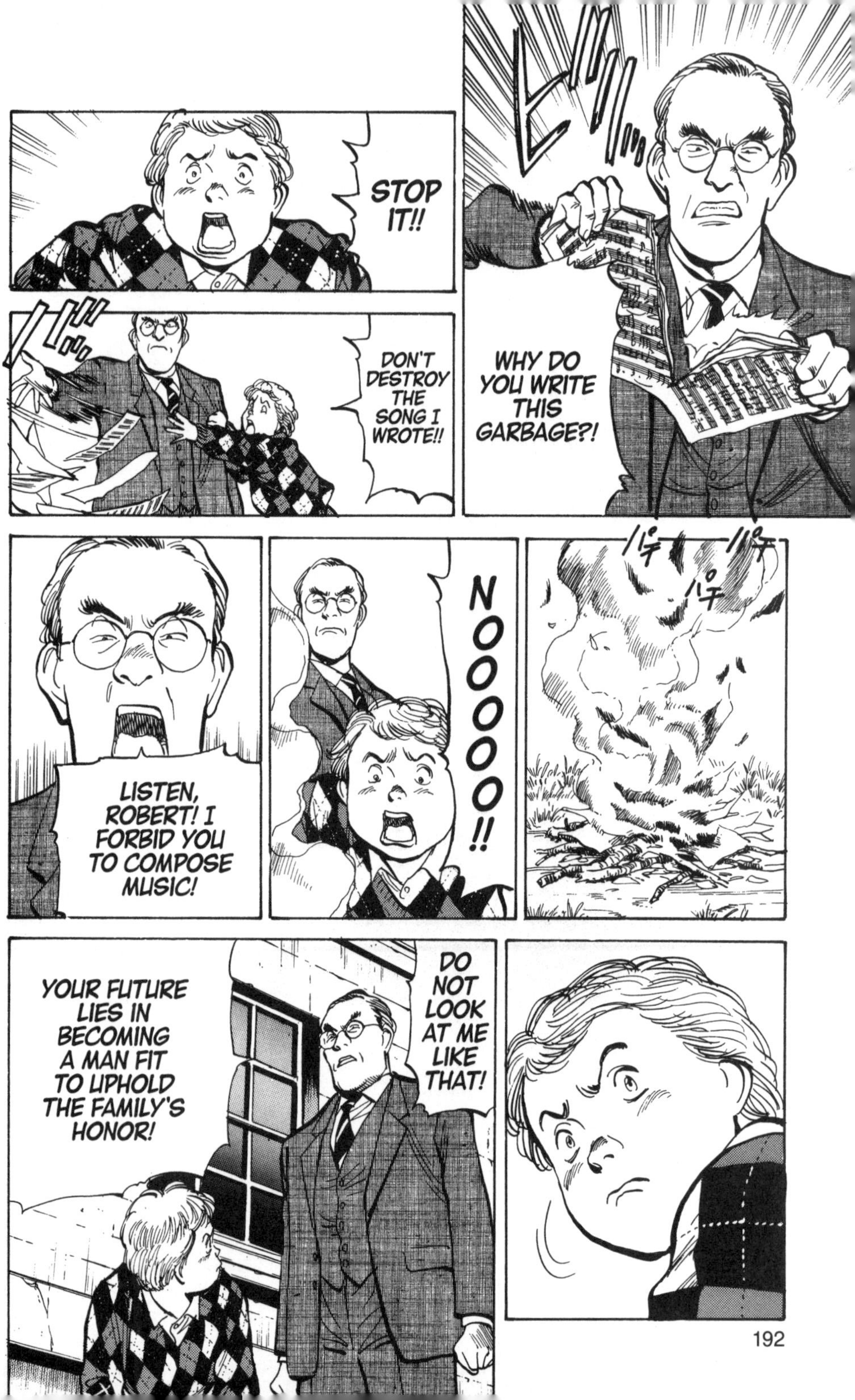
WHY DO YOU WRITE THIS GARBAGE?!
STOP IT!!
DON'T DESTROY THE SONG I WROTE!!
パチ パチ パチ
NOOOOOO!!
LISTEN, ROBERT! I FORBID YOU TO COMPOSE MUSIC!
DO NOT LOOK AT ME LIKE THAT!
YOUR FUTURE LIES IN BECOMING A MAN FIT TO UPHOLD THE FAMILY'S HONOR!

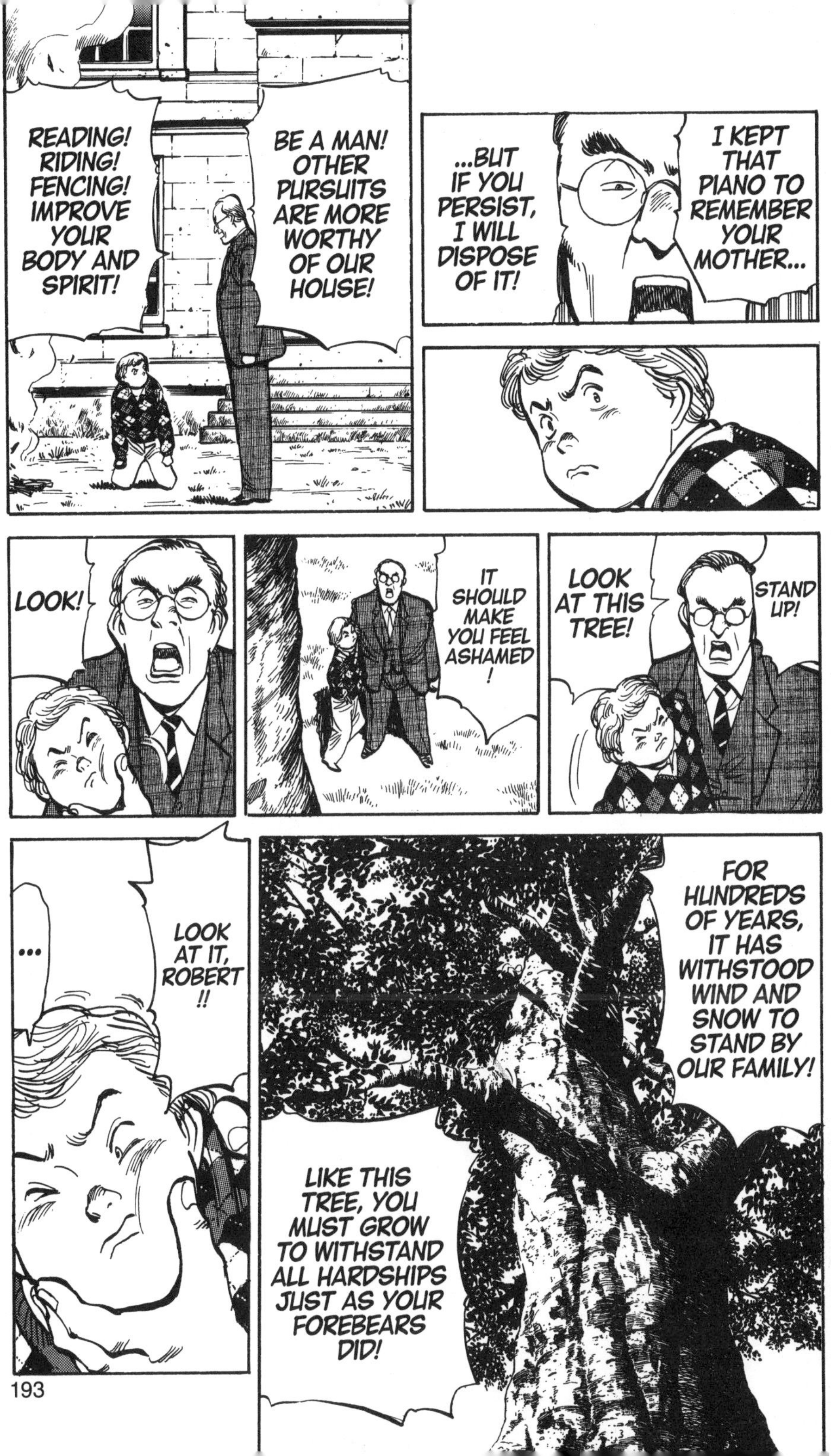
I KEPT THAT PIANO TO REMEMBER YOUR MOTHER...
...BUT IF YOU PERSIST, I WILL DISPOSE OF IT!
BE A MAN! OTHER PURSUITS ARE MORE WORTHY OF OUR HOUSE!
READING! RIDING! FENCING! IMPROVE YOUR BODY AND SPIRIT!
STAND UP!
LOOK AT THIS TREE!
IT SHOULD MAKE YOU FEEL ASHAMED!
LOOK!
FOR HUNDREDS OF YEARS, IT HAS WITHSTOOD WIND AND SNOW TO STAND BY OUR FAMILY!
LIKE THIS TREE, YOU MUST GROW TO WITHSTAND ALL HARDSHIPS JUST AS YOUR FOREBEARS DID!
LOOK AT IT, ROBERT!!
...

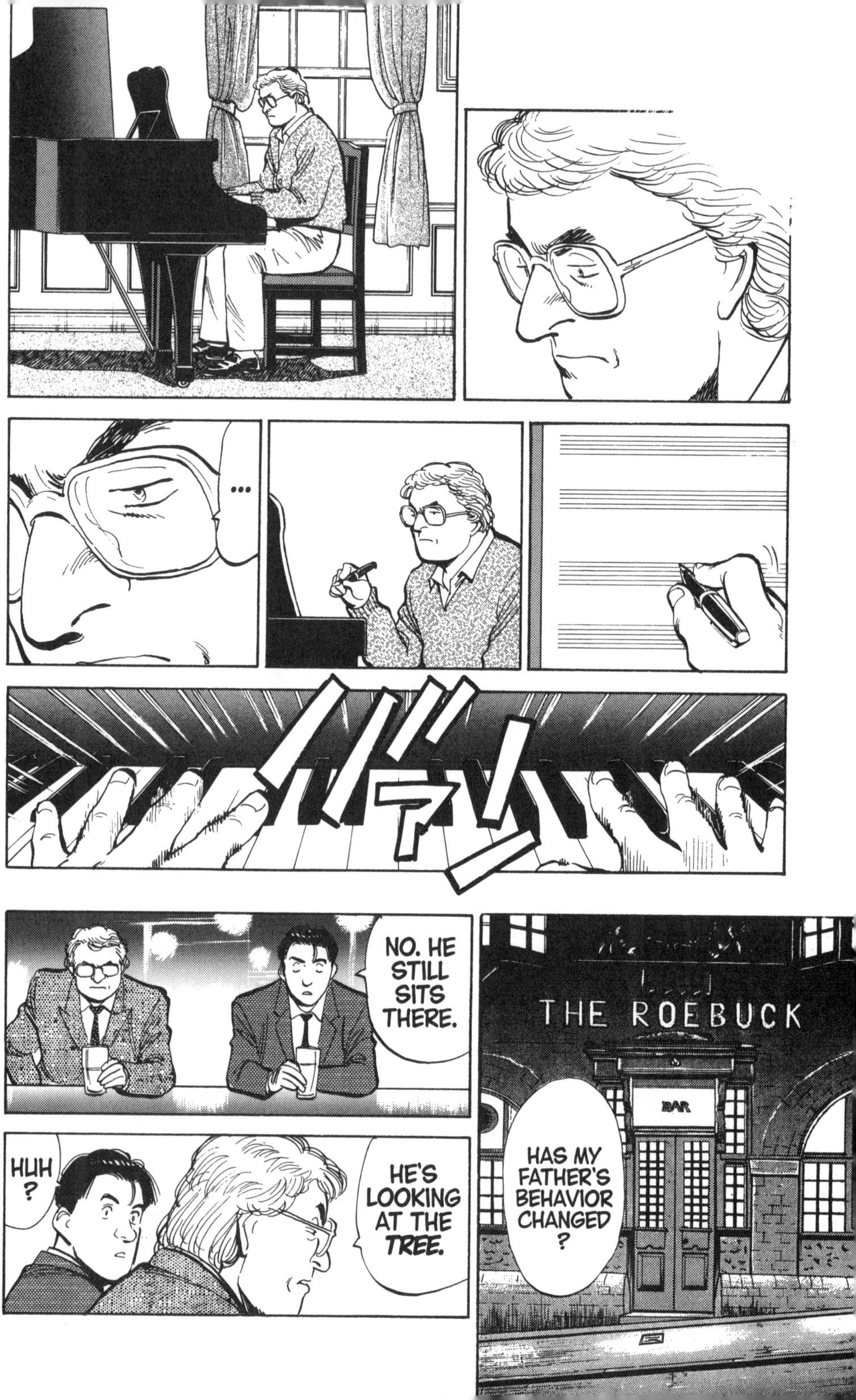
...
バアン
THE ROEBUCK
BAR
HAS MY FATHER'S BEHAVIOR CHANGED?
NO. HE STILL SITS THERE.
HE'S LOOKING AT THE TREE.
HUH?

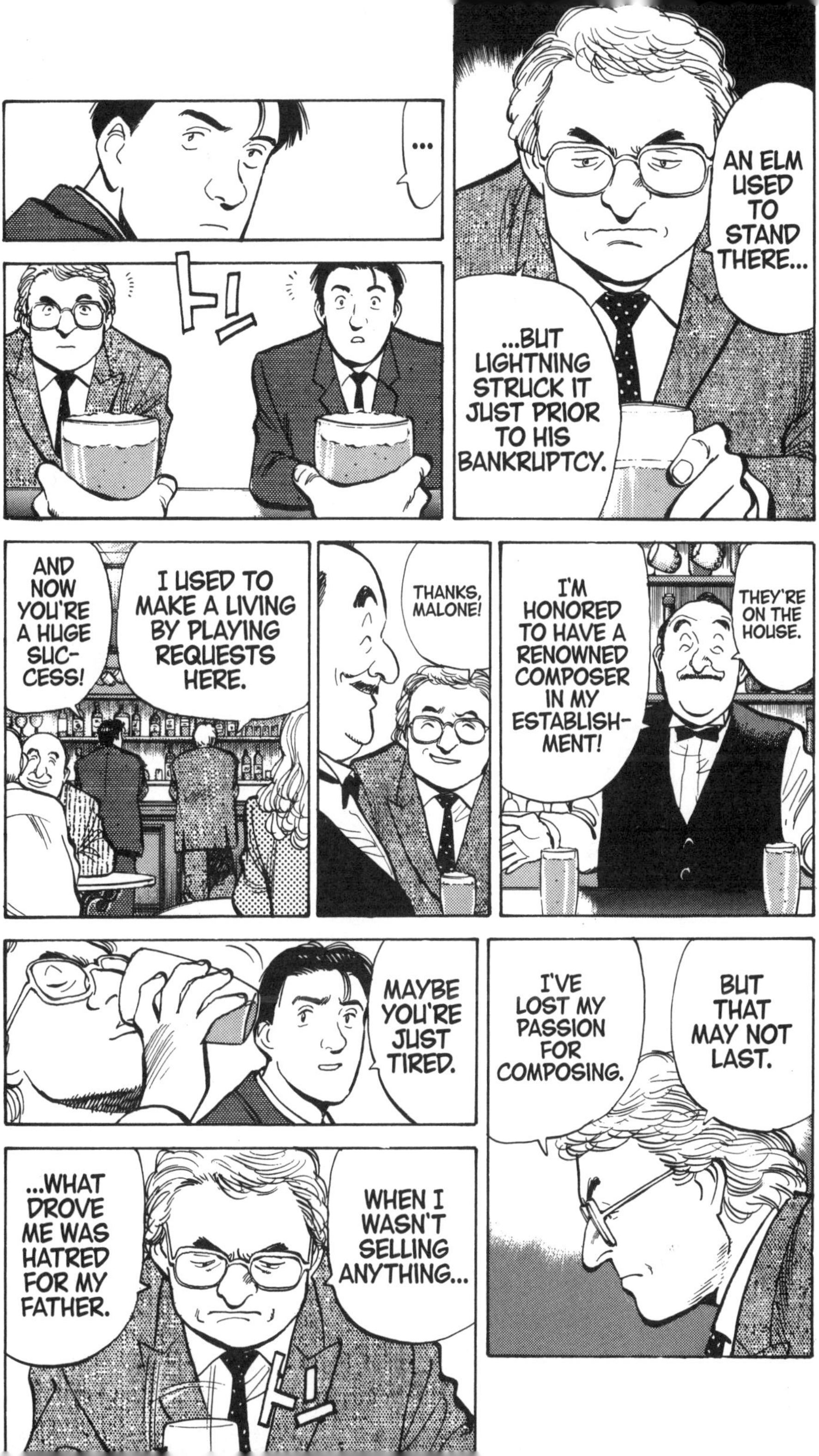
AN ELM USED TO STAND THERE...
...BUT LIGHTNING STRUCK IT JUST PRIOR TO HIS BANKRUPTCY.
...
THEY'RE ON THE HOUSE.
I'M HONORED TO HAVE A RENOWNED COMPOSER IN MY ESTABLISH-MENT!
THANKS, MALONE!
I USED TO MAKE A LIVING BY PLAYING REQUESTS HERE.
AND NOW YOU'RE A HUGE SUC-CESS!
BUT THAT MAY NOT LAST.
I'VE LOST MY PASSION FOR COMPOSING.
MAYBE YOU'RE JUST TIRED.
WHEN I WASN'T SELLING ANYTHING...
...WHAT DROVE ME WAS HATRED FOR MY FATHER.

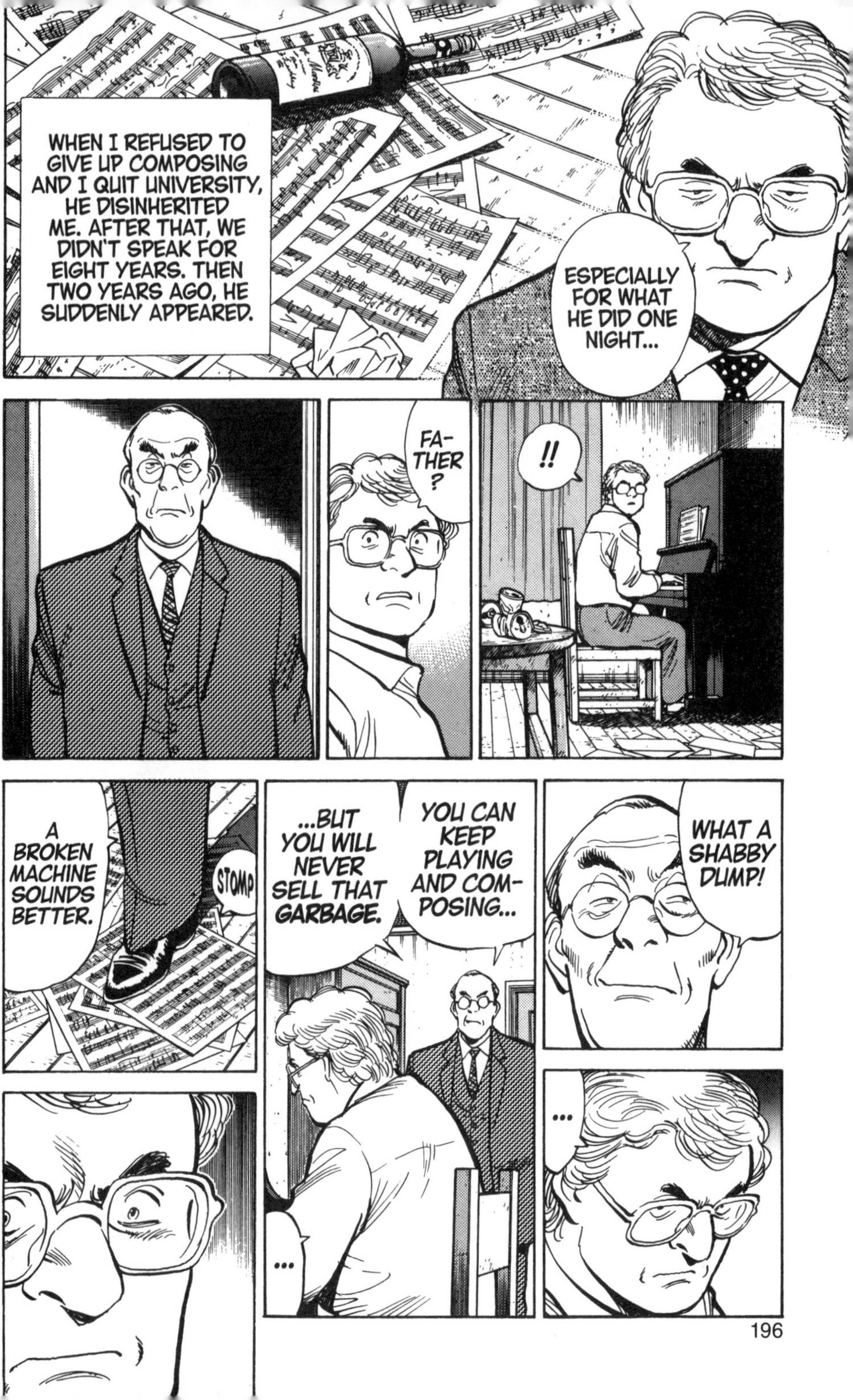
ESPECIALLY FOR WHAT HE DID ONE NIGHT...
WHEN I REFUSED TO GIVE UP COMPOSING AND I QUIT UNIVERSITY, HE DISINHERITED ME. AFTER THAT, WE DIDN'T SPEAK FOR EIGHT YEARS. THEN TWO YEARS AGO, HE SUDDENLY APPEARED.
!!
FA-THER?
WHAT A SHABBY DUMP!
...
YOU CAN KEEP PLAYING AND COM-POSING...
...BUT YOU WILL NEVER SELL THAT GARBAGE.
...
STOMP
A BROKEN MACHINE SOUNDS BETTER.

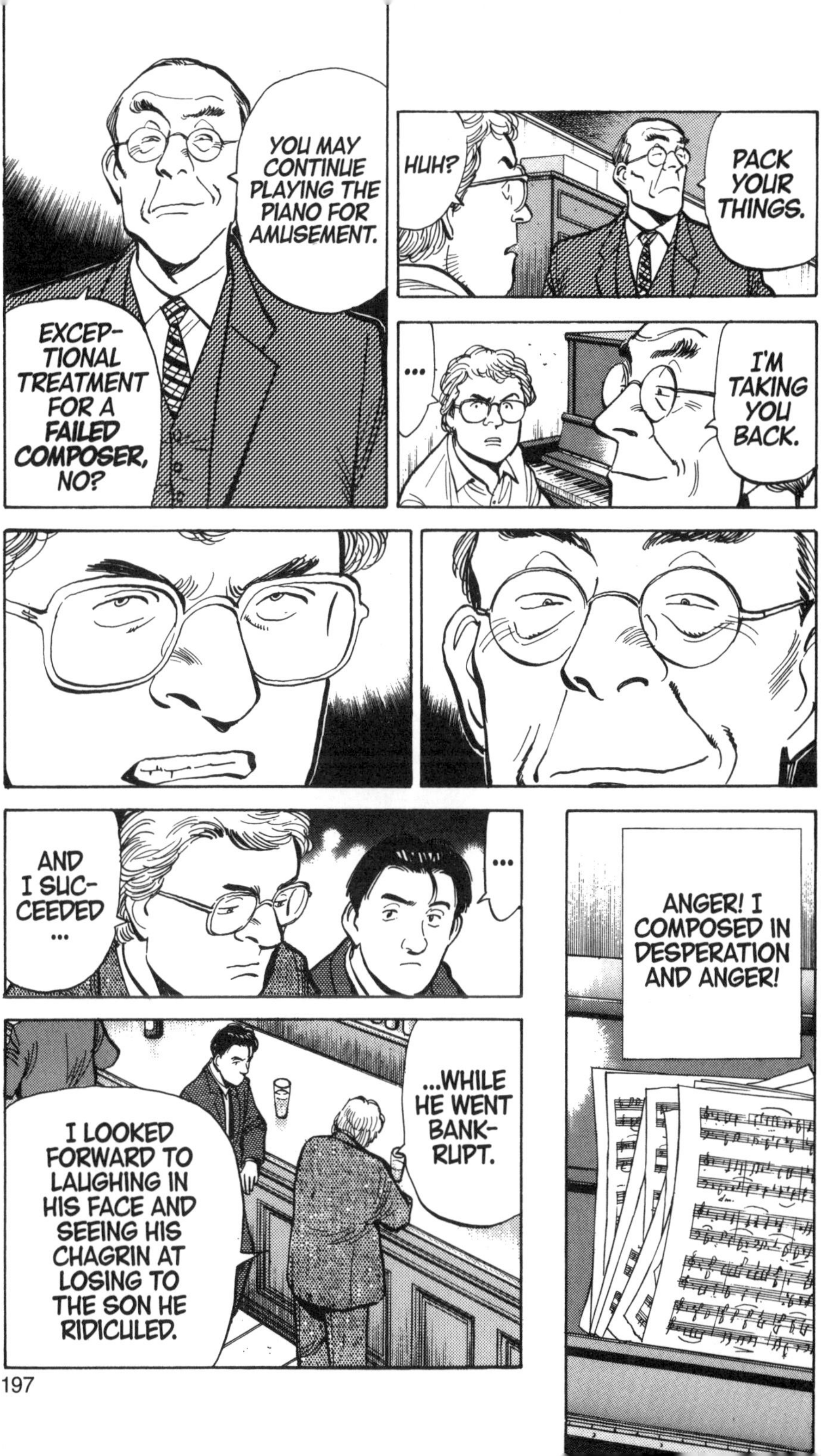
PACK YOUR THINGS.
HUH?
I'M TAKING YOU BACK.
...
YOU MAY CONTINUE PLAYING THE PIANO FOR AMUSEMENT.
EXCEP-TIONAL TREATMENT FOR A FAILED COMPOSER, NO?
ANGER! I COMPOSED IN DESPERATION AND ANGER!
...
AND I SUC-CEEDED ...
...WHILE HE WENT BANK-RUPT.
I LOOKED FORWARD TO LAUGHING IN HIS FACE AND SEEING HIS CHAGRIN AT LOSING TO THE SON HE RIDICULED.

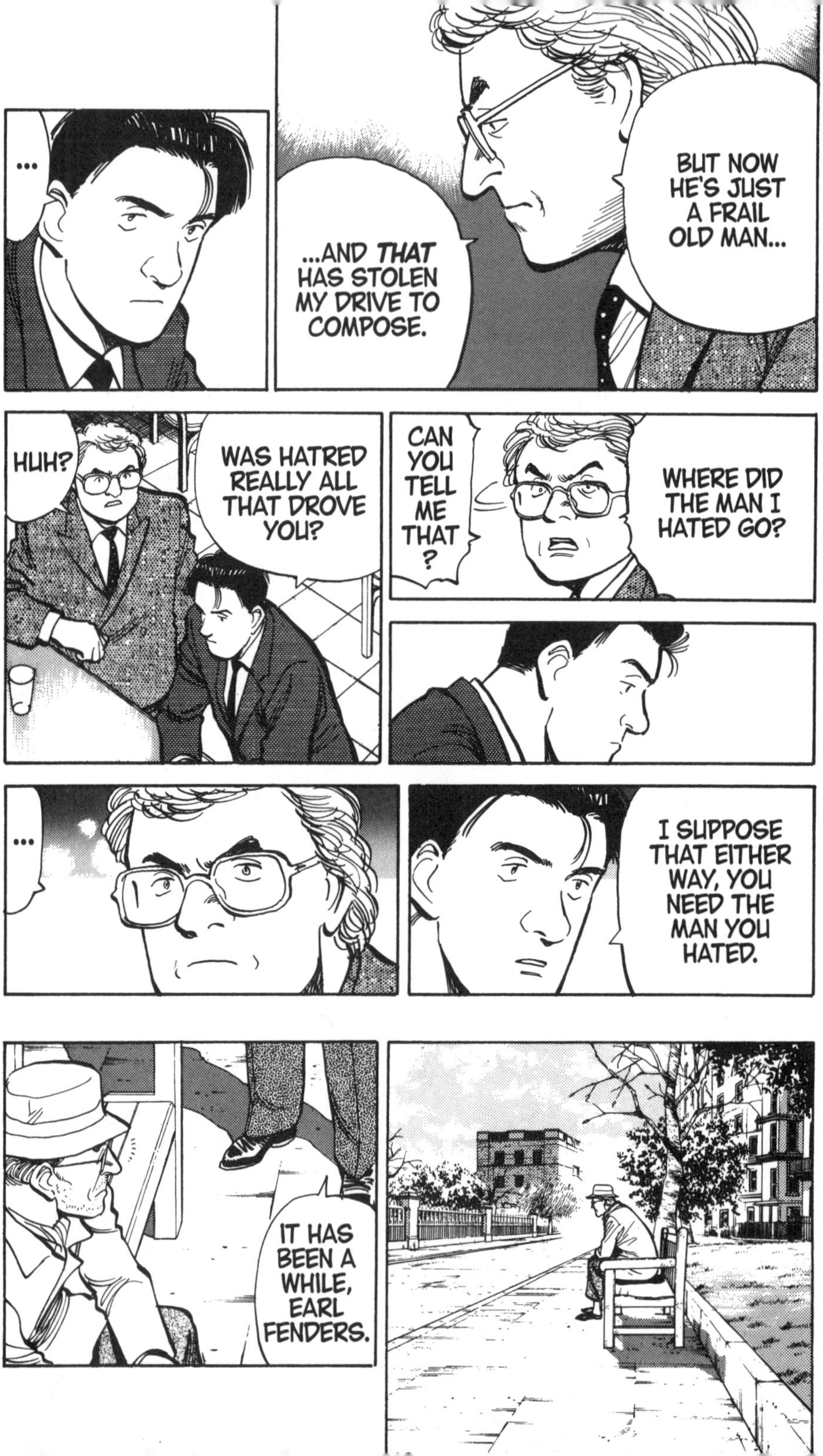
BUT NOW HE'S JUST A FRAIL OLD MAN...
...AND *THAT* HAS STOLEN MY DRIVE TO COMPOSE.
...
WHERE DID THE MAN I HATED GO?
CAN YOU TELL ME THAT?
WAS HATRED REALLY ALL THAT DROVE YOU?
HUH?
I SUPPOSE THAT EITHER WAY, YOU NEED THE MAN YOU HATED.
...
IT HAS BEEN A WHILE, EARL FENDERS.

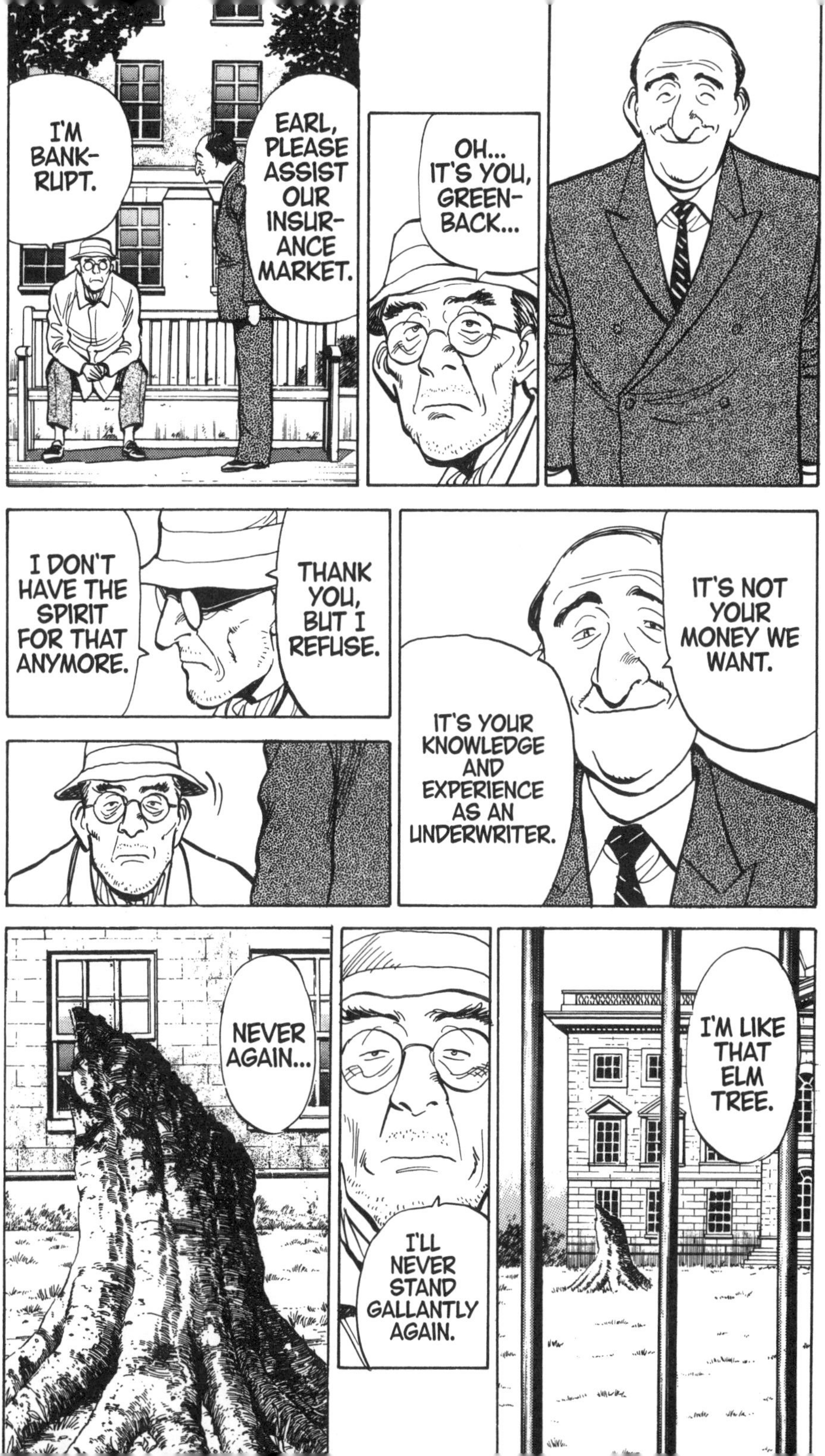
OH... IT'S YOU, GREEN-BACK...
EARL, PLEASE ASSIST OUR INSURANCE MARKET.
I'M BANKRUPT.
IT'S NOT YOUR MONEY WE WANT.
IT'S YOUR KNOWLEDGE AND EXPERIENCE AS AN UNDERWRITER.
THANK YOU, BUT I REFUSE.
I DON'T HAVE THE SPIRIT FOR THAT ANYMORE.
I'M LIKE THAT ELM TREE.
I'LL NEVER STAND GALLANTLY AGAIN.
NEVER AGAIN...

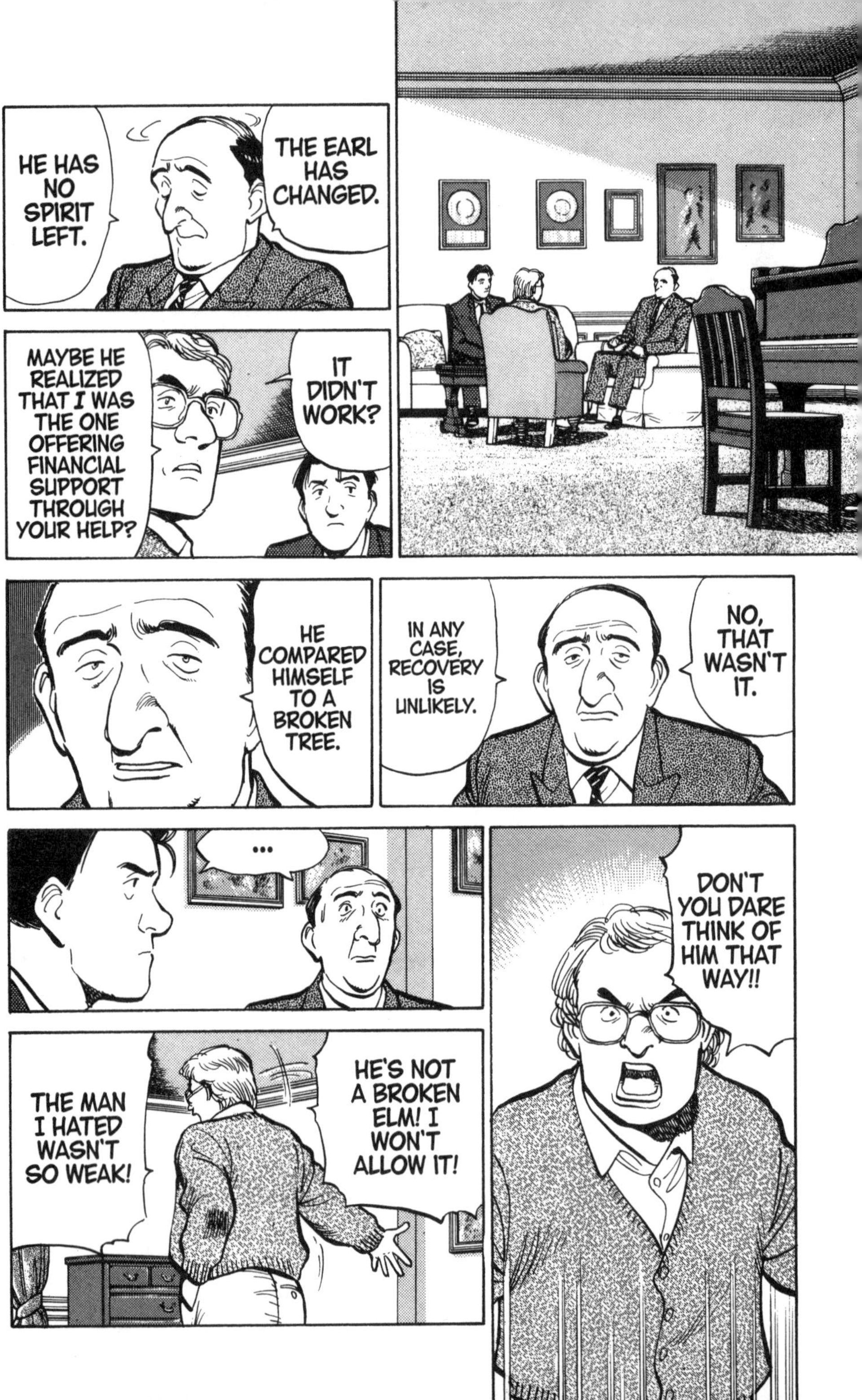
THE EARL HAS CHANGED.
HE HAS NO SPIRIT LEFT.
IT DIDN'T WORK?
MAYBE HE REALIZED THAT I WAS THE ONE OFFERING FINANCIAL SUPPORT THROUGH YOUR HELP?
NO, THAT WASN'T IT.
IN ANY CASE, RECOVERY IS UNLIKELY.
HE COMPARED HIMSELF TO A BROKEN TREE.
DON'T YOU DARE THINK OF HIM THAT WAY!!
...
HE'S NOT A BROKEN ELM! I WON'T ALLOW IT!
THE MAN I HATED WASN'T SO WEAK!

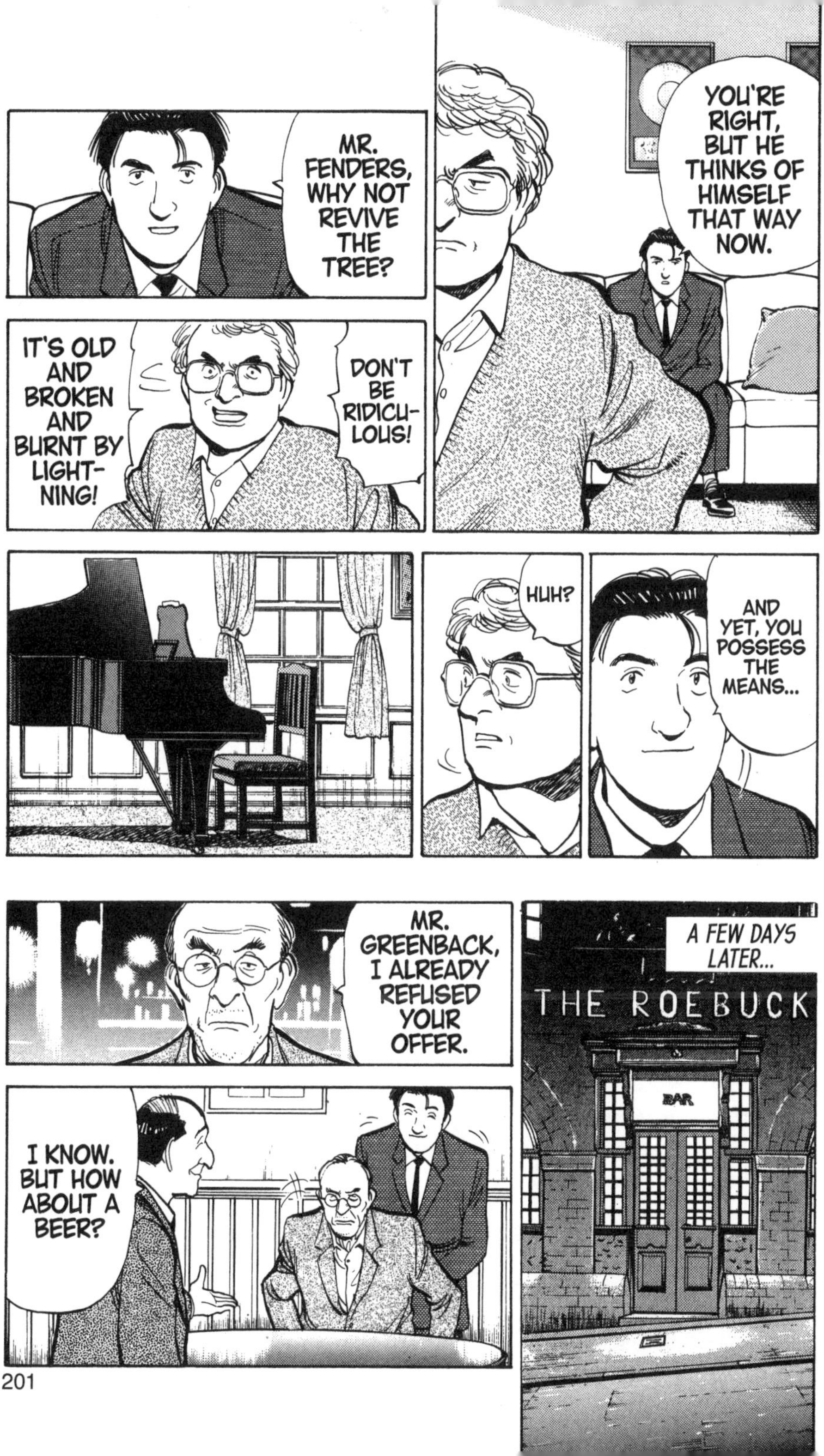
YOU'RE RIGHT, BUT HE THINKS OF HIMSELF THAT WAY NOW.
MR. FENDERS, WHY NOT REVIVE THE TREE?
DON'T BE RIDICULOUS!
IT'S OLD AND BROKEN AND BURNT BY LIGHT-NING!
AND YET, YOU POSSESS THE MEANS...
HUH?
A FEW DAYS LATER...
THE ROEBUCK
BAR
MR. GREENBACK, I ALREADY REFUSED YOUR OFFER.
I KNOW. BUT HOW ABOUT A BEER?

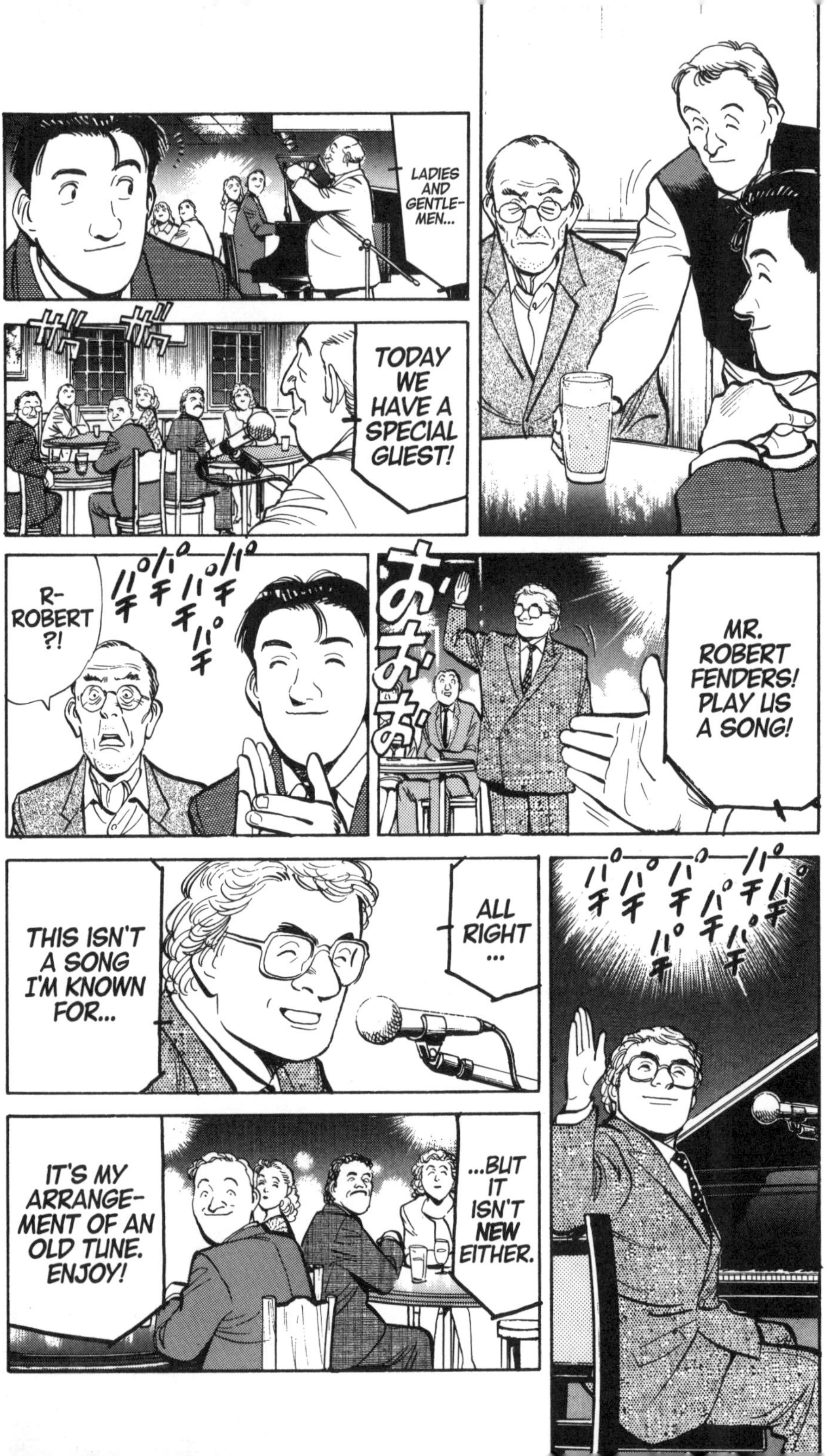
LADIES AND GENTLEMEN...
ザワ ザワ
TODAY WE HAVE A SPECIAL GUEST!
MR. ROBERT FENDERS! PLAY US A SONG!
おおお
R-ROBERT?!
パチパチパチパチパチ
パチパチパチパチパチパチ
ALL RIGHT...
THIS ISN'T A SONG I'M KNOWN FOR...
...BUT IT ISN'T NEW EITHER.
IT'S MY ARRANGEMENT OF AN OLD TUNE. ENJOY!

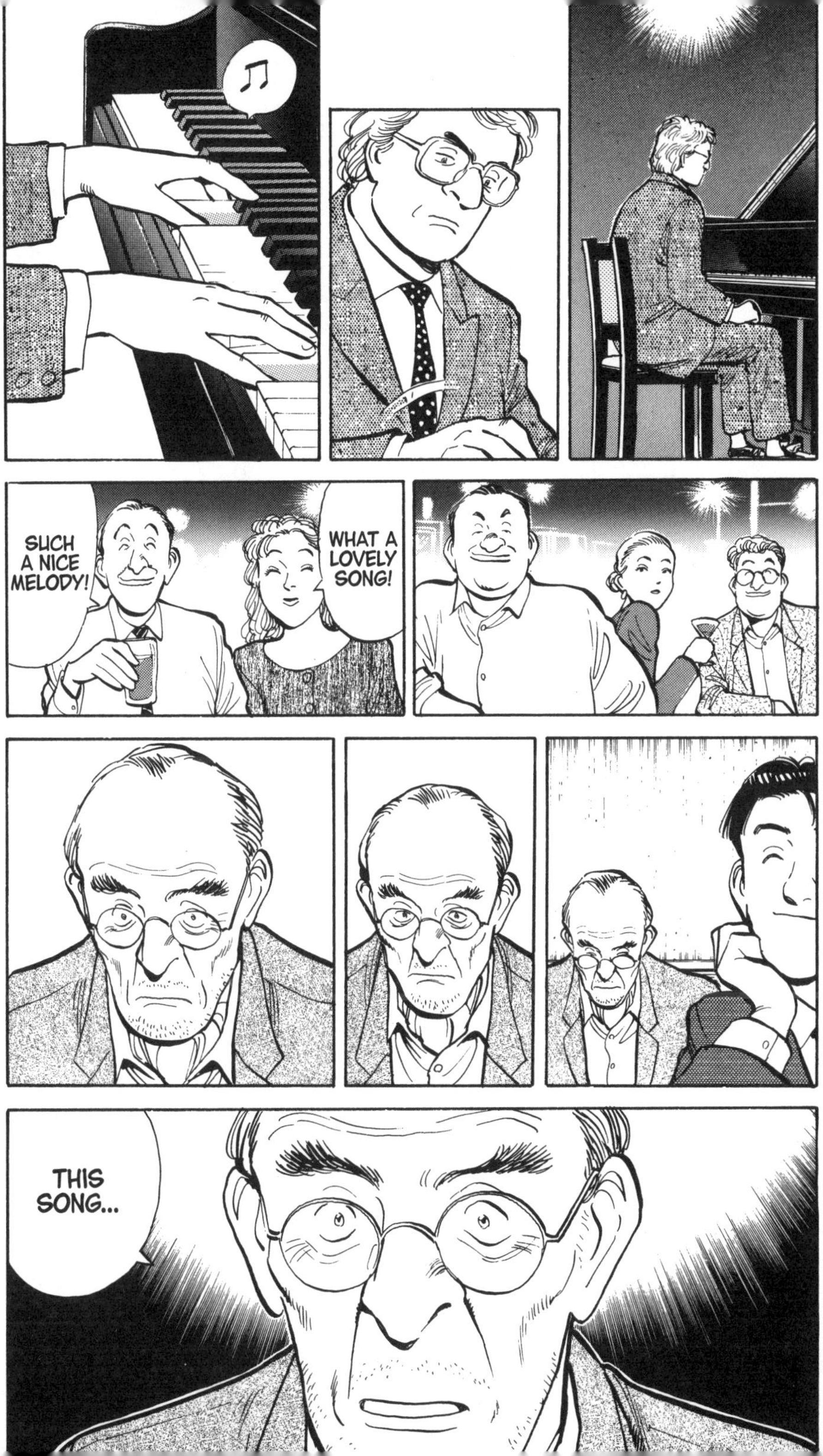
WHAT A LOVELY SONG!
SUCH A NICE MELODY!
THIS SONG...

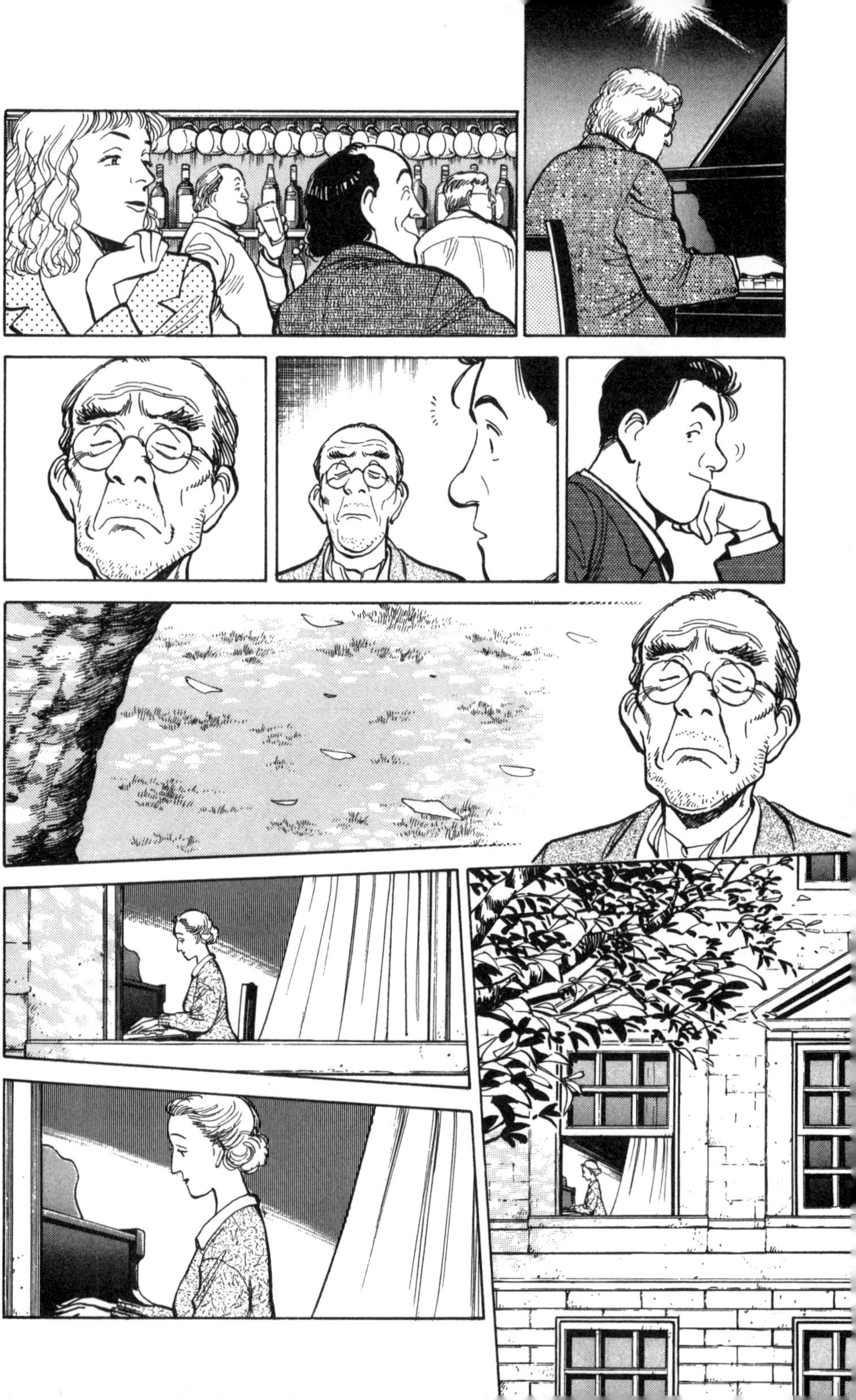

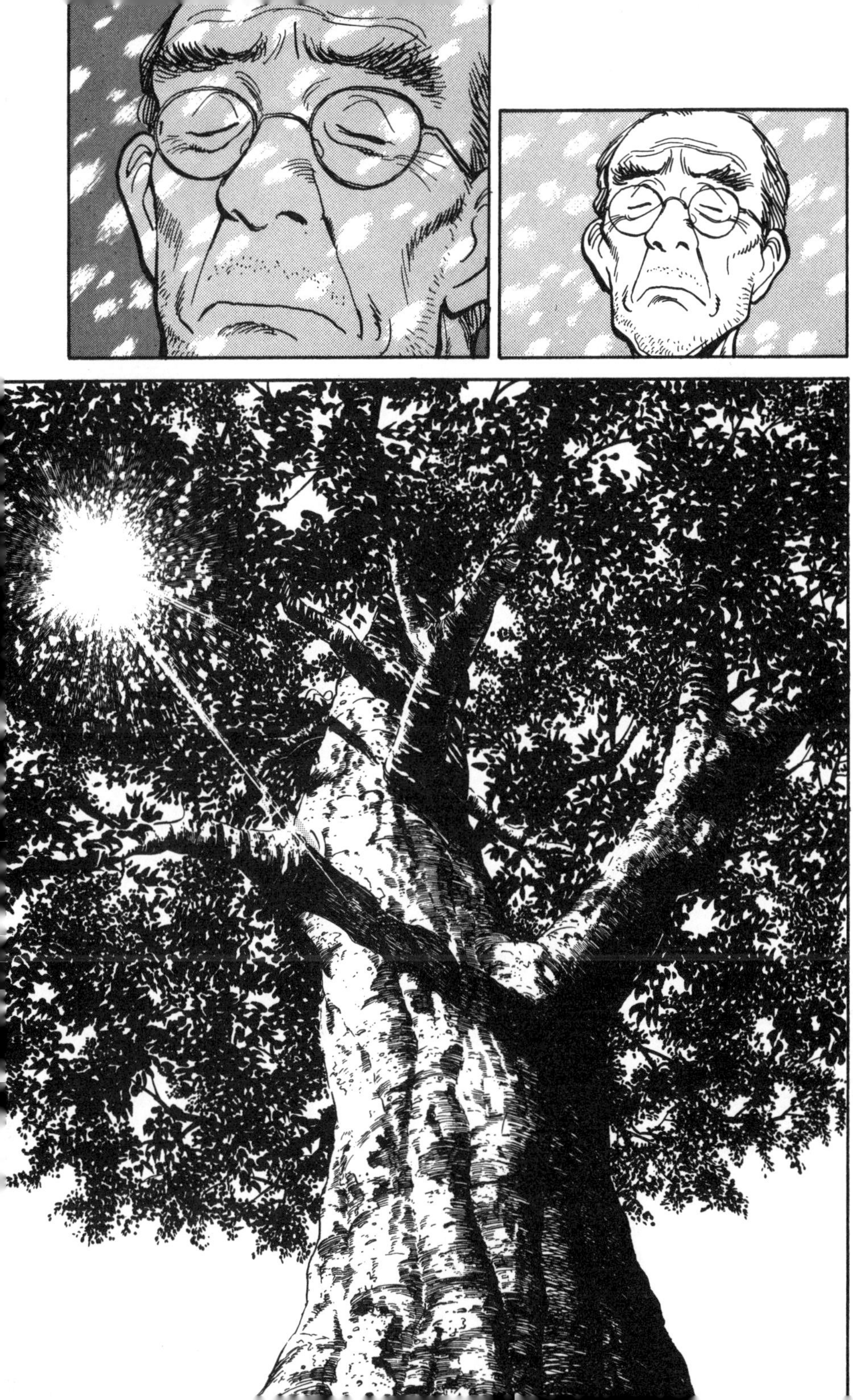

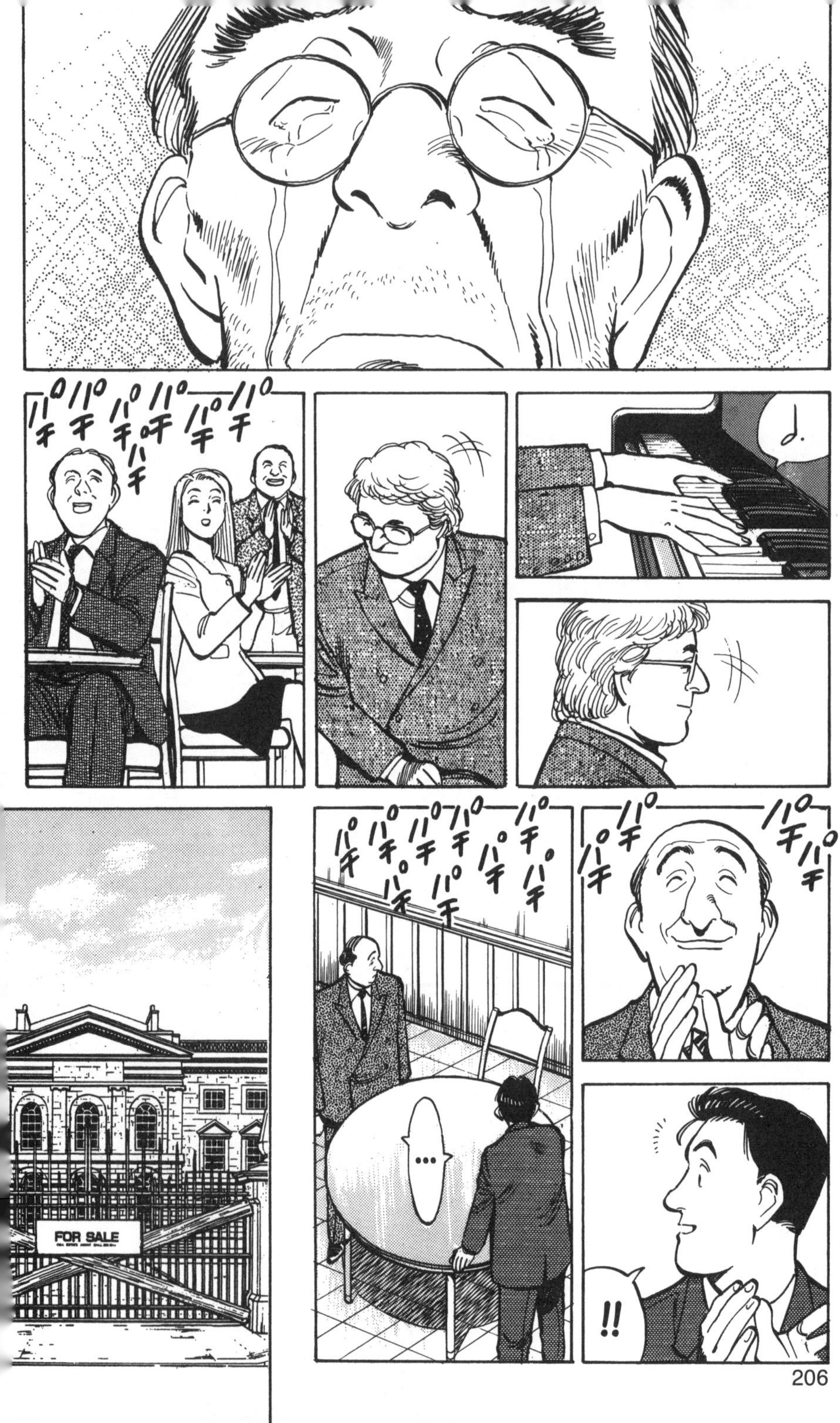
♪
パチパチパチパチ
パチパチパチパチ
パチパチ
パチパチ
!!
...
パチパチパチパチパチパチパチパチパチパチ
FOR SALE

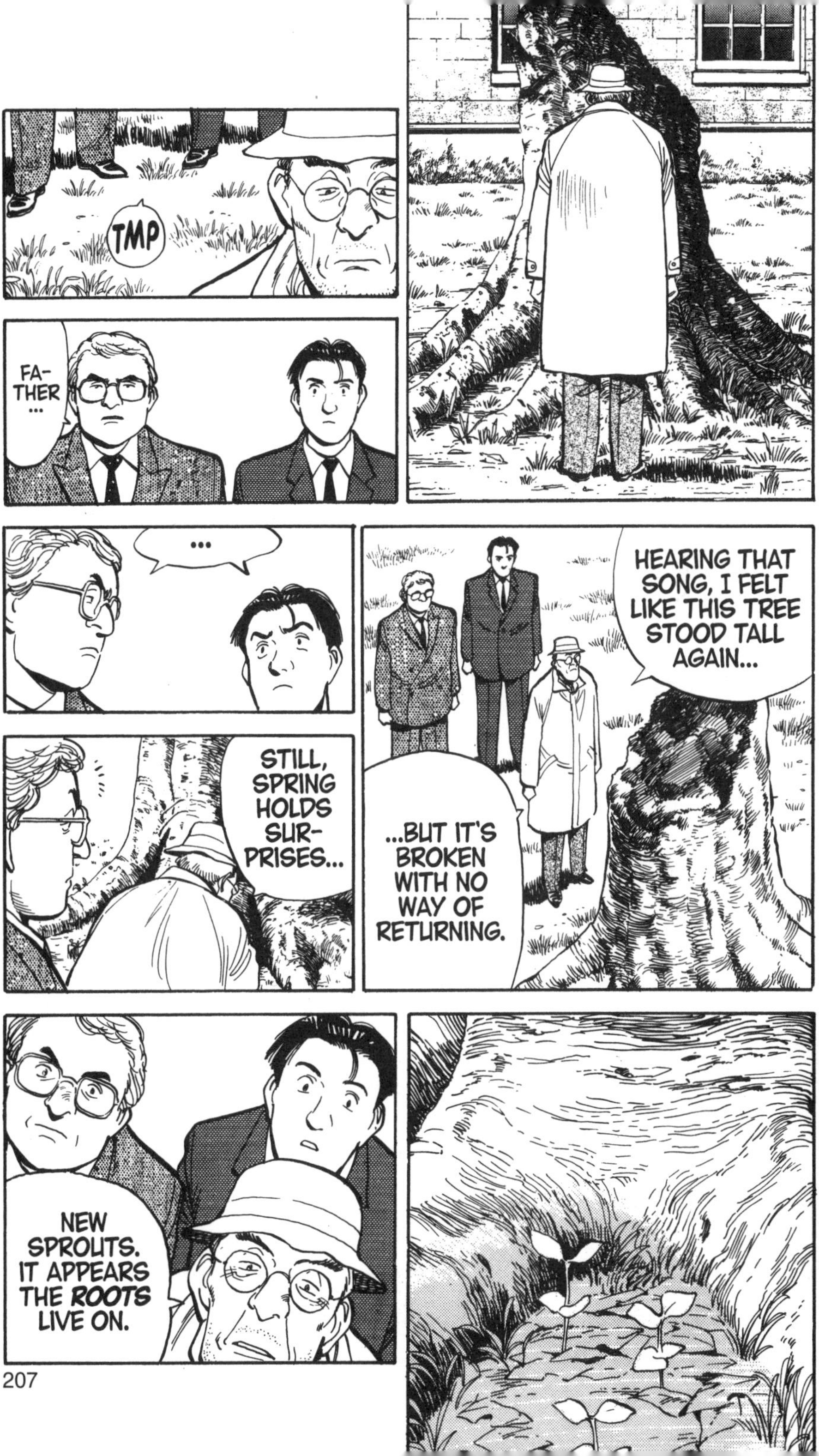
TMP
FA-THER ...
HEARING THAT SONG, I FELT LIKE THIS TREE STOOD TALL AGAIN...
...BUT IT'S BROKEN WITH NO WAY OF RETURNING.
...
STILL, SPRING HOLDS SUR-PRISES...
NEW SPROUTS. IT APPEARS THE *ROOTS* LIVE ON.

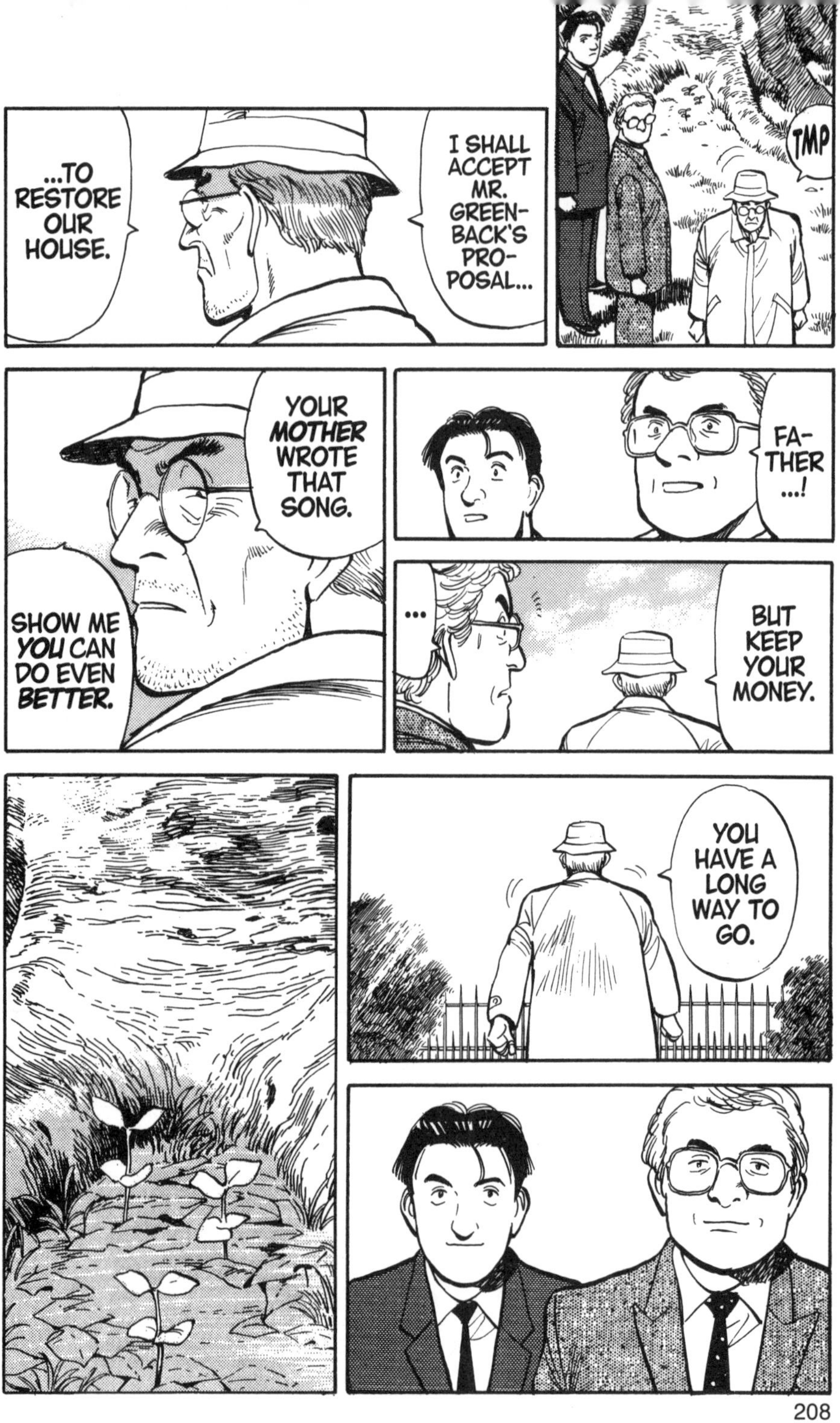
TMP
I SHALL ACCEPT MR. GREEN-BACK'S PRO-POSAL...
...TO RESTORE OUR HOUSE.
FA-THER ...!
BUT KEEP YOUR MONEY.
...
YOUR *MOTHER* WROTE THAT SONG.
SHOW ME *YOU* CAN DO EVEN *BETTER.*
YOU HAVE A LONG WAY TO GO.

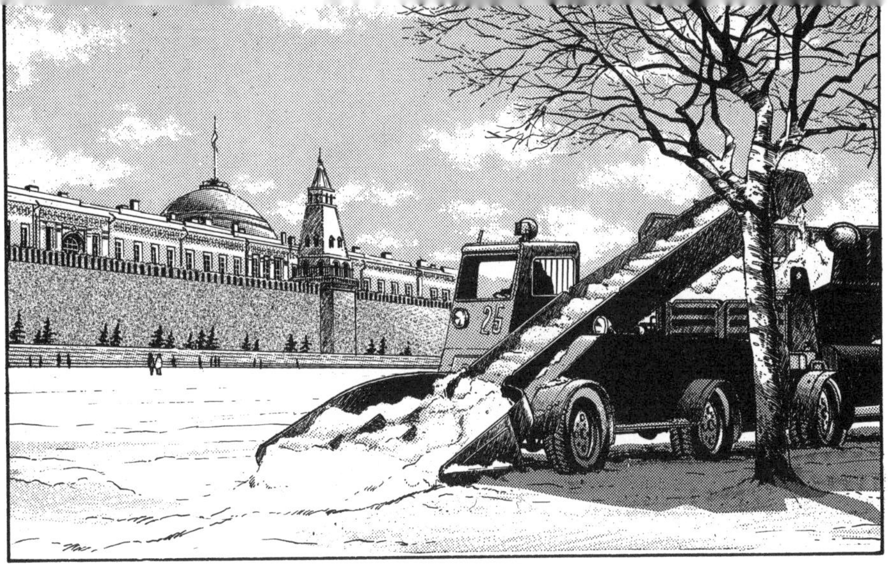
25

Chapter 9

Crimson Wind

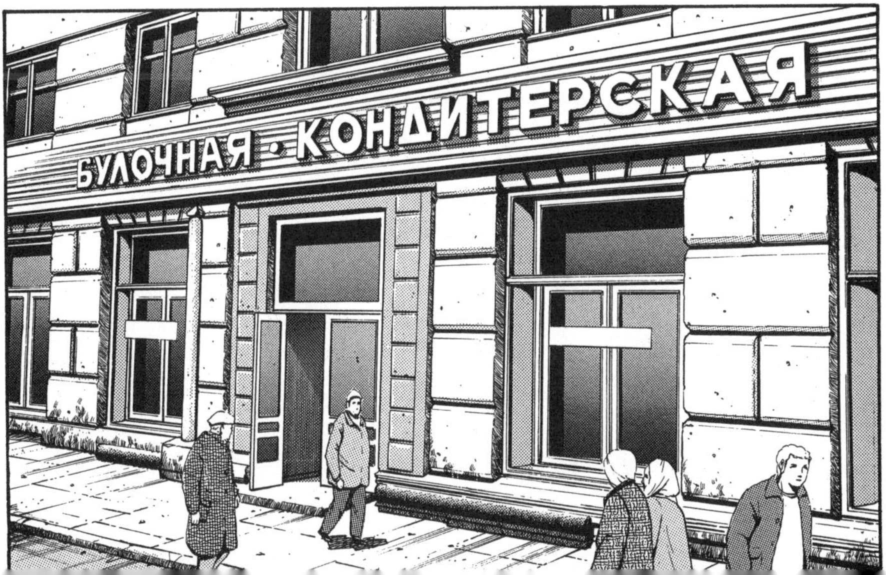
БУЛОЧНАЯ · КОНДИТЕРСКАЯ

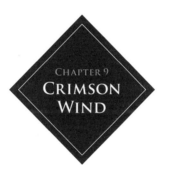

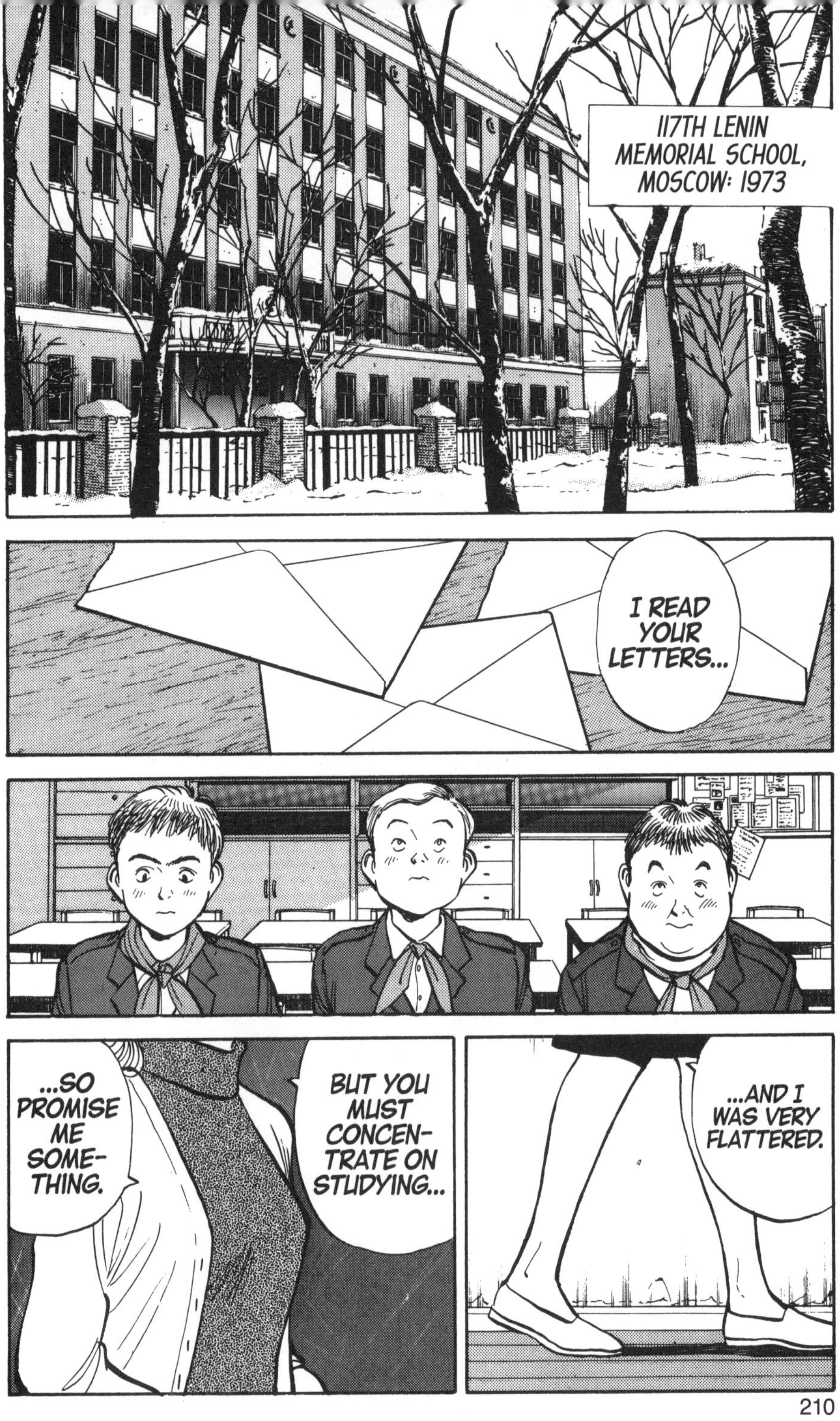
117TH LENIN MEMORIAL SCHOOL, MOSCOW: 1973
I READ YOUR LETTERS...
...AND I WAS VERY FLATTERED.
BUT YOU MUST CONCENTRATE ON STUDYING...
...SO PROMISE ME SOMETHING.

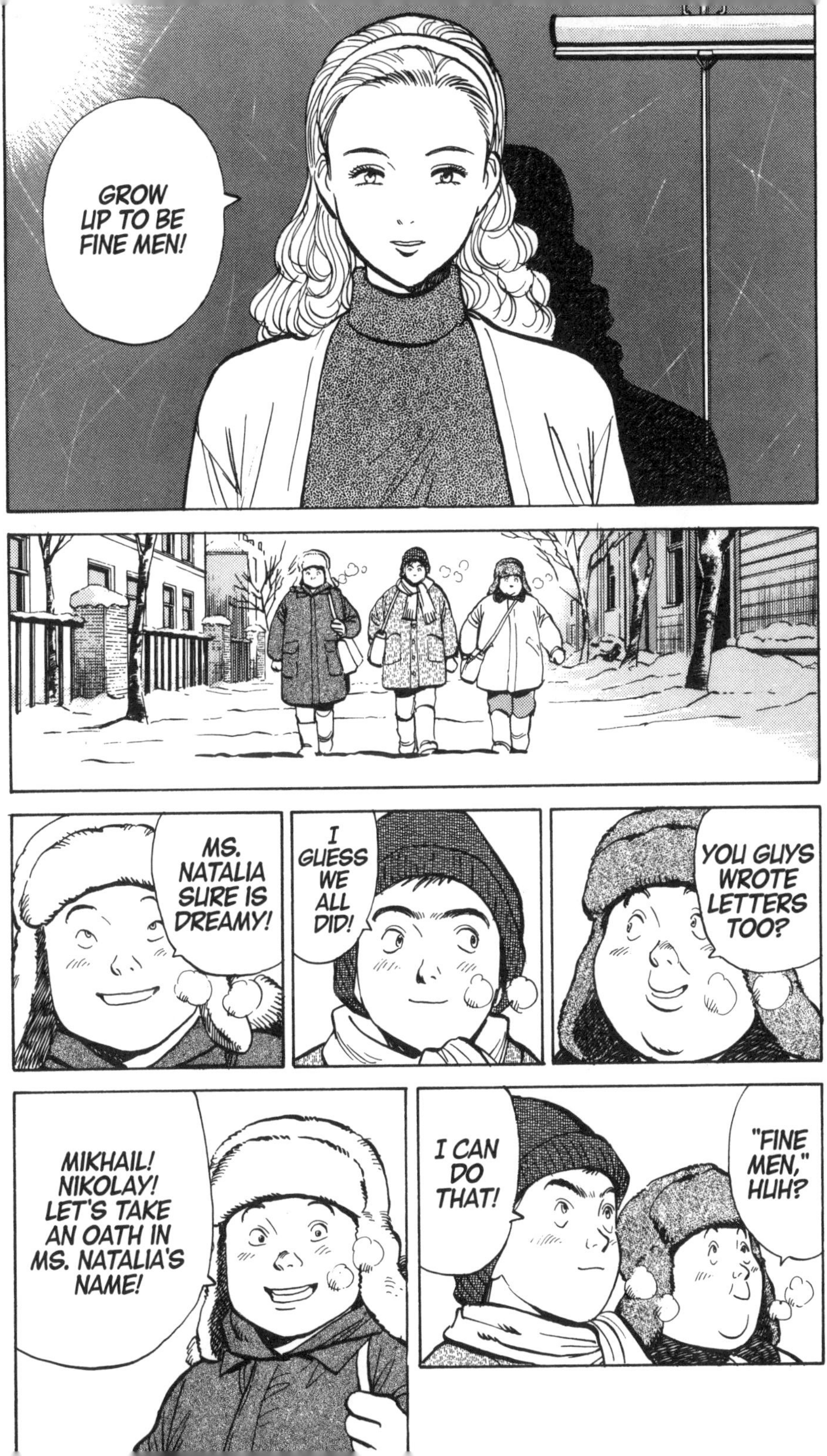
GROW UP TO BE FINE MEN!
YOU GUYS WROTE LETTERS TOO?
I GUESS WE ALL DID!
MS. NATALIA SURE IS DREAMY!
"FINE MEN," HUH?
I CAN DO THAT!
MIKHAIL! NIKOLAY! LET'S TAKE AN OATH IN MS. NATALIA'S NAME!

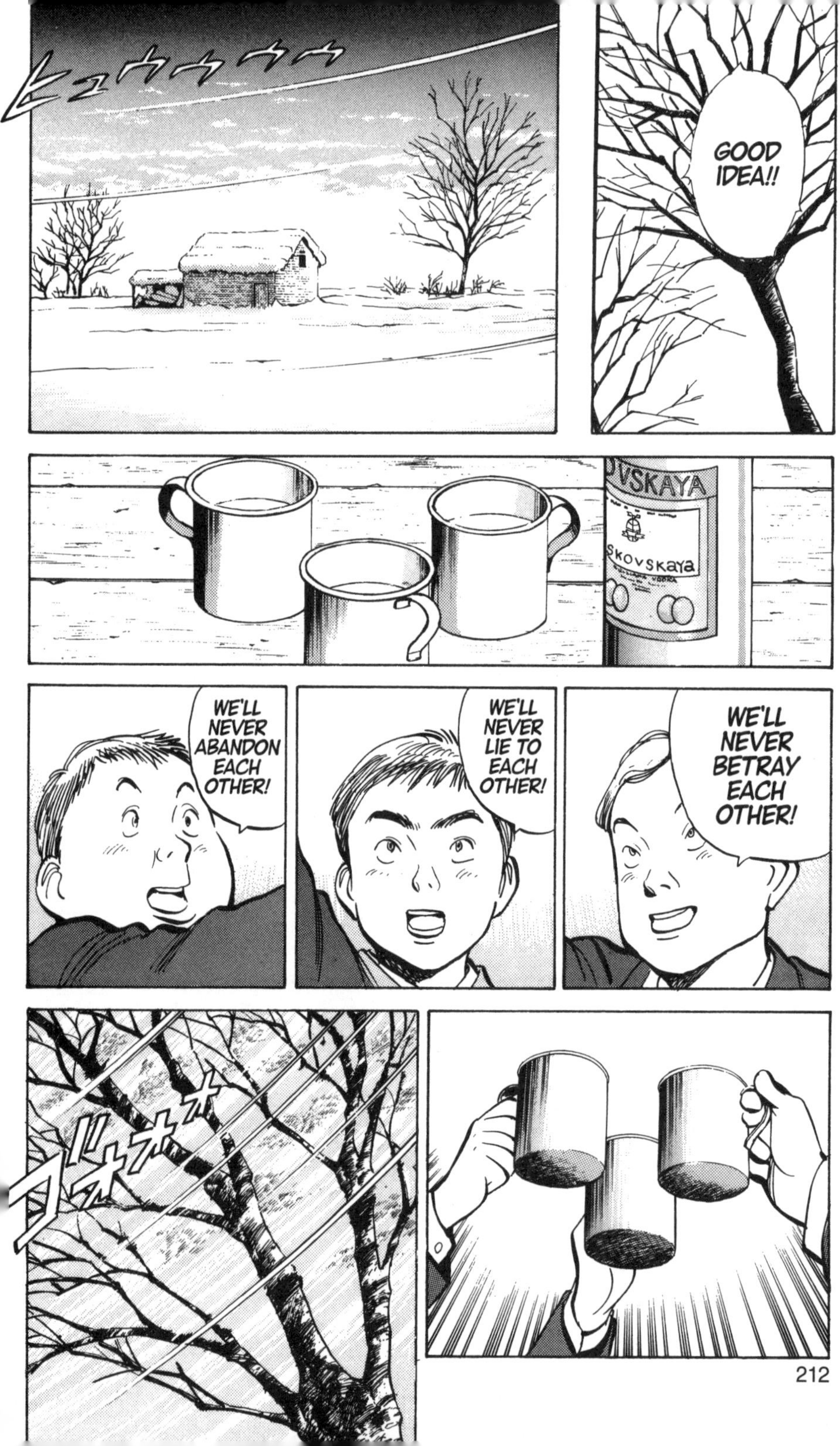
GOOD IDEA!!
ヒュウウウウ
SKOVSKAYA
WE'LL NEVER BETRAY EACH OTHER!
WE'LL NEVER LIE TO EACH OTHER!
WE'LL NEVER ABANDON EACH OTHER!
ゴォオオ

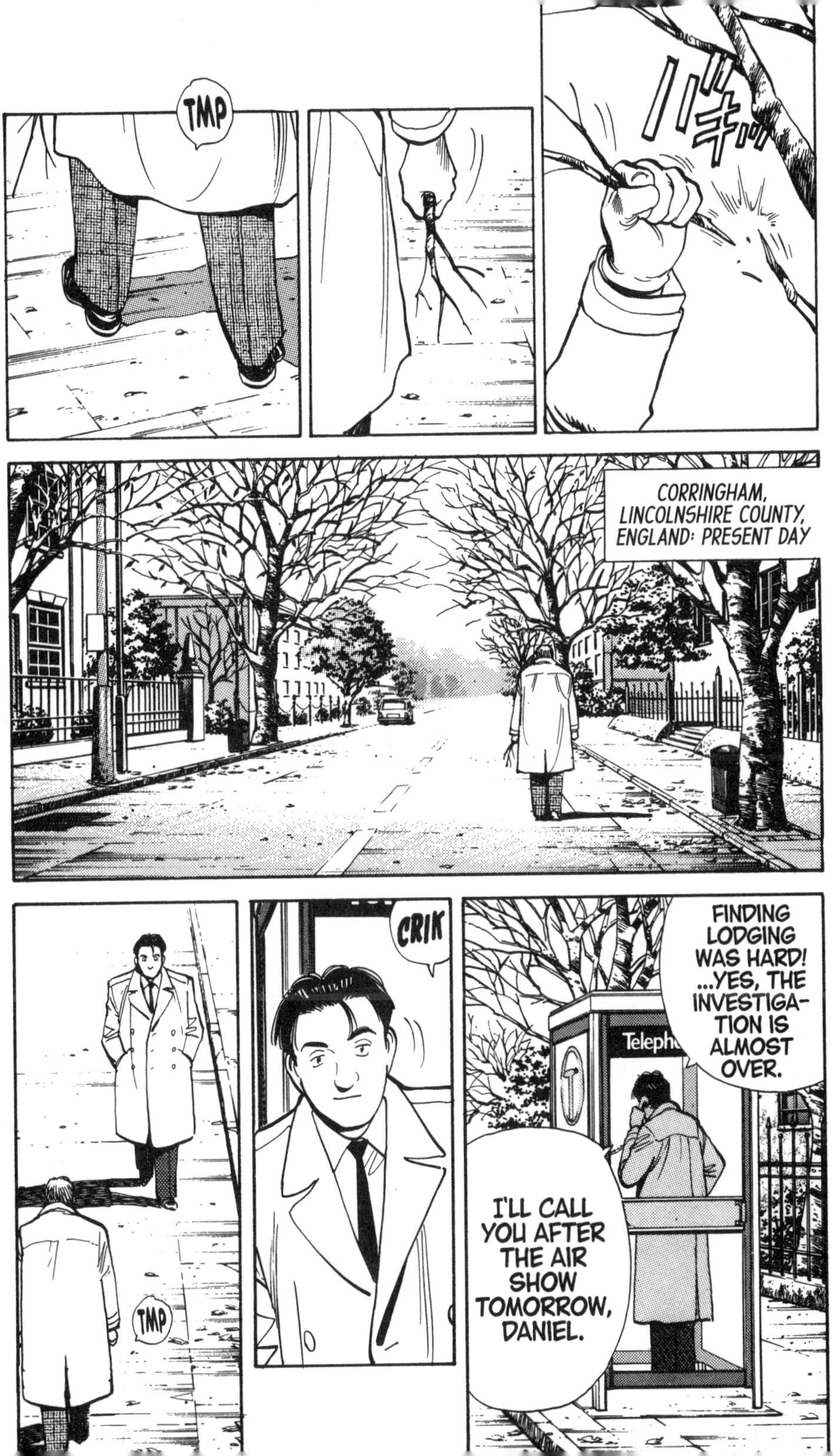
バキッ
TMP
CORRINGHAM, LINCOLNSHIRE COUNTY, ENGLAND: PRESENT DAY
FINDING LODGING WAS HARD! ...YES, THE INVESTIGA-TION IS ALMOST OVER.
I'LL CALL YOU AFTER THE AIR SHOW TOMORROW, DANIEL.
CRIK
TMP

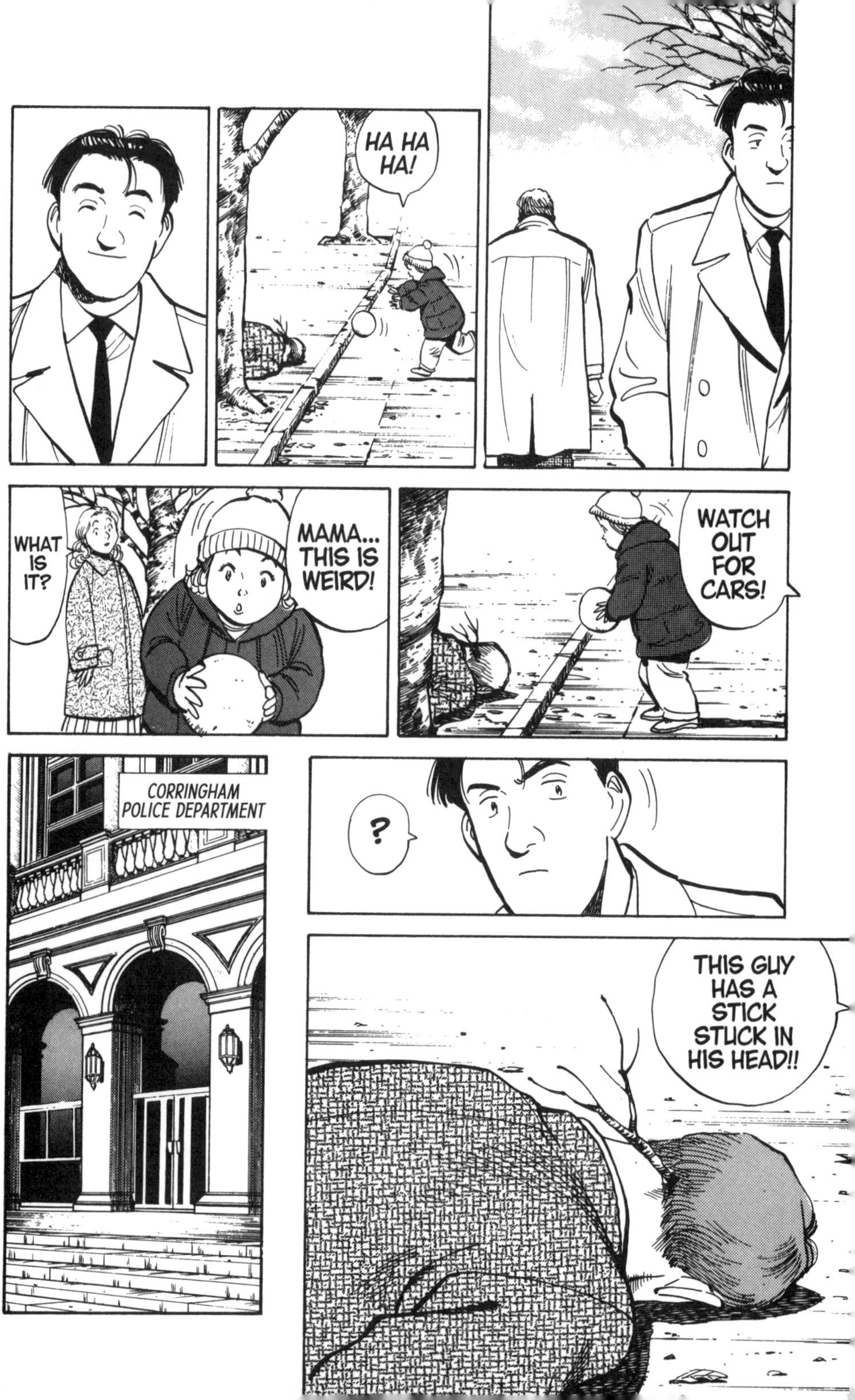
HA HA HA!
WATCH OUT FOR CARS!
MAMA... THIS IS WEIRD!
WHAT IS IT?
?
THIS GUY HAS A STICK STUCK IN HIS HEAD!!
CORRINGHAM POLICE DEPARTMENT

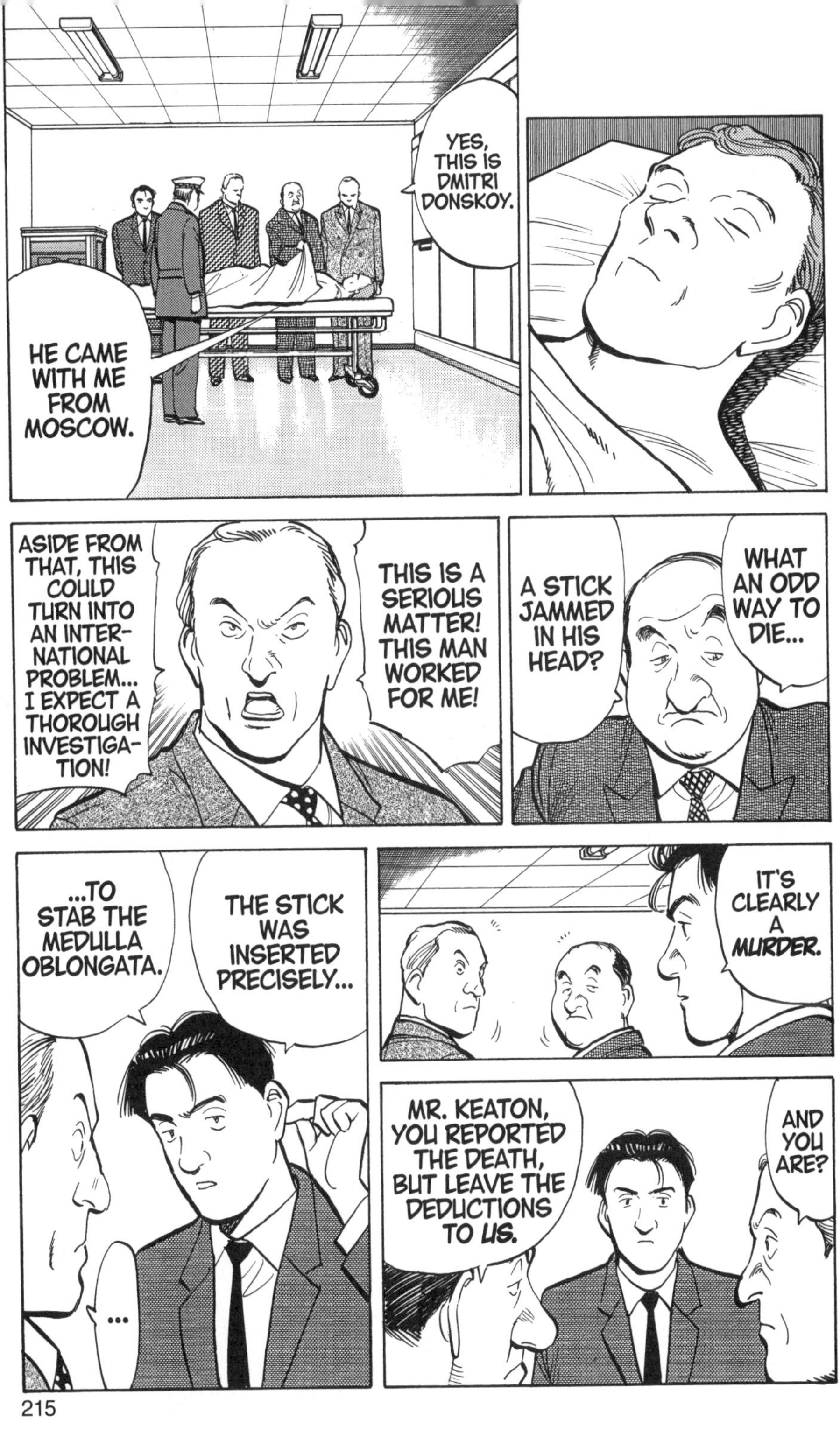
YES, THIS IS DMITRI DONSKOY.
HE CAME WITH ME FROM MOSCOW.
WHAT AN ODD WAY TO DIE...
A STICK JAMMED IN HIS HEAD?
THIS IS A SERIOUS MATTER! THIS MAN WORKED FOR ME!
ASIDE FROM THAT, THIS COULD TURN INTO AN INTER-NATIONAL PROBLEM... I EXPECT A THOROUGH INVESTIGA-TION!
IT'S CLEARLY A *MURDER.*
AND YOU ARE?
MR. KEATON, YOU REPORTED THE DEATH, BUT LEAVE THE DEDUCTIONS TO *US.*
THE STICK WAS INSERTED PRECISELY...
...TO STAB THE MEDULLA OBLONGATA.
...

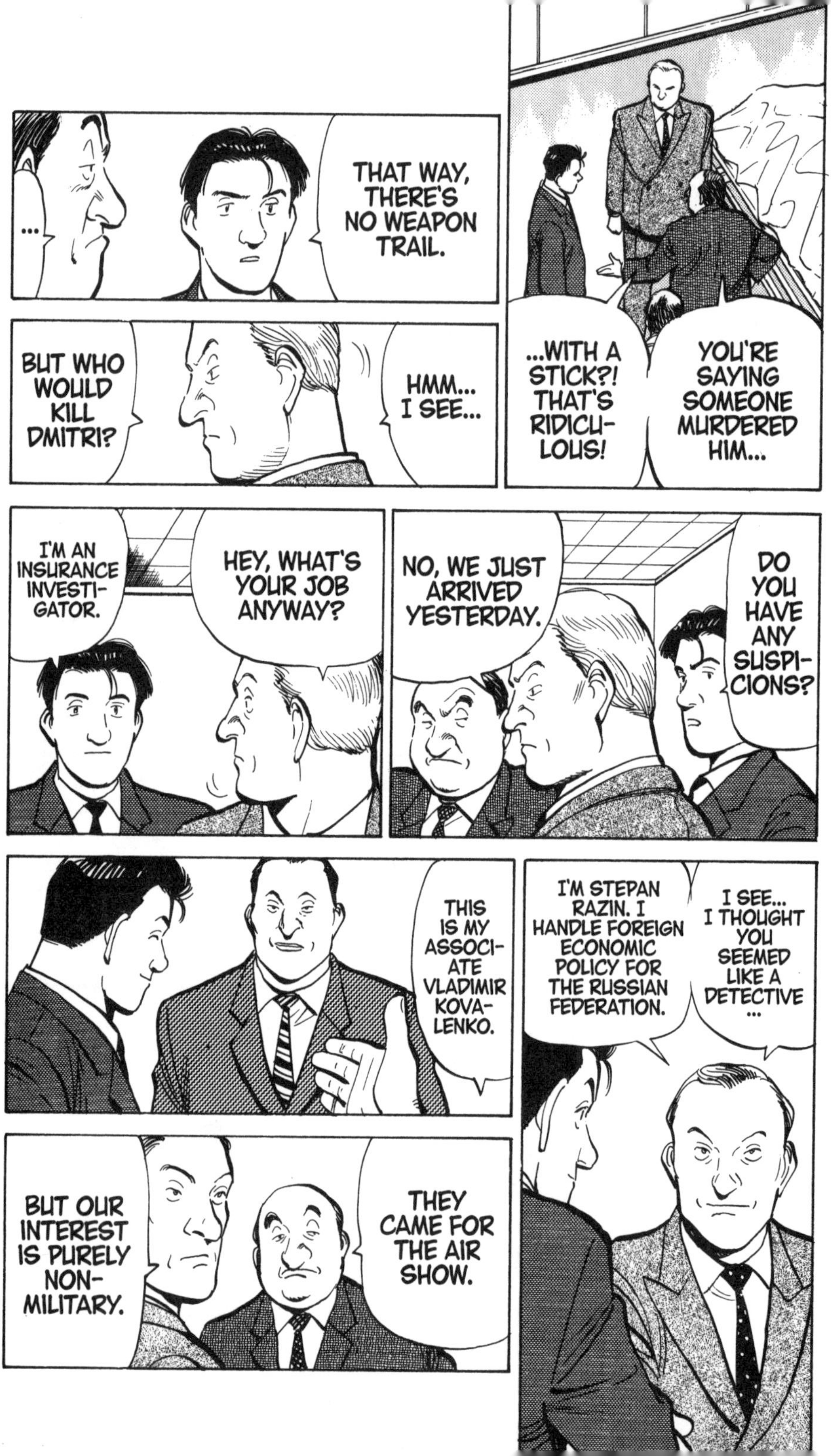
YOU'RE SAYING SOMEONE MURDERED HIM...
...WITH A STICK?! THAT'S RIDICULOUS!
THAT WAY, THERE'S NO WEAPON TRAIL.
...
HMM... I SEE...
BUT WHO WOULD KILL DMITRI?
DO YOU HAVE ANY SUSPICIONS?
NO, WE JUST ARRIVED YESTERDAY.
HEY, WHAT'S YOUR JOB ANYWAY?
I'M AN INSURANCE INVESTIGATOR.
I SEE... I THOUGHT YOU SEEMED LIKE A DETECTIVE ...
I'M STEPAN RAZIN. I HANDLE FOREIGN ECONOMIC POLICY FOR THE RUSSIAN FEDERATION.
THIS IS MY ASSOCIATE VLADIMIR KOVALENKO.
THEY CAME FOR THE AIR SHOW.
BUT OUR INTEREST IS PURELY NON-MILITARY.

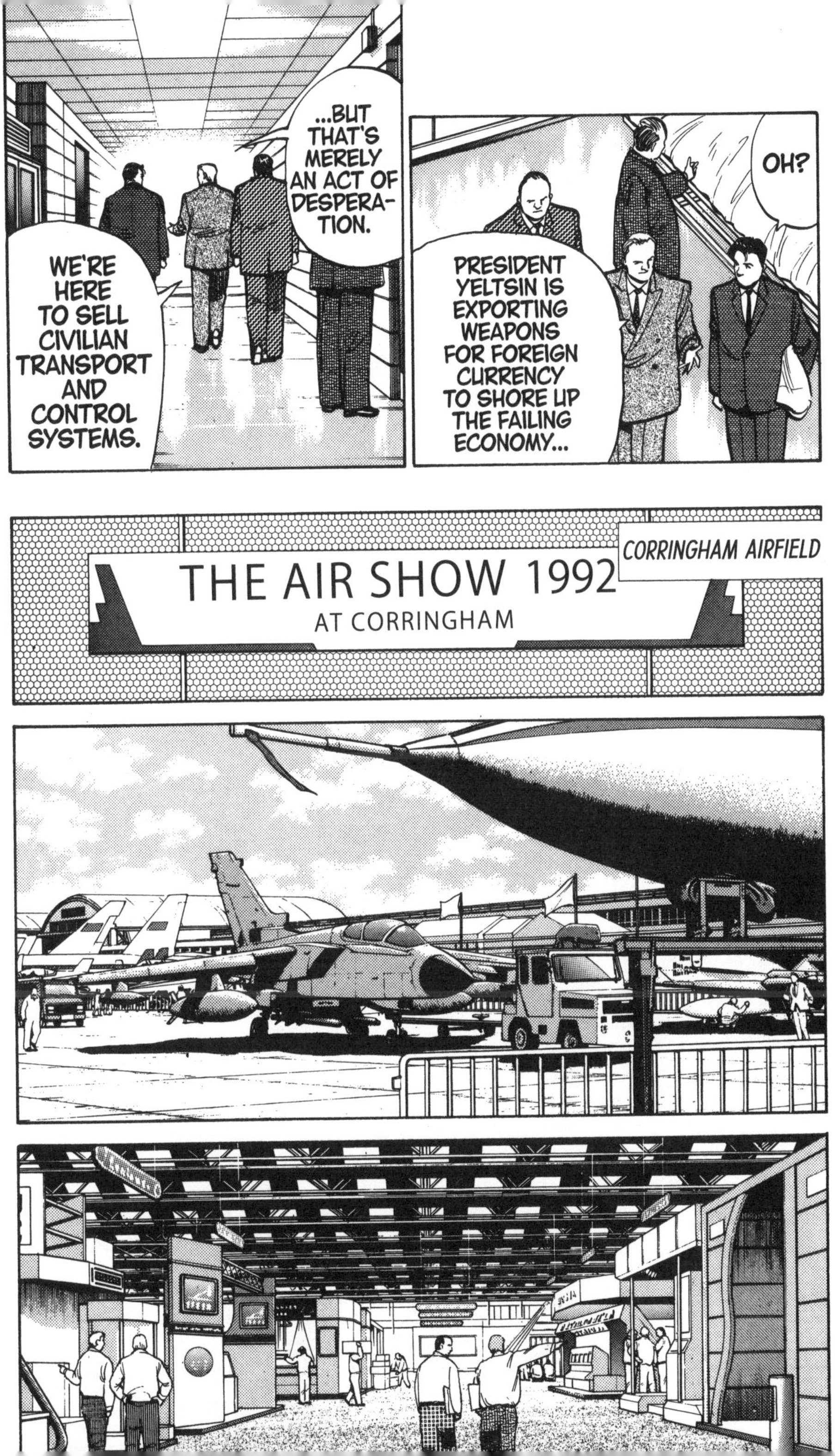
OH?
PRESIDENT YELTSIN IS EXPORTING WEAPONS FOR FOREIGN CURRENCY TO SHORE UP THE FAILING ECONOMY...
...BUT THAT'S MERELY AN ACT OF DESPERA-TION.
WE'RE HERE TO SELL CIVILIAN TRANSPORT AND CONTROL SYSTEMS.
CORRINGHAM AIRFIELD
THE AIR SHOW 1992
AT CORRINGHAM

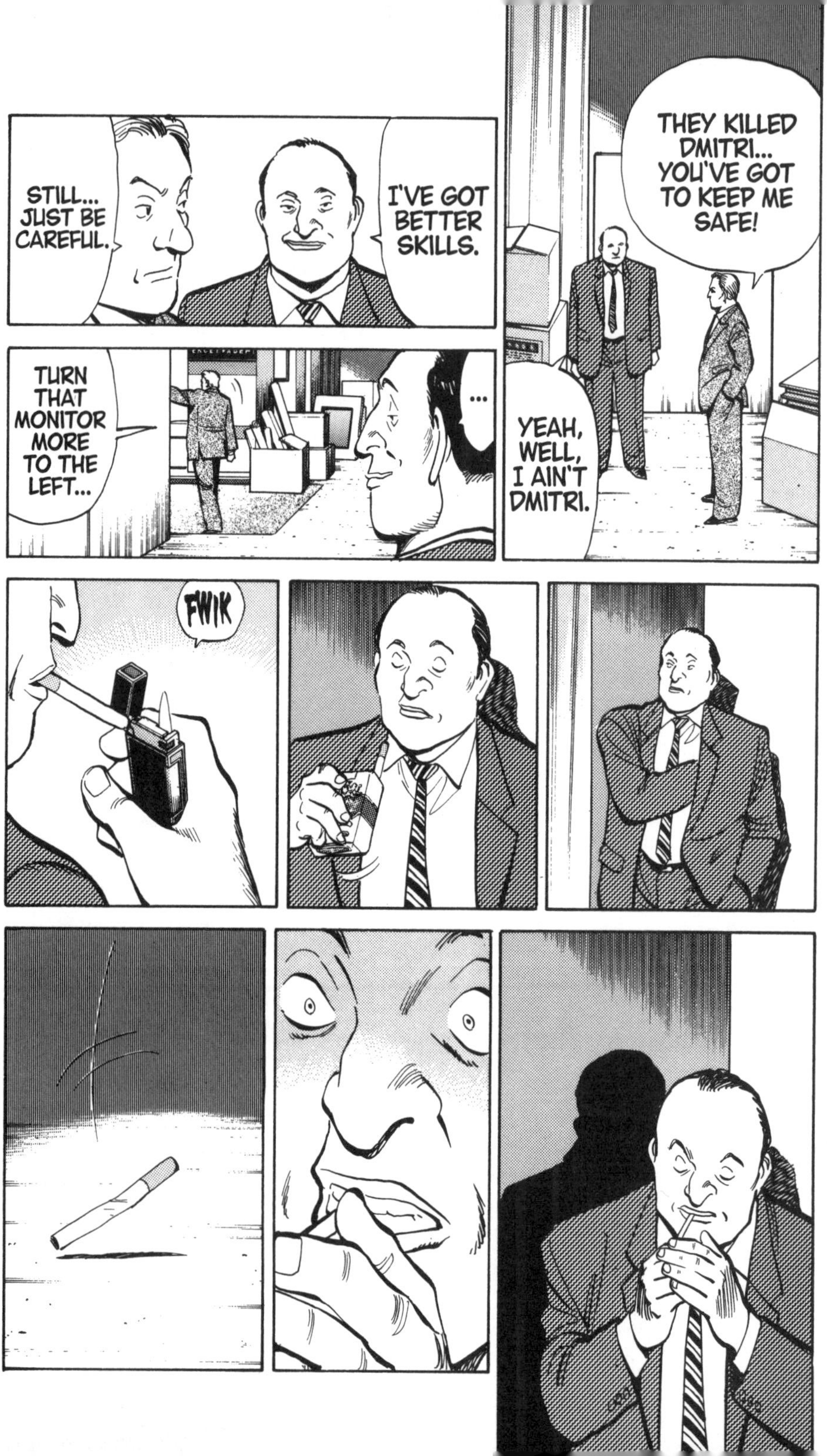
THEY KILLED DMITRI... YOU'VE GOT TO KEEP ME SAFE!
YEAH, WELL, I AIN'T DMITRI.
I'VE GOT BETTER SKILLS.
STILL... JUST BE CAREFUL.
...
TURN THAT MONITOR MORE TO THE LEFT...
FWIK

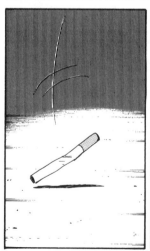

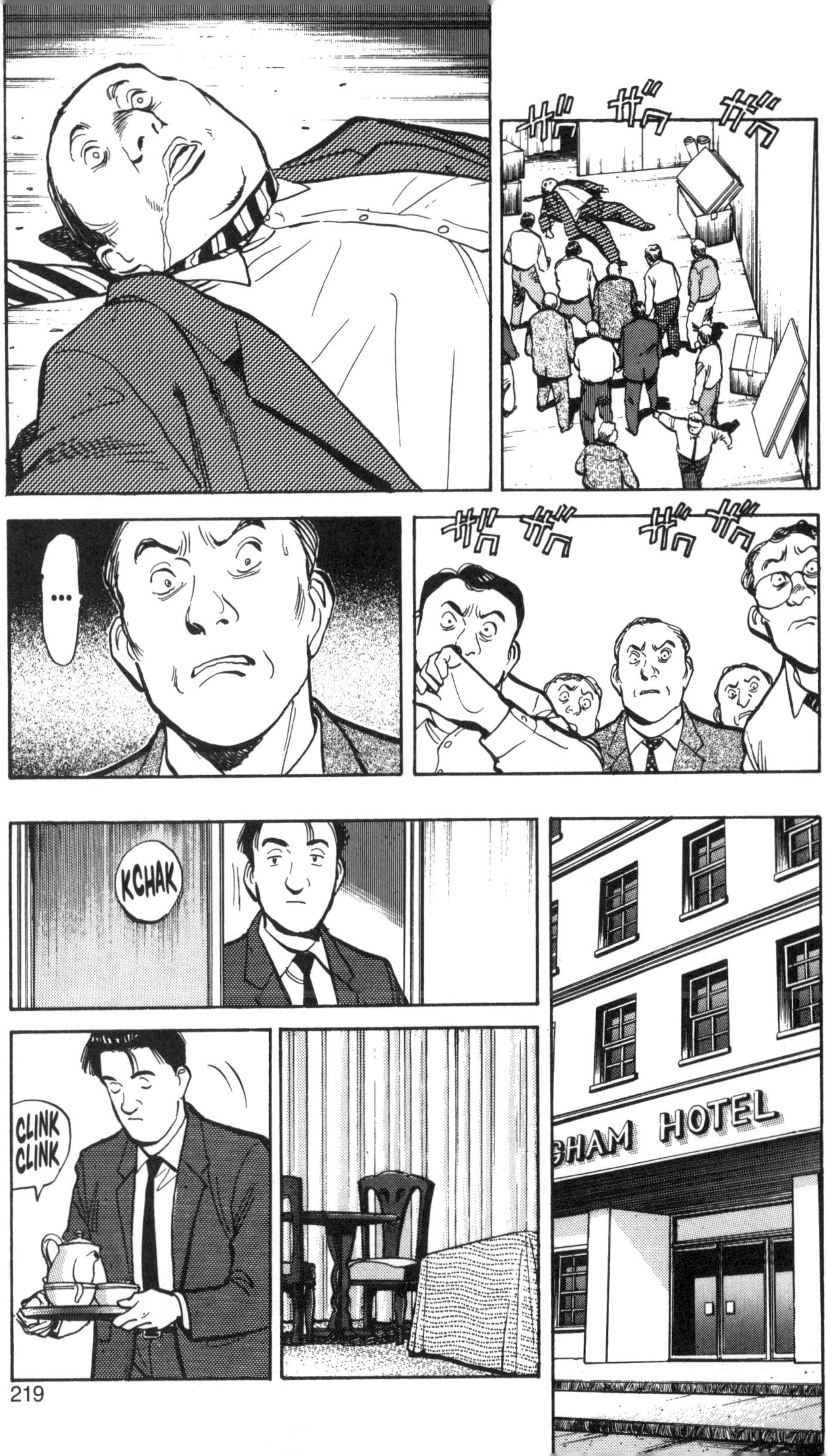
...
GHAM HOTEL
KCHAK
CLINK
CLINK

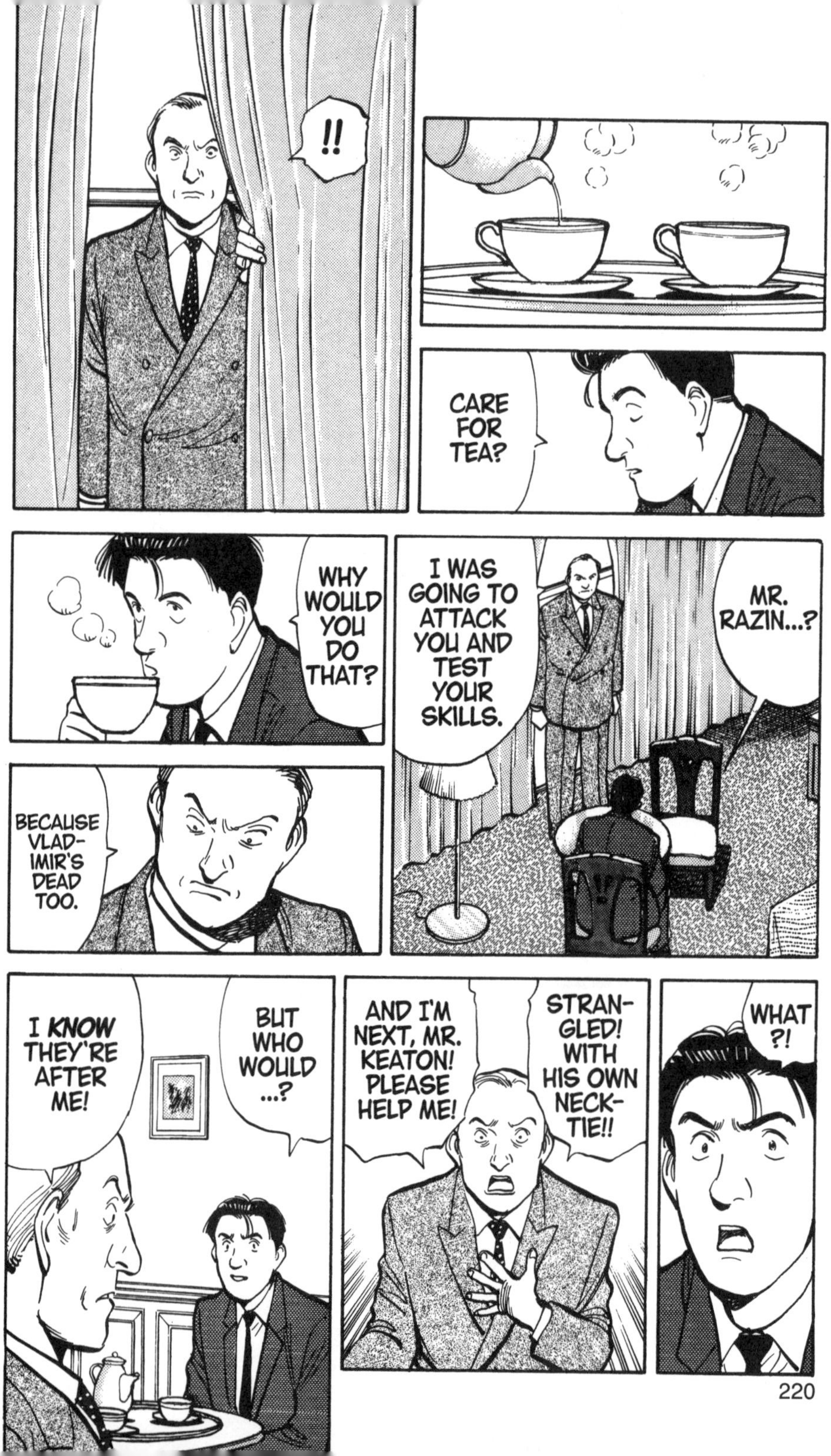
CARE FOR TEA?
!!
MR. RAZIN...?
I WAS GOING TO ATTACK YOU AND TEST YOUR SKILLS.
WHY WOULD YOU DO THAT?
BECAUSE VLADIMIR'S DEAD TOO.
WHAT?!
STRANGLED! WITH HIS OWN NECKTIE!!
AND I'M NEXT, MR. KEATON! PLEASE HELP ME!
BUT WHO WOULD...?
I *KNOW* THEY'RE AFTER ME!

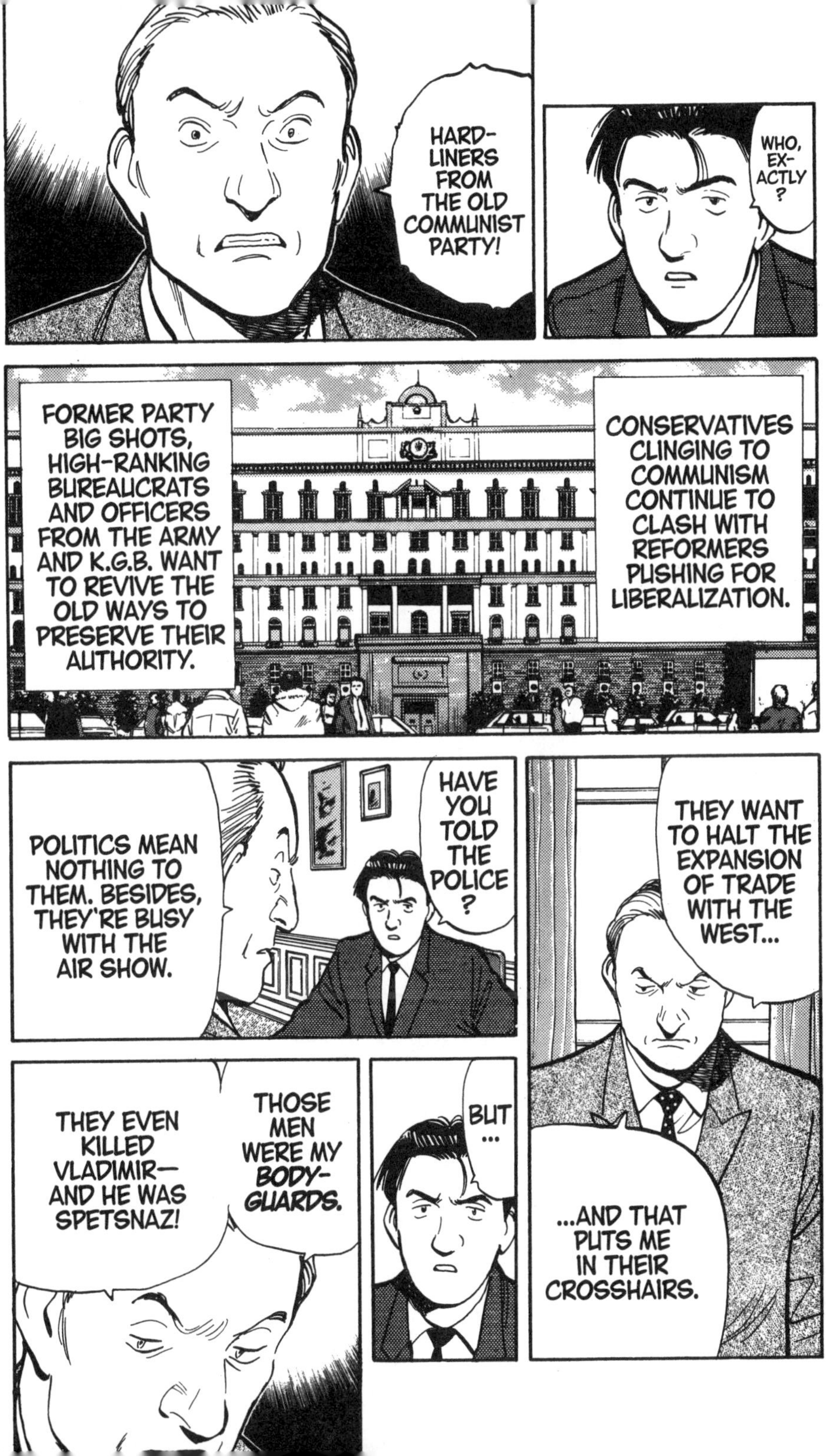
WHO, EX-ACTLY?
HARD-LINERS FROM THE OLD COMMUNIST PARTY!
CONSERVATIVES CLINGING TO COMMUNISM CONTINUE TO CLASH WITH REFORMERS PUSHING FOR LIBERALIZATION.
FORMER PARTY BIG SHOTS, HIGH-RANKING BUREAUCRATS AND OFFICERS FROM THE ARMY AND K.G.B. WANT TO REVIVE THE OLD WAYS TO PRESERVE THEIR AUTHORITY.
THEY WANT TO HALT THE EXPANSION OF TRADE WITH THE WEST...
...AND THAT PUTS ME IN THEIR CROSSHAIRS.
HAVE YOU TOLD THE POLICE?
POLITICS MEAN NOTHING TO THEM. BESIDES, THEY'RE BUSY WITH THE AIR SHOW.
BUT...
THOSE MEN WERE MY *BODY-GUARDS.*
THEY EVEN KILLED VLADIMIR—AND HE WAS SPETSNAZ!

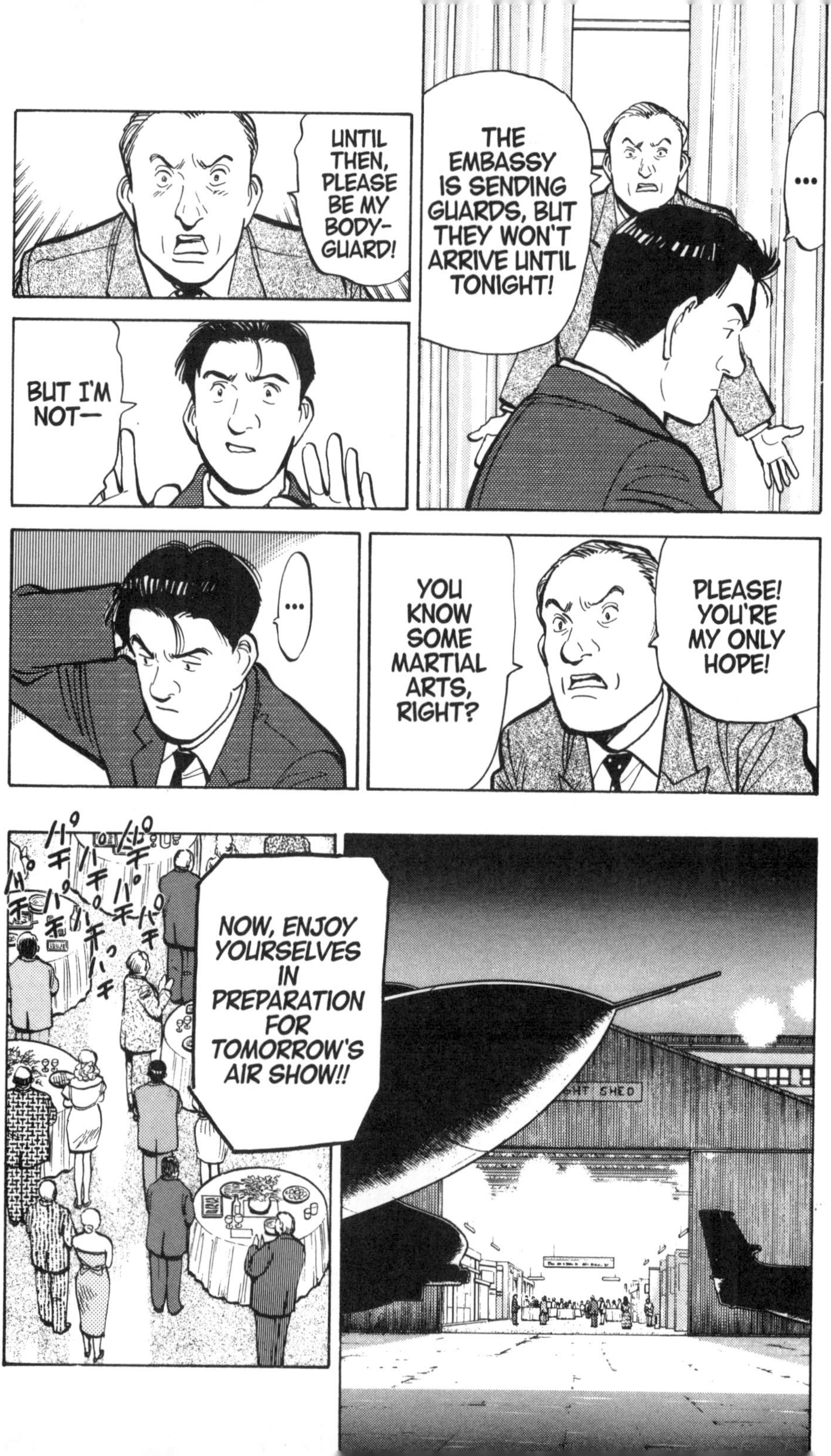
...
THE EMBASSY IS SENDING GUARDS, BUT THEY WON'T ARRIVE UNTIL TONIGHT!
UNTIL THEN, PLEASE BE MY BODY-GUARD!
BUT I'M NOT—
PLEASE! YOU'RE MY ONLY HOPE!
YOU KNOW SOME MARTIAL ARTS, RIGHT?
...
NOW, ENJOY YOURSELVES IN PREPARATION FOR TOMORROW'S AIR SHOW!!

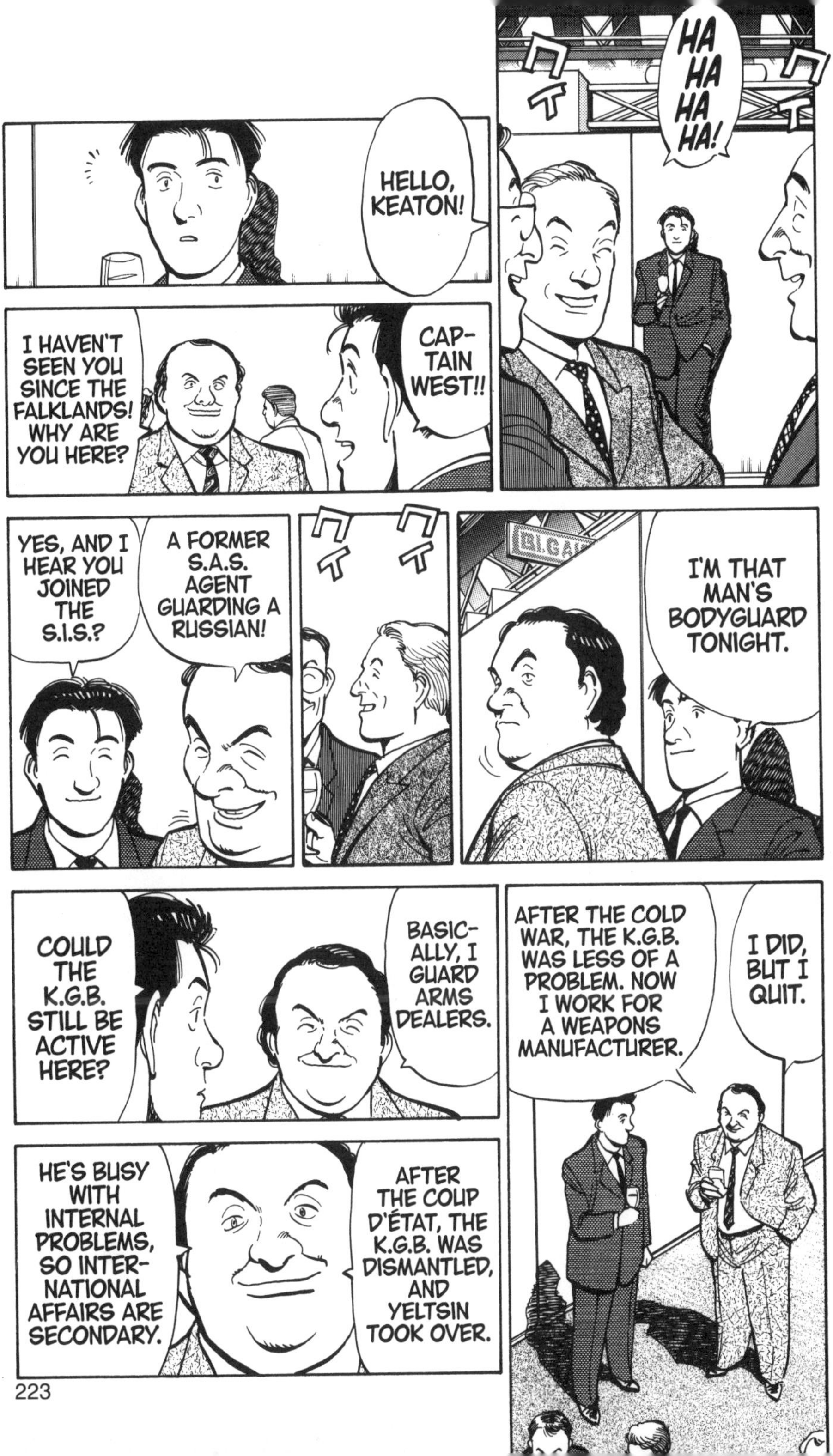
HA HA HA HA!
HELLO, KEATON!
CAP-TAIN WEST!!
I HAVEN'T SEEN YOU SINCE THE FALKLANDS! WHY ARE YOU HERE?
I'M THAT MAN'S BODYGUARD TONIGHT.
A FORMER S.A.S. AGENT GUARDING A RUSSIAN!
YES, AND I HEAR YOU JOINED THE S.I.S.?
I DID, BUT I QUIT.
AFTER THE COLD WAR, THE K.G.B. WAS LESS OF A PROBLEM. NOW I WORK FOR A WEAPONS MANUFACTURER.
BASIC-ALLY, I GUARD ARMS DEALERS.
COULD THE K.G.B. STILL BE ACTIVE HERE?
AFTER THE COUP D'ÉTAT, THE K.G.B. WAS DISMANTLED, AND YELTSIN TOOK OVER.
HE'S BUSY WITH INTERNAL PROBLEMS, SO INTER-NATIONAL AFFAIRS ARE SECONDARY.

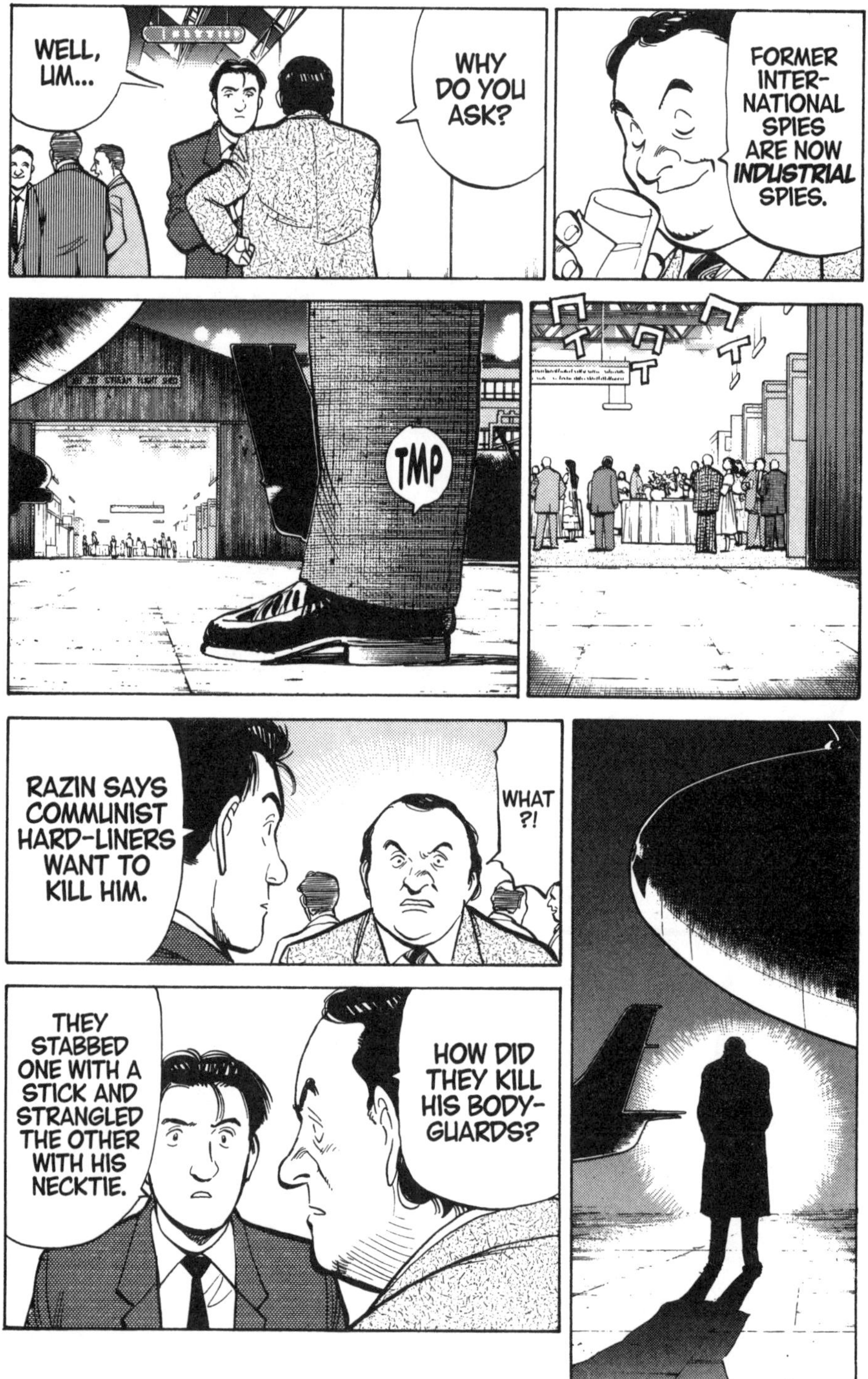
FORMER INTER-NATIONAL SPIES ARE NOW INDUSTRIAL SPIES.
WHY DO YOU ASK?
WELL, UM...
TMP
WHAT?!
RAZIN SAYS COMMUNIST HARD-LINERS WANT TO KILL HIM.
HOW DID THEY KILL HIS BODY-GUARDS?
THEY STABBED ONE WITH A STICK AND STRANGLED THE OTHER WITH HIS NECKTIE.

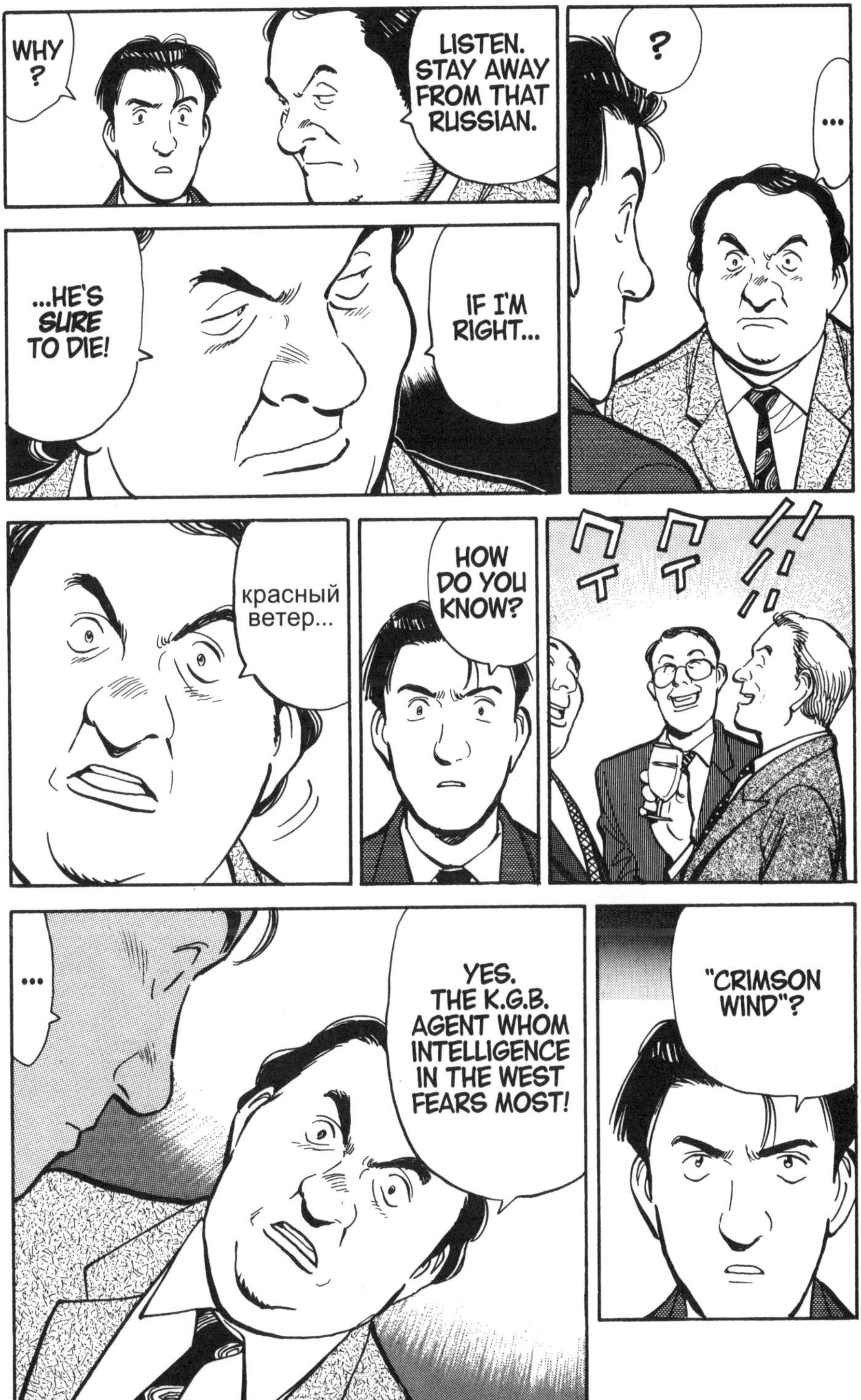
...
?
LISTEN. STAY AWAY FROM THAT RUSSIAN.
WHY?
IF I'M RIGHT...
...HE'S **SURE** TO DIE!
HOW DO YOU KNOW?
красный ветер...
"CRIMSON WIND"?
YES. THE K.G.B. AGENT WHOM INTELLIGENCE IN THE WEST FEARS MOST!
...

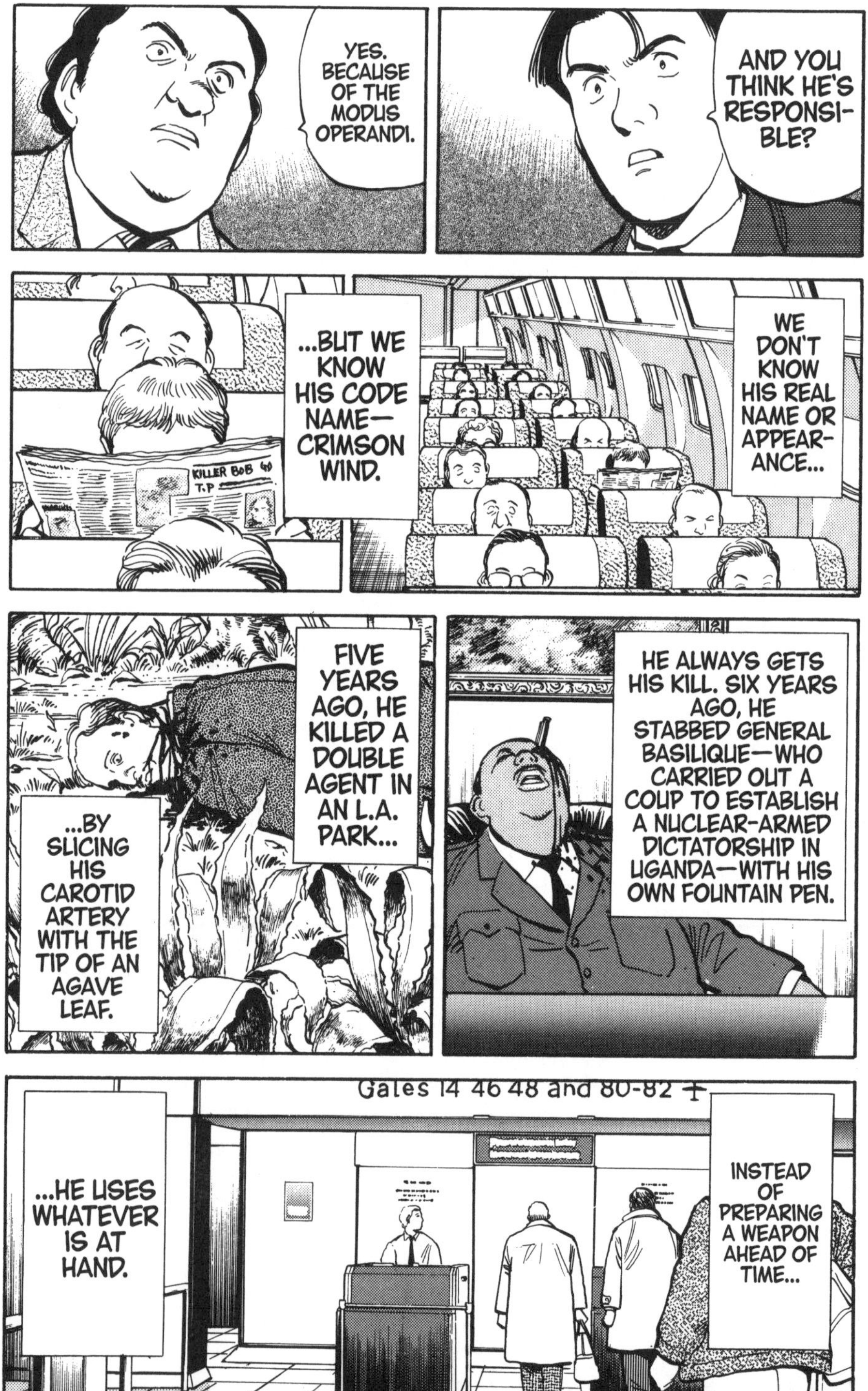
AND YOU THINK HE'S RESPONSI-BLE?
YES. BECAUSE OF THE MODUS OPERANDI.
WE DON'T KNOW HIS REAL NAME OR APPEAR-ANCE...
...BUT WE KNOW HIS CODE NAME—CRIMSON WIND.
HE ALWAYS GETS HIS KILL. SIX YEARS AGO, HE STABBED GENERAL BASILIQUE—WHO CARRIED OUT A COUP TO ESTABLISH A NUCLEAR-ARMED DICTATORSHIP IN UGANDA—WITH HIS OWN FOUNTAIN PEN.
FIVE YEARS AGO, HE KILLED A DOUBLE AGENT IN AN L.A. PARK...
...BY SLICING HIS CAROTID ARTERY WITH THE TIP OF AN AGAVE LEAF.
Gales 14 46 48 and 80-82
INSTEAD OF PREPARING A WEAPON AHEAD OF TIME...
...HE USES WHATEVER IS AT HAND.

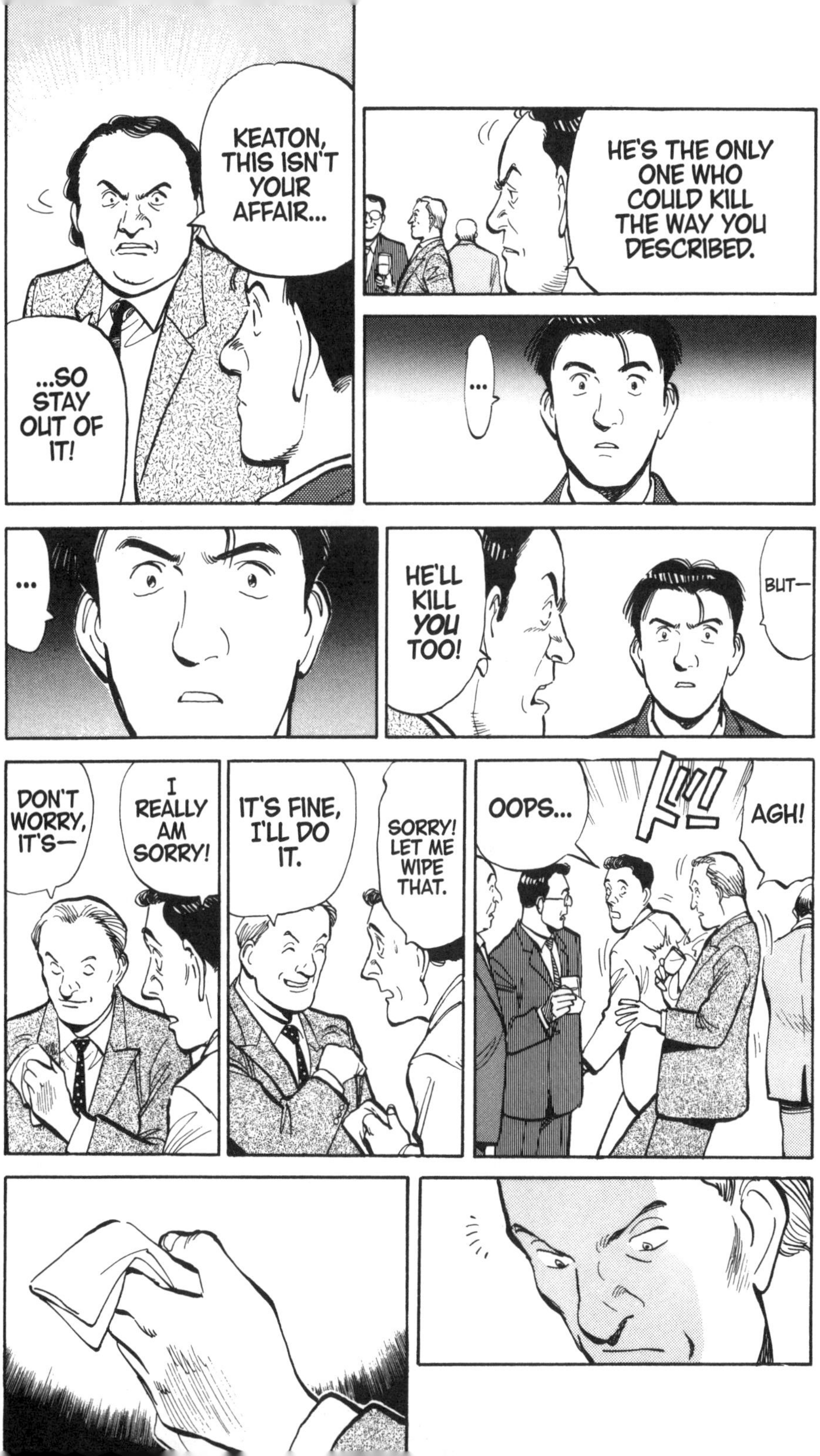
HE'S THE ONLY ONE WHO COULD KILL THE WAY YOU DESCRIBED.
...
KEATON, THIS ISN'T YOUR AFFAIR...
...SO STAY OUT OF IT!
BUT—
HE'LL KILL *YOU* TOO!
...
AGH!
OOPS...
SORRY! LET ME WIPE THAT.
IT'S FINE, I'LL DO IT.
I REALLY AM SORRY!
DON'T WORRY, IT'S—

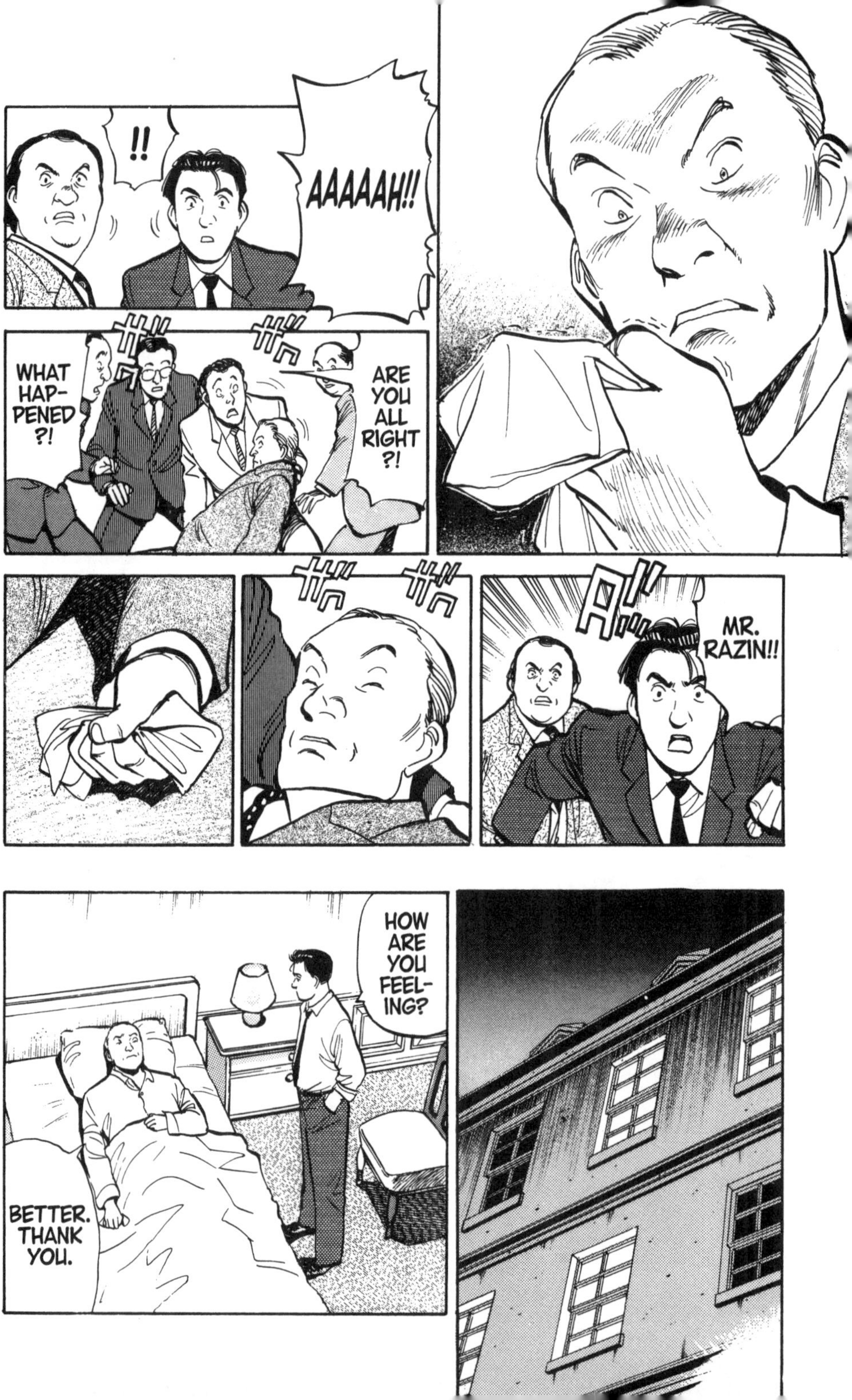
AAAAAH!!
!!
ARE YOU ALL RIGHT?!
WHAT HAPPENED?!
MR. RAZIN!!
HOW ARE YOU FEELING?
BETTER. THANK YOU.

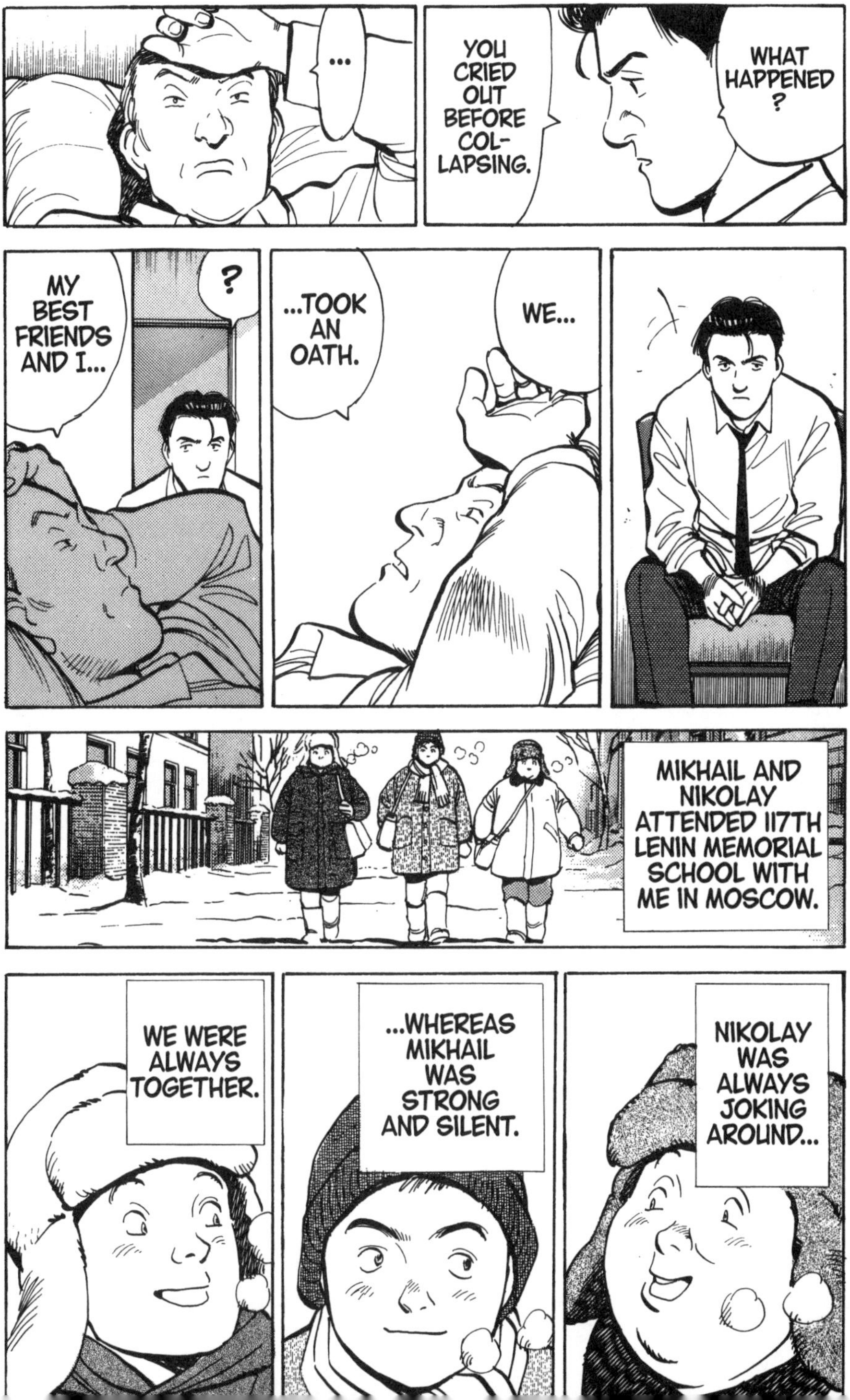
WHAT HAPPENED?
YOU CRIED OUT BEFORE COL-LAPSING.
...
WE...
...TOOK AN OATH.
?
MY BEST FRIENDS AND I...
MIKHAIL AND NIKOLAY ATTENDED 117TH LENIN MEMORIAL SCHOOL WITH ME IN MOSCOW.
NIKOLAY WAS ALWAYS JOKING AROUND...
...WHEREAS MIKHAIL WAS STRONG AND SILENT.
WE WERE ALWAYS TOGETHER.

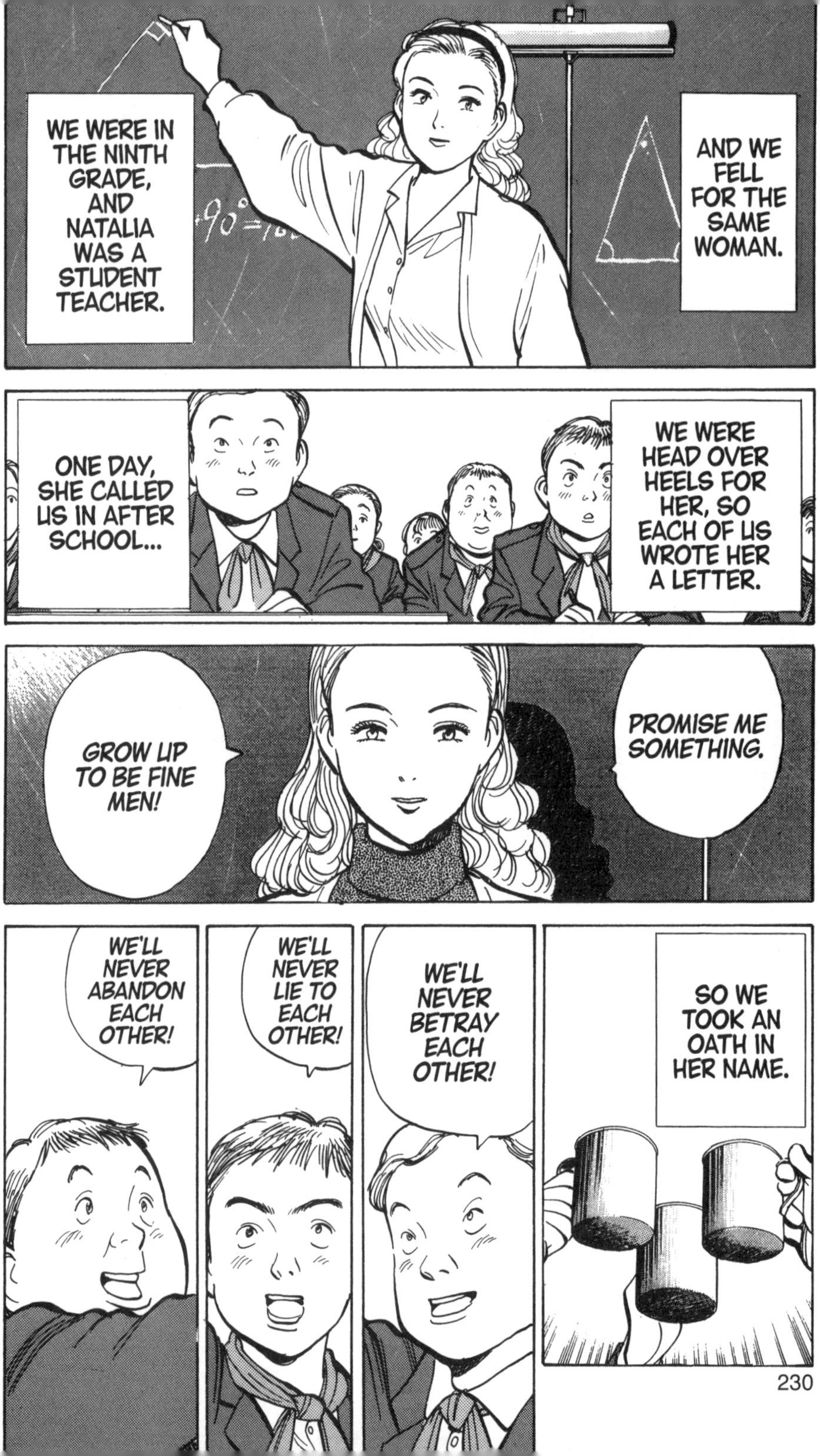
AND WE FELL FOR THE SAME WOMAN.
WE WERE IN THE NINTH GRADE, AND NATALIA WAS A STUDENT TEACHER.
WE WERE HEAD OVER HEELS FOR HER, SO EACH OF US WROTE HER A LETTER.
ONE DAY, SHE CALLED US IN AFTER SCHOOL...
PROMISE ME SOMETHING.
GROW UP TO BE FINE MEN!
SO WE TOOK AN OATH IN HER NAME.
WE'LL NEVER BETRAY EACH OTHER!
WE'LL NEVER LIE TO EACH OTHER!
WE'LL NEVER ABANDON EACH OTHER!

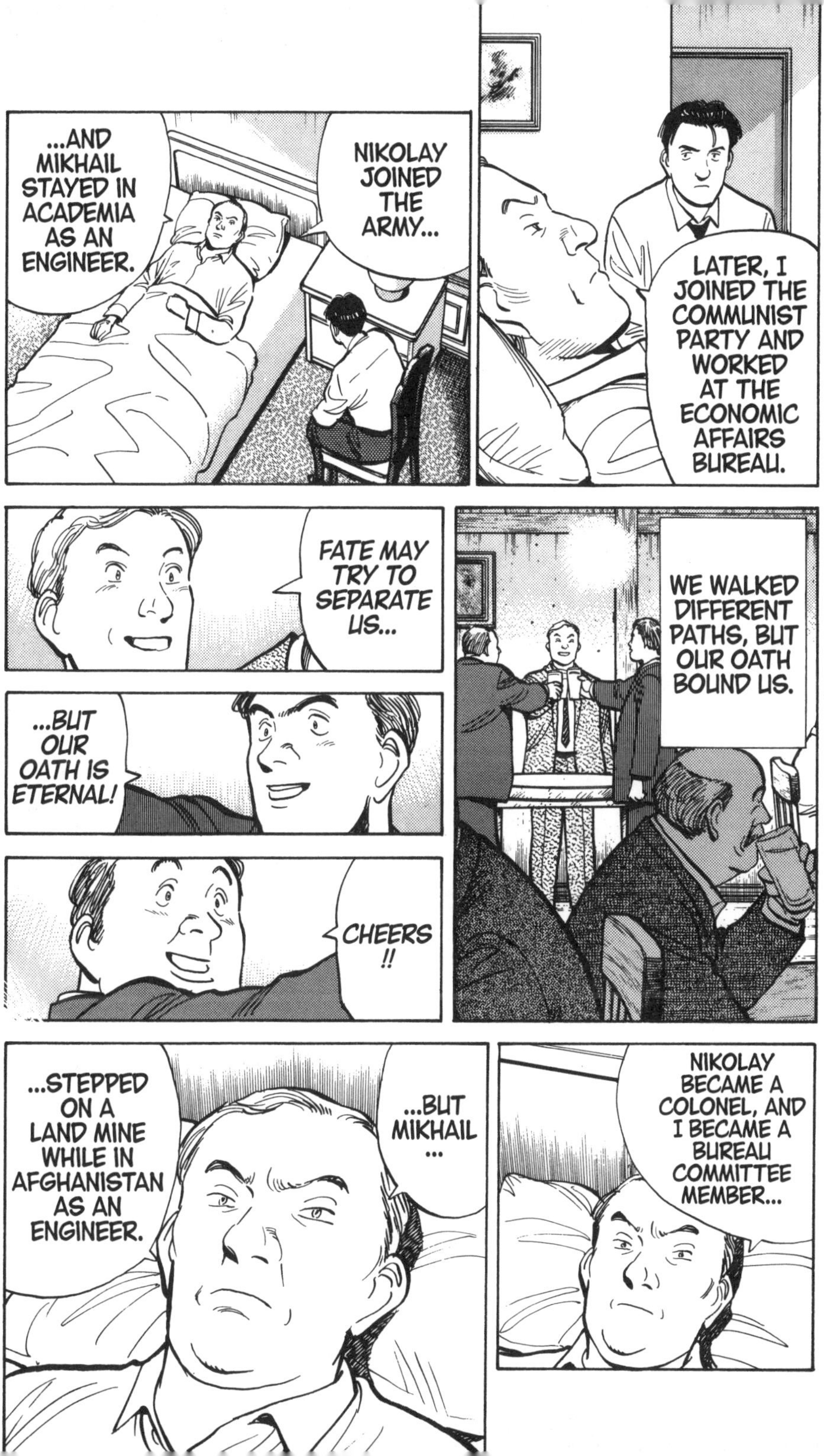
LATER, I JOINED THE COMMUNIST PARTY AND WORKED AT THE ECONOMIC AFFAIRS BUREAU.
NIKOLAY JOINED THE ARMY...
...AND MIKHAIL STAYED IN ACADEMIA AS AN ENGINEER.
WE WALKED DIFFERENT PATHS, BUT OUR OATH BOUND US.
FATE MAY TRY TO SEPARATE US...
...BUT OUR OATH IS ETERNAL!
CHEERS !!
NIKOLAY BECAME A COLONEL, AND I BECAME A BUREAU COMMITTEE MEMBER...
...BUT MIKHAIL ...
...STEPPED ON A LAND MINE WHILE IN AFGHANISTAN AS AN ENGINEER.

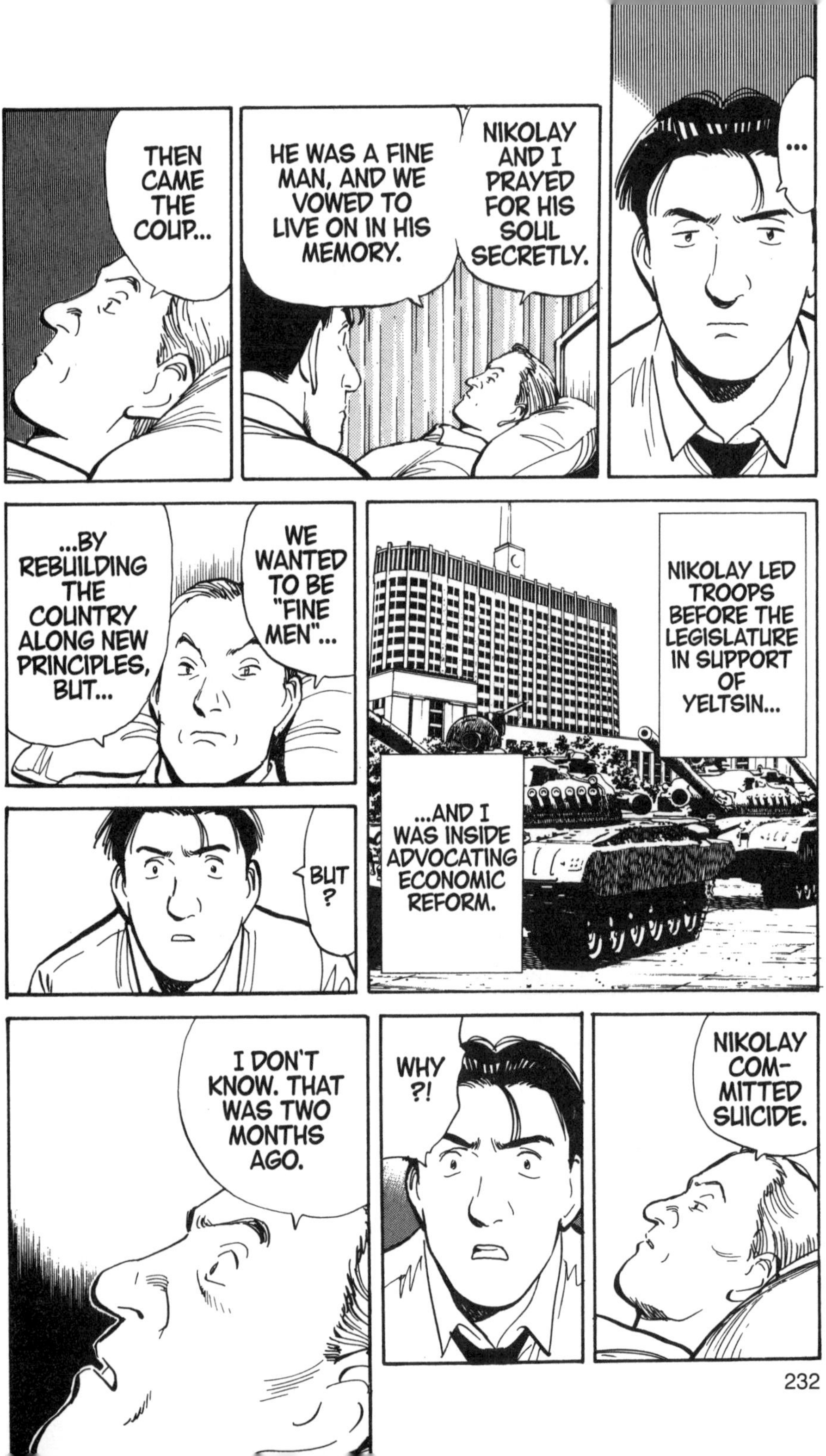
...
NIKOLAY AND I PRAYED FOR HIS SOUL SECRETLY.
HE WAS A FINE MAN, AND WE VOWED TO LIVE ON IN HIS MEMORY.
THEN CAME THE COUP...
NIKOLAY LED TROOPS BEFORE THE LEGISLATURE IN SUPPORT OF YELTSIN...
...AND I WAS INSIDE ADVOCATING ECONOMIC REFORM.
WE WANTED TO BE "FINE MEN"...
...BY REBUILDING THE COUNTRY ALONG NEW PRINCIPLES, BUT...
BUT ?
NIKOLAY COM-MITTED SUICIDE.
WHY ?!
I DON'T KNOW. THAT WAS TWO MONTHS AGO.

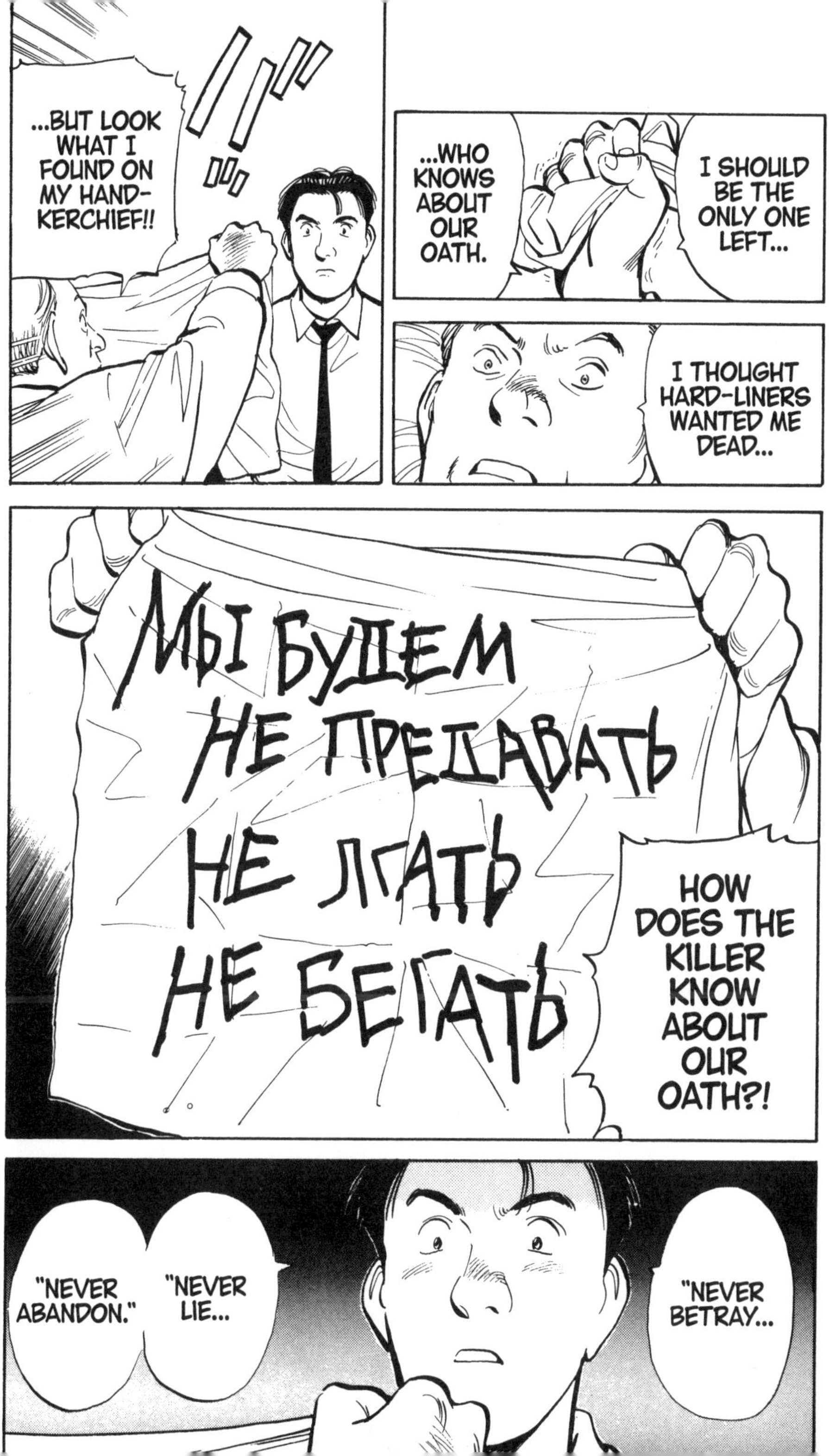
I SHOULD BE THE ONLY ONE LEFT...
...WHO KNOWS ABOUT OUR OATH.
I THOUGHT HARD-LINERS WANTED ME DEAD...
...BUT LOOK WHAT I FOUND ON MY HAND-KERCHIEF!!
МЫ БУДЕМ
НЕ ПРЕДАВАТЬ
НЕ ЛГАТЬ
НЕ БЕГАТЬ
HOW DOES THE KILLER KNOW ABOUT OUR OATH?!
"NEVER BETRAY...
"NEVER LIE...
"NEVER ABANDON."

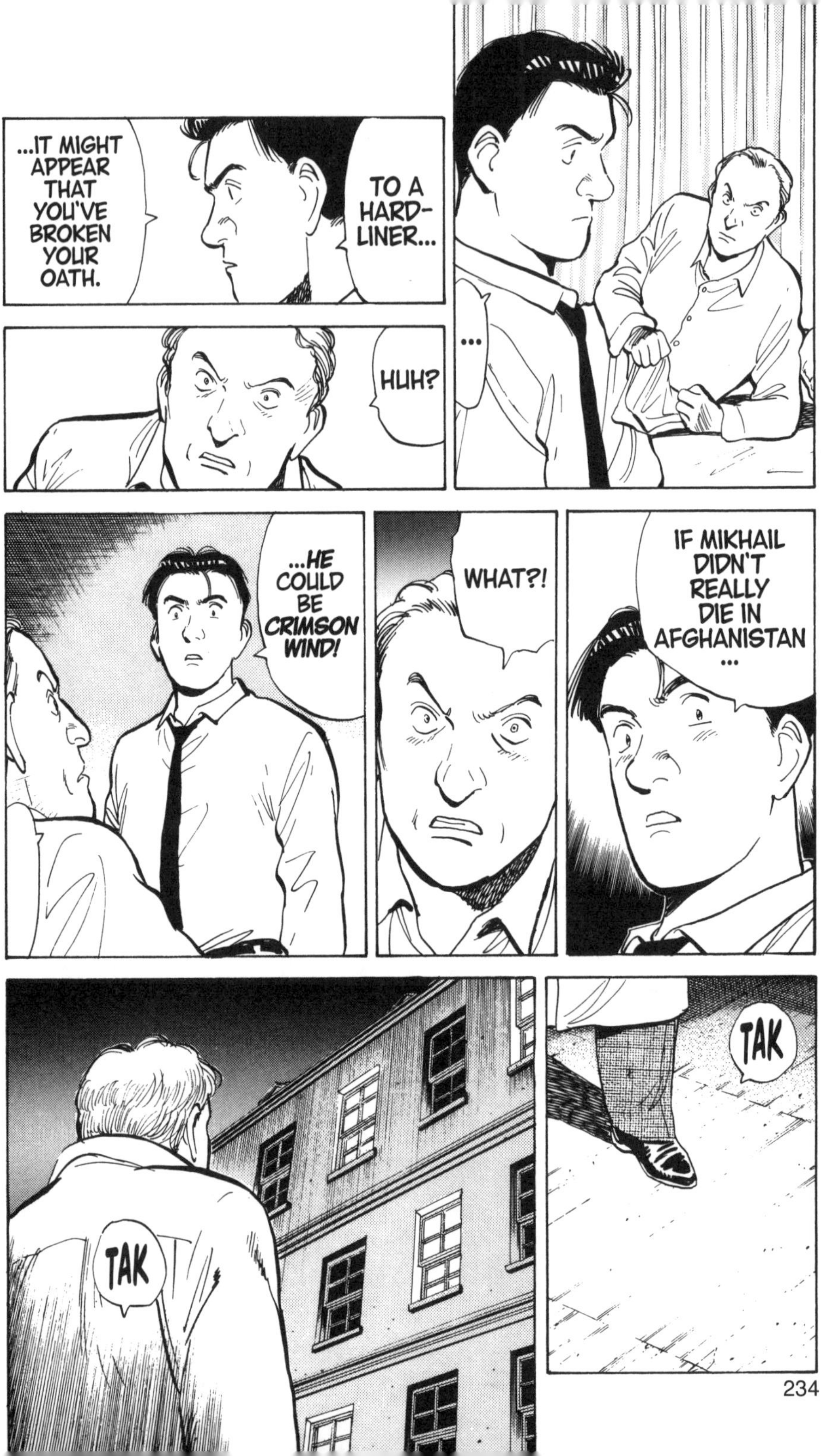
...
TO A HARD-LINER...
...IT MIGHT APPEAR THAT YOU'VE BROKEN YOUR OATH.
HUH?
IF MIKHAIL DIDN'T REALLY DIE IN AFGHANISTAN ...
WHAT?!
...HE COULD BE CRIMSON WIND!
TAK
TAK

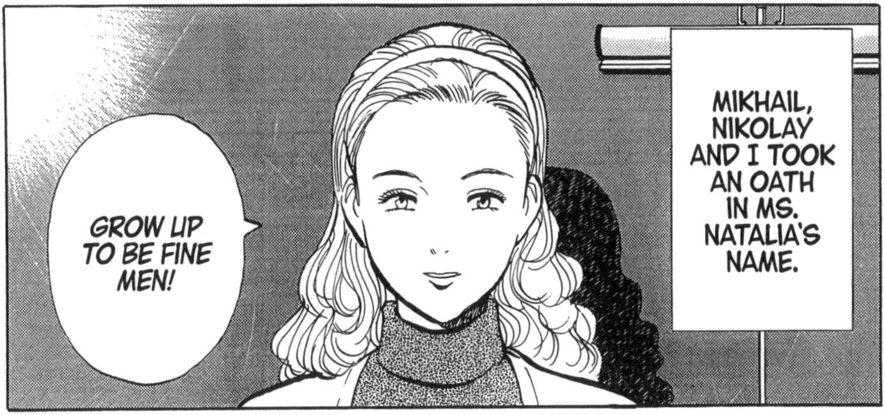
MIKHAIL, NIKOLAY AND I TOOK AN OATH IN MS. NATALIA'S NAME.
GROW UP TO BE FINE MEN!

Chapter 10
Scarlet Sadness

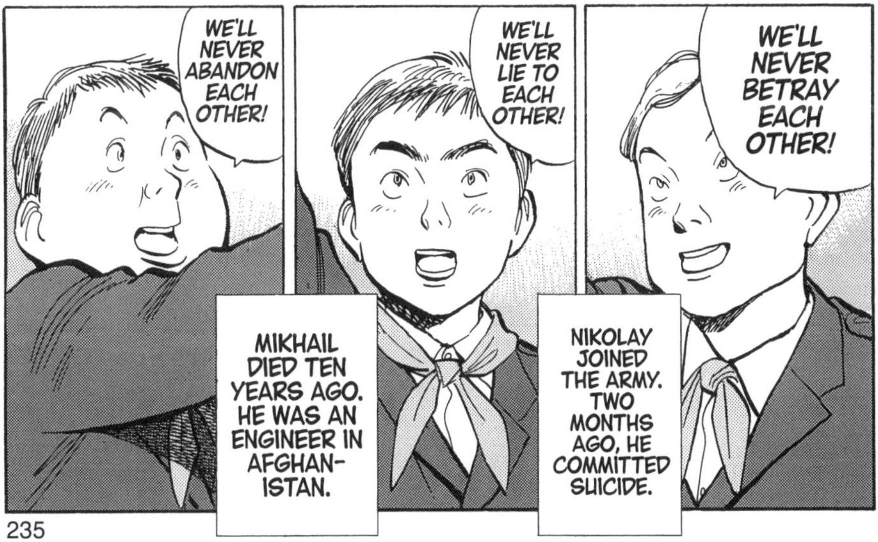
WE'LL NEVER BETRAY EACH OTHER!
WE'LL NEVER LIE TO EACH OTHER!
NIKOLAY JOINED THE ARMY. TWO MONTHS AGO, HE COMMITTED SUICIDE.
WE'LL NEVER ABANDON EACH OTHER!
MIKHAIL DIED TEN YEARS AGO. HE WAS AN ENGINEER IN AFGHAN-ISTAN.

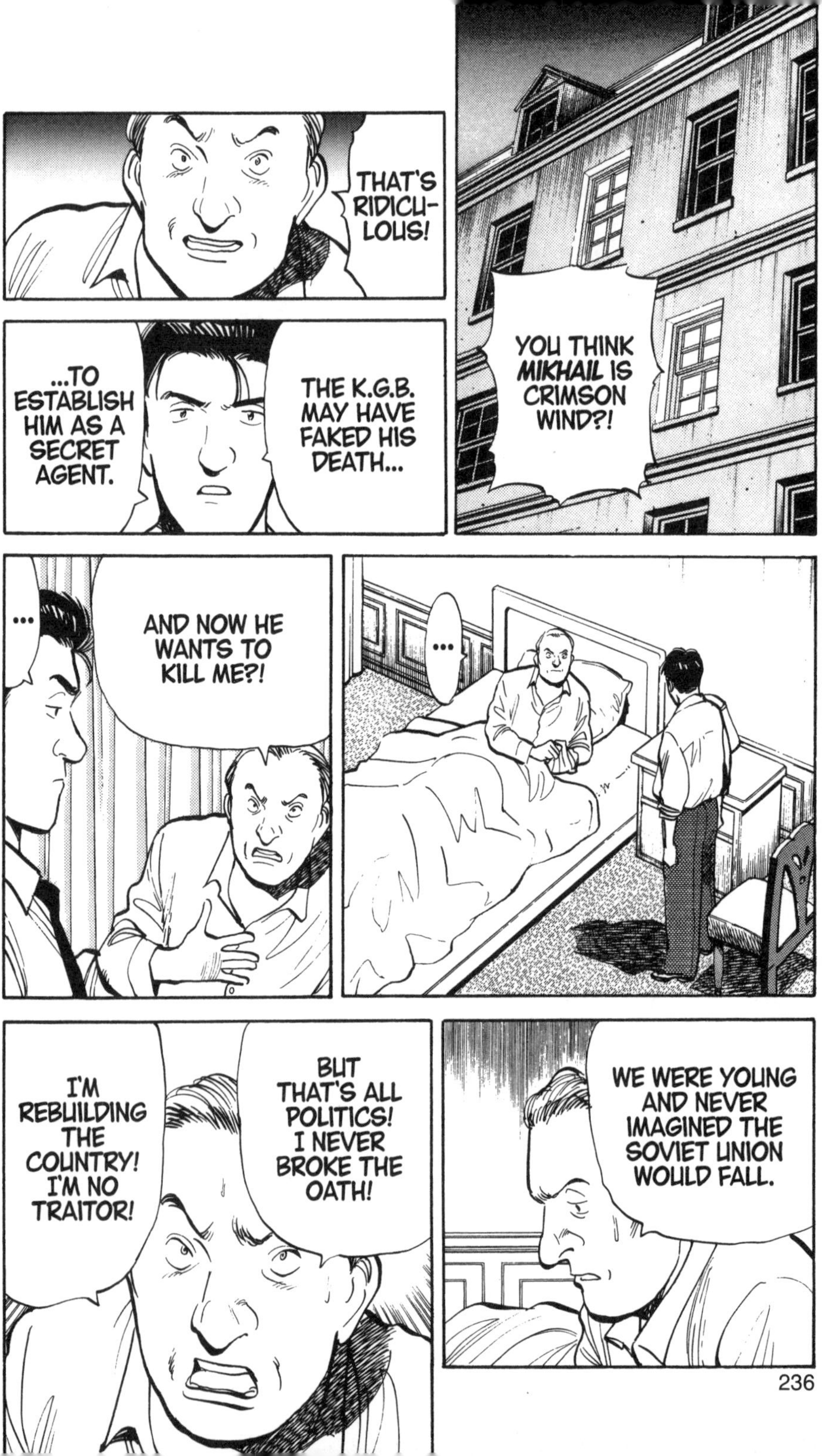
YOU THINK MIKHAIL IS CRIMSON WIND?!
THAT'S RIDICU-LOUS!
THE K.G.B. MAY HAVE FAKED HIS DEATH...
...TO ESTABLISH HIM AS A SECRET AGENT.
...
AND NOW HE WANTS TO KILL ME?!
...
WE WERE YOUNG AND NEVER IMAGINED THE SOVIET UNION WOULD FALL.
BUT THAT'S ALL POLITICS! I NEVER BROKE THE OATH!
I'M REBUILDING THE COUNTRY! I'M NO TRAITOR!

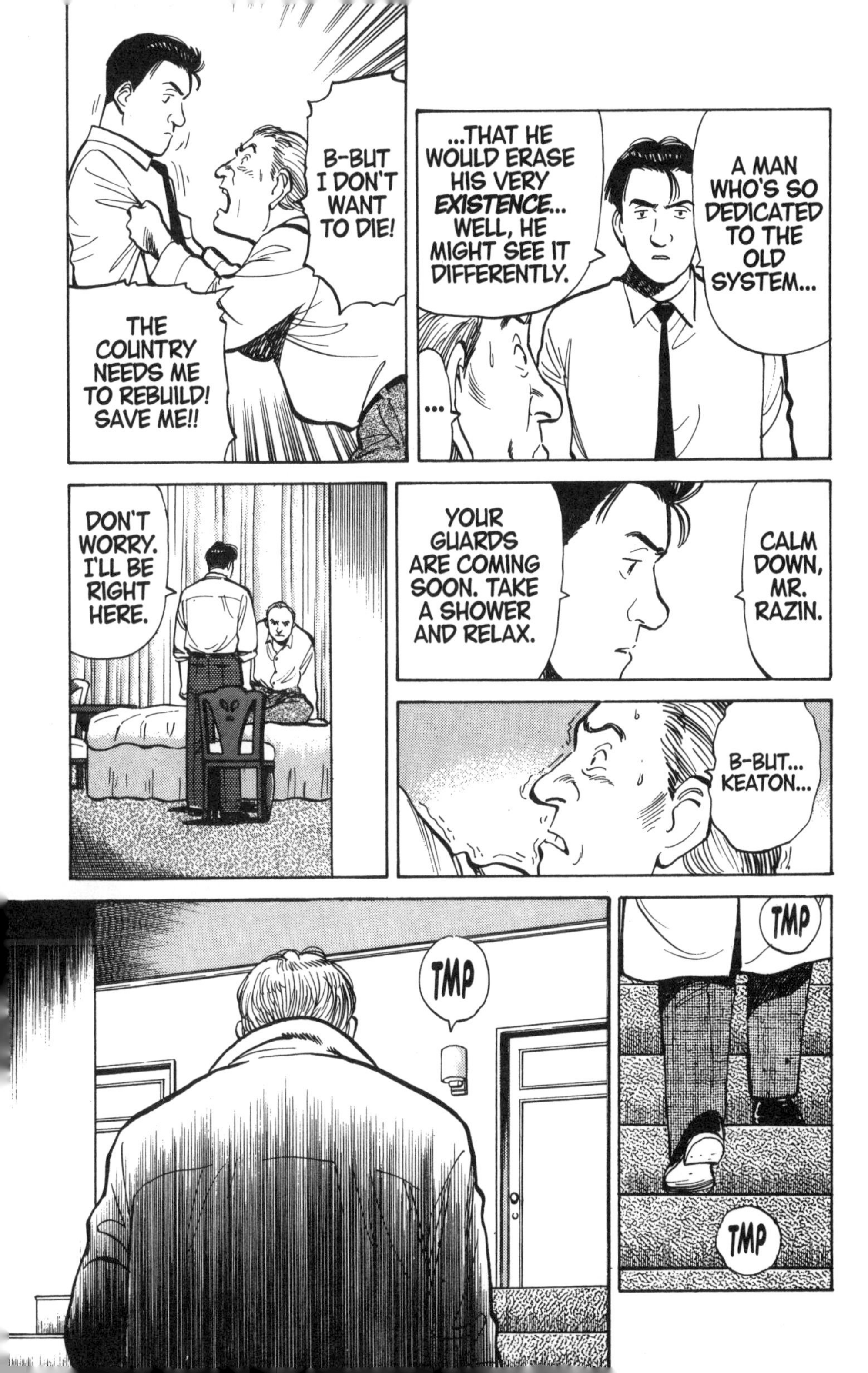
A MAN WHO'S SO DEDICATED TO THE OLD SYSTEM...
...THAT HE WOULD ERASE HIS VERY *EXISTENCE*... WELL, HE MIGHT SEE IT DIFFERENTLY.
...
B-BUT I DON'T WANT TO DIE!
THE COUNTRY NEEDS ME TO REBUILD! SAVE ME!!
CALM DOWN, MR. RAZIN.
YOUR GUARDS ARE COMING SOON. TAKE A SHOWER AND RELAX.
B-BUT... KEATON...
DON'T WORRY. I'LL BE RIGHT HERE.
TMP
TMP
TMP

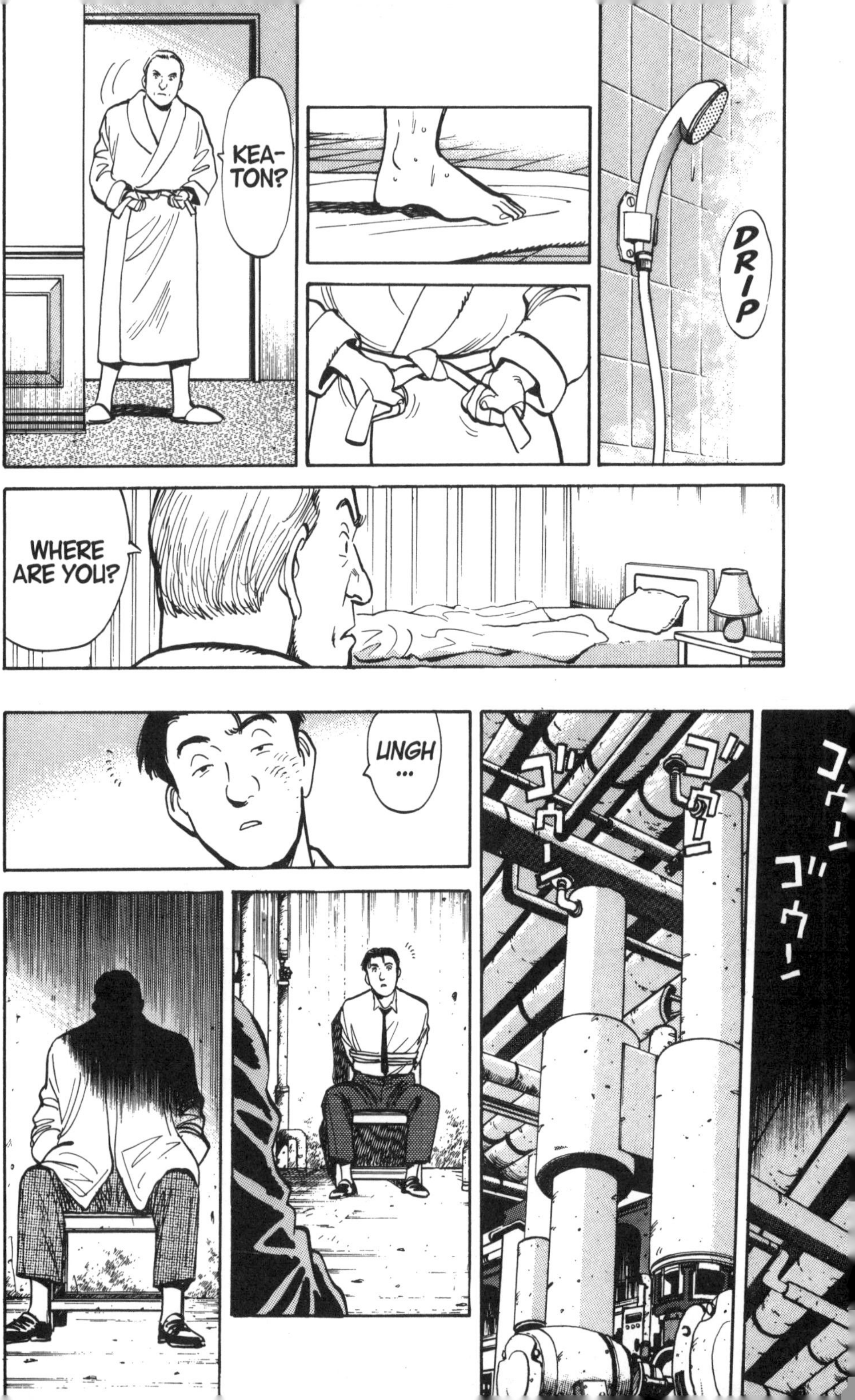
DRIP
KEA-TON?
WHERE ARE YOU?
ゴウーン ゴウーン
ゴウーン ゴウーン
UNGH ...

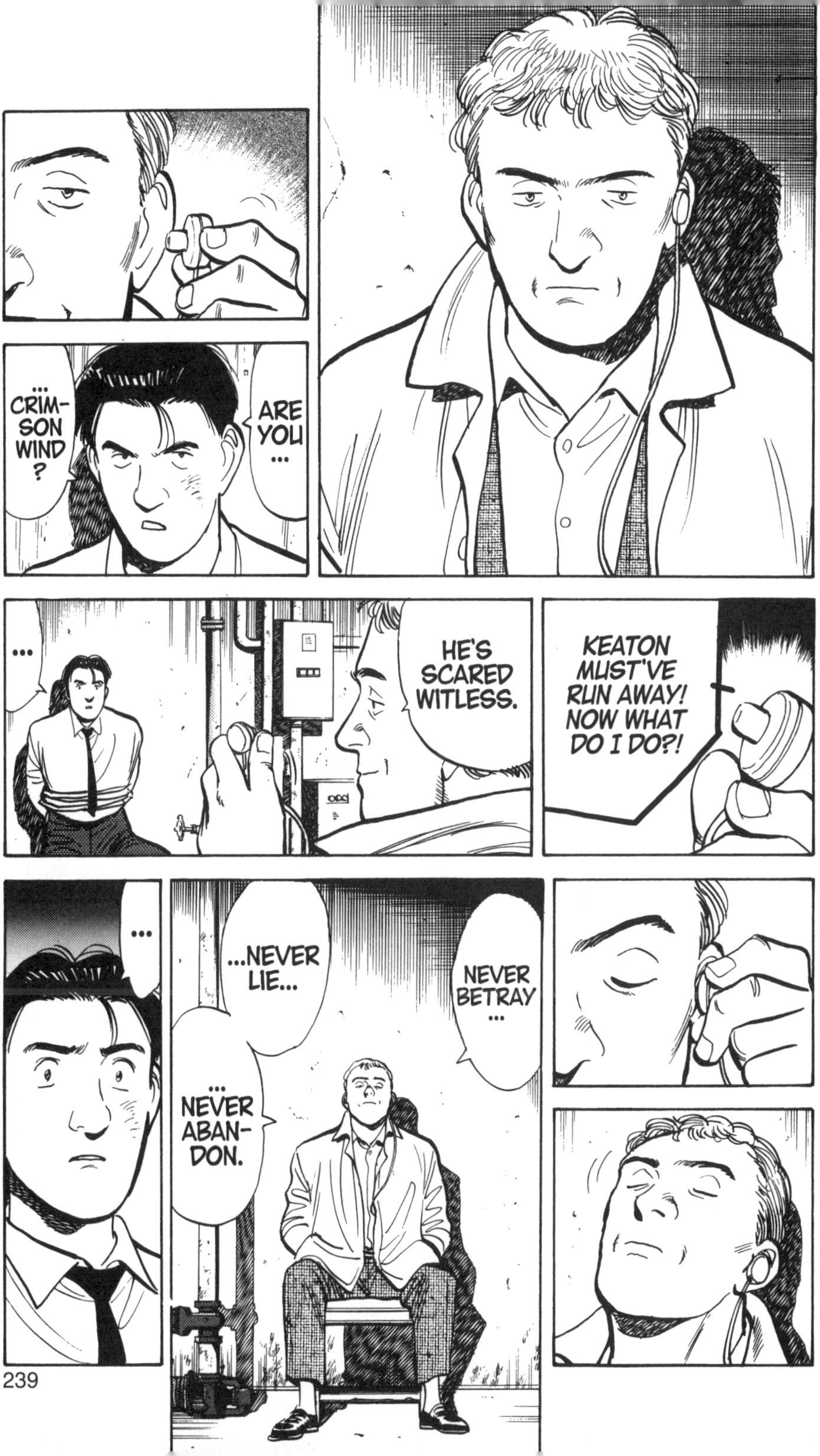
ARE YOU...
...CRIMSON WIND?
KEATON MUST'VE RUN AWAY! NOW WHAT DO I DO?!
HE'S SCARED WITLESS.
...
NEVER BETRAY...
...NEVER LIE...
...NEVER ABANDON.
...

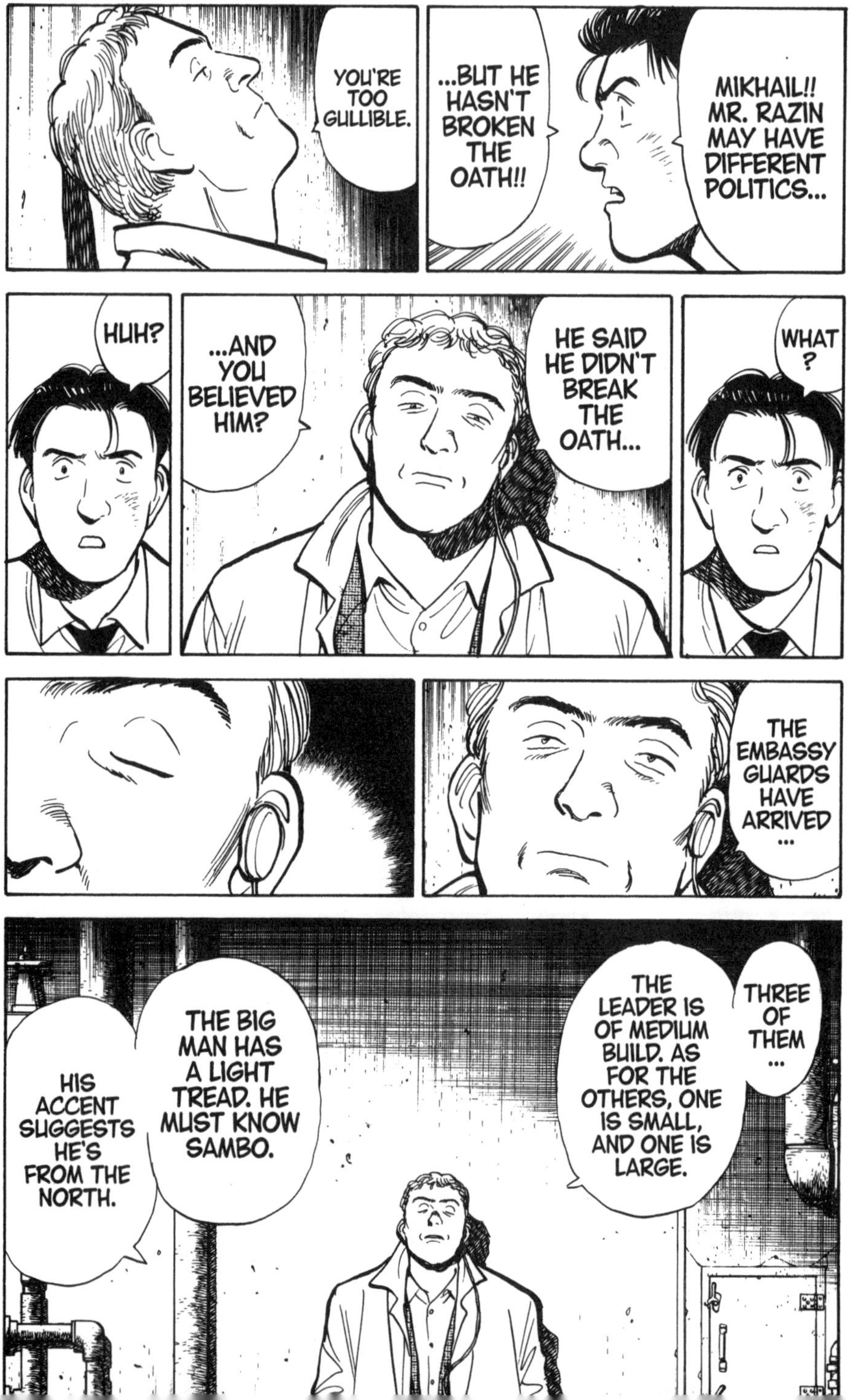
MIKHAIL!! MR. RAZIN MAY HAVE DIFFERENT POLITICS...
...BUT HE HASN'T BROKEN THE OATH!!
YOU'RE TOO GULLIBLE.
WHAT?
HE SAID HE DIDN'T BREAK THE OATH...
...AND YOU BELIEVED HIM?
HUH?
THE EMBASSY GUARDS HAVE ARRIVED...
THREE OF THEM...
THE LEADER IS OF MEDIUM BUILD. AS FOR THE OTHERS, ONE IS SMALL, AND ONE IS LARGE.
THE BIG MAN HAS A LIGHT TREAD. HE MUST KNOW SAMBO.
HIS ACCENT SUGGESTS HE'S FROM THE NORTH.

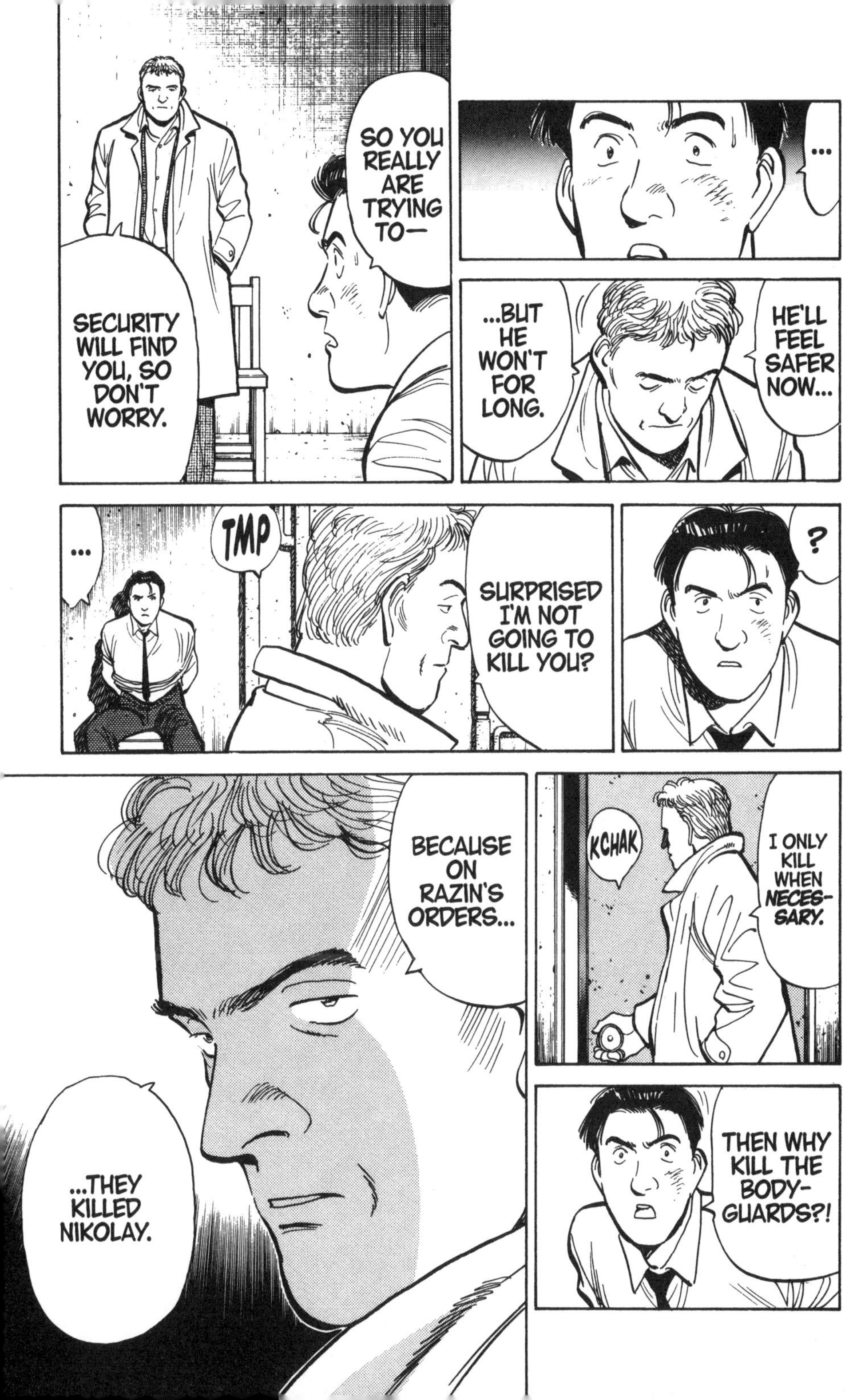
...
HE'LL FEEL SAFER NOW...
...BUT HE WON'T FOR LONG.
SO YOU REALLY ARE TRYING TO—
SECURITY WILL FIND YOU, SO DON'T WORRY.
?
SURPRISED I'M NOT GOING TO KILL YOU?
TMP
...
I ONLY KILL WHEN NECES-SARY.
KCHAK
THEN WHY KILL THE BODY-GUARDS?!
BECAUSE ON RAZIN'S ORDERS...
...THEY KILLED NIKOLAY.

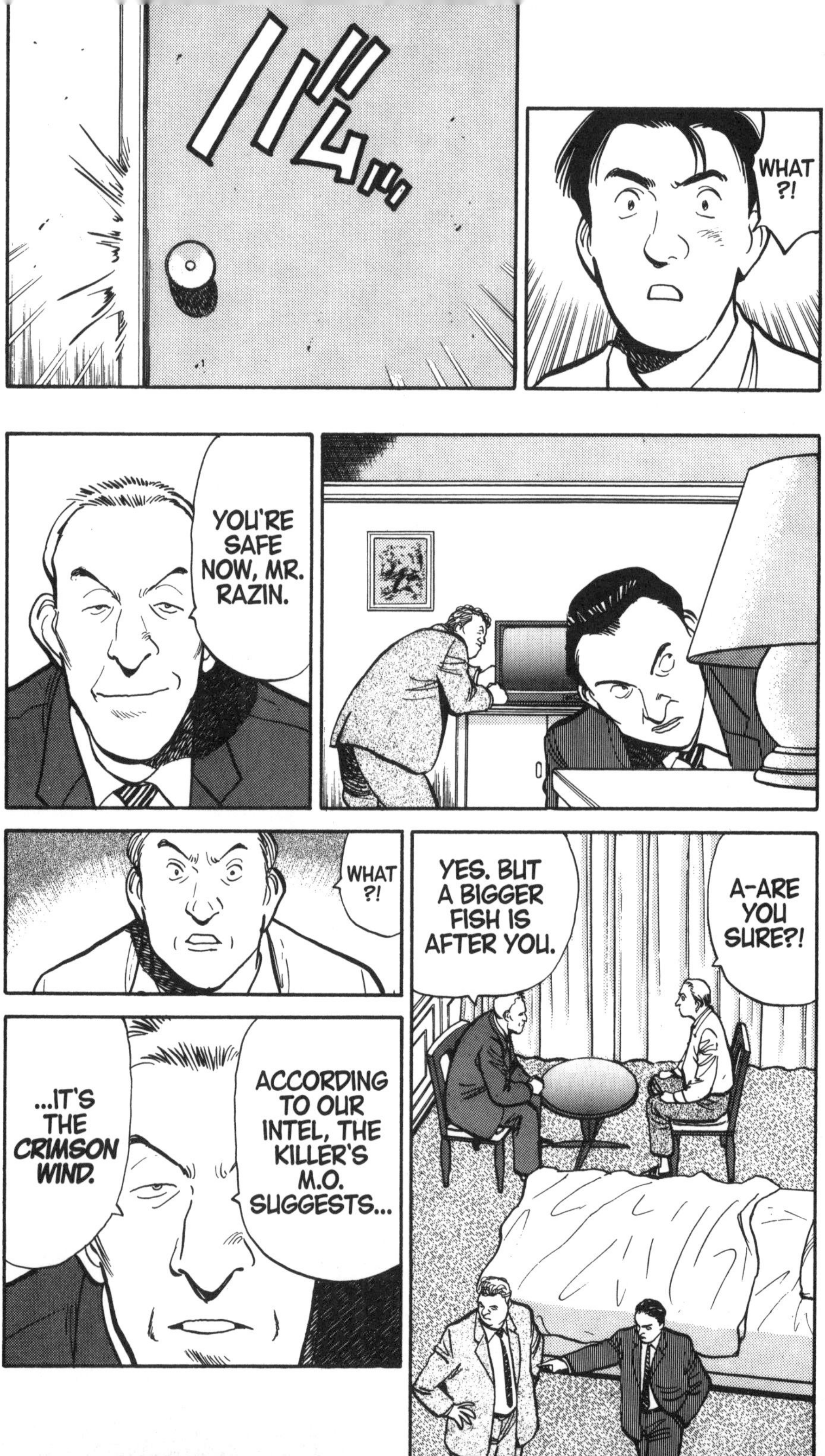
WHAT ?!
YOU'RE SAFE NOW, MR. RAZIN.
A-ARE YOU SURE?!
YES. BUT A BIGGER FISH IS AFTER YOU.
WHAT ?!
ACCORDING TO OUR INTEL, THE KILLER'S M.O. SUGGESTS...
...IT'S THE CRIMSON WIND.

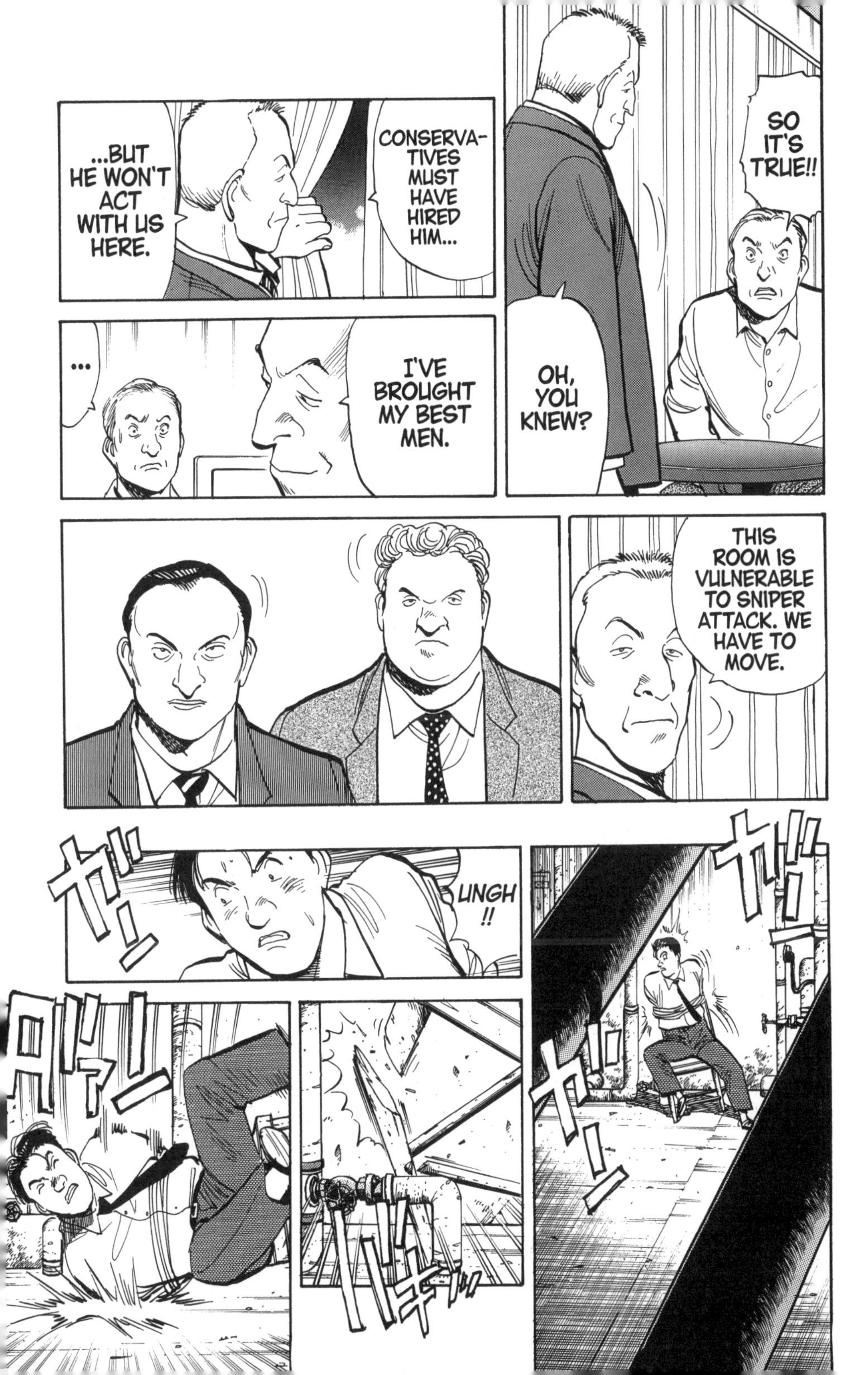
SO IT'S TRUE!!
OH, YOU KNEW?
CONSERVA-TIVES MUST HAVE HIRED HIM...
...BUT HE WON'T ACT WITH US HERE.
I'VE BROUGHT MY BEST MEN.
...
THIS ROOM IS VULNERABLE TO SNIPER ATTACK. WE HAVE TO MOVE.
UNGH !!

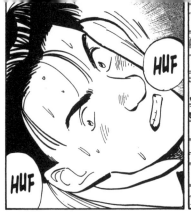

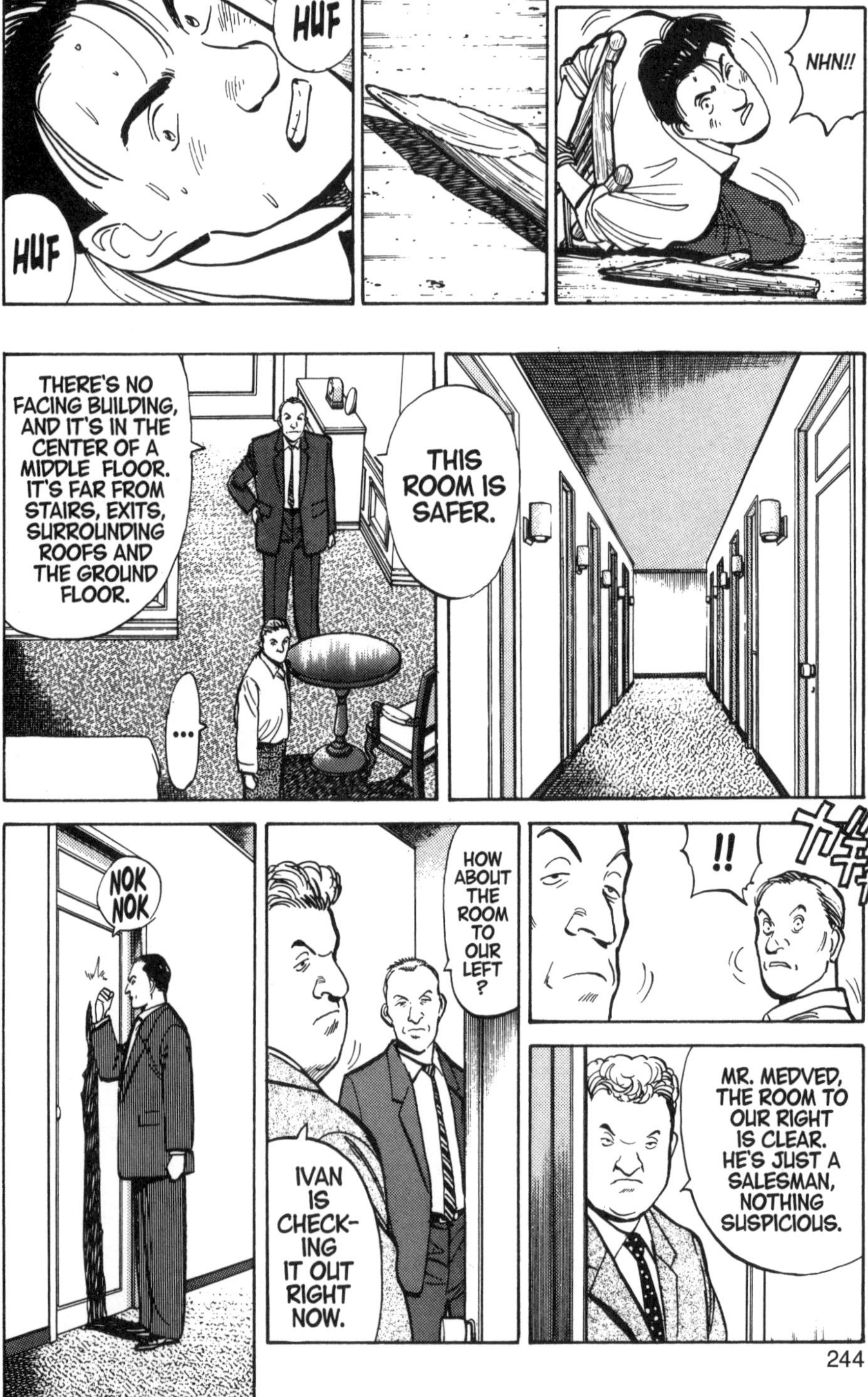
NHN!!
HUF
HUF
THIS ROOM IS SAFER.
THERE'S NO FACING BUILDING, AND IT'S IN THE CENTER OF A MIDDLE FLOOR. IT'S FAR FROM STAIRS, EXITS, SURROUNDING ROOFS AND THE GROUND FLOOR.
...
!!
MR. MEDVED, THE ROOM TO OUR RIGHT IS CLEAR. HE'S JUST A SALESMAN, NOTHING SUSPICIOUS.
HOW ABOUT THE ROOM TO OUR LEFT?
IVAN IS CHECKING IT OUT RIGHT NOW.
NOK NOK

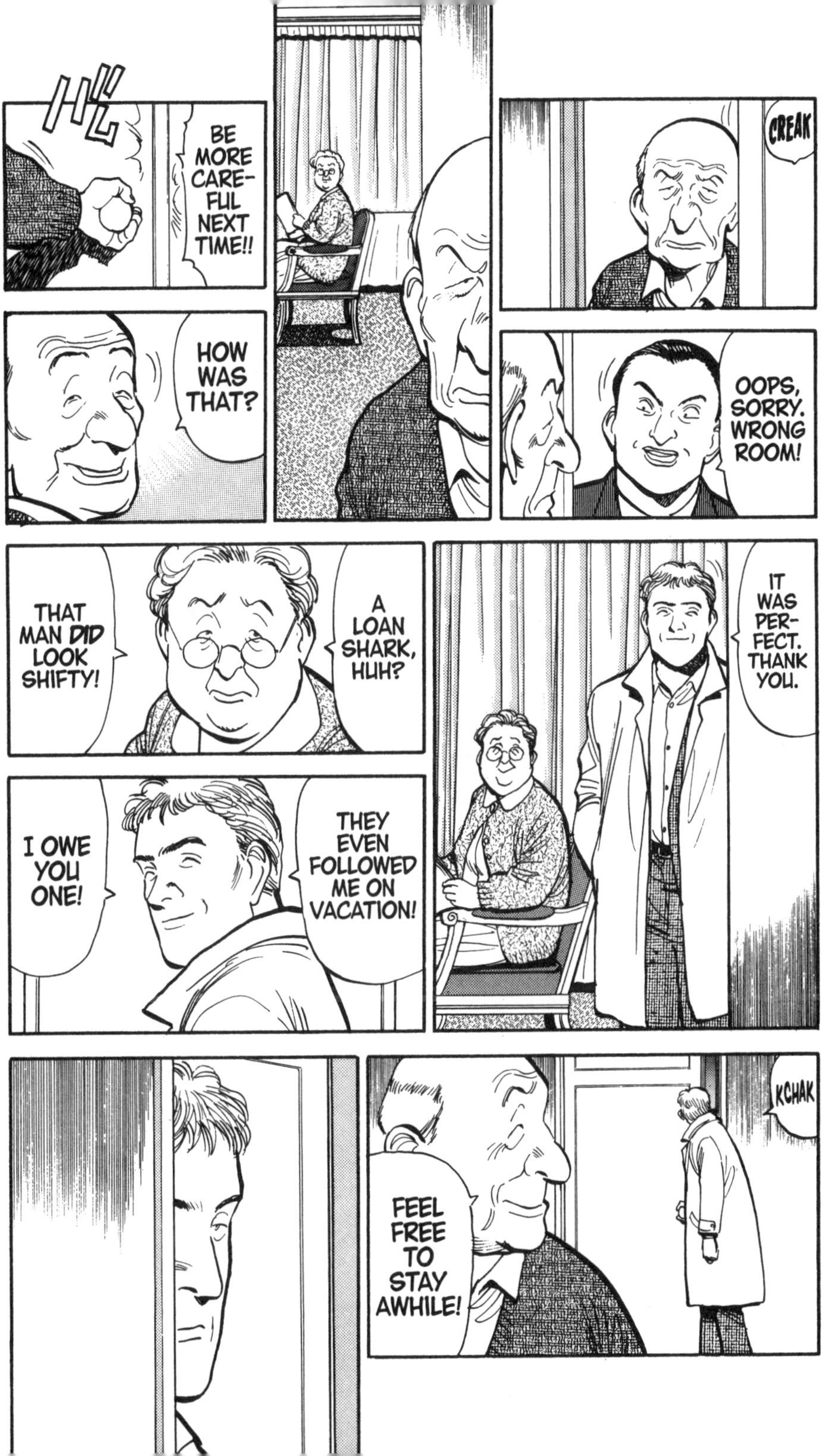
CREAK
OOPS, SORRY. WRONG ROOM!
BE MORE CAREFUL NEXT TIME!!
HOW WAS THAT?
IT WAS PERFECT. THANK YOU.
A LOAN SHARK, HUH?
THAT MAN **DID** LOOK SHIFTY!
THEY EVEN FOLLOWED ME ON VACATION!
I OWE YOU ONE!
KCHAK
FEEL FREE TO STAY AWHILE!

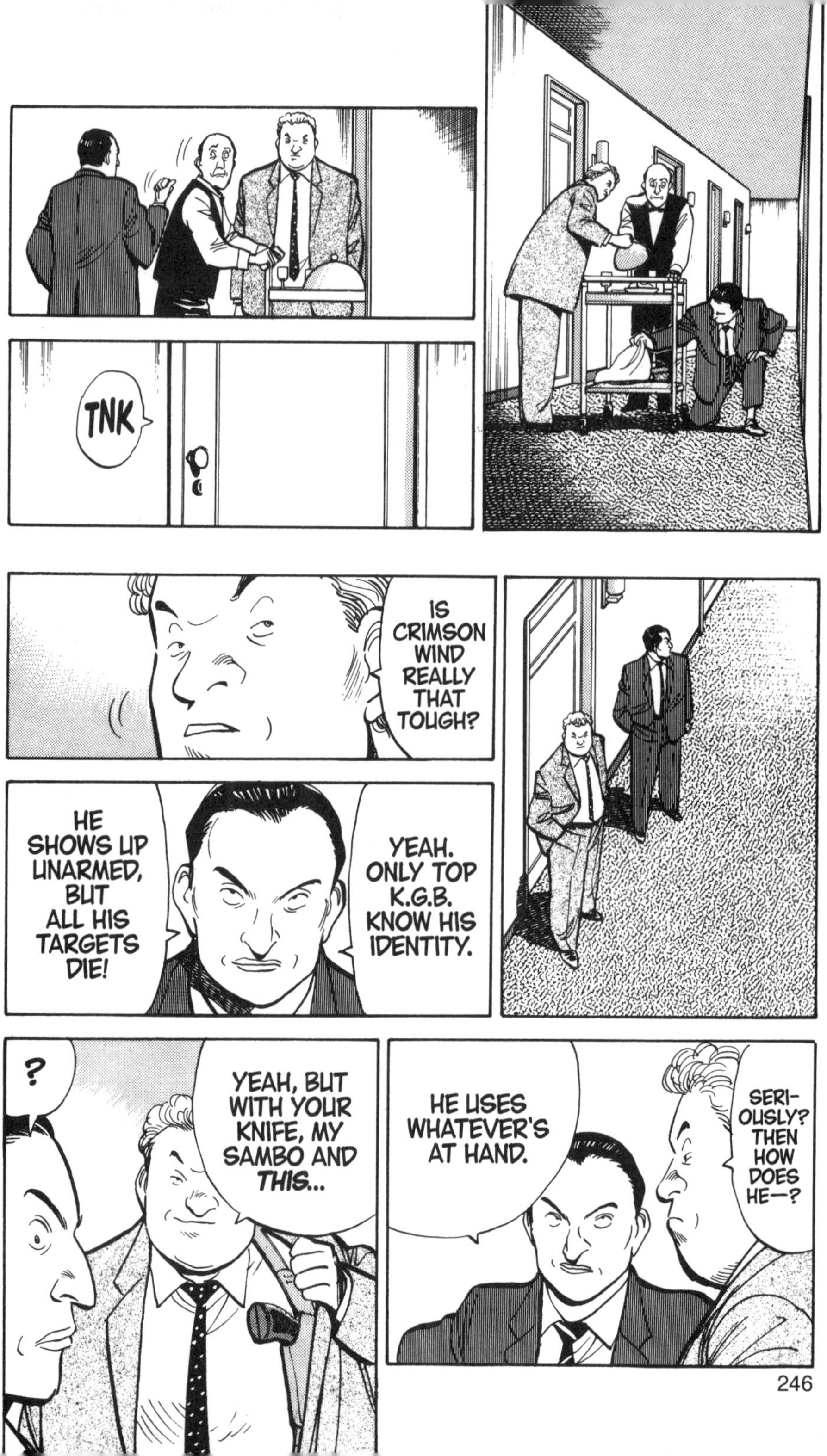
TNK
IS CRIMSON WIND REALLY THAT TOUGH?
YEAH. ONLY TOP K.G.B. KNOW HIS IDENTITY.
HE SHOWS UP UNARMED, BUT ALL HIS TARGETS DIE!
SERI-OUSLY? THEN HOW DOES HE—?
HE USES WHATEVER'S AT HAND.
YEAH, BUT WITH YOUR KNIFE, MY SAMBO AND *THIS*...
?

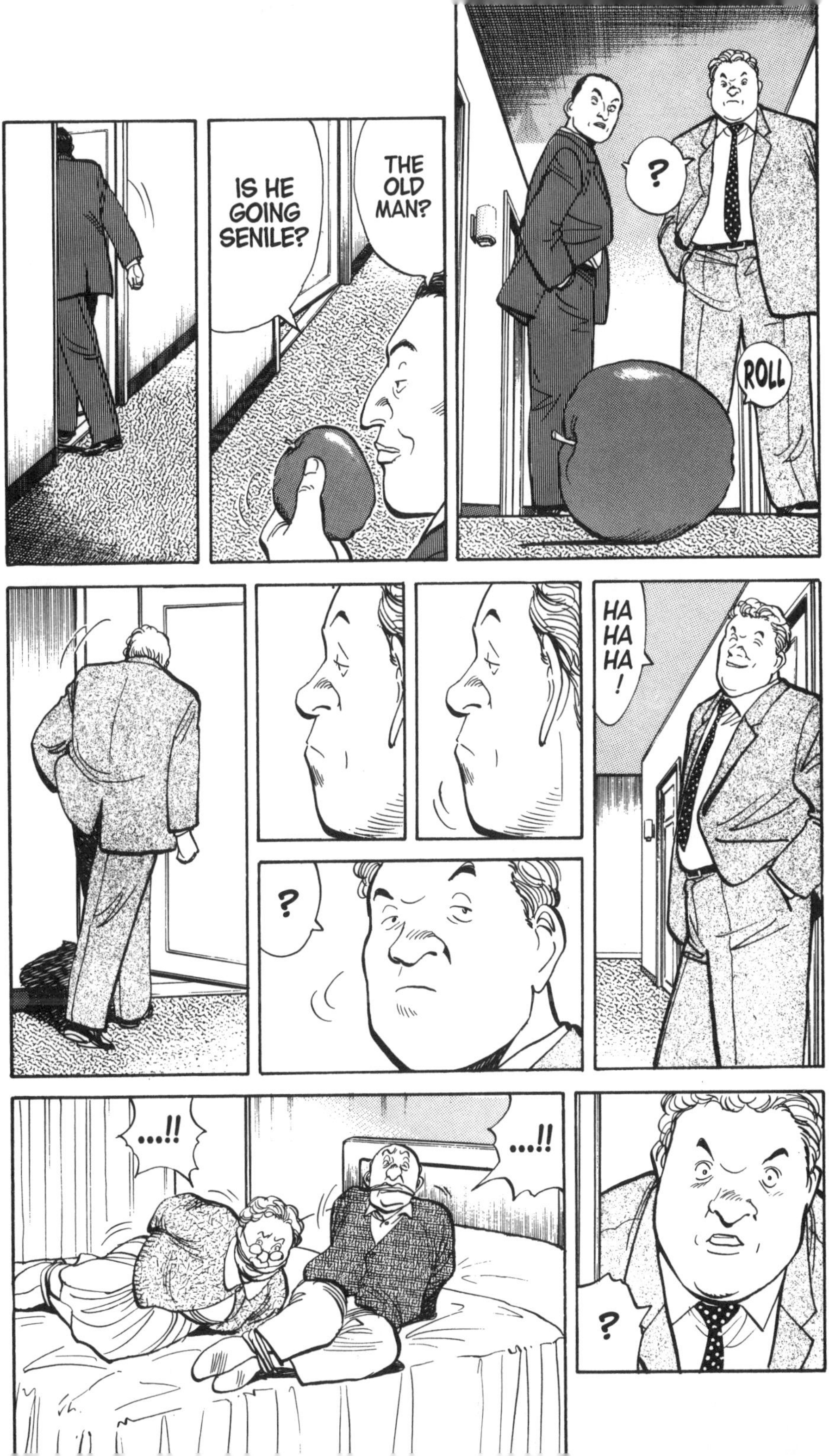
?
ROLL
THE OLD MAN?
IS HE GOING SENILE?
HA HA HA!
?
?
...!!
...!!

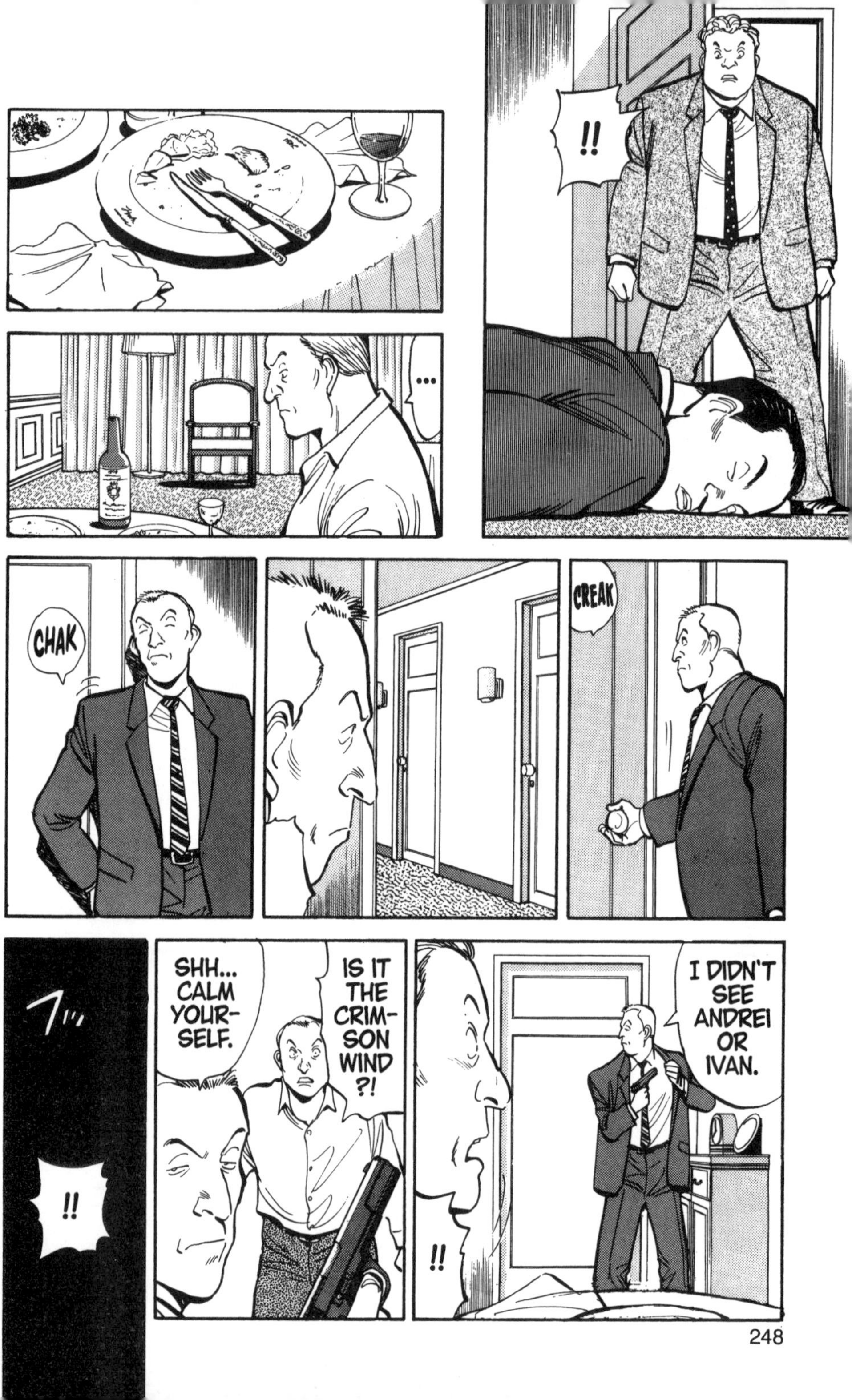
!!
...
CREAK
CHAK
I DIDN'T SEE ANDREI OR IVAN.
!!
IS IT THE CRIM-SON WIND ?!
SHH... CALM YOUR-SELF.
フッ
!!

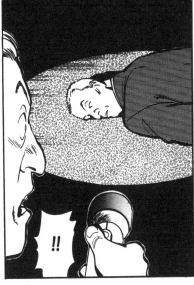

FWIK

MEDVED!!

WHERE ARE YOU?!

GAH!!

M-MIK-HAIL?!

STEPAN... HOW LONG HAS IT BEEN?

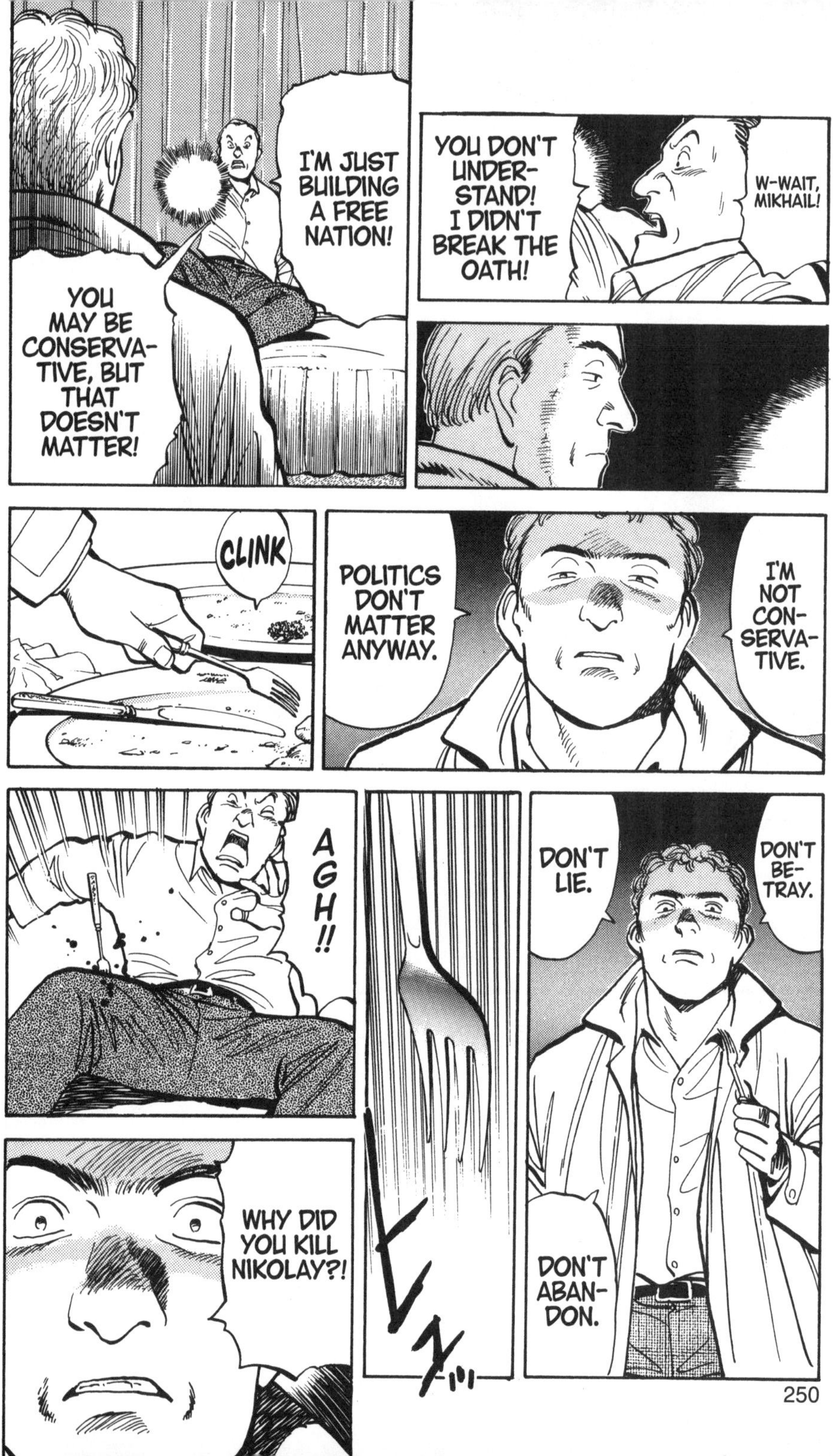
W-WAIT, MIKHAIL!
YOU DON'T UNDER-STAND! I DIDN'T BREAK THE OATH!
I'M JUST BUILDING A FREE NATION!
YOU MAY BE CONSERVA-TIVE, BUT THAT DOESN'T MATTER!
I'M NOT CON-SERVA-TIVE.
POLITICS DON'T MATTER ANYWAY.
CLINK
DON'T BE-TRAY.
DON'T LIE.
DON'T ABAN-DON.
AGH!!
WHY DID YOU KILL NIKOLAY?!

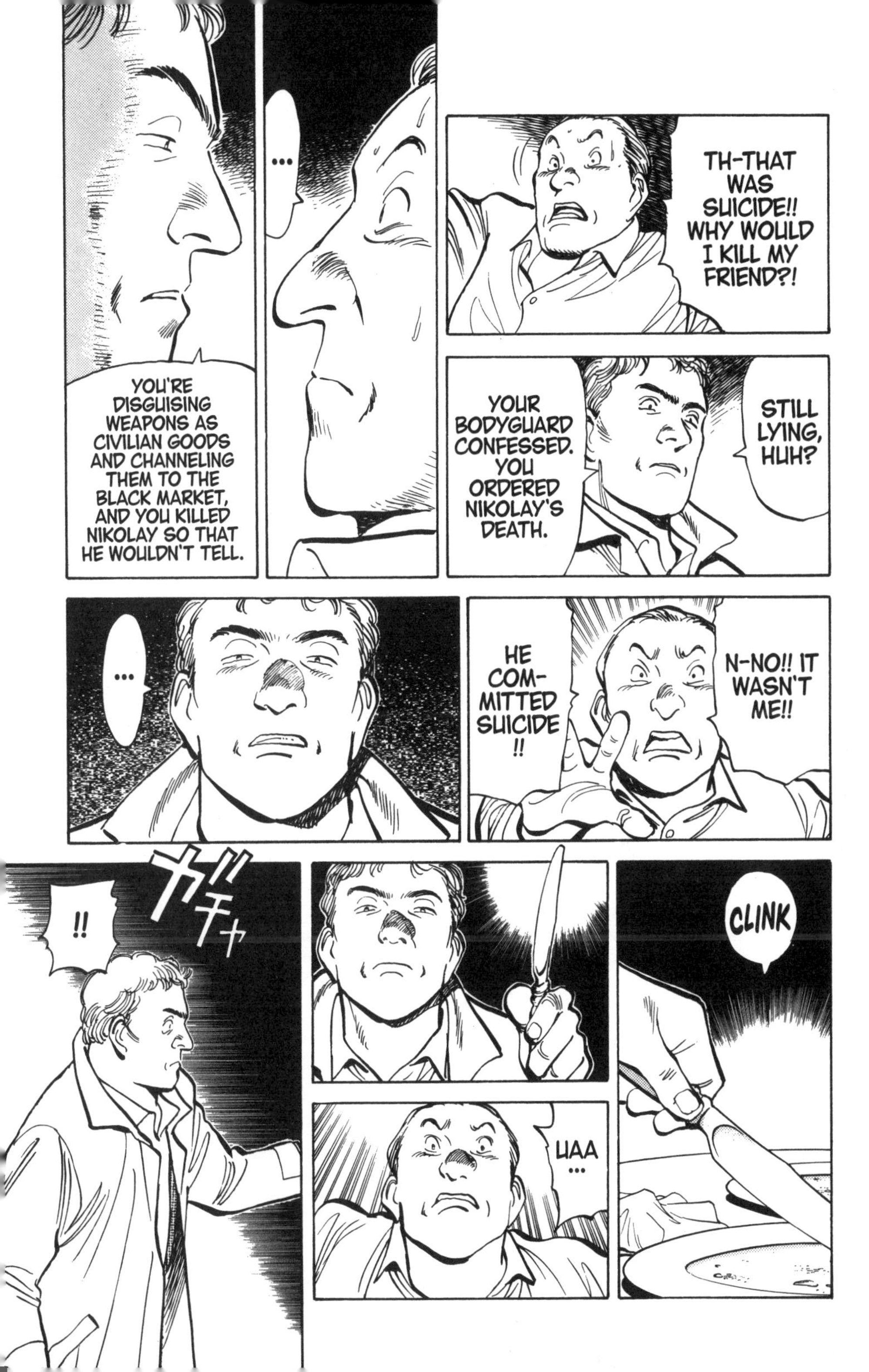
TH-THAT WAS SUICIDE!! WHY WOULD I KILL MY FRIEND?!
STILL LYING, HUH?
YOUR BODYGUARD CONFESSED. YOU ORDERED NIKOLAY'S DEATH.
...
YOU'RE DISGUISING WEAPONS AS CIVILIAN GOODS AND CHANNELING THEM TO THE BLACK MARKET, AND YOU KILLED NIKOLAY SO THAT HE WOULDN'T TELL.
N-NO!! IT WASN'T ME!!
HE COM-MITTED SUICIDE!!
...
CLINK
UAA ...
ガチャ
!!

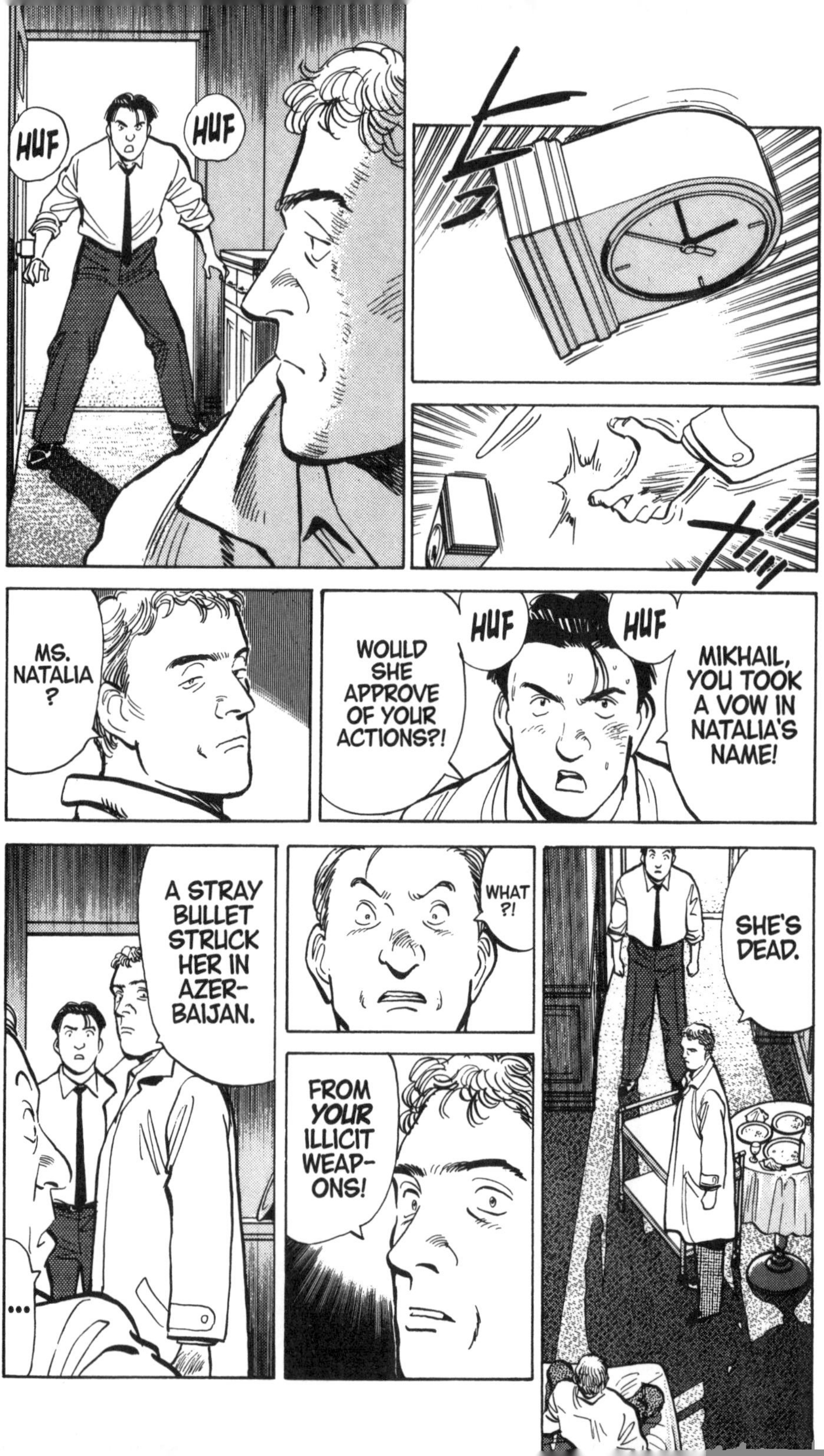
HUF
HUF
HUF
HUF
MIKHAIL, YOU TOOK A VOW IN NATALIA'S NAME!
WOULD SHE APPROVE OF YOUR ACTIONS?!
MS. NATALIA?
SHE'S DEAD.
WHAT?!
FROM YOUR ILLICIT WEAP-ONS!
A STRAY BULLET STRUCK HER IN AZER-BAIJAN.
...

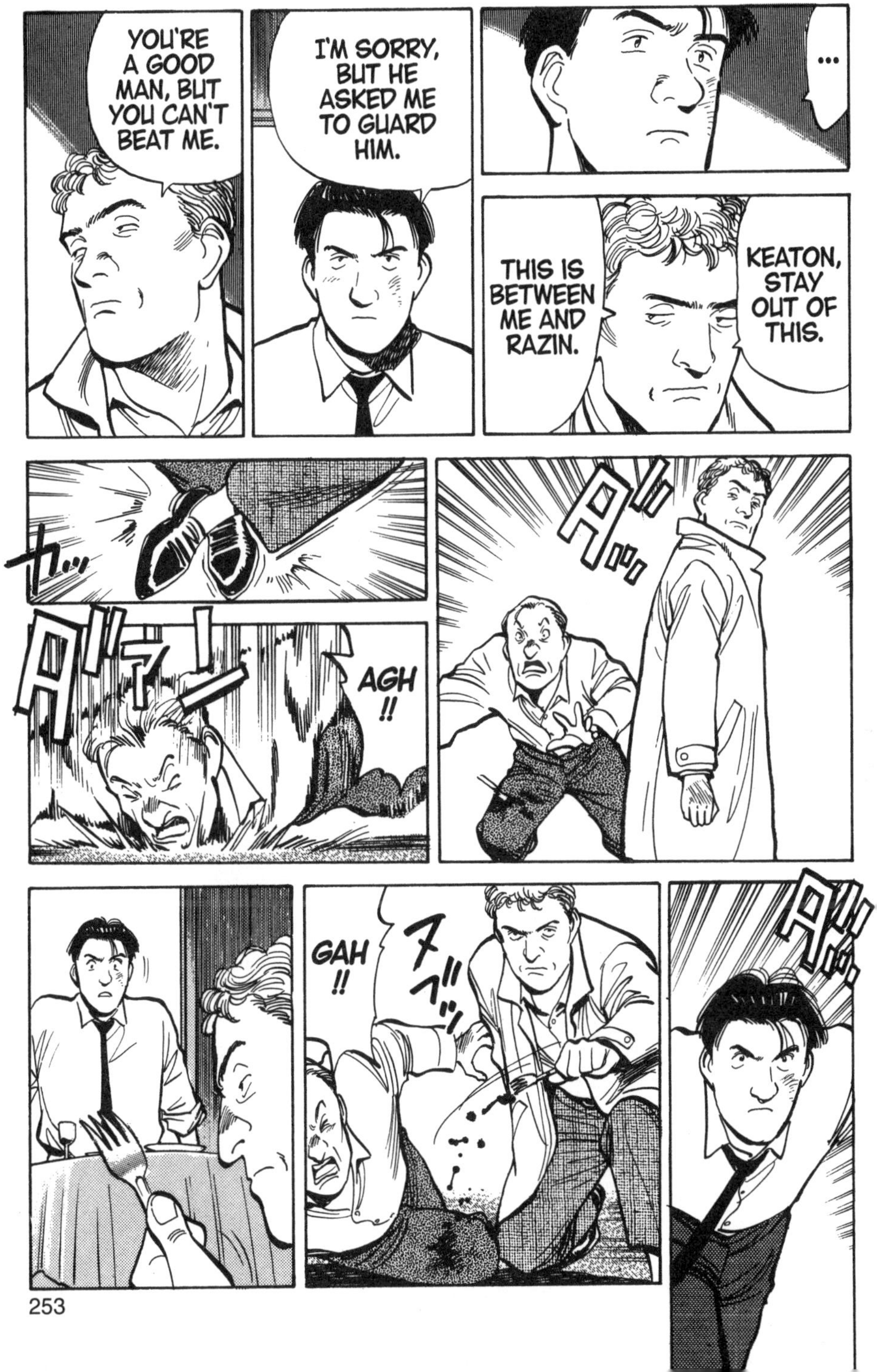
...
KEATON, STAY OUT OF THIS.
THIS IS BETWEEN ME AND RAZIN.
I'M SORRY, BUT HE ASKED ME TO GUARD HIM.
YOU'RE A GOOD MAN, BUT YOU CAN'T BEAT ME.
AGH !!
GAH !!

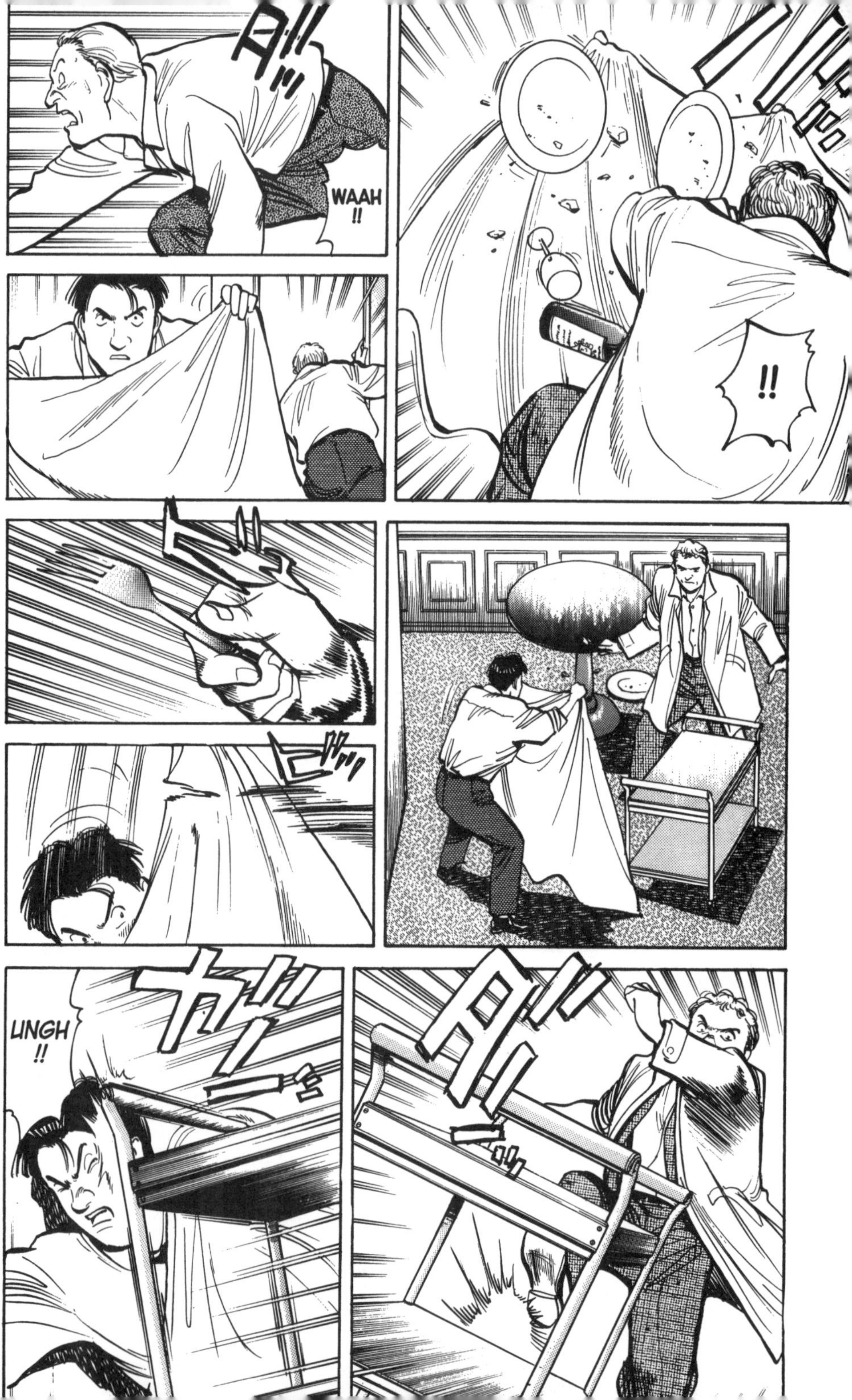
!!
WAAH !!
UNGH !!

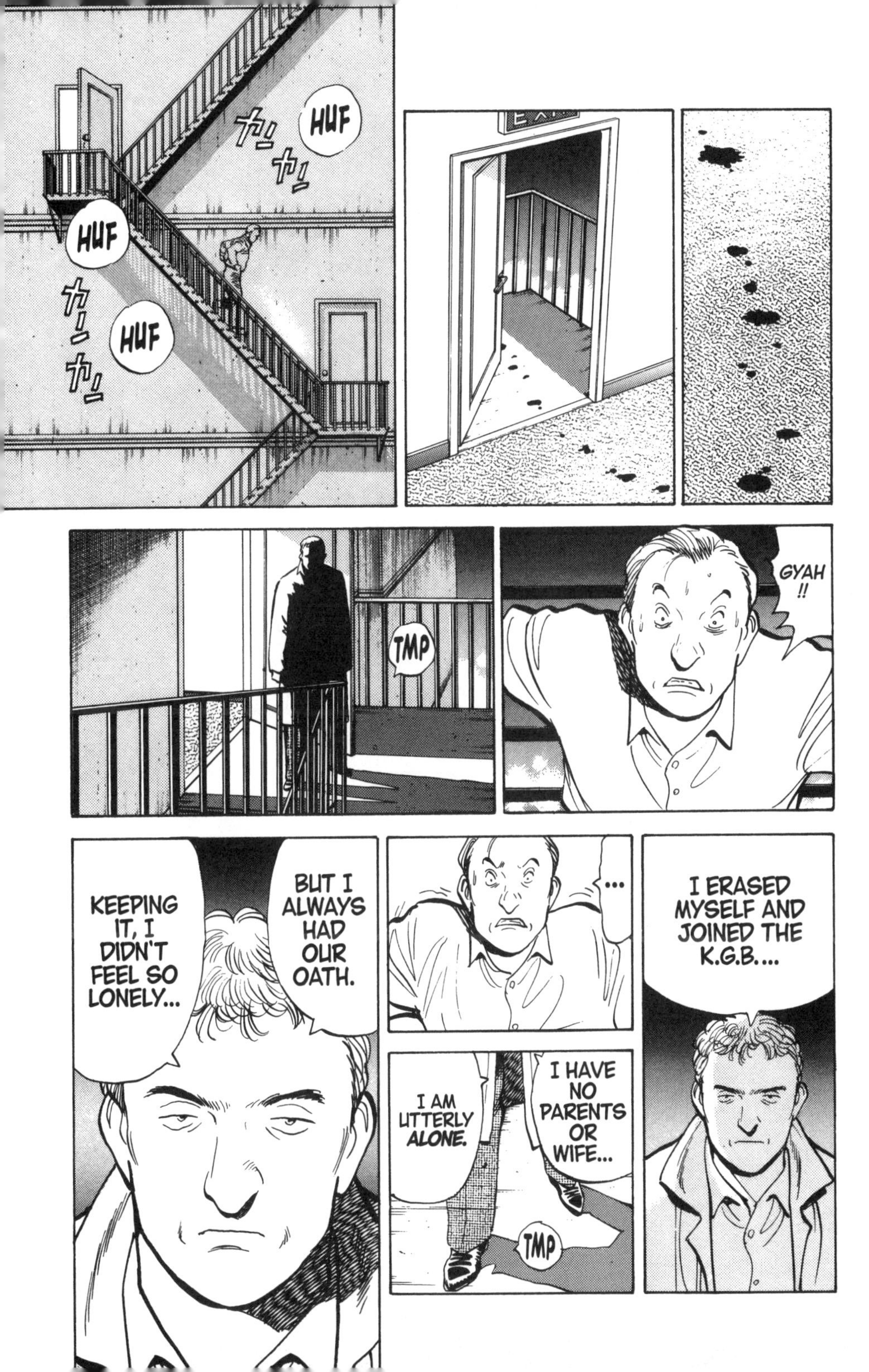
HUF
HUF
HUF
GYAH !!
TMP
I ERASED MYSELF AND JOINED THE K.G.B....
...
I HAVE NO PARENTS OR WIFE...
I AM UTTERLY ALONE.
TMP
BUT I ALWAYS HAD OUR OATH.
KEEPING IT, I DIDN'T FEEL SO LONELY...

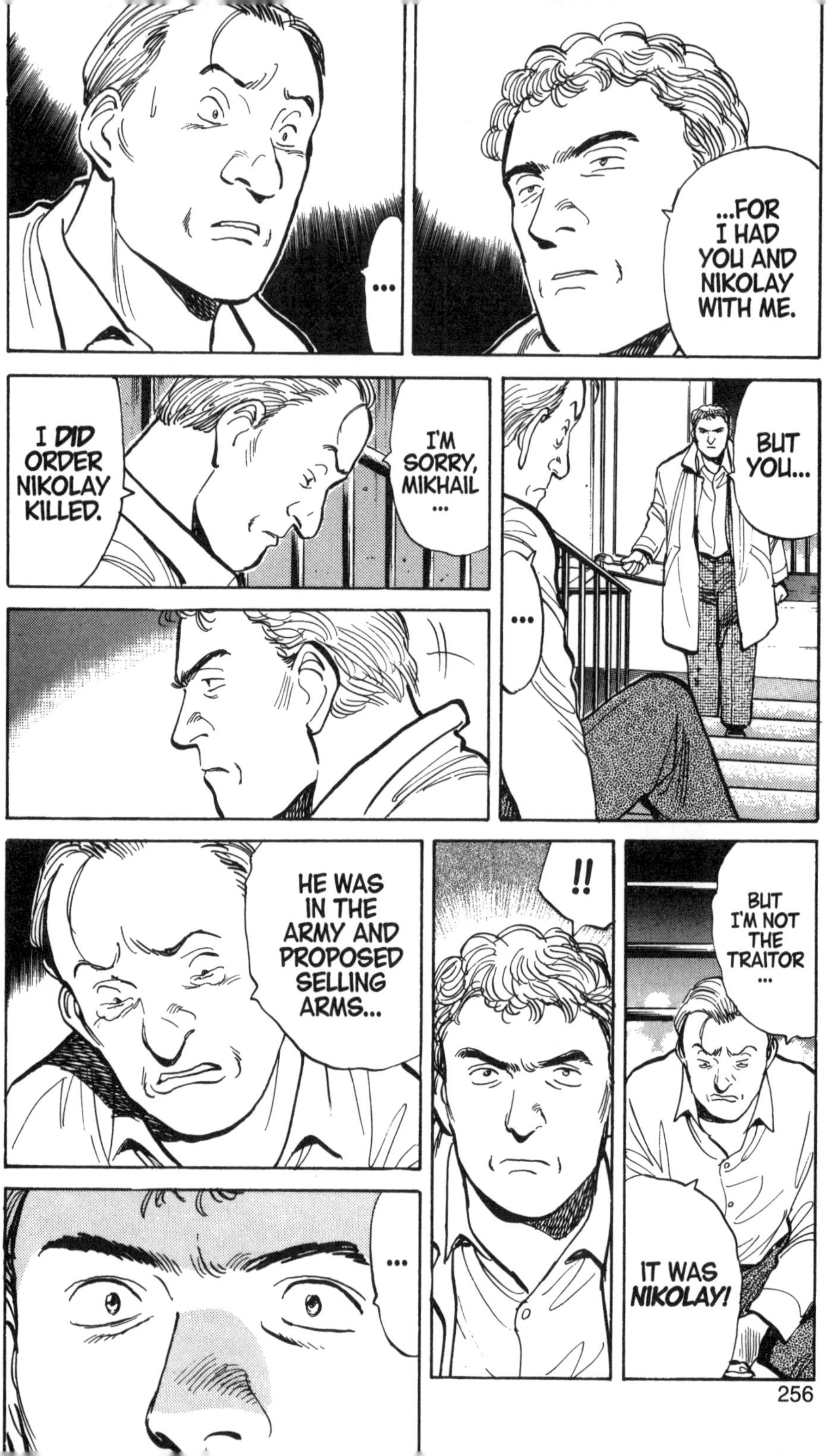
...FOR I HAD YOU AND NIKOLAY WITH ME.
...
BUT YOU...
...
I'M SORRY, MIKHAIL...
I DID ORDER NIKOLAY KILLED.
BUT I'M NOT THE TRAITOR...
IT WAS NIKOLAY!
!!
HE WAS IN THE ARMY AND PROPOSED SELLING ARMS...
...

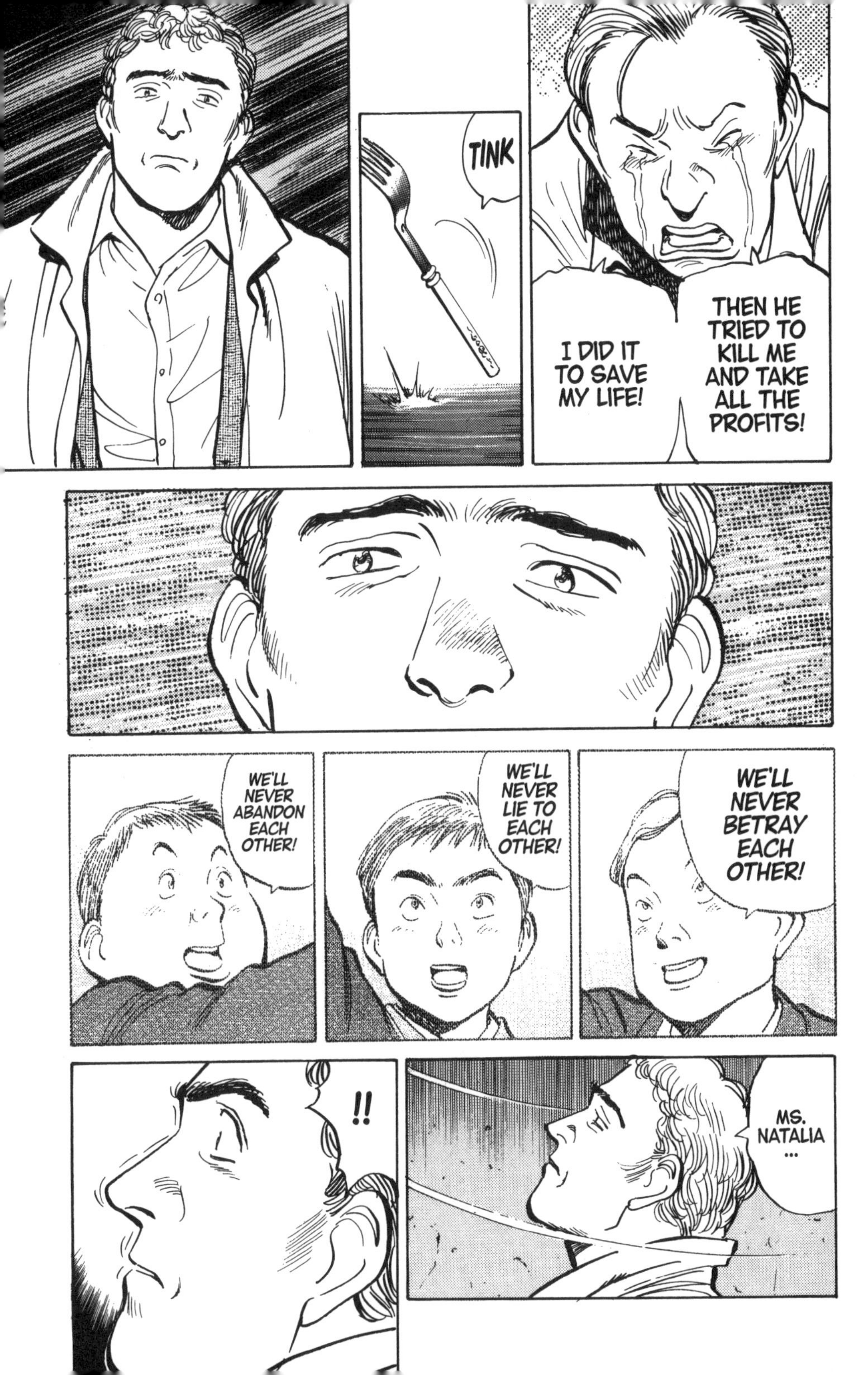
THEN HE TRIED TO KILL ME AND TAKE ALL THE PROFITS!
I DID IT TO SAVE MY LIFE!
TINK
WE'LL NEVER BETRAY EACH OTHER!
WE'LL NEVER LIE TO EACH OTHER!
WE'LL NEVER ABANDON EACH OTHER!
MS. NATALIA ...
!!

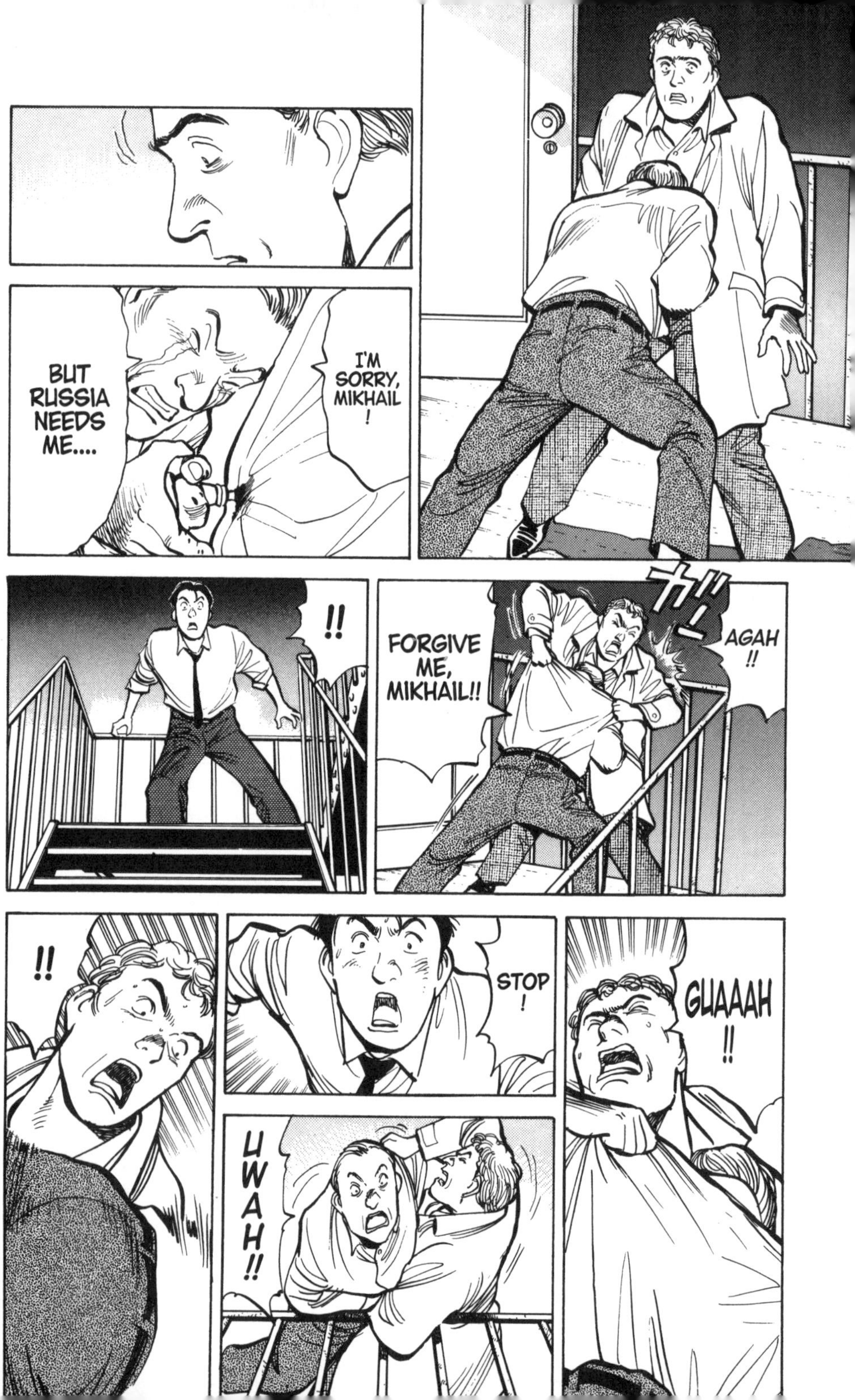
I'M SORRY, MIKHAIL!
BUT RUSSIA NEEDS ME....
ガッ
AGAH!!
FORGIVE ME, MIKHAIL!!
!!
GUAAAH!!
STOP!
UWAH!!
!!

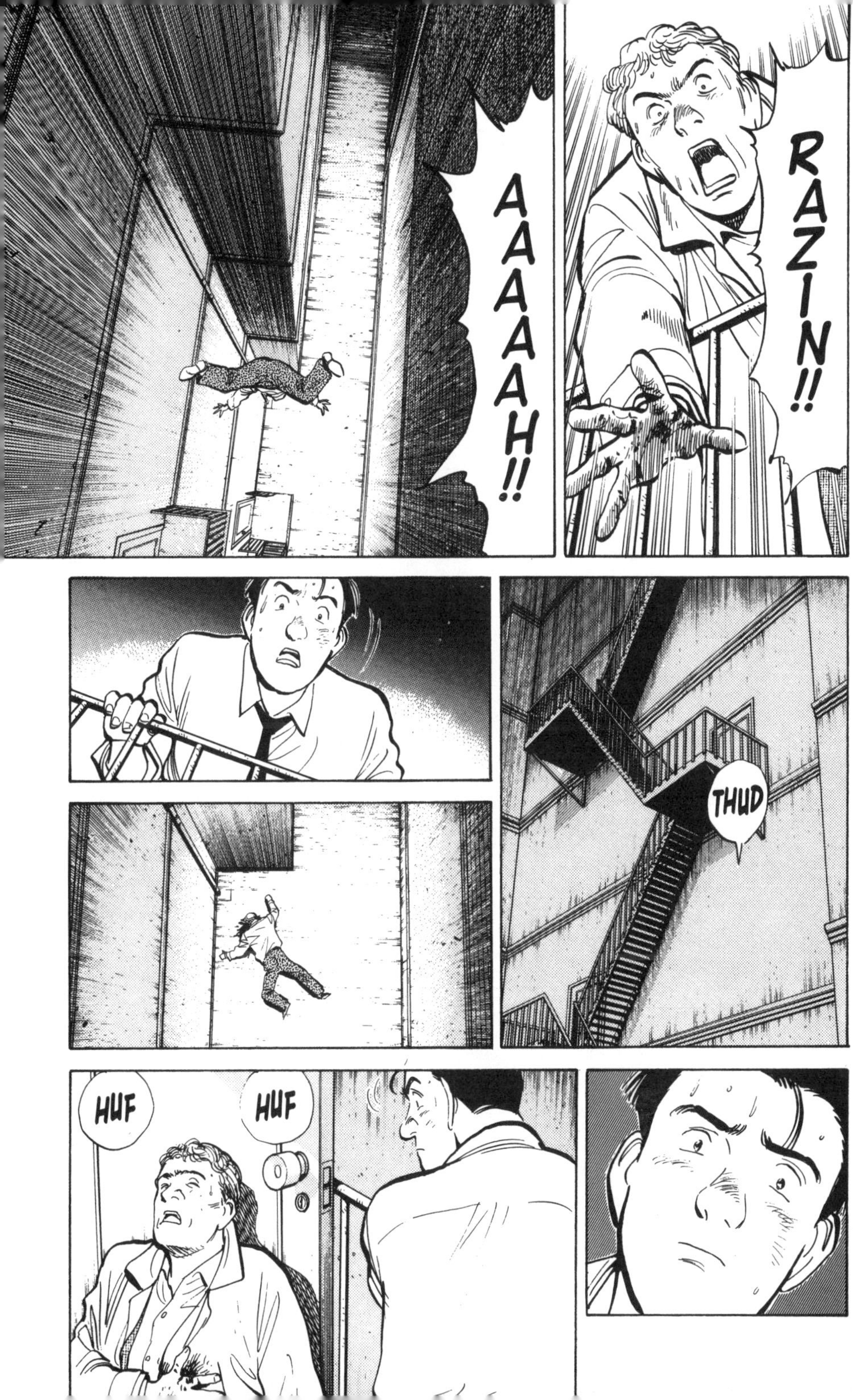
RAZIN!!
AAAAAAH!!
THUD
HUF
HUF

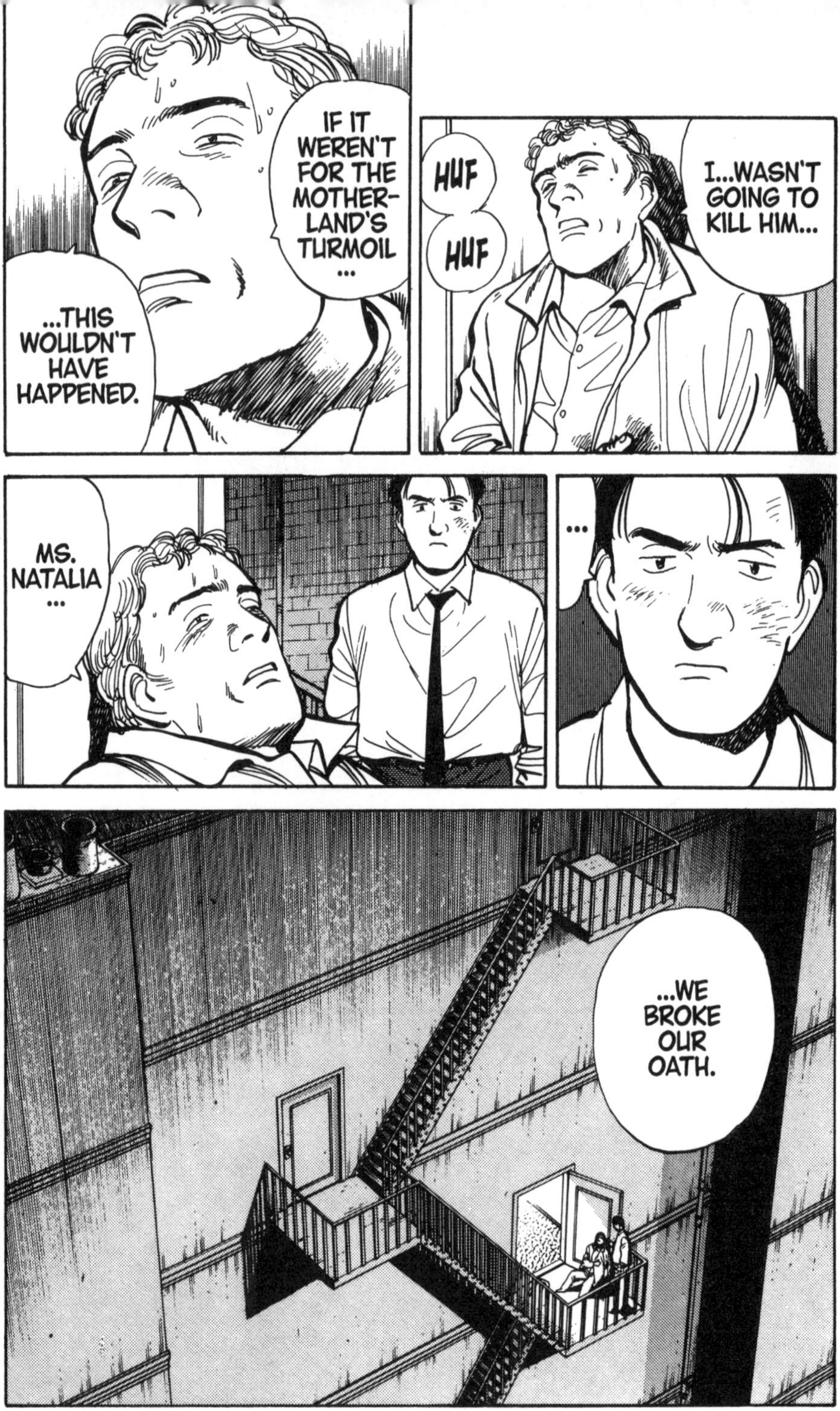
I...WASN'T GOING TO KILL HIM...
HUF
HUF
IF IT WEREN'T FOR THE MOTHER-LAND'S TURMOIL...
...THIS WOULDN'T HAVE HAPPENED.
...
MS. NATALIA...
...WE BROKE OUR OATH.

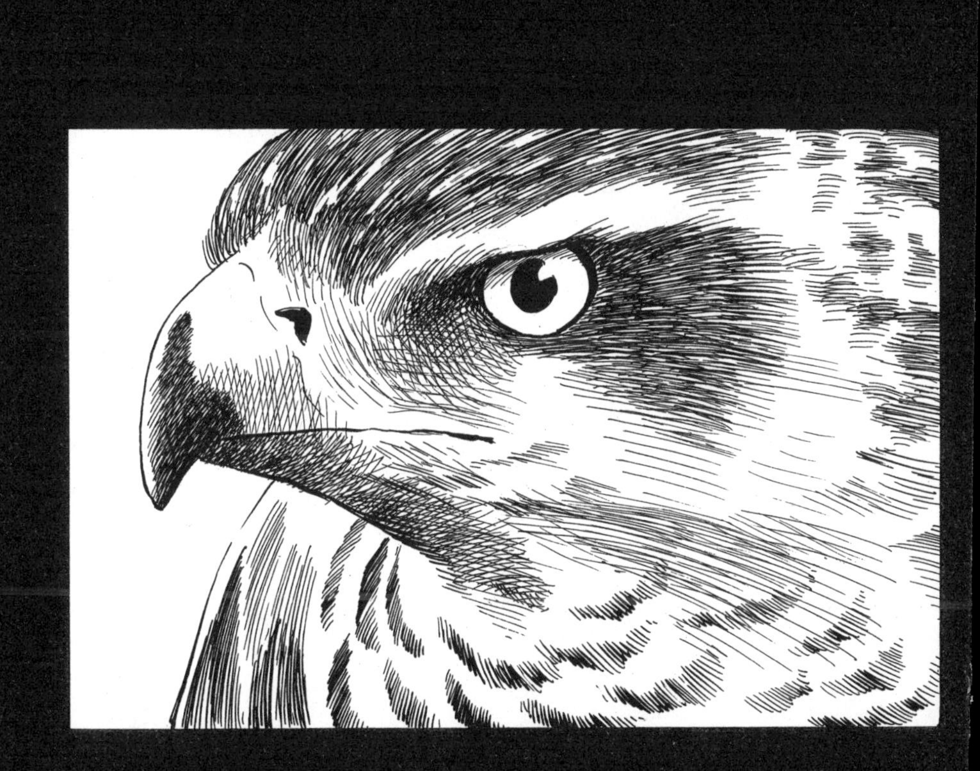

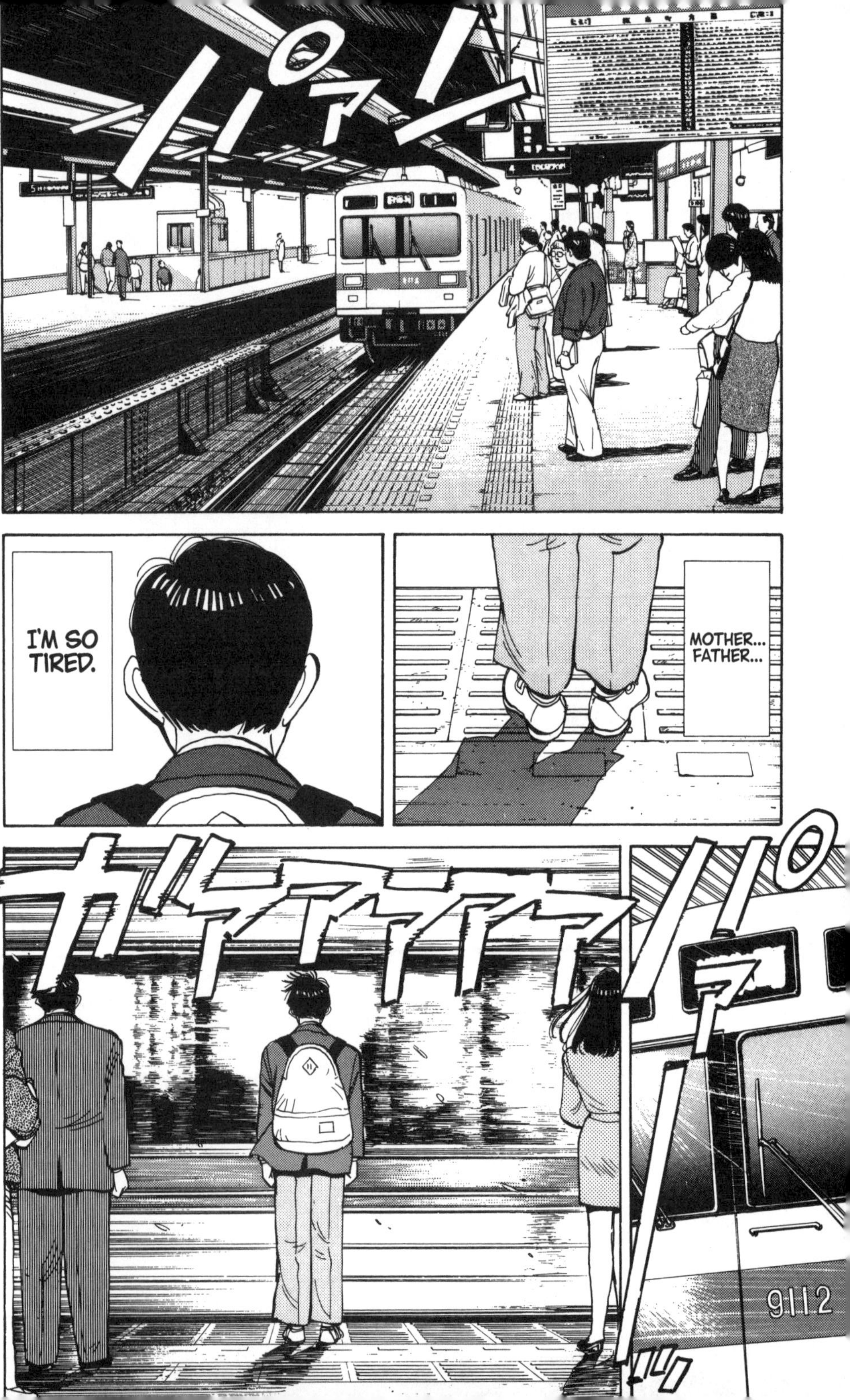
パァーン
MOTHER... FATHER...
I'M SO TIRED.
ガァァァァ
パァ
9112

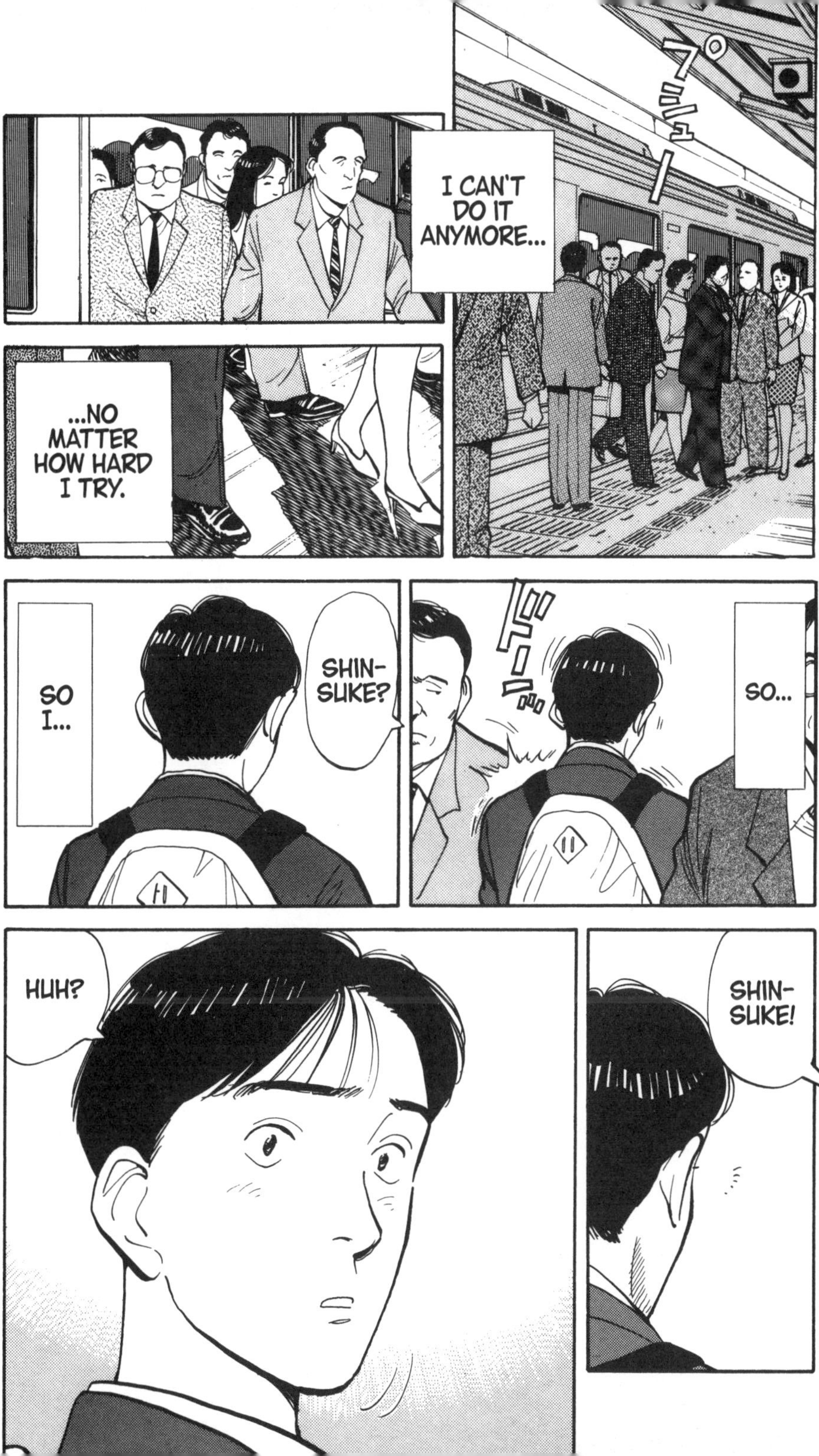
プシュー
I CAN'T DO IT ANYMORE...
...NO MATTER HOW HARD I TRY.
SO...
SHIN-SUKE?
SO I...
SHIN-SUKE!
HUH?

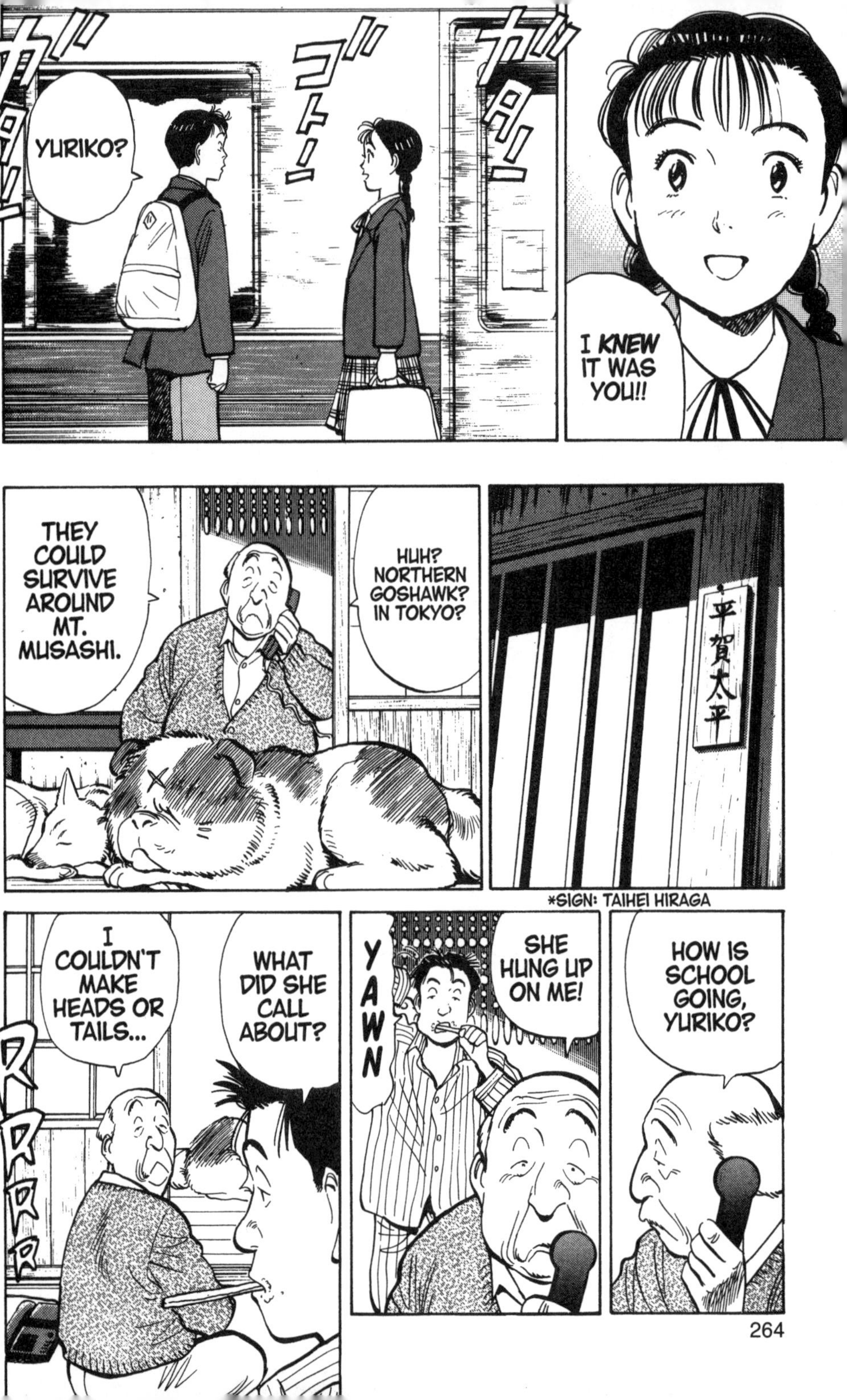
I KNEW IT WAS YOU!!
YURIKO?
平賀太平
*SIGN: TAIHEI HIRAGA
HUH? NORTHERN GOSHAWK? IN TOKYO?
THEY COULD SURVIVE AROUND MT. MUSASHI.
HOW IS SCHOOL GOING, YURIKO?
SHE HUNG UP ON ME!
YAWN
WHAT DID SHE CALL ABOUT?
I COULDN'T MAKE HEADS OR TAILS...
RRRRR

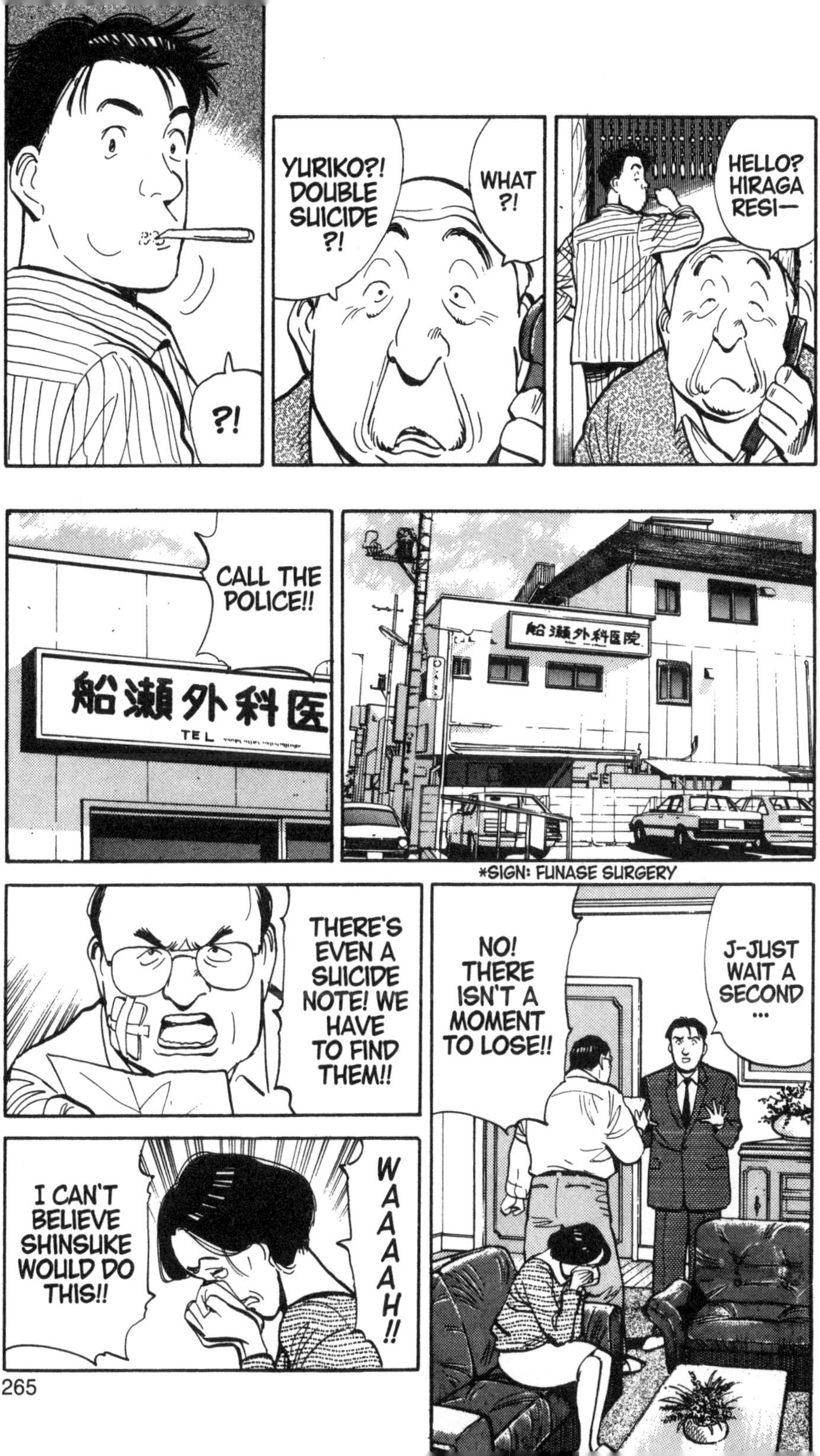
HELLO? HIRAGA RESI—
WHAT ?!
YURIKO?! DOUBLE SUICIDE ?!
?!
船瀬外科医院
CALL THE POLICE!!
船瀬外科医
TEL
J-JUST WAIT A SECOND ...
NO! THERE ISN'T A MOMENT TO LOSE!!
THERE'S EVEN A SUICIDE NOTE! WE HAVE TO FIND THEM!!
WAAAAAH!!
I CAN'T BELIEVE SHINSUKE WOULD DO THIS!!

*SIGN: FUNASE SURGERY

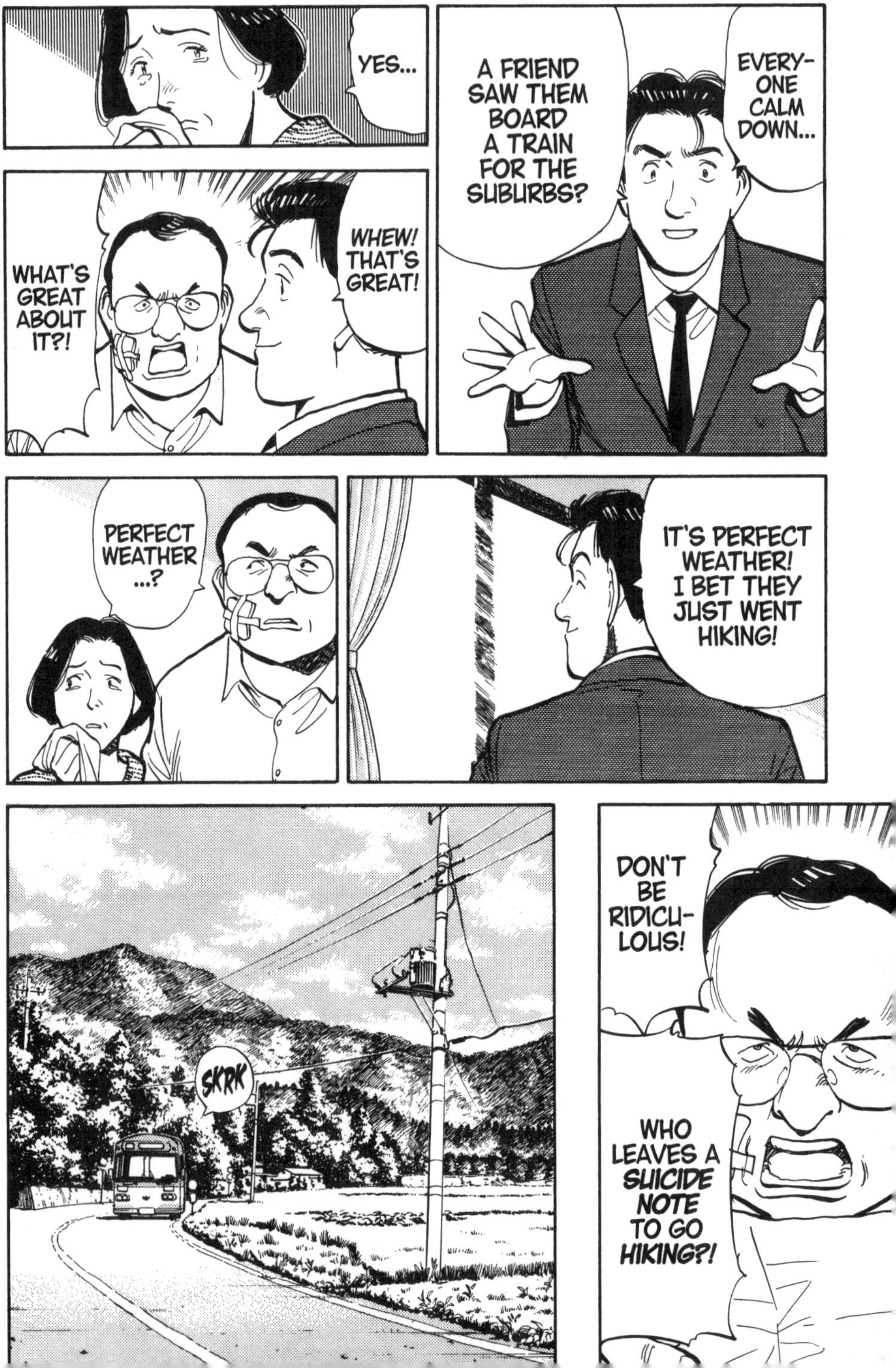
EVERY-ONE CALM DOWN...
A FRIEND SAW THEM BOARD A TRAIN FOR THE SUBURBS?
YES...
WHEW! THAT'S GREAT!
WHAT'S GREAT ABOUT IT?!
IT'S PERFECT WEATHER! I BET THEY JUST WENT HIKING!
PERFECT WEATHER ...?
DON'T BE RIDICU-LOUS!
WHO LEAVES A SUICIDE NOTE TO GO HIKING?!
SKRK

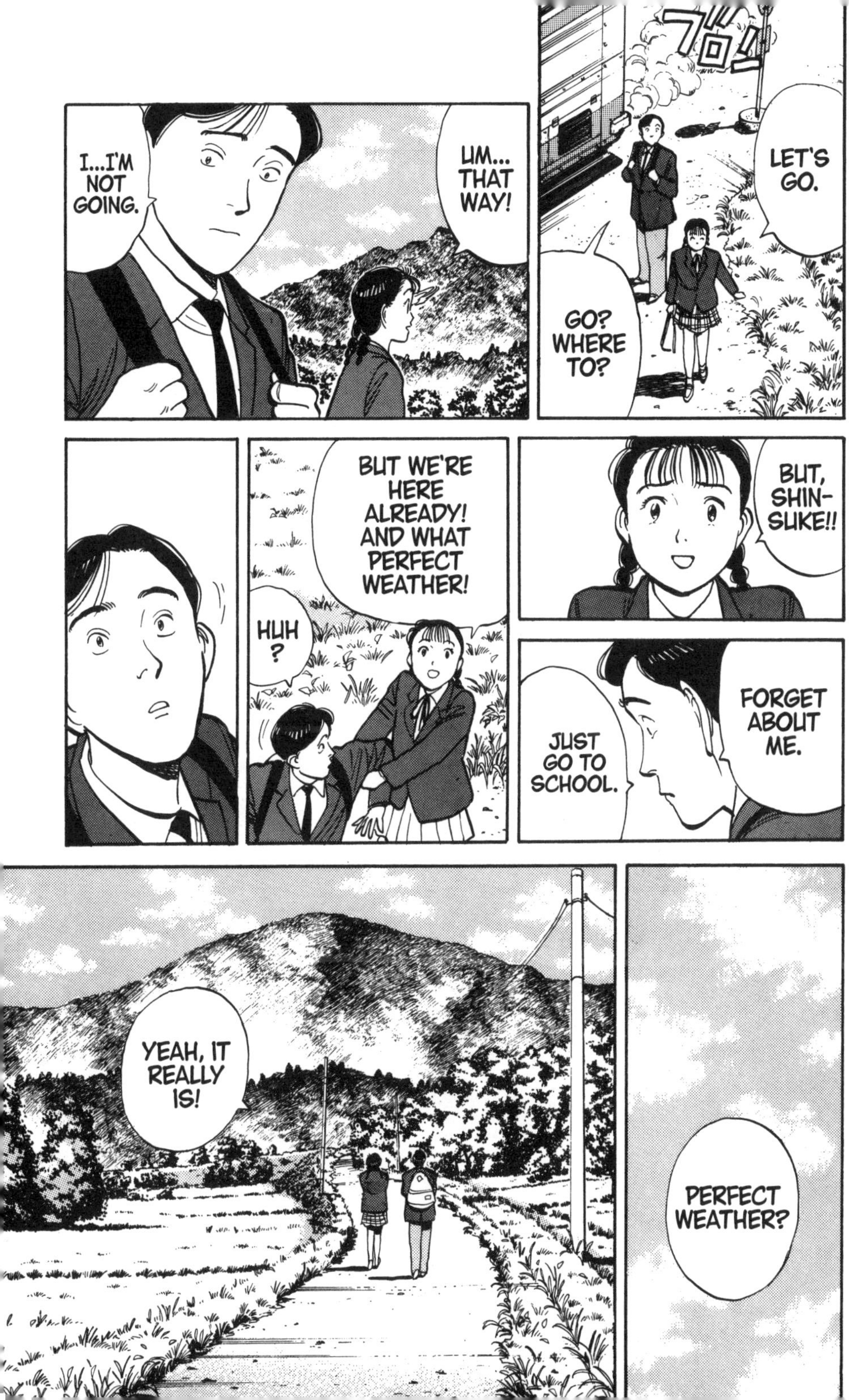
ブロ!
LET'S GO.
GO? WHERE TO?
UM... THAT WAY!
I...I'M NOT GOING.
BUT, SHIN-SUKE!!
FORGET ABOUT ME.
JUST GO TO SCHOOL.
BUT WE'RE HERE ALREADY! AND WHAT PERFECT WEATHER!
HUH?
PERFECT WEATHER?
YEAH, IT REALLY IS!

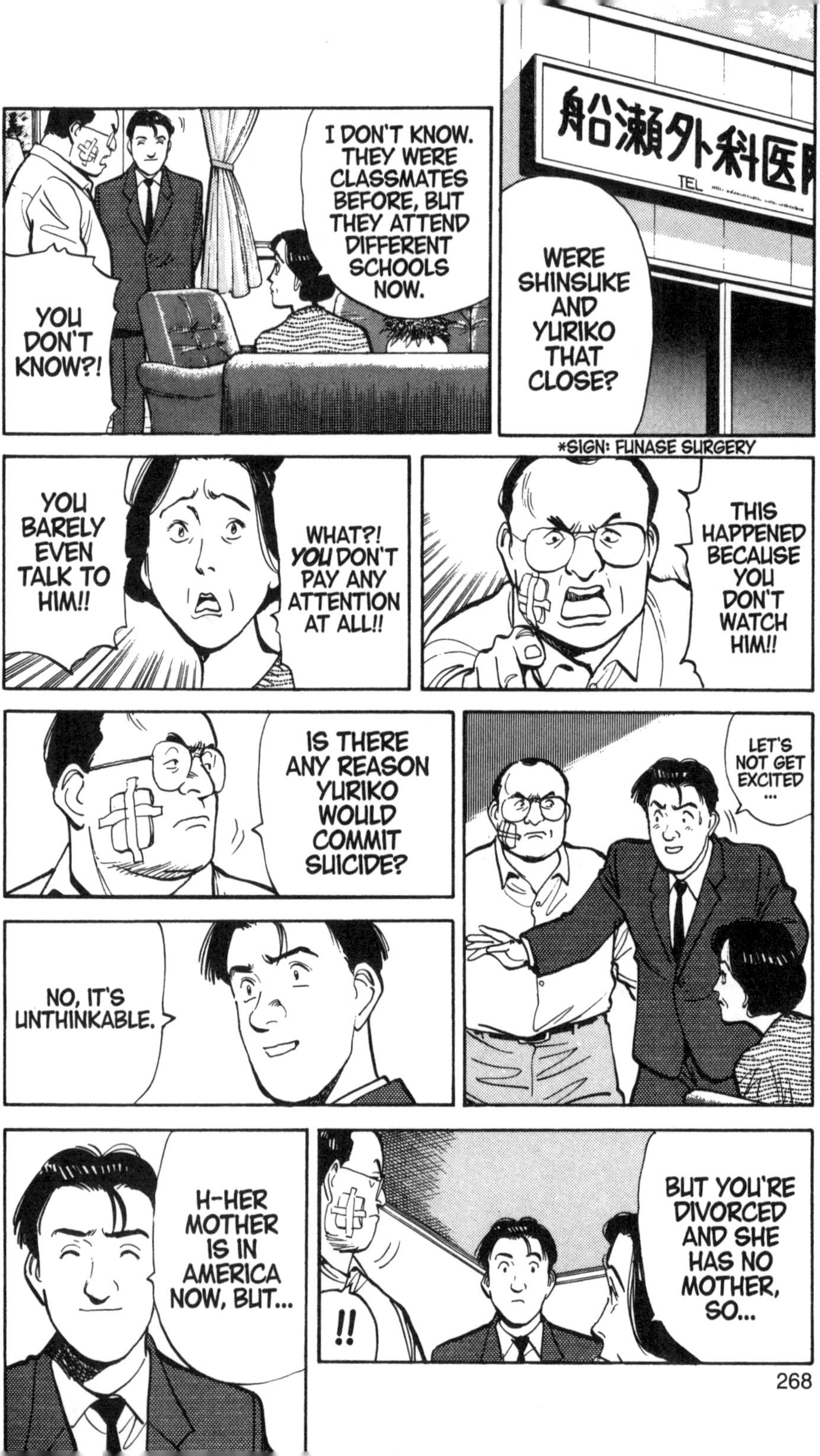
船瀬外科医
TEL
WERE SHINSUKE AND YURIKO THAT CLOSE?
*SIGN: FUNASE SURGERY
I DON'T KNOW. THEY WERE CLASSMATES BEFORE, BUT THEY ATTEND DIFFERENT SCHOOLS NOW.
YOU DON'T KNOW?!
THIS HAPPENED BECAUSE YOU DON'T WATCH HIM!!
WHAT?! *YOU* DON'T PAY ANY ATTENTION AT ALL!!
YOU BARELY EVEN TALK TO HIM!!
LET'S NOT GET EXCITED...
IS THERE ANY REASON YURIKO WOULD COMMIT SUICIDE?
NO, IT'S UNTHINKABLE.
BUT YOU'RE DIVORCED AND SHE HAS NO MOTHER, SO...
!!
H-HER MOTHER IS IN AMERICA NOW, BUT...

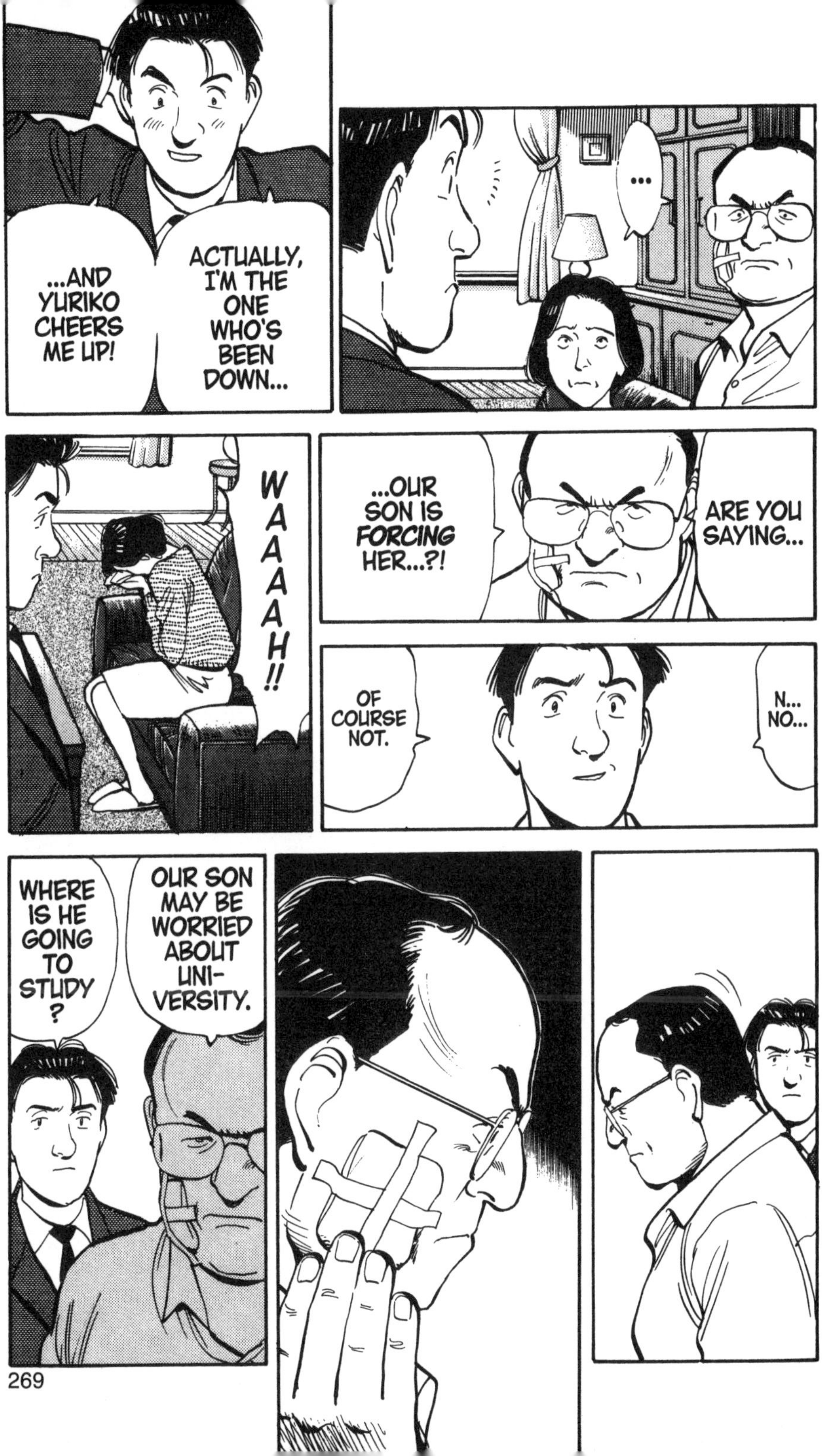
...
ACTUALLY, I'M THE ONE WHO'S BEEN DOWN...
...AND YURIKO CHEERS ME UP!
ARE YOU SAYING...
...OUR SON IS *FORCING* HER...?!
N... NO...
OF COURSE NOT.
WAAAAAH!!
OUR SON MAY BE WORRIED ABOUT UNI-VERSITY.
WHERE IS HE GOING TO STUDY?

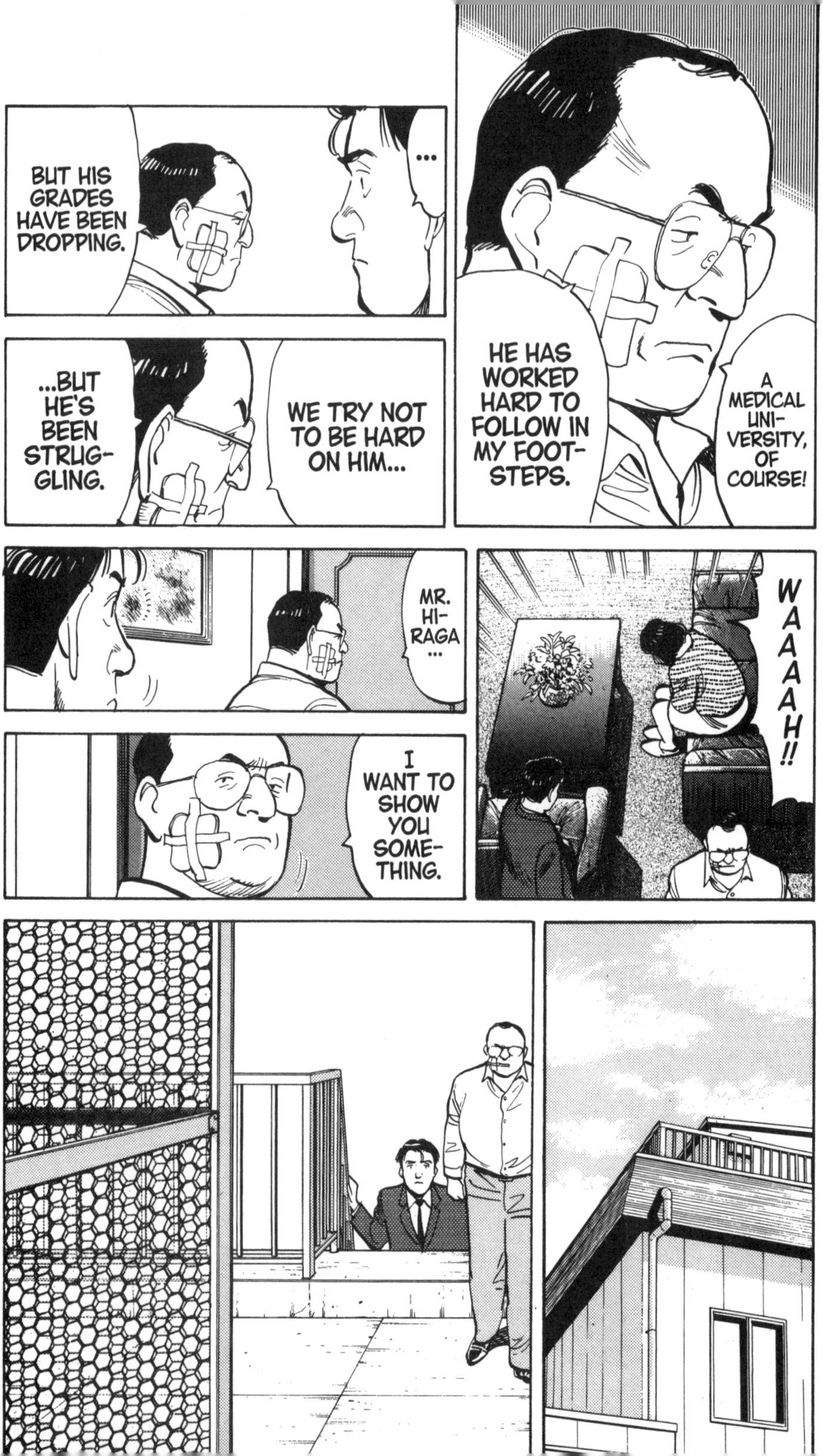
HE HAS WORKED HARD TO FOLLOW IN MY FOOT-STEPS.
A MEDICAL UNI-VERSITY, OF COURSE!
...
BUT HIS GRADES HAVE BEEN DROPPING.
WE TRY NOT TO BE HARD ON HIM...
...BUT HE'S BEEN STRUG-GLING.
WAAAAAH!!
MR. HI-RAGA...
I WANT TO SHOW YOU SOME-THING.

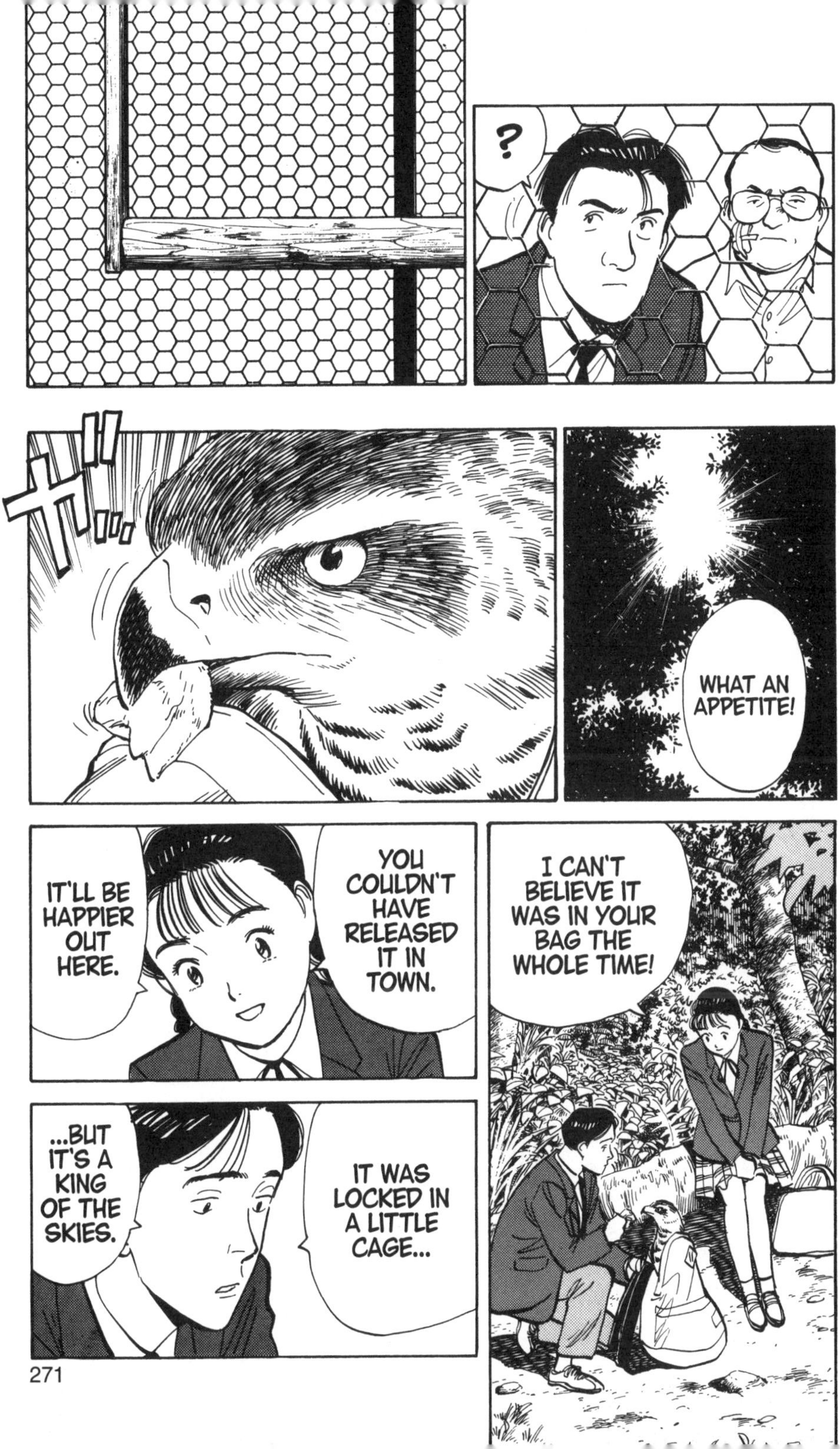
?
WHAT AN APPETITE!
I CAN'T BELIEVE IT WAS IN YOUR BAG THE WHOLE TIME!
YOU COULDN'T HAVE RELEASED IT IN TOWN.
IT'LL BE HAPPIER OUT HERE.
IT WAS LOCKED IN A LITTLE CAGE...
...BUT IT'S A KING OF THE SKIES.

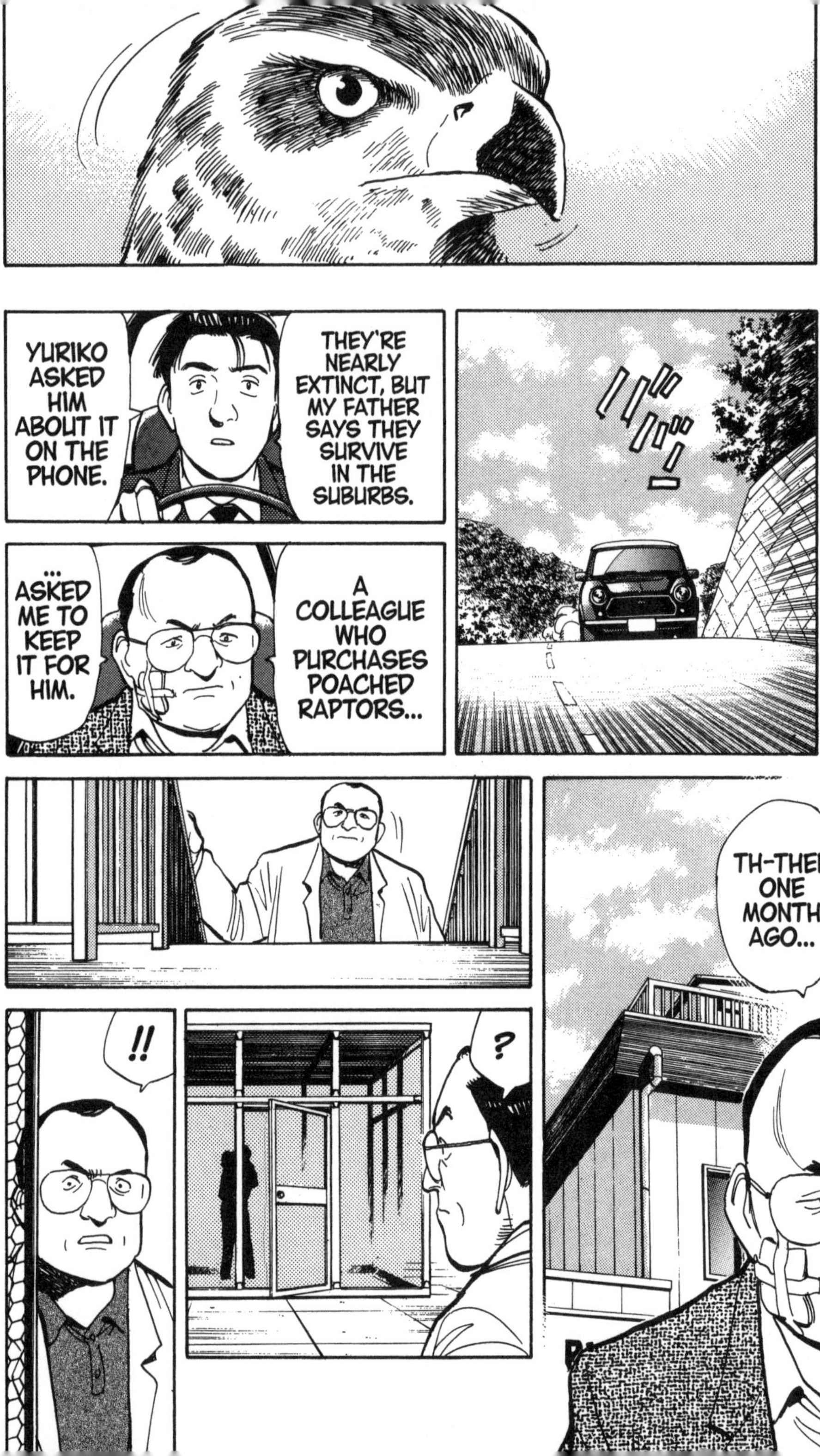
THEY'RE NEARLY EXTINCT, BUT MY FATHER SAYS THEY SURVIVE IN THE SUBURBS.
YURIKO ASKED HIM ABOUT IT ON THE PHONE.
A COLLEAGUE WHO PURCHASES POACHED RAPTORS...
... ASKED ME TO KEEP IT FOR HIM.
TH-THEN ONE MONTH AGO...
?
!!

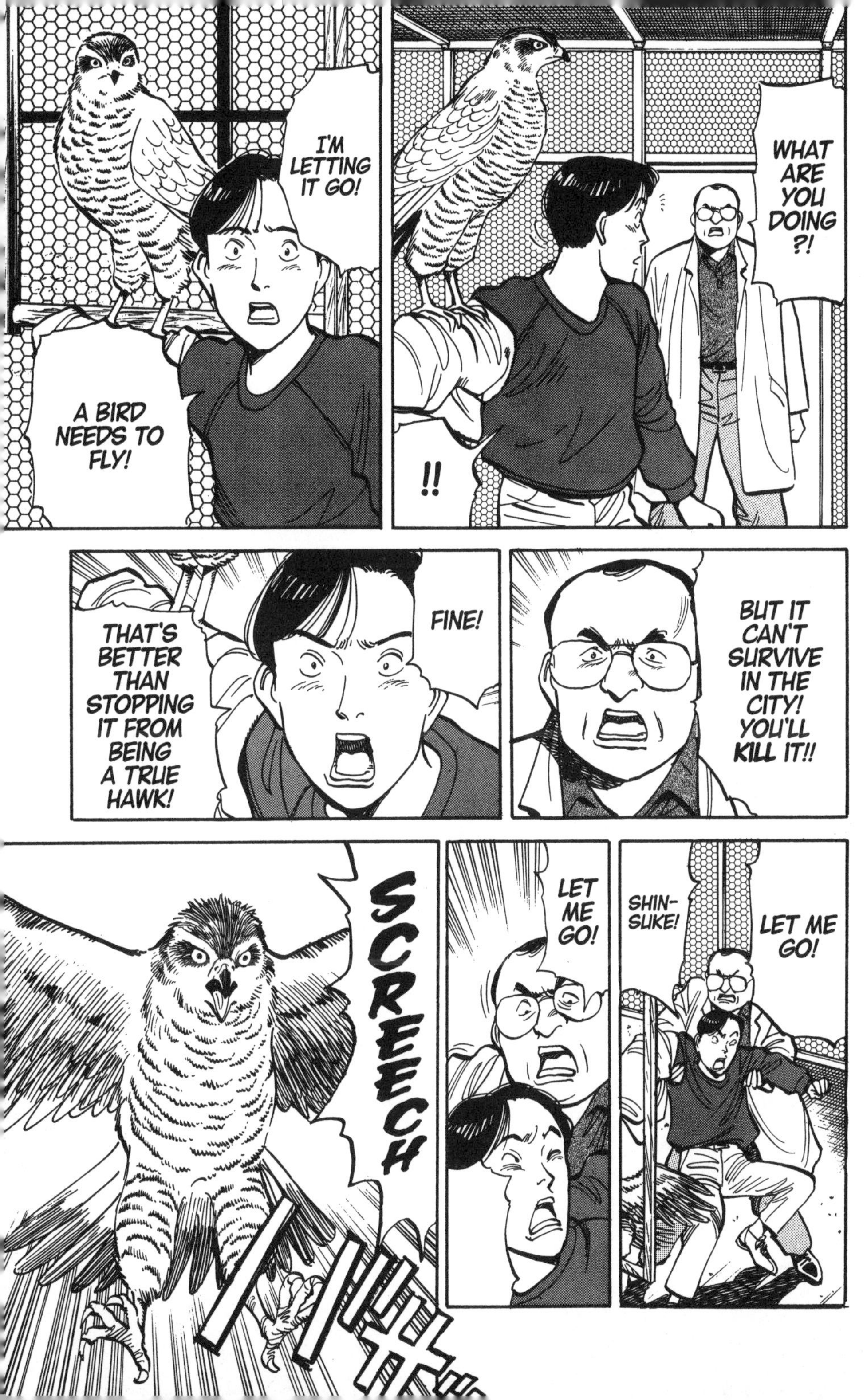
WHAT ARE YOU DOING?!
!!
I'M LETTING IT GO!
A BIRD NEEDS TO FLY!
BUT IT CAN'T SURVIVE IN THE CITY! YOU'LL KILL IT!!
FINE!
THAT'S BETTER THAN STOPPING IT FROM BEING A TRUE HAWK!
LET ME GO!
SHIN-SUKE!
LET ME GO!
SCREECH

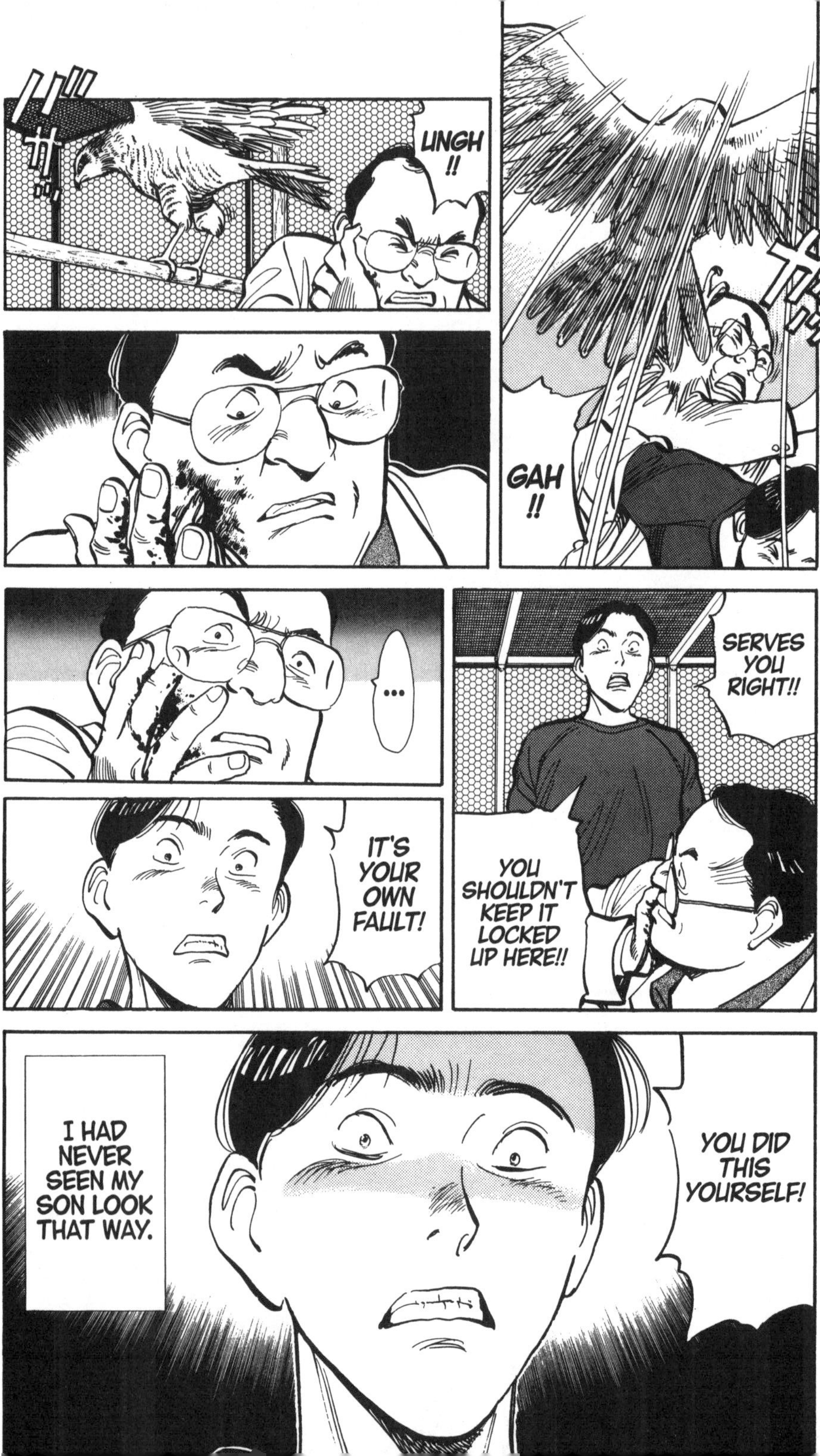
GAH!!
UNGH!!
SERVES YOU RIGHT!!
YOU SHOULDN'T KEEP IT LOCKED UP HERE!!
...
IT'S YOUR OWN FAULT!
YOU DID THIS YOURSELF!
I HAD NEVER SEEN MY SON LOOK THAT WAY.

I DON'T KNOW WHAT HE'S THINKING...

THERE'S THE MOUNTAIN.

!!

YOU MUST BE WORRIED.

I'M SORRY MY SON INVOLVED YURIKO.

THAT'S WHERE GOSHAWKS LIVE...

...AND WHERE OUR CHILDREN MAY HAVE GONE.

NO, IT WILL WORK OUT.

NO PARTICULAR REASON.

YOU'RE SO CALM. WHY IS THAT?

...I ALWAYS IMAGINE HER SMILING.

BUT WHENEVER I THINK OF MY DAUGHTER...

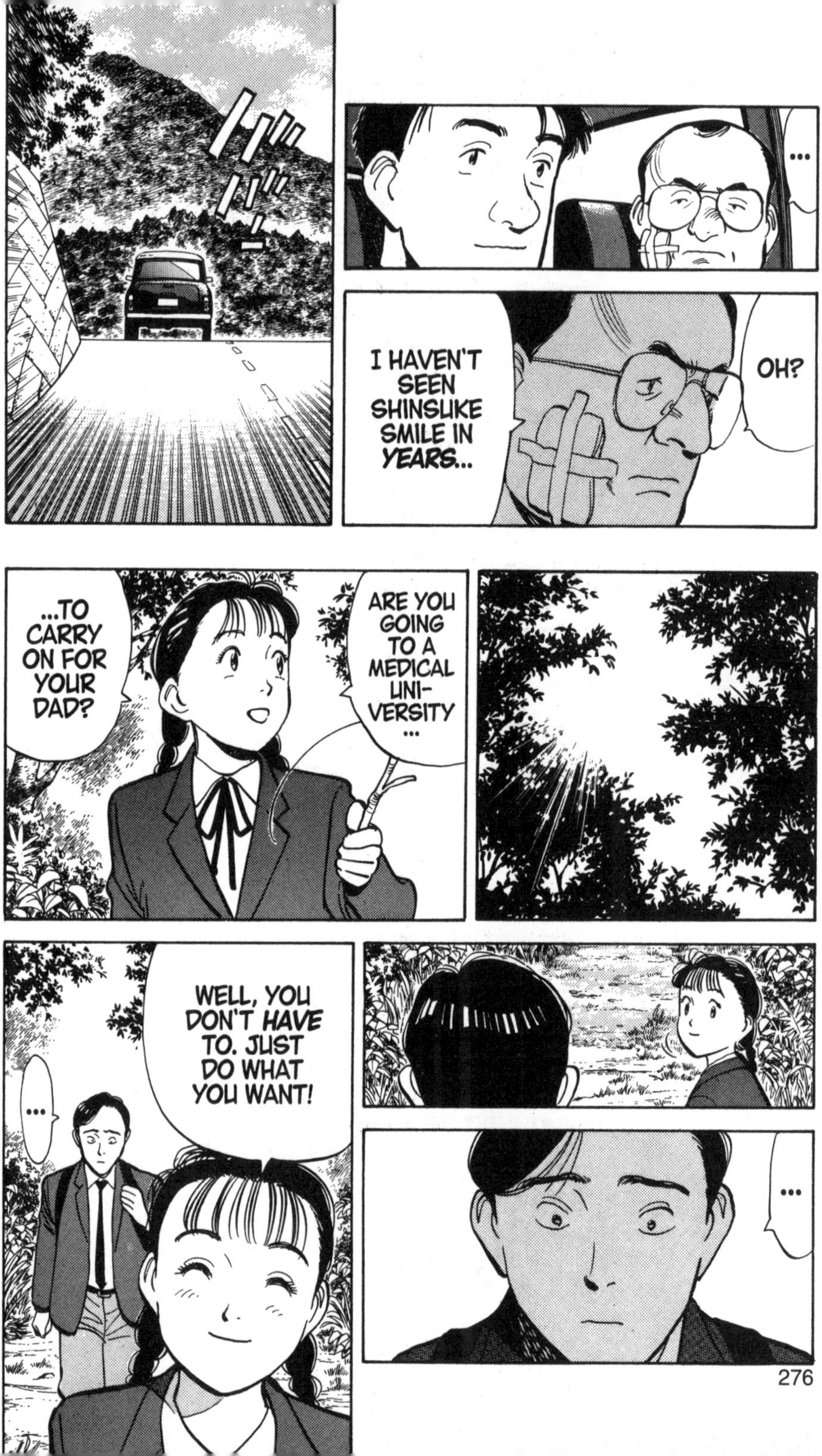
...
OH?
I HAVEN'T SEEN SHINSUKE SMILE IN *YEARS*...
ARE YOU GOING TO A MEDICAL UNI-VERSITY...
...TO CARRY ON FOR YOUR DAD?
...
WELL, YOU DON'T *HAVE* TO. JUST DO WHAT YOU WANT!
...

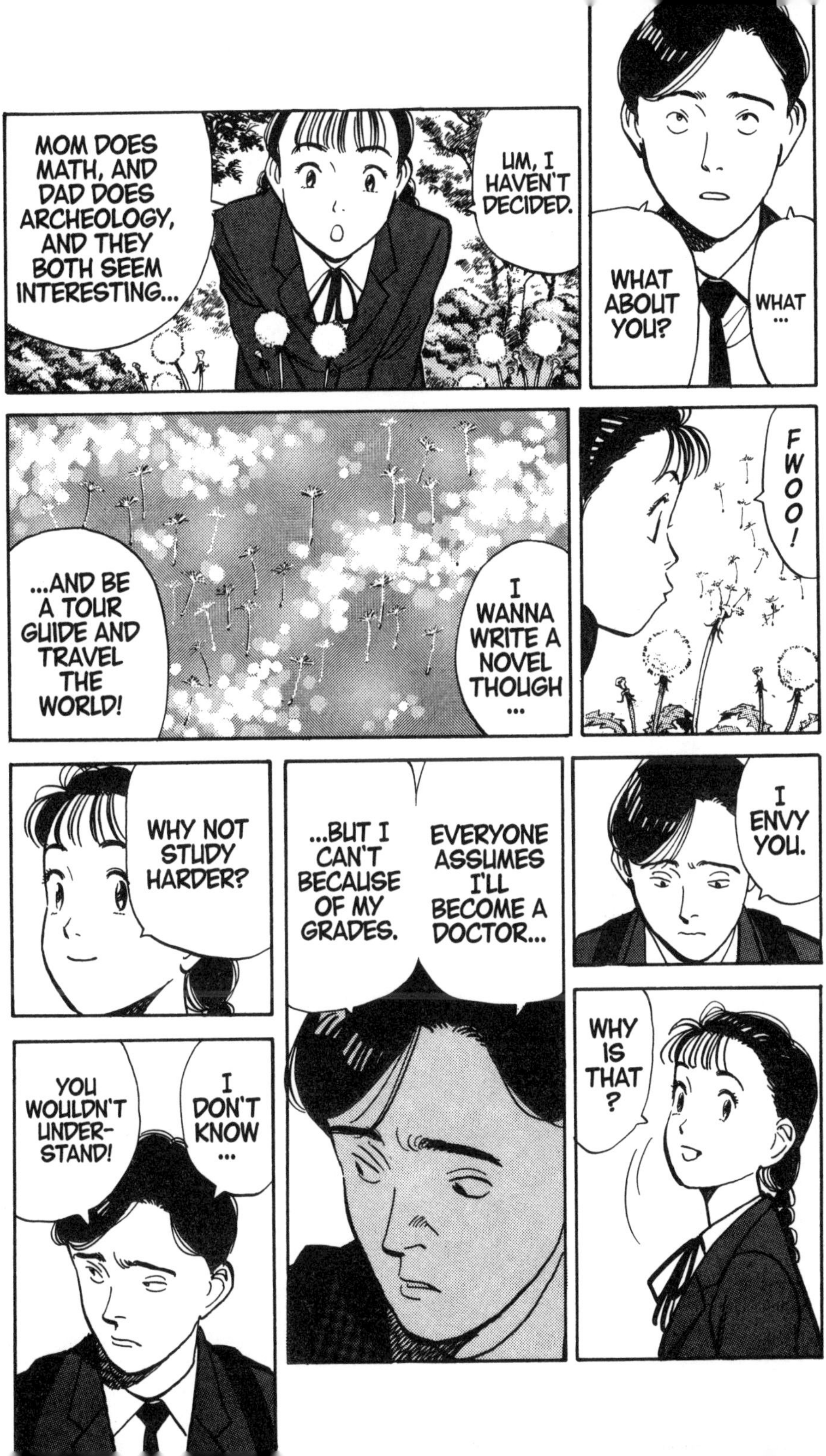
WHAT ...
WHAT ABOUT YOU?
UM, I HAVEN'T DECIDED.
MOM DOES MATH, AND DAD DOES ARCHEOLOGY, AND THEY BOTH SEEM INTERESTING...
FWOO!
I WANNA WRITE A NOVEL THOUGH ...
...AND BE A TOUR GUIDE AND TRAVEL THE WORLD!
I ENVY YOU.
WHY IS THAT?
EVERYONE ASSUMES I'LL BECOME A DOCTOR...
...BUT I CAN'T BECAUSE OF MY GRADES.
WHY NOT STUDY HARDER?
I DON'T KNOW ...
YOU WOULDN'T UNDER-STAND!

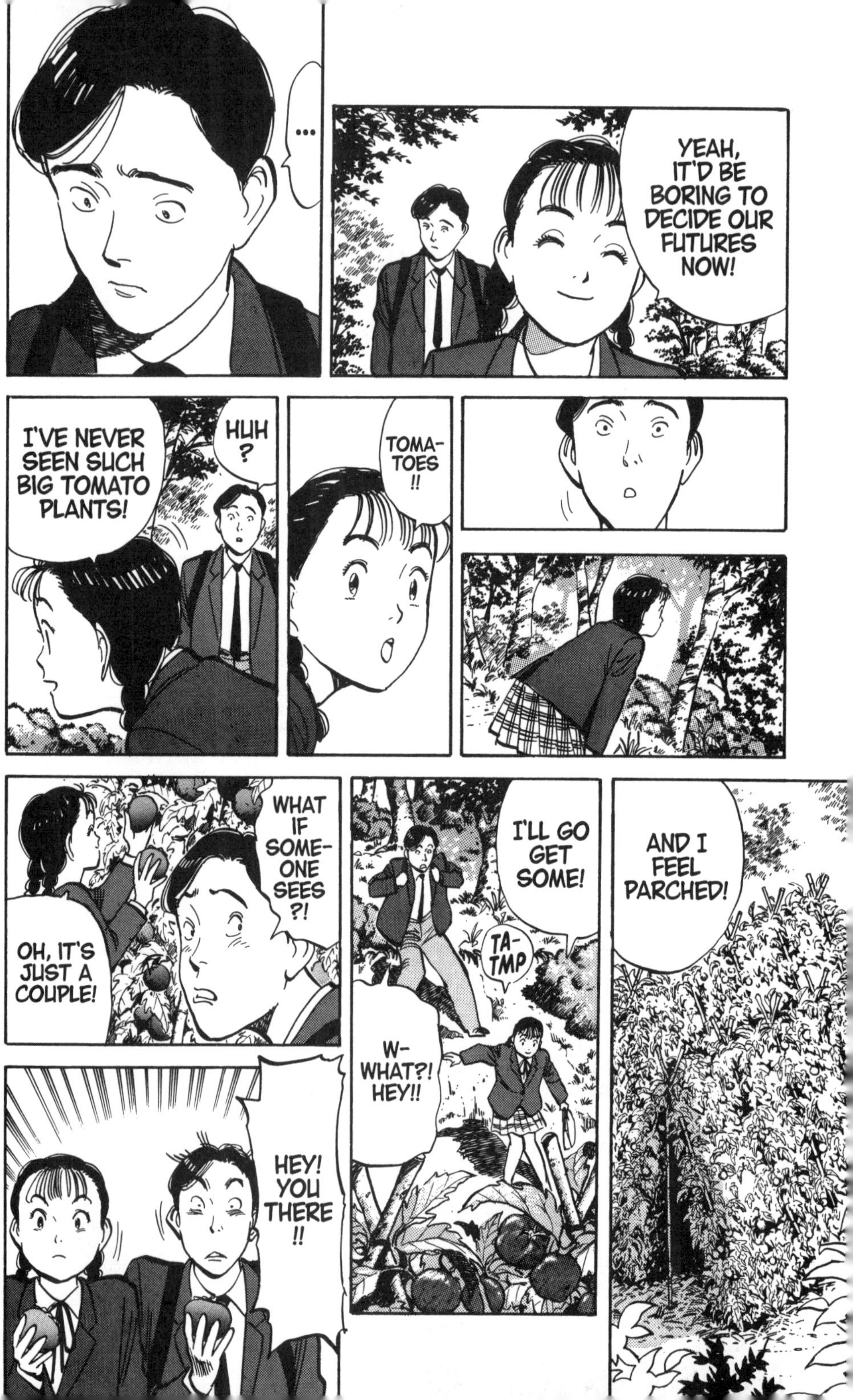
YEAH, IT'D BE BORING TO DECIDE OUR FUTURES NOW!
...
TOMA-TOES !!
HUH ?
I'VE NEVER SEEN SUCH BIG TOMATO PLANTS!
AND I FEEL PARCHED!
I'LL GO GET SOME!
TA-TMP
W-WHAT?! HEY!!
WHAT IF SOME-ONE SEES ?!
OH, IT'S JUST A COUPLE!
HEY! YOU THERE !!

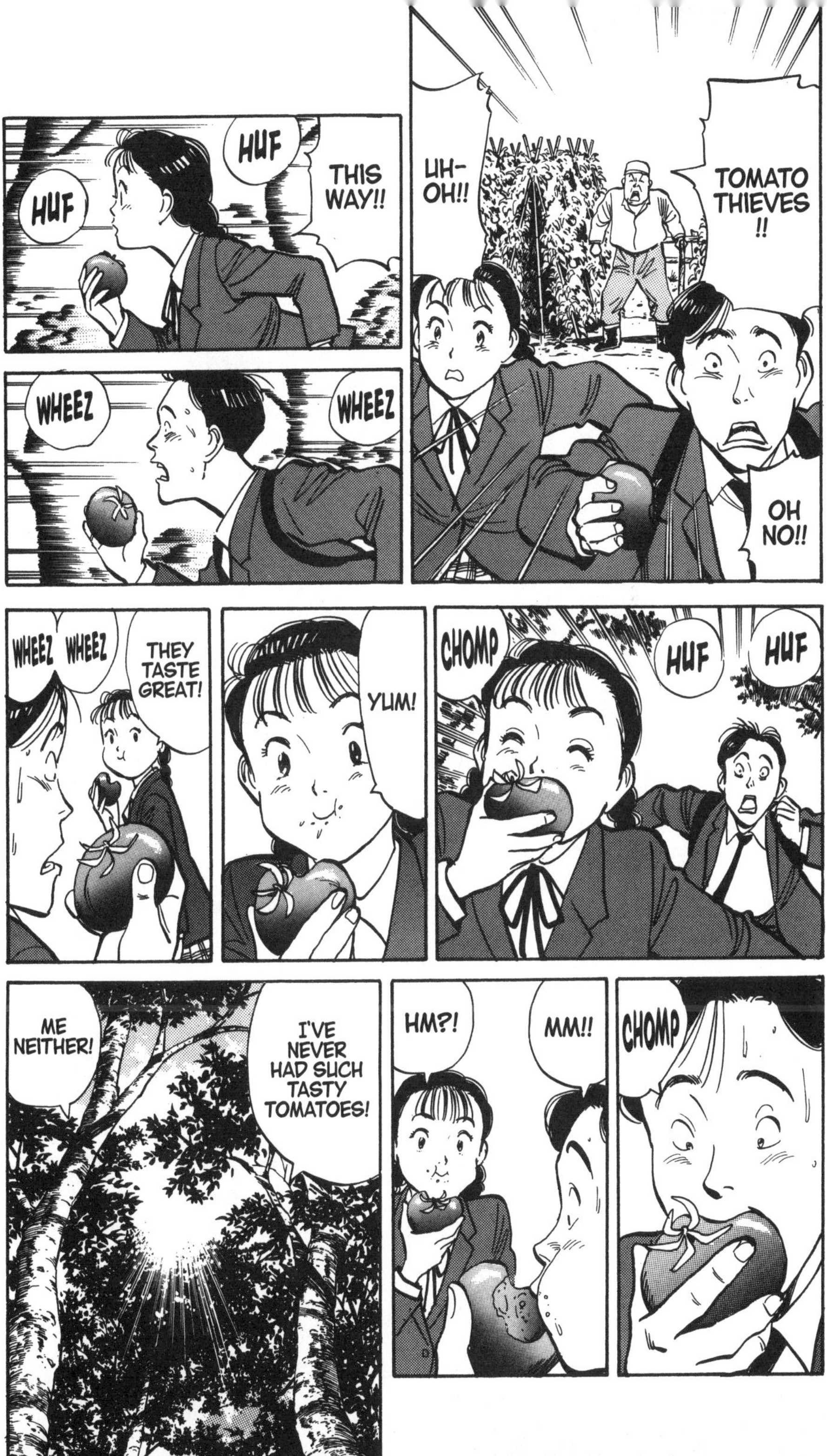
TOMATO THIEVES!!
UH-OH!!
OH NO!!
THIS WAY!!
HUF
HUF
WHEEZ
WHEEZ
HUF
HUF
CHOMP
YUM!
THEY TASTE GREAT!
WHEEZ
WHEEZ
CHOMP
MM!!
HM?!
I'VE NEVER HAD SUCH TASTY TOMATOES!
ME NEITHER!

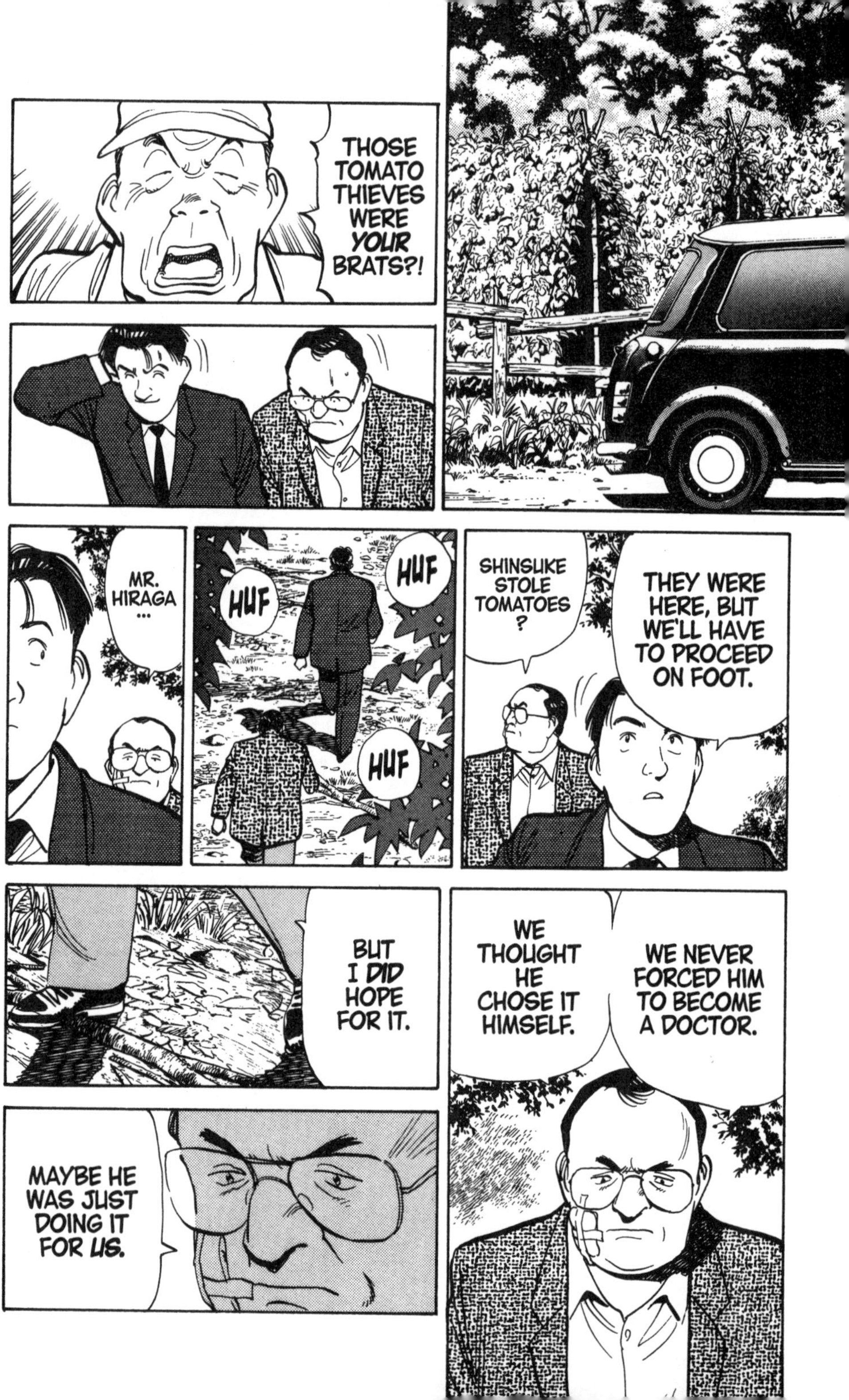
THOSE TOMATO THIEVES WERE YOUR BRATS?!
THEY WERE HERE, BUT WE'LL HAVE TO PROCEED ON FOOT.
SHINSUKE STOLE TOMATOES?
HUF
HUF
HUF
MR. HIRAGA ...
WE NEVER FORCED HIM TO BECOME A DOCTOR.
WE THOUGHT HE CHOSE IT HIMSELF.
BUT I DID HOPE FOR IT.
MAYBE HE WAS JUST DOING IT FOR US.

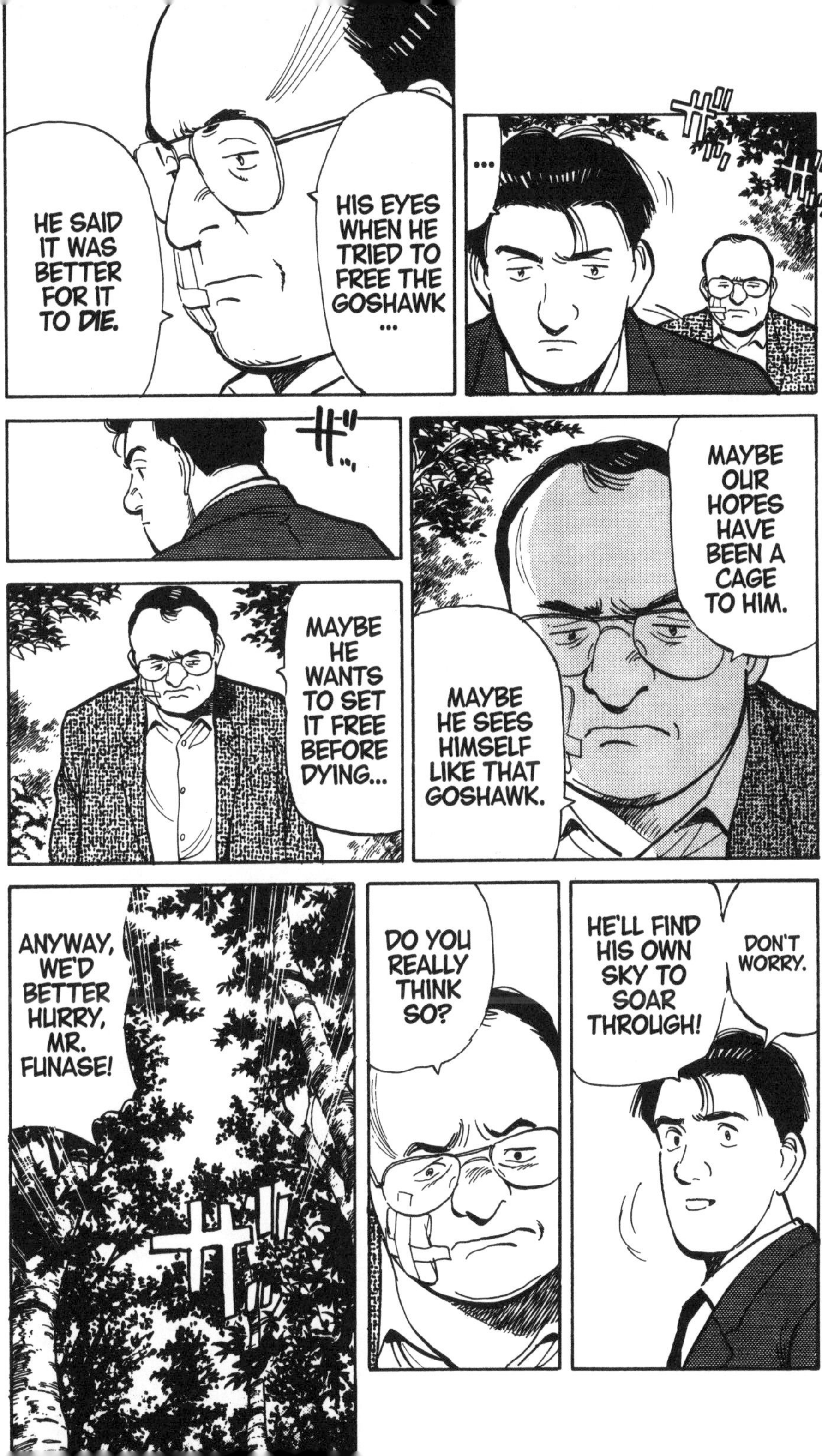
...
HIS EYES WHEN HE TRIED TO FREE THE GOSHAWK ...
HE SAID IT WAS BETTER FOR IT TO DIE.
MAYBE OUR HOPES HAVE BEEN A CAGE TO HIM.
MAYBE HE SEES HIMSELF LIKE THAT GOSHAWK.
MAYBE HE WANTS TO SET IT FREE BEFORE DYING...
DON'T WORRY.
HE'LL FIND HIS OWN SKY TO SOAR THROUGH!
DO YOU REALLY THINK SO?
ANYWAY, WE'D BETTER HURRY, MR. FUNASE!

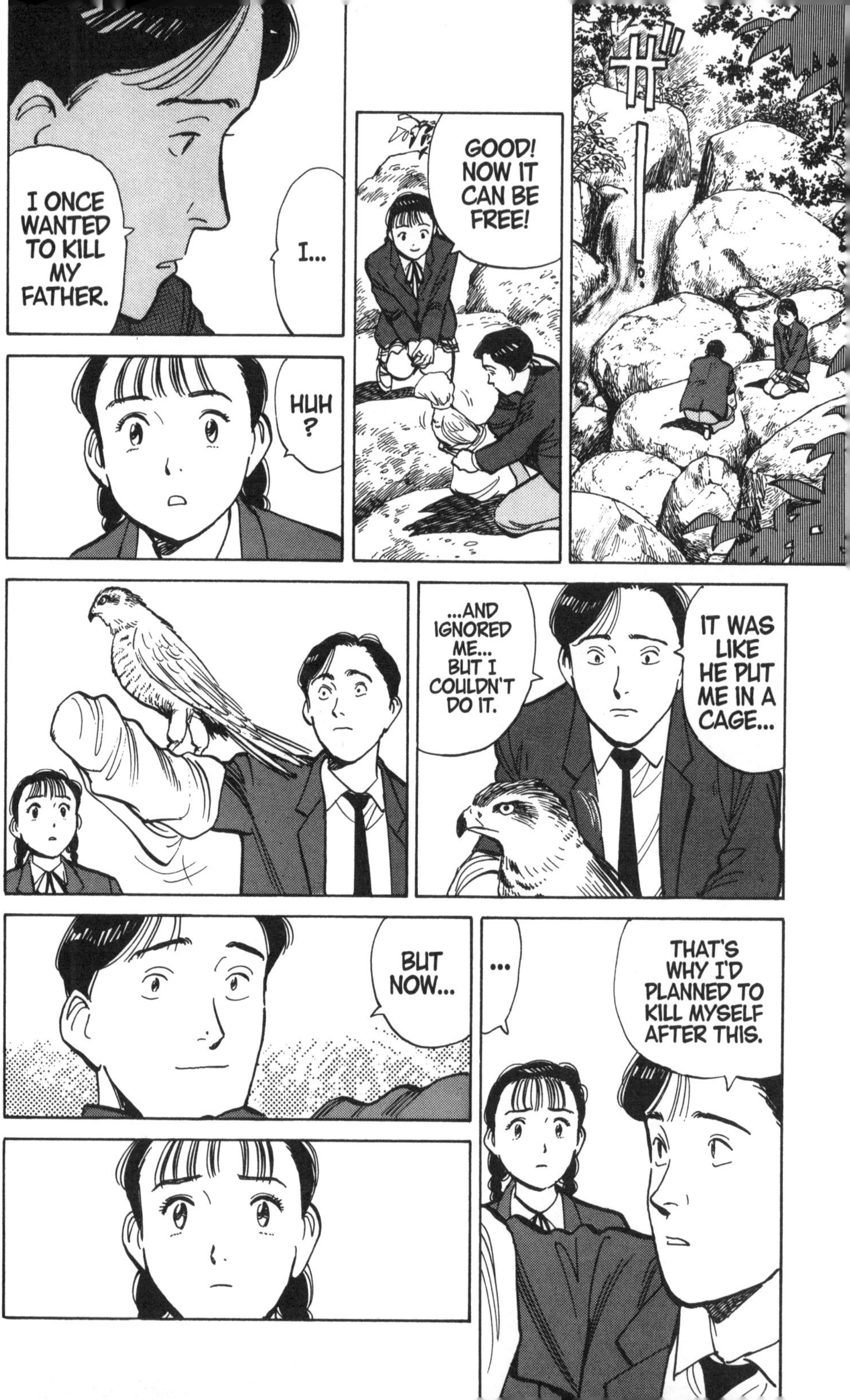
GOOD! NOW IT CAN BE FREE!
I...
I ONCE WANTED TO KILL MY FATHER.
HUH?
IT WAS LIKE HE PUT ME IN A CAGE...
...AND IGNORED ME... BUT I COULDN'T DO IT.
THAT'S WHY I'D PLANNED TO KILL MYSELF AFTER THIS.
...
BUT NOW...

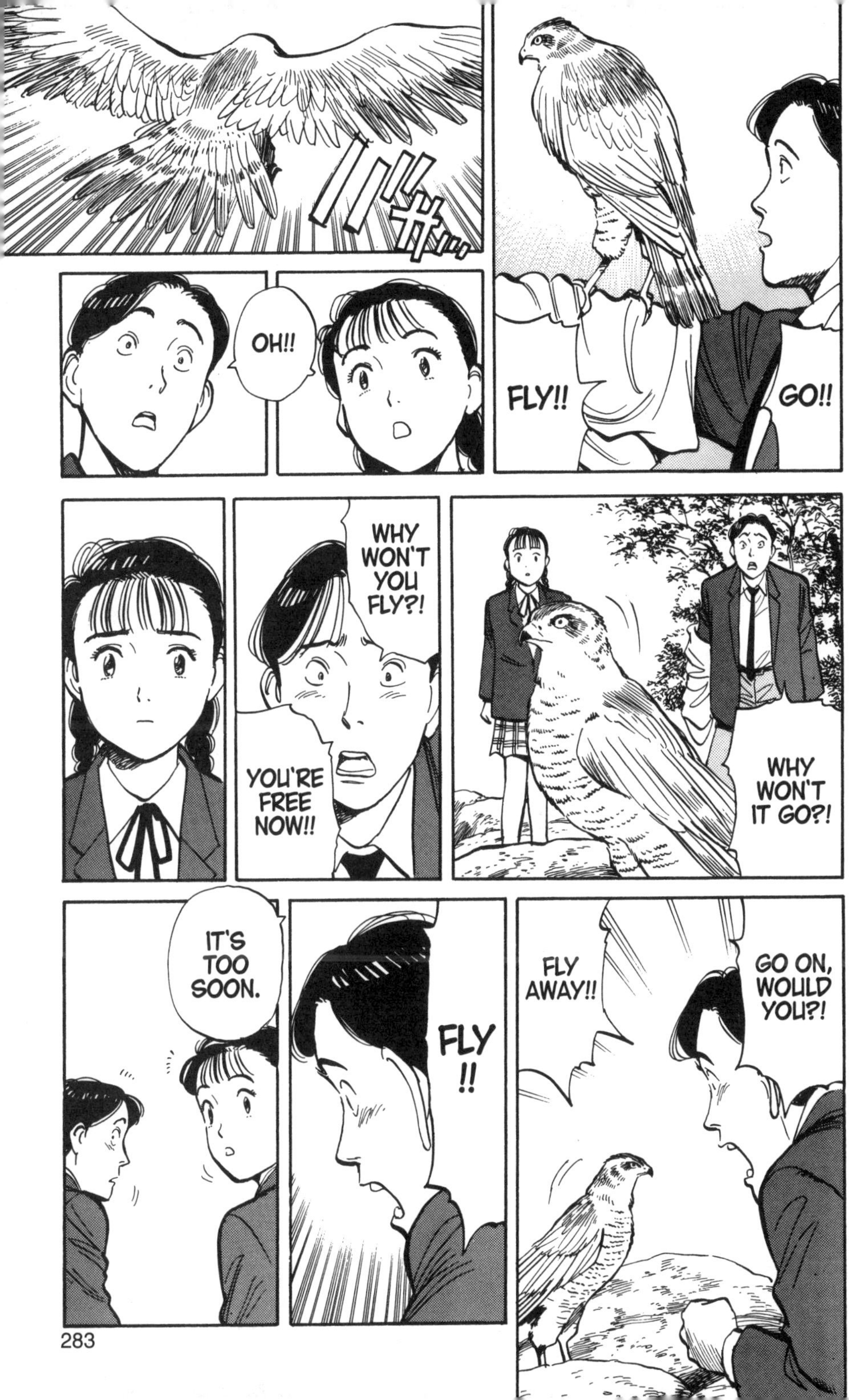
GO!!
FLY!!
OH!!
WHY WON'T IT GO?!
WHY WON'T YOU FLY?!
YOU'RE FREE NOW!!
GO ON, WOULD YOU?!
FLY AWAY!!
FLY !!
IT'S TOO SOON.

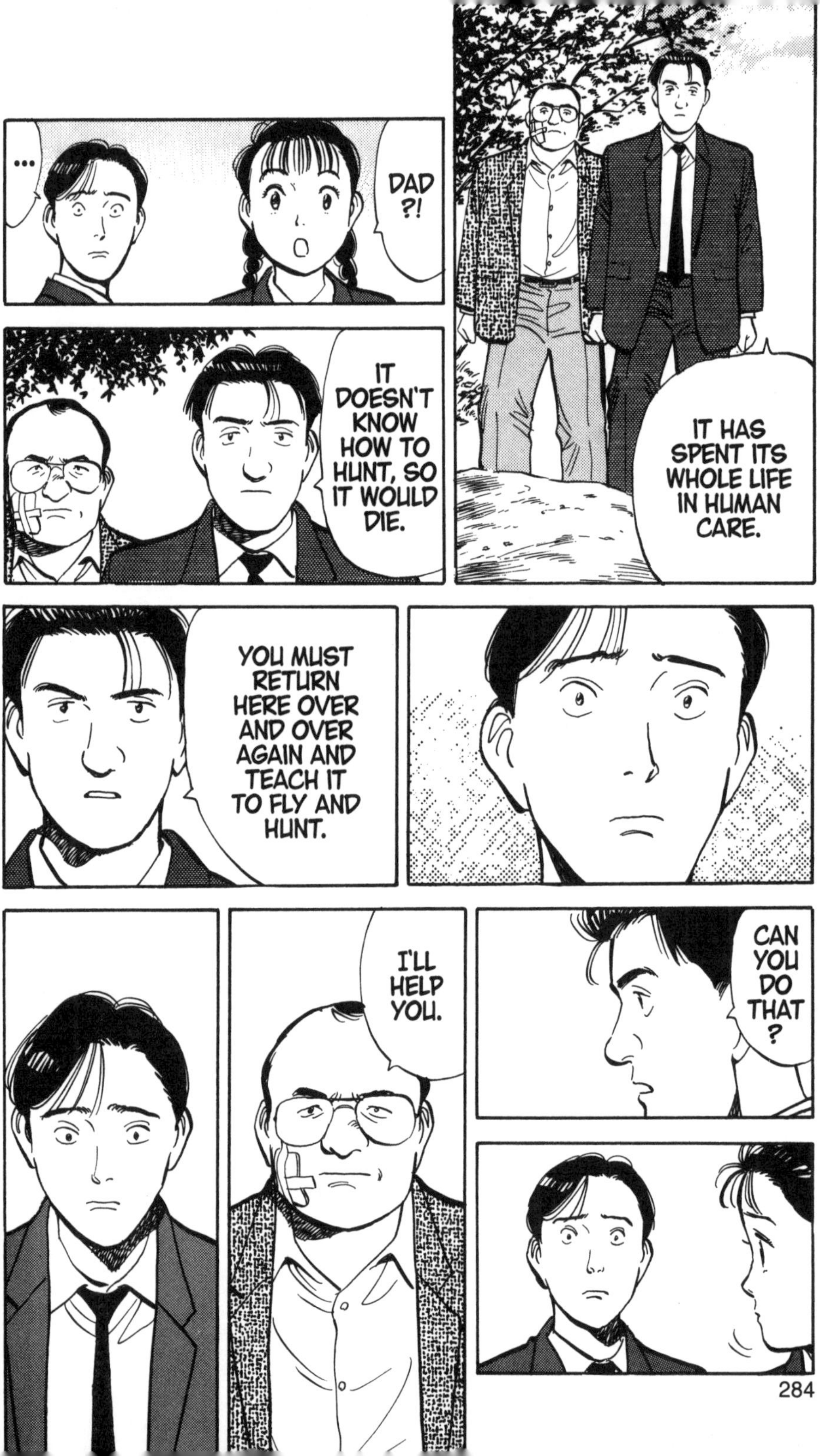
IT HAS SPENT ITS WHOLE LIFE IN HUMAN CARE.
DAD ?!
...
IT DOESN'T KNOW HOW TO HUNT, SO IT WOULD DIE.
YOU MUST RETURN HERE OVER AND OVER AGAIN AND TEACH IT TO FLY AND HUNT.
CAN YOU DO THAT ?
I'LL HELP YOU.

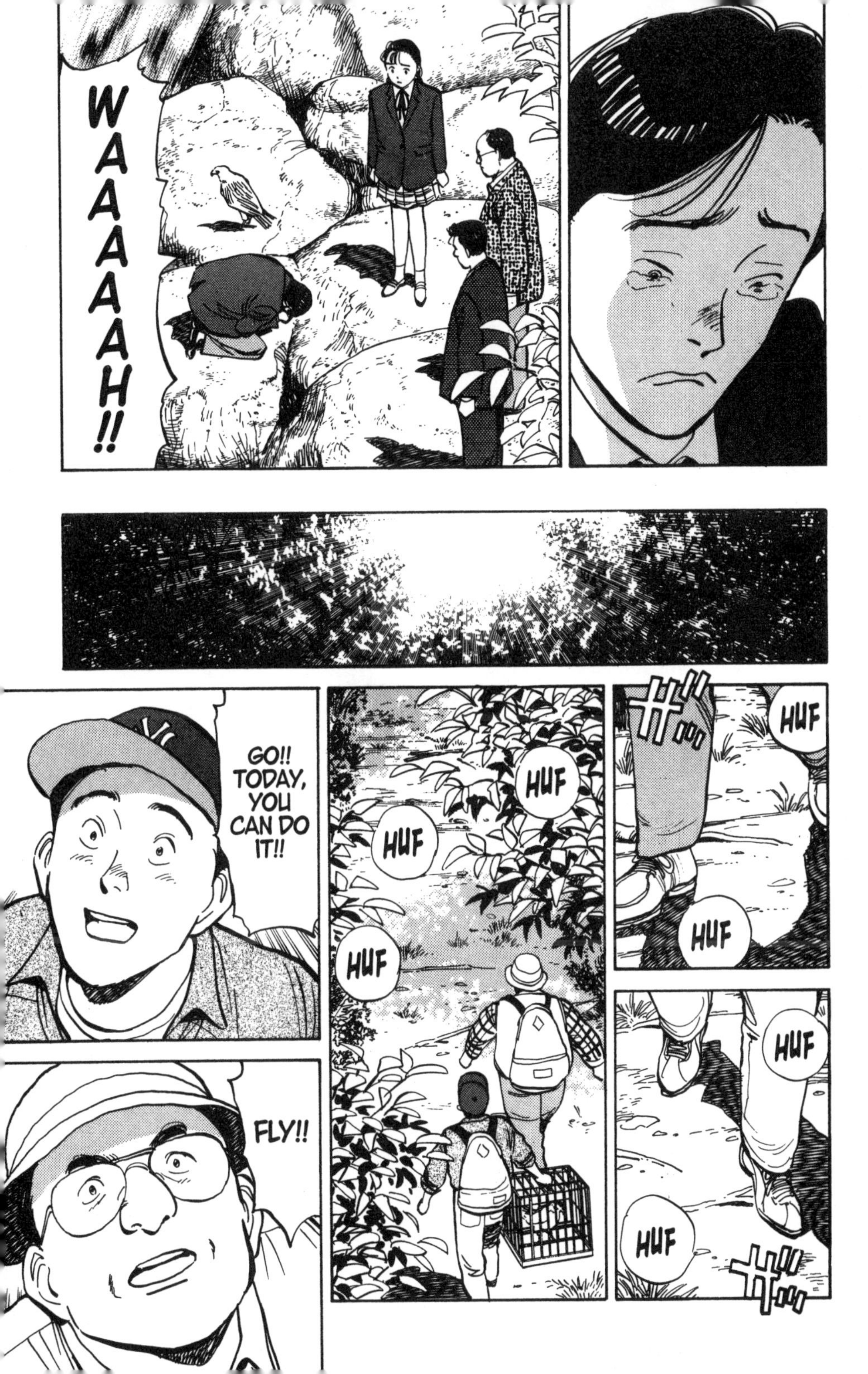
WAAAAAAH!!
HUF
HUF
HUF
HUF
HUF
HUF
HUF
GO!! TODAY, YOU CAN DO IT!!
FLY!!

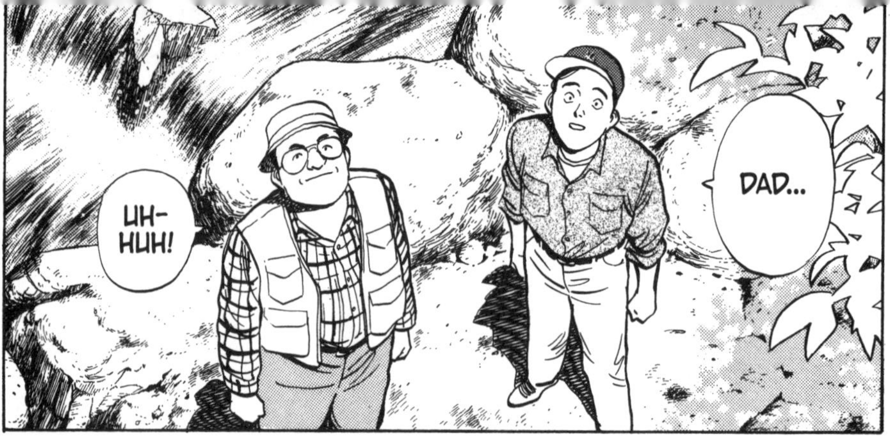
DAD...
UH-HUH!

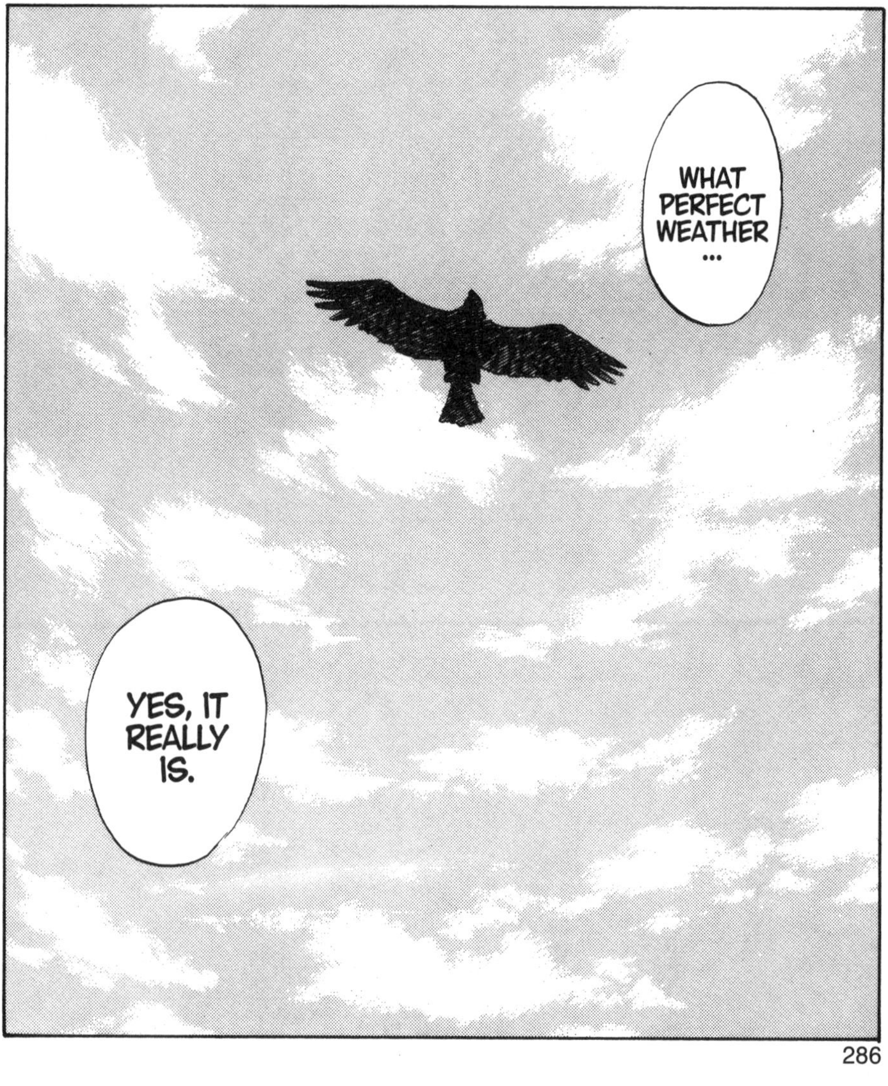
WHAT PERFECT WEATHER ...
YES, IT REALLY IS.

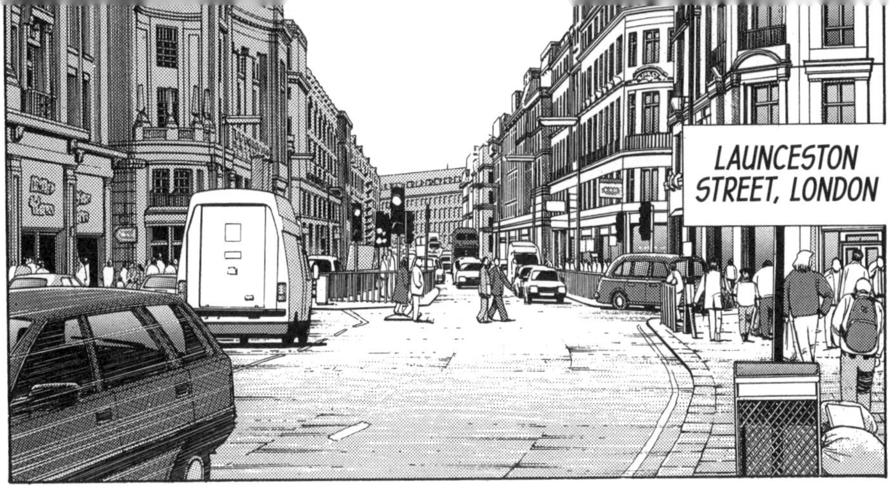
LAUNCESTON STREET, LONDON

Chapter 12
Shoes and Violin

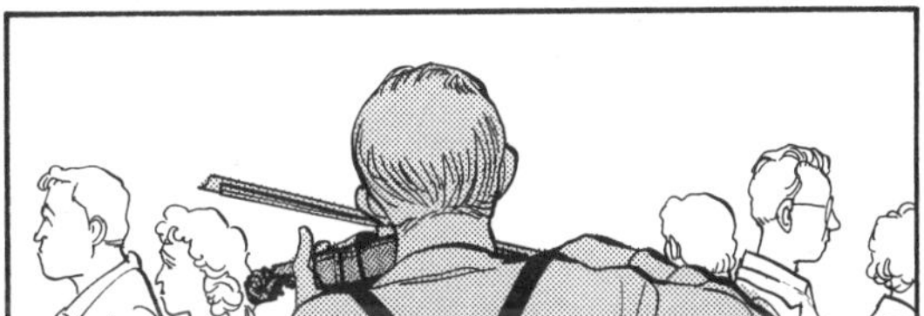

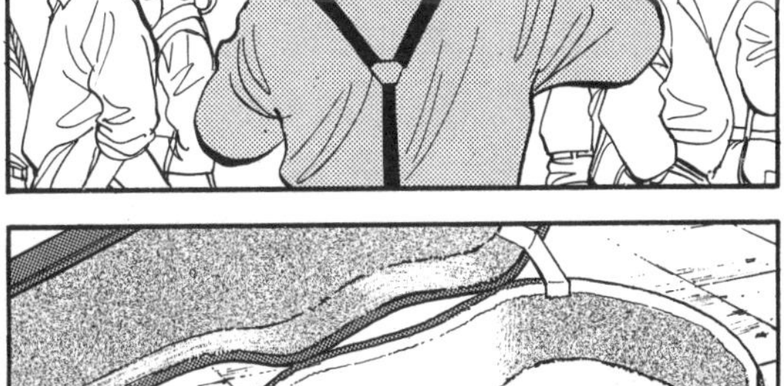

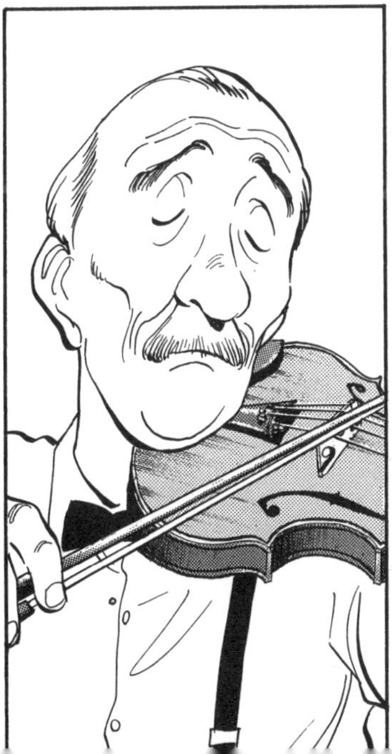

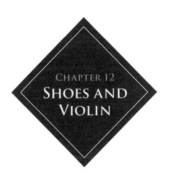

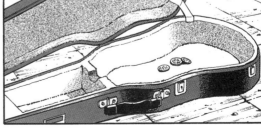

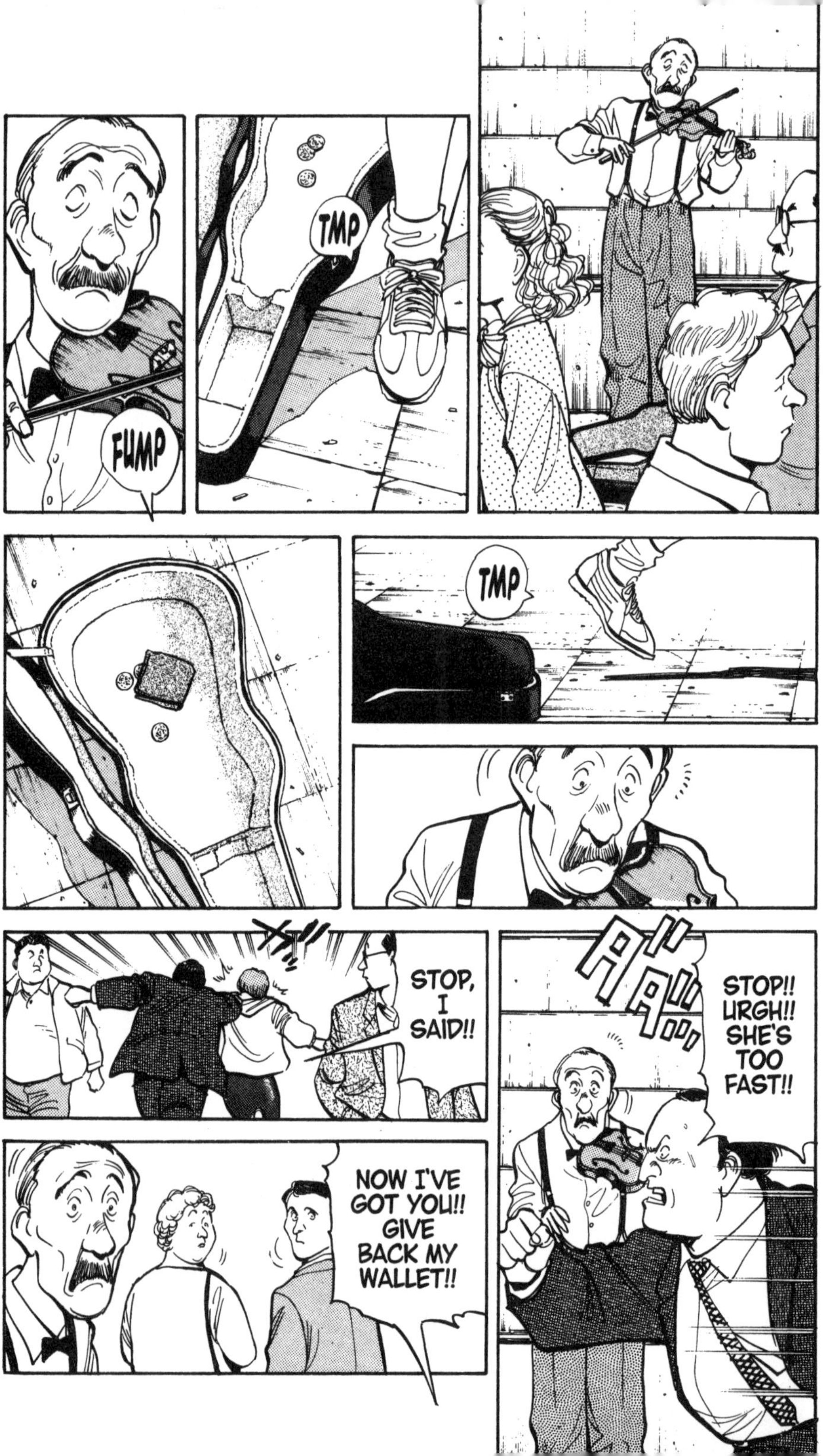
TMP
FUMP
TMP
STOP!! URGH!! SHE'S TOO FAST!!
STOP, I SAID!!
NOW I'VE GOT YOU!! GIVE BACK MY WALLET!!

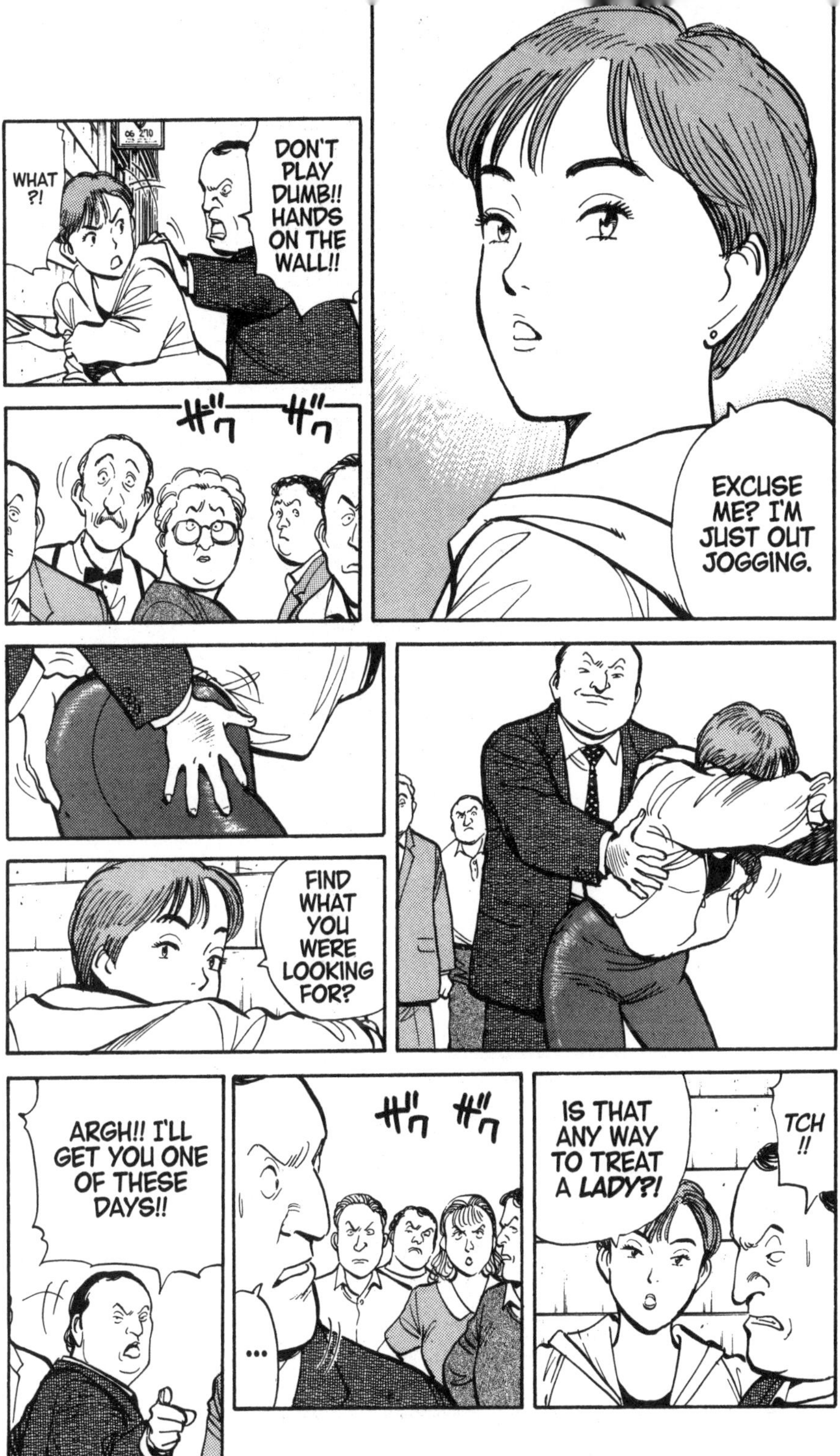
EXCUSE ME? I'M JUST OUT JOGGING.
DON'T PLAY DUMB!! HANDS ON THE WALL!!
WHAT?!
ザク ザク
FIND WHAT YOU WERE LOOKING FOR?
TCH!!
IS THAT ANY WAY TO TREAT A LADY?!
ザク ザク
...
ARGH!! I'LL GET YOU ONE OF THESE DAYS!!

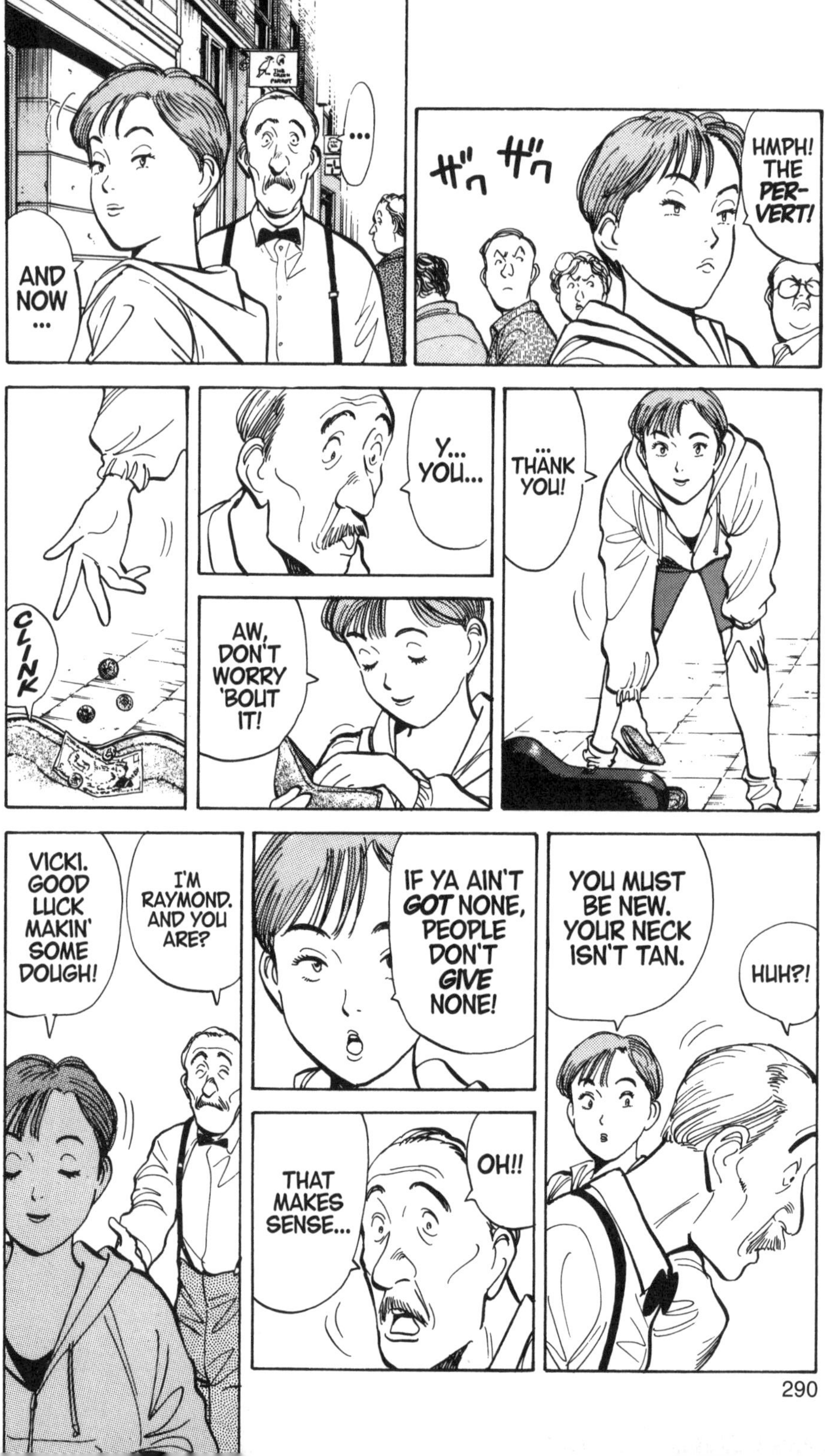
ザク ザク
HMPH! THE PER-VERT!
...
AND NOW ...
... THANK YOU!
Y... YOU...
AW, DON'T WORRY 'BOUT IT!
CLINK
HUH?!
YOU MUST BE NEW. YOUR NECK ISN'T TAN.
IF YA AIN'T GOT NONE, PEOPLE DON'T GIVE NONE!
OH!!
THAT MAKES SENSE...
I'M RAYMOND. AND YOU ARE?
VICKI. GOOD LUCK MAKIN' SOME DOUGH!

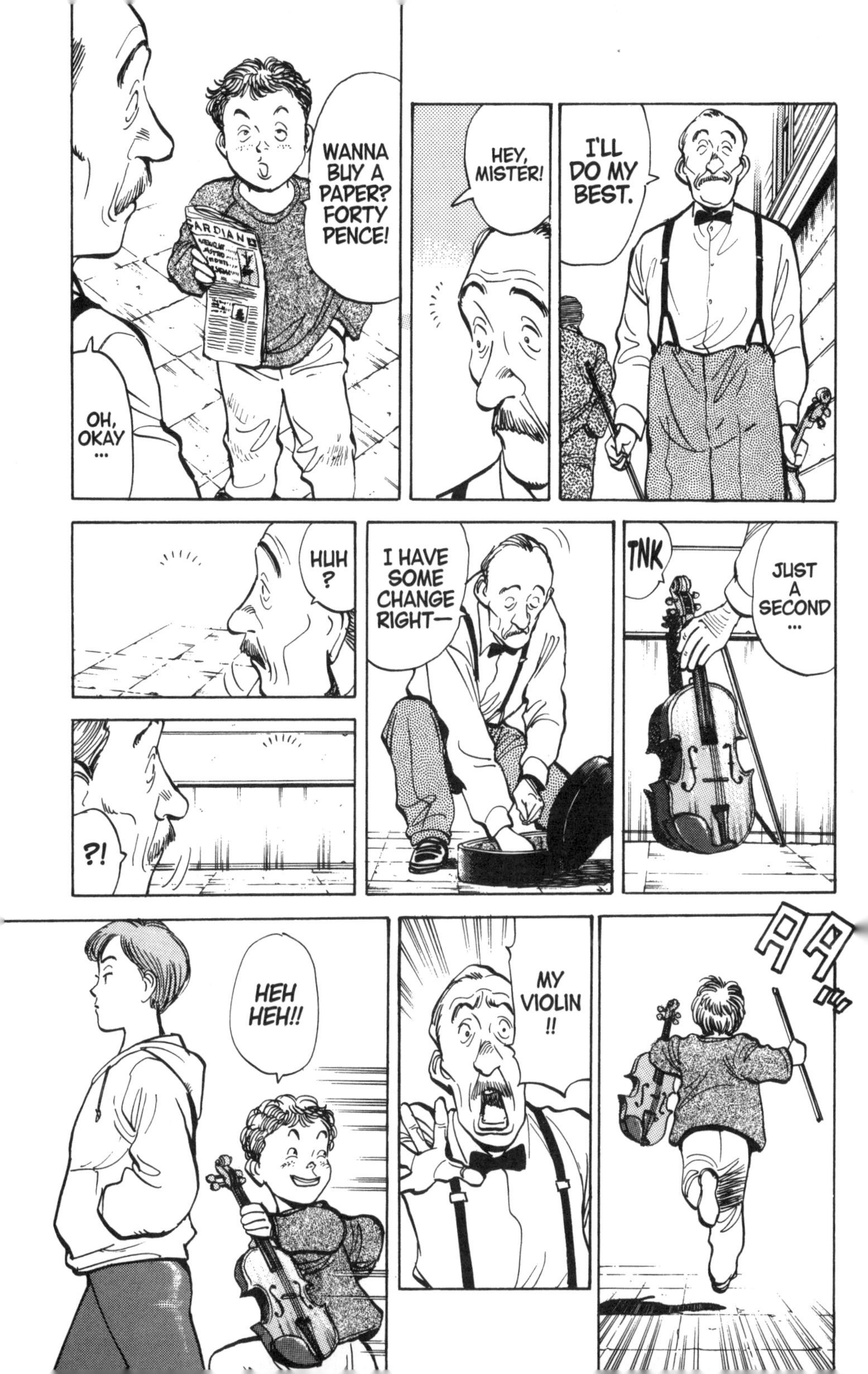
I'LL DO MY BEST.
HEY, MISTER!
WANNA BUY A PAPER? FORTY PENCE!
OH, OKAY...
TNK
JUST A SECOND...
I HAVE SOME CHANGE RIGHT—
HUH?
?!
MY VIOLIN!!
HEH HEH!!

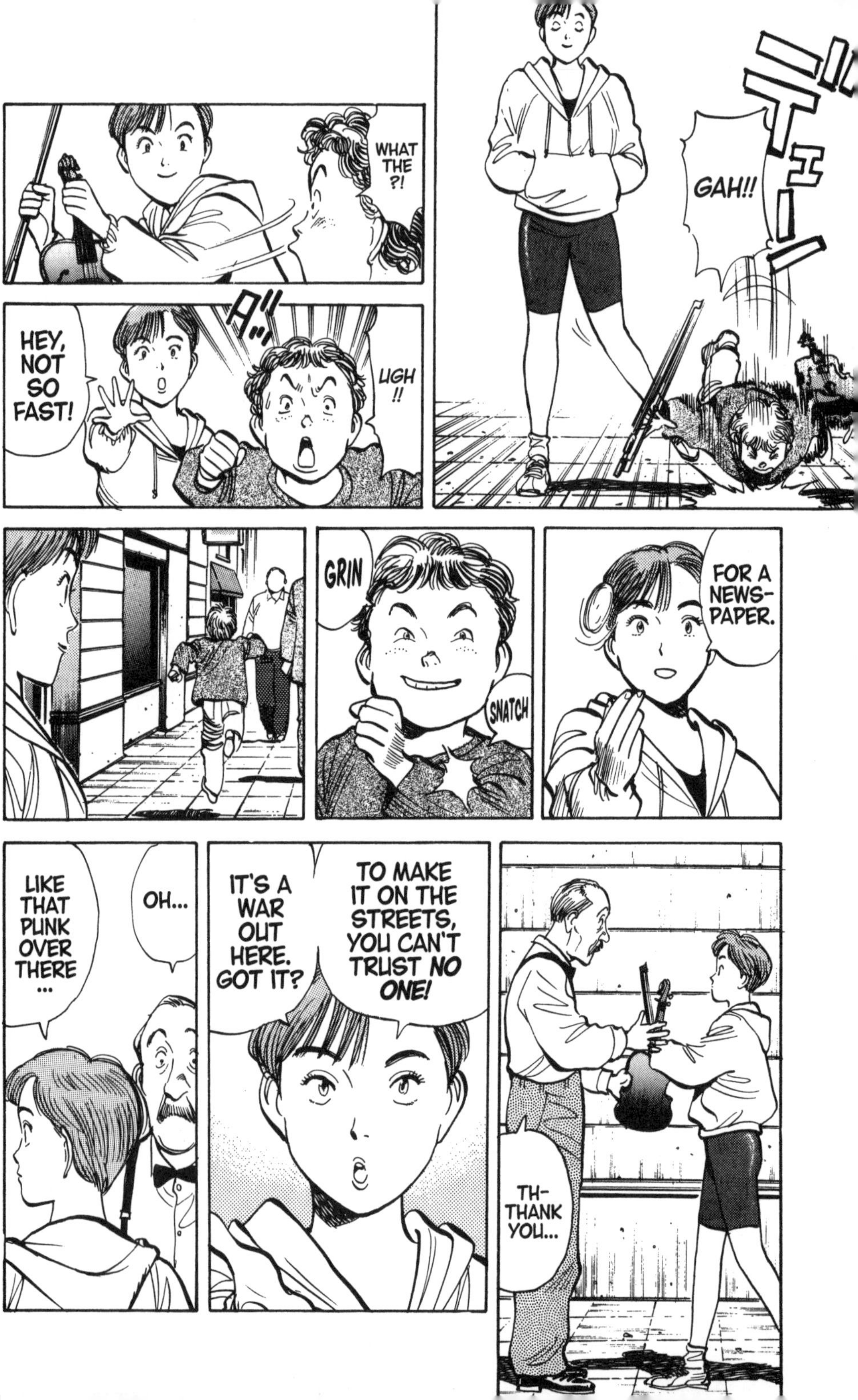
GAH!!
WHAT THE ?!
UGH !!
HEY, NOT SO FAST!
FOR A NEWS-PAPER.
GRIN
SNATCH
TH-THANK YOU...
TO MAKE IT ON THE STREETS, YOU CAN'T TRUST NO ONE!
IT'S A WAR OUT HERE. GOT IT?
OH...
LIKE THAT PUNK OVER THERE ...

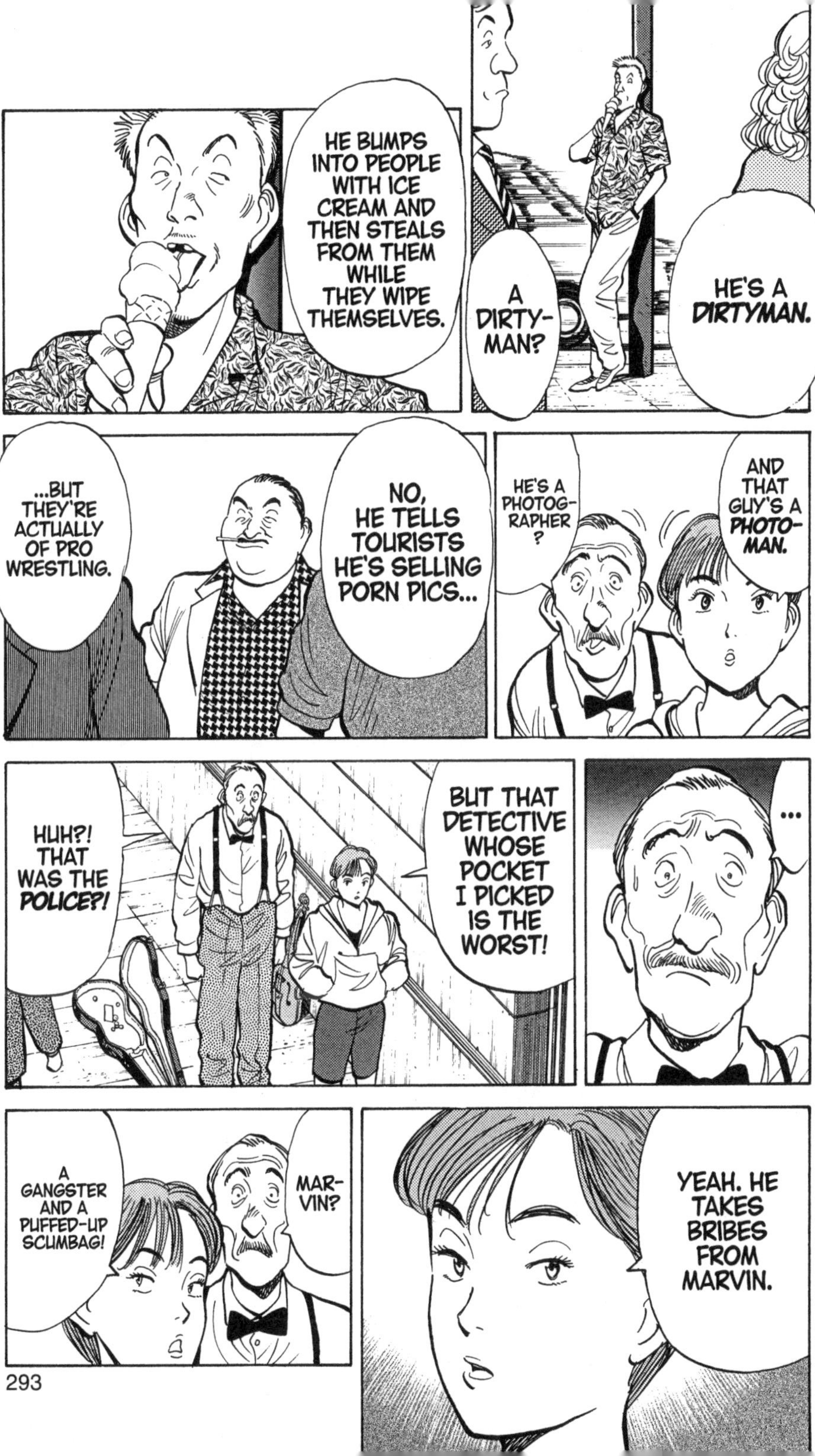

HE'S A DIRTYMAN.
A DIRTY-MAN?
HE BUMPS INTO PEOPLE WITH ICE CREAM AND THEN STEALS FROM THEM WHILE THEY WIPE THEMSELVES.
AND THAT GUY'S A PHOTO-MAN.
HE'S A PHOTOG-RAPHER?
NO, HE TELLS TOURISTS HE'S SELLING PORN PICS...
...BUT THEY'RE ACTUALLY OF PRO WRESTLING.
...
BUT THAT DETECTIVE WHOSE POCKET I PICKED IS THE WORST!
HUH?! THAT WAS THE POLICE?!
YEAH. HE TAKES BRIBES FROM MARVIN.
MAR-VIN?
A GANGSTER AND A PUFFED-UP SCUMBAG!

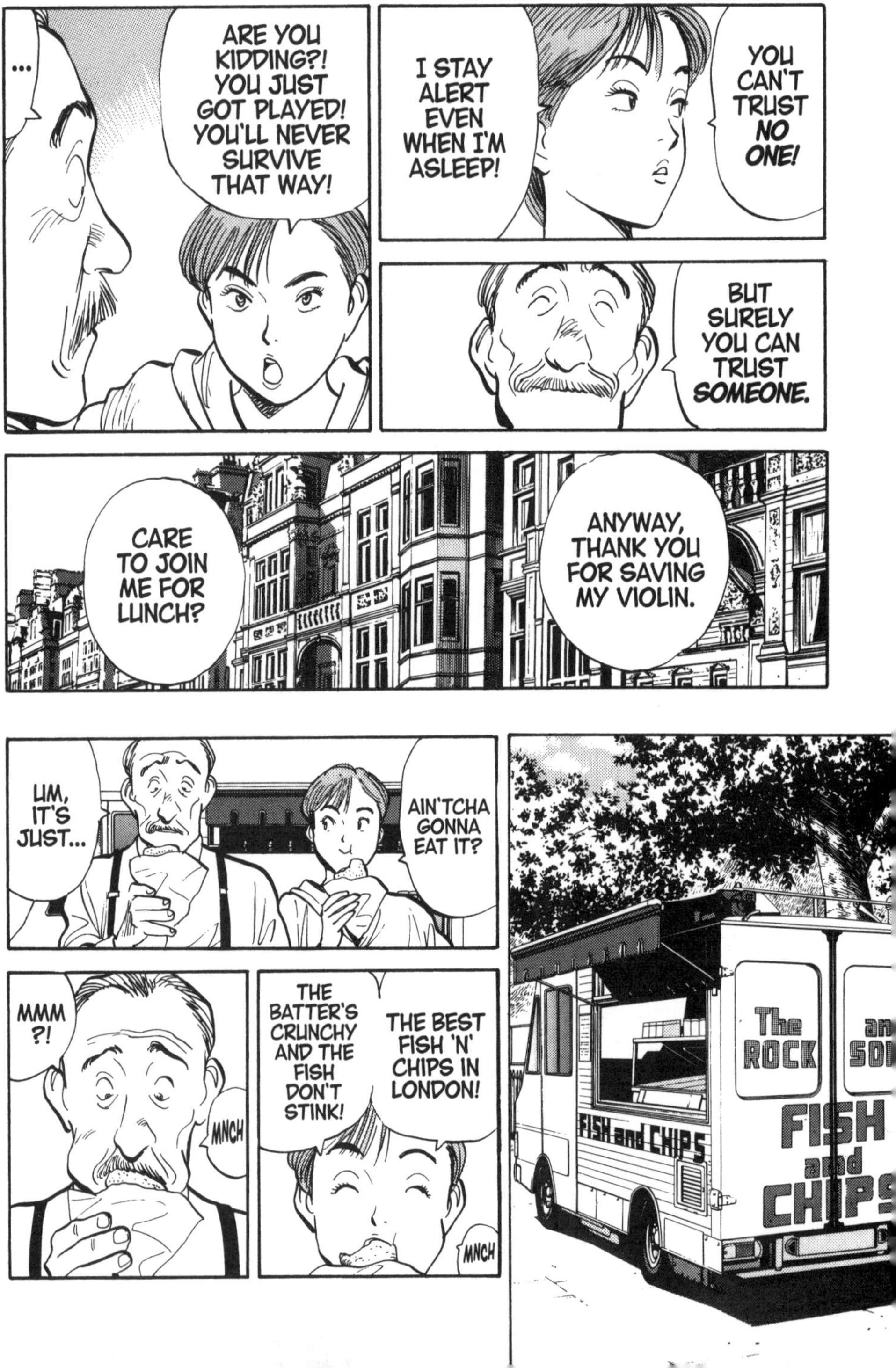
YOU CAN'T TRUST NO ONE!
I STAY ALERT EVEN WHEN I'M ASLEEP!
BUT SURELY YOU CAN TRUST SOMEONE.
ARE YOU KIDDING?! YOU JUST GOT PLAYED! YOU'LL NEVER SURVIVE THAT WAY!
...
ANYWAY, THANK YOU FOR SAVING MY VIOLIN.
CARE TO JOIN ME FOR LUNCH?
The ROCK
FISH and CHIPS
FISH and CHIPS
AIN'TCHA GONNA EAT IT?
UM, IT'S JUST...
THE BEST FISH 'N' CHIPS IN LONDON!
THE BATTER'S CRUNCHY AND THE FISH DON'T STINK!
MNCH
MNCH
MMM ?!

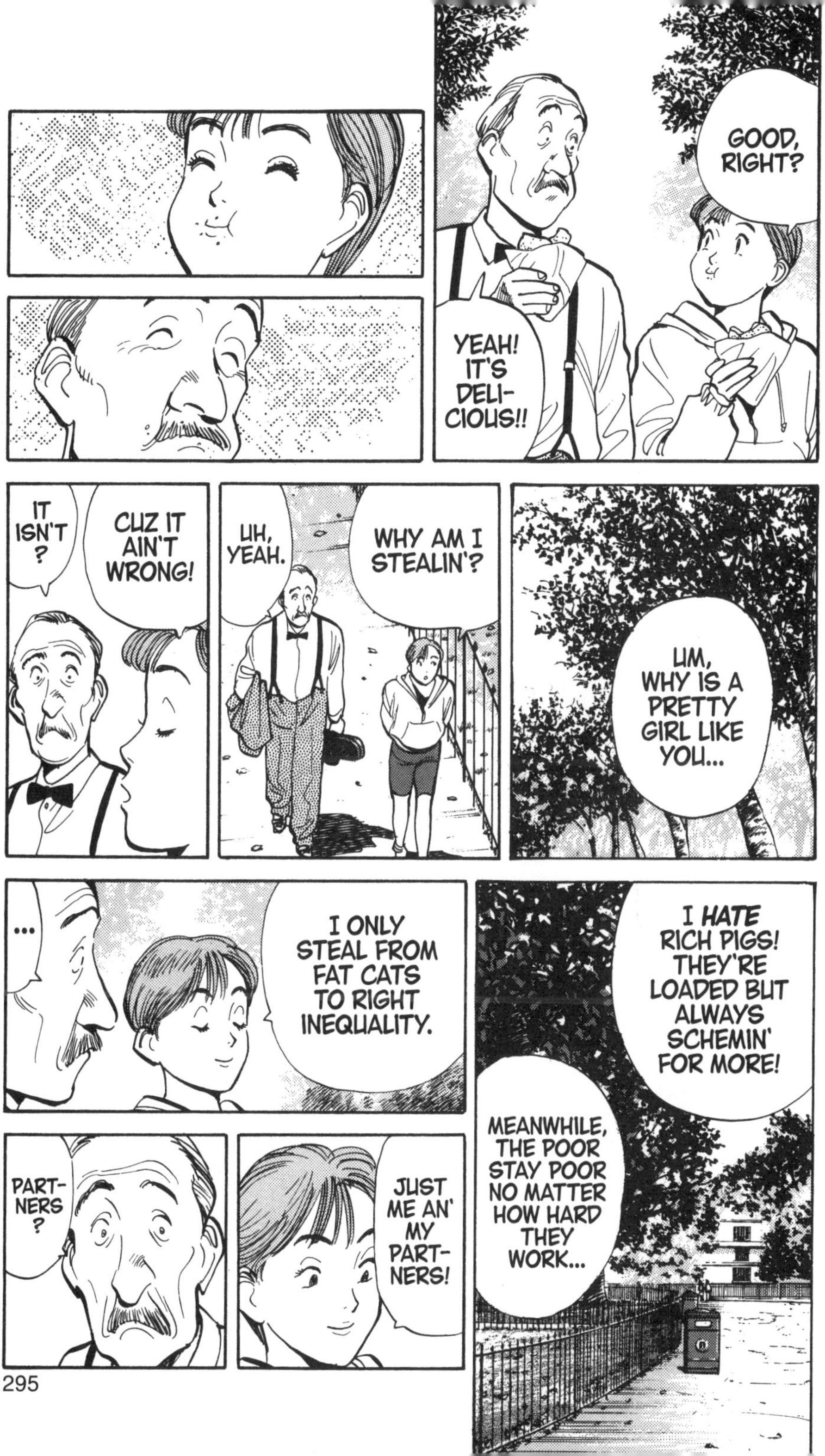
GOOD, RIGHT?
YEAH! IT'S DELICIOUS!!
UM, WHY IS A PRETTY GIRL LIKE YOU...
WHY AM I STEALIN'?
UH, YEAH.
CUZ IT AIN'T WRONG!
IT ISN'T?
I *HATE* RICH PIGS! THEY'RE LOADED BUT ALWAYS SCHEMIN' FOR MORE!
MEANWHILE, THE POOR STAY POOR NO MATTER HOW HARD THEY WORK...
I ONLY STEAL FROM FAT CATS TO RIGHT INEQUALITY.
...
JUST ME AN' MY PARTNERS!
PARTNERS?

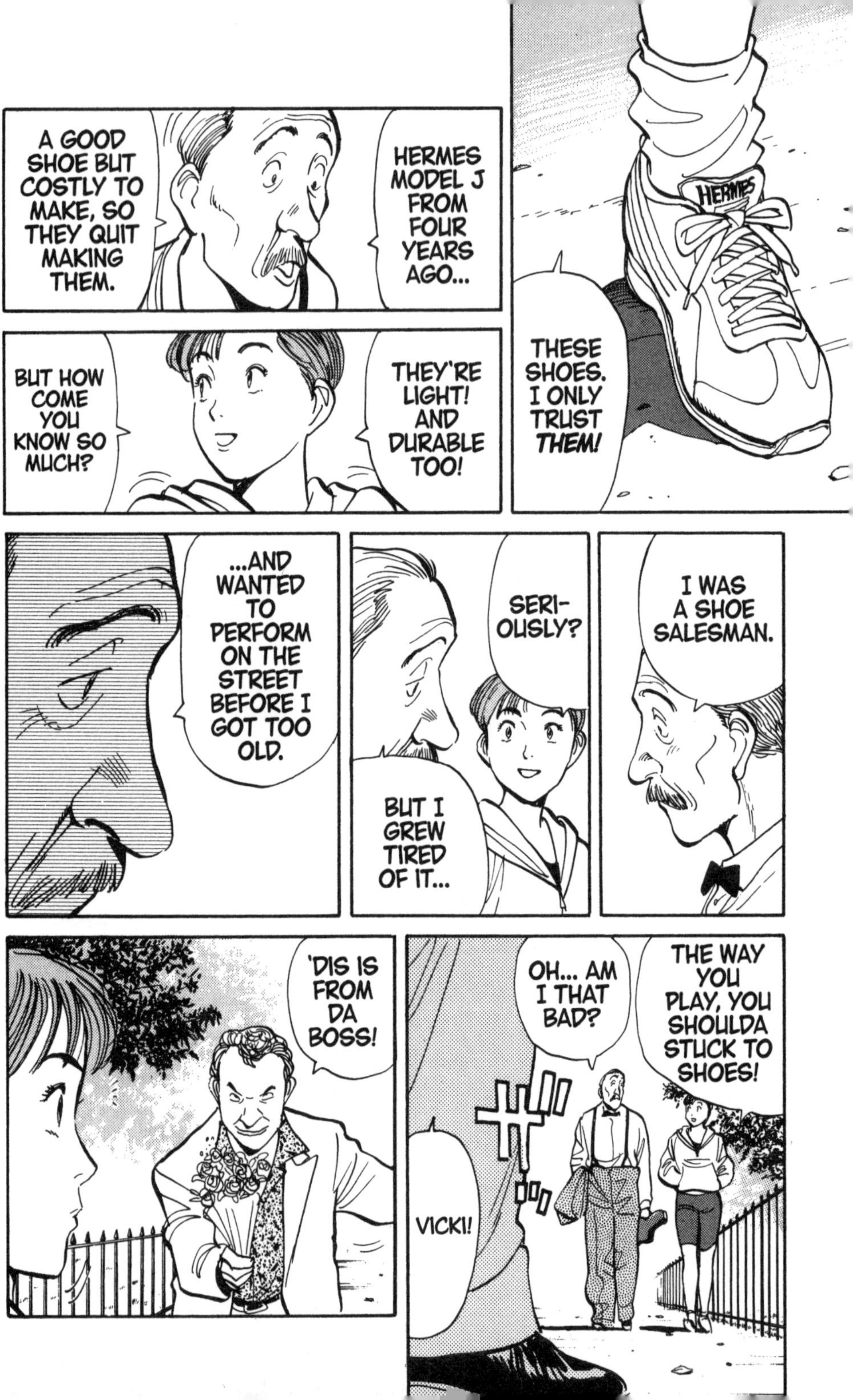
THESE SHOES. I ONLY TRUST *THEM!*
HERMES MODEL J FROM FOUR YEARS AGO...
A GOOD SHOE BUT COSTLY TO MAKE, SO THEY QUIT MAKING THEM.
THEY'RE LIGHT! AND DURABLE TOO!
BUT HOW COME YOU KNOW SO MUCH?
I WAS A SHOE SALESMAN.
SERI-OUSLY?
BUT I GREW TIRED OF IT...
...AND WANTED TO PERFORM ON THE STREET BEFORE I GOT TOO OLD.
THE WAY YOU PLAY, YOU SHOULDA STUCK TO SHOES!
OH... AM I THAT BAD?
VICKI!
'DIS IS FROM DA BOSS!

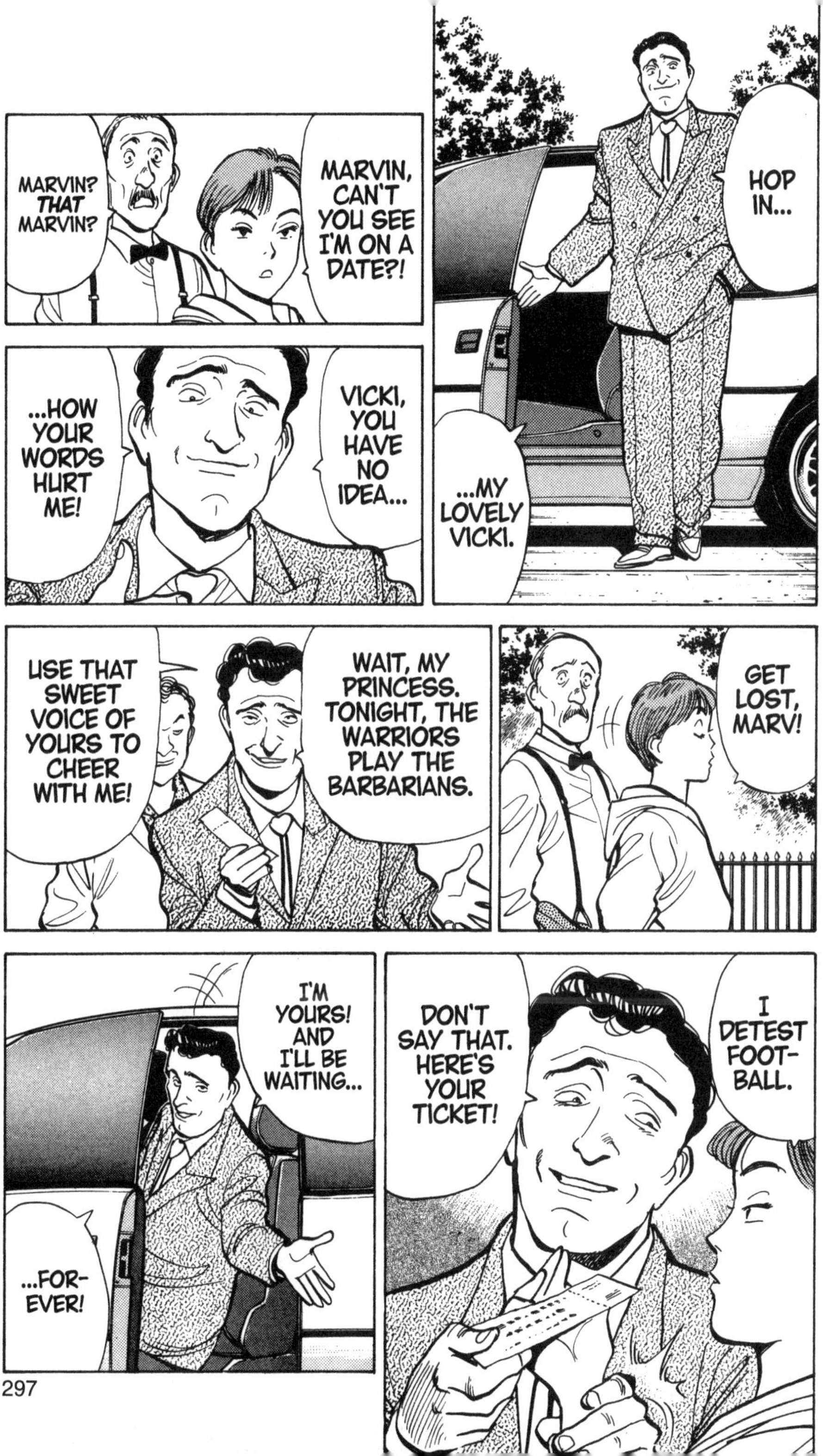
HOP IN...
...MY LOVELY VICKI.
MARVIN, CAN'T YOU SEE I'M ON A DATE?!
MARVIN? *THAT* MARVIN?
VICKI, YOU HAVE NO IDEA...
...HOW YOUR WORDS HURT ME!
GET LOST, MARV!
WAIT, MY PRINCESS. TONIGHT, THE WARRIORS PLAY THE BARBARIANS.
USE THAT SWEET VOICE OF YOURS TO CHEER WITH ME!
I DETEST FOOT-BALL.
DON'T SAY THAT. HERE'S YOUR TICKET!
I'M YOURS! AND I'LL BE WAITING...
...FOR-EVER!

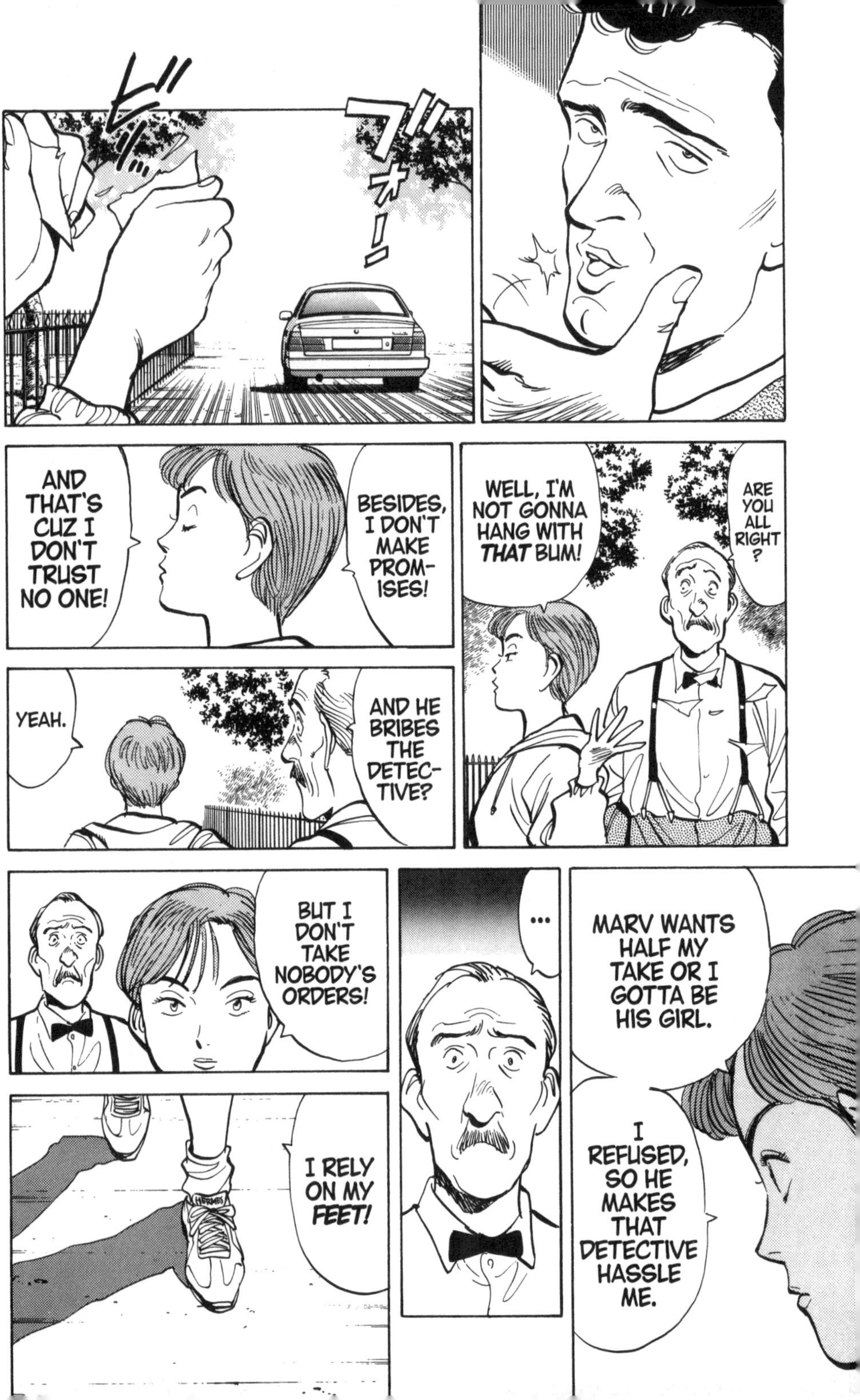
ブォ!
ARE YOU ALL RIGHT?
WELL, I'M NOT GONNA HANG WITH *THAT* BUM!
BESIDES, I DON'T MAKE PROMISES!
AND THAT'S CUZ I DON'T TRUST NO ONE!
AND HE BRIBES THE DETECTIVE?
YEAH.
MARV WANTS HALF MY TAKE OR I GOTTA BE HIS GIRL.
I REFUSED, SO HE MAKES THAT DETECTIVE HASSLE ME.
...
BUT I DON'T TAKE NOBODY'S ORDERS!
I RELY ON MY *FEET*!

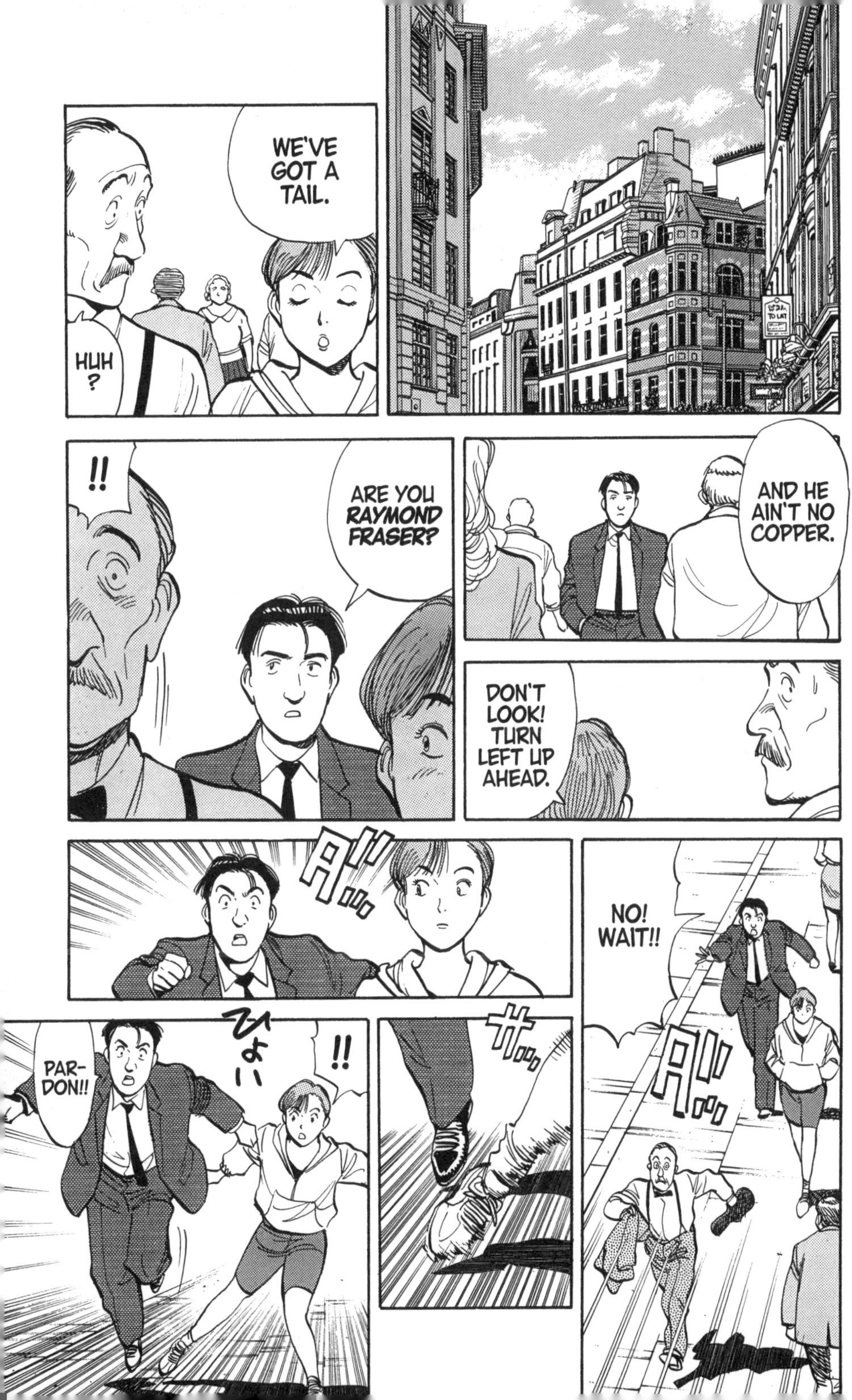
WE'VE GOT A TAIL.
HUH ?
AND HE AIN'T NO COPPER.
DON'T LOOK! TURN LEFT UP AHEAD.
ARE YOU RAYMOND FRASER?
!!
NO! WAIT!!
ダッ
ダッ
ザッ
!!
ひょい
PAR-DON!!

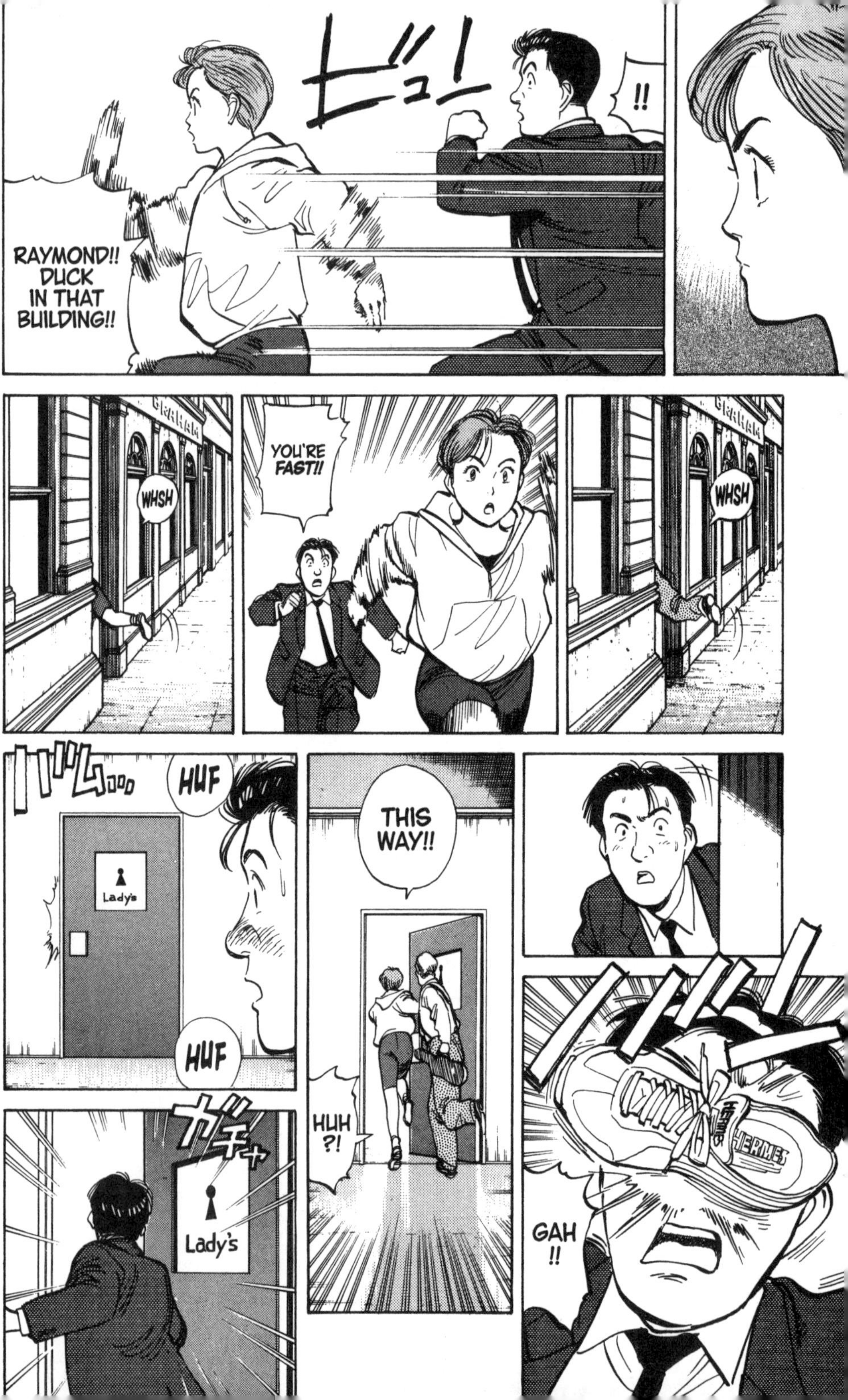
!!
ビュ!
RAYMOND!! DUCK IN THAT BUILDING!!
WHSH
YOU'RE FAST!!
WHSH
GAH!!
THIS WAY!!
HUH?!
HUF
Lady's
HUF
ガチャ
Lady's

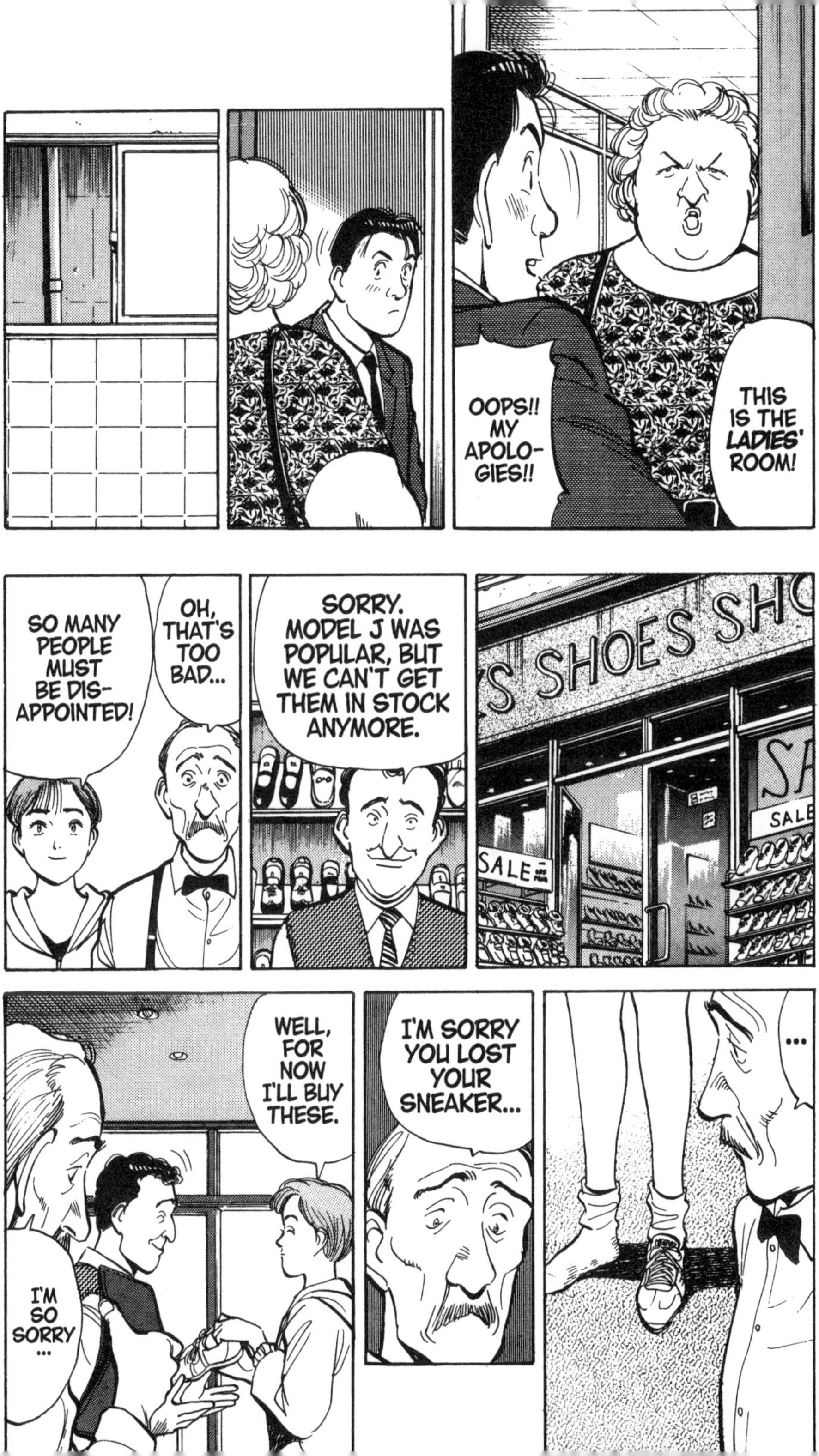
THIS IS THE LADIES' ROOM!
OOPS!! MY APOLOGIES!!
SHOES SHO
SALE
SALE
SORRY. MODEL J WAS POPULAR, BUT WE CAN'T GET THEM IN STOCK ANYMORE.
OH, THAT'S TOO BAD...
SO MANY PEOPLE MUST BE DISAPPOINTED!
...
I'M SORRY YOU LOST YOUR SNEAKER...
WELL, FOR NOW I'LL BUY THESE.
I'M SO SORRY...

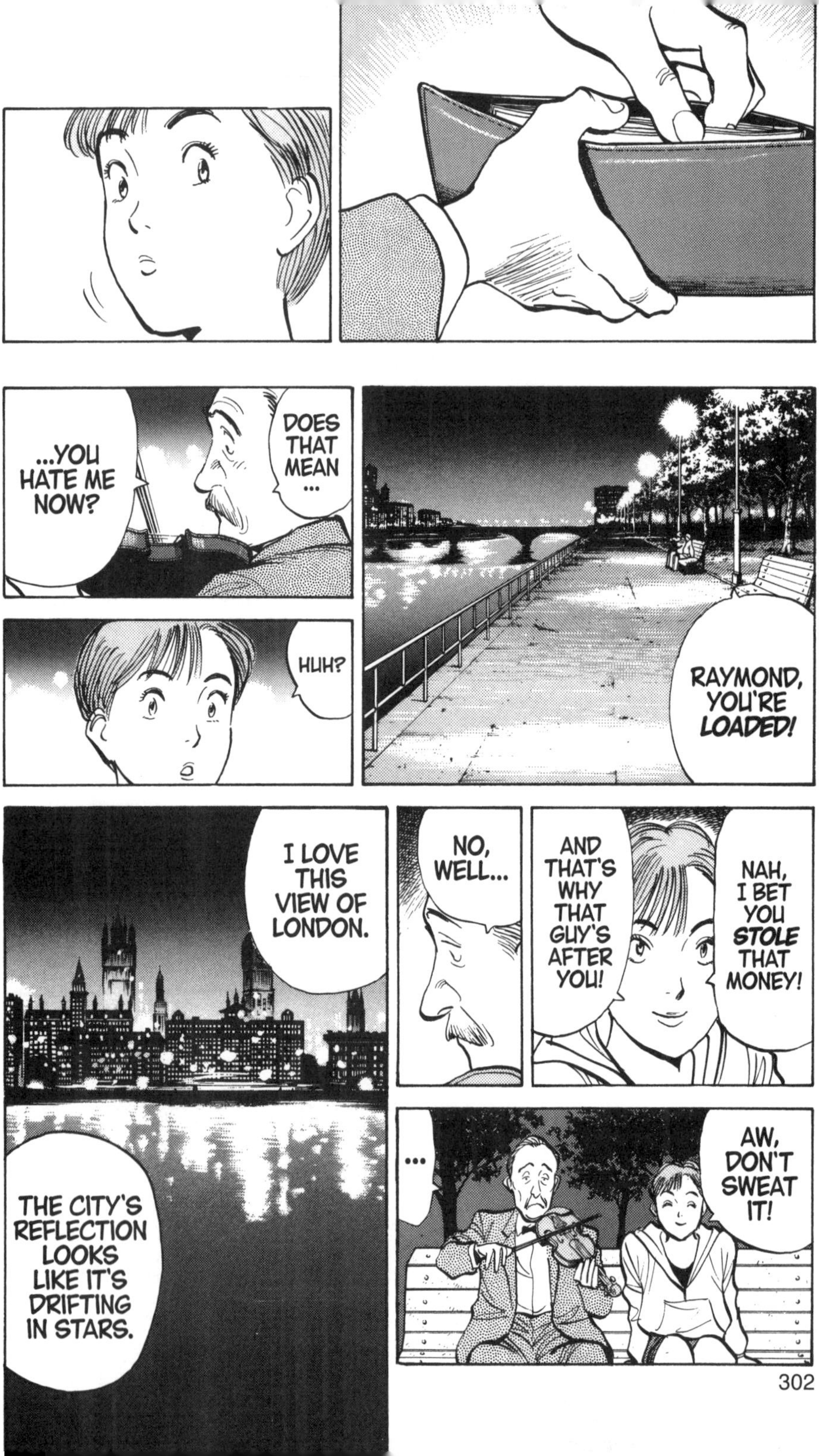
RAYMOND, YOU'RE LOADED!
DOES THAT MEAN...
...YOU HATE ME NOW?
HUH?
NAH, I BET YOU STOLE THAT MONEY!
AND THAT'S WHY THAT GUY'S AFTER YOU!
NO, WELL...
AW, DON'T SWEAT IT!
...
I LOVE THIS VIEW OF LONDON.
THE CITY'S REFLECTION LOOKS LIKE IT'S DRIFTING IN STARS.

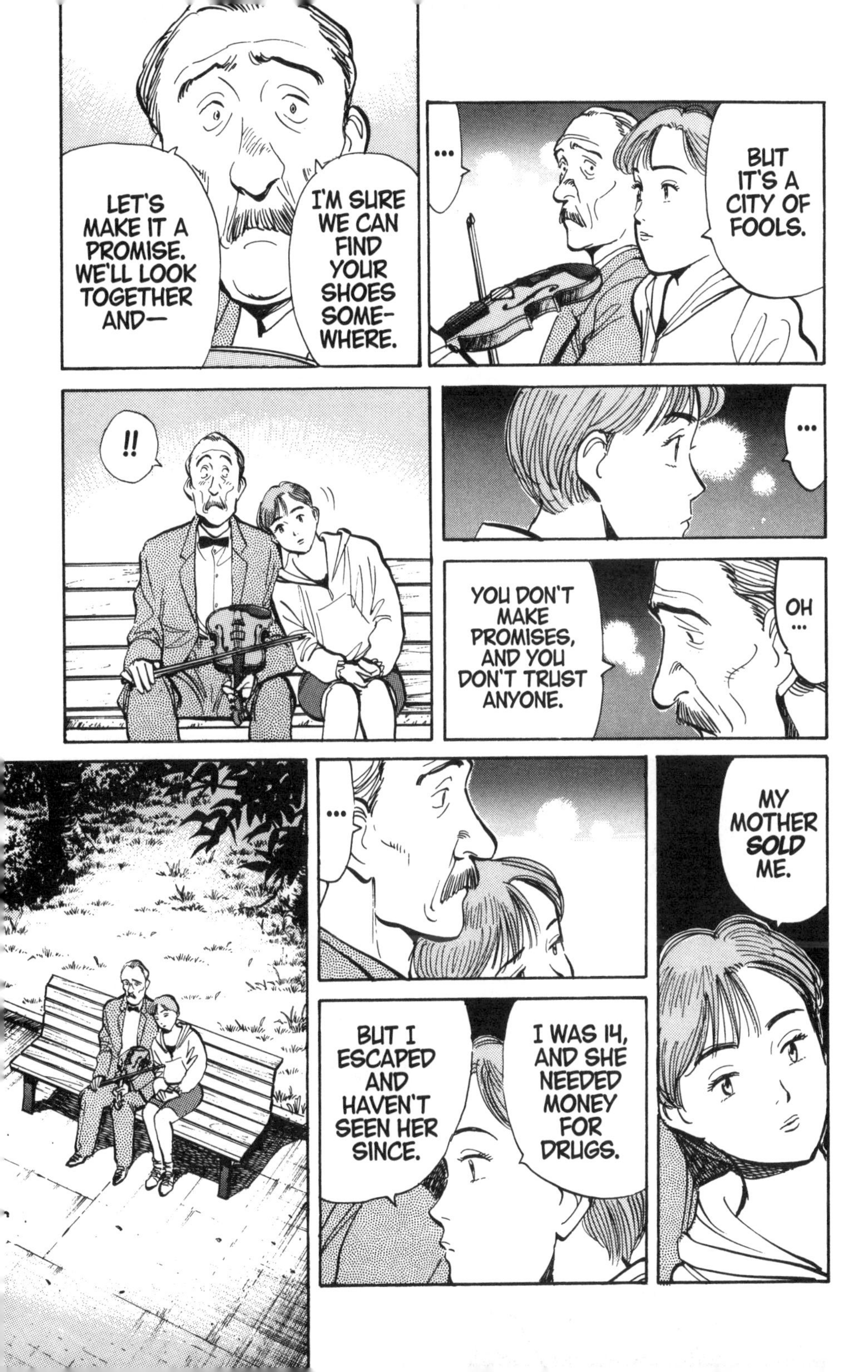
BUT IT'S A CITY OF FOOLS.
...
I'M SURE WE CAN FIND YOUR SHOES SOME-WHERE.
LET'S MAKE IT A PROMISE. WE'LL LOOK TOGETHER AND—
...
OH ...
YOU DON'T MAKE PROMISES, AND YOU DON'T TRUST ANYONE.
!!
MY MOTHER *SOLD* ME.
...
I WAS 14, AND SHE NEEDED MONEY FOR DRUGS.
BUT I ESCAPED AND HAVEN'T SEEN HER SINCE.

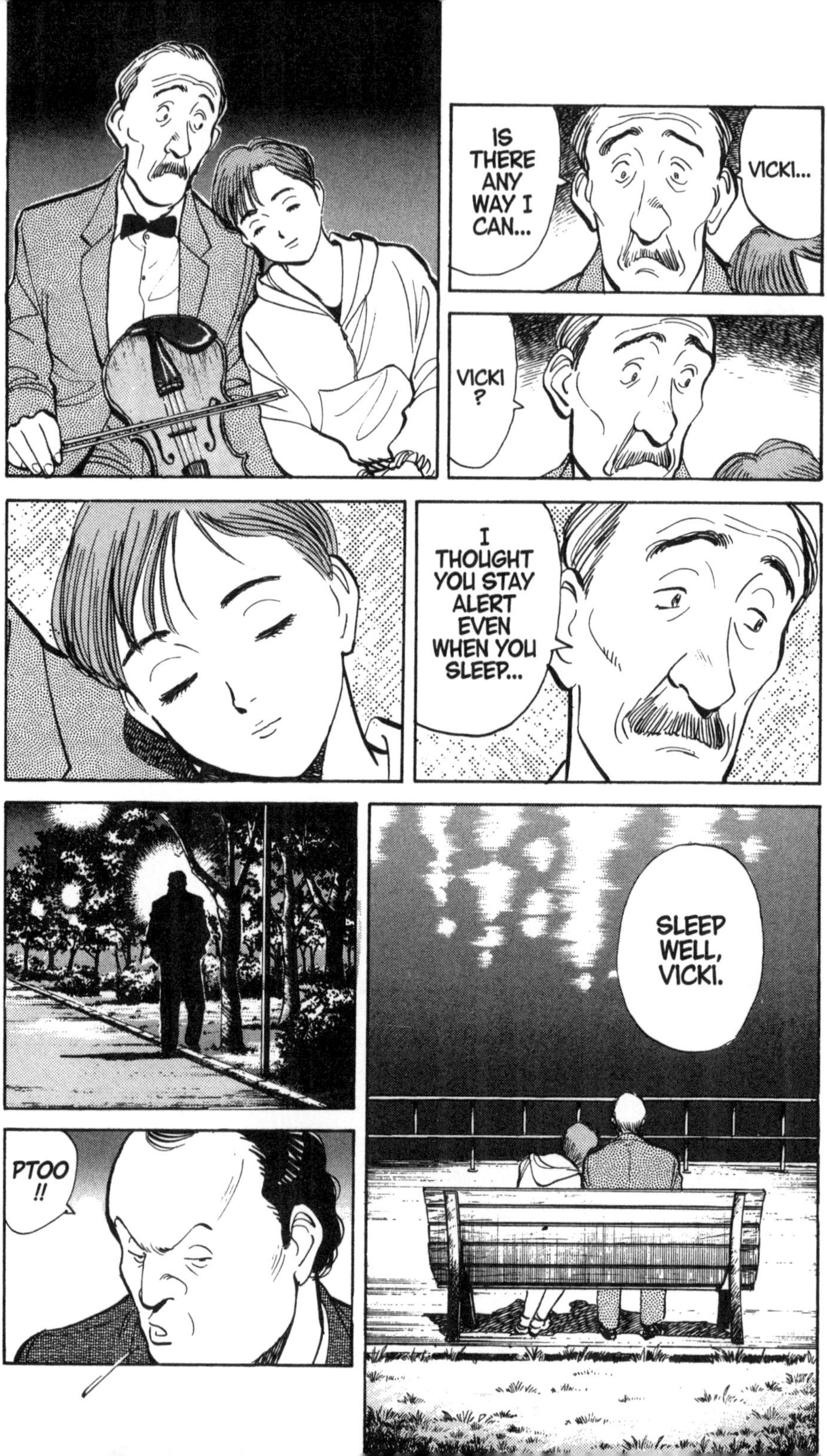
VICKI...
IS THERE ANY WAY I CAN...
VICKI ?
I THOUGHT YOU STAY ALERT EVEN WHEN YOU SLEEP...
SLEEP WELL, VICKI.
PTOO !!

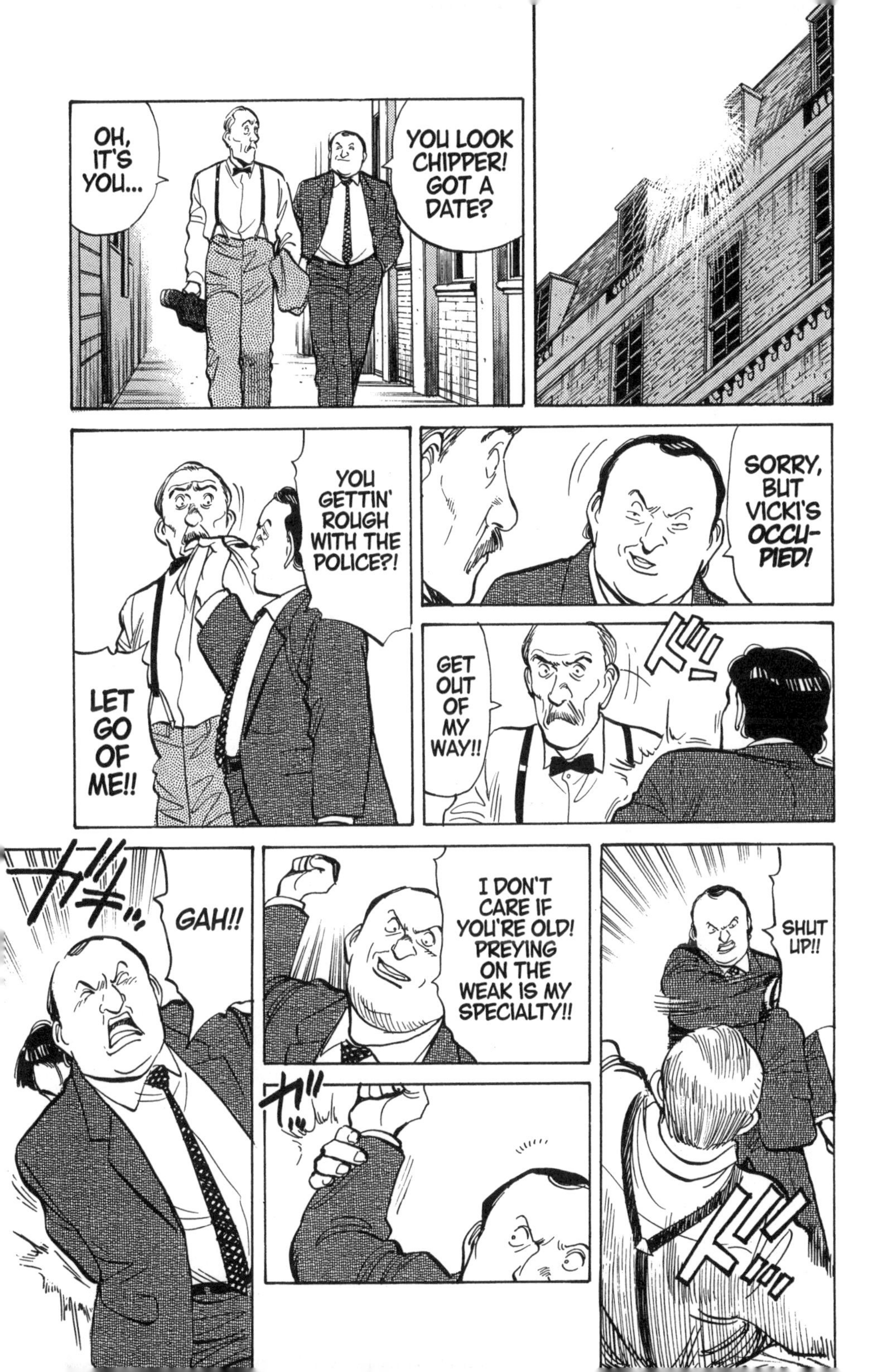
YOU LOOK CHIPPER! GOT A DATE?
OH, IT'S YOU...
SORRY, BUT VICKI'S OCCU-PIED!
GET OUT OF MY WAY!!
YOU GETTIN' ROUGH WITH THE POLICE?!
LET GO OF ME!!
SHUT UP!!
I DON'T CARE IF YOU'RE OLD! PREYING ON THE WEAK IS MY SPECIALTY!!
GAH!!

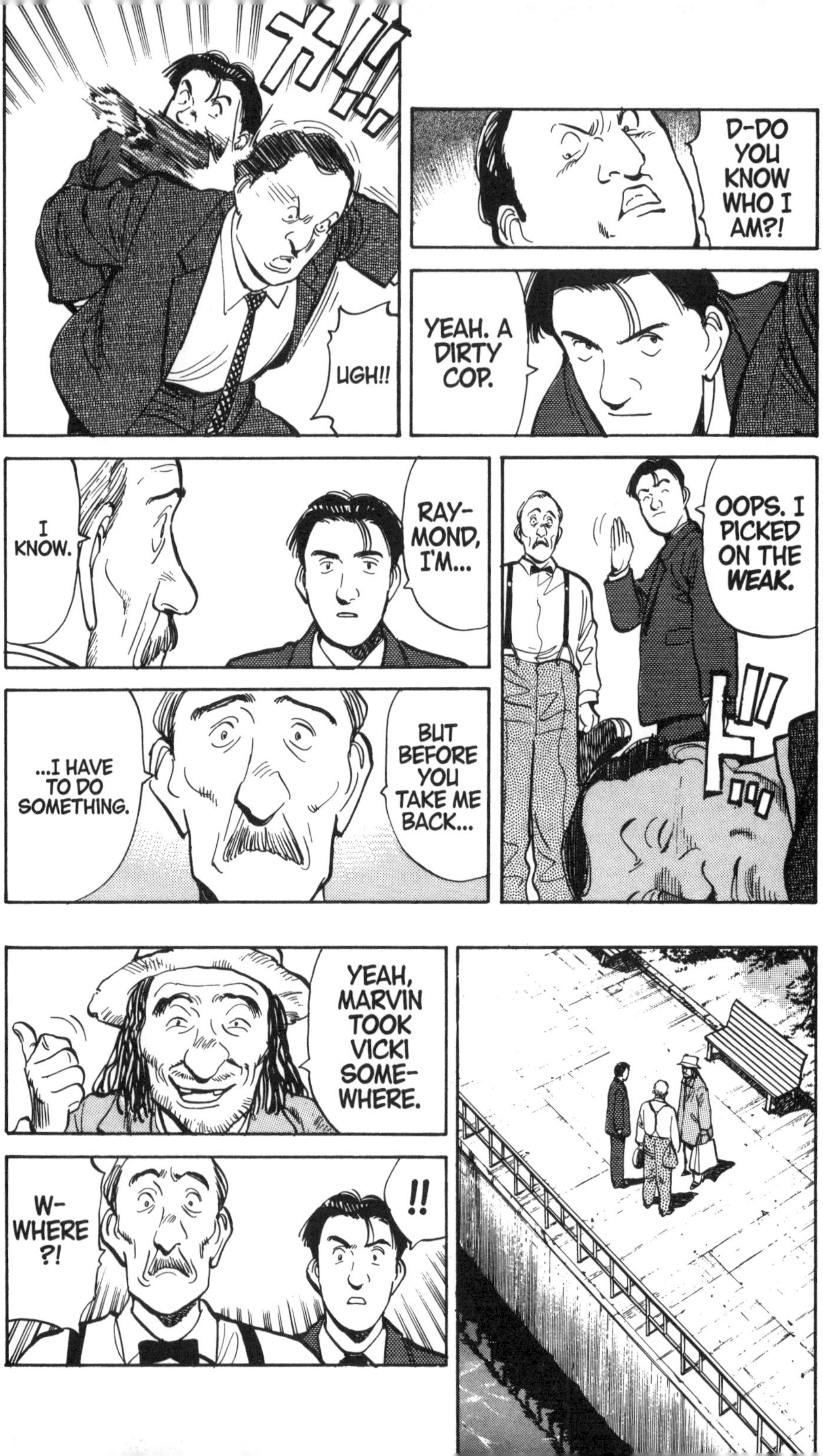
D-DO YOU KNOW WHO I AM?!
YEAH. A DIRTY COP.
UGH!!
OOPS. I PICKED ON THE WEAK.
RAY-MOND, I'M...
I KNOW.
BUT BEFORE YOU TAKE ME BACK...
...I HAVE TO DO SOMETHING.
YEAH, MARVIN TOOK VICKI SOME-WHERE.
!!
W-WHERE ?!

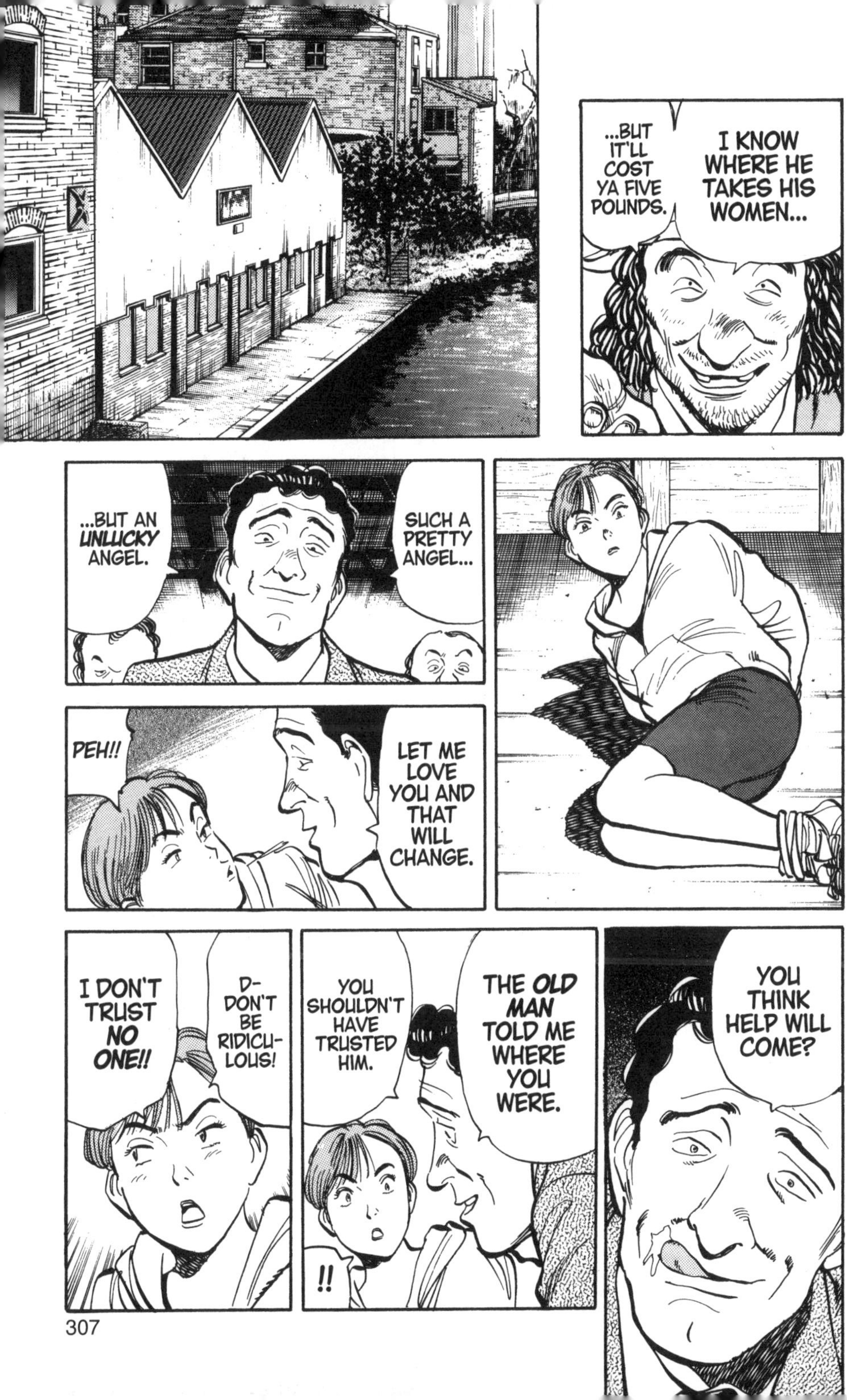
I KNOW WHERE HE TAKES HIS WOMEN...
...BUT IT'LL COST YA FIVE POUNDS.
SUCH A PRETTY ANGEL...
...BUT AN *UNLUCKY* ANGEL.
LET ME LOVE YOU AND THAT WILL CHANGE.
PEH!!
YOU THINK HELP WILL COME?
THE *OLD MAN* TOLD ME WHERE YOU WERE.
YOU SHOULDN'T HAVE TRUSTED HIM.
!!
D-DON'T BE RIDICULOUS!
I DON'T TRUST *NO ONE*!!

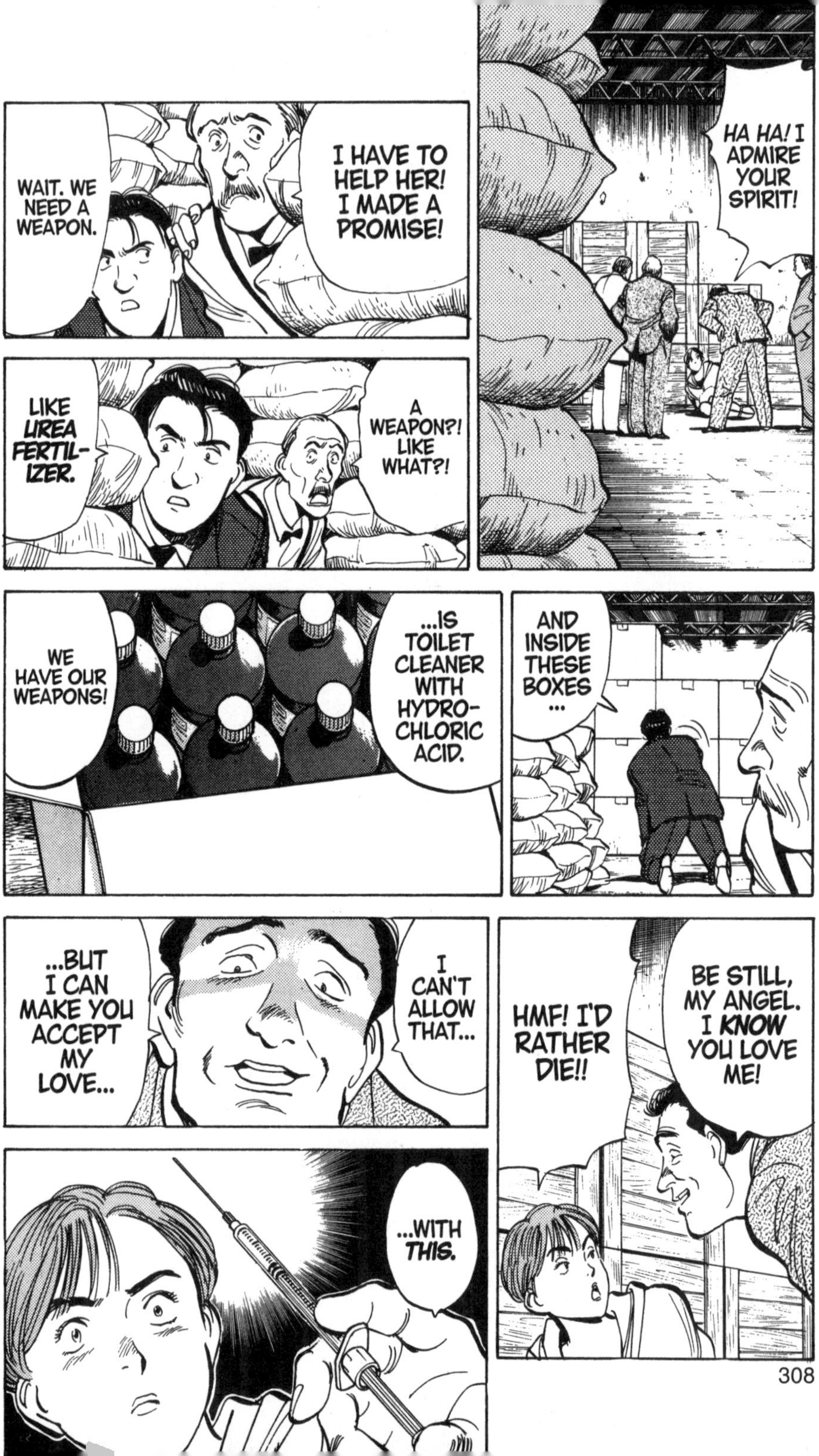
HA HA! I ADMIRE YOUR SPIRIT!
I HAVE TO HELP HER! I MADE A PROMISE!
WAIT. WE NEED A WEAPON.
A WEAPON?! LIKE WHAT?!
LIKE UREA FERTILIZER.
AND INSIDE THESE BOXES...
...IS TOILET CLEANER WITH HYDROCHLORIC ACID.
WE HAVE OUR WEAPONS!
BE STILL, MY ANGEL. I KNOW YOU LOVE ME!
HMF! I'D RATHER DIE!!
I CAN'T ALLOW THAT...
...BUT I CAN MAKE YOU ACCEPT MY LOVE...
...WITH THIS.

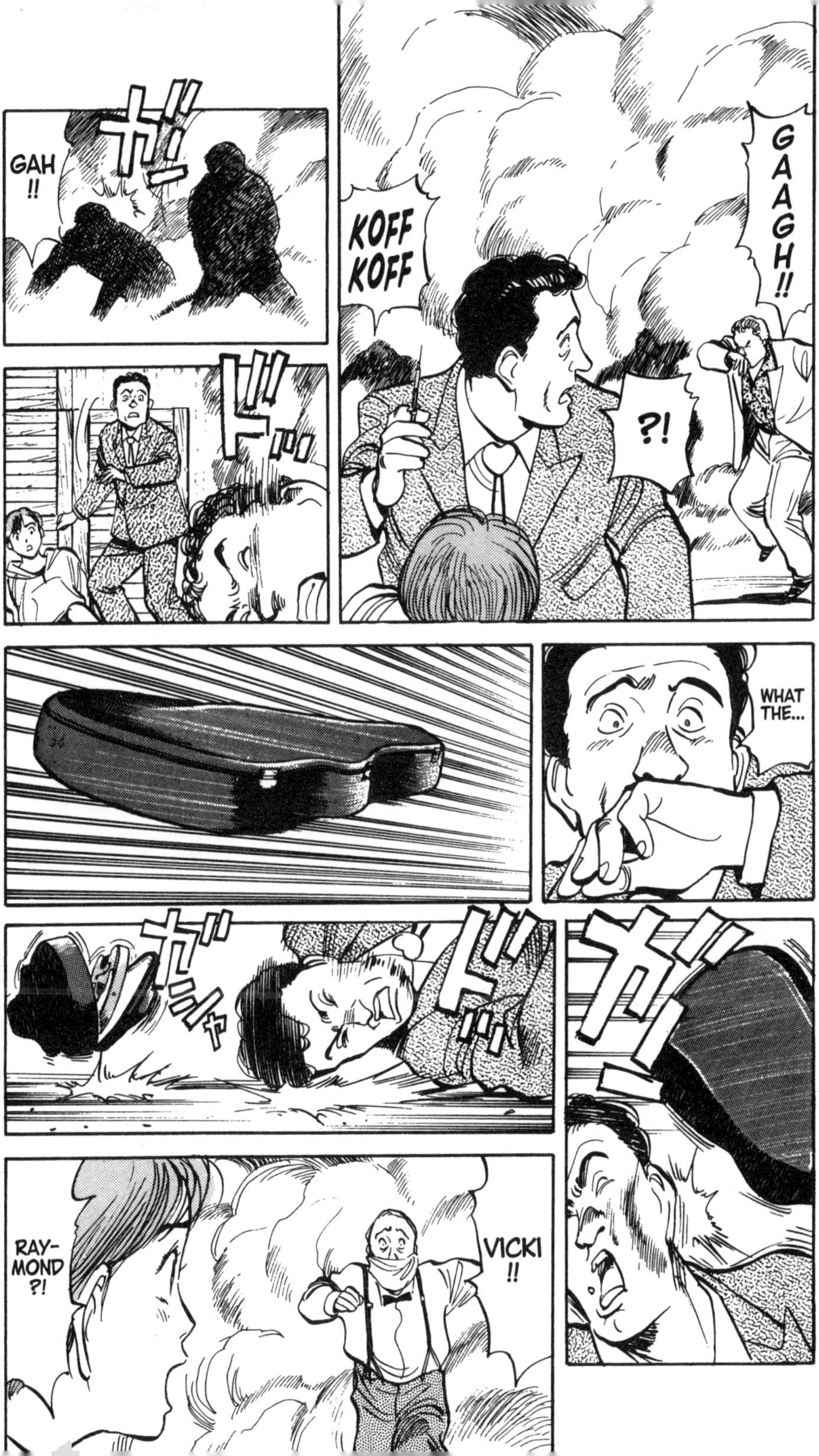
GAAGH!!
KOFF KOFF
?!
GAH!!
WHAT THE...
VICKI!!
RAY-MOND?!

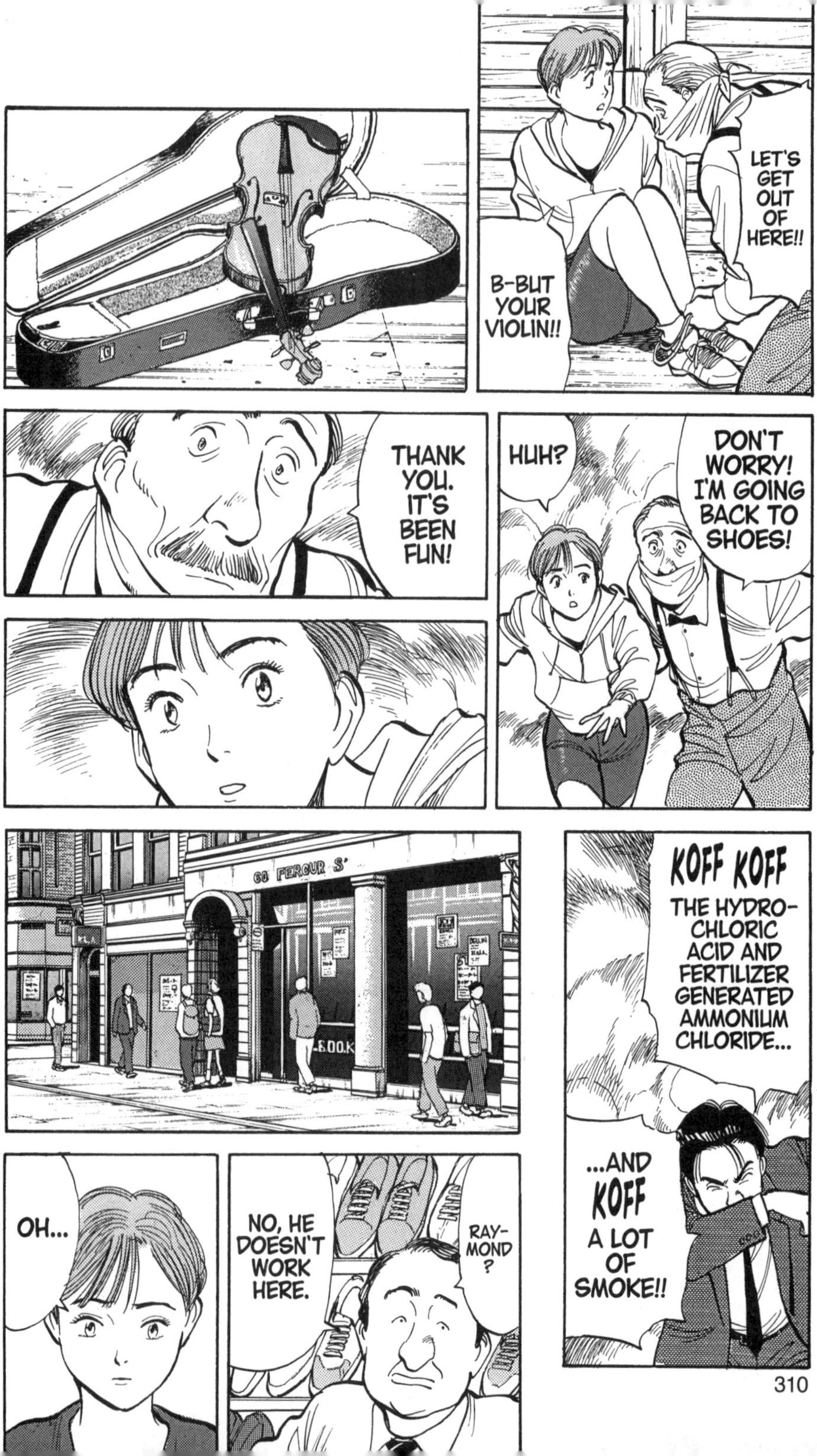
LET'S GET OUT OF HERE!!
B-BUT YOUR VIOLIN!!
DON'T WORRY! I'M GOING BACK TO SHOES!
HUH?
THANK YOU. IT'S BEEN FUN!
KOFF KOFF
THE HYDRO-CHLORIC ACID AND FERTILIZER GENERATED AMMONIUM CHLORIDE...
...AND KOFF A LOT OF SMOKE!!
RAY-MOND?
NO, HE DOESN'T WORK HERE.
OH...

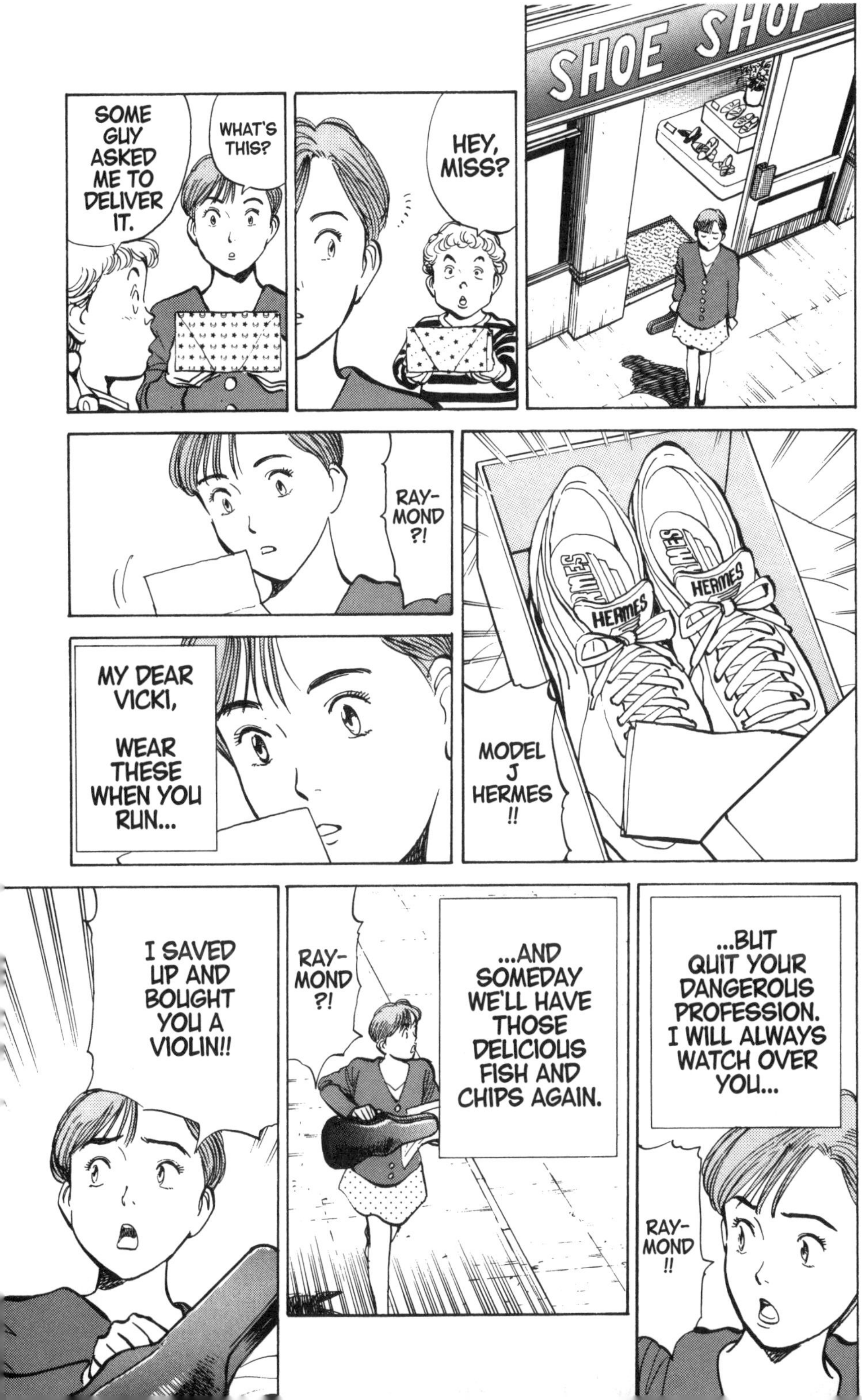
SHOE SHOP
HEY, MISS?
WHAT'S THIS?
SOME GUY ASKED ME TO DELIVER IT.
HERMES
HERMES
MODEL J HERMES !!
RAY-MOND ?!
MY DEAR VICKI,
WEAR THESE WHEN YOU RUN...
I SAVED UP AND BOUGHT YOU A VIOLIN!!
RAY-MOND ?!
...AND SOMEDAY WE'LL HAVE THOSE DELICIOUS FISH AND CHIPS AGAIN.
...BUT QUIT YOUR DANGEROUS PROFESSION. I WILL ALWAYS WATCH OVER YOU...
RAY-MOND !!

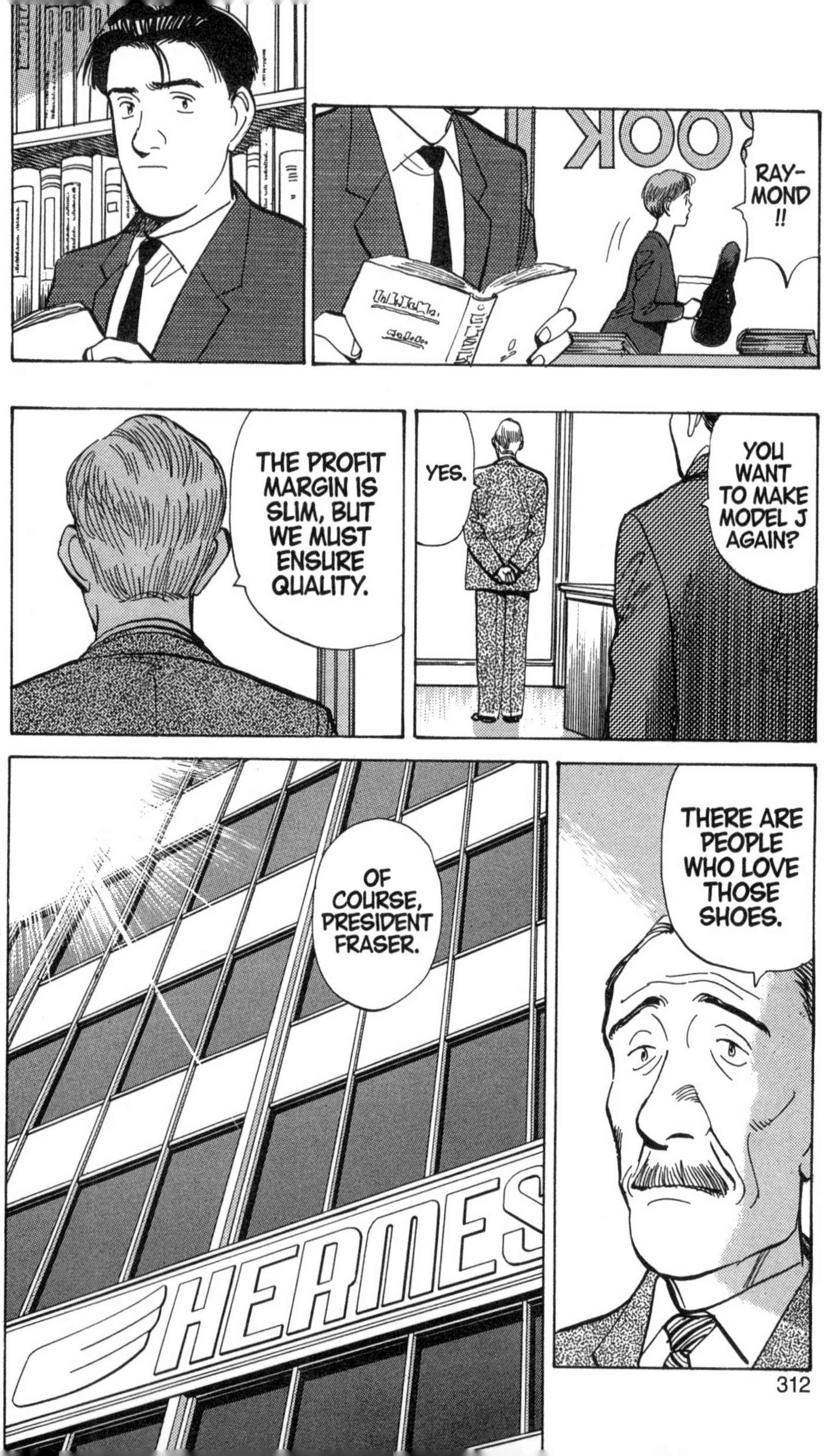
RAY-
MOND
!!
YOU WANT TO MAKE MODEL J AGAIN?
YES.
THE PROFIT MARGIN IS SLIM, BUT WE MUST ENSURE QUALITY.
THERE ARE PEOPLE WHO LOVE THOSE SHOES.
OF COURSE, PRESIDENT FRASER.
HERMES

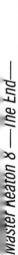

Sound Effects Glossary

The sound effects in *Master Keaton* have been preserved in their original Japanese format. To avoid additional lettering cluttering up the panels, a list of the sound effects (FX) is provided here. Each FX is listed by page and panel number. For example, "8.2" means the FX is on page 8, panel 2.

5.4 – clap clap clap clap clap clap clap clap
    (pachi pachi pachi pachi pachi pachi pachi pachi:
    clapping)
5.7 – tump (za: footstep)
9.5 – tump (za: footstep)
9.6 – tump (za: footstep)
9.7 – tump tump (za za: footsteps)
9.8 – thud (do: falling)
10.2 – splash splash (basha basha: struggling)
10.5 – spwash (zabaan: splash)
10.6 – sloosh (basha: swimming)
10.7 – splash (basha: splash)
16.4 – raaah (waaaa: cheers)
16.5 – yaay yaay (waa waa: cheers)
17.4 – raaah (waa: cheers)
17.5 – yaay yaay (waa waa: cheers)
20.2 – murmur murmur (zawa zawa: talking)
20.3 – rrring (jirirriri: bell)
20.4 – chatter chatter (zawa zawa: talking)
20.6 – swip (za: standing and saluting)
23.2 – tunk (bamu: car door closing)
23.4 – honk (papaa: car horn)
23.4 – vroom (buoon: car engine)
25.5 – smash (gashaan: breaking the glass)
26.3 – bwam (ba: colliding)
26.4 – fwump (do: falling)
26.5 – shunk (zaku: stabbing)
28.8 – raah raah (waa waa: cheers)
29.1 – chatter chatter (wai wai: talking)
30.3 – whsh (da: running)
30.8 – tump (ta: footstep)
30.10 – bwam (don: car hitting)
30.10 – screech (kikii: car braking)
35.3 – yaaay yaaay (waa waa: cheers)
35.4 – chatter chatter (wai wai: talking)
35.5 – chatter chatter (wai wai: talking)
33.3 – tak tak (ka ka: footsteps)
33.8 – bump (don: bumping)
37.7 – chatter chatter chatter (wai wai wai: talking)
39.3 – raaaaah (waaaa: cheers)
44.3 – fwash (ka: light)
7.1 – kabooooo (goooooo: explosion)
44.1 – ooommmmm (ooooooo: explosion)
44.5 – chak (batamu: door closing)
44.10 – creak (gi: door opening)
45.2 – hug (ga: hugging)
45.3 – chak (batan: door closing)
45.4 – chak (gata: standing up)
45.6 – bam bam (don don: hitting the door)
45.7 – bam bam (don don: hitting the door)
45.8 – crik (gi: door opening)
45.9 – slam (bamu: door closing)
54.4 – vroom (buoon: car)
57.2 – bam (bamu: car door closing)
57.3 – vroom (buon: car)
64-5 – vrooom (buoon oon: car)
7.2 – whok (gan: elbowing)

8.2 – clank (gashaan: dropping pan)
14.9 – munch munch (hagu hagu: eating)
15.3 – rrring (RRRR: phone)
17.4 – tump (za: footstep)
34.8 – chatter chatter (zawa zawa: talking)
37.3 – ha ha ha ha (daa ha ha ha: laughter)
37.4 – ha ha ha (ha ha ha: laughter)
37.5 – thok (gan: hitting)
37.6 – thud (daan: falling)
38.1 – whsh (da: running)
48.5 – krrnk krrnk (goton gogon: moving the statue)
50.5 – krrnk krrnk (gogon gogo: moving the statue)
58.4 – totter totter (hyoko hyoko: walking unsteadily)
61.3 – stagger stagger (yoro yoro: walking unsteadily)
61.7 – wobble (gara: rock moving)
61.7 – twist (guki: spraining his ankle)
61.8 – fwam (do: falling)
65.5 – slip (za: sliding)
65.7 – skiddd (zaza: sliding)
65.9 – zwip (shaa: rope sliding)
68.3 – gwoooo (goooooo: wind)
69.7 – gwooo (gooooo: wind)
69.9 – hwoooo (hyuuuu: wind)
70.4 – gwoooooo (goooooo: wind)
70.5 – hwoooo (hyuuuu: wind)
72.1 – chatter chatter chatter chatter
    (wai wai wai wai: talking)
72.6 – gwoooooo (goooooo: wind)
73.1 – bwooooo (byuuuuu: wind)
73.3 – tump (za: footstep)
73.6 – gwooooo (gooooo: wind)
74.4 – whsh (za: skiing)
75.4 – whsh (zaa: skiing)
76.3 – rrmmm (gogogogogo: avalanche)
76.4 – dadoom (dododoo: avalanche)
79.1 – yaaay (waa: cheers)
79.3 – yaaay (waaa: cheers)
80.1-3 – yaaaay (waaaaa: cheers)
80.8 – ha ha ha (ha ha ha: laughter)
82.4 – bwoooooo (byuuuuu: wind)
84.4 – slam (batan: door closing)
86.4 – whsh (ba: moving quickly)
86.5 – wham (za: falling)
87.9 – tatump (za: leaving)
88.4 – clap clap clap clap clap clap clap clap clap
    (pachi pachi pachi pachi pachi pachi pachi pachi
    pachi: clapping)
88.4 – yahoo (waa: cheers)
91.3 – clomp (za: footsteps)
91.6 – krash (gashaan: window breaking)
94.1 – whok (doka: kneeing)
94.2 – fwam (za: falling)
94.4 – thonk (bashi: icicle striking)
94.6 – shunk (zan: icicles falling)
94.8 – hwsh (hyu: icicles flying)
95.1 – thud thud (zaku zaku: icicles falling)
95.3 – tatump (za: leaving)

223.1 – chatter chatter (wai wai: talking)
223.5 – chatter chatter (wai wai: talking)
224.3 – chatter chatter chatter (wai wai wai: talking)
225.4 – ha ha ha (ha ha ha: laughter)
225.4 – chatter chatter (wai wai: talking)
227.6 – bwump (don: bumping)
228.3 – chatter chatter (zawa zawa: talking)
228.4 – whsh (da: running)
228.5 – chatter chatter (zawa zawa: talking)
233.3 – fwup (ba: showing)
238.6 – klunk klunk (goun goun: machinery)
238.7 – vmm vmm (goun goun: machinery)
242.2 – slam (bamu: door closing)
243.6 – bam bam (gan gan hitting)
243.7 – bam (gan: hitting)
243.8 – krak (baki: chair breaking)
243.9 – fwam (daan: falling)
244.6 – kchak (gacha: door opening)
245.4 – slam (bamu: door closing)
248.9 – fwsh (fu: lights going out)
250.7 – fwing (hyu: throwing)
251.10 – kchak (gacha: door opening)
252.1 – hwsh (hyu: throwing)
252.2 – thock (ga: hitting)
253.5 – whsh (da: running)
253.6 – thwup (ka: tripping)
253.7 – thwud (daan: falling)
253.8 – whsh (da: running)
253.9 – shuk (nubu: pulling out the knife)
254.1 – fwup (ba: pulling the tablecloth)
254.2 – whsh (da: running)
254.5 – fwing (byu: throwing)
254.6 – swik (bi: cutting)
254.7 – whok (dan: kicking)
254.8 – wham (gan: hitting)
255.3 – tunk tunk tunk tunk
    (kan kan kan kan: footsteps)
258.4 – wham (gan: hitting the railing)
262.1 – bwonk (paan: train horn)
262.4 – bwonk (paan: train)
262.5 – vwooosh (gaaaaa: train)
263.1 – pshht (pushuu: doors opening)
263.4 – bwump (don: bumping)
264.2 – klik klak klik (gatan goton gatan: train)
264.7 – rrring (RRRR: phone)
267.1 – vroom (buron: bus)
271.4 – chomp (ga: biting)
272.2 – vroom (baban: car)
273.7 – fwap (basa: wings flapping)
274.1 – skrak (ga: attacking)
275.2 – skrik (ki: car stopping)
275.8 – vroom (buon: car)
276.3 – vroom (baban: car)
281.1 – tump tump (za za: footsteps)
281.4 – tump (za: footstep)
281.8 – whsh (za: hurrying)
282.1 – spshhh (zaa: waterfall)
283.2 – fwap (basa: wings flapping)
285.4 – tump (za: footstep)
285.5 – tump (za: footstep)
288.7 – tatump (dada: running)
288.8 – grab (ga: grasping)
289.3 – murmur murmur (zawa zawa: talking)
289.8 – grumble grumble (zawa zawa: talking)
290.1 – chatter chatter (zawa zawa: talking)

145.3 – thump (do: falling)
146.1 – vrooom (buoon: cars)
146.2 – swerve (gya: cutting off)
146.2 – screeech (kikii: car braking)
146.3 – tatump (ba: stepping out)
146.4 – swik (sa: pointing a gun)
146.5 – kchak (gi: doors opening)
146.7 – fwip (ba: raising the cover)
151.3 – blam (don: gunshot)
151.6 – splash (basha: falling)
151.9 – blam blam (don don: gunshots)
152.2 – zing zang (chun chuun: bullets flying)
152.6 – blam blam (don don: gunshots)
152.7 – crackle crackle (bachi bachi: electricity)
152.8 – grab (ga: holding)
152.9 – splish splash (basha basha: walking)
152.10 – tug (gui: pulling)
153.1 – zak (bon: shocking)
153.2 – splash splash (basha basha: falling)
153.9 – blam (don: gunshot)
159.1 – shukk (za: digging)
159.2 – tok tok (kan kan: hammering)
159.2 – shuk shuk (za za: digging)
159.2 – tunk tunk (kon kon: tapping)
178.5 – grab (ga: grasping)
178.9 – grab (ga: grasping)
179.2 – bash (gan: hitting)
179.8 – whok (doka: kicking)
180.1 – konk (gan: hitting his head)
180.2 – whsh (da: running)
180.10 – kasmash (gashaan: hitting and breaking)
181.1 – wrnch (ga: twisting his arm)
182.7 – slam (batamu: door closing)
187.9 – chak (batan: door closing)
191.4 – vroom (buoon: car)
191.5 – vroom (oon: car)
192.1 – rrip (biri: ripping)
192.3 – toss (ba: scattering)
192.4 – crackle crackle crackle
    (pachi pachi pachi: burning)
194.6 – bam (baan: hitting)
195.3 – tunk (ton: setting down cups)
202.3 – murmur murmur (zawa zawa: talking)
202.4 – ohhh (oou: marveling)
202.5 – clap clap clap clap clap
    (pachi pachi pachi pachi pachi: clapping)
202.6 – clap clap clap clap clap clap clap clap (pachi pac...
    pachi pachi pachi pachi pachi pachi: clapping)
206.5 – clap clap clap clap clap clap clap clap
    (pachi pachi pachi pachi pachi pachi pach...
    clapping)
206.6 – clap clap clap clap
    (pachi pachi pachi pachi: clapping)
206.7 – clap clap clap clap clap clap clap clap (pac...
    pachi pachi pachi pachi pachi pachi pachi:
    clapping)
212.2 – hwooooo (hyuuuuu: wind)
212.8 – gwoooo (goooo: wind)
213.1 – snap (baki: breaking)
219.1 – chatter chatter chatter (zawa zawa zawa: talki...
219.3 – chatter chatter chatter chatter
    (zawa zawa zawa zawa: talking)
222.7 – clap clap clap clap clap clap clap clap clap
    (pachi pachi pachi pachi pachi pachi pachi pach...
    pachi: clapping)

291.8 – whsh (tata: running)
292.1 – thwud (deen: falling)
292.3 – whsh (da: footstep)
296.7 – tump (za: footstep)
298.2 – vroom (buoon: car)
298.2 – rrip (biri: ripping)
299.6 – whsh (da: running)
299.7 – whsh (da: running)
299.8 – swip (sa: tripping)
299.9 – hwip (hyoi: dodging)
300.2 – hwoosh (byun: running past)
300.7 – thupp (ban: shoe striking)
300.9 – slam (bamu: door closing)
300.10 – chak (gacha: door opening)
305.4 – bwump (don: bumping)
305.6 – fump (do: falling)
305.8 – grab (ga: grasping)
305.9 – crik (gaki: twisting his arm)
306.3 – whok (ga: hitting)
306.4 – thud (do: falling)
309.2 – thok (gan: hitting)
309.3 – thud (do: falling)
309.6 – whack (gan: hitting)
309.7– thud (do: falling)
309.7 – ktunk (gasha: dropping)

MASTER KEATON: THE PERFECT EDITION
Volume 8
VIZ Signature Edition

by NAOKI URASAWA
Story by HOKUSEI KATSUSHIKA, NAOKI URASAWA

Translation & English Adaptation/John Werry
Lettering/Steve Dutro
Cover & Interior Design/Yukiko Whitley
Editor/Amy Yu

MASTER KEATON Vol.8
by Naoki URASAWA, Hokusei KATSUSHIKA
© 1989 Naoki URASAWA/Studio Nuts, Hokusei KATSUSHIKA, Takashi NAGASAKI
All rights reserved.
Original Japanese edition published by SHOGAKUKAN.
English translation rights in the United States of America, Canada, the United Kingdom,
Ireland, Australia and New Zealand arranged with SHOGAKUKAN.
Original Art Direction by Kazuo UMINO
Original cover design by Mikiyo KOBAYASHI + Bay Bridge Studio

Printed in the U.S.A.

Published by VIZ Media, LLC
P.O. Box 77010
San Francisco, CA 94107

10 9 8 7 6 5 4 3 2 1
First printing, September 2016

www.viz.com

VIZ SIGNATURE